Elasticsearch: A Complete Guide

End-to-end Search and Analytics

A course in three modules

BIRMINGHAM - MUMBAI

Elasticsearch: A Complete Guide

Copyright © 2017 Packt Publishing

All rights reserved. No part of this course may be reproduced, stored in a retrieval system, or transmitted in any form or by any means, without the prior written permission of the publisher, except in the case of brief quotations embedded in critical articles or reviews.

Every effort has been made in the preparation of this course to ensure the accuracy of the information presented. However, the information contained in this course is sold without warranty, either express or implied. Neither the authors, nor Packt Publishing, and its dealers and distributors will be held liable for any damages caused or alleged to be caused directly or indirectly by this course.

Packt Publishing has endeavored to provide trademark information about all of the companies and products mentioned in this course by the appropriate use of capitals. However, Packt Publishing cannot guarantee the accuracy of this information.

Published on: January 2017

Production reference: 1100317

Published by Packt Publishing Ltd.
Livery Place
35 Livery Street
Birmingham B3 2PB, UK.

ISBN 978-1-78728-854-6

www.packtpub.com

Credits

Authors
Bharvi Dixit
Rafał Kuć
Marek Rogoziński
Saurabh Chhajed

Reviewers
Alberto Paro
Hüseyin Akdoğan
Julien Duponchelle
Marcelo Ochoa
Isra El Isa
Anthony Lapenna
Blake Praharaj

Content Development Editor
Mayur Pawanikar

Production Coordinator
Nilesh Mohite

Preface

Elasticsearch is a modern, fast, distributed, scalable, fault tolerant, open source search and analytics engine. It provides a new level of control over how you can index and search even huge sets of data. This course will take you from basics of Elasticsearch to using Elasticsearch in the Elastic stack, and in production. You will start with very basics of understanding Elasticsearch terminologies and installation & configuration. After this, you will understand the basic analytics and indexing, search, and querying. You will also learn about creating various maps and visualization. You will also get a quick understanding of cluster scaling, search and bulk operations, and more. You will also learn about backups and security. After this, you will dig your teeth deeper into Elasticsearch's internal functionalities including caches, Apache Lucene library, and its monitoring capabilities. You'll learn about practical usage of Elasticsearch configuration parameters and how to use the monitoring API. You will learn how to improve user search experience, index distribution, segment statistics, merging, and more. Once you are a master, it would be time to move on. You will dive into end-to-end visualize-analyze-log techniques with Elastic Stack (also known as the ELK stack). You will look at Elasticsearch, Logstash, and Kibana, and how to make them work together to build amazing insights and business metrics out of data. You will know how to effectively use Elasticsearch with other De facto components and get the most out of Elasticsearch. You will have developed a full-fledged data pipeline by the end of this course.

What this learning path covers

Module 1, Elasticsearch Essentials, this module provides a complete coverage of working with Elasticsearch using Python and as well as Java APIs to perform CRUD operations, aggregation-based analytics, handling document relationships, working with geospatial data, and controlling search relevancy.

Module 2, Mastering Elasticsearch, in this module we start with an introduction to the world of Lucene and Elasticsearch. We will discuss topics such as different scoring algorithms, choosing the right store mechanism, what the differences between them are, and why choosing the proper one matters. We touch the administration part of Elasticsearch by discussing discovery and recovery modules and the human-friendly Cat API.

Module 3, Learning ELK Stack, this module is aimed at introducing building your own ELK Stack data pipeline using the open source technologies stack of Elasticsearch, Logstash, and Kibana. This module covers the core concepts of each of the components of the stack and quickly using them to build your own log analytics solutions.

What you need for this learning path

Module 1:

This book was written using Elasticsearch version 2.0.0, and all the examples and functions should work with it. Using Oracle Java 1.7u55 and above is recommended for creating Elasticsearch clusters. In addition to this, you'll need a command that allows you to send HTTP requests, such as curl, which is available for most operating systems. In addition to this, this book covers all the examples using Python and Java.

For Java examples, you will need to have Java JDK (Java Development Kit) installed and an editor that will allow you to develop your code (or a Java IDE such as Eclipse). Apache Maven have been used to build Java codes.

For running Python examples, you will need Python 2.7 and above and also need to install Elasticsearch-Py, the official Python client for Elasticsearch.

In addition to this, some chapters may require additional software such as Elasticsearch plugins and other software but it has been explicitly mentioned when certain types of software are needed.

Module 2:

This book was written for Elasticsearch users and enthusiasts who are already familiar with the basics concepts of this great search server and want to extend their knowledge when it comes to Elasticsearch itself as well as topics such as how Apache Lucene or the JVM garbage collector works. In addition to that, readers who want to see how to improve their query relevancy and learn how to extend Elasticsearch with their own plugin may find this book interesting and useful.

If you are new to Elasticsearch and you are not familiar with basic concepts such as querying and data indexing, you may find it hard to use this book, as most of the chapters assume that you have this knowledge already. In such cases, we suggest that you look at our previous book about Elasticsearch— Elasticsearch Server, Second Edition, Packt Publishing.

Module 3:

You will need the following as a requisite for this module:

> Unix Operating System (Any flavor)
>
> Elasticsearch 1.5.2
>
> Logstash 1.5.0
>
> Kibana 4.0.2

Who this learning path is for

This course appeals to anyone who wants to build efficient search and analytics applications. Some development experience is expected.

Reader feedback

Feedback from our readers is always welcome. Let us know what you think about this course—what you liked or disliked. Reader feedback is important for us as it helps us develop titles that you will really get the most out of.

To send us general feedback, simply e-mail feedback@packtpub.com, and mention the course's title in the subject of your message.

If there is a topic that you have expertise in and you are interested in either writing or contributing to a course, see our author guide at www.packtpub.com/authors.

Customer support

Now that you are the proud owner of a Packt course, we have a number of things to help you to get the most from your purchase.

Downloading the example code

You can download the example code files for this course from your account at `http://www.packtpub.com`. If you purchased this course elsewhere, you can visit `http://www.packtpub.com/support` and register to have the files e-mailed directly to you.

You can download the code files by following these steps:

1. Log in or register to our website using your e-mail address and password.
2. Hover the mouse pointer on the **SUPPORT** tab at the top.
3. Click on **Code Downloads & Errata**.
4. Enter the name of the course in the **Search** box.
5. Select the course for which you're looking to download the code files.
6. Choose from the drop-down menu where you purchased this course from.
7. Click on **Code Download**.

You can also download the code files by clicking on the **Code Files** button on the course's webpage at the Packt Publishing website. This page can be accessed by entering the course's name in the **Search** box. Please note that you need to be logged in to your Packt account.

Once the file is downloaded, please make sure that you unzip or extract the folder using the latest version of:

- WinRAR / 7-Zip for Windows
- Zipeg / iZip / UnRarX for Mac
- 7-Zip / PeaZip for Linux

The code bundle for the course is also hosted on GitHub at `https://github.com/PacktPublishing/ElasticSearch-A-Complete-Guide`. We also have other code bundles from our rich catalog of books, videos and courses available at `https://github.com/PacktPublishing/`. Check them out!

Errata

Although we have taken every care to ensure the accuracy of our content, mistakes do happen. If you find a mistake in one of our books—maybe a mistake in the text or the code—we would be grateful if you could report this to us. By doing so, you can save other readers from frustration and help us improve subsequent versions of this course. If you find any errata, please report them by visiting http://www.packtpub.com/submit-errata, selecting your course, clicking on the **Errata Submission Form** link, and entering the details of your errata. Once your errata are verified, your submission will be accepted and the errata will be uploaded to our website or added to any list of existing errata under the Errata section of that title.

To view the previously submitted errata, go to https://www.packtpub.com/books/content/support and enter the name of the book in the search field. The required information will appear under the **Errata** section.

Piracy

Piracy of copyrighted material on the Internet is an ongoing problem across all media. At Packt, we take the protection of our copyright and licenses very seriously. If you come across any illegal copies of our works in any form on the Internet, please provide us with the location address or website name immediately so that we can pursue a remedy.

Please contact us at copyright@packtpub.com with a link to the suspected pirated material.

We appreciate your help in protecting our authors and our ability to bring you valuable content.

Questions

If you have a problem with any aspect of this course, you can contact us at questions@packtpub.com, and we will do our best to address the problem.

Module 1: Elasticsearch Essentials

Chapter 1: Getting Started with Elasticsearch — 3
- Introducing Elasticsearch — 3
- Installing and configuring Elasticsearch — 9
- Basic operations with Elasticsearch — 15
- Summary — 22

Chapter 2: Understanding Document Analysis and Creating Mappings — 23
- Text search — 24
- Document analysis — 26
- Elasticsearch mapping — 31
- Summary — 42

Chapter 3: Putting Elasticsearch into Action — 43
- CRUD operations using elasticsearch-py — 43
- CRUD operations using Java — 50
- Creating a search database — 53
- Elasticsearch Query-DSL — 55
- Understanding Query-DSL parameters — 56
- Search requests using Python — 66
- Search requests using Java — 67
- Sorting your data — 69
- Document routing — 71
- Summary — 71

Chapter 4: Aggregations for Analytics — 73
- Introducing the aggregation framework — 73
- Metric aggregations — 77

Table of Contents

Bucket aggregations	84
Combining search, buckets, and metrics	96
Memory pressure and implications	100
Summary	101
Chapter 5: Data Looks Better on Maps: Master Geo-Spatiality	**103**
Introducing geo-spatial data	103
Working with geo-point data	104
Geo-aggregations	112
Geo-shapes	116
Summary	123
Chapter 6: Document Relationships in NoSQL World	**125**
Relational data in the document-oriented NoSQL world	126
Working with nested objects	129
Parent-child relationships	137
Considerations for using document relationships	142
Summary	143
Chapter 7: Different Methods of Search and Bulk Operations	**145**
Introducing search types in Elasticsearch	145
Cheaper bulk operations	147
Multi get and multi search APIs	152
Data pagination	156
Practical considerations for bulk processing	161
Summary	162
Chapter 8: Controlling Relevancy	**163**
Introducing relevant searches	163
The Elasticsearch out-of-the-box tools	164
Controlling relevancy with custom scoring	167
Summary	177
Chapter 9: Cluster Scaling in Production Deployments	**179**
Node types in Elasticsearch	180
Introducing Zen-Discovery	182
Node upgrades without downtime	184
Upgrading Elasticsearch version	185
Best Elasticsearch practices in production	186
Creating a cluster	188
Scaling your clusters	190
Summary	194

Chapter 10: Backups and Security	195
Introducing backup and restore mechanisms	195
Securing Elasticsearch	204
Summary	210

Module 2: Mastering Elasticsearch

Chapter 1: Introduction to Elasticsearch	213
Introducing Apache Lucene	214
Introducing Elasticsearch	221
The story	230
Summary	232
Chapter 2: Power User Query DSL	**233**
Default Apache Lucene scoring explained	233
Query rewrite explained	240
Query templates	248
Handling filters and why it matters	255
Choosing the right query for the job	265
Summary	289
Chapter 3: Not Only Full Text Search	**291**
Query rescoring	291
Controlling multimatching	297
Significant terms aggregation	306
Documents grouping	320
Relations between documents	326
Scripting changes between Elasticsearch versions	336
Summary	355
Chapter 4: Improving the User Search Experience	**357**
Correcting user spelling mistakes	358
Improving the query relevance	387
Summary	406
Chapter 5: The Index Distribution Architecture	**409**
Choosing the right amount of shards and replicas	410
Routing explained	413
Altering the default shard allocation behavior	424
Query execution preference	434
Summary	437

Chapter 6: Low-level Index Control — 439
- Altering Apache Lucene scoring — 439
- Choosing the right directory implementation – the store module — 446
- NRT, flush, refresh, and transaction log — 450
- Segment merging under control — 455
- When it is too much for I/O – throttling explained — 462
- Understanding Elasticsearch caching — 465
- Summary — 481

Chapter 7: Elasticsearch Administration — 483
- Discovery and recovery modules — 483
- The human-friendly status API – using the Cat API — 501
- Backing up — 506
- Federated search — 511
- Summary — 518

Chapter 8: Improving Performance — 519
- Using doc values to optimize your queries — 520
- Knowing about garbage collector — 524
- Benchmarking queries — 535
- Very hot threads — 542
- Scaling Elasticsearch — 545
- Summary — 573

Chapter 9: Developing Elasticsearch Plugins — 575
- Creating the Apache Maven project structure — 575
- Understanding the basics — 576
- Creating custom REST action — 581
- Creating the custom analysis plugin — 589
- Summary — 600

Module 3: Learning ELK Stack

Chapter 1: Introduction to ELK Stack — 605
- The need for log analysis — 605
- Challenges in log analysis — 607
- The ELK Stack — 609
- ELK data pipeline — 612
- ELK Stack installation — 612
- Summary — 626

Chapter 2: Building Your First Data Pipeline with ELK — 627
Input dataset — 627
Configuring Logstash input — 629
Filtering and processing input — 630
Putting data to Elasticsearch — 633
Visualizing with Kibana — 636
Summary — 645

Chapter 3: Collect, Parse and Transform Data with Logstash — 647
Configuring Logstash — 648
Logstash plugins — 649
Summary — 676

Chapter 4: Creating Custom Logstash Plugins — 677
Logstash plugin management — 677
Plugin lifecycle management — 678
Structure of a Logstash plugin — 680
Summary — 689

Chapter 5: Why Do We Need Elasticsearch in ELK? — 691
Why Elasticsearch? — 691
Elasticsearch basic concepts — 692
Document — 692
Exploring the Elasticsearch API — 694
Elasticsearch Query DSL — 700
Elasticsearch plugins — 707
Summary — 709

Chapter 6: Finding Insights with Kibana — 711
Kibana 4 features — 711
Kibana interface — 713
Summary — 721

Chapter 7: Kibana – Visualization and Dashboard — 723
Visualize page — 723
Dashboard page — 735
Summary — 737

Chapter 8: Putting It All Together — 739
Input dataset — 739
Configuring Logstash input — 740
Visualizing with Kibana — 743
Summary — 753

Chapter 9: ELK Stack in Production — 755
Prevention of data loss — 755
Data protection — 756
System scalability — 758
Data retention — 759
ELK Stack implementations — 760
ELK at SCA — 763
ELK at Cliffhanger Solutions — 764
Kibana demo – Packetbeat dashboard — 766
Summary — 769
Chapter 10: Expanding Horizons with ELK — 771
Elasticsearch plugins and utilities — 771
ELK roadmap — 778
Summary — 780
Bibliography — 781
Index — 783

Module 1

Elasticsearch Essentials

Harness the power of ElasticSearch to build and manage scalable search and analytics solutions with this fast-paced guide

Getting Started with Elasticsearch

Nowadays, search is one of the primary functionalities needed in every application; it can be fulfilled by Elasticsearch, which also has many other extra features. Elasticsearch, which is built on top of Apache Lucene, is an open source, distributable, and highly scalable search engine. It provides extremely fast searches and makes data discovery easy.

In this chapter, we will cover the following topics:

- Concepts and terminologies related to Elasticsearch
- Rest API and the JSON data structure
- Installing and configuring Elasticsearch
- Installing the Elasticsearch plugins
- Basic operations with Elasticsearch

Introducing Elasticsearch

Elasticsearch is a distributed, full text search and analytic engine that is build on top of Lucene, a search engine library written in Java, and is also a base for Solr. After its first release in 2010, Elasticsearch has been widely adopted by large as well as small organizations, including NASA, Wikipedia, and GitHub, for different use cases. The latest releases of Elasticsearch are focusing more on resiliency, which builds confidence in users being able to use Elasticsearch as a data storeage tool, apart from using it as a full text search engine. Elasticsearch ships with sensible default configurations and settings, and also hides all the complexities from beginners, which lets everyone become productive very quickly by just learning the basics.

The primary features of Elasticsearch

Lucene is a blazing fast search library but it is tough to use directly and has very limited features to scale beyond a single machine. Elasticsearch comes to the rescue to overcome all the limitations of Lucene. Apart from providing a simple HTTP/JSON API, which enables language interoperability in comparison to Lucene's bare Java API, it has the following main features:

- **Distributed**: Elasticsearch is distributed in nature from day one, and has been designed for scaling horizontally and not vertically. You can start with a single-node Elasticsearch cluster on your laptop and can scale that cluster to hundreds or thousands of nodes without worrying about the internal complexities that come with distributed computing, distributed document storage, and searches.

- **High Availability**: Data replication means having multiple copies of data in your cluster. This feature enables users to create highly available clusters by keeping more than one copy of data. You just need to issue a simple command, and it automatically creates redundant copies of the data to provide higher availabilities and avoid data loss in the case of machine failure.

- **REST-based**: Elasticsearch is based on REST architecture and provides API endpoints to not only perform CRUD operations over HTTP API calls, but also to enable users to perform cluster monitoring tasks using REST APIs. REST endpoints also enable users to make changes to clusters and indices settings dynamically, rather than manually pushing configuration updates to all the nodes in a cluster by editing the `elasticsearch.yml` file and restarting the node. This is possible because each resource (index, document, node, and so on) in Elasticsearch is accessible via a simple URI.

- **Powerful Query DSL**: Query DSL (domain-specific language) is a JSON interface provided by Elasticsearch to expose the power of Lucene to write and read queries in a very easy way. Thanks to the Query DSL, developers who are not aware of Lucene query syntaxes can also start writing complex queries in Elasticsearch.

- **Schemaless**: Being schemaless means that you do not have to create a schema with field names and data types before indexing the data in Elasticsearch. Though it is one of the most misunderstood concepts, this is one of the biggest advantages we have seen in many organizations, especially in e-commerce sectors where it's difficult to define the schema in advance in some cases. When you send your first document to Elasticsearch, it tries its best to parse every field in the document and creates a schema itself. Next time, if you send another document with a different data type for the same field, it will discard the document. So, Elasticsearch is not completely schemaless but its dynamic behavior of creating a schema is very useful.

There are many more features available in Elasticsearch, such as multitenancy and percolation, which will be discussed in detail in the next chapters.

Understanding REST and JSON

Elasticsearch is based on a REST design pattern and all the operations, for example, document insertion, deletion, updating, searching, and various monitoring and management tasks, can be performed using the REST endpoints provided by Elasticsearch.

What is REST?

In a REST-based web API, data and services are exposed as resources with URLs. All the requests are routed to a resource that is represented by a path. Each resource has a resource identifier, which is called as URI. All the potential actions on this resource can be done using simple request types provided by the HTTP protocol. The following are examples that describe how CRUD operations are done with REST API:

- To create the user, use the following:

    `POST /user`

    `fname=Bharvi&lname=Dixit&age=28&id=123`

- The following command is used for retrieval:

    `GET /user/123`

- Use the following to update the user information:

    `PUT /user/123`

    `fname=Lavleen`

- To delete the user, use this:

    `DELETE /user/123`

 Many Elasticsearch users get confused between the `POST` and `PUT` request types. The difference is simple. `POST` is used to create a new resource, while `PUT` is used to update an existing resource. The `PUT` request is used during resource creation in some cases but it must have the complete URI available for this.

What is JSON?

All the real-world data comes in object form. Every entity (object) has some properties. These properties can be in the form of simple key value pairs or they can be in the form of complex data structures. One property can have properties nested into it, and so on.

Elasticsearch is a document-oriented data store where objects, which are called as documents, are stored and retrieved in the form of JSON. These objects are not only stored, but also the content of these documents gets indexed to make them searchable.

JavaScript Object Notation (JSON) is a lightweight data interchange format and, in the NoSQL world, it has become a standard data serialization format. The primary reason behind using it as a standard format is the language independency and complex nested data structure that it supports. JSON has the following data type support:

Array, Boolean, Null, Number, Object, and String

The following is an example of a JSON object, which is self-explanatory about how these data types are stored in key value pairs:

```
{
  "int_array": [1, 2,3],
  "string_array": ["Lucene" ,"Elasticsearch","NoSQL"],
  "boolean": true,
  "null": null,
  "number": 123,
  "object": {
    "a": "b",
    "c": "d",
    "e": "f"
  },
  "string": "Learning Elasticsearch"
}
```

Elasticsearch common terms

The following are the most common terms that are very important to know when starting with Elasticsearch:

- **Node**: A single instance of Elasticsearch running on a machine.
- **Cluster**: A cluster is the single name under which one or more nodes/instances of Elasticsearch are connected to each other.
- **Document**: A document is a JSON object that contains the actual data in key value pairs.

- **Index**: A logical namespace under which Elasticsearch stores data, and may be built with more than one Lucene index using shards and replicas.
- **Doc types**: A doc type in Elasticsearch represents a class of similar documents. A type consists of a name, such as a user or a blog post, and a mapping, including data types and the Lucene configurations for each field. (An index can contain more than one type.)
- **Shard**: Shards are containers that can be stored on a single node or multiple nodes and are composed of Lucene segments. An index is divided into one or more shards to make the data distributable.

> A shard can be either primary or secondary. A primary shard is the one where all the operations that change the index are directed. A secondary shard is the one that contains duplicate data of the primary shard and helps in quickly searching the data as well as for high availability; in a case where the machine that holds the primary shard goes down, then the secondary shard becomes the primary automatically.

- **Replica**: A duplicate copy of the data living in a shard for high availability.

Understanding Elasticsearch structure with respect to relational databases

Elasticsearch is a search engine in the first place but, because of its rich functionality offerings, organizations have started using it as a NoSQL data store as well. However, it has not been made for maintaining the complex relationships that are offered by traditional relational databases.

If you want to understand Elasticsearch in relational database terms then, as shown in the following image, an index in Elasticsearch is similar to a database that consists of multiple types. A single row is represented as a document, and columns are similar to fields.

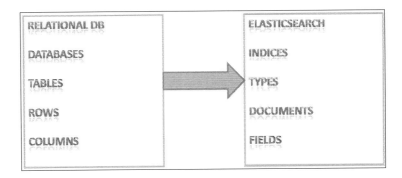

Elasticsearch does not have the concept of referential integrity constraints such as foreign keys. But, despite being a search engine and NoSQL data store, it does allow us to maintain some relationships among different documents, which will be discussed in the upcoming chapters.

With these theoretical concepts, we are good to go with learning the practical steps with Elasticsearch.

First of all, you need to be aware of the basic requirements to install and run Elasticsearch, which are listed as follows:

- Java (Oracle Java 1.7u55 and above)
- RAM: Minimum 2 GB
- Root permission to install and configure program libraries

> Please go through the following URL to check the JVM and OS dependencies of Elasticsearch: https://www.elastic.co/subscriptions/matrix.

The most common error that comes up if you are using an incompatible Java version with Elasticsearch, is the following:

```
Exception in thread "main" java.lang.UnsupportedClassVersionError: org/elasticsearch/bootstrap/Elasticsearch : Unsupported major.minor version 51.0
    at java.lang.ClassLoader.defineClass1(Native Method)
    at java.lang.ClassLoader.defineClassCond(ClassLoader.java:637)
    at java.lang.ClassLoader.defineClass(ClassLoader.java:621)
    at java.security.SecureClassLoader.defineClass(SecureClassLoader.java:141)
    at java.net.URLClassLoader.defineClass(URLClassLoader.java:283)
    at java.net.URLClassLoader.access$000(URLClassLoader.java:58)
    at java.net.URLClassLoader$1.run(URLClassLoader.java:197)
    at java.security.AccessController.doPrivileged(Native Method)
    at java.net.URLClassLoader.findClass(URLClassLoader.java:190)
    at java.lang.ClassLoader.loadClass(ClassLoader.java:306)
    at sun.misc.Launcher$AppClassLoader.loadClass(Launcher.java:301)
    at java.lang.ClassLoader.loadClass(ClassLoader.java:247)
```

If you see the preceding error while installing/working with Elasticsearch, it is most probably because you have an incompatible version of JAVA set as the JAVA_HOME variable or not set at all. Many users install the latest version of JAVA but forget to set the JAVA_HOME variable to the latest installation. If this variable is not set, then Elasticsearch looks into the following listed directories to find the JAVA and the first existing directory is used:

```
/usr/lib/jvm/jdk-7-oracle-x64, /usr/lib/jvm/java-7-oracle, /usr/lib/jvm/java-7-openjdk, /usr/lib/jvm/java-7-openjdk-amd64/, /usr/lib/jvm/java-7-openjdk-armhf, /usr/lib/jvm/java-7-openjdk-i386/, /usr/lib/jvm/default-java
```

Installing and configuring Elasticsearch

I have used the Elasticsearch Version 2.0.0 in this book; you can choose to install other versions, if you wish to. You just need to replace the version number with 2.0.0. You need to have an administrative account to perform the installations and configurations.

Installing Elasticsearch on Ubuntu through Debian package

Let's get started with installing Elasticsearch on Ubuntu Linux. The steps will be the same for all Ubuntu versions:

1. Download the Elasticsearch Version 2.0.0 Debian package:

   ```
   wget https://download.elastic.co/elasticsearch/elasticsearch/elasticsearch-2.0.0.deb
   ```

2. Install Elasticsearch, as follows:

   ```
   sudo dpkg -i elasticsearch-2.0.0.deb
   ```

3. To run Elasticsearch as a service (to ensure Elasticsearch starts automatically when the system is booted), do the following:

   ```
   sudo update-rc.d elasticsearch defaults 95 10
   ```

Installing Elasticsearch on Centos through the RPM package

Follow these steps to install Elasticsearch on Centos machines. If you are using any other Red Hat Linux distribution, you can use the same commands, as follows:

1. Download the Elasticsearch Version 2.0.0 RPM package:

   ```
   wget https://download.elastic.co/elasticsearch/elasticsearch/elasticsearch-2.0.0.rpm
   ```

2. Install Elasticsearch, using this command:

   ```
   sudo rpm -i elasticsearch-2.0.0.rpm
   ```

3. To run Elasticsearch as a service (to ensure Elasticsearch starts automatically when the system is booted), use the following:

   ```
   sudo systemctl daemon-reload
   sudo systemctl enable elasticsearch.service
   ```

Understanding the Elasticsearch installation directory layout

The following table shows the directory layout of Elasticsearch that is created after installation. These directories, have some minor differences in paths depending upon the Linux distribution you are using.

Description	Path on Debian/Ubuntu	Path on RHEL/Centos
Elasticsearch home directory	/usr/share/elasticsearch	/usr/share/elasticsearch
Elasticsearch and Lucene jar files	/usr/share/elasticsearch/lib	/usr/share/elasticsearch/lib
Contains plugins	/usr/share/elasticsearch/plugins	/usr/share/elasticsearch/plugins
The locations of the binary scripts that are used to start an ES node and download plugins	usr/share/elasticsearch/bin	usr/share/elasticsearch/bin

Description	Path on Debian/Ubuntu	Path on RHEL/Centos
Contains the Elasticsearch configuration files: (`elasticsearch.yml` and `logging.yml`)	`/etc/elasticsearch`	`/etc/elasticsearch`
Contains the data files of the index/shard allocated on that node	`/var/lib/elasticsearch/data`	`/var/lib/elasticsearch/data`
The startup script for Elasticsearch (contains environment variables including HEAP SIZE and file descriptors)	`/etc/init.d/elasticsearch`	`/etc/sysconfig/elasticsearch` Or `/etc/init.d/elasticsearch`
Contains the log files of Elasticsearch.	`/var/log/elasticsearch/`	`/var/log/elasticsearch/`

During installation, a user and a group with the `elasticsearch` name are created by default. Elasticsearch does not get started automatically just after installation. It is prevented from an automatic startup to avoid a connection to an already running node with the same cluster name.

> It is recommended to change the cluster name before starting Elasticsearch for the first time.

Configuring basic parameters

1. Open the `elasticsearch.yml` file, which contains most of the Elasticsearch configuration options:

   `sudo vim /etc/elasticsearch/elasticsearch.yml`

2. Now, edit the following ones:
   - `cluster.name`: The name of your cluster
   - `node.name`: The name of the node
   - `path.data`: The path where the data for the ES will be stored

> Similar to `path.data`, we can change `path.logs` and `path.plugins` as well. Make sure all these parameters values are inside double quotes.

3. After saving the `elasticsearch.yml` file, start Elasticsearch:

   `sudo service elasticsearch start`

   Elasticsearch will start on two ports, as follows:
   - **9200**: This is used to create HTTP connections
   - **9300**: This is used to create a TCP connection through a JAVA client and the node's interconnection inside a cluster

   > Do not forget to uncomment the lines you have edited. Please note that if you are using a new data path instead of the default one, then you first need to change the owner and the group of that data path to the user, *elasticsearch*.
   >
   > The command to change the directory ownership to *elasticsearch* is as follows:
   >
   > `sudo chown -R elasticsearch:elasticsearch data_directory_path`

4. Run the following command to check whether Elasticsearch has been started properly:

   `sudo service elasticsearch status`

   If the output of the preceding command is shown as **elasticsearch is not running**, then there must be some configuration issue. You can open the log file and see what is causing the error.

The list of possible issues that might prevent Elasticsearch from starting is:

- A Java issue, as discussed previously
- Indention issues in the `elasticsearch.yml` file
- At least 1 GB of RAM is not free to be used by Elasticsearch
- The ownership of the data directory path is not changed to *elasticsearch*
- Something is already running on port 9200 or 9300

Adding another node to the cluster

Adding another node in a cluster is very simple. You just need to follow all the steps for installation on another system to install a new instance of Elasticsearch. However, keep the following in mind:

- In the `elasticsearch.yml` file, `cluster.name` is set to be the same on both the nodes
- Both the systems should be reachable from each other over the network.
- There is no firewall rule set for Elasticsearch port blocking
- The Elasticsearch and JAVA versions are the same on both the nodes

You can optionally set the `network.host` parameter to the IP address of the system to which you want Elasticsearch to be bound and the other nodes to communicate.

Installing Elasticsearch plugins

Plugins provide extra functionalities in a customized manner. They can be used to query, monitor, and manage tasks. Thanks to the wide Elasticsearch community, there are several easy-to-use plugins available. In this book, I will be discussing some of them.

The Elasticsearch plugins come in two flavors:

- **Site plugins**: These are the plugins that have a site (web app) in them and do not contain any Java-related content. After installation, they are moved to the site directory and can be accessed using `es_ip:port/_plugin/plugin_name`.
- **Java plugins**: These mainly contain `.jar` files and are used to extend the functionalities of Elasticsearch. For example, the Carrot2 plugin that is used for text-clustering purposes.

Elasticsearch ships with a plugin script that is located in the `/user/share/elasticsearch/bin` directory, and any plugin can be installed using this script in the following format:

`bin/plugin --install plugin_url`

> Once the plugin is installed, you need to restart that node to make it active. In the following image, you can see the different plugins installed inside the Elasticsearch node. Plugins need to be installed separately on each node of the cluster.

Getting Started with Elasticsearch

The following is the layout of the plugin directory of Elasticsearch:

```
bharvi@grownout:~$ cd /usr/share/elasticsearch/plugins/
bharvi@grownout:/usr/share/elasticsearch/plugins$ ls
carrot2  head  marvel
bharvi@grownout:/usr/share/elasticsearch/plugins$ cd carrot2/
bharvi@grownout:/usr/share/elasticsearch/plugins/carrot2$ ls
attributes-binder-1.2.2.jar       guava-18.0.jar                  jackson-databind-2.5.3.jar    _site
carrot2-mini-3.10.1.jar            hppc-0.7.1.jar                  mahout-collections-1.0.jar    slf4j-api-1.7.12.jar
commons-lang-2.6.jar               jackson-annotations-2.5.3.jar   mahout-math-0.6.jar           slf4j-log4j12-1.7.12.jar
elasticsearch-carrot2-1.9.0.jar    jackson-core-2.5.3.jar          simple-xml-2.7.jar
```

Checking for installed plugins

You can check the log of your node that shows the following line at start up time:

```
[2015-09-06 14:16:02,606][INFO ][plugins                  ] [Matt
Murdock] loaded [clustering-carrot2, marvel], sites [marvel, carrot2,
head]
```

Alternatively, you can use the following command:

```
curl XGET 'localhost:9200/_nodes/plugins'?pretty
```

Another option is to use the following URL in your browser:

```
http://localhost:9200/_nodes/plugins
```

Installing the Head plugin for Elasticsearch

The Head plugin is a web front for the Elasticsearch cluster that is very easy to use. This plugin offers various features such as showing the graphical representations of shards, the cluster state, easy query creations, and downloading query-based data in the CSV format.

The following is the command to install the Head plugin:

```
sudo /usr/share/elasticsearch/bin/plugin -install mobz/elasticsearch-head
```

Restart the Elasticsearch node with the following command to load the plugin:

```
sudo service elasticsearch restart
```

Once Elasticsearch is restarted, open the browser and type the following URL to access it through the Head plugin:

```
http://localhost:9200/_plugin/head
```

> More information about the Head plugin can be found here:
> https://github.com/mobz/elasticsearch-head

Installing Sense for Elasticsearch

Sense is an awesome tool to query Elasticsearch. You can add it to your latest version of Chrome, Safari, or Firefox browsers as an extension.

Now, when Elasticsearch is installed and running in your system, and you have also installed the plugins, you are good to go with creating your first index and performing some basic operations.

Basic operations with Elasticsearch

We have already seen how Elasticsearch stores data and provides REST APIs to perform the operations. In next few sections, we will be performing some basic actions using the command line tool called CURL. Once you have grasped the basics, you will start programming and implementing these concepts using Python and Java in upcoming chapters.

 When we create an index, Elasticsearch by default creates five shards and one replica for each shard (this means five primary and five replica shards). This setting can be controlled in the `elasticsearch.yml` file by changing the `index.number_of_shards` properties and the `index.number_of_replicas` settings, or it can also be provided while creating the index.

Once the index is created, the number of shards can't be increased or decreased; however, you can increase or decrease the number of replicas at any time after index creation. So it is better to choose the number of required shards for an index at the time of index creation.

Creating an Index

Let's begin by creating our first index and give this index a name, which is `book` in this case. After executing the following command, an index with five shards and one replica will be created:

`curl -XPUT 'localhost:9200/books/'`

 Uppercase letters and blank spaces are not allowed in index names.

Indexing a document in Elasticsearch

Similar to all databases, Elasticsearch has the concept of having a unique identifier for each document that is known as `_id`. This identifier is created in two ways, either you can provide your own unique ID while indexing the data, or if you don't provide any id, Elasticsearch creates a default id for that document. The following are the examples:

```
curl -XPUT 'localhost:9200/books/elasticsearch/1' -d '{
"name":"Elasticsearch Essentials",
"author":"Bharvi Dixit",
"tags":["Data Analytics","Text Search","Elasticsearch"],
"content":"Added with PUT request"
}'
```

On executing above command, Elasticsearch will give the following response:

```
{"_index":"books","_type":"elasticsearch","_id":"1","_version":1,"created":true}
```

However, if you do not provide an id, which is `1` in our case, then you will get the following error:

`No handler found for uri [/books/elasticsearch] and method [PUT]`

The reason behind the preceding error is that we are using a `PUT` request to create a document. However, Elasticsearch has no idea where to store this document (no existing URI for the document is available).

If you want the _id to be auto generated, you have to use a POST request. For example:

```
curl -XPOST 'localhost:9200/books/elasticsearch' -d '{
"name":"Elasticsearch Essentials",
"author":"Bharvi Dixit",
"tags":["Data Anlytics","Text Search","Elasticsearch"],
"content":"Added with POST request"
}'
```

The response from the preceding request will be as follows:

```
{"_index":"books","_type":"elasticsearch","_id":"AU-ityC8xdEEi6V7cMV5","_version":1,"created":true}
```

If you open the `localhost:9200/_plugin/head` URL, you can perform all the CRUD operations using the HEAD plugin as well:

Some of the stats that you can see in the preceding image are these:

- Cluster name: `elasticsearch_cluster`
- Node name: `node-1`
- Index name: books
- No. of primary shards: 5
- No. of docs in the index: 2
- No. of unassigned shards (replica shards): 5

>
> **Cluster states in Elasticsearch**
>
> An Elasticsearch cluster can be in one of the three states: GREEN, YELLOW, or RED. If all the shards, meaning primary as well as replicas, are assigned in the cluster, it will be in the GREEN state. If any one of the replica shards is not assigned because of any problem, then the cluster will be in the YELLOW state. If any one of the primary shards is not assigned on a node, then the cluster will be in the RED state. We will see more on these states in the upcoming chapters. Elasticsearch never assigns a primary and its replica shard on the same node.

Fetching documents

We have stored documents in Elasticsearch. Now we can fetch them using their unique ids with a simple GET request.

Get a complete document

We have already indexed our document. Now, we can get the document using its document identifier by executing the following command:

```
curl -XGET 'localhost:9200/books/elasticsearch/1'?pretty
```

The output of the preceding command is as follows:

```
{
  "_index" : "books",
  "_type" : "elasticsearch",
  "_id" : "1",
  "_version" : 1,
  "found" : true,
  "_source":{"name":"Elasticsearch Essentials","author":"Bharvi Dixit","tags":["Data Anlytics","Text Search","ELasticsearch"],"content":"Added with PUT request"}
}
```

>
> pretty is used in the preceding request to make the response nicer and more readable.

As you can see, there is a `_source` field in the response. This is a special field reserved by Elasticsearch to store all the JSON data. There are options available to not store the data in this field since it comes with an extra disk space requirement. However, this also helps in many ways while returning data from ES, re-indexing data, or doing partial document updates. We will see more on this field in the next chapters.

If the document did not exist in the index, the `_found` field would have been marked as false.

Getting part of a document

Sometimes you need only some of the fields to be returned instead of returning the complete document. For these scenarios, you can send the names of the fields to be returned inside the `_source` parameter with the GET request:

```
curl -XGET 'localhost:9200/books/elasticsearch/1'?_source=name,author
```

The response of Elasticsearch will be as follows:

```
{
"_index":"books",
"_type":"elasticsearch",
"_id":"1",
"_version":1,
"found":true,
"_source":{"author":"Bharvi Dixit","name":"Elasticsearch Essentials"}
}
```

Updating documents

It is possible to update documents in Elasticsearch, which can be done either completely or partially, but updates come with some limitations and costs. In the next sections, we will see how these operations can be performed and how things work behind the scenes.

Updating a whole document

To update a whole document, you can use a similar PUT/POST request, which we had used to create a new document:

```
curl -XPUT 'localhost:9200/books/elasticsearch/1' -d '{
"name":"Elasticsearch Essentials",
"author":"Bharvi Dixit",
"tags":["Data Analytics","Text Search","Elasticsearch"],
"content":"Updated document",
"publisher":"pact-pub"
}'
```

The response of Elasticsearch looks like this:

```
{"_index":"books","_type":"elasticsearch","_id":"1","_version":2,"created":false}
```

If you look at the response, it shows `_version` is 2 and `created` is `false`, meaning the document is updated.

Updating documents partially

Instead of updating the whole document, we can use the `_update` API to do partial updates. As shown in the following example, we will add a new field, `updated_time`, to the document for which a script parameter has been used. Elasticsearch uses Groovy scripting by default.

 Scripting is by default disabled in Elasticsearch, so to use a script you need to enable it by adding the following parameter to your `elasticsearch.yml` file:

`script.inline: on`

```
curl -XPOST 'localhost:9200/books/elasticsearch/1/_update' -d '{

   "script" : "ctx._source.updated_time= \"2015-09-09T00:00:00\""

}'
```

The response of the preceding request will be this:

```
{"_index":"books","_type":"elasticsearch","_id":"1","_version":3}
```

It shows that a new version has been created in Elasticsearch.

Elasticsearch stores data in indexes that are composed of Lucene segments. These segments are immutable in nature, meaning that, once created, they can't be changed. So, when we send an update request to Elasticsearch, it does the following things in the background:

- Fetches the JSON data from the `_source` field for that document
- Makes changes in the `_source` field
- Deletes old documents
- Creates a new document

All these data re-indexing tasks can be done by the user; however, if you are using the `UPDATE` method, it is done using only one request. These processes are the same when doing a whole document update as for a partial update. The benefit of a partial update is that all operations are done within a single shard, which avoids network overhead.

Deleting documents

To delete a document using its identifier, we need to use the `DELETE` request:

```
curl -XDELETE 'localhost:9200/books/elasticsearch/1'
```

The following is the response of Elasticsearch:

```
{"found":true,"_index":"books","_type":"elasticsearch","_id":"1","_version":4}
```

If you are from a Lucene background, then you must know how segment merging is done and how new segments are created in the background with more documents getting indexed. Whenever we delete a document from Elasticsearch, it does not get deleted from the file system right away. Rather, Elasticsearch just marks that document as deleted, and when you index more data, segment merging is done. At the same time, the documents that are marked as deleted are indeed deleted based on a merge policy. This process is also applied while the document is updated.

The space from deleted documents can also be reclaimed with the `_optimize` API by executing the following command:

```
curl -XPOST http://localhost:9200/_optimize?only_expunge_deletes=true'
```

Checking documents' existence

While developing applications, some scenarios require you to check whether a document exists or not in Elasticsearch. In these scenarios, rather than querying the documents with a `GET` request, you have the option of using another `HTTP` request method called `HEAD`:

```
curl -i -XHEAD 'localhost:9200/books/elasticsearch/1'
```

The following is the response of the preceding command:

```
HTTP/1.1 200 OK
Content-Type: text/plain; charset=UTF-8
Content-Length: 0
```

In the preceding command, I have used the `-i` parameter that is used to show the header information of an `HTTP` response. It has been used because the `HEAD` request only returns headers and not any content. If the document is found, then status code will be `200`, and if not, then it will be `400`.

Summary

A lot of things have been covered in this chapter. You have got to know about the Elasticsearch architecture and its workings. Then, you have learned about the installations of Elasticsearch and its plugins. Finally, basic operations with Elasticsearch were done.

With all these, you are ready to learn about data analysis phases and mappings in the next chapter.

2
Understanding Document Analysis and Creating Mappings

Search is hard, and it becomes harder when both speed and relevancy are required together. There are lots of configurable options Elasticsearch provides out-of-the-box to take control before you start putting the data into it. *Elasticsearch is schemaless*. I gave a brief idea in the previous chapter of why it is not completely schemaless and how it creates a schema right after indexing the very first document for all the fields existing in that document. However, the schema matters a lot for a better and more relevant search. Equally important is understanding the theory behind the phases of document indexing and search.

In this chapter, we will cover the following topics:

- Full text search and inverted indices
- Document analysis
- Introducing Lucene analyzers
- Creating custom analyzers
- Elasticsearch mappings

Text search

Searching is broadly divided into two types: **exact term search** and **full text search**. An exact term search is something in which we look out for the exact terms; for example, any named entity such as the name of a person, location, or organization or date. These searches are easier to make since the search engine simply looks out for a yes or no and returns the documents.

However, full text search is different as well as challenging. Full text search refers to the search within text fields, where the text can be unstructured as well as structured. The text data can be in the form of any human language and based on the natural languages, which are very hard for a machine to understand and give relevant results. The following are some examples of full text searches:

- Find all the documents with *search* in the title or content fields, and return the results with matches in titles with the higher score
- Find all the tweets in which people are talking about *terrorism* and *killing* and return the results sorted by the tweet creation time

While doing these kinds of searches, we not only want relevant results but also expect that the search for a keyword matches all of its synonyms, root words, and spelling mistakes. For example, terrorism should match terorism and terror, while killing should match kills, kill, and killed.

To serve all these queries, the text-based fields go through an analysis phase before indexing, and based on this analysis, inverted indexes are built. At the time of querying, the same analysis process is applied to the terms that are sent within the queries to match those terms stored in the inverted indexes.

TF-IDF

TF-IDF stands for **term frequencies-inverse document frequencies**, and it is an important parameter used inside Lucene's standard similarity algorithm, **Vector Space Model** (**VSM**). The weight calculated by TF-IDF is the statistical measure to evaluate how important a word is to a document in a collection of documents.

Let's see how a TF-IDF weight is calculated to find our term's relevancy:

- **TF (term)**: (The number of times a term appears in a document) / (The total number of terms in the document)
- **IDF (term)**: $\log_e$ (The total number of documents / The number of documents with the t term in it)

> While calculating IDF, the log is taken because terms such as *the*, *that*, and *is* may appear too many times, and we need to weigh down these frequently appearing terms while increasing the importance of rare terms.

The weight of TF-IDF is a product of *TF(term)*IDF(term)*.

In information retrieval, one of the simplest relevancy ranking functions is implemented by summing the TF-IDF weight for each query term. Based on the combined weights for all the terms appearing in a single query, a score is calculated that is used to return the results in a sorted order.

Inverted indexes

Inverted index is the heart of search engines. The primary goal of a search engine is to provide speedy searches while finding the documents in which our search terms occur. Relevancy comes second.

Let's see with an example how inverted indexes are created and why they are so fast. In this example, we have two documents with each content field containing the following texts:

- I hate when spiders sit on the wall and act like they pay rent
- I hate when spider just sit there

While indexing, these texts are tokenized into separate terms and all the unique terms are stored inside the index with information such as in which document this term appears and what is the term position in that document.

The inverted index built with the preceding document texts looks like this:

Term	Document:Position
I	1:1, 2:1
Hate	1:2, 2:2
When	1:3, 2:3
Spiders	1:4
Sit	1:5, 2:5
On	1:6
Wall	1:7
Spider	2:4

Term	Document:Position
Just	2:5
There	2:6

When you search for the term spider OR spiders, the query is executed against the inverted index and the terms are looked out for, and the documents where these terms appear are quickly identified. If you search for spider AND spiders, you will not get any results because when we use AND queries, both the terms used in the queries must be present in the document. However, spiders and spider are different for the search engine unless they are normalized into their root forms. For all these term normalizations, Elasticsearch has a document analysis phase that we will see in the upcoming sections.

Document analysis

When we index documents into Elasticsearch, it goes through an analysis phase that is necessary in order to create inverted indexes. It is a series of steps performed by Lucene, which is depicted in the following image:

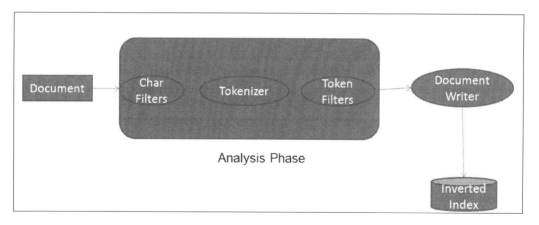

The analysis phase is performed by analyzers that are composed of one or more char filters, a single tokenizer, and one or more token filters. You can declare separate analyzers for each field in your document depending on the need. For the same field, the analyzers can be the same for both indexing and searching or they can be different.

- **Character Filters**: The job of character filters is to do cleanup tasks such as stripping out HTML tags.

- **Tokenizers**: The next step is to split the text into terms that are called tokens. This is done by a tokenizer. The splitting can be done based on any rule such as whitespace. More details about tokenizers can be found at this URL: `https://www.elastic.co/guide/en/elasticsearch/reference/current/analysis-tokenizers.html`.

- **Token filters**: Once the tokens are created, they are passed to token filters that normalize the tokens. Token filters can change the tokens, remove the terms, or add terms to new tokens.

The most used token filters are: the lowercase token filter, which converts a token into lowercase: the stop token filter, which removes the stop word tokens such as to, be, a, an, the, and so on: and the ASCII folding token filter, which converts Unicode characters into their ASCII equivalent. A long list of token filters can be found here: `https://www.elastic.co/guide/en/elasticsearch/reference/current/analysis-tokenfilters.html`.

Introducing Lucene analyzers

Lucene has a wide range of built-in analyzers. We will see the most important ones here:

- **Standard analyzer**: This is the default analyzer used by Elasticsearch unless you mention any other analyzer to be used explicitly. This is best suited for any language. A standard analyzer is composed of a standard tokenizer (which splits the text as defined by Unicode Standard Annex), a standard token filter, a lowercase token filter, and a stop token filter.

> A standard tokenizer uses a stop token filter but it defaults to an empty stopword list, so it does not remove any stop words by default. If you need to remove stopwords, you can either use the stop analyzer or you can provide a stopword list to the standard analyzer setting.

- **Simple analyzer**: A simple analyzer splits the token wherever it finds a non-letter character and lowercases all the terms using the lowercase token filter.

- **Whitespace analyzer**: As the name suggests, it splits the text at white spaces. However, unlike simple and standard analyzers, it does not lowercase tokens.

- **Keyword analyzer**: A keyword analyzer creates a single token of the entire stream. Similar to the whitespace analyzer, it also does not lowercase tokens. This analyzer is good for fields such as zip codes and phone numbers. It is mainly used for either exact terms matching, or while doing aggregations. However, it is beneficial to use `not_analyzed` for these kinds of fields.

- **Language analyzer**: There are lots of ready-made analyzers available for many languages. These analyzers understand the grammatical rules and the stop words of corresponding languages, and create tokens accordingly. To know more about language specific analyzers, visit the following URL: https://www.elastic.co/guide/en/elasticsearch/reference/current/analysis-lang-analyzer.html.

Elasticsearch provides an easy way to test the analyzers with the `_analyze` REST endpoint. Just create a test index, as follows:

```
curl -XPUT 'localhost:9200/test'
```

Use the following command by passing the text through the `_analyze` API to test the analyzer regarding how your tokens will be created:

```
curl -XGET 'localhost:9200/test/_analyze?analyzer=whitespace&text=testing, Analyzers&pretty'
```

You will get the following response:

```
{
  "tokens" : [ {
    "token" : "testing,",
    "start_offset" : 0,
    "end_offset" : 8,
    "type" : "word",
    "position" : 1
  }, {
    "token" : "Analyzers",
    "start_offset" : 9,
    "end_offset" : 18,
    "type" : "word",
    "position" : 2
  } ]
}
```

You can see in the response how Elasticsearch splits the `testing` and `Analyzers` text into two tokens based on white spaces. It also returns the token positions and the offsets. You can hit the preceding request in your favorite browser too using this: `localhost:9200/test/_analyze?analyzer=whitespace&text=testing, Analyzers&pretty`.

The following image explains how different analyzers split a token and how many tokens they produce for the same stream of text:

Standard Analyzers	Analyzed Text
	i HATE when spiders sit on the wall and act like they pay 1000$ rent
standard	i 1, hate 2, when 3, spiders 4, sit 5, on 6, the 7, wall 8, and 9, act 10, like 11, they 12, pay 13, 1000 14, rent 15
simple	i 1, hate 2, when 3, spiders 4, sit 5, on 6, the 7, wall 8, and 9, act 10, like 11, they 12, pay 13, rent 14
whitespace	i 1, HATE 2, when 3, spiders 4, sit 5, on 6, the 7, wall 8, and 9, act 10, like 11, they 12, pay 13, 1000$ 14, rent 15
stop	i 1, hate 2, when 3, spiders 4, sit 5, wall 8, act 10, like 11, pay 13, rent 14
keyword	i HATE when spiders sit on the wall and act like they pay 1000$ rent 1

Creating custom analyzers

In the previous section, we saw in-built analyzers. Sometimes, they are not good enough to serve our purpose. We need to customize the analyzers using built-in tokenizers and token/char filters. For example, the keyword analyzer by default does not use a lowercase filter, but we need it so that data is indexed in the lowercase form and is searched using either lowercase or uppercase.

To achieve this purpose, Elasticsearch provides a custom analyzer that's type is custom and can be combined with one tokenizer with zero or more token filters and zero or more char filters.

Custom analyzers always take the following form:

```
{
  "analysis": {
    "analyzer": {}, //Where we put our custom analyzers
    "filters": {} //where we put our custom filters.
  }
}
```

Let's create a custom analyzer now with the name `keyword_tokenizer` using the keyword tokenizer and lowercase and asciifolding token filters:

```
"keyword_tokenizer": {
  "type": "custom",
    "filter": [
      "lowercase",
      "asciifolding"
    ],
    "tokenizer": "keyword"
}
```

Similarly, we can create one more custom analyzer with the name `url_analyzer` for creating tokens of URLs and e-mail addresses:

```
"url_analyzer": {
    "type": "custom",
    "filter": [
       "lowercase",
       "stop"
    ],
    "tokenizer": "uax_url_email"
}
```

Changing a default analyzer

You have all the control to define the type of analyzer to be used for each field while creating mapping. However, what about those dynamic fields that you do not know about while creating mappings. By default, these fields will be indexed with a standard analyzer. But in case you want to change this default behavior, you can do it in the following way.

A default analyzer always has the name default and is created using a custom type:

```
"default": {
    "filter": [
      "standard",
      "lowercase",
      "asciifolding"
    ],
    "type": "custom",
    "tokenizer": "keyword"
}
```

In the preceding setting, the name of the `analyzer` is default, which is created with the keyword tokenizer

Putting custom analyzers into action

We have learned to create custom analyzers but we have to tell Elasticsearch about our custom analyzers so that they can be used. This can be done via the `_settings` API of Elasticsearch, as shown in the following example:

```
curl -XPUT 'localhost/index_name/_settings' -d '{
  "analysis": {
    "analyzer": {
      "default": {
        "filter": [
          "standard",
          "lowercase",
          "asciifolding"
        ],
        "type": "custom",
        "tokenizer": "keyword"
      }
    },
    "keyword_tokenizer": {
      "filter": [
        "lowercase",
        "asciifolding"
      ],
      "type": "custom",
      "tokenizer": "keyword"
    }
  }
}'
```

> If an index already exists and needs to be updated with new custom analyzers, then the index first needs to be closed before updating the analyzers. It can be done using `curl -XPOST 'localhost:9200/index_name/_close'`. After updating, the index can be opened again using `curl -XPOST 'localhost:9200/index_name/_open'`.

Elasticsearch mapping

We have seen in the previous chapter how an index can have one or more types and each type has its own mapping.

Mappings are like database schemas that describe the fields or properties that the documents of that type may have. For example, the data type of each field, such as a string, integer, or date, and how these fields should be indexed and stored by Lucene.

One more thing to consider is that unlike a database, you cannot have a field with the same name with different types in the same index; otherwise, you will break `doc_values`, and the sorting/searching is also broken. For example, create `myIndex` and also index a document with a `valid` field that contains an integer value inside the `type1` document type:

```
curl -XPOST localhost:9200/myIndex/type1/1 -d '{"valid":5}'
```

Now, index another document inside `type2` in the same index with the `valid` field. This time the `valid` field contains a string value:

```
curl -XPOST localhost/myIndex/type2/1 -d '{"valid":"40"}'
```

In this scenario, the sort and aggregations on the `valid` field are broken because they are both indexed as `valid` fields in the same index!

Document metadata fields

When a document is indexed into Elasticsearch, there are several metadata fields maintained by Elasticsearch for that document. The following are the most important metadata fields you need to know in order to control your index structure:

- `_id`: `_id` is a unique identifier for the document and can be either auto-generated or can be set while indexing or can be configured in the mapping to be parsed automatically from a field.

- `_source`: This is a special field generated by Elasticsearch that contains the actual JSON data in it. Whenever we execute a search request, the `_source` field is returned by default. By default, it is enabled, but it can be disabled using the following configuration while creating a mapping:

    ```
    PUT index_name/_mapping/doc_type
        {"_source":{"enabled":false}}
    ```

> Be careful while disabling the `_source` field, as there are lots of features you can't with it disabled. For example, highlighting is dependent on the `_source` field. Documents can only be searched and not returned; documents can't be re-indexed and can't be updated.

- `_all`: When a document is indexed, values from all the fields are indexed separately as well as in a special field called `_all`. This is done by Elasticsearch by default to make a search request on the content of the document without specifying the field name. It comes with an extra storage cost and should be disabled if searches need to be made against field names. For disabling it completely, use the following configuration in you mapping file:

    ```
    PUT index_name/_mapping/doc_type
        {"_all": { "enabled": true  }}
    ```

    However, there are some cases where you do not want to include all the fields to be included in `_all` where only certain fields. You can achieve it by setting the `include_in_all` parameter to `false`:

    ```
    PUT index_name/_mapping/doc_type
        {
            "_all": {
            "enabled": true
            },
            "properties": {
              "first_name": {
              "type": "string",
              "include_in_all": false
              },
              "last_name": {
              "type": "string"
              }
            }
        }
    ```

    In the preceding example, only the last name will be included inside the `_all` field.

- `_ttl`: There are some cases when you want the documents to be automatically deleted from the index. For example, the logs. `_ttl` (time to live) field provides the options you can set when the documents should be deleted automatically. By default, it is disabled and can be enabled using the following configuration:

    ```
    PUT index_name/_mapping/doc_type
    {
      "_ttl": {
        "enabled": true,
        "default": "1w"
        }
    }
    ```

Inside the default field, you can use time units such as m (minutes), d (days), w (weeks), M (months), and ms (milliseconds). The default is milliseconds.

> Please note that the _ttl field has been deprecated since the Elasticsearch 2.0.0 beta 2 release and might be removed from the upcoming versions. Elasticsearch will provide a new replacement for this field in future versions.

- dynamic: There are some scenarios in which you want to restrict the dynamic fields to be indexed. You only allow the fields that are defined by you in the mapping. This can be done by setting the dynamic property to be strict, in the following way:

```
PUT index_name/_mapping/doc_type
{
    "dynamic": "strict",
    "properties": {
      "first_name": {
      "type": "string"
      },
      "last_name": {
      "type": "string"
      }
    }
}
```

Data types and index analysis options

Lucene provides several options to configure each and every field separately depending on the use case. These options slightly differ based on the data types for a field.

Configuring data types

Data types in Elasticsearch are segregated in two forms:

- **Core types**: These include string, number, date, boolean, and binary
- **Complex data types**: These include arrays, objects, multi fields, geo points, geo shapes, nested, attachment, and IP

> Since Elasticsearch understands JSON, all the data types supported by JSON are also supported in Elasticsearch, along with some extra data types such as geopoint and attachment.

The following are the common attributes for the core data types:

- `index`: The values can be from `analyzed`, `no`, or `not_analyzed`. If set to `analyzed`, the text for that field is analyzed using a specified analyzer. If set to `no`, the values for that field do not get indexed and thus, are not searchable. If set to `not_analyzed`, the values are indexed as it is; for example, `Elasticsearch Essentials` will be indexed as a single term and thus, only exact matches can be done while querying.
- `store`: This takes values as either yes or no (default is `no` but `_source` is an exception). Apart from indexing the values, Lucene does have an option to store the data, which comes in handy when you want to extract the data from the field. However, since Elasticsearch has an option to store all the data inside the `_source` field, it is usually not required to store individual fields in Lucene.
- `boost`: This defaults to `1`. This specifies the importance of the field inside doc.
- `null_value`: Using this attribute, you can set a default value to be indexed if a document contains a null value for that field. The default behavior is to omit the field that contains null.

> One should be careful while configuring default values for null. The default value should always be of the type corresponding to the data type configured for that field, and it also should not be a real value that might appear in some other document.

Let's start with the configuration of the core as well as complex data types.

String

In addition to the common attributes, the following attributes can also be set for string-based fields:

- `term_vector`: This property defines whether the Lucene term vectors should be calculated for that field or not. The values can be `no` (the default one), `yes`, `with_offsets`, `with_positions`, and `with_positions_offsets`.

> A term vector is the list of terms in the document and their number of occurrences in that document. Term vectors are mainly used for Highlighting and MorelikeThis (searching for similar documents) queries. A very nice blog on term vectors has been written by Adrien Grand, which can be read here: http://blog.jpountz.net/post/41301889664/putting-term-vectors-on-a-diet.

- `omit_norms`: This takes values as `true` or `false`. The default value is `false`. When this attribute is set to `true`, it disables the Lucene norms calculation for that field (and thus you can't use index-time boosting).
- `analyzer`: A globally defined analyzer name for the index is used for indexing and searching. It defaults to the standard analyzer, but can be controlled also, which we will see in the upcoming section.
- `index_analyzer`: The name of the analyzer used for indexing. This is not required if the analyzer attribute is set.
- `search_analyzer`: The name of the analyzer used for searching. This is not required if the analyzer attribute is set.
- `ignore_above`: This specifies the maximum size of the field. If the character count is above the specified limit, that field won't be indexed. This setting is mainly used for the `not_analyzed` fields. Lucene has a term byte-length limit of 32,766. This means a single term cannot contain more than 10,922 characters (one UTF-8 character contains at most 3 bytes).

An example mapping for two string fields, `content` and `author_name`, is as follows:

```
{
  "contents": {
    "type": "string",
    "store": "yes",
    "index": "analyzed",
    "include_in_all": false,
    "analyzer": "simple"
  },
  "author_name": {
    "type": "string",
    "index": "not_analyzed",
    "ignore_above": 50
  }
}
```

Number

The number data types are: `byte`, `short`, `integer`, `long`, `floats`, and `double`. The fields that contain numeric values need to be configured with the appropriate data type. Please go through the storage type requirements for all the types under a number before deciding which type you should actually use. In case the field does not contain bigger values, choosing long instead of integer is a waste of space.

An example of configuring numeric fields is shown here:

```
{"price":{"type":"float"},"age":{"type":"integer"}}
```

Date

Working with dates usually comes with some extra challenges because there are so many data formats available and you need to decide the correct format while creating a mapping. Date fields usually take two parameters: type and format. However, you can use other analysis options too.

Elasticsearch provides a list of formats to choose from depending on the date format of your data. You can visit the following URL to learn more about it: http://www.elasticsearch.org/guide/reference/mapping/date-format.html.

The following is an example of configuring date fields:

```
{
  "creation_time": {
    "type": "date",
    "format": "YYYY-MM-dd"
  },
  "updation_time": {
    "type": "date",
    "format": "yyyy/MM/dd HH:mm:ss||yyyy/MM/dd"
  },
  "indexing_time": {
    "type": "date",
    "format": "date_optional_time"
  }
}
```

Please note the different date formats used for different date fields in the preceding mapping. The `updation_time` field contains a special format with an || operator, which specifies that it will work for both `yyyy/MM/dd HH:mm:ss` and `yyyy/MM/dd` date formats. Elasticsearch uses `date_optional_time` as the default date parsing format, which is an ISO datetime parser.

Boolean

While indexing data, a Boolean type field can contain only two values: `true` or `false`, and it can be configured in a mapping in the following way:

```
{"is_verified":{"type":"boolean"}}
```

Arrays

By default, all the fields in Lucene and thus in Elasticsearch are multivalued, which means that they can store multiple values. In order to send such fields for indexing to Elasticsearch, we use the JSON array type, which is nested within opening and closing square brackets []. Some considerations need to be taken care of while working with array data types:

- All the values of an array must be of the same data type.
- If the data type of a field is not explicitly defined in a mapping, then the data type of the first value inside the array is used as the type of that field.
- The order of the elements is not maintained inside the index, so do not get upset if you do not find the desired results while querying. However, this order is maintained inside the _source field, so when you return the data after querying, you get the same JSON as you had indexed.

Objects

JSON documents are hierarchical in nature, which allows them to define inner *objects*. Elasticsearch completely understands the nature of these inner objects and can map them easily by providing query support for their inner fields.

> Once a field is declared as an object type, you can't put any other type of data into it. If you try to do so, Elasticsearch will throw an exception.

```
{
  "features": {
    "type": "object",
    "properties": {
      "name": {
        "type": "string"
      },
      "sub_features": {
        "dynamic": false,
        "type": "object",
        "properties": {
          "name": {
            "type": "string"
          },
          "description": {
            "type": "string"
```

```
            }
          }
        }
      }
    }
}
```

If you look carefully in the previous mapping, there is a `features` root object field and it contains two properties: `name` and `sub_features`. Further, `sub_features`, which is an inner object, also contains two properties: `name` and `description`, but it has an extra setting: `dynamic: false`. Setting this property to `false` for an object changes the dynamic behavior of Elasticsearch, and you cannot index any other fields inside that object apart from the one that is declared inside the mapping. Therefore, you can index more fields in future inside the features object, but not inside the `sub_features` object.

Indexing the same field in different ways

If you need to index the same field in different ways, the following is the way to create a mapping for it. You can define as many fields with the `fields` parameter as you want:

```
{
  "name": {
    "type": "string",
    "fields": {
      "raw": {
        "type": "string",
        "index": "not_analyzed"
      }
    }
  }
}
```

With the preceding mapping, you just need to index data into the `name` field, and Elasticsearch will index the data into the `name` field using the standard analyzer that can be used for a full text search, and the data in the `name.raw` field without analyzing the tokens; which can be used for an exact term matching. You do not have to send data into the `name.raw` field explicitly.

 Please note that this option is only available for core data types and not for the objects.

Putting mappings in an index

There are two ways of putting mappings inside an index:

- Using a `post` request at the time of index creation:

    ```
    curl -XPOST 'localhost:9200/index_name' -d '{
      "settings": {
        "number_of_shards": 1,
        "number_of_replicas": 0
      },
      "mappings": {
        "type1": {
          "_all": {
            "enabled": false
          },
          "properties": {
            "field1": {
              "type": "string",
              "index": "not_analyzed"
            }
          }
        },
        "type2": {
          "properties": {
            "field2": {
              "type": "string",
              "index": "analyzed",
              "analyzer":"keyword"
            }
          }
        }
      }
    }'
    ```

- Using a `PUT` request using the `_mapping` API. The index must exist before creating a mapping in this way:

    ```
    curl -XPUT 'localhost:9200/index_name/index_type/_mapping' -d '{
    "_all": {
            "enabled": false
      },
      "properties": {
        "field1": {
          "type": "integer"
        }
      }
    }'
    ```

The mappings for the fields are enclosed inside the `properties` object, while all the metadata fields will appear outside the properties object.

 It is highly recommended to use the same configuration for the same field names across different types and indexes in a cluster. For instance, the data types and analysis options must be the same; otherwise, you will face weird outputs.

Viewing mappings

Mappings can be viewed easily with the `_mapping` API:

- To view the mapping of all the types in an index, use the following URL: `curl -XGET localhost:9200/index_name/_mapping?pretty`
- To view the mapping of a single type, use the following URL: `curl -XGET localhost:9200/index_name/type_name/_mapping?pretty`

Updating mappings

If you want to add mapping for some new fields in the mapping of an existing type, or create a mapping for a new type, you can do it later using the same `_mapping` API.

For example, to add a new field in our existing type, we only need to specify the mapping for the new field in the following way:

```
curl -XPUT 'localhost:9200/index_name/index_type/_mapping' -d '{
  "properties": {
    "new_field_name": {
      "type": "integer"
    }
  }
}'
```

Please note that the mapping definition of an existing field cannot be changed.

>
> **Dealing with a long JSON data to be sent in request body**
>
> While creating indexes with settings, custom analyzers, and mappings, you must have noted that all the JSON configurations are passed using -d, which stands for data. This is used to send a request body. While creating settings and mappings, it usually happens that the JSON data becomes so large that it gets difficult to use them in a command line using `curl`. The easy solution is to create a file with the `.json` extension and provide the path of the file while working with those settings or mappings. The following is an example command:
>
> ```
> curl -XPUT 'localhost:9200/index_name/_settings' -d @path/setting.json
> curl -XPUT 'localhost:9200/index_name/index_type/_mapping' -d @path/mapping.json
> ```

Summary

In this chapter, we covered a lot of ground involving inverted indexes, document analysis phases, the working of analyzers, and creating custom analyzers. We also learned about creating and working with mappings of different data types.

In the next chapter, we will start pushing data into Elasticsearch and will learn how to perform operations with Elasticsearch using Python and Java API.

3
Putting Elasticsearch into Action

We have covered a lot of ground on Elasticsearch architecture, indexes, analyzers, and mappings. It's time to start learning about the indexing of data and the querying of Elasticsearch using its rich *Query-DSL*.

In this chapter, we will cover the following topics:

- CRUD operations using the Elasticsearch Python client
- CRUD operations using the Elasticsearch Java client
- Creating a search database
- Introducing Query-DSL
- Search requests using Python
- Search requests using Java
- Sorting data
- Document routing

CRUD operations using elasticsearch-py

Elasticsearch is written in Java but it is interoperable with non-JVM languages too. In this book, we will use its Python client, `elasticsearch-py`, as well as its Java client to perform all the operations. The best part of this Python client library is that it communicates over HTTP and gives you the freedom to write your settings, mappings, and queries using plain JSON objects, and allows them to pass into the body parameters of the requests. To read more about this client, you can visit this URL: `http://elasticsearch-py.readthedocs.org/en/master/`.

All the examples used in this book are based on Python 2.7. However, they are compatible with Python version 3 also.

Setting up the environment

In this section, you will learn how to set up Python environments on Ubuntu using `pip` and `virtualenv`.

Installing Pip

`Pip` is a package installer for Python modules. It can be installed using the following commands:

```
sudo apt-get install python-pip python-dev build-essential
sudo pip install --upgrade pip
```

Installing virtualenv

While developing programs using Python, it is good practice to create `virtualenv`. A `virtualenv` command creates a directory that stores a private copy of Python and all the default Python packages. Virtual environments are of great help while working with several projects and different versions of Python on a single system. You can create separate virtual environments for each project and enable them for each corresponding project. To install `virtualenv`, use the following command:

```
sudo pip install --upgrade virtualenv
```

Once the virtual environment is installed, you can create a directory and copy existing Python packages to it using this command:

```
mkdir venv
```
```
virtualenv venv
```

After this, you can activate this environment with the following command:

```
source venv
```

Once this environment is activated, all the packages that you install will be inside this `venv` directory. A virtual environment can be deactivated using just the `deactivate` command.

Installing elasticsearch-py

`elasticsearch-py` can be easily installed using `pip` in the following way:

`pip install elasticsearch`

You can verify the installation using the following command:

`pip freeze | grep elasticsearch`

You will get to know which version of the Elasticsearch client has been installed:

`elasticsearch==1.6.0`

> The version can be different depending on the latest release. The preceding command installs the latest version. If you want to install a specific version, then you can specify the version using the `==` operator. For example, `pip install elasticsearch==1.5`.

Performing CRUD operations

You will learn to perform CRUD operations in the upcoming sections, but before that, let's start with the creation of indexes using Python code.

> Since `elasticsearch-py` communicates over HTTP, it takes JSON data (setting, mapping, and queries) in the body parameters of the requests. It is advisable to use a `sense` plugin (which comes with `Marvel` or as an extension too) to write queries, settings, mappings, and all other requests, because `sense` offers a lot of help with its autosuggestion functionality. Once the correct JSON data is created, you can simply store it inside a variable in your Python code and use it inside a function's body parameter.

Request timeouts

The default timeout for any request sent to Elasticsearch is 10 seconds but there are chances for requests not to get completed within 10 seconds due to the complexity of the queries, the load on Elasticsearch, or network latencies. You have two options to control the timeouts:

- **Global timeout**: This involves using the `timeout` parameter while creating a connection.
- **Per-request timeout**: This involves using the `request_timeout` parameter (in seconds) while hitting separate requests. When `request_timeout` is used, it overrides the global `timeout` value for that particular request.

Putting Elasticsearch into Action

Creating indexes with settings and mappings

Create a Python file with index settings and mappings and save it with the name `config.py`. It will have two variables, `index_settings` and `doc_mappings`:

```
index_settings = {
"number_of_shards": 1,
"number_of_replicas": 1,
"index": {
"analysis": {
"analyzer": {
"keyword_analyzed": {
"type": "custom",
"filter": [
"lowercase",
"asciifolding"
],
"tokenizer": "keyword"
}
            }
          }
        }
     }
doc_mapping = {
"_all": {
"enabled": False
},
"properties": {
"skills": {
"type": "string",
"index": "analyzed",
"analyzer": "standard",
      }
   }
}
```

Now create another file, `es_operations.py`, and follow these steps:

1. Import the `Elasticsearch` module to your Python file:

    ```
    from elasticsearch import Elasticsearch
    from time import time
    ```

2. Import the `index_setting` and `mapping` variables from the `config` file:

    ```
    from config import index_settings, doc_mapping
    ```

3. Initialize the client:

   ```
   es = Elasticsearch('localhost:9200')
   ```

4. Declare variables for the index name, doc type, and body. The body will contain the settings and the mapping:

   ```
   index_name='books'
   doc_type='search'
   body = {}
   mapping = {}
   mapping[doc_type] = doc_mapping
   body['settings'] = index_settings
   body['mappings'] = mapping
   ```

5. Check whether the index exists; otherwise, create the index:

   ```
   if not es.indices.exists(index = index_name):
   print 'index does not exist, creating the index'
   es.indices.create(index = index_name, body = body)
       time.sleep(2)
   print 'index created successfully'
   else:
   print 'An index with this name already exists'
   ```

Indexing documents

Let's create a document and store it inside a `doc1` variable, which is a dictionary:

```
doc1 = {
'name' : 'Elasticsearch Essentials',
'category' : ['Big Data', 'search engines', 'Analytics'],
'Publication' : 'Packt-Pub',
'Publishing Date' : '2015-31-12'
}
```

Once the document is created, it can be indexed using the `index` function:

```
es.index(index = index_name, doc_type = doc_type, body = doc1, id = '123')
```

> If you want the unique ID to be autogenerated, use the `None` keyword inside the `id` parameter.

[47]

Retrieving documents

Document retrieval is done using a `GET` request that takes the following parameter:

```
response = es.get(index=index_name, doc_type=doc_type, id='1',
ignore=404)
print response
```

The `ignore` parameter is used to avoid exceptions in case the document does not exist in the index. The response will look as follows:

```
{u'_type': u'1', u'_source': {u'category': [u'Big Data', u'search engines', u'Analytics'], u'name': u'Elasticsearch Essentials', u'Publishing Date': u'2015-31-12', u'Publication': u'Packt-Pub'}, u'_index': u'1', u'_version': 1, u'found': True, u'_id': u'1'}
[u'Big Data', u'search engines', u'Analytics']
```

> In the response, all the field names start with u that denotes Unicode. In normal scenarios, this format does not affect when any task is performed with the response data. However, in some cases, you might require this to be in the form of a plain JSON format. To do this, simply import the JSON module of Python in your code and call the `json.dumps(response)` function with the response object inside its parameter.

All the fields are returned inside the `_source` object and a particular field can be accessed using this:

```
response.get('_source').get(field_name)
```

Updating documents

As we have seen in *Chapter 1, Getting Started with Elasticsearch*, a partial document update can be done using scripts with the `_update` API. With a Python client, it can be done using the `update` function. We can do an update in two scenarios; either to completely replace the value for a field, or to append the value inside that field. To use scripts to update the documents, make sure you have dynamic scripting enabled.

Replacing the value of a field completely

To replace the value of an existing field, you need to simply pass the new value inside the `_source` of the document in the following way:

```
script ={"script" : "ctx._source.category= \"data analytics\""}
es.update(index=index_name, doc_type=doc_type, body=script, id='1',
ignore=404)
```

After this request, the `category` field will contain only one value, `data analytics`.

Appending a value in an array

Sometimes you need to preserve the original value and append some new data inside it. Groovy scripting supports the use of parameters with the `param` attribute inside scripts, which helps us to achieve this task:

```
script =  {"script" : "ctx._source.category += tag",
"params" : {
"tag" : "Python"
}
        }
es.update(index=index_name, doc_type=doc_type, body=script, id='1', ignore=404)
```

After this request, the `category` field will contain two values: `data analytics` and `Python`.

Updates using doc

Partial updates can be done using the `doc` parameter instead of `body`, where `doc` is a dictionary object that holds the partial fields that are to be updated. This is the preferable method to do partial updates. It can be done as shown in the following example:

```
es.update(index=index_name, doc_type=doc_type, 'doc': {'new_field': 'doing partial update with a new field'}, id='1', ignore=404)
```

> In most cases, where many documents need to be updated, document re-indexing makes more sense than updating it through a script or with `doc`.

Checking document existence

If it is required to check whether a document exists, you can use the `exists` function that returns either `true` or `false` in its response:

```
es.exists(index=index_name, doc_type=doc_type, id='1'):
```

Deleting a document

Document deletion can be done using the `delete` function in the following way:

```
es.delete(index=index_name, doc_type=doc_type, id='1', ignore=404)
```

CRUD operations using Java

In this section, we will go through the Elasticsearch Java client to perform the CRUD operations. To use a Java client of Elasticsearch, you can either build a Maven project (recommended) or simply add Elasticsearch jar files, which ship with the Elasticsearch installation file, into your project classpath.

You can include an Elasticsearch dependency in your Maven project by adding the following code to the project's `pom.xml` file:

```xml
<dependency>
    <groupId>org.elasticsearch</groupId>
    <artifactId>elasticsearch</artifactId>
    <version>2.0.0</version>
</dependency>
```

Connecting with Elasticsearch

To connect with Elasticsearch using its transport client, you need to add the following imports:

```java
import org.elasticsearch.client.Client;
import org.elasticsearch.client.transport.TransportClient;
import org.elasticsearch.common.settings.Settings;
import org.elasticsearch.common.transport.InetSocketTransportAddress;
```

After this, a connection can be created with the following code snippet:

```java
static Client client;
static Settings settings;
public static Client getEsConnection()
  {
  settings = Settings.settingsBuilder().put("cluster.name", "elasticsearch").put("path.home", "/").put("client.transport.ping_timeout","10s").build();
   try {
     client = TransportClient.builder().settings(settings)
          .addTransportAddress(new InetSocketTransportAddress(InetAddress.getByName("localhost"), 9300));
   } catch (UnknownHostException e) {
     e.printStackTrace();
   }
   return client;
  }
```

[50]

To connect with more than one node of a single cluster, you can add more transport addresses in this way:

```
client = TransportClient.builder().settings(settings).build()
    .addTransportAddress(new InetSocketTransportAddress(InetAddress.getByName("localhost"), 9300))
    .addTransportAddress(new InetSocketTransportAddress(InetAddress.getByName("some_other_host"), 9300));
```

Note that to create a connection with Elasticsearch using Java API, you need to first create settings by specifying the cluster name and can optionally provide a timeout that defaults to 5s.

This setting is then used by the transport client to create a connection with the Elasticsearch cluster over the TCP port 9300.

Indexing a document

To index a single document at once (sequential indexing), you can create documents in multiple ways, such as using plain JSON strings, or using Jackson API or your familiar HashMap. The following example shows the use of HashMap to create a document:

1. The first import will be as follows:

   ```
   import org.elasticsearch.action.index.IndexResponse;
   ```

2. Then create the document:

   ```
   Map<String, Object> document1= new HashMap<String, Object>();
       document1.put("screen_name", "d_bharvi");
       document1.put("followers_count", 2000);
       document1.put("create_at", "2015-09-20");
   ```

3. The preceding document can be indexed with the following code, assuming you have an object of the client available in your code:

   ```
   IndexResponse response = client.prepareIndex()
       .setIndex("IndexName").setType("docType")
       .setId("1").setSource(document1)
       .execute().actionGet();
   ```

   In the preceding code, the setIndex and setType methods take the index name and the name of the document type correspondingly.

   - The setSource method takes the actual data for indexing.
   - The setId method takes the unique document identifier. This is optional; Elasticsearch will generate it dynamically if it is not set.

There are many other methods available, which will see in the upcoming chapter.

Putting Elasticsearch into Action

Fetching a document

To fetch a document from Elasticsearch, you need its document ID. Once you know the document ID, it is simple to fetch it. Just add the following import:

```
import org.elasticsearch.action.get.GetResponse;
```

Then, you can get the document using `prepareGet`:

```
GetResponse response = client.prepareGet()
    .setIndex(indexName).setType(docType)
    .setId("1").execute().actionGet();
```

Updating a document

As you are aware, documents can be updated in two ways; first using `doc`, and the other way is to use script. In both cases, you need to import `UpdateResponse` to you, code:

```
import org.elasticsearch.action.delete.UpdateResponse;
```

Updating a document using doc

To do a partial update, you can create the object to be appended or replace an existing value for a field:

```
Map<String, Object> partialDoc1= new HashMap<String, Object>();
partialDoc1.put("user_name", "Bharvi Dixit");
```

Then, you can send it to Elasticsearch using the `prepareUpdate` method by setting the partial document inside the `setDoc` method:

```
UpdateResponse response = client.prepareUpdate()
  .setIndex(indexName).setType(docType)
  .setId("1").setDoc(partialDoc1)
  .execute().actionGet();
```

Updating a document using script

To use scripts for updating, first you need to make sure that you have enabled dynamic scripting in your `elasticsearch.yml` file. Then, you need to import the following classes into your code:

```
import org.elasticsearch.script.Script;
import org.elasticsearch.script.ScriptService.ScriptType;
```

Once the import is done, you can do the update in the following way:

```
String script = "ctx._source.user_name = \"Alberto Paro\"";
UpdateResponse response = client.prepareUpdate()
  .setIndex(indexName).setType(docType)
  .setScript(new Script(script, ScriptType.INLINE, "groovy", null)).
setId("1").execute().actionGet();
```

Note that in this example, the `INLINE` scripts have been used. You can also use file scripts or indexed scripts . You can find more about scripting here: https://www.elastic.co/guide/en/elasticsearch/reference/2.0/modules-scripting.html.

Deleting documents

To delete a single document in a single request, import the following line of code:

```
import org.elasticsearch.action.delete.DeleteResponse;
```

You can delete the document with the `prepareDelete` method using the document ID:

```
DeleteResponse response = client.prepareDelete()
    .setIndex(indexName).setType(docType)
    .setId("1").execute().actionGet();
```

Creating a search database

It's always good to have some practical examples with real data sets, and what could be better than real-time social media data? In this section, we will write the code that will fetch tweets from Twitter in real time based on the search keywords provided. There are three dependencies of the code written in this section:

- `tweepy` is a Python client for Twitter.
- `elasticsearch` is a Python client for Elasticsearch that we have already installed.
- For Twitter API access token keys, please follow the instructions at this link. https://dev.twitter.com/oauth/overview/application-owner-access-tokens, to create a sample Twitter application and get all the four keys that are needed to interact with the Twitter API. These four tokens are named: **Access Token**, **Access Token Secret**, **Consumer Key**, and **Consumer Secret**.

Putting Elasticsearch into Action

After generating the `auth` tokens and keys stored it inside `config.py` with the variable names: `consumer_key`, `consumer_secret`, `access_token`, and `access_token_secret`. The next step is to install `tweepy` using this command:

`pip install tweepy`

 If you get any error during the installation of `tweepy`, the version of `pip` may need to be upgraded. To upgrade the `pip` version use the following command: `pip install 'pip>1.5' --upgrade`.

It's good to do some hands-on while creating mappings. For this, first you need to understand the JSON data of Twitter. You can view a sample on the following URL and accordingly create mappings with the appropriate field types and analyzers: https://gist.github.com/bharvidixit/0d35b7ac907127860e58.

Once the mapping is created, write the code to start fetching tweets and indexing them in our index with the name `twitter`, and type `tweet`:

```
from tweepy import OAuthHandler
from tweepy import Stream
from tweepy.streaming import StreamListener
from elasticsearch import Elasticsearch
import config
import json

es = Elasticsearch('localhost:9200')

class StdOutListener(StreamListener):
    """A listener handles tweets that are received from the stream.
    This listener dumps the tweets into elasticsearch
    """
    counter = 0
    total_docs_to_be_indexed = 10000

    def on_data(self, data):
        print data
        while self.total_docs_to_be_indexed > self.counter:

            tweet = json.loads(data)
            self.index_tweet(tweet)
            self.counter += 1
            return True

    def index_tweet(self, tweet):
```

```
        es.index(index='twitter', doc_type='tweets',id=tweet['id_str'],
body=tweet)

def on_error(self, status):
        print status
    pass

#code execution starts here
if __name__ == '__main__':
    listener = StdOutListener()
    auth = OAuthHandler(config.consumer_key, config.consumer_secret)
    auth.set_access_token(config.access_token, config.access_token_
secret)
    stream = Stream(auth, listener)
#set the terms for tracking and fetching tweets from Twitter
    stream.filter(track=['crime', 'blast', 'earthquake', 'riot',
'politics'])
```

Elasticsearch Query-DSL

Query-DSL is a JSON interface provided by Elasticsearch to write queries in the JSON format. It allows you to write any query that you may write in Lucene. The queries can be as simple as just matching simple terms, or they can be very complex.

Until now, to retrieve documents from Elasticsearch we used a `GET` request that was dependent on the ID to search and retrieve the document. You can extend the searches in similar way; for example: `localhost:9200/index_name/doc_type/_search?q=category:databases`.

The preceding query is a typical Lucene `query string` that searches for the `databases` word inside the `category` field. Submitting queries to Elasticsearch in this way is very limited, so you will learn about Query-DSL now.

Syntax:

The Query-DSL follows the following syntax:

```
{
  "query": {},
  "from": 0,
  "size": 20,
  "_source": ["field1","field2"]
}
```

Understanding Query-DSL parameters

- `query`: The `query` object contains all the queries that need to be passed to Elasticsearch. For example, the query to find all the documents that belong to a search category can written as follows:

  ```
  GET index_name/doc_type/_search
  {
    "query": {
      "query_string": {
    "default_field": "category",
        "query": "search"
      }
    }
  }
  ```

- `from` and `size`: These parameters control the pagination and the result size to be returned after querying. The `from` parameter is used to specify the starting point from which document the results will be returned. It defaults to `0`. The `size` parameter, which defaults to `10`, specifies how many top documents will be returned from the total matched documents in a corpus.

- `_source`: This is an optional parameter that takes field names in an array format, which are to be returned in the query results. It by default returns all the fields stored inside the `_source` field. If you do not want to return any field, you can specify `_source: false`.

Elasticsearch queries majorly fall into two categories:

- **Basic Queries**: These queries include normal keyword searching inside indexes.
- **Compound Queries**: These queries combine multiple basic queries together with Boolean clauses.

 We will be using our Twitter dataset to perform all the queries in this and the upcoming chapters.

Query types

At the abstract level, there are two major categories of queries in Elasticsearch:

- **Full-Text Search Queries**: These are the queries that usually run over text fields like a tweet text. These queries understand the field mapping, and depending on the field type and analyzer used for that field and query, the text goes through an analysis phase (similar to indexing) to find the relevant documents.
- **Term-based search queries**: Unlike full-text queries, term-based queries do not go through an analysis process. These queries are used to match the exact terms stored inside an inverted index.

> There exist a few other categories of queries such as **Compound Queries**, **Geo Queries**, and **Relational Queries**. We will cover **Compound Queries** in this chapter and the rest will be covered in the subsequent chapters.

Full-text search queries

The most important queries in this category are the following:

- `match_all`
- `match`
- `match_phrase`
- `multi_match`
- `query_string`

match_all

The simplest query in Elasticsearch is `match_all` query that matches all the documents. It gives a generous `_score` of `1.0` to each document in the index. The syntax of the `match_all` query is as follows:

```
{
   "query": {
      "match_all": {}
   }
}
```

match query

The text passed inside a `match` query goes through the analysis phase and, depending on the operator (which defaults to `OR`), documents are matched. For example:

```
{
  "query": {
    "match": {
      "text": "Build Great Web Apps",
      "operator" : "and"
    }
  }
}
```

The preceding query will match the documents that contain the `Build`, `Great`, `Web`, and `Apps` terms in the `text` field. If we had used the `OR` operator, it would have matched the documents containing any of these terms.

> If you want the exact matches, you need to pass the text in the following way so that the text is not broken into tokens:
>
> ```
> {
>   "query": {
>     "match": {
>       "text": "\"Build Great Web Apps\""
>     }
>   }
> }
> ```
>
> The preceding query will match the documents in which `Build Great Web Apps` appear together exactly in the same order.

Phrase search

`Match` query provides an option to search phrases with the `type` parameter in the following way:

```
{
  "query": {
    "match": {
      "text": "Build Great Web Apps",
      "type" : "phrase"
    }
  }
}
```

multi match

The `multi_match` query is similar to the `match` query but it provides options to search the same terms in more than one field at one go. For example:

```
{
  "query": {
  "multi_match": {
    "query": "Build Great Web Apps",
    "fields": ["text","retweeted_status.text"]
  }
  }
}
```

The preceding query will search the words `Build`, `Great`, `Web`, and `Apps` inside the two fields `text` and `retweeted_status.text`, and will return the relevant results in a sorted order based on the score each document gets. If you want to match only those documents in which all the terms are present, then use the `and` keyword in the `operator` parameter.

query_string

In comparison to all the other queries available in Elasticsearch, the `query_string` query provides a full Lucene syntax to be used in it. It uses a query parser to construct an actual query out of the provided text. Similar to the `match` query, it also goes through the analysis phase. The following is the syntax for `query_string`:

```
{
  "query": {
    "query_string": {
      "default_field": "text",
      "query": "text:analytics^2 +text:data -user.name:d_bharvi"
    }
  }
}
```

The `match` query that we used in the previous section can be written using a query string in the following way:

```
{
  "query": {
    "query_string": {
      "default_field": "text",
      "query": "Build Great Web Apps"
    }
  }
}
```

Term-based search queries

The most important queries in this category are the following:

- Term query
- Terms query
- Range query
- Exists query
- Missing query

Term query

The `term` query does an exact term matching in a given field. So, you need to provide the exact term to get the correct results. For example, if you have used a lowercase filter while indexing, you need to pass the terms in lowercase while querying with the `term` query.

The syntax for a `term` query is as follows:

```
{
  "query": {
    "term": {
      "text": "elasticsearch"
    }
  }
}
```

Terms query

If you want to search more than one term in a single field, you can use the `terms` query. For example, to search all the tweets in which the hashtags used are either `bomb` or `blast`, you can write a query like this:

```
{
  "query": {
    "terms": {
      "entities.hashtags": [
        "bomb",
        "blast"
      ],
      "minimum_match": 1
    }
  }
}
```

The `minimum_match` specifies the number of minimum terms that should match in each document. This parameter is optional.

Range queries

`Range` queries are used to find data within a certain range. The syntax of a `range` query is as follows and is the same for date fields as well as number fields such as `integer`, `long`, and so on:

```
{
  "query": {
    "range": {
      "user.followers_count": {
        "gte": 100,
        "lte": 200
      }
    }
  }
}
```

The preceding query will find all the tweets created by users whose follower count is between 100 and 200. The parameters supported in the range queries are: `gt`, `lt`, `gte`, and `lte`.

> Please note that if you use `range` queries on string fields, you will get weird results as strings. String ranges are calculated lexicographically or alphabetically, so a string stored as 50 will be lesser than 6. In addition, doing `range` queries on strings is a heavier operation in comparison to numbers.

`Range` queries on dates allow date math operations. So, for example, if you want to find all the tweets from the last one hour, you can use the following query:

```
{
  "query": {
    "range": {
      "created_at": {
        "gt": "now-1h"
      }
    }
  }
}
```

Similarly, months (`M`), minutes (`m`), years (`y`), and seconds (`s`) are allowed in the query.

Exists queries

The `exists` query matches documents that have at least one non-value in a given field. For example, the following query will find all the tweets that are replies to any other tweet:

```
{
  "query":{
    "constant_score":{
      "filter":{
        "exists":{"field":"in_reply_to_user_id"}
      }
    }
  }
}
```

Missing queries

`Missing` queries are the opposite of `exists` queries. They are used to find the documents that contain null values. For instance, the following query finds all the tweets that do not contain any hashtags:

```
{
  "query":{
    "constant_score":{
      "filter":{
        "missing":{"field":"hashtags"}
      }
    }
  }
}
```

> **The story of filters**
>
> Before version 2.0.0, Elasticsearch used to have two different objects for querying data: **Queries** and **Filters**. Both used to differ in functionality and performance.
>
> Queries were used to find out how relevant a document was to a particular query by calculating a score for each document, whereas filters were used to match certain criteria and were cacheable to enable faster execution. This means that if a filter matched 1,000 documents, with the help of bloom filters, Elasticsearch used to cache them in the memory to get them quickly in case the same filter was executed again.
>
>
>
> However, with the release of Lucene 5.0, which is used by Elasticsearch version 2.0.0, things have completely changed and both the queries and filters are now the same internal object. Users need not worry about caching and performance anymore, as Elasticsearch will take care of it. However, one must be aware of the contextual difference between a query and a filter that was listed in the previous paragraph.
>
> In the query context, put the queries that ask the questions about document relevance and score calculations, while in the filter context, put the queries that need to match a simple yes/no question.
>
> If you have been using an Elasticsearch version below 2.0.0, please go through the breaking changes here: `https://www.elastic.co/guide/en/elasticsearch/reference/2.0/breaking-changes-2.0.html`, and migrate your application code accordingly since there have been a lot of changes, including the removal of various filters.

Compound queries

Compound queries are offered by Elasticsearch to connect multiple simple queries together to make your search better. A compound query clause can combine any number of queries including compound ones that allow you to write very complex logic for your searches. You will need them at every step while creating any search application.

>
>
> In the previous chapter, we saw how Lucene calculates a score based on the TF/IDF formula. This score is calculated for each and every query we send to Elasticsearch. Thus, when we combine queries in a compound form, the scores of all the queries are combined to calculate the overall score of the document.

The primary compound queries are as follows:

- `Bool` query
- `Not` query
- `Function score` query (will be discussed in *Chapter 8, Controlling Relevancy*)

Bool queries

`Bool` queries allow us to wrap up many queries clauses together including `bool` clauses. The documents are matched based on the combinations of these Boolean clauses that are listed as follows:

- `must`: The queries that are written inside this clause must match in order to return the documents.
- `should`: The queries written inside the `should` clause may or may not have a match but if the `bool` query has no `must` clause inside it, then at least one `should` condition needs to be matched in order to return the documents.
- `must_not`: The queries wrapped inside this clause must not appear in the matching documents.
- `filter`: A query wrapped inside this clause must appear in the matching documents. However, this does not contribute to scoring. The structure of `bool` queries is as follows:

  ```
  {
    "query":{
    "bool":{
      "must":[{}],
      "should":[{}],
      "must_not":[{}]
      "filter":[{}]
      }
    }
  }
  ```

There are some additional parameters supported by bool queries that are listed here:

- `boost`: This parameter controls the score of each query, which is wrapped inside the `must` or `should` clause.
- `minimum_should_match`: This is only used for the `should` clauses. Using this, we can specify how many `should` clauses must match in order to return a document.

- `disable_coord`: The bool queries by default use query coordination for all the `should` clauses; it is a good thing to have since the more clauses get matched, the higher the score a document will get. However, look at the following example where we may need to disable this:

```
{
"query":{
  "bool":{
    "disable_coord":true,
    "should":[
       {"term":{"text":{"value":"turmoil"}}},
       {"term":{"text":{"value":"riot"}}}
       ]
    }
  }
}
```

In the preceding example, inside the text field, we are looking for the terms `turmoil` and `riot`, which are synonyms of each other. In these cases, we do not care how many synonyms are present in the document since all have the same meaning. In these kinds of scenarios, we can disable query coordination by setting `disable_coord` to `true`, so that similar clauses do not impact the score factor computation.

Not queries

The `not` query is used to filter out the documents that match the query. For example, we can use the following to get the tweets that are not created within a certain range of time:

```
{
  "filter": {
    "not": {
      "filter": {
        "range": {
          "created_at": {
            "from": "2015-10-01",
            "to": "2010-10-30"
          }
        }
      }
    }
  }
}
```

Please note that any filter can be used inside bool queries with the `must`, `must_not`, or `should` blocks.

Search requests using Python

All the queries that we have discussed can be performed with the Elasticsearch Python client using the `search` function. To do this, first store the query inside a variable that is `query` in the following example:

```
query = {
    "query": {
        "match_all": {}
    },
}
```

Call the `search` function with all the parameters including the index name, document type, and query. The size parameter used in the following search request can also be included inside the query itself:

```
response = es.search(index='twitter', doc_type='tweets', body=query,
size=2, request_timeout=20)
```

> To search against more than one index, instead of using a string value, you need to use a list of index names. The same applies for document types too.

The response data comes in the following format:

```
{
  "hits": {
    "hits": [
      {
        "_score": 1,
        "_type": "tweets",
        "_id": "649956033515773953",
        "_source": {
          "contributors": null,
          "truncated": false,
          "text": "RT @lexcanroar: \"No mass shootings in the past 30 years have been stopped by an armed civilian.\""
             .
             .
             .
      },
      {
         ...
```

```
      }
        "_index": "twitter"
      }
    ],
    "total": 124,
    "max_score": 1
  },
  "_shards": {
    "successful": 5,
    "failed": 0,
    "total": 5
  },
  "took": 5,
  "timed_out": false
}
```

The response contains an object hit that has an array of hits containing all the documents. Further, each hit inside an array of hits contains the following fields in it:

- _score: The document score with respect to the query
- _index: The index name to which the document belongs
- _type: The document type to which the document belongs
- _id: The unique ID of the document
- _source: This contains all the fields and values

The documents inside _source can be accessed with the following code:

```
for hit in response['hits']['hits']:
      print hit.get('_source')
```

Search requests using Java

While it's easy to write a JSON query and directly use it with the Python client, using Java client requires a bit of expertise to create queries using Elasticsearch Java APIs.

In Java, there is the `QueryBuilder` class that helps you in constructing queries. Once the queries are created, you can execute that query with the client's `prepareSearch` method.

First of all, you need the following imports in your code:

```
import org.elasticsearch.index.query.QueryBuilder;
import org.elasticsearch.index.query.QueryBuilders;
import org.elasticsearch.search.SearchHit;
```

Then you can start building queries and executing them:

```
QueryBuilder query = QueryBuilders.termQuery("screen_name", "d_
bharvi");
SearchResponse response = client.prepareSearch()
    .setIndices(indexName).setTypes(docType)
    .setQuery(query).setFrom(0).setSize(10)
    .execute().actionGet();
```

The preceding code shows an example of creating term queries where we search for a term, d_bharvi, inside the screen_name field.

Similarly, you can create all types of query against the QueryBuilders class. To take another example, a match_all query can be created by this:

```
QueryBuilders.matchAllQuery();
```

The other parameters are as follows:

- setIndices: This is required as search requests support a single search query to be executed against more than one index. You can specify comma-separated index names if you want to do so.
- setTypes: Similar to searching inside more than one index, a search can be executed inside more than one document type. Here, you can provide comma-separated type names if needed.
- setQuery: This method takes the actual query built using QueryBuilder.
- setFrom and setSize: These parameters are used for pagination purposes and to specify the number of documents that need to be returned.

Parsing search responses

A search response contains multiple document hits inside it that can be iterated by converting the response hits into a SearchHit array:

```
SearchHit[] results = response.getHits().getHits();
    for (SearchHit hit : results) {
        System.out.println(hit.getSource());
        //process documents
    }
```

There are many other methods supported for search requests. A full list can be found at this gist: https://gist.github.com/bharvidixit/357367e30cea59bb5d62.

Sorting your data

Data in Elasticsearch is by default sorted by a relevance score, which is computed using the Lucene scoring formula, TF/IDF. This relevance score is a floating point value that is returned with search results inside the `_score` parameter. By default, results are sorted in descending order.

> Sorting on nested and geo-points fields will be covered in the upcoming chapters.

See the following query for an example:

```
{
  "query": {
    "match": {
      "text": "data analytics"
    }
  }
}
```

We are searching for tweets that contain the `data` or `analytics` terms in their text fields. In some cases, however, we do not want the results to be sorted based on `_score`. Elasticsearch provides a way to sort documents in various ways. Let's explore how this can be done.

Sorting documents by field values

This section covers the sorting of documents based on the fields that contain a single value such as `created_at`, or `followers_count`. Please note that we are not talking about sorting string-based fields here.

Suppose we want to sort tweets that contain `data` or `analytics` in their text field based on their creation time in ascending order:

```
{
  "query":{
    "match":{"text":"data analytics"}
  },
  "sort":[
    {"created_at":{"order":"asc"}}
  ]
}
```

Putting Elasticsearch into Action

In the response of the preceding query, `max_score` and `_score` will have null as values. They are not calculated because `_score` is not used for sorting. You will see an additional field, `sort`. This field contains the date value in the long format, which has been used for sorting.

Sorting on more than one field

In scenarios where it is required to sort documents based on more than one field, one can use the following syntax for sorting:

```
"sort": [
{"created_at":{"order":"asc"},"followers_count":{"order":"asc"}}
]
```

With the above query, the results will be sorted first using tweet creation time, and if two tweets have the same tweet creation time, then they will be sorted using the followers count.

Sorting multivalued fields

Multivalued fields such as arrays of dates contain more than one value, and you cannot specify on which value to sort. So in this case, the single value needs to be calculated first using `mode` parameter that takes `min`, `max`, `avg`, `median`, or `sum` as a value. For example, in the following query the sorting will be done on the maximum value inside the `price` field of each document:

```
"sort" : [
     {"price" : {"order" : "asc", "mode" : "max"}}
  ]
```

Sorting on string fields

The `analyzed` string fields are also multivalued fields since they contain multiple tokens and because of performance considerations; do not use sorting on analyzed fields.

The string field on which sorting is to be done must be `not_analyzed` or keyword tokenized so that the field contains only one single token.

> Sorting is an expensive process. All the values for the field on which sorting is to be performed are loaded into memory. So, you should have an ample amount of memory on the node to perform sorting. The data type of the field should also be chosen carefully while creating mapping. For example, `short` can be used in place of `integer` or `long` if the value is not going to be bigger.

Document routing

Document routing is the concept of indexing a document to a particular shard. By default, Elasticsearch tries to evenly distribute the documents among all the shards in an index. For this, it uses the following formula:

shard = hash(routing) % number_of_primary_shards

Here, `shard` is the shard number in which the document will be indexed and routing is the `_id` of a document.

We can explicitly specify the routing value while indexing, updating, fetching, or searching data in Elasticsearch. Custom routing yields faster indexing as well as faster searches. However, it is more about designing for scale that we will study in the following chapters.

Summary

In this chapter, you learned how to use Python and Java clients for Elasticsearch and perform CRUD operations using it. We also covered Elasticsearch Query-DSL, various queries, and data sorting techniques in this chapter.

In the next chapter, we will take a deep dive into the Elasticsearch aggregation framework.

4
Aggregations for Analytics

Elasticsearch is a search engine at the core but what makes it more usable is its ability to make complex data analytics in an easy and simple way. The volume of data is growing rapidly and companies want to perform analysis on data in real time. Whether it is log, real-time streaming of data, or static data, Elasticsearch works wonderfully in getting a summarization of data through its aggregation capabilities.

In this chapter, we will cover the following topics:

- Introducing the aggregation framework
- Metric and bucket aggregations
- Combining search, buckets, and metrics
- Memory pressure and implications

Introducing the aggregation framework

The aggregation functionality is completely different from search and enables you to ask sophisticated questions of the data. The use cases of aggregation vary from building analytical reports to getting real-time analysis of data and taking quick actions.

Also, despite being different in functionality, aggregations can operate along the usual search requests. Therefore, you can search or filter your data, and at the same time, you can also perform aggregation on the same datasets matched by search/filter criteria in a single request. A simple example can be to *find the maximum number of hashtags used by users related to tweets that has crime in the text field*. Aggregations enable you to calculate and summarize data about the current query on the fly. They can be used for all sorts of tasks such as dynamic counting of result values to building a histogram.

Aggregations come in two flavors: **metrics** and **buckets**.

- **Metrics**: Metrics are used to do statistics calculations, such as min, max, average, on a field of a document that falls into a certain criteria. An example of a metric can be to find the maximum count of followers among the user's follower counts.
- **Buckets**: Buckets are simply the grouping of documents that meet a certain criteria. They are used to categorize documents, for example:
    - The category of loans can fall into the buckets of home loan or personal loan
    - The category of an employee can be either male or female

Elasticsearch offers a wide variety of buckets to categorize documents in many ways such as by days, age range, popular terms, or locations. However, all of them work on the same principle: **document categorization based on some criteria**.

The most interesting part is that bucket aggregations can be nested within each other. This means that a bucket can contain other buckets within it. Since each of the buckets defines a set of documents, one can create another aggregation on that bucket, which will be executed in the context of its parent bucket. For example, a country-wise bucket can include a state-wise bucket, which can further include a city-wise bucket.

In SQL terms, metrics are simply functions such as `MIN()`, `MAX()`, `SUM()`, `COUNT()`, and `AVG()`, where buckets group the results using `GROUP BY` queries.

Aggregation syntax

Aggregation follows the following syntax:

```
"aggregations" : {
    "<aggregation_name>" : {
        "<aggregation_type>" : {
            <aggregation_body>
        }
        [,"aggregations" : { [<sub_aggregation>]+ } ]?
    }
    [,"<aggregation_name_2>" : { ... } ]*
}
```

Let's understand how the preceding structure works:

- **aggregations**: The aggregations objects (which can also be replaced with agg) in the preceding structure holds the aggregations that have to be computed. There can be more than one aggregation inside this object.
- **<aggregation_name>**: This is a user-defined logical name for the aggregations that are held by the aggregations object (for example, if you want to compute the average age of users in the index, it makes sense to give the name as avg_age). These logical names will also be used to uniquely identify the aggregations in the response.
- **<aggregation_type>**: Each aggregation has a specific type, for example, terms, sum, avg, min, and so on.
- **<aggregation_body>**: Each type of aggregation defines its own body depending on the nature of the aggregation (for example, an avg aggregation on a specific field will define the field on which the average will be calculated).
- **<sub_aggregation>**: The sub aggregations are defined on the bucketing aggregation level and are computed for all the buckets built by the bucket aggregation. For example, if you define a set of aggregations under the range aggregation, the sub aggregations will be computed for the range buckets that are defined.

Look at the following JSON structure to understand a more simple structure of aggregations:

```
{
  "aggs": {
    "NAME1": {
      "AGG_TYPE": {},
      "aggs": {
        "NAME": {
          "AGG_TYPE": {}
        }
      }
    },
    "NAME2": {
      "AGG_TYPE": {}
    }
  }
}
```

Extracting values

Aggregations typically work on the values extracted from the aggregated document set. These values can be extracted either from a specific field using the field key inside the aggregation body or can also be extracted using a script.

While it's easy to define a field to be used to aggregate data, the syntax of using scripts needs some special understanding. The benefit of using scripts is that one can combine the values from more than one field to use as a single value inside an aggregation.

> Using scripting requires much more computation power and slows down the performance on bigger datasets.

The following are the examples of extracting values from a script:

Extracting a value from a single field:

```
{ "script" : "doc['field_name'].value" }
```

Extracting and combining values from more than one field:

```
"script": "doc['author.first_name'].value + ' ' + doc['author.last_name'].value"
```

The scripts also support the use of parameters using the param keyword. For example:

```
{
  "avg": {
    "field": "price",
    "script": {
      "inline": "_value * correction",
      "params": {
        "correction": 1.5
      }
    }
  }
}
```

The preceding aggregation calculates the average price after multiplying each value of the price field with 1.5, which is used as an inline function parameter.

Returning only aggregation results

Elasticsearch by default computes aggregations on a complete set of documents using the `match_all` query and returns 10 documents by default along with the output of the aggregation results.

If you do not want to include the documents in the response, you need to set the value of the size parameter to 0 inside your query. Note that you do not need to use the from parameter in this case. This is a very useful parameter because it avoids document relevancy calculation and the inclusion of documents in the response, and only returns the aggregated data.

Metric aggregations

As explained in the previous sections, metric aggregations allow you to find out the statistical measurement of the data, which includes the following:

- Computing basic statistics
    - Computing in a combined way: `stats` aggregation
    - Computing separately : `min`, `max`, `sum`, `value_count`, aggregations
- Computing extended statistics: `extended_stats` aggregation
- Computing distinct counts: `cardinality` aggregation

> Metric aggregations are fundamentally categorized in two forms:
> - **single-value metric**: `min`, `max`, `sum`, `value_count`, `avg`, and `cardinality` aggregations
> - **multi-value metric**: `stats` and `extended_stats` aggregations

Computing basic stats

The basic statistics include: `min`, `max`, `sum`, `count`, and `avg`. These statistics can be computed in the following two ways and can only be performed on numeric fields.

Combined stats

All the stats mentioned previously can be calculated with a single aggregation query.

Python example

```
query = {
 "aggs": {
   "follower_counts_stats": {
     "stats": {
       "field": "user.followers_count"
     }
   }
  }
}
res = es.search(index='twitter', doc_type='tweets', body=query)
print resp
```

The response would be as follows:

```
"aggregations": {
    "follower_counts_stats": {
        "count": 124,
        "min": 2,
        "max": 38121,
        "avg": 2102.814516129032,
        "sum": 260749
    }
}
```

In the preceding response, count is the total values on which the aggregation is executed.

- `min` is the minimum follower count of a user
- `max` is the maximum follower count of a user
- `avg` is the average count of followers
- `Sum` is the addition of all the followers count

Java example

 In Java, all the metric aggregations can be created using the `MetricsAggregationBuilder` and `AggregationBuilders` classes. However, you need to import a specific package into your code to parse the results.

To build and execute a `stats` aggregation in Java, first do the following imports in the code:

```
import org.elasticsearch.search.aggregations.metrics.stats.Stats;
```

Then build the aggregation in the following way:

```
MetricsAggregationBuilder aggregation =
        AggregationBuilders
              .stats("follower_counts_stats")
              .field("user.followers_count");
```

This aggregation can be executed with the following code snippet:

```
SearchResponse response = client.prepareSearch(indexName).
setTypes(docType).setQuery(QueryBuilders.matchAllQuery())
   .addAggregation(aggregation)
   .execute().actionGet();
```

The `stats` aggregation response can be parsed as follows:

```
Stats agg = sr.getAggregations().get("follower_counts_stats");
long min = agg.getMin();
long max = agg.getMax();
double avg = agg.getAvg();
long sum = agg.getSum();
long count = agg.getCount();
```

Computing stats separately

In addition to computing these basic stats in a single query, Elasticsearch provides multiple aggregations to compute them one by one. The following are the aggregation types that fall into this category:

- `value_count`: This counts the number of values that are extracted from the aggregated documents
- `min`: This finds the minimum value among the numeric values extracted from the aggregated documents

- `max`: This finds the maximum value among the numeric values extracted from the aggregated documents
- `avg`: This finds the average value among the numeric values extracted from the aggregated documents
- `sum`: This finds the sum of all the numeric values extracted from the aggregated documents

To perform these aggregations, you just need to use the following syntax:

```
{
  "aggs": {
    "aggaregation_name": {
      "aggrigation_type": {
        "field": "name_of_the_field"
      }
    }
  }
}
```

Python example

```
query = {
  "aggs": {
    "follower_counts_stats": {
      "sum": {
        "field": "user.followers_count"
      }
    }
  },"size": 0
}
res = es.search(index='twitter', doc_type='tweets', body=query)
```

We used the `sum` aggregation type in the preceding query; for other aggregations such as `min`, `max`, `avg`, and `value_count`, just replace the type of aggregation in the query.

Java example

To perform these aggregations using the Java client, you need to follow this syntax:

```
MetricsAggregationBuilder aggregation =
        AggregationBuilders
                .sum("follower_counts_stats")
                .field("user.followers_count");
```

Note that in the preceding aggregation, instead of sum, you just need to call the corresponding aggregation type to build other types of metric aggregations such as, min, max, count, and avg. The rest of the syntax remains the same.

For parsing the responses, you need to import the correct package according to the aggregation type. The following are the imports that you will need:

- **For min aggregation**:

    ```
    import org.elasticsearch.search.aggregations.metrics.min.Min;
    ```

    The parsing response will be as follows:

    ```
    Min agg = response.getAggregations().get("follower_counts_stats");
    double value = agg.getValue();
    ```

- **For max aggregation**:

    ```
    import org.elasticsearch.search.aggregations.metrics.min.Max;
    ```

    The parsing response will be:

    ```
    Max agg = response.getAggregations().get("follower_counts_stats");
    double value = agg.getValue();
    ```

- **For avg aggregation**:

    ```
    import org.elasticsearch.search.aggregations.metrics.min.Avg;
    ```

    The parsing response will be this:

    ```
    Avg agg = response.getAggregations().get("follower_counts_stats");
    double value = agg.getValue();
    ```

- **For sum aggregation**:

    ```
    import org.elasticsearch.search.aggregations.metrics.min.Sum;
    ```

    This will be the parsing response:

    ```
    Sum agg = response.getAggregations().get("follower_counts_stats");
    double value = agg.getValue();
    ```

> Stats aggregations cannot contain sub aggregations. However, they can be a part of the sub aggregations of buckets.

Computing extended stats

The `extended_stats` aggregation is the extended version of `stats` aggregation and provides advanced statistics of the data, which include sum of square, variance, standard deviation, and standard deviation bounds.

So, if we hit the query with the `extended_stats` aggregation on the followers count field, we will get the following data:

```
"aggregations": {
    "follower_counts_stats": {
        "count": 124,
        "min": 2,
        "max": 38121,
        "avg": 2102.814516129032,
        "sum": 260749,
        "sum_of_squares": 3334927837,
        "variance": 22472750.441402186,
        "std_deviation": 4740.543264374051,
        "std_deviation_bounds": {
            "upper": 11583.901044877135,
            "lower": -7378.272012619071
        }
    }
}
```

Python example

```
query = {
    "aggs": {
      "follower_counts_stats": {
        "extended_stats": {
          "field": "user.followers_count"
        }
      }
    }
},"size": 0
res = es.search(index='twitter', doc_type='tweets', body=query)
```

Java example

An extended aggregation is build using the Java client in the following way:

```
MetricsAggregationBuilder aggregation =
        AggregationBuilders
            .extendedStats("agg_name")
            .field("user.follower_count");
```

To parse the response of the `extended_stats` aggregation in Java, you need to have the following `import` statement:

```
import org.elasticsearch.search.aggregations.metrics.stats.extended.ExtendedStats;
```

Then the response can parsed in the following way:

```
ExtendedStats agg = response.getAggregations().get("agg_name");
double min = agg.getMin();
double max = agg.getMax();
double avg = agg.getAvg();
double sum = agg.getSum();
long count = agg.getCount();
double stdDeviation = agg.getStdDeviation();
double sumOfSquares = agg.getSumOfSquares();
double variance = agg.getVariance();
```

Finding distinct counts

The count of a distinct value of a field can be calculated using the cardinality aggregation. For example, we can use this to calculate unique users:

```
{
  "aggs": {
    "unique_users": {
      "cardinality": {
        "field": "user.screen_name"
      }
    }
  }
}
```

The response will be as follows:

```
"aggregations": {
    "unique_users": {
        "value": 122
    }
}
```

Java example

Cardinality aggregation is built using the Java client in the following way:

```
MetricsAggregationBuilder aggregation =
        AggregationBuilders
                .cardinality("unique_users")
                .field("user.screen_name");
```

To parse the response of the cardinality aggregation in Java, you need to have the following `import` statement:

```
import org.elasticsearch.search.aggregations.metrics.cardinality.Cardinality;
```

Then the response can parsed in the following way:

```
Cardinality agg = response.getAggregations().get("unique_users");
long value = agg.getValue();
```

Bucket aggregations

Similar to metric aggregations, `bucket` aggregations are also categorized into two forms: **Single buckets** that contain only a single bucket in the response, and **multi buckets** that contain more than one bucket in the response.

The following are the most important aggregations that are used to create buckets:

- Multi bucket aggregations
    - Terms aggregation
    - Range aggregation
    - Date range aggregation
    - Histogram aggregation
    - Date histogram aggregation

- Single bucket aggregation

    ○ Filter-based aggregation

 We will cover a few more aggregations such as `nested` and `geo` aggregations in subsequent chapters.

`Buckets` aggregation response formats are different from the response formats of metric aggregations. The response of a `bucket` aggregation usually comes in the following format:

```
"aggregations": {

    "aggregation_name": {
       "buckets": [
          {
             "key": value,
             "doc_count": value
          },
          ......
       ]
    }
}
```

 All the bucket aggregations can be created in Java using the `AggregationBuilder` and `AggregationBuilders` classes. You need to have the following classes imported inside your code for the same:

```
org.elasticsearch.search.aggregations.
AggregationBuilder;
```

```
org.elasticsearch.search.aggregations.
AggregationBuilders;
```

Also, all the aggregation queries can be executed with the following code snippet:

```
SearchResponse response =    client.
prepareSearch(indexName).setTypes(docType)
   .setQuery(QueryBuilders.matchAllQuery())
   .addAggregation(aggregation)
   .execute().actionGet();
```

The `setQuery()` method can take any type of Elasticsearch query, whereas the `addAggregation()` method takes the aggregation built using `AggregationBuilder`.

Terms aggregation

Terms aggregation is the most widely used aggregation type and returns the buckets that are dynamically built using one per unique value.

Let's see how to find the top 10 hashtags used in our Twitter index in descending order.

Python example

```
query = {
  "aggs": {
    "top_hashtags": {
      "terms": {
        "field": "entities.hashtags.text",
        "size": 10,
        "order": {
          "_term": "desc"
        }
      }
    }
  }
}
```

In the preceding example, the size parameter controls how many buckets are to be returned (defaults to 10) and the order parameter controls the sorting of the bucket terms (defaults to asc):

```
res = es.search(index='twitter', doc_type='tweets', body=query)
```

The response would look like this:

```
"aggregations": {
    "top_hashtags": {
        "doc_count_error_upper_bound": 0,
        "sum_other_doc_count": 44,
        "buckets": [
           {
              "key": "politics",
              "doc_count": 2
           },
           ….............
        ]
    }
}
```

Java example

`Terms` aggregation can be built as follows:

```
AggregationBuilder aggregation =
        AggregationBuilders.terms("agg").field(fieldName)
        .size(10);
```

Here, `agg` is the aggregation bucket name and `fieldName` is the field on which the aggregation is performed.

The response object can be parsed as follows:

To parse the terms aggregation response, you need to import the following class:

```
import org.elasticsearch.search.aggregations.bucket.terms.Terms;
```

Then, the response can be parsed with the following code snippet:

```
Terms screen_names = response.getAggregations().get("agg");
    for (Terms.Bucket entry : screen_names.getBuckets()) {
      entry.getKey();      // Term
      entry.getDocCount(); // Doc count
    }
```

Range aggregation

With range aggregation, a user can specify a set of ranges, where each range represents a bucket. Elasticsearch will put the document sets into the correct buckets by extracting the value from each document and matching it against the specified ranges.

Python example

```
    query = "aggs": {
      "status_count_ranges": {
        "range": {
          "field": "user.statuses_count",
          "ranges": [
            {
              "to": 50
            },
            {
              "from": 50,
              "to": 100
            }
```

Aggregations for Analytics

```
            ]
          }
        }
    },"size": 0
}
res = es.search(index='twitter', doc_type='tweets', body=query)
```

 The range aggregation always discards the *to* value for each range and only includes the from value.

The response for the preceding query request would look like this:

```
"aggregations": {
    "status_count_ranges": {
        "buckets": [
            {
                "key": "*-50.0",
                "to": 50,
                "to_as_string": "50.0",
                "doc_count": 3
            },
            {
                "key": "50.0-100.0",
                "from": 50,
                "from_as_string": "50.0",
                "to": 100,
                "to_as_string": "100.0",
                "doc_count": 3
            }
        ]
    }
}
```

Java example

Building range aggregation:

```
AggregationBuilder aggregation =
  AggregationBuilders
    .range("agg")
    .field(fieldName)
    .addUnboundedTo(1)      // from -infinity to 1 (excluded)
    .addRange(1, 100)       // from 1 to 100(excluded)
    .addUnboundedFrom(100); // from 100 to +infinity
```

Here, `agg` is the aggregation bucket name and `fieldName` is the field on which the aggregation is performed. The `addUnboundedTo` method is used when you do not specify the `from` parameter and the `addUnboundedFrom` method is used when you don't specify the `to` parameter.

Parsing the response

To parse the `range` aggregation response, you need to import the following class:

```
import org.elasticsearch.search.aggregations.bucket.range.Range;
```

Then, the response can be parsed with the following code snippet:

```
Range agg = response.getAggregations().get("agg");
for (Range.Bucket entry : agg.getBuckets()) {
    String key = entry.getKeyAsString();      // Range as key
    Number from = (Number) entry.getFrom();   // Bucket from
    Number to = (Number) entry.getTo();       // Bucket to
    long docCount = entry.getDocCount();      // Doc count
}
```

Date range aggregation

The `date range` aggregation is dedicated for date fields and is similar to range aggregation. The only difference between range and date range aggregation is that the latter allows you to use a `date math` expression inside the from and to fields. The following table shows an example of using math operations in Elasticsearch. The supported time units for the math operations are: y (year), M (month), w (week), d (day), h (hour), m (minute), and s (second):

Operation	Description
Now	Current time
Now+1h	Current time plus 1 hour
Now-1M	Current time minus 1 month
Now+1h+1m	Current time plus 1 hour plus one minute
Now+1h/d	Current time plus 1 hour rounded to the nearest day
2016-01-01||+1M/d	2016-01-01 plus 1 month rounded to the nearest day

Python example

```
query = {
    "aggs": {
        "tweets_creation_interval": {
```

```
            "range": {
              "field": "created_at",
              "format": "yyyy",
              "ranges": [
                {
                  "to": 2000
                },
                {
                  "from": 2000,
                  "to": 2005
                },
                {
                  "from": 2005
                }
              ]
            }
          }
       },"size": 0
     }
    res = es.search(index='twitter', doc_type='tweets', body=query)
    print res
```

Java example

Building date range aggregation:

```
AggregationBuilder aggregation =
  AggregationBuilders
   .dateRange("agg")
   .field(fieldName)
   .format("yyyy")
   .addUnboundedTo("2000")    // from -infinity to 2000 (excluded)
   .addRange("2000", "2005")  // from 2000 to 2005 (excluded)
   .addUnboundedFrom("2005"); // from 2005 to +infinity
```

Here, `agg` is the aggregation `bucket` name and `fieldName` is the field on which the aggregation is performed. The `addUnboundedTo` method is used when you do not specify the `from` parameter and the `addUnboundedFrom` method is used when you don't specify the `to` parameter.

Parsing the response:

To parse the `date range` aggregation response, you need to import the following class:

```
import org.elasticsearch.search.aggregations.bucket.range.Range;
import org.joda.time.DateTime;
```

Then, the response can be parsed with the following code snippet:

```
Range agg = response.getAggregations().get("agg");
for (Range.Bucket entry : agg.getBuckets()) {
  String key = entry.getKeyAsString();      // Date range as key
  DateTime fromAsDate = (DateTime) entry.getFrom(); // Date bucket from as a Date
  DateTime toAsDate = (DateTime) entry.getTo(); // Date bucket to as a Date
  long docCount = entry.getDocCount();         // Doc count
}
```

Histogram aggregation

A `histogram` aggregation works on numeric values extracted from documents and creates fixed-sized buckets based on those values. Let's see an example for creating buckets of a user's favorite tweet counts:

Python example

```
query = {
  "aggs": {
    "favorite_tweets": {
      "histogram": {
        "field": "user.favourites_count",
        "interval": 20000
      }
    }
  },"size": 0
}
res = es.search(index='twitter', doc_type='tweets', body=query)
for bucket in res['aggregations']['favorite_tweets']['buckets']:
    print bucket['key'], bucket['doc_count']
```

The response for the preceding query will look like the following, which says that 114 users have favorite tweets between `0` to `20000` and 8 users have more than `20000` as their favorite tweets:

```
"aggregations": {
    "favorite_tweets": {
        "buckets": [
            {
                "key": 0,
                "doc_count": 114
            },
```

```
            {
                "key": 20000,
                "doc_count": 8
            }
        ]
    }
}
```

 While executing the `histogram` aggregation, the values of the documents are rounded off and they fall into the closest bucket; for example, if the favorite tweet count is 72 and the bucket size is set to 5, it will fall into the bucket with the key 70.

Java example

Building histogram aggregation:

```
AggregationBuilder aggregation =
        AggregationBuilders
        .histogram("agg")
        .field(fieldName)
        .interval(5);
```

Here, `agg` is the aggregation `bucket` name and `fieldName` is the field on which aggregation is performed. The `interval` method is used to pass the interval for generating the buckets.

Parsing the response:

To parse the histogram aggregation response, you need to import the following class:

```
import org.elasticsearch.search.aggregations.bucket.histogram.
Histogram;
```

Then, the response can be parsed with the following code snippet:

```
Range agg = response.getAggregations().get("agg");
for (Histogram.Bucket entry : agg.getBuckets()) {
    Long key = (Long) entry.getKey();        // Key
    long docCount = entry.getDocCount();     // Doc coun
}
```

Date histogram aggregation

Date histogram is similar to the `histogram` aggregation but it can only be applied to date fields. The difference between the two is that date histogram allows you to specify intervals using date/time expressions.

The following values can be used for intervals:

- year, quarter, month, week, day, hour, minute, and second

You can also specify fractional values, such as 1h (1 hour), 1m (1 minute) and so on.

Date histograms are mostly used to generate time-series graphs in many applications.

Python example

```
query = {
    "aggs": {
      "tweet_histogram": {
        "date_histogram": {
          "field": "created_at",
          "interval": "hour"
        }
      }
    }, "size": 0
}
```

The preceding aggregation will generate an hourly-based tweet timeline on the field, `created_at`:

```
res = es.search(index='twitter', doc_type='tweets', body=query)
for bucket in res['aggregations']['tweet_histogram']['buckets']:
    print bucket['key'], bucket['key_as_string'], bucket['doc_count']
```

Java example

Building date histogram aggregation:

```
AggregationBuilder aggregation =
      AggregationBuilders
        .histogram("agg")
        .field(fieldName)
        .interval(DateHistogramInterval.YEAR);
```

Here, `agg` is the aggregation `bucket` name and `fieldname` is the field on which the aggregation is performed. The `interval` method is used to pass the interval to generate buckets. For interval in days, you can do this: `DateHistogramInterval.days(10)`

Parsing the response:

To parse the `date histogram` aggregation response, you need to import the following class:

```
import org.elasticsearch.search.aggregations.bucket.histogram.
DateHistogramInterval;
```

The response can be parsed with this code snippet:

```
Histogram agg = response.getAggregations().get("agg");
for (Histogram.Bucket entry : agg.getBuckets()) {
   DateTime key = (DateTime) entry.getKey();    // Key
   String keyAsString = entry.getKeyAsString(); // Key as String
   long docCount = entry.getDocCount();         // Doc count
   }
```

Filter-based aggregation

Elasticsearch allows filters to be used as aggregations too. Filters preserve their behavior in the aggregation context as well and are usually used to narrow down the current aggregation context to a specific set of documents. You can use any filter such as `range`, `term`, `geo`, and so on.

To get the count of all the tweets done by the user, `d_bharvi`, use the following code:

Python example

```
query = {
  "aggs": {
    "screename_filter": {
      "filter": {
        "term": {
          "user.screen_name": "d_bharvi"
        }
      }
    }
  },"size": 0
}
```

In the preceding request, we have used a term filter to narrow down the bucket of tweets done by a particular user:

```
res = es.search(index='twitter', doc_type='tweets', body=query)
    for bucket in res['aggregations']['screename_filter']['buckets']:
        print bucket['doc_count']
```

The response would look like this:

```
"aggregations": {
    "screename_filter": {
        "doc_count": 100
    }
  }
}
```

Java example

Building filter-based aggregation:

```
AggregationBuilder aggregation =
  AggregationBuilders
  .filter("agg")
  .filter(QueryBuilders.termQuery("user.screen_name ", "d_bharvi"));
```

Here, agg is the aggregation bucket name under the first filter method and the second filter method takes a query to apply the filter.

Parsing the response:

To parse a filter-based aggregation response, you need to import the following class:

```
import org.elasticsearch.search.aggregations.bucket.histogram.
DateHistogramInterval;
```

The response can be parsed with the following code snippet:

```
Filter agg = response.getAggregations().get("agg");
    agg.getDocCount(); // Doc count
```

Aggregations for Analytics

Combining search, buckets, and metrics

We can always combine searches, filters bucket aggregations, and metric aggregations to get a more and more complex analysis. Until now, we have seen single levels of aggregations; however, as explained in the aggregation syntax section earlier, an aggregation can contain multiple levels of aggregations within. However, metric aggregations cannot contain further aggregations within themselves. Also, when you run an aggregation, it is executed on all the documents in the index for a document type if specified on a match_all query context, but you can always use any type of Elasticsearch query with an aggregation. Let's see how we can do this in Python and Java clients.

Python example

```
query = {
  "query": {
    "match": {
      "text": "crime"
    }
  },
  "aggs": {
    "hourly_timeline": {
      "date_histogram": {
        "field": "created_at",
        "interval": "hour"
      },
      "aggs": {
        "top_hashtags": {
          "terms": {
            "field": "entities.hashtags.text",
            "size": 1
          },
          "aggs": {
            "top_users": {
              "terms": {
                "field": "user.screen_name",
                "size": 1
              },
              "aggs": {
                "average_tweets": {
                  "avg": {
                    "field": "user.statuses_count"
                  }
                }
              }
```

```
                    }
                  }
                }
              }
            }
          }
        } ,"size": 0
    }
    res = es.search(index='twitter', doc_type='tweets', body=query)
```

Parsing the response data:

```
    for timeline_bucket in res['aggregations']['hourly_timeline']
    ['buckets']:
        print 'time range', timeline_bucket['key_as_string']
        print 'tweet count ',timeline_bucket['doc_count']
        for hashtag_bucket in timeline_bucket['top_hashtags']['buckets']:
            print 'hashtag key ', hashtag_bucket['key']
            print 'hashtag count ', hashtag_bucket['doc_count']
            for user_bucket in hashtag_bucket['top_users']['buckets']:
                print 'screen_name ', user_bucket['key']
                print 'count', user_bucket['doc_count']
                print 'average tweets', user_bucket['average_tweets']
    ['value']
```

And you will find the output as below:

time_range 2015-10-14T10:00:00.000Z
tweet_count   1563
  hashtag_key   crime
  hashtag_count   42
    screen_name   andresenior
    count 2
    average_tweets 9239.0
  ....

Understanding the response in the context of our search of the term crime in a text field:

- **time_range**: The key of the `daywise_timeline` bucket
- **tweet_count**: The number of tweets happening per hour
- **hashtag_key**: The name of the hashtag used by users within the specified time bucket

Aggregations for Analytics

- **hashtag_count**: The count of each hashtag within the specified time bucket
- **screen_name**: The screen name of the user who has tweeted using that hashtag
- **count**: The number of times that user tweeted using a corresponding hashtag
- **average_tweets**: The average number of tweets done by users in their lifetime who have used this particular hashtag

Java example

Writing multilevel aggregation queries (as we just saw) in Java seems quite complex, but once you learn the basics of structuring aggregations, it becomes fun.

Let's see how we write the previous query in Java:

Building the query using QueryBuilder:

```
QueryBuilder query = QueryBuilders.matchQuery("text", "crime");
```

Building the aggregation:

The syntax for a multilevel aggregation in Java is as follows:

```
AggregationBuilders
       .aggType("aggs_name")
       //aggregation_definition
       .subAggregation(AggregationBuilders
          .aggType("aggs_name")
          //aggregation_definition
         .subAggregation(AggregationBuilders
          .aggType("aggs_name")
          //aggregation_definition……..
```

You can relate the preceding syntax with the aggregation syntax you learned in the beginning of this chapter.

The exact aggregation for our Python example will be as follows:

```
AggregationBuilder aggregation =
       AggregationBuilders
        .dateHistogram("hourly_timeline")
        .field("@timestamp")
        .interval(DateHistogramInterval.YEAR)
        .subAggregation(AggregationBuilders
            .terms("top_hashtags")
            .field("entities.hashtags.text")
        .subAggregation(AggregationBuilders
```

```
            .terms("top_users")
                .field("user.screen_name")
            .subAggregation(AggregationBuilders
                .avg("average_status_count")
                .field("user.statuses_count"))));
```

Let's execute the request by combining the query and aggregation we have built:

```
SearchResponse response = client.prepareSearch(indexName).
setTypes(docType)
        .setQuery(query).addAggregation(aggregation)
        .setSize(0)
        .execute().actionGet();
```

Parsing multilevel aggregation responses:

Since multilevel aggregations are nested inside each other, you need to iterate accordingly to parse each level of aggregation response in loops.

The response for our request can be parsed with the following code:

```
//Get first level of aggregation data
Histogram agg = response.getAggregations().get("hourly_timeline");
//for each entry of hourly histogram
for (Histogram.Bucket entry : agg.getBuckets()) {
  DateTime key = (DateTime) entry.getKey();
  String keyAsString = entry.getKeyAsString();
  long docCount = entry.getDocCount();
  System.out.println(key);
  System.out.println(docCount);

    //Get second level of aggregation data
    Terms topHashtags = entry.getAggregations().get("top_hashtags");
    //for each entry of top hashtags
    for (Terms.Bucket hashTagEntry : topHashtags.getBuckets()) {
        String hashtag = hashTagEntry.getKey().toString();
        long hashtagCount = hashTagEntry.getDocCount();
System.out.println(hashtag);
        System.out.println(hashtagCount);

        //Get 3rd level of aggregation data
        Terms topUsers = hashTagEntry.getAggregations()
            .get("top_users");
        //for each entry of top users
        for (Terms.Bucket usersEntry : topUsers.getBuckets()) {
```

```
            String screenName = usersEntry.getKey().toString();
    long userCount = usersEntry.getDocCount();            System.out.
println(screenName);
            System.out.println(userCount);

            //Get 4th level of aggregation data
            Avg average_status_count = usersEntry
                        .getAggregations()
            .get("average_status_count");
            double max = average_status_count.getValue();
            System.out.println(max);
            }
        }
    }
```

As you saw, building these types of aggregations and going for a drill down on data sets to do complex analytics can be fun. However, one has to keep in mind the pressure on memory that Elasticsearch bears while doing these complex calculations. The next section covers how we can avoid these memory implications.

Memory pressure and implications

Aggregations are awesome! However, they bring a lot of memory pressure on Elasticsearch. They work on an in-memory data structure called **fielddata**, which is the biggest consumer of HEAP memory in a Elasticsearch cluster. Fielddata is not only used for aggregations, but also used for sorting and scripts. The in-memory fielddata is slow to load, as it has to read the whole inverted index and un-invert it. If the fielddata cache fills up, old data is evicted causing heap churn and bad performance (as fielddata is reloaded and evicted again.)

The more unique terms exist in the index, the more terms will be loaded into memory and the more pressure it will have. If you are using an Elasticsearch version below 2.0.0 and above 1.0.0, then you can use the `doc_vlaues` parameter inside the mapping while creating the index to avoid the use of fielddata using the following syntax:

```
PUT /index_name/_mapping/index_type
{
  "properties": {
    "field_name": {
      "type": "string",
      "index": "not_analyzed",
      "doc_values": true
    }
  }
}
```

> `doc_values` have been enabled by default from Elasticsearch version 2.0.0 onwards.

The advantages of using `doc_values` are as follows:

- Less heap usage and faster garbage collections
- No longer limited by the amount of fielddata that can fit into a given amount of heap—instead the file system caches can make use of all the available RAM
- Fewer latency spikes caused by reloading a large segment into memory

The other important consideration to keep in mind is not to have a huge number of buckets in a nested aggregation. For example, finding the total order value for a country during a year with an interval of one week will generate 100*51 buckets with the sum value. It is a big overhead that is not only calculated in data nodes, but also in the co-ordinating node that aggregates them. A big JSON also gives problems on parsing and loading on the "frontend". It will easily kill a server with wide aggregations.

Summary

In this chapter, we learned about one of the most powerful features of Elasticsearch, that is, aggregation frameworks. We went through the most important metric and bucket aggregations along with examples of doing analytics on our Twitter dataset with Python and Java API.

This chapter covered many fundamental as well complex examples of the different facets of analytics, which can be built using a combination of full-text searches, term-based searches, and multilevel aggregations. Elasticsearch is awesome for analytics but one should always keep in mind the memory implications, which we covered in the last section of this chapter, to avoid the over killing of nodes.

In the next chapter, we will learn to work with geo spatial data in Elasticsearch and we will also cover analytics with `geo` aggregations.

5
Data Looks Better on Maps: Master Geo-Spatiality

The world is getting smarter day by day and searches based on locations have become an integral part of our daily life. Be it searching for shopping centers, hospitals, restaurants, or any locations, we always look out for information such as distance and other information about the area. Elasticsearch is helpful in combining geo-location data with full-text search, structured search, and also in doing analytics.

In this chapter, we will cover the following topics:

- Introducing geo-spatial data
- Geo-location data types
- Working with geo-point data
- Geo aggregations
- Working with geo-shapes

Introducing geo-spatial data

Geo-spatial data is information of any object on the earth and is presented by numeric values called latitude-longitude (lat-lon) that are presented on geographical systems. Apart from lat-lon, a geo-spatial object also contains other information about that object such as name, size, and shape. Elasticsearch is very helpful when working with such kinds of data. It doesn't only provide powerful geo-location searches, but also has functionalities such as sorting with geo distance, creating geo clusters, scoring based on location, and working with arbitrary geo-shapes.

Elasticsearch has two data types to solely work on geo-spatial data; they are as follows:

- **geo_point**: This is a combination of latitude-longitude pairs that defines a single location point
- **geo_shape**: This works on latitude-longitudes, but with complex shapes such as points, multi-points, lines, circles, polygons, and multi-polygons defined by a geo-JSON data structure

Working with geo-point data

Geo-points are single location points defined by a latitude-longitude pair on the surface of the earth. Using geo-points you can do the following things:

- Calculate the distance between two points
- Find the document that falls in a specified rectangular area
- Sort documents based on distance and score results based on it
- Create clusters of geo-points using aggregations

Mapping geo-point fields

Unlike all the data types in Elasticsearch, geo-point fields can't be determined dynamically. So, you have to define the mapping in advance before indexing data. The mapping for a geo-point field can be defined in the following format:

```
"location": {
    "type": "geo_point"
}
```

A `geo_point` mapping indexes a single field (the location in our example) in the `lat-lon` format. You can optionally index `.lat` and `.lon` separately by setting the `lat-lon` parameter to `true`.

Indexing geo-point data

Elasticsearch supports the following three formats to index `geo_point` data with the same mapping that we defined in the previous section:

```
lat-lon as a string   : "location" : "28.61, 77.23"
lat-lon as an object  : "location": {
                          "lat": 28.61,
                          "lon": 77.23
                      }
lat-lon as an array   : "location" : [77.23, 28.61]
```

The order of latitude-longitude differs in an array format. It takes longitude first and then latitude.

Python example

In this section, we will see how to index the `geo_point` data in all the three formats using Python:

- Using string format:

```
doc ={"location": "28.61, 77.23"}
es.index(index=index_name, doc_type=doc_type, body=doc)
```

- Using object format:

```
location = dict()
location['lat'] = 28.61
location['lon'] = 77.23
doc['location'] = location
es.index(index=index_name, doc_type=doc_type, body=doc)
```

- Using array format:

```
location = list()
location.append(77.23)
location.append(28.6)
doc['location'] = location
es.index(index=index_name, doc_type=doc_type, body=doc)
```

Java example

- Using string format:

```
Map<String, Object> document1= new HashMap<String, Object>();
    document1.put("location", "29.9560, 78.1700");
    document1.put("name", "delhi");
    document1.put("dish_name", "chinese");
client.prepareIndex().setIndex(indexName).setType(docType)
        .setSource(document1).execute().actionGet();
```

- Using object format:

```
Map<String, Object> document3 = new HashMap<String, Object>();
Map<String, Object> locationMap = new HashMap<String, Object>();
    locationMap.put("lat", 29.9560);
    locationMap.put("lon", 78.1700);
    document3.put("location", locationMap);
    document3.put("name", "delhi");
    document3.put("dish_name", "chinese");
client.prepareIndex().setIndex(indexName).setType(docType)
        .setSource(document3).execute().actionGet();
```

- Using array format:

```
Map<String, Object> document2= new HashMap<String, Object>();
List<Double> geoPoints = new ArrayList<Double>();
    geoPoints.add(77.42);
    geoPoints.add(28.67);
  document2.put("location", geoPoints);
  document2.put("name", "delhi");
  document2.put("dish_name", "chinese");
client.prepareIndex().setIndex(indexName).setType(docType)
      .setSource(document2).execute().actionGet();
```

Querying geo-point data

The following are the query types available to query data with the `geo_point` field type:

- Geo distance query
- Geo distance range query
- Geo bounding box query

Geo distance query

The geo distance query is used to filter documents that exist within a specified distance from a given field. Let's see an example of how can we find out the best places to visit within a 200 km distance from Delhi.

Python example

```
query = {
  "query": {
    "bool": {
      "must": {
        "match_all": {}
      },
      "filter": {
        "geo_distance": {
          "distance": "200km",
          "location": {
            "lat": 28.67,
            "lon": 77.42
          }
        }
      }
    }
```

```
            }
        }
    }
    response = es.search(index=index_name, doc_type=doc_type, body=query)
```

In the preceding query, we have used locations `lat-lon` in the object form; however, you always have an option to use string or array formats in the query without worrying about the format in which your data has been indexed.

The distance can be specified in various time-unit formats, such as the following:

- mi or miles for mile
- yd or yards for yard
- ft or feet for feet
- in or inch for inch
- km or kilometers for kilometer
- m or meters for meter
- cm or centimeters for centimeter
- mm or millimeters for millimeter
- NM, nmi or nauticalmiles for nautical mile

Java example

Apart from importing `QueryBuilders`, you need to have the following import in you code:

```
import org.elasticsearch.common.unit.DistanceUnit;
```

`DistanceUnit` is an Enum type that provides all the distance units that can be used.

Build the search query as follows:

```
QueryBuilder query = QueryBuilders.matchAllQuery();
```

Now, the geo distance query can be built like this:

```
QueryBuilder geoDistanceQuery =
        QueryBuilders.geoDistanceQuery("location")
        .lat(28.67).lon(77.42)
        .distance(12, DistanceUnit.KILOMETERS);
```

Combine both the queries to make a final query. Note that our geo distance query is part of a `boolQuery` that comes under the `must` block:

```
QueryBuilder finalQuery = QueryBuilders.boolQuery()
        .must(query).filter(geoDistanceQuery);
```

Here is the final execution:

```
SearchResponse response =
        client.prepareSearch(indexName).setTypes(docType)
        .setQuery(finalQuery)
        .execute().actionGet();
```

Geo distance range query

In *Chapter 3*, Putting *Elasticsearch into Action* we saw range and date range queries. The geo distance range query has the same concept. It is used to filter out documents that fall in a specified range with respect to a given point of location. For example, with the following query, you can find out the documents that fall in the range of 2,000 to 400 km from Delhi:

```
{
  "query": {
    "bool": {
      "must": {
        "match_all": {}
      },
      "filter": {
        "geo_distance_range": {
          "from": "200km",
          "to": "400km",
          "location": [77.42,28.67]
        }
      }
    }
  }
}
```

All the distance units that we have seen for the `geo_distance` query can be applied to this query too. This query also supports the common parameters for a range (`lt`, `lte`, `gt`, `gte`, `from`, `to`, `include_upper`, and `include_lower`).

Java example

The following example is an implementation of the same JSON query that we have seen for Python:

```
QueryBuilder query = QueryBuilders.matchAllQuery();
QueryBuilder geoDistanceRangeQuery =
        QueryBuilders.geoDistanceRangeQuery("location")
        .lon(28.67).lat(77.42)
        .from("100km").to("4000km");
QueryBuilder finalQuery = QueryBuilders.boolQuery()
```

```
        .must(query).filter(geoDistanceRangeQuery);

SearchResponse response =
        client.prepareSearch(indexName).setTypes(docType)
        .setQuery(finalQuery).execute().actionGet();
```

Geo bounding box query

This query works based on the points of a rectangle also called as bounding box. You provide the top, bottom, left, and right coordinates of the rectangle and the query compares the latitude with the left and right coordinates and the longitude with the top and bottom coordinates:

```
{
  "query": {
    "bool": {
      "must": {
        "match_all": {}
      },
      "filter": {
        "geo_bounding_box": {
          "location": {
            "top_left": {
              "lat":76.9771,
              "lon": 28.7965
            },
            "bottom_right": {
              "lat": 28.4301,
              "lon": 77.5717
            }
          }
        }
      }
    }
  }
}
```

See the special parameters, `top_left` and `bottom_right`, that are points of a rectangle.

These keys can also be used in an array format:

```
"top_left" : [28.7965,76.9771],
"bottom_right" : [77.5717, 28.4301]
```

They can be used in a string format as well:

```
"top_left" : "76.9771, 28.7965",
"bottom_right" : "28.4301, 77.5717"
```

Understanding bounding boxes

Initially it could be a little hard to understand and create the bounding boxes but this section will guide you in understanding and creating bounding boxes to enable you to use them in queries.

Please visit http://www.openstreetmap.org/ and on the top-left corner, click the **Export** button.

Now you can either search for a place or can manually select an area (Delhi and related areas in our example) using the corners, as shown in the following image:

In the preceding image, you can see four points that depict the corners of the rectangle that we have drawn. The top_left point in the preceding image is 76.9771, 28.7965, whereas the **bottom_right** point is 28.4301, 77.5717.

Java example

You need to import the following additional classes in your code first:

```
import org.elasticsearch.common.geo.GeoPoint;
```

Note that Geopoint is a class in Elasticsearch that is used to create geo-points. If you do not choose to use it, you always have the lat() and lon() methods available to set the latitude and longitude points in the queries, as we have seen in the previous examples. However, for your knowledge, this example uses the GeoPoint class:

```
GeoPoint topLeft= new GeoPoint(68.91,35.60);
GeoPoint bottomRight= new GeoPoint(7.80,97.29);

QueryBuilder query = QueryBuilders.matchAllQuery();
QueryBuilder geoDistanceRangeQuery =
        QueryBuilders.geoBoundingBoxQuery("location")
        .topLeft(topLeft).bottomRight(bottomRight);
QueryBuilder finalQuery = QueryBuilders.boolQuery()
        .must(query).filter(geoDistanceRangeQuery);
SearchResponse response =
        client.prepareSearch(indexName).setTypes(docType)
        .setQuery(finalQuery)
        .execute().actionGet();
```

Sorting by distance

In the previous chapters, we saw how default sorting works on _score calculated by Elasticsearch, and we also saw how we can use the values of a field to influence the sorting of documents. Elasticsearch allows the sorting of documents by distance using the _geo_distance parameter.

For example, you want to find all the restaurants in a sorted order with respect to your current location and those that have Chinese cuisine in a list of restaurants available in your index.

Python example

```
query = {
    "query": {
      "term": {
        "dish_name": {
          "value": "chinese"
        }
      }
    },
    "sort": [
      {
        "_geo_distance": {
          "location": [
            28.67,
            77
          ],
          "order": "asc",
          "unit": "km"
        }
```

```
            }
        ]
    }
response = es.search(index=index_name, doc_type=doc_type, body=query)
```

Java example

The same preceding query can be written in Java in the following way; however, first you need to import some extra classes:

```
import org.elasticsearch.search.sort.SortBuilder;
import org.elasticsearch.search.sort.SortBuilders;
import org.elasticsearch.search.sort.SortOrder;
import org.elasticsearch.common.unit.DistanceUnit;
```

We have already covered the explanation of `DistanceUnit`. `SortOrder` is also an Enum that provides different values such as `ASC` and `DESC` that can be used for sorting purposes.

Our other import, `SortBuilder`, is not only used for gro sorting, but can be also used to do sorting on other types of fields:

```
QueryBuilder query = QueryBuilders.termQuery("dish_name", "chinese");
SortBuilder sortingQuery =   SortBuilders.geoDistanceSort("location")
        .point(28.67, 77).unit(DistanceUnit.KILOMETERS)
        .order(SortOrder.ASC);
SearchResponse response =
        client.prepareSearch(indexName).setTypes(docType)
        .setQuery(query)
        .addSort(sortingQuery)
        .execute().actionGet();
```

> Please note that sorting by distance is a memory- and CPU-intensive task, so if you have a lot of documents in your index, it's better to use filters such as bounding box or queries to minimize the search context.

Geo-aggregations

Sometimes searches may return too many results but you might be just interested in finding out how many documents exist in a particular range of a location. A simple example can be to see how many news events related to crime occurred in an area by plotting them on a map or by generating a heatmap cluster of the events on the map, as shown in the following image:

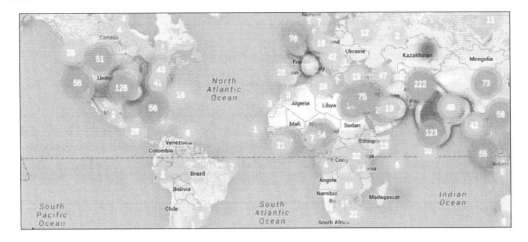

Elasticsearch offers both metric and bucket aggregations for geo_point fields.

Geo distance aggregation

Geo distance aggregation is an extension of range aggregation. It allows you to create buckets of documents based on specified ranges. Let's see how this can be done using an example.

Python example

```
query = {
  "aggs": {
    "news_hotspots": {
      "geo_distance": {
        "field": "location",
        "origin": "28.61, 77.23",
    "unit": "km",
    "distance_type": "plane",
        "ranges": [
          {
            "to": 50
          },
          {
            "from": 50, "to": 200
          },
          {
            "from": 200
          }
        ]
      }
```

Executing the query, as follows:

```
response = es.search(index=index_name, doc_type=doc_type, body=query, search_type='count')
```

The preceding query creates buckets of documents with the following ranges with respect to the specified origin point:

- The count of the news events that happened in 0 to 50 km of range
- The count of the news events that happened in 50 to 200 km of range
- The count of the news events that happened outside the 200 km range

The query parameters are as follows:

- **origin**: This accepts lat-lon in all three formats: object, string or array.
- **unit**: This defaults to m (meters), but accepts other distance units as well, such as km.
- **distance_type**: This is used to specify how the distance needs to be calculated. It is an optional parameter, which defaults to `sloppy_arc` (faster but less accurate), but can also be set to `arc` (slower but most accurate) or `plane` (fastest but least accurate). Because of high error margins, plane should be used only for small geographic areas.

Java example

We covered aggregation in detail in the previous chapter, where you saw range aggregation. Geo distance aggregation is similar to it and only takes the following extra parameters:

Point, distance unit, and distance type, which we have already covered in the previous section.

For the distance type, `import org.elasticsearch.common.geo.GeoDistance;`.

```
AggregationBuilder aggregation =
  AggregationBuilders.geoDistance("news_hotspots").field(fieldName).
point(new GeoPoint(28.61, 77.23))
        .unit(DistanceUnit.KILOMETERS)
        .distanceType(GeoDistance.PLANE)
        .addUnboundedTo(50)
        .addRange(50, 100)
        .addUnboundedFrom(200);
```

```
SearchResponse response =   client.prepareSearch(indexName).
setTypes(docType)
      .setQuery(QueryBuilders.matchAllQuery())
      .addAggregation(aggregation)
      .setSize(0).execute().actionGet();
Range agg = response.getAggregations().get("news_hotspots");

for (Range.Bucket entry : agg.getBuckets()) {
     String key = entry.getKeyAsString();
     Number from = (Number) entry.getFrom();
     Number to = (Number) entry.getTo();
     long docCount = entry.getDocCount();       System.out.
println("key: "+key + " from: "+from+" to: "+to+" doc count: "+docCount);
}
```

Using bounding boxes with geo distance aggregation

The following is an example of using a bounding box query to limit the scope of our searches and then performing aggregation.

Python example

```
query= {
  "query": {
    "bool": {
      "must": {
        "match_all": {}
      },
      "filter": {
        "geo_bounding_box": {
          "location": {
            "top_left": {"lat": 68.91, "lon": 35.6},
            "bottom_right": {"lat": 7.8, "lon": 97.29}
          }
        }
      }
    }
  },
  "aggs": {
    "news_hotspots": {
      "geo_distance": {
        "field": "location",
```

```
        "origin": "28.61, 77.23",
        "unit": "km",
        "distance_type": "plane",
        "ranges": [
          {"from": 0, "to": 50 },
          {"from": 50, "to": 200 }
        ]
      }
    }
  }
}
response = es.search(index=index_name, doc_type=doc_type, body=query)
print 'total documents found', response['hits']['total']
for hit in response['hits']['hits']:
    print hit.get('_source')
```

The preceding query finds all the news documents within India (specified using the bounding box query) and creates buckets from 0 to 50 km and from 50 to 200 km in the national capital region of Delhi.

To build this query in Java, you can use the geo bounding box query in combination with geo distance aggregation examples.

Geo-shapes

Geo-shapes are completely different from geo-points. Until now we have worked with simple geo-location and rectangle searches. However, with geo-shapes, the sky is the limit. On a map, you can simply draw a line, polygon, or circle and ask Elasticsearch to populate the data according to the co-ordinates of your queries, as seen in the following image:

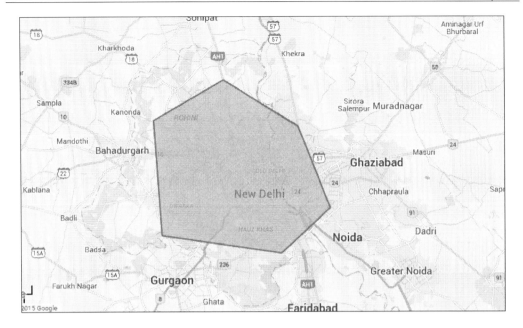

Let's see some of the most important geo-shapes.

Point

A point is a single geographical coordinate, such as your current location shown by your smart-phone. A point in Elasticsearch is represented as follows:

```
{
    "location" : {
        "type" : "point",
        "coordinates" : [28.498564, 77.0812823]
    }
}
```

Linestring

A `linestring` can be defined in two ways. If it contains two coordinates, it will be a straight line, but if it contains more than two points, it will be an arbitrary path:

```
{
    "location" : {
        "type" : "linestring",
        "coordinates" : [[-77.03653, 38.897676], [-77.009051, 38.889939]]
    }
}
```

Circles

A circle contains a coordinate as its centre point and a radius. For example:

```
{
    "location" : {
        "type" : "circle",
        "coordinates" : [-45.0, 45.0],
        "radius" : "500m"
    }
}
```

Polygons

A polygon is composed of a list of points with the condition that its first and last points are the same, to make it closed. For example:

```
{
  "location": {
    "type": "polygon",
    "coordinates": [
      [
        [-5.756836, 49.991408],
        [-7.250977, 55.124723],
        [1.845703, 51.500194],
        [-5.756836, 49.991408]
      ]
    ]
  }
}
```

Envelops

An envelope is a bounding rectangle and is created by specifying only the top-left and bottom-right points. For example:

```
{"location":
  {
    "type":"envelope",
    "coordinates":[[-45,45],[45,-45]]
  }
}
```

Mappings geo-shape fields

Similar to geo-points, geo-shapes are also not dynamically identified by Elasticsearch, and a mapping needs to be defined before putting in the data.

The mapping for a geo-point field can be defined in the following format:

```
"location": {
    "type": "geo_shape",
    "tree": " quadtree "
}
```

The `tree` parameter defines which kind of grid encoding is to be used for geo-shapes. It defaults to `geo_hash`, but can also be set to `quadtree`.

> **Geohash versus Quadtree**
>
> **Geohashes** transform a two-dimension spatial point (latitude-longitude) into an alphanumerical string or hash and is used by Elasticsearch as a default encoding scheme for geo-point data. Geohashes divide the world into a grid of 32 cells, and each cell is given an alphanumeric character.
>
> **Quadtrees** are similar to geohashes, except that they are built on a quadrant that is, there are only four cells at each level instead of 32. As per my experience with geo data, quadtrees are faster and provide more performance in comparison to geohashes.

Indexing geo-shape data

Indexing a geo-shape value in a point form is easier and follows this syntax:

```
location": {
  "type": "Point",
   "coordinates": [13.400544, 52.530286]
    }
```

Python example

The same previous location data can be used for indexing with Python in the following way:

```
doc = dict()
location = dict()
location['coordinates'] = [13.400544, 52.530286]
doc['location'] = location
doc['location']['type'] = 'Point'
es.index(index=index_name, doc_type=doc_type, body=doc)
```

Java example

```
List<Double> coordinates = new ArrayList<Double>();
coordinates.add(13.400544);
coordinates.add(52.530286);
Map<String, Object> location = new HashMap<String, Object>();
location.put("coordinates", coordinates);
location.put("type", "Point");
Map<String, Object> document = new HashMap<String, Object>();
document.put("location", location);
IndexResponse response = client.prepareIndex().setIndex(indexName).
setType(docType)
    .setSource(document).setId("1").execute().actionGet();
```

Querying geo-shape data

> Java programmers need to add the following dependencies in the pom.
> xml file to be able to work with geo-spatial data. If you are using Jar
> files in your class path, the Spatial4J and JTS Jar files can be found
> under Elasticsearch home's lib directory:
>
> ```xml
> <dependency>
>     <groupId>com.spatial4j</groupId>
>     <artifactId>spatial4j</artifactId>
>     <version>0.4.1</version>
> </dependency>
> <dependency>
>     <groupId>com.vividsolutions</groupId>
>     <artifactId>jts</artifactId>
>     <version>1.13</version>
>     <exclusions>
>         <exclusion>
>             <groupId>xerces</groupId>
>             <artifactId>xercesImpl</artifactId>
>         </exclusion>
>     </exclusions></dependency>
> ```

The data we have stored previously can be queried using any geo shape type.
Let's see a few examples to search the previous document in both Python and Java
languages.

Python example

Searching on `linestring` is done as follows:

```
query = {
    "query": {
      "bool": {
        "must": {
          "match_all": {}
        },
        "filter": {
          "geo_shape": {
            "location": {
              "shape": {
                "type": "linestring",
                "coordinates": [[ 13.400544,52.530286],[13.4006,52.5303]]
              }
            }
          }
        }
      }
    }
}
response = es.search(index=index_name, doc_type=doc_type, body=query)
```

Searching inside an envelope is done like this:

```
query = {
    "query": {
      "bool": {
        "must": {
          "match_all": {}
        },
        "filter": {
          "geo_shape": {
            "location": {
              "shape": {
                "type": "envelope",
                "coordinates": [[13,53],[14,52]]
              }
            }
          }
        }
      }
    }
}
```

```
        }
    }
    response = es.search(index=index_name, doc_type=doc_type,
body=query)
```

Similarly, you can search all type of shapes by specifying the type and the corresponding coordinates for that shape.

Java example

To search using `linestring`:

Apart from `QueryBuilder`, you also need to import the following statement that is used to build various geo shape queries:

```
import org.elasticsearch.common.geo.builders.ShapeBuilder;
```

Then you can build the query, as follows:

```
QueryBuilder lineStringQuery =
    QueryBuilders.boolQuery()
    .must(QueryBuilders.matchAllQuery())
    .filter(QueryBuilders.geoShapeQuery(geoShapeFieldName,
        ShapeBuilder.newLineString()
        .point(13.400544, 52.530286)
        .point(13.4006,   52.5303)));
SearchResponse response =
    client.prepareSearch(indexName)
    .setTypes(docType)
    .setQuery(lineStringQuery)
    .execute().actionGet();
```

To search using `Envelope`:

```
QueryBuilder envelopQuery =
    QueryBuilders.boolQuery()
    .must(QueryBuilders.matchAllQuery())
    .filter(QueryBuilders.geoShapeQuery(geoShapeFieldName,
        ShapeBuilder.newEnvelope()
        .topLeft(13.0, 53.0)
        .bottomRight(14.0, 52.0)));
```

As shown in the preceding code, an envelope takes top-left and bottom-right points similar to what we saw for bounding box queries:

```
SearchResponse response =
     client.prepareSearch(indexName).setTypes(docType)
    .setQuery(envelopQuery)
    .execute().actionGet();
```

Summary

In this chapter, we learned about geo data concepts and covered the rich geo search functionalities offered by Elasticsearch, including creating mappings for geo-points and geo-shapes, indexing documents, geo-aggregations, and sorting data based on geo-distance. We also covered code examples for the most widely used geo-queries in both Python and Java.

In the next chapter, you will learn how document relationships can be managed in Elasticsearch using nested and parent-child relationships.

6
Document Relationships in NoSQL World

We have all grown up learning about relational data and databases. However, relational databases have their limitations, especially when providing full-text searches. Because of the limitations faced with relational databases, the world is adapting quickly to NoSQL solutions, and despite of there being so many NoSQL databases in the market, Elasticsearch has an upper hand because it offers the handling of relationships among different entities in combination with a powerful full-text search.

In this chapter, we will cover the following topics:

- Managing relational data in Elasticsearch
- Working with nested objects
- Introducing parent-child relationships
- Considerations for using document relationships

Relational data in the document-oriented NoSQL world

Relational databases have a lot of problems when it comes to dealing with a massive amount of data. Be it speed, efficient processing, effective parallelization, scalability, or costs, relational databases fail when the volume of data starts growing. The other challenge of relational databases is that relationships and schemas must be defined upfront. To overcome these problems, people started with normalizing data, dropping constraints, and relaxing transactional guarantees. Eventually, by compromising on these features, relational databases started resembling a NoSQL product. NoSQL is a combination of two terms, No and SQL. Some people say that it means no relational or no RDBMS, whereas other people say that it is "not only SQL". Whatever the meaning is, one thing is for sure, NoSQL is all about not following the rules of relational databases.

There is no doubt that document-oriented NoSQL databases have succeeded a lot in overcoming the issues faced in relational databases, but one thing cannot be missed out while working with any kind of data: **relationships**.

Managing relational data in Elasticsearch

Elasticsearch is also a NoSQL document data store. However, despite being a NoSQL data store, Elasticsearch offers a lot of help in managing relational data to an extent. It does support SQL-like joins and works awesomely on nested and related data entities.

For blog posts and comments, or an employee and their experiences, the data is always relational. With Elasticsearch, you can work very easily by preserving the association with different entities along with a powerful full-text search and analytics. Elasticsearch makes this possible by introducing two types of document relation models:

- Nested relationships
- Parent-child relationships

Both types of relationship work on the same model, **one to many relationship**. There is one root/parent object that can have one or more child objects.

The following image is a visual representation of how nested and parent-child documents look into Elasticsearch:

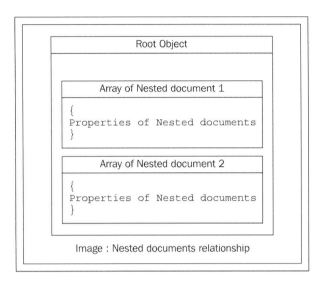

As shown in the preceding image, in a nested relationship, there is a one root object, which is the main document that we have, and it contains an array of sub-documents called nested documents. There is no limit to the level of nesting of documents inside a root object. For example, look at the following JSON for a multilevel nesting:

```
{
    "location_id": "axdbyu",
    "location_name": "gurgaon",
    "company": [
      {
        "name": "honda",
        "modelName": [
           { "name": "honda cr-v", "price": "2 million" }
        ]
      },
      {
        "name": "bmw",
        "modelName": [
           { "name": "BMW 3 Series", "price": "2 million"},
           { "name": "BMW 1 Series", "price": "3 million" }
        ]
      }
    ]
}
```

The preceding example shows that we are dealing with data in which each location can have multiple companies and each company has different models. So, indexing this kind of data without a nested type will not solve our purpose if we have to find a particular model with the name or price of a particular company at a given location. This type of relational data with a one to many relationship can be handled in Elasticsearch using nested types.

Nested fields are used to index arrays of objects, in which each object can be queried (with the nested query) as an independent document; however, in a nested structure, everything is stored in the same Lucene block. This has the advantage of fast joins while querying, but also a disadvantage of the storage of the data.

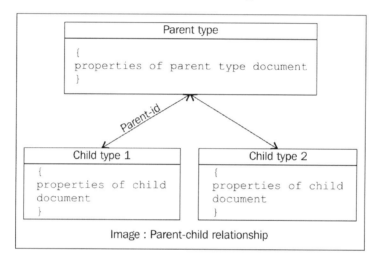

Image : Parent-child relationship

The parent-child relational model overcomes the storage problems of a nested model as the related documents here are not stored in the same lucene block, rather they are stored in the same shard. The parent and child are completely different documents. Elasticsearch maintains an internal data structure by mapping child document IDs to parent document IDs (similar to a foreign key that we use to define in relational databases).

Working with nested objects

Nested objects look similar to plain objects but they differ in mapping and the way they are stored internally in Elasticsearch.

We will work with the same Twitter data but this time we will index it in a nested structure. We will have a user as our root object and every user can have multiple tweets as nested documents. Indexing this kind of data without using nested mapping will lead to problems, as shown in the following example:

```
PUT /twitter/tweet/1
{
  "user": {
    "screen_name": "d_bharvi",
    "followers_count": "2000",
    "created_at": "2012-06-05"
  },
  "tweets": [
    {
      "id": "121223221",
      "text": "understanding nested relationships",
      "created_at": "2015-09-05"
    },
    {
      "id": "121223222",
      "text": "NoSQL databases are awesome",
      "created_at": "2015-06-05"
    }
  ]
}

PUT /twitter/tweet/2
{
  "user": {
    "screen_name": "d_bharvi",
    "followers_count": "2000",
    "created_at": "2012-06-05"
  },
  "tweets": [
    {
      "id": "121223223",
      "text": "understanding nested relationships",
      "created_at": "2015-09-05"
    },
```

```
    {
      "id": "121223224",
      "text": "NoSQL databases are awesome",
      "created_at": "2015-09-05"
    }
  ]
}
```

Now, if we want to query all the tweets that are about NoSQL and have been created on `2015-09-05`, we would use the following code:

```
GET twitter/tweets/_search
{
  "query": {
    "bool": {
      "must": [
        {
          "match": {
            "tweets.text": "NoSQL"
          }
        },
        {
          "term": {
            "tweets.created_at": "2015-09-05"
          }
        }
      ]
    }
  }
}
```

The preceding query will return both the documents in the response. The reason is that Elasticsearch internally stores objects in the following way:

```
{tweets.id : ["121223221","121223222","121223223","121223224"],
tweets.text : ["understanding nested relationships",........],
tweets.created_at : ["2015-09-05","2015-06-05","2015-09-05","2015-09-
05"]}
```

All the fields of the tweet objects are flattened into an array format, which leads to loosing the association between the tweet texts and tweet creation dates, and because of this, the previous query returned the wrong results.

Creating nested mappings

The mapping for nested objects can be defined in the following way:

```
PUT twitter_nested/users/_mapping
{
  "properties": {
    "user": {
      "type": "object",
      "properties": {
        "screen_name": {
          "type": "string"
        },
        "followers_count": {
          "type": "integer"
        },
        "created_at": {
          "type": "date"
        }
      }
    },
    "tweets": {
      "type": "nested",
      "properties": {
        "id": {
          "type": "string"
        },
        "text": {
          "type": "string"
        },
        "created_at": {
          "type": "date"
        }
      }
    }
  }
}
```

In the previous mapping, `user` is a simple object field but the `tweets` field is defined as a `nested` type object, which contains `id`, `text`, and `created_at` as its properties.

Indexing nested data

You can use the same JSON documents that we used in the previous section to index users and their tweets, as indexing nested fields is similar to indexing object fields and does not require any extra effort in the code. However, Elasticsearch considers all the nested documents as separate documents and stores them internally in the following format, which preserves the relationships between tweet texts and dates:

```
{tweets.id : "121223221",tweets.text : "understanding nested
relationships", tweets.created_at : "2015-09-05"}
{tweets.id : "121223221",tweets.text : "understanding nested
relationships", tweets.created_at : "2015-09-05"}
{tweets.id : "121223221",tweets.text : "understanding nested
relationships", tweets.date : "2015-09-05"}
```

Querying nested type data

To query a nested field, Elasticsearch offers a `nested` query, which has the following syntax:

```
"query": {
   "nested": {
      "path": "path_to_nested_doc",
      "query": {}
   }
}
```

Let's understand the `nested` query syntax:

- The top most `query` parameter wraps all the queries inside it.
- The `nested` parameter tells Elasticsearch that this query is of the nested type
- The `path` parameter specifies the path of the nested field
- The internal `query` object contains all the queries supported by Elasticsearch

Now let's run the nested query to search all the tweets that are about NoSQL and have been created on `2015-09-05`.

Python example

```
query = {
  "query": {
    "nested": {
      "path": "tweets",
      "query": {
```

```
          "bool": {
            "must": [
              {
                "match": {
                  "tweets.text": "NoSQL"
                }
              },
              {
                "term": {
                  "tweets.created_at": "2015-09-05"
                }
              }
            ]
          }
        }
      }
    }
  }
}
res = es.search(index='twitter_nested', doc_type= 'users', body=query)
```

Java example

```
SearchResponse response = client.prepareSearch("twitter_nested")
  .setTypes("users")
  .setQuery(QueryBuilders
  .nestedQuery(nestedField, QueryBuilders
  .boolQuery()
    .must(QueryBuilders
      .matchQuery("tweets.text", "Nosql Databases"))
    .must(QueryBuilders
      .termQuery("tweets.created_at", "2015-09-05"))))
      .execute().actionGet();
```

The response object contains the output returned from Elasticsearch, which will have one matching document in the response this time.

Nested aggregations

Nested aggregations allow you to perform aggregations on nested fields. There are two types of nested aggregations available in Elasticsearch. The first one (nested aggregation) allows you to aggregate the `nested` fields, whereas the second one (reverse `nested` aggregation) allows you to aggregate the fields that fall outside the `nested` scope.

Nested aggregation

A `nested` aggregation allows you to perform all the aggregations on the fields inside a `nested` object. The syntax is as follows:

```
{
  "aggs": {
    "NAME": {
      "nested": {
        "path": "path_to_nested_field"
      },
      "aggs": {}
    }
  }
}
```

Understanding nested aggregation syntax:

The syntax of a `nested` aggregation is similar to the other aggregations but here we need to specify the path of the topmost `nested` field as we have learnt to do in the `nested` queries. Once the path is specified, you can perform any aggregation on the nested documents using the inner `aggs` object. Let's see an example of how to do it:

Python example

```
query = {
  "aggs": {
    "NESTED_DOCS": {
      "nested": {
        "path": "tweets"
      },"aggs": {
        "TWEET_TIMELINE": {
          "date_histogram": {
            "field": "tweets.created_at",
            "interval": "day"
          }
        }
      }
    }
  }
}
res = es.search(index='twitter_nested', doc_type= 'users', body=query, size=0)
```

The preceding aggregation query creates a bucket of `nested` aggregation, which further contains the date histogram of tweets (the number of tweets created per day). Please note that we can combine `nested` aggregation with full-text search queries in a similar way to how we saw in *Chapter 4, Aggregations for Analytics*.

Java example

The following example requires this extra import in your code:

```
org.elasticsearch.search.aggregations.bucket.histogram.
DateHistogramInterval
```

You can build the aggregation in the following way:

```
SearchResponse response = client.prepareSearch("twitter_nested")
.setTypes("users")
.addAggregation(AggregationBuilders.nested("NESTED_DOCS")
.path(nestedField)
.subAggregation(AggregationBuilders
.dateHistogram("TWEET_TIMELINE")
.field("tweets.created_at")
.interval(DateHistogramInterval.DAY)
)).setSize(0).execute().actionGet();
```

> The `DateHistogramInterval` class offers the final static variables (DAY in our example) to define the intervals of buckets. The possible values are SECOND, MINUTE, HOUR, DAY, WEEK, MONTH, QUARTER, and YEAR.

The output for the preceding query will look like the following:

```
"aggregations" : {
    "NESTED_DOCS" : {
        "doc_count" : 2,
        "TWEET_TIMELINE" : {
            "buckets" : [ {
                "key_as_string" : "2015-09-05T00:00:00.000Z",
                "key" : 1441411200000,
                "doc_count" : 2
            } ]
        }
    }
}
```

In the output, `NESTED_DOCS` is the name of our nested aggregations that shows `doc_count` as 2 because our document was composed using an array of two nested tweet documents. The `TWEET_TIMELINE` buckets show two documents because we have two tweets in one document.

Reverse nested aggregation

Nested aggregation has the limitation that it can only access the fields within the nested scope. Reverse nested aggregations overcome this scenario and allow you to look beyond the nested scope and go back to the root document or other nested documents.

For example, we can find all the unique users who have tweeted in a particular date range with the following reverse nested aggregation:

Python example

```
query = {
  "aggs": {
    "NESTED_DOCS": {
      "nested": {
        "path": "tweets"
      },
      "aggs": {
        "TWEET_TIMELINE": {
          "date_histogram": {
            "field": "tweets.created_at",
            "interval": "day"
          },
          "aggs": {
            "USERS": {
              "reverse_nested": {},
              "aggs": {
                "UNIQUE_USERS": {
                  "cardinality": {
                    "field": "user.screen_name"
                  }
                }
              }
            }
          }
        }
      }
    }
  }
}
resp = es.search(index='twitter_nested', doc_type= 'users', body=query, size=0)
```

Java example

```
SearchResponse response =
        client.prepareSearch(indexName).setTypes(docType)
    .addAggregation(AggregationBuilders.nested("NESTED_DOCS")
    .path(nestedField)
    .subAggregation(AggregationBuilders.dateHistogram("TWEET_TIMELINE")
.field("tweets.created_at").interval(DateHistogramInterval.DAY)
    .subAggregation(AggregationBuilders.reverseNested("USERS")
    .subAggregation(AggregationBuilders.cardinality("UNIQUE_USERS")
.field("user.screen_name")))))
.setSize(0).execute().actionGet();
```

The output for the preceding aggregation will be as follows:

```
{   "aggregations": {
    "NESTED_DOCS": {
      "doc_count": 2,
      "TWEET_TIMELINE": {
        "buckets": [
          {
            "key_as_string": "2015-09-05T00:00:00.000Z",
            "key": 1441411200000,
            "doc_count": 2,
            "USERS": {
              "doc_count": 1,
              "UNIQUE_USERS": {
                "value": 1
    }
   }
  }         ]    }    }  }
```

The preceding output shows the nested docs count as 2, whereas the USERS key specifies that there is only one root document that exists in the given time range. UNIQUE_USERS shows the cardinality aggregation output for the unique users in the index.

Parent-child relationships

Similar to nested types, parent-child relationships also allow you to relate different entities together but they differ in the implementation and behavior. Unlike nested documents, they are not present within the same document, rather parent-child documents are completely separate documents. They follow the one to many relationship principle and allow you to define one type as parent and one or more as the child type.

Creating parent-child mappings

To create a parent-child mapping, you just need to specify which type should be the parent of the child type. You do not need to define anything extra in the parent type mapping but before indexing the data in the child type, you need to specify in the child's mapping who will be its parent.

Let's create a new index, `twitter_parent_child`:

```
PUT /twitter_parent_child
```

Now, put the mapping of the tweets type by specifying that the `user` will be its parent. This is done using the `_parent` keyword inside the mapping, but outside the properties:

```
PUT /twitter_parent_child/tweets/_mapping
{
  "_parent": {
    "type": "users"
  },
  "properties": {
    "text":{"type": "string"},
    "created_at":{"type": "date"}
  }
}
```

Next, put the mapping of the users type:

```
PUT /twitter_parent_child/users/_mapping
{
  "properties": {
    "screen_name":{"type": "string"},
    "created_at":{"type": "date"}
  }
}
```

> One parent can have multiple child types but one child can have only one parent type. It's also important to know the fact that you have to create the mappings for child type and specify the parent before creating the parent type. If you do it in reverse, you will get the exception: "Can't add a `_parent` field that points to an already existing type". Also, note that parents cannot be updated for any child type.

Indexing parent-child documents

Indexing parent documents is similar to what we have followed till now. However, while indexing children, you need to specify the unique ID of the parent document so that Elasticsearch can know which document is the parent of this document.

Python example

Indexing parent document:

A parent document is indexed in a similar way to any other document:

```
parent_doc = {}
parent_doc['screen_name'] = 'd_bharvi'
parent_doc['followers_count"'] = 2000
parent_doc['create_at"'] = '2012-05-30'
es.index(index='twitter_parent_child', doc_type= users, body=parent_doc, id='64995604')
```

Indexing a child document:

Indexing a child document requires specifying the `_id` of the parent document type. In Python, it is done using the `id` parameter inside the `index` function:

```
child_doc = {}
child_doc['text'] = 'learning parent-child concepts'
child_doc['created_at'] = '2015-10-30'
es.index(index='twitter_parent_child', doc_type= 'tweets', body=child_doc, id = '2333', parent='64995604')
```

Java example

Include the following import statements:

```
import org.elasticsearch.action.index.IndexRequestBuilder;
```

The parent document can be indexed in the following way:

```
IndexRequestBuilder index = client.prepareIndex(
"twitter_parent_child", "users");
Map<String, Object> parentDoc= new HashMap<String, Object>();
parentDoc.put("screen_name", "d_bharvi");
parentDoc.put("followers_count", 2000);
parentDoc.put("create_at", "2012-05-30");
index.setId("64995604").setSource(parentDoc)
.execute().actionGet();
```

The child document can be indexed in the following way:

```
IndexRequestBuilder index=client.prepareIndex("twitter_parent_child",
"tweets");
Map<String, Object> childDoc= new HashMap<String, Object>();
childDoc.put("text", "learning parent-child concepts in
elasticsearch");
childDoc.put("create_at", "2015-05-30");
index.setParent("64995604").setId("2333")
.setSource(childDoc).execute().actionGet();
```

Please note that while indexing the child document, we have used the `setParent` method and passed the `_id` of the parent document.

 By specifying the parent ID, we not only create an association between the parent and child documents but also make sure that they reside in the same shard.

Querying parent-child documents

Elasticsearch offers two queries to search parent-child documents:

- The `has_child` query
- The `has_parent` query

has_child query

The `has_child` query allows you to find and return parent documents by querying the child type. For example, we can find all the users who have tweeted about Elasticsearch.

Python example

```
query = {
  "query": {
    "has_child": {
      "type": "tweets",
      "query": {
        "match": {
          "text": "elasticsearch"
        }
      }
    }
  }
```

```
    }
  }
  resp = es.search(index='twitter_parent_child', doc_type= 'users',
  body=query)
```

Java example

The same query can be applied using Java with the following code:

```
  SearchResponse response = client.prepareSearch("twitter_parent_
  child").setTypes("users")
    .setQuery(QueryBuilders.hasChildQuery(childType,   QueryBuilders.mat
  chQuery("text","elasticsearch")))
    .execute().actionGet();
```

> Please see carefully that while using the has_child query, it is applied to the parent type because we have to return the parent documents, while the has_child parameter contains the name of the child type.

has_parent query

The has_parent query works in reverse compared to the has_child query and allows you to find and return child documents by querying on the parent type. For example, we can find all the tweets tweeted by users who have a followers count greater than 200.

Python example

```
  query = {
    "query": {
      "has_parent": {
        "type": "users",
        "query": {
          "range": {
            "followers_count": {
              "gte": 200
            }
          }
        }
      }
    }
  }
  resp = es.search(index='twitter_parent_child', doc_type= 'tweets',
  body=query)
```

Java example

The same query can be applied using Java with the following code:

```
SearchResponse response = client.prepareSearch("twitter_parent_child")
    .setTypes("tweets")
    .setQuery(QueryBuilders
    .hasParentQuery(parentType, QueryBuilders.rangeQuery("followers_count")
    .gt(200))).execute().actionGet();
```

Considerations for using document relationships

Over the years, Elasticsearch has improved a lot in reducing memory pressure by introducing `doc_values`, which is a little slower than the in-memory data structure, fielddata, but still offer reasonable speed and performance. However, because of the way nested and parent-child documents are stored and searched, you should keep the pros and cons in mind before modeling your data. The following is a comparison of nested versus parent-child types, which is nicely outlined by Zachary Tong in one of his articles:

Nested	Parent-Child
Stored in the same Lucene block as each other, which helps in a faster read/query performance. Reading a nested doc is faster than the equivalent parent/child.	Children are stored separately from the parent, but are routed to the same shard. So parent/children performance is slightly less on read/query than nested.
Updating a single field in a nested document (parent or nested children) forces ES to re-index the entire nested document. This can be very expensive for large nested docs.	If you are not using doc_values (which is by default since version 2.0.0), parent/child mappings have a bit extra memory overhead since ES maintains a "join" list in the memory.
This is best suited for data that does not change frequently.	Updating a child doc does not affect the parent or any other children, which can potentially save a lot of indexing on large docs.

Summary

This chapter covered the concepts of handling relational data in Elasticsearch with the help of nested and parent-child types. We learned about creating mappings, indexing, and querying data using Java and Python. This chapter also covered the pros and cons of using these relationships in Elasticsearch.

In the next chapter, we will learn about the different types of search execution offered by Elasticsearch and write code to re-index data from one index to other.

7
Different Methods of Search and Bulk Operations

The use cases of different searches differ according to scenarios, and Elasticsearch provides a lot of flexibility regarding how a user can perform search requests and return the data for efficient processing. The other most important thing to know is the execution of bulk operations, which enables you to finish your tasks quickly and do some other important work in your life.

In this chapter, we will cover the following topics:

- Introducing search types in Elasticsearch
- Cheaper CRUD bulk operations
- Multi get and multi search APIs
- Data pagination and re-indexing
- Practical considerations for bulk processing

Introducing search types in Elasticsearch

Elasticsearch provides the following search types to be executed:

- `query_then_fetch`: This is the default search type available in Elasticsearch. It follows a two-phase search execution. In the first phase (`query`), the query goes to a coordinating node that further forwards the query to all the relevant shards. Each shard searches the documents, sorts them locally, and returns the results to the coordinating node. The coordinating node further merges all the results, sorts them, and returns the result to the caller. The final results are of the maximum size specified in the size parameter with the search request.

- `dfs_query_then_fetch`: This is similar to the `query_then_fetch` search type, but asks Elasticsearch to do some extra processing for more accurate scoring of documents. In the `fetch` phase, all the shards compute the distributed term frequencies.
- `scan`: The scan search type differs from normal search requests because it does not involve any scoring and sorting processing of the documents. `scan` is used for the scenarios where scoring is not required and you need to iterate over a large number of documents from Elasticsearch.

>
> **The deprecated search type: count**
> There used to be another search type, `count`, that was used to return just the count of documents for a given query. It was also used while doing aggregation for excluding documents in a result and only returning the aggregation results. Count has been deprecated from Elasticsearch version 2.0 and will be removed in upcoming releases. You just need to use the `size` parameter of 0 in your query instead of using the `count` search type.

Search types can be specified while executing your search with the `search_type` parameter in the following way:

- Using REST endpoint:

   ```
   GET /search/search_type=scan
   ```

- Using Python client:

   ```
   es.search(index=index_name, doc_type=doc_type, body=query, search_type='scan'
   ```

- Using Java client, first import `SearchType` using the following import statement:

   ```
   import org.elasticsearch.action.search.SearchType;
   ```

- Then, do the following:

   ```
   client.prepareSearch("index_name")
   .setTypes("doc_type")
   .setSearchType(SearchType.SCAN)
   .setQuery(QueryBuilders.matchAllQuery())
   .execute().actionGet();
   ```

Cheaper bulk operations

There are times when you need to perform more than one request on Elasticsearch. For this, Elasticsearch offers a bulk API with the `_bulk` endpoint that allows you to perform bulk operations in a single request, be it indexing, updating, or deleting more than one document, getting more than one document using more than one document ID, or executing more than one query in a single request. The best part is that bulk operations can be executed on more than one `index` and `doc` type in a single request. The Elasticsearch Java client also offers a `BulkProcessor` class, which will be covered in a later section of this chapter. For now, let's explore the bulk requests.

> The Python client provides a helper module to create bulk operations. You need to import this module `from elasticsearch.helpers import bulk`.

Bulk create

`Bulk create` allows to create documents only if they do not already exist in the index. It expects `_source` for each document to be separated with new lines.

Python example:

1. Declare a list to hold the document set, as follows:

   ```
   docs = []
   ```

2. Create documents with the following:

   ```
   doc1 = dict()
   doc1['text'] = 'checking out search types in elasticsearch'
   doc1['created_at'] = datetime.datetime.utcnow()
   doc2 = dict()
   doc2['text'] = 'bulk API is awesome'
   doc2['created_at'] = datetime.datetime.utcnow()
   ```

3. Add both the documents to a list of documents:

   ```
   docs.append(doc1)
   docs.append(doc2)
   ```

4. Declare a list that will hold the actions to be executed in the `bulk`:

   ```
   actions = list()
   ```

5. Create an action for each document and append it to the list of `bulk` actions:

```
for doc in docs:
    action = {
    '_index': index_name,
    '_type': doc_type,
    '_op_type': 'create',
    '_source': doc
    }
    actions.append(action)
```

Please note that if you use `_op_type` as `index`, it will be of the `index` type bulk request. Now, execute the `bulk` method of the Elasticsearch helpers module to index the documents in a single request:

```
try:
    bulk_response = helpers.bulk(es, actions,request_timeout=100)
    print "bulk response:",bulk_response
except Exception as e:
    print str(e)
```

If the bulk size is more than 500, the Python module of Elasticsearch internally breaks the bulk requests into chunks of 500 documents and then indexes them.

Java example:

1. Create an object of the `BulkRequestBuilder` class:

   ```
   BulkRequestBuilder bulkRequests = client.prepareBulk();
   ```

2. Create two documents using `hashmap`, as follows:

   ```
   Map<String, Object> document1= new HashMap<String, Object>();
   Map<String, Object> document2= new HashMap<String, Object>();
   document1.put("screen_name", "d_bharvi");
   document1.put("followers_count", 2000);
   document1.put("create_at", "2015-09-20");
   document2.put("screen_name", "b44nz0r");
   document2.put("followers_count", 6000);
   document2.put("create_at", "2019-09-20");
   ```

3. Create individual index requests and add them to the bulk request:

   ```
   bulkRequests.add(new IndexRequest().index(indexName).
   type(docType).source(document1).opType("create").id("125"));

   bulkRequests.add(new IndexRequest().index(indexName).
   type(docType).source(document1).opType("index").id("123"));
   ```

4. Execute the bulk request, as shown here:

   ```
   BulkResponse bulkResponse =bulkRequests.execute().actionGet();

   if (bulkResponse.hasFailures())
     {
       //handle the failure scenarios
       for (BulkItemResponse bulkItemResponse : bulkResponse) {

       }
     }
   ```

Bulk indexing

Bulk indexing allows you to index multiple documents in a single request, which is similar to indexing a single document as we have seen until now. If the document already exists, it deletes the document and indexes a new document in its place, and if the document does not already exist, it creates a new document. It also expects _source for each document to be separated with new lines.

The code for `bulk index` is the same as for `bulk create`, with only one difference: in Python, you just need to set the `_op_type` value to `index`, and in Java `opType` will take `index` as its parameter. The difference between `index` and `create` is: when the operation is set to `index`, documents get over-ridden if they already exist in the index, whereas a `create` operation is useful when you want to skip the indexing of documents that already exist. Therefore, the `create` operation gives a performance boost in comparison to `index`.

Bulk updating

Bulk updating allows you to perform partial updates on one or more than one document in a single request. Instead of _source, it requires either a `script` parameter or a `doc` parameter to update the documents.

Python example:

1. Declare a list that will hold the actions to be executed in the `bulk`:

    ```
    actions = list()
    ```

2. Create an action for each document and append it to the list of bulk actions:

    ```
    for doc in docs:
        action = {
        '_index': index_name,
        '_type': doc_type,
        '_id': doc_id,
        '_op_type': 'update',
        'doc': {'new_field': 'doing partial update with a new field'}
        }
        actions.append(action)
    ```

As mentioned earlier, a partial update requires `doc` instead of `_source` as a new field to be updated when an ID for the existing documents is provided. The same is shown in the preceding example. For every document, we have created an inline partial `doc` with the field name as `new field`, and once the actions are created, we are all set to execute a bulk update as follows:

```
try:
    bulk_indexed = helpers.bulk(es, actions,request_timeout=100)
    print "bulk response:",bulk_indexed
except Exception as e:
    print str(e)
```

You will get a missing document exception if the document ID does not exist in the index.

Java example

In Java, you can create individual bulk requests using `UpdateRequest` and add them to the object of `BulkRequestBuilder`, using the following code:

```
bulkRequests.add(new UpdateRequest().index(indexName).type(docType).
doc(partialDoc1).id("125"));

bulkRequests.add(new UpdateRequest().index(indexName).type(docType).
doc(partialDoc2).id("123"));
```

Finally, bulk updates can be executed similarly to what we saw for bulk indexing:

```
BulkResponse bulkResponse = bulkRequests.execute().actionGet();

if (bulkResponse.hasFailures())
  {
    //handle the failure scenarios
    for (BulkItemResponse bulkItemResponse : bulkResponse) {

    }
  }
```

Bulk deleting

Bulk deleting allows you to delete one or more than one document in a single request. It does not require any source in the request body and follows the same semantic as a standard `delete` request.

Python example:

Bulk deleting needs the IDs of documents to be deleted, which you can do as follows:

```
del_complete_batch = []
for id in ids_to_delete:
    del_complete_batch.append({
            '_op_type': 'delete',
            '_index': index_name,
            '_type': doc_type,
            '_id': id,
        })
try:
    helpers.bulk(es, del_complete_batch, request_timeout=100)
except Exception as e:
    print str(e)
```

Java example:

Bulk delete requests can be built by creating individual `DeleteRequest` and adding them to the `BulkRequestBuilder` object:

```
bulkRequests.add(new DeleteRequest().index(indexName).type(docType).id("1252"));

bulkRequests.add(new UpdateRequest().index(indexName).type(docType).id("123"));
And once the bulk is ready, then can be executed.
BulkResponse bulkResponse = bulkRequests.execute().actionGet();
```

Please note that the execution might return an exception similar to bulk updates if the documents do not exist in the index.

Multi get and multi search APIs

Until now, you have seen the execution of a single `get` request to fetch a document and hit a single query at a time to search for documents. However, life will be easier with the following two APIs offered by Elasticsearch.

Multi get

`Multi get` is all about combining more than one `get` request in a single request. I remember once I had a requirement to check the existence of multiple documents in an index and create a bulk update request against only those IDs that did not already exist. The one way to do this was by hitting a single HEAD request for each document ID, and based on the response of Elasticsearch, create a bulk update request for the documents that did not exist. However, multi get requests can solve this problem in a single API call instead of multiple HEAD requests.

All you need to do is create an array of document IDs and hit them on Elasticsearch using the `_mget` endpoint of Elasticsearch. The following is a simple `curl` request to show how you can do this:

```
curl 'localhost:9200/index_name/doc_type/_mget' -d '{
    "ids" : ["1", "2"]
}'
```

Here, IDs are the `_id` of the documents to be fetched.

 If an ID does not exist in the index, Elasticsearch returns `found=false` for that document ID.

You have additional options to decide whether you want to return the data of the document or not. If it is not required, just set `_source : false` while hitting the `mget` request. For example:

```
curl 'localhost:9200/index_name/doc_type/_mget' -d '{
    "ids" : ["1", "2"], "_source" : false
}'
```

If you are interested in only returning a particular field, you can do it like this:

```
curl 'localhost:9200/index_name/doc_type/_mget' -d '{
    "ids" : ["1", "2"], "_source" : ["field1", "field2"]
}
```

Here, `field1` and `field2` are the names of the fields required to be returned.

Python example:

Declare an array of IDs to be fetched:

```
document_ids_to_get = ['1','4','12','54','123','543']
```

Create a query by passing an array of `doc` IDs to the ID parameter:

```
query = {"ids": document_ids_to_get}
#Exceute the query using mget endpoint:
exists_resp = es.mget(index=index_name,doc_type=doc_type, body=query, _source=False, request_timeout=100)
```

Java example:

Import the following packages into your source code:

```
import org.elasticsearch.action.get.MultiGetItemResponse;
import org.elasticsearch.action.get.MultiGetResponse;
```

Create a multi get request in the following way:

```
MultiGetResponse responses = client.prepareMultiGet()
    .add(indexName, docType, ids_to_be_fetched)
    .execute().actionGet();
```

The multi get response is parsed in the following way:

```
for (MultiGetItemResponse itemResponse : responses) {
    GetResponse response = itemResponse.getResponse();
    if (response.isExists()) {
        String json = response.getSourceAsString();
        System.out.println(json);
    }
}
```

The `id_to_be_fetched` function is a list of document IDs that need to be fetched.

Different Methods of Search and Bulk Operations

Multi searches

You might have worked with many databases and search engines, but none of them provides the functionality to hit more than one query in a single request. Elasticsearch can do this with its _msearch REST API. For this, it follows a specific request format as shown here:

```
header\n
body\n
.........
.........
header\n
body\n
```

Understanding the preceding search request structure:

- header: This includes the name of the index/indices to be searched upon and optionally includes the search type, search preference nodes (primary, secondary, and so on), and routing
- body: This includes the search request queries

Let's see an example:

1. Create a file, multi_requests, with the following content. Please note that each line is separated with \n (new line):

   ```
   {"index" : "users"}
   {"query" : {"match_all" : {}}, "from" : 0, "size" : 10}
   {"index" : "twitter", "search_type" : "dfs_query_then_fetch"}
   {"query" : {"match_all" : {}}}
   ```

2. Now execute the search request using the _msearch API:

   ```
   curl -XGET localhost:9200/_msearch --data-binary "@ multi_requests"
   ```

   In the preceding curl command, we have used the -data-binary flag to load the multiline content from the file. This is required while executing bulk data indexing too.

> Searches executed with the _msearch API return responses in the responses array form, which includes the search response for each search request that matches its order in the original multi search request. If there is a complete failure for that specific search request, an object with an error message will be returned in the place of the actual search response.

Python example:

1. Create an individual request head with an index name and doc type in the following way:

   ```
   req_head1 = {'index': index_name1, 'type': doc_type1}
   ```

2. Create a `query_request_array` list, which contains the actual queries and the head part of those queries:

   ```
   query_request_array = []
   query_1 = {"query" : {"match_all" : {}}}
   query_request_array.append(req_head1)
   query_request_array.append(query_1)
   ```

3. Create another request with a head and body:

   ```
   req_head2 = {'index': index_name2, 'type': doc_typ2}
   query_2 = {"query" : {"match_all" : {}}}
   query_request_array.append(req_head2)
   query_request_array.append(query_2)
   ```

4. Execute the request using a `msearch` endpoint by passing `query_request_array` into the body; you can optionally set `request_timeout` too:

   ```
   response = es.msearch(body=query_request_array)
   ```

5. The response of a multi search can be parsed in the following way:

   ```
   for resp in response["responses"]:
       if resp.get("hits"):
           for hit in resp.get("hits").get('hits'):
               print hit["_source"]
   ```

Java example:

1. To execute a multi search using Java, you need to import the following packages into your code:

   ```
   import org.elasticsearch.action.search.MultiSearchResponse;
   import org.elasticsearch.action.search.SearchRequestBuilder;
   ```

2. Then, you can create an individual search request using the `SearchRequestBuilder` class:

   ```
   SearchRequestBuilder searchRequest1 = client.
   prepareSearch().setIndices(indexName).setTypes(docType)
   .setQuery(QueryBuilders.queryStringQuery("elasticsearch").
   defaultField("text")).setSize(1);

   SearchRequestBuilder searchRequest2 =
   ```

```
client.prepareSearch().setIndices(indexName).setTypes(docType)
        .setQuery(QueryBuilders.matchQuery("screen_name", "d_
bharvi")).setSize(1);
```

3. These individual search requests can be added to a multi search request and executed in the following way:

```
MultiSearchResponse sr = client.prepareMultiSearch()
            .add(searchRequest1)
            .add(searchRequest1)
            .execute().actionGet();
```

4. You will get all the individual responses from `MultiSearchResponse`, as follows:

```
long nbHits = 0;
for (MultiSearchResponse.Item item : sr.getResponses()) {
    SearchResponse response = item.getResponse();
    nbHits += response.getHits().getTotalHits();
  }
}
```

Data pagination

We have seen that for any query, Elasticsearch by default returns only the top 10 documents after scoring and sorting them. However, they are not always enough to serve the purpose. A user always needs more and more data either to render on a page or to process in the backend. Let's see how we can do this.

Pagination with scoring

In the previous chapters, we discussed how Elasticsearch offers the `from` and `to` parameters to be passed with search requests. So, you always have an option to either increase the `size` parameter to load more results from Elasticsearch or send another query with the changed `from` and `size` values to get more data.

This pagination approach makes sense when you have to fetch a limited number of documents from Elasticsearch. As this approach is too costly and can kill Elasticsearch if you are hitting a request, for example, where `from = 100000` and `size = 100010` to get 10 documents, which have less score than those `1 lac` documents in the index.

Pagination without scoring

While working with Elasticsearch, a functionality that is needed most of the time is: returning a large set of data to process or to simply re-index from one index to another. This type of data fetching does not require any document scoring or sorting. Elasticsearch offers a scan search type to fulfil this requirement.

Scrolling and re-indexing documents using scan-scroll

A scan search type works in the same manner as how you scan a Facebook or Twitter web page with your eyes and scroll to see more content.

Python example:

You can define a query for which you want all the documents to be returned, as follows:

```
query = {"query":{"match_all":{}}}
```

Also, you can create a list that will hold the returned documents:

```
documents = []
```

Then execute the following request to get the scroll ID from Elasticsearch, which will be used to get the actual data in subsequent requests. The scroll parameter (timeout for scrolling) in the following request specifies for how long the scroll will be open. It can be defined using 100s (100 seconds) or 2m (two minutes):

```
resp = es.search(index=source_index, doc_type=source_doc_type,
body=query, search_type="scan", scroll='100s', size=100)
```

Once scroll_id is returned with the preceding request, you can use it inside a while loop, which will run until Elasticsearch returns the entire document for your query:

```
while True:
    print 'scrolling for ',str(scroll_count)+' time'
  #A new scroll id generated for each request. Scroll parameter is
also need to be set for each request.
    resp = es.scroll(resp['_scroll_id'], scroll='100s')
    if len(resp['hits']['hits']) == 0:
        print 'data re-indexing completed..!!'
        break
    else:
      #add the documents to the documents list
        documents.extend(resp['hits']['hits'])
```

Different Methods of Search and Bulk Operations

```
        #send the documens to for re-indexing
         perform_bulk_index(destination_index, destination_doc_type,
documents)
    #Empty your documents list so that it can hold another batch of
response
         documents = []
```

The `perform_bulk_index` function can be implemented in the same way as we have seen in bulk indexing. It will take a set of documents and will be sent to Elasticsearch in bulk:

```
actions = []
for document in documents:
    actions.append({
            '_op_type': 'create',
            '_index': destination_index,
            '_type': destination_doc_type,
            '_id': document['_id'],
            '_source': document['_source']
            })
try:
    helpers.bulk(es, actions, request_timeout=100)
except Exception as e:
    print "bulk index raised exception", str(e)
```

Java Example (using bulk processor):

We have already seen how bulk indexing can be done using `BulkRequestBuilder`. You will now learn how to do bulk indexing using the `BulkProcessor` class.

As mentioned in the Elasticsearch documentation:

> *"A bulk processor is a thread safe bulk processing class, allowing you to easily set when to "flush a new bulk request (either based on number of actions, based on the size, or time), and to easily control the number of concurrent bulk requests allowed to be executed in parallel."*

The most important parameters offered by `BulkProcessor` are as follows:

- **Bulk actions**: This defaults to 1,000. This sets the number of operations to be processed in a single bulk request.
- **Flush interval**: The default for this is not set. Flush is a process of performing a Lucene commit on the disk. Before doing a flush, Elasticsearch stores the data inside a special file called `translog` to prevent data loss.

- **Bulk size**: This defaults to 5 MB. This specifies how much data should be flushed at once. It should be increased wisely according to the capacity of the Elasticsearch cluster.
- **Concurrent Requests**: The default value is 1. (It should not be set to more than the number of available CPU cores where code is running because each concurrent request starts a new thread.)

Let's import the packages into our code to get data through `scan-scroll` and `bulk` processing:

```
import static org.elasticsearch.index.query.QueryBuilders.matchAllQuery;
import java.util.concurrent.TimeUnit;
import org.elasticsearch.action.bulk.BulkProcessor;
import org.elasticsearch.action.bulk.BulkRequest;
import org.elasticsearch.action.bulk.BulkResponse;
import org.elasticsearch.action.index.IndexRequest;
import org.elasticsearch.action.search.SearchResponse;
import org.elasticsearch.action.search.SearchType;
import org.elasticsearch.client.Client;
import org.elasticsearch.common.unit.TimeValue;
import org.elasticsearch.search.SearchHit;
```

The following are the main variables you need to declare to index using a bulk processor:

```
//The maximum time to wait for the bulk requests to complete
    public static final int SCROLL_TIMEOUT_SECONDS = 30;
    //Number of documents to be returned, maximum would be scroll_size*number of shards
    public static final int SCROLL_SIZE = 10;
    //Sets when to flush a new bulk request based on the number of actions currently added. defaults to 1000
    public static final int BULK_ACTIONS_THRESHOLD = 10000;
    //Sets the number of concurrent requests allowed to be executed.
    public static final int BULK_CONCURRENT_REQUESTS = 2;
    //Sets a flush interval flushing (specified in seconds)
    public static final int BULK_FLUSH_DURATION = 30;
```

Create an instance of the `Bulk Processor` class using the previous variables:

```
BulkProcessor bulkProcessor = BulkProcessor.builder(clientTo,
            createLoggingBulkProcessorListener()).
setBulkActions(BULK_ACTIONS_THRESHOLD).setConcurrentRequests(BULK_CONCURRENT_REQUESTS)
        .setFlushInterval(createFlushIntervalTime().build();
```

Getting the data from scan-scroll can be done as follows:

```
SearchResponse searchResponse = clientFrom.prepareSearch(fromIndex)
         .setTypes(sourceDocType)
            .setQuery(matchAllQuery())
            .setSearchType(SearchType.SCAN)
            .setScroll(createScrollTimeoutValue())
            .setSize(SCROLL_SIZE).execute().actionGet();
```

This will return a scroll ID, which will be used to scroll the documents and return them for processing:

```
while (true) {
            searchResponse = clientFrom.prepareSearchScroll(searchResponse.getScrollId())
                    .setScroll(createScrollTimeoutValue()).execute().actionGet();
            if (searchResponse.getHits().getHits().length == 0) {
                System.out.println("Closing the bulk processor");
                bulkProcessor.close();
                break; //Break condition: No hits are returned
            }
            //Add the documents to the bulk processor and depending on the bulk threshold they will be flushed to ES
            for (SearchHit hit : searchResponse.getHits()) {
    IndexRequest request = new IndexRequest(toIndex, destinationDocType, hit.id());
                request.source(hit.getSource());
                bulkProcessor.add(request);
            }
        }
```

The bulk processor has a listener, which flushes the request index depending on the bulk threshold. This listener can be defined in the following way:

```
    private BulkProcessor.Listener createLoggingBulkProcessorListener() {
        return new BulkProcessor.Listener() {
        @Override
        public void beforeBulk(long executionId, BulkRequest request)
{
```

```
            System.out.println("Going to execute new bulk composed "+ 
request.numberOfActions()+" no. of actions");
        }

        @Override
        public void afterBulk(long executionId, BulkRequest request, 
BulkResponse response) {
            System.out.println("Executed bulk composed "+ request.
numberOfActions()+" no. of actions");
        }

        @Override
        public void afterBulk(long executionId, BulkRequest request, 
Throwable failure) {
            System.out.println("Error executing bulk "+ failure);
        }
    };
}
```

You also need to define the following helper function to create time units to be used by bulk processing:

```
private TimeValue createFlushIntervalTime() {
    return new TimeValue(BULK_FLUSH_DURATION, TimeUnit.SECONDS);
}

private TimeValue createScrollTimeoutValue() {
    return new TimeValue(SCROLL_TIMEOUT_SECONDS, TimeUnit.
SECONDS);
}
```

Practical considerations for bulk processing

It's awesome to minimize the requests using the search types and bulk APIs we saw in this chapter, but you also need to think that for a large amount of processing to be done by Elasticsearch, you need to take care of resource utilization and control the size of your requests accordingly. The following are some points that will help you while working with the things you have learned in this chapter.

The most important factor to be taken care of is the size of your documents. Fetching or indexing 1 KB of 1,000 documents in a single request is damn easier than 100 KB of 1,000 documents:

- **Multisearch**: While querying with multi search requests, you should take care of how many queries you are hitting in a single request. You just can't combine 1,000 queries in a single query and execute them in one go. Also, the number of queries should be minimized according to the complexity of queries. So, you can break your query set into multiple multi-search requests in batches of, for example, 100 queries per batch, and execute them. You can combine the results after all the batches are executed. The same rule applies while querying with the `mget` API too.
- **Scan-scroll**: A search with scan and scroll is highly beneficial for performing deep paginations, but the number of documents returned in a single request is usually *scroll_size*number_of_shards*. We have also seen that we need to pass the timeout using a `scroll` parameter because it tells Elasticsearch for how long a search context needs to be open on the server to serve a particular scroll request. Scroll timeouts do not need to be long enough to process all the data — they just need to be long enough to process the previous batch of results. Each scroll request (with the `scroll` parameter) sets a new expiry time. So, you need to set the scroll timeout wisely so that there are not too many open search contexts existing at the same time on your Elasticsearch server. This heavily affects the background merge process of Lucene indexes. Also, the scroll time should not be so small that your request gets a timeout.
- **Bulk indexing and bulk updates**: Sending too much data in a single request can harm your Elasticsearch node if you do not have the optimal resources available. Remember that while data indexing or updating, the merging of Lucene segments is done in the background, and with a large amount of data merging and flushing on the disk, a very high amount of CPU and disk IO is required. So, choose the numbers wisely by benchmarking your requests.

Summary

This chapter provided you some very important functionalities of Elasticsearch, which every programmer needs to know while developing applications in real-time scenarios and working with a large number of datasets. We covered the bulk APIs by combining multiple requests into a single one to reduce the time and number of requests to process large datasets. We also saw some best practices to be kept in mind while working with these APIs, and most importantly, you got practical code examples that will help you through your journey with Elasticsearch.

In the next chapter, you are going to learn about search relevancy and how to control the scoring of your searches.

8
Controlling Relevancy

Getting a search engine to behave can be very hard. It does not matter if you are a newbie or have years of experience with Elasticsearch or Solr, you must have definitely struggled with low-quality search results in your application. The default algorithm of Lucene does not come close to meeting your requirements, and there is always a struggle to deliver the relevant search results.

In this chapter, we will cover the following topics:

- Introducing relevant searches
- Out-of-the-box tools from Elasticsearch
- Controlling relevancy with custom scoring

Introducing relevant searches

Relevancy is the root of a search engine's value proposition and can be defined as the art of ranking content for a user's search based on how much that content satisfies the needs of the user or the business.

In an application, it does not matter how beautiful your user interface looks or how many functionalities you are providing to the user; search relevancy cannot be avoided at any cost. So, despite of the mystical behavior of search engines, you have to find a solution to get relevant results. The relevancy becomes more important because a user does not care about the whole bunch of documents that you have. The user enters their keywords, selects filters, and focuses on a very small amount of data—the relevant results. And if your search engine fails to deliver according to expectations, the user might be annoyed, which might be a loss for your business.

A search engine like Elasticsearch comes with a built-in intelligence. You enter the keyword and within the blink of an eye, it returns to you the results that it thinks are relevant according to its intelligence. However, Elasticsearch does not have a built-in intelligence according to your application domain. The relevancy is not defined by a search engine; rather it is defined by your users, their business needs, and the domains. Take an example of Google or Twitter; they have put in years of engineering experience, but still fail occasionally while providing relevancy. Don't they?

Further, the challenges of searching differ with the domain: the search on an e-commerce platform is about driving sales and bringing positive customer outcomes, whereas in fields such as medicine, it is about the matter of life and death. The lives of search engineers become more complicated because they do not have domain-specific knowledge, which can be used to understand the semantics of user queries.

However, despite of all the challenges, the implementation of search relevancy is up to you, and it depends on what information you can extract from the users, their queries, and the content they see. We continuously take feedback from users, create funnels, or enable loggings to capture the search behavior of users so that we can improve our algorithms to provide relevant results.

The Elasticsearch out-of-the-box tools

Elasticsearch primarily works with two models of information retrieval: the **Boolean model** and the **Vector Space model**. In addition to these, there are other scoring algorithms available in Elasticsearch as well, such as Okapi BM25, **Divergence from Randomness** (**DFR**), and **Information Based** (**IB**). Working with these three models requires extensive mathematical knowledge and needs some extra configurations in Elasticsearch, which are beyond the scope of this book.

The Boolean model uses the AND, OR, and NOT conditions in a query to find all the matching documents. This Boolean model can be further combined with the Lucene scoring formula, TF/IDF (which we have already discussed in *Chapter 2, Understanding Document Analysis and Creating Mappings*), to rank documents.

The vector space model works differently from the Boolean model, as it represents both queries and documents as vectors. In the vector space model, each number in the vector is the weight of a term that is calculated using TF/IDF.

The queries and documents are compared using a cosine similarity in which angles between two vectors are compared to find the similarity, which ultimately leads to finding the relevancy of the documents.

An example: why defaults are not enough

Let's build an index with sample documents to understand the examples in a better way.

First, create an index with the name `profiles`:

```
curl -XPUT 'localhost:9200/profiles'
```

Then, put the mapping with the document type as `candidate`:

```
curl -XPUT 'localhost:9200/profiles/candidate'

{
  "properties": {
    "geo_code": {
      "type": "geo_point",
      "lat_lon": true
    }
  }
}
```

Please note that in the preceding mapping, we are putting mapping only for the `geo` data type. The rest of the fields will be indexed dynamically.

Now, you can create a `data.json` file with the following content in it:

```
{ "index" : { "_index" : "profiles", "_type" : "candidate", "_id" : 1 }}
{ "name" : "Sam", "geo_code" : "12.9545163,77.3500487", "total_experience":5, "skills":["java","python"] }
{ "index" : { "_index" : "profiles", "_type" : "candidate", "_id" : 2 }}
{ "name" : "Robert", "geo_code" : "28.6619678,77.225706", "total_experience":2, "skills":["java"] }
{ "index" : { "_index" : "profiles", "_type" : "candidate", "_id" : 3 }}
{ "name" : "Lavleen", "geo_code" : "28.6619678,77.225706", "total_experience":4, "skills":["java","Elasticsearch"] }
{ "index" : { "_index" : "profiles", "_type" : "candidate", "_id" : 4 }}
{ "name" : "Bharvi", "geo_code" : "28.6619678,77.225706", "total_experience":3, "skills":["java","lucene"] }
{ "index" : { "_index" : "profiles", "_type" : "candidate", "_id" : 5 }}
{ "name" : "Nips", "geo_code" : "12.9545163,77.3500487", "total_experience":7, "skills":["grails","python"] }
{ "index" : { "_index" : "profiles", "_type" : "candidate", "_id" : 6 }}
{ "name" : "Shikha", "geo_code" : "28.4250666,76.8493508", "total_experience":10, "skills":["c","java"] }
```

Controlling Relevancy

> If you are indexing skills, which are separated by spaces or which include non-English characters, that is, C++, C#, or Core Java, you need to create mapping for the `skills` field as `not_analyzed` in advance to have exact term matching.

Once the file is created, execute the following command to put the data inside the index we have just created:

`curl -XPOST 'localhost:9200' --data-binary @data.json`

If you look carefully at the example, the documents contain the data of the candidates who might be looking for jobs. For hiring candidates, a recruiter can have the following criteria:

- Candidates should know about Java
- Candidates should have experience of 3 to 5 years
- Candidates should fall in the distance range of 100 kilometers from the office of the recruiter

You can construct a simple `bool` query in combination with a term query on the `skills` field along with `geo_distance` and range filters on the `geo_code` and `total_experience` fields respectively. However, does this give a relevant set of results? The answer would be NO.

The problem is that if you are restricting the range of experience and distance, you might even get zero results or no suitable candidates. For example, you can put a range of 0 to 100 kilometers of distance but your perfect candidate might be at a distance of 101 kilometers. At the same time, if you define a wide range, you might get a huge number of non-relevant results.

The other problem is that if you search for candidates who know Java, there is a chance that a person who knows only Java and not any other programming language will be at the top, while a person who knows other languages apart from Java will be at the bottom. This happens because during the ranking of documents with TF/IDF, the lengths of the fields are taken into account. If the length of a field is small, the document is more relevant.

Elasticsearch is not intelligent enough to understand the semantic meaning of your queries, but for these scenarios, it offers you the full power to redefine how scoring and document ranking should be done.

Controlling relevancy with custom scoring

In most cases, you are good to go with the default scoring algorithms of Elasticsearch to return the most relevant results. However, some cases require you to have more control on the calculation of a score. This is especially required while implementing domain-specific logic such as finding the relevant candidates for a job, where you need to implement a very specific scoring formula. Elasticsearch provides you with the function_score query to take control of all these things.

This chapter covers the code examples only in Java because a Python client gives you the flexibility to pass the query inside the body parameter of a search function as you have learned in the previous chapters. Python programmers can simply use the example queries in the same way. There is no extra module required to execute these queries. You can still download the Python code for this chapter from the Packt website.

The function_score query

The function_score query allows you to take the complete control of how a score needs to be calculated for a particular query.

The syntax of a function_score query:

```
{
  "query": {"function_score": {
    "query": {},
    "boost": "boost for the whole query",
    "functions": [
      {}
    ],
    "max_boost": number,
    "score_mode": "(multiply|max|...)",
    "boost_mode": "(multiply|replace|...)",
    "min_score" : number
  }}
}
```

The function_score query has two parts: the first is the base query that finds the overall pool of results you want. The second part is the list of functions, which are used to adjust the scoring. These functions can be applied to each document that matches the main query in order to alter or completely replace the original query _score.

Controlling Relevancy

> In a `function_score` query, each function is composed of an optional filter that tells Elasticsearch which records should have their scores adjusted (this defaults to "all records") and a description of how to adjust the score.

The other parameters that can be used with a `functions_score` query are as follows:

- **boost**: An optional parameter that defines the boost for the entire query.
- **max_boost**: The maximum boost that will be applied by a function score.
- **boost_mode**: An optional parameter, which defaults to `multiply`. The `score` mode defines how the combined result of the score functions will influence the final score together with the subquery score. This can be `replace` (only the `function_score` is used; the query `score` is ignored), `max` (the maximum of the query score and the function score), `min` (the minimum of the query score and the function score), `sum` (the query score and the function score are added), `avg`, or `multiply` (the query score and the function score are multiplied).
- **score_mode**: This parameter specifies how the results of individual score functions will be aggregated. The possible values can be `first` (the first function that has a matching filter is applied), `avg`, `max`, `sum`, `min`, and `multiply`.
- **min_score**: The minimum score to be used.

> **Excluding non-relevant documents with min_score**
> To exclude documents that do not meet a certain score threshold, the `min_score` parameter can be set to the desired score threshold.

The following are the built-in functions that are available to be used with the function score query:

- `weight`
- `field_value_factor`
- `script_score`
- The decay functions—`linear`, `exp`, and `gauss`

Let's see them one by one and then you will learn how to combine them in a single query.

weight

A `weight` function allows you to apply a simple boost to each document without the boost being normalized: a weight of 2 results in 2 * _score. For example:

```
GET profiles/candidate/_search
{
  "query": {
    "function_score": {
      "query": {
        "term": {
          "skills": {
            "value": "java"
          }
        }
      },
      "functions": [
        {
          "filter": {
            "term": {
              "skills": "python"
            }
          },
          "weight": 2
        }
      ],
      "boost_mode": "replace"
    }
  }
}
```

The preceding query will match all the candidates who know Java, but will give a higher score to the candidates who also know Python. Please note that `boost_mode` is set to `replace`, which will cause _score to be calculated by a query that is to be overridden by the `weight` function for our particular filter clause. The query output will contain the candidates on top with a _score of 2 who know both Java and Python.

Java example:

The previous query can be implemented in Java in the following way:

1. First, you need to import the following classes into your code:

   ```
   import org.elasticsearch.action.search.SearchResponse;
   import org.elasticsearch.client.Client;
   ```

Controlling Relevancy

```
import org.elasticsearch.index.query.QueryBuilders;
import org.elasticsearch.index.query.functionscore.
FunctionScoreQueryBuilder;
import org.elasticsearch.index.query.functionscore.
ScoreFunctionBuilders;
```

2. Then the following code snippets can be used to implement the query:

```
FunctionScoreQueryBuilder functionQuery = new FunctionScoreQueryBu
ilder(QueryBuilders.termQuery("skills", "java"))
    .add(QueryBuilders.termQuery("skills", "python"),
ScoreFunctionBuilders.weightFactorFunction(2)).
boostMode("replace");


SearchResponse response =
client.prepareSearch().setIndices(indexName)
        .setTypes(docType).setQuery(functionQuery)
        .execute().actionGet();
```

field_value_factor

This uses the value of a field in the document to alter the _score:

```
GET profiles/candidate/_search
{
  "query": {
    "function_score": {
      "query": {
        "term": {
          "skills": {
            "value": "java"
          }
        }
      },
      "functions": [
        {
          "field_value_factor": {
            "field": "total_experience"
          }
        }
      ],
      "boost_mode": "multiply"
    }
  }
}
```

The preceding query finds all the candidates with Java in their skills, but influences the total score depending on the total experience of the candidate. So, the more experience the candidate has, the higher the ranking they will get. Please note that `boost_mode` is set to multiply, which will yield the following formula for the final scoring:

```
_score = _score * doc['total_experience'].value
```

However, there are two issues with the preceding approach: first is the documents that have the total experience value as 0 and will reset the final score to 0. Second, Lucene `_score` usually falls between 0 and 10, so a candidate with an experience of more than 10 years will completely swamp the effect of the full text search score.

To get rid of this problem, apart from using the `field` parameter, the `field_value_factor` function provides you with the following extra parameters to be used:

- `factor`: This is an optional factor to multiply the field value with. This defaults to 1.
- `modifier`: This is a mathematical modifier to apply to the field value. This can be: `none`, `log`, `log1p`, `log2p`, `ln`, `ln1p`, `ln2p`, `square`, `sqrt`, or `reciprocal`. It defaults to `none`.

Java example:

The preceding query can be implemented in Java in the following way:

1. First, you need to import the following classes into your code:
   ```
   import org.elasticsearch.action.search.SearchResponse;
   import org.elasticsearch.client.Client;
   import org.elasticsearch.index.query.QueryBuilders;
   import org.elasticsearch.index.query.functionscore*;
   ```

2. Then the following code snippets can be used to implement the query:
   ```
   FunctionScoreQueryBuilder functionQuery = new FunctionScoreQueryBuilder(QueryBuilders.termQuery("skills", "java"))
       .add(new FieldValueFactorFunctionBuilder("total_experience")).boostMode("multiply");

   SearchResponse response = client.prepareSearch().setIndices("profiles")
           .setTypes("candidate").setQuery(functionQuery)
           .execute().actionGet();
   ```

script_score

script_score is the most powerful function available in Elasticsearch. It uses a custom script to take complete control of the scoring logic. You can write a custom script to implement the logic you need. Scripting allows you to write from a simple to very complex logic. Scripts are cached, too, to allow faster executions of repetitive queries. Let's see an example:

```
{
  "script_score": {
    "script": "doc['total_experience'].value"
  }
}
```

Look at the special syntax to access the field values inside the script parameter. This is how the value of the fields is accessed using Groovy scripting language.

 Scripting is, by default, disabled in Elasticsearch, so to use script score functions, first you need to add this line in your elasticsearch.yml file: script.inline: on.

To see some of the power of this function, look at the following example:

```
GET profiles/candidate/_search
{
  "query": {
    "function_score": {
      "query": {
        "term": {
          "skills": {
            "value": "java"
          }
        }
      },
      "functions": [
        {
          "script_score": {
            "params": {
              "skill_array_provided": [
                "java",
                "python"
              ]
            },
```

```
             "script": "final_score=0; skill_array = doc['skills'].
toArray(); counter=0; while(counter<skill_array.size()){for(skill in
skill_array_provided){if(skill_array[counter]==skill){final_score =
final_score+doc['total_experience'].value};};counter=counter+1;};retu
rn final_score"
            }
          }
      ],
      "boost_mode": "replace"
    }
  }
}
```

Let's understand the preceding query:

- `params` is the placeholder where you can pass the parameters to your function, similar to how you use parameters inside a method signature in other languages. Inside the `script` parameter, you write your complete logic.
- This script iterates through each document that has Java mentioned in the skills, and for each document it fetches all the skills and stores them inside the `skill_array` variable. Finally, each skill that we have passed inside the `params` section is compared with the skills inside `skill_array`. If this matches, the value of the `final_score` variable is incremented with the value of the `total_experience` field of that document. The score calculated by the script score will be used to rank the documents because `boost_mode` is set to replace the original `_score` value.

Do not try to work with the analyzed fields while writing the scripts. You might get weird results. This is because, had our skills field contained a value such as "core java", you could not have got the exact matching for it inside the script section. So, the fields with space-separated values need to be set as `not_analyzed` or the keyword has to be analyzed in advance.

> To write these script functions, you need to have some command over groovy scripting. However, if you find it complex, you can write these scripts in other languages, such as Python, using the language plugin of Elasticsearch. More on this can be found here: https://github.com/elastic/elasticsearch-lang-python.
>
> For fast performance, use Groovy or Java functions. Python and JavaScript code requires the marshalling and unmarshalling of values that kill performance due to more CPU/memory usage.

Controlling Relevancy

Java example:

The previous query can be implemented in Java in the following way:

1. First, you need to import the following classes into your code:

   ```
   import org.elasticsearch.action.search.SearchResponse;
   import org.elasticsearch.client.Client;
   import org.elasticsearch.index.query.QueryBuilders;
   import org.elasticsearch.index.query.functionscore.*;
   import org.elasticsearch.script.Script;
   ```

2. Then, the following code snippets can be used to implement the query:

   ```
   String script = "final_score=0; skill_array = doc['skills'].toArray(); "
           + "counter=0; while(counter<skill_array.size())"
           + "{for(skill in skill_array_provided)"
           + "{if(skill_array[counter]==skill)"
           + "{final_score =    final_score+doc['total_experience'].value};};"
           + "counter=counter+1;};return final_score";

   ArrayList<String> skills = new ArrayList<String>();
     skills.add("java");
     skills.add("python");

   Map<String, Object> params = new HashMap<String, Object>();
     params.put("skill_array_provided",skills);
     FunctionScoreQueryBuilder functionQuery = new

   FunctionScoreQueryBuilder(QueryBuilders.termQuery("skills", "java"))
       .add(new ScriptScoreFunctionBuilder(new Script(script, ScriptType.INLINE, "groovy", params))).boostMode("replace");

   SearchResponse response =   client.prepareSearch().
   setIndices(indexName)
           .setTypes(docType).setQuery(functionQuery)
           .execute().actionGet();
   ```

As you can see, the script logic is a simple string that is used to instantiate the `Script` class constructor inside `ScriptScoreFunctionBuilder`.

Decay functions - linear, exp, and gauss

We have seen the problems of restricting the range of experience and distance that could result in getting zero results or no suitable candidates. Maybe a recruiter would like to hire a candidate from a different province because of a good candidate profile. So, instead of completely restricting with the range filters, we can incorporate sliding-scale values such as `geo_location` or dates into `_score` to prefer documents near a latitude/longitude point or recently published documents.

`function_score` provide to work with this sliding scale with the help of three decay functions: `linear`, `exp` (that is, exponential), and `gauss` (that is, Gaussian). All three functions take the same parameter, as shown in the following code and are required to control the shape of the curve created for the decay function: `origin`, `scale`, `decay`, and `offset`.

The point of origin is used to calculate distance. For date fields, the default is the current timestamp. The `scale` parameter defines the distance from the origin at which the computed score will be equal to the `decay` parameter.

The `origin` and `scale` parameters can be thought of as your `min` and `max` that define a bounding box within which the curve will be defined. If we wanted to give more boosts to the documents that have been published in the past 10 days, it would be best to define the origin as the current timestamp and the scale as 10d.

The `offset` specifies that the decay function will only compute the decay function of documents with a distance greater that the defined offset. The default is 0.

Finally, the `decay` option alters how severely the document is demoted based on its position. The default decay value is 0.5.

All three decay functions work only on numeric, date, and geo-point fields.

```
GET profiles/candidate/_search
{
  "query": {
    "function_score": {
      "query": {
        "match_all": {}
      },
      "functions": [
        {
          "exp": {
            "geo_code": {
```

Controlling Relevancy

```
          "origin": {
            "lat": 28.66,
            "lon": 77.22
          },
          "scale": "100km"
        }
      }
    }
  ],"boost_mode": "multiply"
    }
  }
}
```

In the preceding query, we have used the exponential decay function that tells Elasticsearch to start decaying the score calculation after a distance of 100 km from the given origin. So, the candidates who are at a distance of greater than 100 km from the given origin will be ranked low, but not discarded. These candidates can still get a higher rank if we combine other function score queries such as weight or `field_value_factor` with the decay function and combine the result of all the functions together.

Java example:

The preceding query can be implemented in Java in the following way:

1. First, you need to import the following classes into your code:

   ```
   import org.elasticsearch.action.search.SearchResponse;
   import org.elasticsearch.client.Client;
   import org.elasticsearch.index.query.QueryBuilders;
   import org.elasticsearch.index.query.functionscore.*;
   ```

2. Then, the following code snippets can be used to implement the query:

   ```
   Map<String, Object> origin = new HashMap<String, Object>();
       String scale = "100km";
       origin.put("lat", "28.66");
       origin.put("lon", "77.22");
   FunctionScoreQueryBuilder functionQuery = new
       FunctionScoreQueryBuilder()
       .add(new ExponentialDecayFunctionBuilder("geo_code",origin,
         scale)).boostMode("multiply");
   //For Linear Decay Function use below syntax
   //.add(new LinearDecayFunctionBuilder("geo_code",origin,
     scale)).boostMode("multiply");
   //For Gauss Decay Function use below syntax
   ```

```
//.add(new GaussDecayFunctionBuilder("geo_code",origin,
  scale)).boostMode("multiply");

SearchResponse response =
client.prepareSearch().setIndices(indexName)
        .setTypes(docType).setQuery(functionQuery)
        .execute().actionGet();
```

In the preceding example, we have used the `exp` decay function but, the commented lines show examples of how other decay functions can be used.

Last, as always, remember that Elasticsearch lets you use multiple functions in a single `function_score` query to calculate a score that combines the results of each function.

Summary

This chapter covered the most important aspects of search engines; that is, relevancy. We discussed the powerful scoring capabilities available in Elasticsearch and the practical examples to show how you can control the scoring process according to your needs. Despite the relevancy challenges faced while working with search engines, the out-of-the-box features such as function scores and custom scoring always allow us to tackle challenges with ease.

In the next chapter, you will learn how to set up an Elasticsearch cluster and configure different types of node for production deployments.

Cluster Scaling in Production Deployments

Until now, we have been more focused about the search and data analytics capabilities of Elasticsearch. Now is the time to learn about taking Elasticsearch clusters in production while focusing on best practices.

In this chapter, we will cover the following topics:

- Node types in Elasticsearch
- Introducing Zen-Discovery
- Best Elasticsearch practices in production
- Cluster creation
- Scaling your clusters

Node types in Elasticsearch

In Elasticsearch, you can configure three types of nodes, as shown in the following cluster:

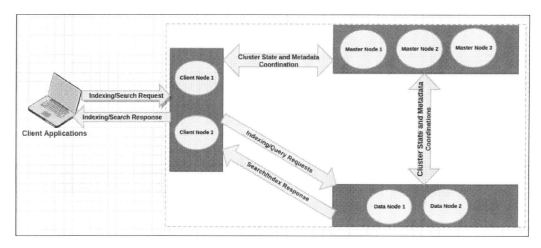

In the preceding cluster diagram, there are two client nodes, three master nodes, and two data nodes. Let's understand how these node types differ in Elasticsearch and how to configure them.

Client node

A client node in Elasticsearch acts as a query router and a load balancer. It does not hold any data. A client node can be used to query as well as index processes. It takes queries and distributes the search to data nodes. Once the data nodes return their respective results, the client node combines all the data to give the final results. Similarly, when you send the data to a client node for indexing, it calculates the sharding key for each document and sends the documents for the respective shards.

A client node can be configured by adding the following lines to the `elasticsearch.yml` file:

- `node.data: false`
- `node.master: false`

Data node

A data node in the Elasticsearch is responsible for holding the data, merging segments, and executing queries. Data nodes are the real work horses of your cluster and need a higher configuration than any other type of node in the cluster.

A data node can be configured by adding the following lines to the `elasticsearch.yml` file:

- `node.data: true`
- `node.master: false`

Master node

A master node is responsible for the management of the complete cluster. It holds the states of all the nodes and periodically distributes the cluster state to all the other nodes in the cluster to make them aware of any new node that has joined the cluster and which nodes have left. A master node periodically sends a ping to all the other nodes to see whether they are alive (other nodes also send pings to the master node). The final major task of the master node is configuration management. It holds the complete meta-data and the mapping of all the indexes in the cluster. If a master leaves, a new master node is chosen from the rest of the master-eligible nodes. If there is no master-eligible node left, the cluster cannot operate at all.

A master node can be configured by adding the following lines to the `elasticsearch.yml` file.

- `node.data: false`
- `node.master: true`

> By default, every node is configured as node.data: true and node.master: true, which means every node is a data node and can also act as a master node.

Introducing Zen-Discovery

Elasticsearch is highly scalable and distributed in nature. This scalability would not have been possible without a reliable centralized co-ordination system. In fact, every distributed system requires a coordination system to maintain configuration information' and provide distributed synchronizations to all the nodes connected in the cluster. If you have worked with SolrCloud, you will know that it uses a coordination service known as **Zookeeper**. Zookeeper is an awesome open source project as a whole and can be used with many distributed systems, even with Elasticsearch by installing the plugin.

At the heart of Elasticsearch, there is no third-party coordination service. However, Elasticsearch does have a built-in centralized coordination mechanism—**Zen Discovery**. One of the primary tasks of Discovery is to choose a master node that looks after the entire cluster.

When you start a node in an Elasticsearch cluster, the first thing that happens is that a node searches for the master node that has the same cluster name. If it finds one, it simply joins the cluster, and if there is no master node available and this newly started node is master eligible (we will see what it means), then it becomes the master node. This process of cluster formation is known as discovery.

Zen-Discovery allows you to have two types of discovery mechanisms: **Multicasting** and **Unicasting**.

Multicasting discovery

In the versions before 2.0, mulitcast used to be the default discovery type in Elasticsearch. However, since version 2.0, this has been changed to unicast discovery.

The reason was that multicasting is good to go in a development environment, but comes with added disadvantages. In multicasting, every node in the cluster sends message packets to all the other nodes for communication and health checks. This not only makes the network congested because of too many message transmissions in the network, it also makes it less secure. Any node that is unwanted and has the same cluster name can automatically join the cluster.

To enable the multicasting discovery type, add the following parameter in all the nodes of your cluster and restart them:

- ```
  discovery.zen.ping.multicast.enabled: true
  ```
  ```

Unicasting discovery

In unicasting discovery, the transmission of a single message is sent over the network to a single host at once. Here, you configure a set of nodes that can receive the messages from the node that wants to join the cluster. The unicasting mechanism is secure too since a node that wants to join the cluster must know the address and port of the master nodes that are responsible for deciding who will join the cluster.

Configuring unicasting discovery

To configure unicasting discovery, there are four properties that need to be configured inside the `elasticsearch.yml` file.

Minimum number of master nodes: preventing split-brain

A split-brain is the situation in which one Elasticsearch cluster divides itself into two clusters, and each cluster has a separate master node. This is mainly caused by network issues or when a cluster becomes unstable because nodes experience long pauses due to slow garbage collections. The subsets of nodes attempt to form their own clusters, and this is known as a **Split-Brain** situation. In this situation, the nodes are diverged and cannot form a single cluster again until you kill the other half of the cluster. Split-brain can be very dangerous and can incur potential data loss. Luckily, the Elasticsearch team has worked hard to prevent the worst scenarios of handling split-brain situations, but the implementation is up to you.

To avoid split-brain, you need to decide the minimum number of master nodes that must be operational in the cluster to keep the cluster running. The size of the minimum number of master nodes depends on the total number of master nodes you have in your cluster. It can be set using the `discovery.zen.minimum_master_nodes` property inside the `elasticsearch.yml` file:

- `discovery.zen.minimum_master_nodes: n`

Here, n is the integer value of the minimum number of master nodes. As per recommendation, this value should be decided based on the formula, *N/2+1*, where N is the total number of master nodes in the cluster. So, if you have three master nodes, this parameter can be set as *3/2+1 = 2* (rounding off to the nearest integer).

An initial list of hosts to ping

Unicasting requires an initial list of hosts to be pinged when a new node is started to form a cluster. Here you need to provide the list of all your master nodes along with an optional TCP port number in the following format:

```
discovery.zen.ping.unicast.hosts: ["masternode1IPAddress:TCP-Port","masternode2IPAddress:TCP-Port", "masternode3IPAddress:TCP-Port"]
```

The TCP port defaults to 9300.

Ping timeout

This, by default, has 3s; within this time the nodes will ping to the master node and the master node will ping back to the other nodes to ensure that all nodes are up. This property should be set to a higher value in a slow network or a congested cluster. It can be configured in the following way:

- `discovery.zen.ping.timeout: 5s`

Node upgrades without downtime

To achieve SLAs, you need highly available systems. However, at the same time, you may need to upgrade or downgrade your machines or even upgrade Elasticsearch to its upgraded release. Both cases require some best practices to be followed because one wrong step can incur data loss or a delay in the completion of the required changes. In both the cases, one thing is for sure, nodes must be stopped one by one. While it's easy to stop the client or the master node and perform maintenance tasks, data nodes require special considerations because they might need a higher shard recovery time.

Every time a data node is restarted, shard re-balancing is done by Elasticsearch, which takes too much time because of some unnecessary data movement and synchronization inside the cluster. To avoid this scenario and for a faster recovery of the data nodes, follow these steps.

Before stopping a data node, set the shard routing allocation to none with the following command:

```
PUT _cluster/settings
{
"transient" : {
"cluster.routing.allocation.enable" : "none"
}
}
```

After starting the data node, set back the shard routing allocation to all with this command:

```
PUT _cluster/settings
{
"transient" : {
"cluster.routing.allocation.enable" : "all"
}
}
```

An Elasticsearch version can't be downgraded to a lower release. So, take data backups before going for a version upgrade. Backup and restores are covered in the next chapter.

Upgrading Elasticsearch version

An Elasticsearch cluster can be upgraded to a higher version in two ways:

- **Rolling upgrade**: This requires one node to stop at once and perform the upgradation.
- **Full cluster restart**: This requires a complete cluster shutdown before proceeding with the upgrade task.

You need to go through the following URL for more information on the supported versions to choose the type of upgrade you need to perform:

https://www.elastic.co/guide/en/elasticsearch/reference/current/setup-upgrade.html

In both cases, to upgrade a node, the following are the easiest steps to upgrade a version node by node:

1. Disable the routing allocation, as discussed in the previous section.
2. Stop the node.
3. Take a backup of the data.
4. Take a backup of the configuration files.
5. Remove Elasticsearch (you can simply purge it to complete the uninstallation of Elasticsearch from the server by running this command: `sudo apt-get purge Elasticsearch`)
6. Install Elasticsearch with the latest release.
7. Change the configuration files according to the previous settings.
8. Upgrade the plugins.
9. Restart the node.

Best Elasticsearch practices in production

This section is dedicated to guide you on following the best practices and considerations to keep in mind when going into production.

Memory

- Always choose ES_HEAP_SIZE 50% of the total available memory. Sorting and aggregations both can be memory hungry, so enough heap space to accommodate these is required. This property is set inside the `/etc/init.d/elasticsearch` file.
- A machine with 64 GB of RAM is ideal; however, 32 GB and 16 GB machines are also common. Less than 8 GB tends to be counterproductive (you end up needing smaller machines), and greater than 64 GB has problems in pointer compression.

CPU

Choose a modern processor with multiple cores. If you need to choose between faster CPUs or more cores, choose more cores. The extra concurrency that multiple cores offer will far outweigh a slightly faster clock speed. The number of threads is dependent on the number of cores. The more cores you have, the more threads you get for indexing, searching, merging, bulk, or other operations.

Disks

- If you can afford SSDs, they are far superior to any spinning media. SSD-backed nodes see boosts in both querying and indexing performance.
- Avoid network-attached storage (NAS) to store data.

Network

- The faster the network you have, the more performance you will get in a distributed system. Low latency helps to ensure that nodes communicate easily, while a high bandwidth helps in shard movement and recovery.
- Avoid clusters that span multiple data centers even if the data centers are collocated in close proximity. Definitely avoid clusters that span large geographic distances.

General consideration

- It is better to prefer medium-to-large boxes. Avoid small machines because you don't want to manage a cluster with a thousand nodes, and the overhead of simply running Elasticsearch is more apparent on such small boxes.
- Always use a Java version greater than JDK1.7 Update 55 from Oracle and avoid using Open JDK.
- A master node does not require much resources. In a cluster with 2 Terabytes of data having 100s of indexes, 2 GB of RAM, 1 Core CPU, and 10 GB of disk space is good enough for the master nodes. In the same scenario, the client nodes with 8 GB of RAM each and 2 Core CPUs is a very good configuration to handle millions of requests. The configuration of data nodes is completely dependent on the speed of indexing, the type of queries, and aggregations. However, they usually need very high configurations such as 64 GB of RAM and 8 Core CPUs.

Some other important configuration changes

- Assign Names: Assign the cluster name and node name.
- Assign Paths: Assign the log path and data path.
- Recovery Settings: Avoid shard shuffles during recovery. The recovery throttling section should be tweaked in large clusters only; otherwise, it comes with very good defaults.

  Disable the deletion of all the indices by a single command:

  ```
  action.disable_delete_all_indices: false
  ```

- Ensure by setting the following property that you do not run more than one Elasticsearch instance from a single installation:

  ```
  max_local_storage_nodes: "1"
  ```

  Disable HTTP requests on all the data and master nodes in the following way:

  ```
  http.enabled: false
  ```

- Plugins installations: Always prefer to install the compatible plugin version according to the Elasticsearch version you are using and after the installation of the plugin, do not forget to restart the node.

- Avoid storing Marvel indexes in the production cluster.
- Clear the cache if the heap fills up when the node start-up and shards refuse to get initialized after going into red state This can be done by executing the following command:
    - To clear the cache of the complete cluster:
      ```
      curl -XPOST 'http://localhost:9200/_cache/clear'
      ```
    - To clear the cache of a single index:
      ```
      curl -XPOST 'http://localhost:9200/index_name/_cache/clear'
      ```
- Use routing wherever beneficial for faster indexing and querying.

Creating a cluster

Since you have learned a major part of cluster configuration, let's begin to create a full-blown production-ready cluster. In this example, we will configure a cluster with three master, two client nodes, and two data nodes.

The example shows a configuration of one master, one data, and one client node. On the rest of nodes, all the configuration will remain the same according to the node category, but only four parameters will be changed:

node.name, path.data, path.log and network.host.

> If you are configuring a new data or log path, make sure that Elasticsearch has the full permission of that directory. You can set the permission with the following command:
> ```
> sudo chown -R elasticsearch:elasticsearch path_of_the_data_directory
> ```

Configuring master nodes

```
cluster.name: "production-cluster"
node.name: "es-master-01"
node.data: false
node.master: true
path.data: "path_to_data_directory"
network.host: "192.168.1.10" (should be changed to a private IP address of this machine or can be left out too, because Elasticsearch, by default, binds itself to the 0.0.0.0 address)
http.enabled: false
transport.tcp.port: 9300
```

```
discovery.zen.minimum_master_nodes: 3
discovery.zen.ping.unicast.hosts: ["es-master-01:6300","es-
master-02:6300", "es-master-03:6300"]
discovery.zen.ping.timeout: 5s
bootstrap.mlockall: true
action.destructive_requires_name: true
#For allowing script execution
script.inline: on
```

Configuring client nodes

```
cluster.name: "production-cluster"
node.name: "es-client-01"
node.data: false
node.master: false
network.host: "192.168.1.10" (should be changed to the private IP
address of this machine)
http.enabled: true
http.port: 9200
transport.tcp.port: 9300
discovery.zen.minimum_master_nodes: 3
discovery.zen.ping.unicast.hosts: ["es-master-01:9300","es-
master-02:9300", "es-master-03:9300"]
discovery.zen.ping.timeout: 5s
bootstrap.mlockall: true
action.destructive_requires_name: true
action.disable_delete_all_indices: false
script.inline: on
#To allow sense and marvel to query elasticsearch
http.cors.enabled: true
http.cors.allow-origin: /http:\/\/localhost(:[0-9]+)?/
http.cors.allow-credentials: true
```

Configuring data nodes

```
cluster.name: "production-cluster"
node.name: "es-data-01"
node.data: true
node.master: false
network.host: "192.168.1.10" (should be changed to the private IP
address of this machine)
http.enabled: false
transport.tcp.port: 9300
discovery.zen.minimum_master_nodes: 3
```

```
discovery.zen.ping.unicast.hosts: ["es-master-01:9300","es-
master-02:9300", "es-master-03:9300"]
discovery.zen.ping.timeout: 5s
bootstrap.mlockall: true
action.destructive_requires_name: true
script.inline: on
```

Scaling your clusters

While it's easy to get started with the launching of nodes and the forming of Elasticsearch clusters, the real challenge comes when the indexing and searching requests increase and your server encounters real pressure. In this section, we will discuss when and how to scale your Elasticsearch clusters.

> Cluster scaling is only possible if you have done some capacity planning in advance and have decided on an optimal number of shards. Always remember that once an index is created, you cannot increase or decrease the number of shards but can always change the number of replicas.

When to scale

Elasticsearch is very good at giving you hints in advance when it starts getting overloaded. The problems can arise in many areas such as slow searches, disk space utilizations, JVM issues, memory pressure, or high CPU utilizations. In any case, scaling should be done before your servers crash.

For timely scaling, the best thing to do is keep a close eye on the monitoring of the metrics provided by Elasticsearch for all resource utilizations. Your biggest friend would be Marvel. It provides very granular statistics of your clusters. However, in case you can't opt for **Marvel** due to any reason, you can use a combination of three approaches: use monitoring plugins such as `Bigdesk`, `HQ`; keep watching the logs and use the monitoring REST APIs to get a clear idea of what is causing the problem; and taking decisions about when to scale.

Metrics to watch

The following are the most important metrics that you need to continuously watch out for in Elasticsearch.

CPU utilization

The performance of Elasticsearch is highly dependent on the type of server on which it has been installed. There are many reasons for spikes in high CPU utilizations, such as higher indexing speed that causes a lot of segment merges in the background or higher garbage collection activities. Look at the following images that have been taken after running the `htop` command on a Ubuntu system:

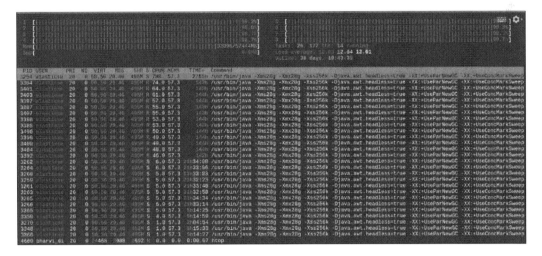

The preceding screenshot is from my server, which has eight CPU cores and 32 GB of RAM (16 GB dedicated to Elasticsearch). You can see Elasticsearch is using almost 800% of CPU because of a higher indexing rate of almost 3,000 documents per second (with a size of 20 KB per document). We were required to increase the indexing rate, but we were not able to because there was no room in the CPU.

The only solution in this scenario was to scale, either vertically (increasing CPU of this server) or horizontally (adding more nodes to allocate some of the shards on a new node), to distribute the load.

The same CPU utilization can be viewed with the help of the `Bigdesk` plugin:

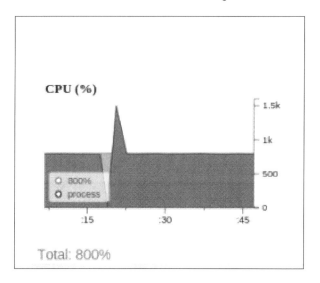

Memory utilization

Elasticsearch is a memory extensive process. It runs in JVM and requires a lot of memory holding objects while performing aggregation, sorting, and caching different kinds of data, such as field cache and filter cache, to give you faster search executions. Many people are worried when they see that Elasticsearch is using almost all the memory of the server. However, this is not always correct. In Elasticsearch, it is good if your server is utilizing all the memory. The actual thing to look for is whether there is any free buffer or cached memory available.

When there is too much memory pressure on an Elasticsearch node, it starts giving warnings in the logs of that particular node, similar to the following one:

```
[2015-11-25 18:13:53,166][WARN ][monitor.jvm] [es-data-1] [gc][ParNew]
[1135087][11248] duration [2.6m], collections [1]/[2.7m], total [2.6m]/
[6.8m], memory [2.4gb]->[2.3gb]/[3.8gb], all_pools {[Code Cache]
[13.7mb]->[13.7mb]/[48mb]}{[Par Eden Space] [109.6mb]->[15.4mb]/[1gb]}
{[Par Survivor Space] [136.5mb]->[0b]/[136.5mb]}{[CMS Old Gen] [2.1gb]-
>[2.3gb]/[2.6gb]}{[CMS Perm Gen] [35.1mb]->[34.9mb]/[82mb]}
```

If you start getting these kinds of warnings in your logs, its time to add more resources.

Disk I/O utilization

If you are working on applications having high writes such as logging and real-time data indexing, you need very high disk I/Ops. Elasticsearch provides options for tuning store-level throttling for segment merging; however, spinning media disks cannot cope with heavy writes. It is best to use SSD for write heavy applications. In our applications, we have seen an almost 10x performance boost after opting for SSD.

Disk low watermark

Look at the following lines of log, which have been taken from the master node of the cluster:

```
[2015-11-21 15:22:52,656][INFO ][cluster.routing.allocation.decider] [es-master-1] low disk watermark [15%] exceeded on [ujhOO-MzR22bJHPUGLtyQA][es-data-1] free: 36.6gb[14.8%], replicas will not be assigned to this node
```

It clearly says that one of the data nodes has less than 15% of disk space available and new shards won't be assigned to this node anymore. This can even be worse if 90% of the disk is full. In this case, your shards will be automatically assigned to other nodes, and if the other nodes also have the same disk space, your cluster will go into hang mode.

However, you can increase the thresholds for low and high watermarks in the following way:

```
curl -XPUT client_node_ip:9200/_cluster/settings -d '{
    "transient" : {
        "cluster.routing.allocation.disk.watermark.low" : "90%",
        "cluster.routing.allocation.disk.watermark.high" : "10gb"
    }
}'
```

As you can see, these parameters take values in the form of percentage as well as gigabytes or megabytes. However, if this is still not enough, you need to add more nodes to move the shards or increase the disk space.

How to scale

Distributed systems such as Elasticsearch, Cassandra, or Mongodb are built for higher scalability. However, it is very important to consider one thing: how you scale your clusters. Scaling can be done either vertically or horizontally. Vertical scaling is the one in which you keep adding more resources to existing machines, whereas in horizontal scaling, you dynamically add more nodes to the cluster. Elasticsearch is built for horizontal scaling. You keep adding more nodes to your cluster, and it can automatically balance the shards/load on the new nodes.

To add new nodes to Elasticsearch, simply launch a new server with Elasticsearch installed on it and similar configuration (cluster name and discovery parameters). It will automatically connect to the existing cluster, if it is able to connect with your master nodes.

There are still some scenarios in which it will be required to go for vertical scaling, such as cost optimizations. In this case, you need to stop the node and increase the resources on it. However, you need to have enough nodes to keep the cluster operational, such as having two client nodes or two data nodes and three master nodes.

Summary

In this chapter, you learned how to configure different types of nodes in Elasticsearch, along with keeping best practices in mind when going for the production deployments of an Elasticsearch cluster. The chapter covered one of the most important aspects of cluster sizing—resource allocation and configuration for different types of nodes.

Finally, we saw some key metrics such as CPU, disk I/Ops, RAM, and utilizations to watch out for when your cluster needs scaling and the best practices to follow for scaling without downtime.

In the next chapter, we will learn about securing clusters and creating data backups.

10
Backups and Security

Data backups and data security are the most important aspects of any organization. It is even more important to design and implement business continuity plans to tackle data loss because of various factors. While Elasticsearch is not a database and it does not provide the backup and security functionalities that you can get in databases, it still offers some way around this. Let's learn how you can create cost effective and robust backup plans for your Elasticsearch clusters.

In this chapter, we will cover the following topics:

- Introducing backup and restore mechanisms
- Securing an Elasticsearch cluster
- Load balancing using Nginx

Introducing backup and restore mechanisms

In Elasticsearch, you can implement a backup and restore functionality in two different ways depending on the requirements and efforts put in. You can either create a script to create manual backups and restoration or you can opt for a more automated and functionality-rich **Backup-Restore** API offered by Elasticsearch.

Backup using snapshot API

A snapshot is the backup of a complete cluster or selected indices. The best thing about snapshots is that they are incremental in nature. So, only data that has been changed since the last snapshot will be taken in the next snapshot.

Life was not so easy before the release of Elasticsearch Version 1.0.0. This release not only introduced powerful aggregation functionalities to Elasticsearch, but also brought in the **Snapshot Restore** API to create backups and restore them on the fly. Initially, only a shared file system was supported by this API, but gradually it has been possible to use this API on AWS to create backups on AWS buckets, Hadoop to create backups inside Hadoop clusters, and Microsoft Azure to create backups on **Azure Storage** with the help of plugins. In the upcoming section, you will learn how to create backups using a shared file system repository. To use cloud and Hadoop plugins, have a look at the following URLs:

`https://github.com/elastic/elasticsearch-cloud-aws#s3-repository`

`https://github.com/elastic/elasticsearch-hadoop/tree/master/repository-hdfs`

`https://github.com/elastic/elasticsearch-cloud-azure#azure-repository`

Creating snapshots using file system repositories requires the repository to be accessible from all the data and master nodes in the cluster. For this, we will be creating an **network file system** (**NFS**) drive in the next section.

Creating an NFS drive

NFS is a distributed file system protocol, which allows you to mount remote directories on your server. The mounted directories look like the local directory of the server, therefore using NFS, multiple servers can write to the same directory.

Let's take an example to create a shared directory using NFS. For this example, there is one host server, which can also be viewed as a backup server of Elasticsearch data, two data nodes, and three master nodes.

The following are the IP addresses of all these nodes:

- Host Server: 10.240.131.44
- Data node 1: 10.240.251.58
- Data node 1: 10.240.251.59
- Master Node 1: 10.240.80.41
- Master Node 2: 10.240.80.42
- Master Node 3: 10.240.80.43

Configuring the NFS host server

The very first step is to install the `nfs-kernel-server` package after updating the local package index:

```
sudo apt-get update
sudo apt-get install nfs-kernel-server
```

Once the package is installed, you can create a directory that can be shared among all the clients. Let's create a directory:

```
sudo mkdir /mnt/shared-directory
```

Give the access permission of this directory to the **nobody** user and the **nogroup** group. They are a special reserved user and group in the Linux operating system that do not need any special permission to run things:

```
sudo chown -R nobody:nogroup /mnt/shared-directory
```

The next step is to configure the **NFS Exports**, where we can specify with which machine this directory will be shared. For this, open the `/etc/exports` file with root permissions:

```
sudo nano /etc/exports
```

Add the following line, which contains the directory to be shared and the space-separated client IP lists:

```
/mnt/shared-directory    10.240.251.58(rw,sync,no_subtree_check) 10.240.251.59(rw,sync,no_subtree_check) 10.240.80.41(rw,sync,no_subtree_check) 10.240.80.42(rw,sync,no_subtree_check) 10.240.80.43(rw,sync,no_subtree_check)
```

Once done, save the file and exit.

The next step is to create an NFS table, which holds the exports of your share by running the following command:

```
sudo exportfs -a
```

Now start the NFS service by running this command:

```
sudo service nfs-kernel-server start
```

After this, your shared directory is available to the clients you have configured on your host machine. It's time to do the configurations on the client machines.

Configuring client machines

First of all, your need to install the NFS client after updating the local package index:

`sudo apt-get update`

`sudo apt-get install nfs-common`

Now, create a directory on the client machine that will be used to mount the remote shared directory:

`sudo mkdir /mnt/nfs`

Mount the shared directory (by specifying the `nfs` server host ip:shared directory name) on the client machine by using the following command:

`sudo mount 10.240.131.44:/mnt/shared-directory /mnt/nfs`

To check whether the mount is successfully done, you can use the following command:

`df -h`

You will see an extra drive mounted on your system, as shown in the following screenshot, which shows the mounted shared directory:

```
bharvi@es-master-1:~$ df -h
Filesystem                                    Size  Used Avail Use% Mounted on
rootfs                                        9.8G  1.4G  7.9G  16% /
udev                                           10M     0   10M   0% /dev
tmpfs                                         171M  148K  171M   1% /run
/dev/disk/by-uuid/906181f7-4e10-4a4e-8fd8-43b20ec980ff  9.8G  1.4G  7.9G  16% /
tmpfs                                         5.0M     0  5.0M   0% /run/lock
tmpfs                                         341M     0  341M   0% /run/shm
10.240.131.44:/mnt/shared-directory           9.8G   23M  9.2G   1% /mnt/nfs
```

Please note that mounting the directories/devices using the mount command only mounts them temporarily. For a permanent mount, open the `/etc/fstab` file:

`sudo nano /etc/fstab`

Add these lines to this file:

`host.domain.com:/mnt/shared-directory   /mnt/nfs/   nfs auto,noatime,nolock,bg,nfsvers=4,sec=krb5p,intr,tcp,actimeo=1800 0 0`

Perform similar steps on all the data and master nodes to mount the shared directory on all of them using NFS.

Creating a snapshot

The following subsections cover the various steps that are performed to create a snapshot.

Registering the repository path

Add the following line inside the `elasticsearch.yml` file, to register the `path.repo` setting on all the master and data nodes:

```
path.repo: ["/mnt/nfs"]
```

After this, restart the nodes one by one to reload the configuration.

Registering the shared file system repository in Elasticsearch

Register the shared file system repository with the name `es-backup`:

```
curl -XPUT 'http://localhost:9200/_snapshot/es-backup' -d '{
    "type": "fs",
    "settings": {
        "location": "/mnt/nfs/es-backup",
        "compress": true
    }
}'
```

In preceding request, the `location` parameter specifies the path of the snapshots and the `compress` parameter turns on the compression of the snapshot files. Compression is applied only to the index metadata files (mappings and settings) and not to the data files.

Create your first snapshot

You can create multiple snapshots of the same cluster within a repository. The following is the command that is used to create a `snapshot_1` snapshot inside the `es-snapshot` repository:

```
curl -XPUT 'http://localhost:9200/_snapshot/es-backup/snapshot_1?wait_for_completion=true'
```

The `wait_for_completion` parameter tells whether the request should return immediately after snapshot initialization (defaults to true) or wait for snapshot completion. During snapshot initialization, information about all previous snapshots is loaded into the memory, which means that in large repositories, it may take several seconds (or even minutes) for this command to return even if the `wait_for_completion` parameter is set to false.

By default, a snapshot of all the open and started indices in the cluster is created. This behavior can be changed by specifying the list of indices in the body of the snapshot request:

```
curl -XPUT 'http://localhost:9200/_snapshot/es-backup/snapshot_1?wait_for_completion=true' -d '{
  "indices": "index_1,index_2",
  "ignore_unavailable": "true",
  "include_global_state": false
}'
```

In the preceding request, the `indices` parameter specifies the names of the indices that need to be included inside the snapshot. The `ignore_unavailable` parameter, if set to true, enables a snapshot request to not fail if any index is not available in the snapshot creation request. The third parameter, `include_global_state`, when set to false, avoids the global cluster state to be stored as a part of the snapshot.

Getting snapshot information

To get the details of a single snapshot, you can run the following command:

```
curl -XPUT 'http://localhost:9200/_snapshot /es-backup/snapshot_1
```

Use comma-separated snapshot names to get the details of more than one snapshot:

```
curl -XPUT 'http://localhost:9200/_snapshot /es-backup/snapshot_1
```

To get the details of all the snapshots, use `_all` in the end, like this:

```
curl -XPUT 'http://localhost:9200/_snapshot /es-backup/_all
```

Deleting snapshots

A snapshot can be deleted using the following command:

```
curl -XDELETE 'http://localhost:9200/_snapshot /es-backup/snapshot_1
```

Restoring snapshots

Restoring a snapshot is very easy and a snapshot can be restored to other clusters too, provided the cluster in which you are restoring is version compatible. You cannot restore a snapshot to a lower version of Elasticsearch.

While restoring snapshots, if the index does not already exist, a new index will be created with the same index name and all the mappings for that index, which was there before creating the snapshot. If the index already exists, then it must be in the closed state and must have the same number of shards as the index snapshot. The restore operation automatically opens the indexes after a successful completion:

Example: restoring a snapshot

To take an example of restoring a snapshot from the `es-backup` repository and the `snapshot_1` snapshot, run the following command against the `_restore` endpoint on the client node:

```
curl -XPOST localhost:9200/_snapshot/es-backup/snapshot_1/_restore
```

This command will restore all the indices of the snapshot.

Elasticsearch offers several options while restoring the snapshots. The following are some of the important ones.

Restoring multiple indices

There might be a scenario in which you do not want to restore all the indices of a snapshot and only a few indices. For this, you can use the following command:

```
curl -XPOST 'localhost:9200/_snapshot/es-backup/snapshot_1/_restore' -d
'{
  "indices": "index_1,index_2",
  "ignore_unavailable": "true"
}'
```

Renaming indices

Elasticsearch does not have any option to rename an index once it has been created, apart from setting aliases. However, it provides you with an option to rename the indices while restoring from the snapshot. For example:

```
curl -XPOST 'localhost:9200/_snapshot/es-backup/snapshot_1/_restore' -d
'{
  "indices": "index_1",
  "ignore_unavailable": "true",
  "rename_replacement": "restored_index"
}'
```

Partial restore

Partial restore is a very useful feature. It comes in handy in scenarios such as creating snapshots, if the snapshots can not be created for some of the shards. In this case, the entire restore process will fail if one or more indices does not have a snapshot of all the shards. In this case, you can use the following command to restore such indices back into cluster:

```
curl -XPOST 'localhost:9200/_snapshot/es-backup/snapshot_1/_restore' -d
'{
  "partial": true
}'
```

Note that you will lose the data of the missing shard in this case, and those missing shards will be created as empty ones after the completion of the restore process.

Changing index settings during restore

During restoration, many of the index settings can be changed, such as the number of replicas and refresh intervals. For example, to restore an index named my_index with a replica size of 0 (for a faster restore process) and a default refresh interval rate, you can run this command:

```
curl -XPOST 'localhost:9200/_snapshot/es-backup/snapshot_1/_restore' -d
'{
  "indices": "my_index",
  "index_settings": {
    "index.number_of_replicas": 0
  },
  "ignore_index_settings": [
    "index.refresh_interval"
  ]
}'
```

The `indices` parameter can contain more than one comma separated `index_name`.

Once restored, the replicas can be increased with the following command:

```
curl -XPUT 'localhost:9200/my_index/_settings' -d '
{
    "index" : {
        "number_of_replicas" : 1
    }
}'
```

Restoring to a different cluster

To restore a snapshot to a different cluster, you first need to register the repository from where the snapshot needs to be restored to a new cluster.

There are some additional considerations that you need to take in this process:

- The version of the new cluster must be the same or greater than the cluster from which the snapshot had been taken
- Index settings can be applied during snapshot restoration
- The new cluster need not be of the same size (the number of nodes and so on) as the old cluster
- An appropriate disk size and memory must be available for restoration
- The plugins that create additional mapping types must be installed on both the clusters (that is, attachment plugins); otherwise, the index will fail to open due to mapping problems.

Manual backups

Manual backups are simple to understand, but difficult to manage with growing datasets and the number of machines inside the cluster. However, you can still give a thought to creating manual backups in small clusters. The following are the steps needed to be performed to create backups:

- Shut down the node.
- Copy the data to a backup directory. You can either take a backup of all the indices available on a node by navigating to the `path_to_data_directory/cluster_name/nodes/0/` directory and copy the complete indices folder or can take a backup of the individual indices too.
- Start the node.

Manual restoration

Manual restorations also require steps similar to those used when the creating backups:

- Shut down the node
- Copy the data from a backup directory to the indices directory of datapath
- Start the node

Securing Elasticsearch

Elasticsearch does not have any default security mechanisms. Anyone can destroy your entire data collection with just a single command. However, with the increasing demand of securing Elasticsearch clusters, the Elastic team has launched a new product called shield that provides you with a complete security solution including authentication, encryption, role-based access control, IP filtering, field- and document-level security, and audit logging. However, if you cannot afford shield, there are other ways to protect Elasticsearch. One way can be to not expose Elasticsearch publicly and put a firewall in front of it to allow access to only a limited number of IPs. The other way is to wrap Elasticsearch in a reverse proxy to enable access control and SSL encryption. In this chapter, we will see how you can secure your Elasticsearch cluster using a basic HTTP authentication behind a reverse proxy.

In the remaining sections, we will go on to learn how to use Nginx to secure an Elasticsearch cluster. The commands used to set up Nginx and Basic Auth work on Ubuntu 12.04 and above. To set up the same on Centos systems, you can get the installation guide at the following URL:

https://gist.github.com/bharvidixit/8b00fdc85f8d31391876

Setting up basic HTTP authentication

HTTP authentication allows you to secure Elasticsearch using username- and password-based access. You can do this by installing the `apache-utils` package:

```
sudo apt-get update
sudo apt-get install apache-utils
```

Now, let's create a password file with this command:

```
sudo htpasswd -c /etc/nginx/.htpasswd username
```

The preceding command will prompt you to create a password for the username user, as shown in the following screenshot:

```
New password:
Re-type new password:
Adding password for user username
```

Once you create the password, a file with the `.htpasswd` name will be created inside the `/etc/nginx` directory in the format of `login:password`.

Setting up Nginx

Run the following command to install Nginx on Ubuntu machines:

```
sudo apt-get install nginx
```

You can find the configuration directory of Nginx inside the `/etc/nginx` directory, which looks similar to this:

```
conf.d            koi-utf   mime.types         naxsi.rules         nginx.conf    scgi_params     sites-enabled   win-utf
fastcgi_params    koi-win   naxsi_core.rules   naxsi-ui.conf.1.4.1 proxy_params  sites-available uwsgi_params
```

Proxy templates are usually created inside the sites-available directory. This can be created with the following command:

```
sudo vi /etc/nginx/sites-available/elastic_proxy
```

Enter the following configuration lines inside this file:

```
server {
    listen 6200;
    server_name es.domainname.com;

    access_log /var/log/nginx/elastic_proxy/access.log;
    error_log /var/log/nginx/elastic_proxy/error.log;

    location / {
        auth_basic "Elasticsearch Authentication";
        auth_basic_user_file /etc/nginx/.htpasswd;

        proxy_pass http://localhost:9200;
        proxy_http_version 1.1;
        proxy_set_header   X-Real-IP  $remote_addr;
        proxy_set_header   X-Forwarded-For $proxy_add_x_forwarded_for;
        proxy_set_header   Host $http_host;
    }
}
```

As you can see, we have configured the Nginx server to listen to port 6200, which is just a custom port number to connect with Elasticsearch. You are no longer required to connect Elasticsearch on its default port 9200 because it is running on localhost. It's also good if you can create a subdomain for your Elasticsearch cluster (`es.domainname.com`, in this example), which points to the public IP of this server. If you do not have any subdomain, but have a public IP available on this server, you can omit the `server_name` parameter.

The main things are written inside the location directive, where we have used the HTTP authentication file you had created. Now only those users who have this user name and password can access this Elasticsearch cluster.

When you are done with the configuration of your template, create a symbolic link of the template to make it available inside the `/etc/sites-enabled` directory that will be finally loaded by Nginx. To do this, run the following command:

```
sudo ln -s /etc/nginx/sites-available/elastic_proxy /etc/nginx/sites-enabled/
```

You also need to create a log directory to store all the access and error logs. You can do it using these commands:

```
sudo mkdir /var/log/nginx/elastic_proxy

sudo touch /var/log/nginx/elastic_proxy/access.log
sudo touch /var/log/nginx/elastic_proxy/error.log
```

Once done, start the Nginx server with the following command:

`sudo service nginx start`

Now, try to access Elasticsearch with this command:

`curl localhost:6200`

You will get the following response:

```
<html>
<head><title>401 Authorization Required</title></head>
<body bgcolor="white">
<center><h1>401 Authorization Required</h1></center>
<hr><center>nginx/1.9.2</center>
</body>
</html>
```

This clearly tells you that to access this URL, you need a valid user name and password. So, it can be accessed using the following command:

`curl username:password@localhost:6200`

Here, the username and password are the ones you have created in the previous section.

Securing critical access

You know very well that Elasticsearch is based on REST and provides the HTTP endpoints for all the tasks, such as `_search`, `_delete`, `_update`, `_stats`, `_settings`, and so on, which essentially works on the HTTP verbs such as GET, PUT, POST, and DELETE.

Nginx is very good for rule-based access by getting the request parameters and putting constraints on the requests. Let's see how you can do this.

Restricting DELETE requests

To keep your data safe by avoiding DELETE requests, you can do the following configurations inside your proxy template:

```
if ($request_method ~ "DELETE") {
            return 403;
            break;
    }
```

Restricting endpoints

To restrict endpoints, such as _shutdown, you can use the following configuration:

```
if ($request_filename ~ _shutdown) {
            return 403;
            break;
    }
```

A final configuration would look like this:

```
server {
    listen 6200;
    server_name es.domainname.com;

    access_log /var/log/nginx/elastic_proxy/access.log;
    error_log /var/log/nginx/elastic_proxy/error.log;

    location / {
        auth_basic "Elasticsearch Authentication";
        auth_basic_user_file /etc/nginx/.htpasswd;

        if ($request_method ~ "DELETE") {
                return 403;
                break;
        }
        if ($request_filename ~ _shutdown) {
                return 403;
                break;
        }

        proxy_pass http://localhost:9200;
        proxy_http_version 1.1;
        proxy_set_header   X-Real-IP        $remote_addr;
        proxy_set_header   X-Forwarded-For  $proxy_add_x_forwarded_for;
        proxy_set_header   Host             $http_host;
    }
}
```

You can add many other constraints using similar `if` statements as shown in the preceding template. Whenever you edit the template inside `/etc/sites-available`, it will automatically reflect the changes inside sites-enabled; however, make sure to reload the changed configurations by running this command:

```
sudo service nginx reload
```

Load balancing using Nginx

If you have more than one client node in your Elasticsearch cluster, you can create connections to all of the client nodes for high availability. However, to load balance the requests in addition to cluster security, you can use the power of Nginx.

For example, you have three client nodes with the IP addresses, 192.168.10.42, 192.168.10.43, and 192.168.10.44. The following is a sample configuration that will listen to your proxy server subdomain or the public IP address (can be a private IP if not an Internet-facing `ES`) and will distribute the load to the Elasticsearch clients in a round-robin fashion:

```
upstream elasticsearch_servers {
    server 192.168.10.42:9200;
    server 192.168.10.43:9200;
    server 192.168.10.44:9200;
}
server {
    listen 6200;
    server_name es.domainname.com;

    access_log /var/log/nginx/elastic_proxy/access.log;
    error_log /var/log/nginx/elastic_proxy/error.log;

    location / {
        auth_basic "Elasticsearch Authentication";
        auth_basic_user_file /etc/nginx/.htpasswd;

        if ($request_method ~ "DELETE") {
                return 403;
                break;
        }
        if ($request_filename ~ _shutdown) {
                return 403;
                break;
        }

        proxy_pass http://elasticsearch_servers;
        proxy_http_version 1.1;
        proxy_set_header   X-Real-IP  $remote_addr;
        proxy_set_header   X-Forwarded-For $proxy_add_x_forwarded_for;
        proxy_set_header   Host $http_host;
    }
}
```

See the upstream directive in the preceding configuration template that holds all the IP and ports of the Elasticsearch clients using the `elasticsearch_servers` name. The `proxy_pass` directive now contains the name of the upstream directive instead of a single client address.

Nginx also provides options to load balance requests such as least connected, weighted, and session persistence. To use them, you can go through the load balancing guide of Nginx at `http://nginx.org/en/docs/http/load_balancing.html` and utilize them to give more power to your Elasticsearch cluster.

Summary

In this chapter, you learned how to create data backups of an Elasticsearch cluster and restore them back into the same or another cluster. You also learned how to secure Elasticsearch clusters and load balance them using Nginx.

Finally, we have reached the end of the book, and we hope that you have had a pleasant reading experience. Elasticsearch is vast, and covering every tiny detail in this book was not possible. However, as per the goal, it covers almost every "essential" topic of Elasticsearch for developers to start from scratch and to be able to manage and scale an Elasticsearch cluster on their own. Most interestingly, this book serves both Java and Python programmers under one hood.

Not only has Elasticsearch matured, but the community around this technology is also much more mature now. If you face any issue, you can post your questions to the official user discussion group: `https://discuss.elastic.co`.

We also suggest you keep visiting the official blog of Elasticsearch at `https://www.elastic.co/blog` to keep yourself updated with the latest and greatest news around this technology.

With all this knowledge and everything you have learned throughout this book, you are now fully equipped to create and manage a full-blown search and analytics solutions based on Elasticsearch. We wish you the best!

Module 2

Mastering Elasticsearch

Further your knowledge of ElasticSearch server by learning more about its internals, querying, and data handling

Introduction to Elasticsearch

Before going further into the book, we would like to emphasize that we are treating this book as an extension to the *Elasticsearch Server Second Edition* book we've written, also published by Packt Publishing. Of course, we start with a brief introduction to both Apache Lucene and Elasticsearch, but this book is not for a person who doesn't know Elasticsearch at all. We treat *Mastering Elasticsearch* as a book that will systematize your knowledge about Elasticsearch and extend it by showing some examples of how to leverage your knowledge in certain situations. If you are looking for a book that will help you start your journey into the world of Elasticsearch, please take a look at *Elasticsearch Server Second Edition* mentioned previously.

That said, we hope that by reading this book, you want to extend and build on basic Elasticsearch knowledge. We assume that you already know how to index data to Elasticsearch using single requests as well as bulk indexing. You should also know how to send queries to get the documents you are interested in, how to narrow down the results of your queries by using filtering, and how to calculate statistics for your data with the use of the faceting/aggregation mechanism. However, before getting to the exciting functionality that Elasticsearch offers, we think we should start with a quick tour of Apache Lucene, which is a full text search library that Elasticsearch uses to build and search its indices, as well as the basic concepts on which Elasticsearch is built. In order to move forward and extend our learning, we need to ensure that we don't forget the basics. This is easy to do. We also need to make sure that we understand Lucene correctly as *Mastering Elasticsearch* requires this understanding. By the end of this chapter, we will have covered the following topics:

- What Apache Lucene is
- What overall Lucene architecture looks like
- How the analysis process is done
- What Apache Lucene query language is and how to use it
- What are the basic concepts of Elasticsearch
- How Elasticsearch communicates internally

Introducing Apache Lucene

In order to fully understand how Elasticsearch works, especially when it comes to indexing and query processing, it is crucial to understand how Apache Lucene library works. Under the hood, Elasticsearch uses Lucene to handle document indexing. The same library is also used to perform a search against the indexed documents. In the next few pages, we will try to show you the basics of Apache Lucene, just in case you've never used it.

Getting familiar with Lucene

You may wonder why Elasticsearch creators decided to use Apache Lucene instead of developing their own functionality. We don't know for sure since we were not the ones who made the decision, but we assume that it was because Lucene is mature, open-source, highly performing, scalable, light and, yet, very powerful. It also has a very strong community that supports it. Its core comes as a single file of Java library with no dependencies, and allows you to index documents and search them with its out-of-the-box full text search capabilities. Of course, there are extensions to Apache Lucene that allow different language handling, and enable spellchecking, highlighting, and much more, but if you don't need those features, you can download a single file and use it in your application.

Overall architecture

Although I would like to jump straight to Apache Lucene architecture, there are some things we need to know first in order to fully understand it, and those are as follows:

- **Document**: It is a main data carrier used during indexing and search, containing one or more fields, that contain the data we put and get from Lucene.
- **Field**: It is a section of the document which is built of two parts: the name and the value.
- **Term**: It is a unit of search representing a word from the text.
- **Token**: It is an occurrence of a term from the text of the field. It consists of term text, start and end offset, and a type.

Apache Lucene writes all the information to the structure called **inverted** index. It is a data structure that maps the terms in the index to the documents, not the other way round like the relational database does. You can think of an inverted index as a data structure, where data is term oriented rather than document oriented.

Let's see how a simple inverted index can look. For example, let's assume that we have the documents with only title field to be indexed and they look like the following:

- Elasticsearch Server (document 1)
- Mastering Elasticsearch (document 2)
- Apache Solr 4 Cookbook (document 3)

So, the index (in a very simple way) could be visualized as shown in the following figure:

Term	Count	Docs
4	1	<3>
Apache	1	<3>
Cooking	1	<3>
Elasticsearch	2	<1><2>
Mastering	1	<1>
Server	1	<1>
Solr	1	<3>

As you can see, each term points to the number of documents it is present in. This allows for a very efficient and fast search such as the term-based queries. In addition to this, each term has a number connected to it: the count, telling Lucene how often it occurs.

Each index is divided into multiple write once and read many time segments. When indexing, after a single segment is written to disk, it can't be updated. For example, the information about deleted documents is stored in a separate file, but the segment itself is not updated.

However, multiple segments can be merged together in a process called **segments merge**. After forcing, segments are merged, or after Lucene decides it is time for merging to be performed, segments are merged together by Lucene to create larger ones. This can be I/O demanding; however, it is needed to clean up some information because during that time some information that is not needed anymore is deleted, for example the deleted documents. In addition to this, searching with the use of one larger segment is faster than searching against multiple smaller ones holding the same data. However, once again, remember that segments merging is an I/O demanding operation and you shouldn't force merging, just configure your merge policy carefully.

If you want to know what files are building the segments and what information is stored inside them, please take a look at Apache Lucene documentation available at http://lucene.apache.org/core/4_10_3/core/org/apache/lucene/codecs/lucene410/package-summary.html.

Getting deeper into Lucene index

Of course, the actual index created by Lucene is much more complicated and advanced, and consists of more than the terms their counts and documents in which they are present. We would like to tell you about a few of those additional index pieces because even though they are internal, it is usually good to know about them as they can be very handy.

Norms

A norm is a factor associated with each indexed document and stores normalization factors used to compute the score relative to the query. Norms are computed on the basis of index time boosts and are indexed along with the documents. With the use of norms, Lucene is able to provide an index time-boosting functionality at the cost of a certain amount of additional space needed for norms indexation and some amount of additional memory.

Term vectors

Term vectors are small inverted indices per document. They consist of pairs—a term and its frequency—and can optionally include information about term position. By default, Lucene and Elasticsearch don't enable term vectors indexing, but some functionality such as the fast vector highlighting requires them to be present.

Posting formats

With the release of Lucene 4.0, the library introduced the so-called codec architecture, giving developers control over how the index files are written onto the disk. One of the parts of the index is the posting format, which stores fields, terms, documents, terms positions and offsets, and, finally, the payloads (a byte array stored at an arbitrary position in Lucene index, which can contain any information we want). Lucene contains different posting formats for different purposes, for example one that is optimized for high cardinality fields like the unique identifier.

Doc values

As we already mentioned, Lucene index is the so-called inverted index. However, for certain features, such as faceting or aggregations, such architecture is not the best one. The mentioned functionality operates on the document level and not the term level and because Elasticsearch needs to uninvert the index before calculations can be done. Because of that, doc values were introduced and additional structure used for faceting, sorting and aggregations. The doc values store uninverted data for a field they are turned on for. Both Lucene and Elasticsearch allow us to configure the implementation used to store them, giving us the possibility of memory-based doc values, disk-based doc values, and a combination of the two.

Analyzing your data

Of course, the question arises of how the data passed in the documents is transformed into the inverted index and how the query text is changed into terms to allow searching. The process of transforming this data is called analysis.

Analysis is done by the analyzer, which is built of tokenizer and zero or more filters, and can also have zero or more character mappers.

A tokenizer in Lucene is used to divide the text into tokens, which are basically terms with additional information, such as its position in the original text and its length. The result of the tokenizer work is a so-called token stream, where the tokens are put one by one and are ready to be processed by filters.

Apart from tokenizer, Lucene analyzer is built of zero or more filters that are used to process tokens in the token stream. For example, it can remove tokens from the stream, change them or even produce new ones. There are numerous filters and you can easily create new ones. Some examples of filters are as follows:

- **Lowercase** filter: It makes all the tokens lowercase
- **ASCII folding** filter: It removes non ASCII parts from tokens
- **Synonyms** filter: It is responsible for changing one token to another on the basis of synonym rules
- **Multiple language stemming** filters: These are responsible for reducing tokens (actually the text part that they provide) into their root or base forms, the stem

Filters are processed one after another, so we have almost unlimited analysis possibilities with adding multiple filters one after another.

The last thing is the character mappings, which is used before tokenizer and is responsible for processing text before any analysis is done. One of the examples of character mapper is the HTML tags removal process.

Indexing and querying

We may wonder how that all affects indexing and querying when using Lucene and all the software that is built on top of it. During indexing, Lucene will use an analyzer of your choice to process the contents of your document; different analyzers can be used for different fields, so the `title` field of your document can be analyzed differently compared to the `description` field.

During query time, if you use one of the provided query parsers, your query will be analyzed. However, you can also choose the other path and not analyze your queries. This is crucial to remember because some of the Elasticsearch queries are being analyzed and some are not. For example, the prefix query is not analyzed and the match query is analyzed.

What you should remember about indexing and querying analysis is that the index should be matched by the query term. If they don't match, Lucene won't return the desired documents. For example, if you are using stemming and lowercasing during indexing, you need to be sure that the terms in the query are also lowercased and stemmed, or your queries will return no results at all.

Lucene query language

Some of the query types provided by Elasticsearch support Apache Lucene query parser syntax. Because of this, it is crucial to understand the Lucene query language.

Understanding the basics

A query is divided by Apache Lucene into terms and operators. A term, in Lucene, can be a single word or a phrase (group of words surrounded by double quote characters). If the query is set to be analyzed, the defined analyzer will be used on each of the terms that form the query.

A query can also contain Boolean operators that connect terms to each other forming clauses. The list of Boolean operators is as follows:

- **AND**: It means that the given two terms (left and right operand) need to match in order for the clause to be matched. For example, we would run a query, such as apache `AND` lucene, to match documents with both apache and lucene terms in a document field.

- **OR**: It means that any of the given terms may match in order for the clause to be matched. For example, we would run a query, such as apache OR lucene, to match documents with apache or lucene (or both) terms in a document field.
- **NOT**: It means that in order for the document to be considered a match, the term appearing after the NOT operator must not match. For example, we would run a query lucene NOT Elasticsearch to match documents that contain lucene term, but not the Elasticsearch term in the document field.

In addition to these, we may use the following operators:

- **+**: It means that the given term needs to be matched in order for the document to be considered as a match. For example, in order to find documents that match lucene term and may match apache term, we would run a query such as +lucene apache.
- **-**: It means that the given term can't be matched in order for the document to be considered a match. For example, in order to find a document with lucene term, but not Elasticsearch term, we would run a query such as +lucene -Elasticsearch.

When not specifying any of the previous operators, the default OR operator will be used.

In addition to all these, there is one more thing: you can use parenthesis to group clauses together for example, with something like the following query:

```
Elasticsearch AND (mastering OR book)
```

Querying fields

Of course, just like in Elasticsearch, in Lucene all your data is stored in fields that build the document. In order to run a query against a field, you need to provide the field name, add the colon character, and provide the clause that should be run against that field. For example, if you would like to match documents with the term Elasticsearch in the title field, you would run the following query:

```
title:Elasticsearch
```

You can also group multiple clauses. For example, if you would like your query to match all the documents having the Elasticsearch term and the mastering book phrase in the title field, you could run a query like the following code:

```
title:(+Elasticsearch +"mastering book")
```

Introduction to Elasticsearch

The previous query can also be expressed in the following way:

```
+title:Elasticsearch +title:"mastering book"
```

Term modifiers

In addition to the standard field query with a simple term or clause, Lucene allows us to modify the terms we pass in the query with modifiers. The most common modifiers, which you will be familiar with, are wildcards. There are two wildcards supported by Lucene, the ? and * terms. The first one will match any character and the second one will match multiple characters.

> Please note that by default these wildcard characters can't be used as the first character in a term because of performance reasons.

In addition to this, Lucene supports fuzzy and proximity searches with the use of the ~ character and an integer following it. When used with a single word term, it means that we want to search for terms that are similar to the one we've modified (the so-called fuzzy search). The integer after the ~ character specifies the maximum number of edits that can be done to consider the term similar. For example, if we would run a query, such as `writer~2`, both the terms `writer` and `writers` would be considered a match.

When the ~ character is used on a phrase, the integer number we provide is telling Lucene how much distance between the words is acceptable. For example, let's take the following query:

```
title:"mastering Elasticsearch"
```

It would match the document with the `title` field containing `mastering Elasticsearch`, but not `mastering book Elasticsearch`. However, if we would run a query, such as `title:"mastering Elasticsearch"~2`, it would result in both example documents matched.

We can also use boosting to increase our term importance by using the ^ character and providing a float number. Boosts lower than one would result in decreasing the document importance. Boosts higher than one will result in increasing the importance. The default boost value is 1. Please refer to the *Default Apache Lucene scoring explained* section in *Chapter 2, Power User Query DSL*, for further information on what boosting is and how it is taken into consideration during document scoring.

In addition to all these, we can use square and curly brackets to allow range searching. For example, if we would like to run a range search on a numeric field, we could run the following query:

```
price:[10.00 TO 15.00]
```

The preceding query would result in all documents with the `price` field between `10.00` and `15.00` inclusive.

In case of string-based fields, we also can run a range query, for example name:`[Adam TO Adria]`.

The preceding query would result in all documents containing all the terms between `Adam` and `Adria` in the `name` field including them.

If you would like your range bound or bounds to be exclusive, use curly brackets instead of the square ones. For example, in order to find documents with the `price` field between `10.00` inclusive and `15.00` exclusive, we would run the following query:

```
price:[10.00 TO 15.00}
```

If you would like your range bound from one side and not bound by the other, for example querying for documents with a price higher than `10.00`, we would run the following query:

```
price:[10.00 TO *]
```

Handling special characters

In case you want to search for one of the special characters (which are +, -, &&, ||, !, (,), { }, [ ], ^, ", ~, *, ?, :, \, /), you need to escape it with the use of the backslash (\) character. For example, to search for the `abc"efg` term you need to do something like `abc\"efg`.

Introducing Elasticsearch

Although we've said that we expect the reader to be familiar with Elasticsearch, we would really like you to fully understand Elasticsearch; therefore, we've decided to include a short introduction to the concepts of this great search engine.

As you probably know, Elasticsearch is production-ready software to build search and analysis-oriented applications. It was originally started by *Shay Banon* and published in February 2010. Since then, it has rapidly gained popularity just within a few years and has become an important alternative to other open source and commercial solutions. It is one of the most downloaded open source projects.

Basic concepts

There are a few concepts that come with Elasticsearch and their understanding is crucial to fully understand how Elasticsearch works and operates.

Index

Elasticsearch stores its data in one or more indices. Using analogies from the SQL world, index is something similar to a database. It is used to store the documents and read them from it. As already mentioned, under the hood, Elasticsearch uses Apache Lucene library to write and read the data from the index. What you should remember is that a single Elasticsearch index may be built of more than a single Apache Lucene index – by using shards.

Document

Document is the main entity in the Elasticsearch world (and also in the Lucene world). At the end, all use cases of using Elasticsearch can be brought at a point where it is all about searching for documents and analyzing them. Document consists of fields, and each field is identified by its name and can contain one or multiple values. Each document may have a different set of fields; there is no schema or imposed structure – this is because Elasticsearch documents are in fact Lucene ones. From the client point of view, Elasticsearch document is a JSON object (see more on the JSON format at http://en.wikipedia.org/wiki/JSON).

Type

Each document in Elasticsearch has its type defined. This allows us to store various document types in one index and have different mappings for different document types. If you would like to compare it to an SQL world, a type in Elasticsearch is something similar to a database table.

Mapping

As already mentioned in the *Introducing Apache Lucene* section, all documents are analyzed before being indexed. We can configure how the input text is divided into tokens, which tokens should be filtered out, or what additional processing, such as removing HTML tags, is needed. This is where mapping comes into play – it holds all the information about the analysis chain. Besides the fact that Elasticsearch can automatically discover field type by looking at its value, in most cases we will want to configure the mappings ourselves to avoid unpleasant surprises.

Node

The single instance of the Elasticsearch server is called a node. A single node in Elasticsearch deployment can be sufficient for many simple use cases, but when you have to think about fault tolerance or you have lots of data that cannot fit in a single server, you should think about multi-node Elasticsearch cluster.

Elasticsearch nodes can serve different purposes. Of course, Elasticsearch is designed to index and search our data, so the first type of node is the **data** node. Such nodes hold the data and search on them. The second type of node is the **master** node—a node that works as a supervisor of the cluster controlling other nodes' work. The third node type is the **tribe** node, which is new and was introduced in Elasticsearch 1.0. The tribe node can join multiple clusters and thus act as a bridge between them, allowing us to execute almost all Elasticsearch functionalities on multiple clusters just like we would be using a single cluster.

Cluster

Cluster is a set of Elasticsearch nodes that work together. The distributed nature of Elasticsearch allows us to easily handle data that is too large for a single node to handle (both in terms of handling queries and documents). By using multi-node clusters, we can also achieve uninterrupted work of our application, even if several machines (nodes) are not available due to outage or administration tasks such as upgrade. Elasticsearch provides clustering almost seamlessly. In our opinion, this is one of the major advantages over competition; setting up a cluster in the Elasticsearch world is really easy.

Shard

As we said previously, clustering allows us to store information volumes that exceed abilities of a single server (but it is not the only need for clustering). To achieve this requirement, Elasticsearch spreads data to several physical Lucene indices. Those Lucene indices are called shards, and the process of dividing the index is called sharding. Elasticsearch can do this automatically and all the parts of the index (shards) are visible to the user as one big index. Note that besides this automation, it is crucial to tune this mechanism for particular use cases because the number of shard index is built or configured during index creation and cannot be changed without creating a new index and re-indexing the whole data.

Replica

Sharding allows us to push more data into Elasticsearch that is possible for a single node to handle. Replicas can help us in situations where the load increases and a single node is not able to handle all the requests. The idea is simple—create an additional copy of a shard, which can be used for queries just as original, primary shard. Note that we get safety for free. If the server with the primary shard is gone, Elasticsearch will take one of the available replicas of that shard and promote it to the leader, so the service work is not interrupted. Replicas can be added and removed at any time, so you can adjust their numbers when needed. Of course, the content of the replica is updated in real time and is done automatically by Elasticsearch.

Key concepts behind Elasticsearch architecture

Elasticsearch was built with a few concepts in mind. The development team wanted to make it easy to use and highly scalable. These core features are visible in every corner of Elasticsearch. From the architectural perspective, the main features are as follows:

- Reasonable default values that allow users to start using Elasticsearch just after installing it, without any additional tuning. This includes built-in discovery (for example, field types) and auto-configuration.
- Working in distributed mode by default. Nodes assume that they are or will be a part of the cluster.
- Peer-to-peer architecture without **single point of failure** (**SPOF**). Nodes automatically connect to other machines in the cluster for data interchange and mutual monitoring. This covers automatic replication of shards.
- Easily scalable both in terms of capacity and the amount of data by adding new nodes to the cluster.
- Elasticsearch does not impose restrictions on data organization in the index. This allows users to adjust to the existing data model. As we noted in type description, Elasticsearch supports multiple data types in a single index, and adjustment to the business model includes handling relationships between documents (although, this functionality is rather limited).
- **Near Real Time** (**NRT**) searching and versioning. Because of the distributed nature of Elasticsearch, it is impossible to avoid delays and temporary differences between data located on the different nodes. Elasticsearch tries to reduce these issues and provide additional mechanisms as versioning.

Workings of Elasticsearch

The following section will include information on key Elasticsearch features, such as bootstrap, failure detection, data indexing, querying, and so on.

The startup process

When Elasticsearch node starts, it uses the discovery module to find the other nodes in the same cluster (the key here is the cluster name defined in the configuration) and connect to them. By default the multicast request is broadcast to the network to find other Elasticsearch nodes with the same cluster name. You can see the process illustrated in the following figure:

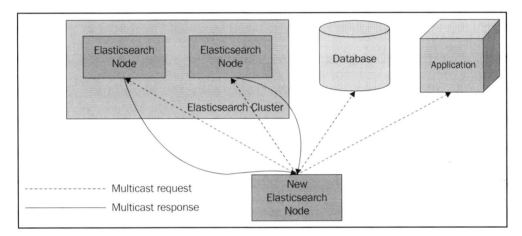

In the preceding figure, the cluster, one of the nodes that is master eligible is elected as master node (by default all nodes are master eligible). This node is responsible for managing the cluster state and the process of assigning shards to nodes in reaction to changes in cluster topology.

Note that a master node in Elasticsearch has no importance from the user perspective, which is different from other systems available (such as the databases). In practice, you do not need to know which node is a master node; all operations can be sent to any node, and internally Elasticsearch will do all the magic. If necessary, any node can send sub-queries in parallel to other nodes and merge responses to return the full response to the user. All of this is done without accessing the master node (nodes operates in peer-to-peer architecture).

The master node reads the cluster state and, if necessary, goes into the recovery process. During this state, it checks which shards are available and decides which shards will be the primary shards. After this, the whole cluster enters into a yellow state.

This means that a cluster is able to run queries, but full throughput and all possibilities are not achieved yet (it basically means that all primary shards are allocated, but not all replicas are). The next thing to do is to find duplicated shards and treat them as replicas. When a shard has too few replicas, the master node decides where to put missing shards and additional replicas are created based on a primary shard (if possible). If everything goes well, the cluster enters into a green state (which means that all primary shards and all their replicas are allocated).

Failure detection

During normal cluster work, the master node monitors all the available nodes and checks whether they are working. If any of them are not available for the configured amount of time, the node is treated as broken and the process of handling failure starts. For example, this may mean rebalancing of shards, choosing new leaders, and so on. As another example, for every primary shard that is present on the failed nodes, a new primary shard should be elected from the remaining replicas of this shard. The whole process of placing new shards and replicas can (and usually should) be configured to match our needs. More information about it can be found in *Chapter 7, Elasticsearch Administration*.

Just to illustrate how it works, let's take an example of a three nodes cluster. One of the nodes is the master node, and all of the nodes can hold data. The master node will send the ping requests to other nodes and wait for the response. If the response doesn't come (actually how many ping requests may fail depends on the configuration), such a node will be removed from the cluster. The same goes in the opposite way — each node will ping the master node to see whether it is working.

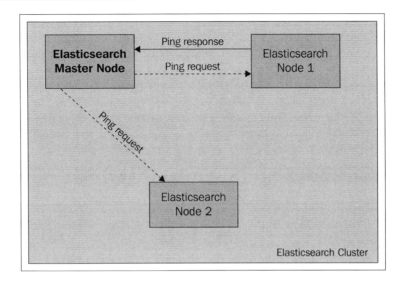

Communicating with Elasticsearch

We talked about how Elasticsearch is built, but, after all, the most important part for us is how to feed it with data and how to build queries. In order to do that, Elasticsearch exposes a sophisticated **Application Program Interface** (**API**). In general, it wouldn't be a surprise if we would say that every feature of Elasticsearch has an API. The primary API is REST based (see `http://en.wikipedia.org/wiki/Representational_state_transfer`) and is easy to integrate with practically any system that can send HTTP requests.

Elasticsearch assumes that data is sent in the URL or in the request body as a JSON document (see `http://en.wikipedia.org/wiki/JSON`). If you use Java or language based on **Java Virtual Machine** (**JVM**), you should look at the Java API, which, in addition to everything that is offered by the REST API, has built-in cluster discovery. It is worth mentioning that the Java API is also internally used by Elasticsearch itself to do all the node-to-node communication. Because of this, the Java API exposes all the features available through the REST API calls.

Indexing data

There are a few ways to send data to Elasticsearch. The easiest way is using the index API, which allows sending a single document to a particular index. For example, by using the `curl` tool (see http://curl.haxx.se/). An example command that would create a new document would look as follows:

```
curl -XPUT http://localhost:9200/blog/article/1 -d '{"title": "New
  version of Elastic Search released!", "tags": ["announce",
  "Elasticsearch", "release"] }'
```

The second way allows us to send many documents using the bulk API and the UDP bulk API. The difference between these methods is the connection type. Common bulk command sends documents by HTTP protocol and UDP bulk sends this using connection less datagram protocol. This is faster but not so reliable. The last method uses plugins, called rivers, but let's not discuss them as the rivers will be removed in future versions of Elasticsearch.

One very important thing to remember is that the indexing will always be first executed at the primary shard, not on the replica. If the indexing request is sent to a node that doesn't have the correct shard or contains a replica, it will be forwarded to the primary shard. Then, the leader will send the indexing request to all the replicas, wait for their acknowledgement (this can be controlled), and finalize the indexation if the requirements were met (like the replica quorum being updated).

The following illustration shows the process we just discussed:

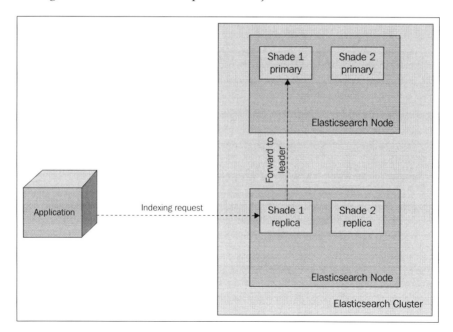

Querying data

The Query API is a big part of Elasticsearch API. Using the Query DSL (JSON-based language for building complex queries), we can do the following:

- Use various query types including simple term query, phrase, range, Boolean, fuzzy, span, wildcard, spatial, and function queries for human readable scoring control
- Build complex queries by combining the simple queries together
- Filter documents, throwing away ones that do not match selected criteria without influencing the scoring, which is very efficient when it comes to performance
- Find documents similar to a given document
- Find suggestions and corrections of a given phrase
- Build dynamic navigation and calculate statistics using aggregations
- Use prospective search and find queries matching a given document

When talking about querying, the important thing is that query is not a simple, single-stage process. In general, the process can be divided into two phases: the scatter phase and the gather phase. The scatter phase is about querying all the relevant shards of your index. The gather phase is about gathering the results from the relevant shards, combining them, sorting, processing, and returning to the client. The following illustration shows that process:

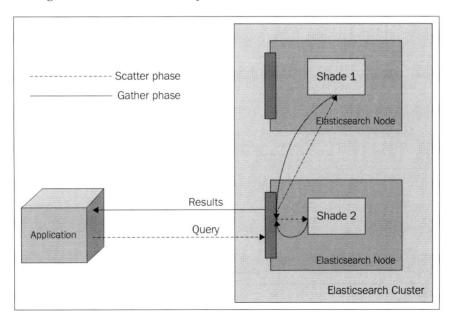

Introduction to Elasticsearch

 You can control the scatter and gather phases by specifying the search type to one of the six values currently exposed by Elasticsearch. We've talked about query scope in our previous book *Elasticsearch Server Second Edition* by *Packt Publishing*.

The story

As we said in the beginning of this chapter, we treat the book you are holding in your hands as a continuation of the *Elasticsearch Server Second Edition* book. Because of this, we would like to continue the story that we've used in that book. In general, we assume that we are implementing and running an online book store, as simple as that.

The mappings for our `library` index look like the following:

```
{
  "book" : {
    "_index" : {
      "enabled" : true
    },
    "_id" : {
      "index": "not_analyzed",
      "store" : "yes"
    },
    "properties" : {
      "author" : {
        "type" : "string"
      },
      "characters" : {
        "type" : "string"
      },
      "copies" : {
        "type" : "long",
        "ignore_malformed" : false
      },
      "otitle" : {
        "type" : "string"
      },
      "tags" : {
        "type" : "string",
        "index" : "not_analyzed"
      },
      "title" : {
        "type" : "string"
```

```
      },
      "year" : {
        "type" : "long",
        "ignore_malformed" : false
      },
      "available" : {
        "type" : "boolean"
      },
      "review" : {
        "type" : "nested",
        "properties" : {
          "nickname" : {
            "type" : "string"
          },
          "text" : {
            "type" : "string"
          },
          "stars" : {
            "type" : "integer"
          }
        }
      }
    }
  }
}
```

The mappings can be found in the `library.json` file provided with the book.

The data that we will use is provided with the book in the `books.json` file. The example documents from that file look like the following:

```
{ "index": {"_index": "library", "_type": "book", "_id": "1"}}
{ "title": "All Quiet on the Western Front","otitle": "Im Westen nichts
  Neues","author": "Erich Maria Remarque","year": 1929,"characters":
["Paul
  Bäumer", "Albert Kropp", "Haie Westhus", "Fredrich Müller",
"Stanislaus
  Katczinsky", "Tjaden"],"tags": ["novel"],"copies": 1, "available":
true,
  "section" : 3}
{ "index": {"_index": "library", "_type": "book", "_id": "2"}}
{ "title": "Catch-22","author": "Joseph Heller","year":
1961,"characters":
```

```
    ["John Yossarian", "Captain Aardvark", "Chaplain Tappman", "Colonel
    Cathcart", "Doctor Daneeka"],"tags": ["novel"],"copies": 6,
"available" :
    false, "section" : 1}
{ "index": {"_index": "library", "_type": "book", "_id": "3"}}
{ "title": "The Complete Sherlock Holmes","author": "Arthur Conan
    Doyle","year": 1936,"characters": ["Sherlock Holmes","Dr. Watson",
"G.
    Lestrade"],"tags": [],"copies": 0, "available" : false, "section" :
12}
{ "index": {"_index": "library", "_type": "book", "_id": "4"}}
{ "title": "Crime and Punishment","otitle": "Преступле́ние и
    наказа́ние","author": "Fyodor Dostoevsky","year": 1886,"characters":
    ["Raskolnikov", "Sofia Semyonovna Marmeladova"],"tags": [],"copies":
0,
    "available" : true}
```

Downloading the example code

You can download the example code files for all Packt books you have purchased from your account at http://www.packtpub.com. If you purchased this book elsewhere, you can visit http://www.packtpub.com/support and register to have the files e-mailed directly to you.

To create the index using the provided mappings and to index the data, we would run the following commands:

```
curl -XPOST 'localhost:9200/library'
curl -XPUT 'localhost:9200/library/book/_mapping' -d @library.json
curl -s -XPOST 'localhost:9200/_bulk' --data-binary @books.json
```

Summary

In this chapter, we looked at the general architecture of Apache Lucene: how it works, how the analysis process is done, and how to use Apache Lucene query language. In addition to that, we discussed the basic concepts of Elasticsearch, its architecture, and internal communication.

In the next chapter, you'll learn about the default scoring formula Apache Lucene uses, what the query rewrite process is, and how it works. In addition to that, we'll discuss some of the Elasticsearch functionality, such as query templates, filters, and how they affect performance, what we can do with that, and how we can choose the right query to get the job done.

2
Power User Query DSL

In the previous chapter, we looked at what Apache Lucene is, how its architecture looks, and how the analysis process is handled. In addition to these, we saw what Lucene query language is and how to use it. We also discussed Elasticsearch, its architecture, and core concepts. In this chapter, we will dive deep into Elasticsearch focusing on the Query DSL. We will first go through how Lucene scoring formula works before turning to advanced queries. By the end of this chapter, we will have covered the following topics:

- How the default Apache Lucene scoring formula works
- What query rewrite is
- What query templates are and how to use them
- How to leverage complicated Boolean queries
- What are the performance implications of large Boolean queries
- Which query you should use for your particular use case

Default Apache Lucene scoring explained

A very important part of the querying process in Apache Lucene is scoring. Scoring is the process of calculating the score property of a document in a scope of a given query. What is a score? A score is a factor that describes how well the document matched the query. In this section, we'll look at the default Apache Lucene scoring mechanism: the **TF/IDF** (term frequency/inverse document frequency) algorithm and how it affects the returned document. Knowing how this works is valuable when designing complicated queries and choosing which queries parts should be more relevant than the others. Knowing the basics of how scoring works in Lucene allows us to tune queries more easily and the results retuned by them to match our use case.

When a document is matched

When a document is returned by Lucene, it means that it matched the query we've sent. In such a case, the document is given a score. Sometimes, the score is the same for all the documents (like for the `constant_score` query), but usually this won't be the case. The higher the score value, the more relevant the document is, at least at the Apache Lucene level and from the scoring formula point of view. Because the score is dependent on the matched documents, query, and the contents of the index, it is natural that the score calculated for the same document returned by two different queries will be different. Because of this, one should remember that not only should we avoid comparing the scores of individual documents returned by different queries, but we should also avoid comparing the maximum score calculated for different queries. This is because the score depends on multiple factors, not only on the boosts and query structure, but also on how many terms were matched, in which fields, the type of matching that was used on query normalization, and so on. In extreme cases, a similar query may result in totally different scores for a document, only because we've used a custom score query or the number of matched terms increased dramatically.

For now, let's get back to the scoring. In order to calculate the score property for a document, multiple factors are taken into account, which are as follows:

- **Document boost**: The boost value given for a document during indexing.
- **Field boost**: The boost value given for a field during querying.
- **Coord**: The coordination factor that is based on the number of terms the document has. It is responsible for giving more value to the documents that contain more search terms compared to other documents.
- **Inverse document frequency**: Term-based factor telling the scoring formula how rare the given term is. The higher the inverse document frequency, the rarer the term is. The scoring formula uses this factor to boost documents that contain rare terms.
- **Length norm**: A field-based factor for normalization based on the number of terms given field contains (calculated during indexing and stored in the index). The longer the field, the lesser boost this factor will give, which means that the Apache Lucene scoring formula will favor documents with fields containing lower terms.
- **Term frequency**: Term-based factor describing how many times a given term occurs in a document. The higher the term frequency, the higher the score of the document will be.

- **Query norm**: Query-based normalization factor that is calculated as a sum of a squared weight of each of the query terms. Query norm is used to allow score comparison between queries, which, as we said, is not always easy and possible.

TF/IDF scoring formula

Since the Lucene version 4.0, contains different scoring formulas and you are probably aware of them. However, we would like to discuss the default TF/IDF formula in greater detail. Please keep in mind that in order to adjust your query relevance, you don't need to understand the following equations, but it is very important to at least know how it works as it simplifies the relevancy tuning process.

Lucene conceptual scoring formula

The conceptual version of the TF/IDF formula looks as follows:

$$score(q,d) = coord(q,d) * queryBoost(q) * \frac{V(q) * V(d)}{|V(q)|} * lengthNorm(d) * docBoost(d)$$

The presented formula is a representation of a Boolean Model of Information Retrieval combined with a Vector Space Model of Information Retrieval. Let's not discuss this and let's just jump into the practical formula, which is implemented by Apache Lucene and is actually used.

> The information about the Boolean Model and Vector Space Model of Information Retrieval are far beyond the scope of this book. You can read more about it at http://en.wikipedia.org/wiki/Standard_Boolean_model and http://en.wikipedia.org/wiki/Vector_Space_Model.

Lucene practical scoring formula

Now, let's look at the following practical scoring formula used by the default Apache Lucene scoring mechanism:

$$score(q,d) = coord(q,d) * queryNorm(q) * \sum_{t\ in\ q} (tf(t\ in\ d) * idf(t)^2 * boost(t) * norm(t,d))$$

Power User Query DSL

As you can see, the score factor for the document is a function of query `q` and document `d`, as we have already discussed. There are two factors that are not dependent directly on query terms, `coord` and `queryNorm`. These two elements of the formula are multiplied by the sum calculated for each term in the query.

The sum, on the other hand, is calculated by multiplying the term frequency for the given term, its inverse document frequency, term boost, and the norm, which is the length norm we've discussed previously.

Sounds a bit complicated, right? Don't worry, you don't need to remember all of that. What you should be aware of is what matters when it comes to document score. Basically, there are a few rules, as follows, which come from the previous equations:

- The rarer the matched term, the higher the score the document will have. Lucene treats documents with unique words as more important than the ones containing common words.
- The smaller the document fields (contain less terms), the higher the score the document will have. In general, Lucene emphasizes shorter documents because there is a greater possibility that those documents are exactly about the topic we are searching for.
- The higher the boost (both given during indexing and querying), the higher the score the document will have because higher boost means more importance of the particular data (document, term, phrase, and so on).

As we can see, Lucene will give the highest score for the documents that have many uncommon query terms matched in the document contents, have shorter fields (less terms indexed), and will also favor rarer terms instead of the common ones.

> If you want to read more about the Apache Lucene TF/IDF scoring formula, please visit Apache Lucene Javadocs for the `TFIDFSimilarity` class available at `http://lucene.apache.org/core/4_9_0/core/org/apache/lucene/search/similarities/TFIDFSimilarity.html`.

Elasticsearch point of view

On top of all this is Elasticsearch that leverages Apache Lucene and thankfully allows us to change the default scoring algorithm by specifying one of the available similarities or by implementing your own. But remember, Elasticsearch is more than just Lucene because we are not bound to rely only on Apache Lucene scoring.

We have different types of queries, where we can strictly control how the score of the documents is calculated, for example, by using the `function_score` query, we are allowed to use scripting to alter score of the documents; we can use the rescore functionality introduced in Elasticsearch 0.90 to recalculate the score of the returned documents, by another query run against top N documents, and so on.

> For more information about the queries from Apache Lucene point of view, please refer to Javadocs, for example, the one available at http://lucene.apache.org/core/4_9_0/queries/org/apache/lucene/queries/package-summary.html.

An example

Till now we've seen how scoring works. Now we would like to show you a simple example of how the scoring works in real life. To do this, we will create a new index called `scoring`. We do that by running the following command:

```
curl -XPUT 'localhost:9200/scoring' -d '{
 "settings" : {
  "index" : {
   "number_of_shards" : 1,
   "number_of_replicas" : 0
  }
 }
}'
```

We will use an index with a single physical shard and no replicas to keep it as simple as it can be (we don't need to bother about distributed document frequency in such a case). Let's start with indexing a very simple document that looks as follows:

```
curl -XPOST 'localhost:9200/scoring/doc/1' -d '{"name":"first document"}'
```

Let's run a simple `match` query that searches for the document term:

```
curl -XGET 'localhost:9200/scoring/_search?pretty' -d '{
 "query" : {
  "match" : { "name" : "document" }
 }
}'
```

Power User Query DSL

The result returned by Elasticsearch would be as follows:

```
{
  "took" : 1,
  "timed_out" : false,
  "_shards" : {
    "total" : 1,
    "successful" : 1,
    "failed" : 0
  },
  "hits" : {
    "total" : 1,
    "max_score" : 0.19178301,
    "hits" : [ {
      "_index" : "scoring",
      "_type" : "doc",
      "_id" : "1",
      "_score" : 0.19178301,
      "_source":{"name":"first document"}
    } ]
  }
}
```

Of course, our document was matched and it was given a score. We can also check how the score was calculated by running the following command:

```
curl -XGET 'localhost:9200/scoring/doc/1/_explain?pretty' -d '{
 "query" : {
  "match" : { "name" : "document" }
 }
}'
```

The results returned by Elasticsearch would be as follows:

```
{
    "_index" : "scoring",
    "_type" : "doc",
    "_id" : "1",
    "matched" : true,
    "explanation" : {
      "value" : 0.19178301,
      "description" : "weight(name:document in 0) [PerFieldSimilarity], result of:",
      "details" : [ {
        "value" : 0.19178301,
```

```
              "description" : "fieldWeight in 0, product of:",
              "details" : [ {
                "value" : 1.0,
                "description" : "tf(freq=1.0), with freq of:",
                "details" : [ {
                  "value" : 1.0,
                  "description" : "termFreq=1.0"
                } ]
              }, {
                "value" : 0.30685282,
                "description" : "idf(docFreq=1, maxDocs=1)"
              }, {
                "value" : 0.625,
                "description" : "fieldNorm(doc=0)"
              } ]
            } ]
          }
        }
```

As we can see, we've got detailed information on how the score has been calculated for our query and the given document. We can see that the score is a product of the term frequency (which is `1` in this case), the inverse document frequency (`0.30685282`), and the field norm (`0.625`).

Now, let's add another document to our index:

```
curl -XPOST 'localhost:9200/scoring/doc/2' -d '{"name":"second
  example document"}'
```

If we run our initial query again, we will see the following response:

```
{
  "took" : 6,
  "timed_out" : false,
  "_shards" : {
    "total" : 1,
    "successful" : 1,
    "failed" : 0
  },
  "hits" : {
    "total" : 2,
    "max_score" : 0.37158427,
    "hits" : [ {
      "_index" : "scoring",
      "_type" : "doc",
      "_id" : "1",
```

```
      "_score" : 0.37158427,
      "_source":{"name":"first document"}
    }, {
      "_index" : "scoring",
      "_type" : "doc",
      "_id" : "2",
      "_score" : 0.2972674,
      "_source":{"name":"second example document"}
    } ]
  }
}
```

We can now compare how the TF/IDF scoring formula works in real life. After indexing the second document to the same shard (remember that we created our index with a single shard and no replicas), the score changed, even though the query is still the same. That's because different factors changed. For example, the inverse document frequency changed and thus the score is different. The other thing to notice is the scores of both the documents. We search for a single word (the `document`), and the query match was against the same term in the same field in case of both the documents. The reason why the second document has a lower score is that it has one more term in the `name` field compared to the first document. As you will remember, we already know that Lucene will give a higher score to the shorter documents.

Hopefully, this short introduction will give you better insight into how scoring works and will help you understand how your queries work when you are in need of relevancy tuning.

Query rewrite explained

We have already talked about scoring, which is valuable knowledge, especially when trying to improve the relevance of our queries. We also think that when debugging your queries, it is valuable to know how all the queries are executed; therefore, it is because of this we decided to include this section on how query rewrite works in Elasticsearch, why it is used, and how to control it.

If you have ever used queries, such as the prefix query and the wildcard query, basically any query that is said to be multiterm, you've probably heard about query rewriting. Elasticsearch does that because of performance reasons. The rewrite process is about changing the original, expensive query to a set of queries that are far less expensive from Lucene's point of view and thus speed up the query execution. The rewrite process is not visible to the client, but it is good to know that we can alter the rewrite process behavior. For example, let's look at what Elasticsearch does with a prefix query.

Prefix query as an example

The best way to illustrate how the rewrite process is done internally is to look at an example and see what terms are used instead of the original query term. Let's say we have the following data in our index:

```
curl -XPUT 'localhost:9200/clients/client/1' -d '{
  "id":"1", "name":"Joe"
}'
curl -XPUT 'localhost:9200/clients/client/2' -d '{
  "id":"2", "name":"Jane"
}'
curl -XPUT 'localhost:9200/clients/client/3' -d '{
  "id":"3", "name":"Jack"
}'
curl -XPUT 'localhost:9200/clients/client/4' -d '{
  "id":"4", "name":"Rob"
}'
```

We would like to find all the documents that start with the j letter. As simple as that, we run the following query against our clients index:

```
curl -XGET 'localhost:9200/clients/_search?pretty' -d '{
 "query" : {
  "prefix" : {
   "name" : {
    "prefix" : "j",
    "rewrite" : "constant_score_boolean"
   }
  }
 }
}'
```

We've used a simple prefix query; we've said that we would like to find all the documents with the j letter in the name field. We've also used the rewrite property to specify the query rewrite method, but let's skip it for now, as we will discuss the possible values of this parameter in the later part of this section.

As the response to the previous query, we've got the following:

```
{
  "took" : 2,
  "timed_out" : false,
  "_shards" : {
```

Power User Query DSL

```
      "total" : 5,
      "successful" : 5,
      "failed" : 0
    },
    "hits" : {
      "total" : 3,
      "max_score" : 1.0,
      "hits" : [ {
        "_index" : "clients",
        "_type" : "client",
        "_id" : "3",
        "_score" : 1.0,
        "_source":{
   "id":"3", "name":"Jack"
}
      }, {
        "_index" : "clients",
        "_type" : "client",
        "_id" : "2",
        "_score" : 1.0,
        "_source":{
   "id":"2", "name":"Jane"
}
      }, {
        "_index" : "clients",
        "_type" : "client",
        "_id" : "1",
        "_score" : 1.0,
        "_source":{
   "id":"1", "name":"Joe"
}
      } ]
    }
}
```

As you can see, in response we've got the three documents that have the contents of the name field starting with the desired character. We didn't specify the mappings explicitly, so Elasticsearch has guessed the name field mapping and has set it to string-based and analyzed. You can check this by running the following command:

```
curl -XGET 'localhost:9200/clients/client/_mapping?pretty'
```

Elasticsearch response will be similar to the following code:

```
{
  "client" : {
    "properties" : {
      "id" : {
        "type" : "string"
      },
      "name" : {
        "type" : "string"
      }
    }
  }
}
```

Getting back to Apache Lucene

Now let's take a step back and look at Apache Lucene again. If you recall what Lucene inverted index is built of, you can tell that it contains a term, a count, and a document pointer (if you can't recall, please refer to the *Introduction to Apache Lucene* section in *Chapter 1, Introduction to Elasticsearch*). So, let's see how the simplified view of the index may look for the previous data we've put to the `clients` index, as shown in the following figure:

Term	Count	Docs
jack	1	<3>
jane	1	<2>
joe	1	<1>
rob	1	<4>

What you see in the column with the term text is quite important. If we look at Elasticsearch and Apache Lucene internals, you can see that our prefix query was rewritten to the following Lucene query:

```
ConstantScore(name:jack name:jane name:joe)
```

We can check the portions of the rewrite using the Elasticsearch API. First of all, we can use the Explain API by running the following command:

```
curl -XGET 'localhost:9200/clients/client/1/_explain?pretty' -d '{
  "query" : {
    "prefix" : {
      "name" : {
```

```
      "prefix" : "j",
      "rewrite" : "constant_score_boolean"
    }
   }
  }
}'
```

The result would be as follows:

```
{
   "_index" : "clients",
   "_type" : "client",
   "_id" : "1",
   "matched" : true,
   "explanation" : {
     "value" : 1.0,
     "description" : "ConstantScore(name:joe), product of:",
     "details" : [ {
       "value" : 1.0,
       "description" : "boost"
     }, {
       "value" : 1.0,
       "description" : "queryNorm"
     } ]
   }
}
```

We can see that Elasticsearch used a constant score query with the `joe` term against the `name` field. Of course, this is on Lucene level; Elasticsearch actually used a cache to get the terms. We can see this by using the Validate Query API with a command that looks as follows:

```
curl -XGET 'localhost:9200/clients/client/_validate/query?explain&pretty' -d '{
 "query" : {
  "prefix" : {
   "name" : {
    "prefix" : "j",
    "rewrite" : "constant_score_boolean"
   }
  }
 }
}'
```

The result returned by Elasticsearch would look like the following:

```
{
  "valid" : true,
  "_shards" : {
    "total" : 1,
    "successful" : 1,
    "failed" : 0
  },
  "explanations" : [ {
    "index" : "clients",
    "valid" : true,
    "explanation" : "filtered(name:j*)->cache(_type:client)"
  } ]
}
```

Query rewrite properties

Of course, the `rewrite` property of multiterm queries can take more than a single `constant_score_boolean` value. We can control how the queries are rewritten internally. To do that, we place the `rewrite` parameter inside the JSON object responsible for the actual query, for example, like the following code:

```
{
  "query" : {
    "prefix" : {
      "name" : "j",
      "rewrite" : "constant_score_boolean"
    }
  }
}
```

The `rewrite` property can take the following values:

- `scoring_boolean`: This rewrite method translates each generated term into a Boolean should clause in a Boolean query. This rewrite method causes the score to be calculated for each document. Because of that, this method may be CPU demanding and for queries that many terms may exceed the Boolean query limit, which is set to `1024`. The default Boolean query limit can be changed by setting the `index.query.bool.max_clause_count` property in the `elasticsearch.yml` file. However, please remember that the more Boolean queries are produced, the lower the query performance may be.

- `constant_score_boolean`: This rewrite method is similar to the `scoring_boolean` rewrite method described previously, but is less CPU demanding because scoring is not computed, and instead of that, each term receives a score equal to the query boost (one by default and can be set using the boost property). Because this rewrite method also results in Boolean should clauses being created, similar to the `scoring_boolean` rewrite method, this method can also hit the maximum Boolean clauses limit.

- `constant_score_filter`: As Apache Lucene Javadocs state, this rewrite method rewrites the query by creating a private filter by visiting each term in a sequence and marking all documents for that term. Matching documents are given a constant score equal to the query boost. This method is faster than the `scoring_boolean` and `constant_score_boolean` methods, when the number of matching terms or documents is not small.

- `top_terms_N`: A rewrite method that translates each generated term into a Boolean should clause in a Boolean query and keeps the scores as computed by the query. However, unlike the `scoring_boolean` rewrite method, it only keeps the N number of top scoring terms to avoid hitting the maximum Boolean clauses limit and increase the final query performance.

- `top_terms_boost_N`: It is a rewrite method similar to the `top_terms_N` one, but the scores are not computed, but instead the documents are given the score equal to the value of the `boost` property (one by default).

> When the `rewrite` property is set to `constant_score_auto` value or not set at all, the value of `constant_score_filter` or `constant_score_boolean` will be used depending on the query and how it is constructed.

For example, if we would like our example query to use the `top_terms_N` with N equal to 2, our query would look like the following:

```
{
  "query" : {
    "prefix" : {
      "name" : {
       "prefix" :"j",
       "rewrite" : "top_terms_2"
      }
     }
    }
  }
}
```

Chapter 2

If you look at the results returned by Elasticsearch, you'll notice that unlike our initial query, the documents were given a score different than the default 1.0:

```
{
  "took" : 3,
  "timed_out" : false,
  "_shards" : {
    "total" : 5,
    "successful" : 5,
    "failed" : 0
  },
  "hits" : {
    "total" : 3,
    "max_score" : 0.30685282,
    "hits" : [ {
      "_index" : "clients",
      "_type" : "client",
      "_id" : "3",
      "_score" : 0.30685282,
      "_source":{
"id":"3", "name":"Jack"
}
    }, {
      "_index" : "clients",
      "_type" : "client",
      "_id" : "2",
      "_score" : 0.30685282,
      "_source":{
"id":"2", "name":"Jane"
}
    }, {
      "_index" : "clients",
      "_type" : "client",
      "_id" : "1",
      "_score" : 0.30685282,
      "_source":{
"id":"1", "name":"Joe"
}
    } ]
  }
}
```

This is because the `top_terms_N` keeps the score for N top scoring terms.

Before we finish the query rewrite section of this chapter, we should ask ourselves one last question: when to use which rewrite types? The answer to this question greatly depends on your use case, but to summarize, if you can live with lower precision and relevancy (but higher performance), you can go for the top N rewrite method. If you need high precision and thus more relevant queries (but lower performance), choose the Boolean approach.

Query templates

When the application grows, it is very probable that the environment will start to be more and more complicated. In your organization, you probably have developers who specialize in particular layers of the application – for example, you have at least one frontend designer and an engineer responsible for the database layer. It is very convenient to have the development divided into several modules because you can work on different parts of the application in parallel without the need of constant synchronization between individuals and the whole team. Of course, the book you are currently reading is not a book about project management, but search, so let's stick to that topic. In general, it would be useful, at least sometimes, to be able to extract all queries generated by the application, give them to a search engineer, and let him/her optimize them, in terms of both performance and relevance. In such a case, the application developers would only have to pass the query itself to Elasticsearch and not care about the structure, query DSL, filtering, and so on.

Introducing query templates

With the release of Elasticsearch 1.1.0, we were given the possibility of defining a template. Let's get back to our example library e-commerce store that we started working on in the beginning of this book. Let's assume that we already know what type of queries should be sent to Elasticsearch, but the query structure is not final – we will still work on the queries and improve them. By using the query templates, we can quickly supply the basic version of the query, let application specify the parameters, and modify the query on the Elasticsearch side until the query parameters change.

Let's assume that one of our queries needs to return the most relevant books from our `library` index. We also allow users to choose whether they are interested in books that are available or the ones that are not available. In such a case, we will need to provide two parameters – the phrase itself and the Boolean that specifies the availability. The first, simplified example of our query could looks as follows:

```
{
  "query": {
    "filtered": {
```

```
    "query": {
     "match": {
      "_all": "QUERY"
     }
    },
    "filter": {
     "term": {
      "available": BOOLEAN
     }
    }
   }
  }
}
```

The QUERY and BOOLEAN are placeholders for variables that will be passed to the query by the application. Of course, this query is too simple for our use case, but as we already said, this is only its first version — we will improve it in just a second.

Having our first query, we can now create our first template. Let's change our query a bit so that it looks as follows:

```
{
  "template": {
   "query": {
    "filtered": {
     "query": {
      "match": {
       "_all": "{{phrase}}"
      }
     },
     "filter": {
      "term": {
       "available": "{{avail}}"
      }
     }
    }
   }
  },
  "params": {
   "phrase": "front",
   "avail": true
  }
}
```

Power User Query DSL

You can see that our placeholders were replaced by `{{phrase}}` and `{{avail}}`, and a new section `params` was introduced. When encountering a section like `{{phrase}}`, Elasticsearch will go to the `params` section and look for a parameter called `phrase` and use it. In general, we've moved the parameter values to the `params` section, and in the query itself we use references using the `{{var}}` notation, where `var` is the name of the parameter from the `params` section. In addition, the query itself is nested in the `template` element. This way we can parameterize our queries.

Let's now send the preceding query to the `/library/_search/template` REST endpoint (not the `/library/_search` as we usually do) using the GET HTTP method. To do this, we will use the following command:

```
curl -XGET 'localhost:9200/library/_search/template?pretty' -d '{
  "template": {
    "query": {
      "filtered": {
        "query": {
          "match": {
            "_all": "{{phrase}}"
          }
        },
        "filter": {
          "term": {
            "available": "{{avail}}"
          }
        }
      }
    }
  },
  "params": {
   "phrase": "front",
   "avail": true
  }
}'
```

[250]

Templates as strings

The template can also be provided as a string value. In such a case, our template will look like the following:

```
{
  "template": "{ \"query\": { \"filtered\": { \"query\": {
  \"match\": { \"_all\": \"{{phrase}}\" } }, \"filter\": {
  \"term\": { \"available\": \"{{avail}}\" } } } } }",
   "params": {
      "phrase": "front",
      "avail": true
   }
}
```

As you can see, this is not very readable or comfortable to write—every quotation needs to be escaped, and new line characters are also problematic and should be avoided. However, you'll be forced to use this notation (at least in Elasticsearch from 1.1.0 to 1.4.0 inclusive) when you want to use Mustache (a template engine we will talk about in the next section) features.

There is a gotcha in the Elasticsearch version used during the writing of this book. If you prepare an incorrect template, the engine detects an error and writes info into the server logs, but from the API point of view, the query is silently ignored and all documents are returned, just like you would send the `match_all` query. You should remember to double-check your template queries until that is changed.

The Mustache template engine

Elasticsearch uses Mustache templates (see: http://mustache.github.io/) to generate resulting queries from templates. As you have already seen, every variable is surrounded by double curly brackets and this is specific to Mustache and is a method of dereferencing variables in this template engine. The full syntax of the Mustache template engine is beyond the scope of this book, but we would like to briefly introduce you to the most interesting parts of it: conditional expression, loops, and default values.

The detailed information about Mustache syntax can be found at http://mustache.github.io/mustache.5.html.

Conditional expressions

The {{val}} expression results in inserting the value of the val variable. The {{#val}} and {{/val}} expressions inserts the values placed between them if the variable called val computes to true.

Let's take a look at the following example:

```
curl -XGET 'localhost:9200/library/_search/template?pretty' -d '{
  "template": "{ {{#limit}}\"size\": 2 {{/limit}}}",
  "params": {
   "limit": false
  }
}'
```

The preceding command returns all documents indexed in the library index. However, if we change the limit parameter to true and send the query once again, we would only get two documents. That's because the conditional would be true and the template would be activated.

Unfortunately, it seems that versions of Elasticsearch available during the writing of this book have problems with conditional expressions inside templates. For example, one of the issues related to that is available at https://github.com/elasticsearch/elasticsearch/issues/8308. We decided to leave the section about conditional expressions with the hope that the issues will be resolved soon. The query templates can be a very handy functionality when used with conditional expressions.

Loops

Loops are defined between exactly the same as conditionals – between expression {{#val}} and {{/val}}. If the variable from the expression is an array, you can insert current values using the {{.}} expression.

For example, if we would like the template engine to iterate through an array of terms and create a terms query using them, we could run a query using the following command:

```
curl -XGET 'localhost:9200/library/_search/template?pretty' -d '{
  "template": {
    "query": {
     "terms": {
```

```
      "title": [
       "{{#title}}",
       "{{.}}",
       "{{/title}}"
      ]
    }
   }
  },
  "params": {
   "title": [ "front", "crime" ]
  }
}'
```

Default values

The default value tag allows us to define what value (or whole part of the template) should be used if the given parameter is not defined. The syntax for defining the default value for a variable called var is as follows:

```
{{var}}{{^var}}default value{{/var}}
```

For example, if we would like to have the default value of crime for the phrase parameter in our template query, we could send a query using the following command:

```
curl -XGET 'localhost:9200/library/_search/template?pretty' -d '{
  "template": {
    "query": {
      "term": {
        "title": "{{phrase}}{{^phrase}}crime{{/phrase}}"
      }
    }
  },
  "params": {
    "phrase": "front"
  }
}'
```

The preceding command will result in Elasticsearch finding all documents with term `front` in the `title` field. However, if the `phrase` parameter was not defined in the `params` section, the term `crime` will be used instead.

Storing templates in files

Regardless of the way we defined our templates previously, we were still a long way from decoupling them from the application. We still needed to store the whole query in the application, we were only able to parameterize the query. Fortunately, there is a simple way to change the query definition so it can be read dynamically by Elasticsearch from the `config/scripts` directory.

For example, let's create a file called `bookList.mustache` (in the `config/scripts/` directory) with the following contents:

```
{
 "query": {
  "filtered": {
   "query": {
    "match": {
     "_all": "{{phrase}}"
    }
   },
   "filter": {
    "term": {
     "available": "{{avail}}"
    }
   }
  }
 }
}
```

We can now use the contents of that file in a query by specifying the template name (the name of the template is the name of the file without the `.mustache` extension). For example, if we would like to use our `bookList` template, we would send the following command:

```
curl -XGET 'localhost:9200/library/_search/template?pretty' -d '{
  "template": "bookList",
  "params": {
   "phrase": "front",
   "avail": true
  }
}'
```

> The very convenient fact is that Elasticsearch can see the changes in the file without the need of a node restart. Of course, we still need to have the template file stored on all Elasticsearch nodes that are capable of handling the query execution. Starting from Elasticsearch 1.4.0, you can also store templates in a special index called .scripts. For more information please refer to the official Elasticsearch documentation available at http://www.elasticsearch.org/guide/en/elasticsearch/reference/current/search-template.html.

Handling filters and why it matters

Let's have a look at the filtering functionality provided by Elasticsearch. At first it may seem like a redundant functionality because almost all the filters have their query counterpart present in Elasticsearch Query DSL. But there must be something special about those filters because they are commonly used and they are advised when it comes to query performance. This section will discuss why filtering is important, how filters work, and what type of filtering is exposed by Elasticsearch.

Filters and query relevance

The first difference when comparing queries to filters is the influence on the document score. Let's compare queries and filters to see what to expect. We will start with the following query:

```
curl -XGET "http://127.0.0.1:9200/library/_search?pretty" -d'
{
    "query": {
        "term": {
            "title": {
                "value": "front"
            }
        }
    }
}'
```

The results for that query are as follows:

```
{
  "took" : 1,
  "timed_out" : false,
  "_shards" : {
```

```
      "total" : 5,
      "successful" : 5,
      "failed" : 0
    },
    "hits" : {
      "total" : 1,
      "max_score" : 0.11506981,
      "hits" : [ {
        "_index" : "library",
        "_type" : "book",
        "_id" : "1",
        "_score" : 0.11506981,
        "_source":{ "title": "All Quiet on the Western
        Front","otitle": "Im Westen nichts Neues","author": "Erich
        Maria Remarque","year": 1929,"characters": ["Paul Bäumer",
        "Albert Kropp", "Haie Westhus", "Fredrich Müller",
        "Stanislaus Katczinsky", "Tjaden"],"tags":
        ["novel"],"copies": 1,
        "available": true, "section" : 3}
      } ]
    }
  }
```

There is nothing special about the preceding query. Elasticsearch will return all the documents having the front value in the title field. What's more, each document matching the query will have its score calculated and the top scoring documents will be returned as the search results. In our case, the query returned one document with the score equal to 0.11506981. This is normal behavior when it comes to querying.

Now let's compare a query and a filter. In case of both query and filter cases, we will add a fragment narrowing the documents to the ones having a single copy (the copies field equal to 1). The query that doesn't use filtering looks as follows:

```
curl -XGET "http://127.0.0.1:9200/library/_search?pretty" -d'
{
   "query": {
      "bool": {
         "must": [
            {
               "term": {
                  "title": {
                     "value": "front"
                  }
```

```
            }
        },
        {
            "term": {
                "copies": {
                    "value": "1"
                }
            }
        }
        ]
    }
}
}'
```

The results returned by Elasticsearch are very similar and look as follows:

```
{
  "took" : 1,
  "timed_out" : false,
  "_shards" : {
    "total" : 5,
    "successful" : 5,
    "failed" : 0
  },
  "hits" : {
    "total" : 1,
    "max_score" : 0.98976034,
    "hits" : [ {
      "_index" : "library",
      "_type" : "book",
      "_id" : "1",
      "_score" : 0.98976034,
      "_source":{ "title": "All Quiet on the Western
      Front","otitle": "Im Westen nichts Neues","author": "Erich
      Maria Remarque","year": 1929,"characters": ["Paul Bäumer",
      "Albert Kropp", "Haie Westhus", "Fredrich Müller",
      "Stanislaus Katczinsky", "Tjaden"],"tags":
      ["novel"],"copies": 1,
      "available": true, "section" : 3}
    } ]
  }
}
```

The `bool` query in the preceding code is built of two `term` queries, which have to be matched in the document for it to be a match. In the response we again have the same document returned, but the score of the document is `0.98976034` now. This is exactly what we suspected after reading the *Default Apache Lucene scoring explained* section of this chapter—both terms influenced the score calculation.

Now let's look at the second case—the query for the value `front` in the `title` field and a filter for the `copies` field:

```
curl -XGET "http://127.0.0.1:9200/library/_search?pretty" -d'
{
    "query": {
        "term": {
            "title": {
                "value": "front"
            }
        }
    },
    "post_filter": {
        "term": {
            "copies": {
                "value": "1"
            }
        }
    }
}'
```

Now we have the simple `term` query, but in addition we are using the `term` filter. The results are the same when it comes to the documents returned, but the score is different now, as we can look in the following code:

```
{
  "took" : 1,
  "timed_out" : false,
  "_shards" : {
    "total" : 5,
    "successful" : 5,
    "failed" : 0
  },
  "hits" : {
    "total" : 1,
```

Chapter 2

```
      "max_score" : 0.11506981,
      "hits" : [ {
        "_index" : "library",
        "_type" : "book",
        "_id" : "1",
        "_score" : 0.11506981,
        "_source":{ "title": "All Quiet on the Western
        Front","otitle": "Im Westen nichts Neues","author": "Erich
        Maria Remarque","year": 1929,"characters": ["Paul Bäumer",
        "Albert Kropp", "Haie Westhus", "Fredrich Müller",
        "Stanislaus Katczinsky", "Tjaden"],"tags":
        ["novel"],"copies": 1,
        "available": true, "section" : 3}
      } ]
    }
  }
```

Our single document has got a score of `0.11506981` now—exactly as the base query we started with. This leads to the main conclusion—filtering does not affect the score.

> Please note that previous Elasticsearch versions were using `filter` for the filters section instead of the `post_filter` used in the preceding query. In the 1.x versions of Elasticsearch, both versions can be used, but please remember that `filter` can be removed in the future.

In general, there is a single main difference between how queries and filters work. The only purpose of filters is to narrow down results with certain criteria. The queries not only narrow down the results, but also care about their score, which is very important when it comes to relevancy, but also has a cost—the CPU cycles required to calculate the document score. Of course, you should remember that this is not the only difference between them, and the rest of this section will focus on how filters work and what is the difference between different filtering methods available in Elasticsearch.

How filters work

We already mentioned that filters do not affect the score of the documents they match. This is very important because of two reasons. The first reason is performance. Applying a filter to a set of documents hold in the index is simple and can be very efficient. The only significant information filter holds about the document is whether the document matches the filter or not—a simple flag.

Filters provide this information by returning a structure called `DocIdSet` (`org.`

[259]

apache.lucene.search.DocIdSet). The purpose of this structure is to provide the view of the index segment with the filter applied on the data. It is possible by providing implementation of the Bits interface (org.apache.lucene.util.Bits), which is responsible for random access to information about documents in the filter (basically allows to check whether the document inside a segment matches the filter or not). The Bits structure is very effective because CPU can perform filtering using bitwise operations (and there is a dedicated CPU piece to handle such operations, you can read more about circular shifts at http://en.wikipedia.org/wiki/Circular_shift). We can also use the DocIdSetIterator on an ordered set of internal document identifiers, also provided by the DocIdSet.

The following figure shows how the classes using the Bits work:

doc	bits.get(doc)	Result
1	FALSE	
2	FALSE	
3	TRUE	3
4	TRUE	4

Lucene (and Elasticsearch) have various implementation of DocIdSet suitable for various cases. Each of the implementations differs when it comes to performance. However, choosing the correct implementation is the task of Lucene and Elasticsearch and we don't have to care about it, unless we extend the functionality of them.

> Please remember that not all filters use the Bits structure. The filters that don't do that are numeric range filters, script ones, and the whole group of geographical filters. Instead, those filters put data into the field data cache and iterate over documents filtering as they operate on a document. This means that the next filter in the chain will only get documents allowed by the previous filters. Because of this, those filters allow optimizations, such as putting the heaviest filters on the end of the filters, execution chain.

Bool or and/or/not filters

We talked about filters in *Elasticsearch Server Second Edition*, but we wanted to remind you about one thing. You should remember that `and`, `or`, and `not` filters don't use `Bits`, while the `bool` filter does. Because of that you should use the `bool` filter when possible. The `and`, `or`, and `not` filters should be used for scripts, geographical filtering, and numeric range filters. Also, remember that if you nest any filter that is not using `Bits` inside the `and`, `or`, or `not` filter, `Bits` won't be used.

Basically, you should use the `and`, `or`, and `not` filters when you combine filters that are not using `Bits` with other filters. And if all your filters use `Bits`, then use the `bool` filter to combine them.

Performance considerations

In general, filters are fast. There are multiple reasons for this—first of all, the parts of the query handled by filters don't need to have a score calculated. As we have already said, scoring is strongly connected to a given query and the set of indexed documents.

There is one thing when it comes to filtering. With the release of Elasticsearch 1.4.0, the bitsets used for nested queries execution are loaded eagerly by default. This is done to allow faster nested queries execution, but can lead to memory problems. To disable this behavior we can set the `index.load_fixed_bitset_filters_eagerly` to `false`. The size of memory used for fixed bitsets can be checked by using the `curl -XGET 'localhost:9200/_cluster/stats?human&pretty'` command and looking at the `fixed_bit_set_memory_in_bytes` property in the response.

When using a filter, the result of the filter does not depend on the query, so the result of the filter can be easily cached and used in the subsequent queries. What's more, the filter cache is stored as per Lucene segment, which means that the cache doesn't have to be rebuilt with every commit, but only on segment creation and segment merge.

Of course, as with everything, there are also downsides of using filters. Not all filters can be cached. Think about filters that depend on the current time, caching them wouldn't make much sense. Sometimes caching is not worth it because of too many unique values that can be used and poor cache hit ratio, an example of this can be filters based on geographical location.

Post filtering and filtered query

If someone would say that the filter will be quicker comparing to the same query, it wouldn't be true. Filters have fewer things to care about and can be reused between queries, but Lucene is already highly optimized and the queries are very fast, even considering that scoring has to be performed. Of course, for a large number of results, filter will be faster, but there is always something we didn't tell you yet. Sometimes, when using post_filter, the query sent to Elasticsearch won't be as fast and efficient as we would want it to be. Let's assume that we have the following query:

```
curl -XGET 'http://127.0.0.1:9200/library/_search?pretty' -d '{
 "query": {
  "terms": {
   "title": [ "crime", "punishment", "complete", "front" ]
  }
 },
 "post_filter" : {
  "term": {
   "available": {
    "value": true,
    "_cache": true
   }
  }
 }
}'
```

The following figure shows what is going on during query execution:

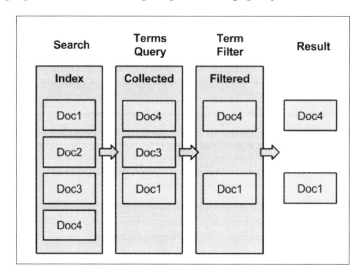

Of course, filtering matters for higher amounts of data, but for the purpose of this example, we've used our data. In the preceding figure, our index contains four documents. Our example `terms` query matches three documents: `Doc1`, `Doc3`, and `Doc4`. Each of them is scored and ordered on the basis of the calculated score. After that, our `post_filter` starts its work. From all of our documents in the whole index, it passes only two of them—`Doc1` and `Doc4`. As you can see from the three documents passed to the filter, only two of them were returned as the search result. So why are we bothering about calculating the score for the `Doc3`? In this case, we lost some CPU cycles for scoring a document that are not valid in terms of query. For a large number of documents returned, this can become a performance problem.

Please note that in the example we've used the `term` filter, which was cached by default until Elasticsearch 1.5. That behavior changed starting with Elasticsearch 1.5 (see https://github.com/elasticsearch/elasticsearch/pull/7583). Because of that, we decided to use the `term` filter in the example, but with forced caching.

Let's modify our query and let's filter the documents before the `Scorer` calculates the score for each document. The query that does that looks as follows:

```
curl -XGET 'http://127.0.0.1:9200/library/_search?pretty' -d '{
  "query": {
   "filtered": {
    "query": {
     "terms": {
      "title": [ "crime", "punishment", "complete", "front" ]
     }
    },
    "filter": {
     "term": {
      "available": {
       "value": true,
       "_cache": true
      }
     }
    }
   }
  }
}'
```

In the preceding example, we have used the `filtered` query. The results returned by the preceding query will be exactly the same, but the execution of the query will be a little bit different, especially when it comes to filtering. Let's look at the following figure showing the logical execution of the query:

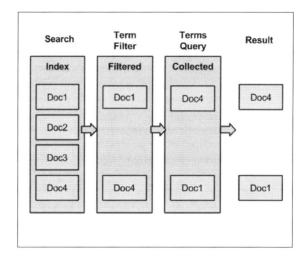

Now the initial work is done by the `term` filter. If it was already used, it will be loaded from the cache, and the whole document set will be narrowed down to only two documents. Finally, those documents are scored, but now the scoring mechanism has less work to do. Of course, in the example, our query matches the documents returned by the filter, but this is not always true.

Technically, our filter is wrapped by query, and internally Lucene library collects results only from documents that meet the enclosed filter criteria. And, of course, only the documents matching the filter are forwarded to the main query. Thanks to filter, the scoring process has fewer documents to look at.

Choosing the right filtering method

If you read the preceding explanations, you may think that you should always use the `filtered` query and run away from post filtering. Such statement will be true for most use cases, but there are exceptions to this rule. The rule of thumb says that the most expensive operations should be moved to the end of query processing. If the filter is fast, cheap, and easily cacheable, then the situation is simple—use `filtered` query. On the other hand, if the filter is slow, CPU-intensive, and hard to cache (i.e., because of too many distinct values), use post filtering or try to optimize the filter by simplifying it and making it more cache friendly, for example by reducing the resolution in case of time-based filters.

Choosing the right query for the job

In our *Elasticsearch Server Second Edition*, we described the full query language, the so-called **Query DSL** provided by Elasticsearch. A JSON structured query language that allows us to virtually build as complex queries as we can imagine. What we didn't talk about is when the queries can be used and when they should be used. For a person who doesn't have much prior experience with a full text search engine, the number of queries exposed by Elasticsearch can be overwhelming and very confusing. Because of that, we decided to extend what we wrote in the second edition of our first Elasticsearch book and show you, the reader, what you can do with Elasticsearch.

We decided to divide the following section into two distinct parts. The first part will try to categorize the queries and tell you what to expect from a query in that category. The second part will show you an example usage of queries from each group and will discuss the differences. Please take into consideration that the following section is not a full reference for the Elasticsearch Query DSL, for such reference please see *Elasticsearch Server Second Edition* from Packt Publishing or official Elasticsearch documentation available at `http://www.elasticsearch.org/guide/en/elasticsearch/reference/current/query-dsl.html`.

Query categorization

Of course, categorizing queries is a hard task and we don't say that the following list of categories is the only correct one. We would even say that if you would ask other Elasticsearch users, they would provide their own categories or say that each query can be assigned to more than a single category. What's funny—they would be right. We also think that there is no single way of categorizing the queries; however, in our opinion, each Elasticsearch query can be assigned to one (or more) of the following categories:

- **Basic queries**: Category that groups queries allowing searching for a part of the index, either in an analyzed or a non-analysed manner. The key point in this category is that you can nest queries inside a basic query. An example of a basic query is the `term` query.

- **Compound queries**: Category grouping queries that allow us to combine multiple queries or filters inside them, for example a `bool` or `dismax` queries.

- **Not analyzed queries**: Category for queries that don't analyze the input and send it as is to Lucene index. An example of such query is the `term` query.

- **Full text search queries**: Quite a large group of queries supporting full text searching, analysing their content, and possibly providing Lucene query syntax. An example of such query is the `match` query.

- **Pattern queries**: Group of queries providing support for various wildcards in queries. For example, a `prefix` query can be assigned to this particular group.
- **Similarity supporting queries**: Group of queries sharing a common feature—support for match of similar words of documents. An example of such query is the `fuzzy_like_this` or the `more_like_this` query.
- **Score altering queries**: Very important group of queries, especially when combined with full text searching. This group includes queries that allow us to modify the score calculation during query execution. An example query that we can assign to this group is the `function_score` query, which we will talk about in detail in *Chapter 3, Not Only Full Text Search*.
- **Position aware queries**: Queries that allow us to use term position information stored in the index. A very good example of such queries is the `span_term` query.
- **Structure aware queries**: Group of queries that can work on structured data such as the parent-child documents. An example query from this group is the `nested one`.

Of course, we didn't talk about the filters at all, but you can use the same logic as for queries, so let's put the filters aside for now. Before going into examples for each type of query, let's briefly describe the purpose of each of the query category.

Basic queries

Queries that are not able to group any other queries, but instead they are used for searching the index only. Queries in this group are usually used as parts of the more complex queries or as single queries sent against Elasticsearch. You can think about those queries as bricks for building structures—more complex queries. For example, when you need to match a certain phrase in a document without any additional requirements, you should look at the basic queries—in such a case, the `match` query will be a good opportunity for this requirement and it doesn't need to be added by any other query.

Some examples of the queries from basic category are as follows:

- `Match`: A Query (actually multiple types of queries) used when you need a full text search query that will analyze the provided input. Usually, it is used when you need analysis of the provided text, but you don't need full Lucene syntax support. Because this query doesn't go through the query parsing process, it has a low chance of resulting in a parsing error, and because of this it is a good candidate for handling text entered by the user.

- `match_all`: A simple query matching all documents useful for situations when we need all the whole index contents returned for aggregations.
- `term`: A simple, not analyzed query that allows us to search for an exact word. An example use case for the `term` query is searching against non-analyzed fields, like ones storing `tags` in our example data. The `term` query is also used commonly combined with filtering, for example filtering on category field from our example data.

The queries from the complex category are: `match`, `multi_match`, `common`, `fuzzy_like_this`, `fuzzy_like_this_field`, `geoshape`, `ids`, `match_all`, `query_string`, `simple_query_string`, `range`, `prefix`, `regexp`, `span_term`, `term`, `terms`, `wildcard`.

Compound queries

Compound queries are the ones that we can use for grouping other queries together and this is their only purpose. If the simple queries were bricks for building houses, the complex queries are joints for those bricks. Because we can create a virtually indefinite level of nesting of the compound queries, we are able to produce very complex queries, and the only thing that limits us is performance.

Some examples of the compound queries and their usage are as follows:

- `bool`: One of the most common compound query that is able to group multiple queries with Boolean logical operator that allows us to control which part of the query must match, which can and which should not match. For example, if we would like to find and group together queries matching different criteria, then the `bool` query is a good candidate. The `bool` query should also be used when we want the score of the documents to be a sum of all the scores calculated by the partial queries.
- `dis_max`: A very useful query when we want the score of the document to be mostly associated with the highest boosting partial query, not the sum of all the partial queries (like in the `bool` query). The `dis_max` query generates the union of the documents returned by all the subqueries and scores the documents by the simple equation max (score of the matching clauses) + tie_breaker * (sum of scores of all the other clauses that are not max scoring ones). If you want the max scoring subquery to dominate the score of your documents, then the `dis_max` query is the way to go.

The queries from that category are: `bool`, `boosting`, `constant_score`, `dis_max`, `filtered`, `function_score`, `has_child`, `has_parent`, `indices`, `nested`, `span_first`, `span_multi`, `span_first`, `span_multi`, `span_near`, `span_not`, `span_or`, `span_term`, `top_children`.

Not analyzed queries

These are queries that are not analyzed and instead the text we provide to them is sent directly to Lucene index. This means that we either need to be aware exactly how the analysis process is done and provide a proper term, or we need to run the searches against the non-analyzed fields. If you plan to use Elasticsearch as NoSQL store this is probably the group of queries you'll be using, they search for the exact terms without analysing them, i.e., with language analyzers.

The following examples should help you understand the purpose of not analyzed queries:

- `term`: When talking about the not analyzed queries, the term query will be the one most commonly used. It provides us with the ability to match documents having a certain value in a field. For example, if we would like to match documents with a certain tag (tags field in our example data), we would use the term query.
- `Prefix`: Another type of query that is not analyzed. The prefix query is commonly used for autocomplete functionality, where the user provides a text and we need to find all the documents having terms that start with the given text. It is good to remember that even though the prefix query is not analyzed, it is rewritten by Elasticsearch so that its execution is fast.

The queries from that category are: `common`, `ids`, `prefix`, `span_term`, `term`, `terms`, `wildcard`.

Full text search queries

A group that can be used when you are building your Google-like search interface. Those queries analyze the provided input using the information from the mappings, support Lucene query syntax, support scoring capabilities, and so on. In general, if some part of the query you are sending comes from a user entering some text, you'll want to use one of the full text search queries such as the `query_string`, `match` or `simple_query_string` queries.

A Simple example of the full text search queries use case can be as follows:

- simple_query_string: A query built on top of Lucene SimpleQueryParser (http://lucene.apache.org/core/4_9_0/queryparser/org/apache/lucene/queryparser/simple/SimpleQueryParser.html) that was designed to parse human readable queries. In general, if you want your queries not to fail when a query parsing error occurs and instead figure out what the user wanted to achieve, this is a good query to consider.

The queries from that category are: `match`, `multi_match`, `query_string`, `simple_query_string`.

Pattern queries

Elasticsearch provides us with a few queries that can handle wildcards directly or indirectly, for example the `wildcard` query and the `prefix` query. In addition to that, we are allowed to use the `regexp` query that can find documents that have terms matching given patterns.

We've already discussed an example using the `prefix` query, so let's focus a bit on the `regexp` query. If you want a query that will find documents having terms matching a certain pattern, then the `regexp` query is probably the only solution for you. For example, if you store logs in your Elasticsearch indices and you would like to find all the logs that have terms starting with the `err` prefix, then having any number of characters and ending with `memory`, the `regexp` query will be the one to look for. However, remember that all the wildcard queries that have expressions matching large number of terms will be expensive when it comes to performance.

The queries from that category are: `prefix`, `regexp`, `wildcard`.

Similarity supporting queries

We like to think that the similarity supporting queries is a family of queries that allow us to search for similar terms or documents to the one we passed to the query. For example, if we would like to find documents that have terms similar to `crimea` term, we could run a `fuzzy` query. Another use case for this group of queries is providing us with "did you mean" like functionality. If we would like to find documents that have titles similar to the input we've provided, we would use the `more_like_this` query. In general, you would use a query from this group whenever you need to find documents having terms or fields similar to the provided input.

The queries from that category are: `fuzzy_like_this`, `fuzzy_like_this_field`, `fuzzy`, `more_like_this`, `more_like_this_field`.

Score altering queries

A group of queries used for improving search precision and relevance. They allow us to modify the score of the returned documents by providing not only a custom boost factor, but also some additional logic. A very good example of a query from this group is the `function_score` query that provides us with a possibility of using functions, which result in document score modification based on mathematical equations. For example, if you would like the documents that are closer to a given geographical point to be scored higher, then using the `function_score` query provides you with such a possibility.

The queries from that category are: `boosting`, `constant_score`, `function_score`, `indices`.

Position aware queries

These are a family of queries that allow us to match not only certain terms but also the information about the terms' positions. The most significant queries from this group are all the span queries in Elasticsearch. We can also say that the `match_phrase` query can be assigned to this group as it also looks at the position of the indexed terms, at least to some extent. If you want to find groups of words that are a certain distance in the index from other words, like "find me the documents that have `mastering` and `Elasticsearch` terms near each other and are followed by `second` and `edition` terms no further than three positions away," then span queries is the way to go. However, you should remember that span queries will be removed in future versions of Lucene library and thus from Elasticsearch as well. This is because those queries are resource-intensive and require vast amount of CPU to be properly handled.

The queries from that category are: `match_phrase`, `span_first`, `span_multi`, `span_near`, `span_not`, `span_or`, `span_term`.

Structure aware queries

The last group of queries is the structure aware queries. The queries that can be assigned to this group are as follows:

- `nested`
- `has_child`
- `has_parent`
- `top_children`

Basically, all the queries that allow us to search inside structured documents and don't require us to flatten the data can be classified as the structure aware queries. If you are looking for a query that will allow you to search inside the children document, nested documents, or for children having certain parents, then you need to use one of the queries that are mentioned in the preceding terms. If you want to handle relationships in the data, this is the group of queries you should look for; however, remember that although Elasticsearch can handle relations, it is still not a relational database.

The use cases

As we already know which groups of queries can be responsible for which tasks and what can we achieve using queries from each group, let's have a look at example use cases for each of the groups so that we can have a better view of what the queries are useful for. Please note that this is not a full and comprehensive guide to all the queries available in Elasticsearch, but instead a simple example of what can be achieved.

Example data

For the purpose of the examples in this section, we've indexed two additional documents to our `library` index.

First, we need to alter the index structure a bit so that it contains nested documents (we will need them for some queries). To do that, we will run the following command:

```
curl -XPUT 'http://localhost:9200/library/_mapping/book' -d '{
 "book" : {
  "properties" : {
   "review" : {
    "type" : "nested",
    "properties": {
     "nickname" : { "type" : "string" },
     "text" : { "type" : "string" },
     "stars" : { "type" : "integer" }
    }
   }
  }
 }
}'
```

The commands used for indexing two additional documents are as follows:

```
curl -XPOST 'localhost:9200/library/book/5' -d '{
 "title" : "The Sorrows of Young Werther",
  "author" : "Johann Wolfgang von Goethe",
   "available" : true,
    "characters" : ["Werther",
    "Lotte","Albert",
      " Fräulein von B"],
      "copies" : 1,
      "otitle" : "Die Leiden des jungen Werthers",
      "section" : 4,
    "tags" : ["novel", "classics"],
    "year" : 1774,
  "review" : [{"nickname" : "Anna","text" : "Could be good, but not
  my style","stars" : 3}]
}'
```

```
curl -XPOST 'localhost:9200/library/book/6' -d '{
 "title" : "The Peasants",
  "author" : "Władysław Reymont",
   "available" : true,
   "characters" : ["Maciej Boryna","Jankiel","Jagna Paczesiówna",
   "Antek Boryna"],
    "copies" : 4,
    "otitle" : "Chłopi",
     "section" : 4,
     "tags" : ["novel", "polish", "classics"],
    "year" : 1904,
  "review" : [{"nickname" : "anonymous","text" : "awsome
  book","stars" : 5},{"nickname" : "Jane","text" : "Great book, but
  too long","stars" : 4},{"nickname" : "Rick","text" : "Why bother,
  when you can find it on the internet","stars" : 3}]
}'
```

Basic queries use cases

Let's look at simple use cases for the basic queries group.

Searching for values in range

One of the simplest queries that can be run is a query matching documents in a given range of values. Usually, such queries are a part of a larger query or a filter. For example, a query that would return books with the number of copies from 1 to 3 inclusive would look as follows:

```
curl -XGET 'localhost:9200/library/_search?pretty' -d '{
 "query" : {
  "range" : {
   "copies" : {
    "gte" : 1,
    "lte" : 3
   }
  }
 }
}'
```

Simplified query for multiple terms

Imagine a situation where your users can show a number of tags the books returned by what the query should contain. The thing is that we require only 75 percent of the provided tags to be matched if the number of tags provided by the user is higher than three, and all the provided tags to be matched if the number of tags is three or less. We could run a `bool` query to allow that, but Elasticsearch provides us with the `terms` query that we can use to achieve the same requirement. The command that sends such query looks as follows:

```
curl -XGET 'localhost:9200/library/_search?pretty' -d '{
 "query" : {
  "terms" : {
   "tags" : [ "novel", "polish", "classics", "criminal", "new" ],
   "minimum_should_match" : "3<75%"
  }
 }
}'
```

Compound queries use cases

Let's now see how we can use compound queries to group other queries together.

Boosting some of the matched documents

One of the simplest examples is using the `bool` query to boost some documents by including not mandatory query part that is used for boosting. For example, if we would like to find all the books that have at least a single copy and boost the ones that are published after 1950, we could use the following query:

```
curl -XGET 'localhost:9200/library/_search?pretty' -d '{
 "query" : {
  "bool" : {
   "must" : [
    {
     "range" : {
      "copies" : {
       "gte" : 1
      }
     }
    }
```

```
    ],
    "should" : [
     {
      "range" : {
       "year" : {
        "gt" : 1950
       }
      }
     }
    ]
   }
  }
}'
```

Ignoring lower scoring partial queries

The `dis_max` query, as we have already covered, allows us to control how influential the lower scoring partial queries are. For example, if we only want to assign the score of the highest scoring partial query for the documents matching `crime punishment` in the `title` field or `raskolnikov` in the `characters` field, we would run the following query:

```
curl -XGET 'localhost:9200/library/_search?pretty' -d '{
 "fields" : [ "_id", "_score" ],
 "query" : {
  "dis_max" : {
   "tie_breaker" : 0.0,
   "queries" : [
    {
     "match" : {
      "title" : "crime punishment"
     }
    },
    {
     "match" : {
      "characters" : "raskolnikov"
     }
    }
```

```
      ]
    }
  }
}'
```

The result for the preceding query should look as follows:

```
{
  "took" : 3,
  "timed_out" : false,
  "_shards" : {
    "total" : 5,
    "successful" : 5,
    "failed" : 0
  },
  "hits" : {
    "total" : 1,
    "max_score" : 0.2169777,
    "hits" : [ {
      "_index" : "library",
      "_type" : "book",
      "_id" : "4",
      "_score" : 0.2169777,
      "fields" : {
        "_id" : "4"
      }
    } ]
  }
}
```

Now let's see the score of the partial queries alone. To do that we will run the partial queries using the following commands:

```
curl -XGET 'localhost:9200/library/_search?pretty' -d '{
 "fields" : [ "_id", "_score" ],
 "query" : {
  "match" : {
   "title" : "crime punishment"
  }
 }
}'
```

The response for the preceding query is as follows:

```
{
  "took" : 2,
  "timed_out" : false,
  "_shards" : {
    "total" : 5,
    "successful" : 5,
    "failed" : 0
  },
  "hits" : {
    "total" : 1,
    "max_score" : 0.2169777,
    "hits" : [ {
      "_index" : "library",
      "_type" : "book",
      "_id" : "4",
      "_score" : 0.2169777,
      "fields" : {
        "_id" : "4"
      }
    } ]
  }
}
```

And the next command is as follows:

```
curl -XGET 'localhost:9200/library/_search?pretty' -d '{
 "fields" : [ "_id", "_score" ],
 "query" : {
  "match" : {
   "characters" : "raskolnikov"
  }
 }
}'
```

And the response is as follows:

```
{
  "took" : 1,
  "timed_out" : false,
  "_shards" : {
    "total" : 5,
    "successful" : 5,
```

```
      "failed" : 0
    },
    "hits" : {
      "total" : 1,
      "max_score" : 0.15342641,
      "hits" : [ {
        "_index" : "library",
        "_type" : "book",
        "_id" : "4",
        "_score" : 0.15342641,
        "fields" : {
          "_id" : "4"
        }
      } ]
    }
}
```

As you can see, the score of the document returned by our `dis_max` query is equal to the score of the highest scoring partial query (the first partial query). That is because we've set the `tie_breaker` property to 0.0.

Not analyzed queries use cases

Let's look at two example use cases for queries that are not processed by any of the defined analyzers.

Limiting results to given tags

One of the simplest examples of the not analyzed query is the `term` query provided by Elasticsearch. You'll probably very rarely use the `term` query alone; however, it may be commonly used in compound queries. For example, let's assume that we would like to search for all the books with the `novel` value in the `tags` field. To do that, we would run the following command:

```
curl -XGET 'localhost:9200/library/_search?pretty' -d '{
 "query" : {
  "term" : {
   "tags" : "novel"
  }
 }
}'
```

Efficient query time stopwords handling

Elasticsearch provides the common terms query, which allows us to handle query time stopwords in an efficient way. It divides the query terms into two groups—more important terms and less important terms. The more important terms are the ones that have a lower frequency; the less important terms are the opposite. Elasticsearch first executes the query with important terms and calculates the score for those documents. Then, a second query with the less important terms is executed, but the score is not calculated and thus the query is faster.

For example, the following two queries should be similar in terms of results, but not in terms of score computation. Please also note that to see the differences in scoring we would have to use a larger data sample and not use index time stopwords:

```
curl -XGET 'localhost:9200/library/_search?pretty' -d '{
 "query" : {
  "common" : {
   "title" : {
    "query" : "the western front",
    "cutoff_frequency" : 0.1,
    "low_freq_operator": "and"
   }
  }
 }
}'
```

And the second query would be as follows:

```
curl -XGET 'localhost:9200/library/_search?pretty' -d '{
 "query" : {
  "bool" : {
   "must" : [
    {
     "term" : { "title" : "western" }
    },
    {
     "term" : { "title" : "front" }
    }
   ],
   "should" : [
    {
     "term" : { "title" : "the" }
    }
   ]
  }
 }
}'
```

Full text search queries use cases

Full text search is a broad topic and so are the use cases for the full text queries. However, let's look at two simple examples of queries from that group.

Using Lucene query syntax in queries

Sometimes, it is good to be able to use Lucene query syntax as it is. We talked about this syntax in the *Lucene query language* section in *Chapter 1, Introduction to Elasticsearch*. For example, if we would like to find books having `sorrows` and `young` terms in their title, `von goethe` phrase in the `author` field and not having more than five copies we could run the following query:

```
curl -XGET 'localhost:9200/library/_search?pretty' -d '{
 "query" : {
  "query_string" : {
   "query" : "+title:sorrows +title:young +author:\"von goethe\" -copies:{5 TO *]"
  }
 }
}'
```

As you can see, we've used the Lucene query syntax to pass all the matching requirements and we've let query parser construct the appropriate query.

Handling user queries without errors

Sometimes, queries coming from users can contain errors. For example, let's look at the following query:

```
curl -XGET 'localhost:9200/library/_search?pretty' -d '{
 "query" : {
  "query_string" : {
   "query" : "+sorrows +young \"",
   "default_field" : "title"
  }
 }
}'
```

The response would contain the following:

```
    "error" : "SearchPhaseExecutionException[Failed to execute phase
      [query]
```

This means that the query was not properly constructed and parse error happened. That's why the `simple_query_string` query was introduced. It uses a query parser that tries to handle user mistakes and tries to guess how the query should look. Our query using that parser would look as follows:

```
curl -XGET 'localhost:9200/library/_search?pretty' -d '{
 "query" : {
  "simple_query_string" : {
   "query" : "+sorrows +young \"",
   "fields" : [ "title" ]
  }
 }
}'
```

If you run the preceding query, you would see that the proper document has been returned by Elasticsearch, even though the query is not properly constructed.

Pattern queries use cases

There are multiple use cases for the wildcard queries; however, we wanted to show you the following two.

Autocomplete using prefixes

A very common use case provides autocomplete functionality on the indexed data. As we know, the prefix query is not analyzed and works on the basis of terms indexed in the field. So the actual functionality depends on what tokens are produced during indexing. For example, let's assume that we would like to provide autocomplete functionality on any token in the `title` field and the user provided `wes` prefix. A query that would match such a requirement looks as follows:

```
curl -XGET 'localhost:9200/library/_search?pretty' -d '{
 "query" : {
  "prefix" : {
   "title" : "wes"
  }
 }
}'
```

Pattern matching

If we need to match a certain pattern and our analysis chain is not producing tokens that allow us to do so, we can turn into the regexp query. One should remember, though, that this kind of query can be expensive during execution and thus should be avoided. Of course, this is not always possible. One thing to remember is that the performance of the regexp query depends on the chosen regular expression. If you choose a regular expression that will be rewritten into a high number of terms, then performance will suffer.

Let's now see the example usage of the regexp query. Let's assume that we would like to find documents that have a term starting with wat, then followed by two characters and ending with the n character, and those terms should be in the characters field. To match this requirement, we could use a regexp query like the one used in the following command:

```
curl -XGET 'localhost:9200/library/_search?pretty' -d '{
  "query" : {
   "regexp" : {
    "characters" : "wat..n"
   }
  }
}'
```

Similarity supporting queries use cases

Let's look at a couple of simple use cases about how we can find similar documents and terms.

Finding terms similar to a given one

A very simple example is using the fuzzy query to find documents having a term similar to a given one. For example, if we would like to find all the documents having a value similar to crimea, we could run the following query:

```
curl -XGET 'localhost:9200/library/_search?pretty' -d '{
  "query" : {
   "fuzzy" : {
    "title" : {
     "value" : "crimea",
     "fuzziness" : 3,
     "max_expansions" : 50
    }
```

```
      }
    }
}'
```

Finding documents with similar field values

Another example of similarity queries is a use case when we want to find all the documents having field values similar to what we provided in a query. For example, if we would like to find books having a title similar to the `western front battles` name, we could run the following query:

```
curl -XGET 'localhost:9200/library/_search?pretty' -d '{
 "query" : {
  "fuzzy_like_this_field" : {
   "title" : {
    "like_text" : "western front battles",
    "max_query_terms" : 5
   }
  }
 }
}'
```

The result of the preceding query would be as follows:

```
    {
      "took" : 10,
      "timed_out" : false,
      "_shards" : {
        "total" : 5,
        "successful" : 5,
        "failed" : 0
      },
      "hits" : {
        "total" : 2,
        "max_score" : 1.0162667,
        "hits" : [ {
          "_index" : "library",
          "_type" : "book",
          "_id" : "1",
          "_score" : 1.0162667,
```

```
      "_source":{ "title": "All Quiet on the Western
      Front","otitle": "Im Westen nichts Neues","author": "Erich
      Maria Remarque","year": 1929,"characters": ["Paul B⊢Aumer",
      "Albert Kropp", "Haie Westhus", "Fredrich M⊢ller",
      "Stanislaus Katczinsky", "Tjaden"],"tags":
      ["novel"],"copies": 1,
      "available": true, "section" : 3}
    }, {
      "_index" : "library",
      "_type" : "book",
      "_id" : "5",
      "_score" : 0.4375,
      "_source":{"title" : "The Sorrows of Young Werther","author"
      : "Johann Wolfgang von Goethe","available" :
      true,"characters" : ["Werther","Lotte","Albert","Fraulein
      von B"],"copies" : 1, "otitle" : "Die Leiden des jungen
      Werthers","section" : 4,"tags" : ["novel",
      "classics"],"year" : 1774,"review" : [{"nickname" :
      "Anna","text" : "Could be good, but not my style","stars" :
      3}]}
    } ]
  }
}
```

As you can see, sometimes the results are not as obvious as we would expect (look at the second book title). This is because of what Elasticsearch thinks is similar to each other. In the case of the preceding query, Elasticsearch will take all the terms, run a fuzzy search on them, and choose a number of best differentiating terms for documents matching.

Score altering queries use cases

When it comes to relevancy, Elasticsearch provides us with a few queries that we can use to alter the score as per our need. Of course, in addition to this, most queries allow us to provide boost, which gives us even more control. Let's now look at two example use cases of score altering queries.

Favoring newer books

Let's assume that we would like to favor books that are newer, so that a book from the year 1986 is higher in the results list than a book from 1870. The query that would match that requirement looks as follows:

```
curl -XGET 'localhost:9200/library/_search?pretty' -d '{
 "query" : {
  "function_score" : {
```

```
    "query" : {
     "match_all" : {}
    },
    "score_mode" : "multiply",
    "functions" : [
     {
      "gauss" : {
       "year" : {
        "origin" : 2014,
        "scale" : 2014,
        "offset" : 0,
        "decay": 0.5
       }
      }
     }
    ]
   }
  }
}'
```

We will discuss the `function_score` query in *Chapter 3, Not Only Full Text Search*. For now, if you look at the results returned by the preceding query, you can see that the newer the book, the higher in the results it will be.

Decreasing importance of books with certain value

Sometimes, it is good to be able to decrease the importance of certain documents, while still showing them in the results list. For example, we may want to show all books, but put the ones that are not available on the bottom of the results list by lowering their score. We don't want sorting on availability because sometimes use may know what he or she is looking for and the score of a full text search query should be also important. However, if our use case is that we want the books that are not available on the bottom of the results list, we could use the following command to get them:

```
curl -XGET 'localhost:9200/library/_search?pretty' -d '{
 "query" : {
  "boosting" : {
   "positive" : {
```

```
    "match_all" : {}
  },
  "negative" : {
    "term" : {
      "available" : false
    }
  },
  "negative_boost" : 0.2
 }
}
}'
```

Pattern queries use cases

Not very commonly used because of how resource hungry they are, pattern aware queries allow us to match documents having phrases and terms in the right order. Let's look at some examples.

Matching phrases

The simplest position aware query possible and the most performing one from the queries assigned in this group. For example, a query that would only match document `leiden des jungen` phrase in the `otitle` field would look as follows:

```
curl -XGET 'localhost:9200/library/_search?pretty' -d '{
 "query" : {
  "match_phrase" : {
    "otitle" : "leiden des jungen"
  }
 }
}'
```

Spans, spans everywhere

Of course, the phrase query is very simple when it comes to position handling. What if we would like to run a query to find documents that have `des jungen` phrase not more than two positions after the `die` term and just before the `werthers` term? This can be done with span queries, and the following command shows how such a query could look:

```
curl -XGET 'localhost:9200/library/_search?pretty' -d '{
 "query" : {
  "span_near" : {
```

```
"clauses" : [
 {
  "span_near" : {
   "clauses" : [
    {
     "span_term" : {
      "otitle" : "die"
     }
    },
    {
     "span_near" : {
      "clauses" : [
       {
        "span_term" : {
         "otitle" : "des"
        }
       },
       {
        "span_term" : {
         "otitle" : "jungen"
        }
       }
      ],
      "slop" : 0,
      "in_order" : true
     }
    }
   ],
   "slop" : 2,
   "in_order" : false
  }
 },
 {
  "span_term" : {
   "otitle" : "werthers"
  }
 }
],
"slop" : 0,
"in_order" : true
```

```
      }
    }
}'
```

Please note that span queries are not analyzed. We can see that by looking at the response of the Explain API. To see that response, we should run the same request body (our query) to the `/library/book/5/_explain` REST endpoint. The interesting part of the output looks as follows:

```
"description" : "weight(spanNear([spanNear([otitle:die,
  spanNear([otitle:des, otitle:jungen], 0, true)], 2, false),
  otitle:werthers], 0, true) in 1) [PerFieldSimilarity], result
  of:",
```

Structure aware queries use cases

When it comes to the nested documents or the parent–child relationship, structure aware queries are the ones that will be needed sooner or later. Let's look at the following two examples of where the structure query can be used.

Returning parent documents having a certain nested document

The first example will be a very simple one. Let's return all the books that have at least a single review that was given four stars or more. The query that does that looks as follows:

```
curl -XGET 'localhost:9200/library/_search?pretty' -d '{
  "query" : {
    "nested" : {
      "path" : "review",
      "query" : {
        "range" : {
          "stars" : {
            "gte" : 4
          }
        }
      }
    }
  }
}'
```

[287]

Affecting parent document score with the score of nested documents

Let's assume that we want to find all the available books that have reviews and let's sort them on the maximum number of stars given in the review. The query that would fill such a requirement looks as follows:

```
curl -XGET 'localhost:9200/library/_search?pretty' -d '{
 "query" : {
  "nested" : {
   "path" : "review",
   "score_mode" : "max",
   "query" : {
    "function_score" : {
     "query" : { "match_all" : {} },
     "score_mode" : "max",
     "boost_mode" : "replace",
     "field_value_factor" : {
      "field" : "stars",
      "factor" : 1,
      "modifier" : "none"
     }
    }
   }
  }
 }
}'
```

Summary

In this chapter, we've looked at how the default Apache Lucene scoring works and we've discussed the query rewrite process—how it is done and why is it needed. We've discussed how query templates work and how they can simplify your queries. We've also looked at different query filtering methods, how they differ in comparison to each other, and when they can be used. Finally, we've assigned queries to different groups, we've learned when which query group can be used, and we've seen some example queries for each of the groups.

In the next chapter, we'll step away from full text search and focus on other search functionalities. We will start by extending our knowledge about the rescore functionality and the ability to recalculate the score for top documents in the results. After that we will look at how to load significant terms and add documents grouping using aggregations. We will also compare parent–child relationships to the nested documents, we will use function queries and, finally, we will learn how to efficiently page documents.

3
Not Only Full Text Search

In the previous chapter, we extensively talked about querying in Elasticsearch. We started by looking at how default Apache Lucene scoring works, through how filtering works, and we've finished with looking at which query to use in a particular situation. In this chapter, we will continue with discussions regarding some of the Elasticsearch functionalities connected to both querying and data analysis. By the end of this chapter, we will have covered the following areas:

- What query rescoring is and how you can use it to optimize your queries and recalculate the score for some documents
- Controlling multimatch queries
- Analyzing your data to get significant terms from it
- Grouping your documents in buckets using Elasticsearch
- Differences in relationship handling when using object, nested documents, and parent–child functionality
- Extended information regarding Elasticsearch scripting such as Groovy usage and Lucene expressions

Query rescoring

One of the great features provided by Elasticsearch is the ability to change the ordering of documents after they were returned by a query. Actually, Elasticsearch does a simple trick—it recalculates the score of top matching documents, so only part of the document in the response is reordered. The reasons why we want to do that can vary. One of the reasons may be performance—for example, calculating target ordering is very costly because scripts are used and we would like to do this on the subset of documents returned by the original query. You can imagine that rescore gives us many great opportunities for business use cases. Now, let's look at this functionality and how we can benefit from using it.

What is query rescoring?

Rescore in Elasticsearch is the process of recalculating the score for a defined number of documents returned by the query. This means that Elasticsearch first takes N documents for a given query (or the `post_filter` phase) and calculates their score using a provided rescore definition. For example, if we would take a `term` query and ask for all the documents that are available, we can use rescore to recalculate the score for 100 documents only, not for all documents returned by the query. Please note that the rescore phase will not be executed when using `search_type` of `scan` or `count`. This means that rescore won't be taken into consideration in such cases.

An example query

Let's start with a simple query that looks as follows:

```
{
 "fields" : ["title", "available"],
 "query" : {
  "match_all" : {}
 }
}
```

It returns all the documents from the index the query is run against. Every document returned by the query will have the score equal to `1.0` because of the `match_all` query. This is enough to show how rescore affects our result set.

Structure of the rescore query

Let's now modify our query so that it uses the rescore functionality. Basically, let's assume that we want the score of the document to be equal to the value of the `year` field. The query that does that would look as follows:

```
{
    "fields": ["title", "available"],
    "query": {
       "match_all": {}
    },
    "rescore": {
       "query": {
          "rescore_query": {
             "function_score": {
                "query": {
                   "match_all": {}
                },
```

Chapter 3

```
            "script_score": {
                "script": "doc['year'].value"
            }
          }
        }
      }
    }
  }
}
```

> Please note that you need to specify the `lang` property with the `groovy` value in the preceding query if you are using Elasticsearch 1.4 or older. What's more, the preceding example uses dynamic scripting which was enabled in Elasticsearch until versions 1.3.8 and 1.4.3 for groovy and till 1.2 for MVEL. If you would like to use dynamic scripting with groovy you should add `script.groovy.sandbox.enabled` property and set it to `true` in your `elasticsearch.yml` file. However, please remember that this is a security risk.

Let's now look at the preceding query in more detail. The first thing you may have noticed is the `rescore` object. The mentioned object holds the query that will affect the scoring of the documents returned by the query. In our case, the logic is very simple – just assign the value of the `year` field as the score of the document. Please also note, that when using curl you need to escape the script value, so the `doc['year'].value` would look like `doc[\"year\"].value`

> In the preceding example, in the `rescore` object, you can see a `query` object. When this book was written, a `query` object was the only option, but in future versions, we may expect other ways to affect the resulting score.

If we save this query in the `query.json` file and send it using the following command:

```
curl localhost:9200/library/book/_search?pretty -d @query.json
```

The document that Elasticsearch should return should be as follows (please note that we've omitted the structure of the response so that it is as simple as it can be):

```
{
  "took" : 1,
  "timed_out" : false,
  "_shards" : {
    "total" : 5,
    "successful" : 5,
    "failed" : 0
  },
```

```
"hits" : {
  "total" : 6,
  "max_score" : 1962.0,
  "hits" : [ {
    "_index" : "library",
    "_type" : "book",
    "_id" : "2",
    "_score" : 1962.0,
    "fields" : {
      "title" : [ "Catch-22" ],
      "available" : [ false ]
    }
  }, {
    "_index" : "library",
    "_type" : "book",
    "_id" : "3",
    "_score" : 1937.0,
    "fields" : {
      "title" : [ "The Complete Sherlock Holmes" ],
      "available" : [ false ]
    }
  }, {
    "_index" : "library",
    "_type" : "book",
    "_id" : "1",
    "_score" : 1930.0,
    "fields" : {
      "title" : [ "All Quiet on the Western Front" ],
      "available" : [ true ]
    }
  }, {
    "_index" : "library",
    "_type" : "book",
    "_id" : "6",
    "_score" : 1905.0,
    "fields" : {
      "title" : [ "The Peasants" ],
      "available" : [ true ]
    }
  }, {
    "_index" : "library",
    "_type" : "book",
    "_id" : "4",
    "_score" : 1887.0,
    "fields" : {
      "title" : [ "Crime and Punishment" ],
      "available" : [ true ]
    }
```

```
    }, {
      "_index" : "library",
      "_type" : "book",
      "_id" : "5",
      "_score" : 1775.0,
      "fields" : {
        "title" : [ "The Sorrows of Young Werther" ],
        "available" : [ true ]
      }
    } ]
  }
}
```

As we can see, Elasticsearch found all the documents from the original query. Now look at the score of the documents. Elasticsearch took the first N documents and applied the second query to them. In the result, the score of those documents is the sum of the score from the first and second queries.

As you know, scripts execution can be demanding when it comes to performance. That's why we've used it in the rescore phase of the query. If our initial `match_all` query would return thousands of results, calculating script-based scoring for all those can affect query performance. Rescore gave us the possibility to only calculate such scoring on the top N documents and thus reduce the performance impact.

> In our example, we have only seen a single rescore definition. Since Elasticsearch 1.1.0, there is a possibility of defining multiple rescore queries for a single result set. Thanks to this, you can build multilevel queries when the top N documents are reordered and this result is an input for the next reordering.

Now let's see how to tune rescore functionality behavior and what parameters are available.

Rescore parameters

In the query under the `rescore` object, we are allowed to use the following parameters:

- `window_size` (defaults to the sum of the `from` and `size` parameters): The number of documents used for rescoring on every shard

- `query_weight` (defaults to `1`): The resulting score of the original query will be multiplied by this value before adding the score generated by rescore
- `rescore_query_weight` (defaults to `1`): The resulting score of the rescore will be multiplied by this value before adding the score generated by the original query

To sum up, the target score for the document is equal to:

```
original_query_score * query_weight + rescore_query_score * rescore_query_weight
```

Choosing the scoring mode

By default, the score from the original query part and the score from the rescored part are added together. However, we can control that by specifying the `score_mode` parameter. The available values for it are as follows:

- `total`: Score values are added together (the default behavior)
- `multiply`: Values are multiplied by each other
- `avg`: The result score is an average of enclosed scores
- `max`: The result is equals of greater score value
- `min`: The result is equals of lower score value

To sum up

Sometimes, we want to show results, where the ordering of the first documents on the page is affected by some additional rules. Unfortunately, this cannot be achieved by the rescore functionality. The first idea points to the `window_size` parameter, but this parameter, in fact, is not connected with the first documents on the result list but with the number of results returned on every shard. In addition, the `window_size` value cannot be less than page size (Elasticsearch will set the `window_size` value to the value of the `size` property, when `window_size` is lower than `size`). Also, one very important thing, rescoring cannot be combined with sorting because sorting is done before the changes to the documents, score are done by rescoring, and thus sorting won't take the newly calculated score into consideration.

Controlling multimatching

Until Elasticsearch 1.1, we had limited control over the `multi_match` query. Of course, we had the possibility to specify the fields we want our query to be run against; we could use disjunction max queries (by setting the `use_dis_max` property to `true`). Finally, we could inform Elasticsearch about the importance of each field by using boosting. Our example query run against multiple fields could look as follows:

```
curl -XGET 'localhost:9200/library/_search?pretty' -d '{
 "query" : {
  "multi_match" : {
   "query" : "complete conan doyle",
   "fields" : [ "title^20", "author^10", "characters" ]
  }
 }
}'
```

A simple query that will match documents having given tokens in any of the mentioned fields. In addition to that required query, the `title` field is more important than the `author` field, and finally the `characters` field.

Of course, we could also use the disjunction max query:

```
curl -XGET 'localhost:9200/library/_search?pretty' -d '{
 "query" : {
  "multi_match" : {
   "query" : "complete conan doyle",
   "fields" : [ "title^20", "author^10", "characters" ],
   "use_dis_max" : true
  }
 }
}'
```

But apart from the score calculation for the resulting documents, using disjunction max didn't change much.

Multimatch types

With the release of Elasticsearch 1.1, the `use_dis_max` property was deprecated and Elasticsearch developers introduced a new property—the `type`. This property allows control over how the `multi_match` query is internally executed. Let's now look at the possibilities of controlling how Elasticsearch runs queries against multiple fields.

 Please note that the `tie_breaker` property was not deprecated and we can still use it without worrying about future compatibility.

Best fields matching

To use the best fields type matching, one should set the `type` property of the `multi_match` query to the `best_fields` query. This type of multimatching will generate a match query for each field specified in the `fields` property and it is best used for searching for multiple words in the same, best matching field. For example, let's look at the following query:

```
curl -XGET 'localhost:9200/library/_search?pretty' -d '{
 "query" : {
  "multi_match" : {
   "query" : "complete conan doyle",
   "fields" : [ "title", "author", "characters" ],
   "type" : "best_fields",
   "tie_breaker" : 0.8
  }
 }
}'
```

The preceding query would be translated into a query similar to the following one:

```
curl -XGET 'localhost:9200/library/_search?pretty' -d '{
 "query" : {
  "dis_max" : {
   "queries" : [
    {
     "match" : {
      "title" : "complete conan doyle"
     }
```

```
      },
      {
        "match" : {
          "author" : "complete conan doyle"
        }
      },
      {
        "match" : {
          "characters" : "complete conan doyle"
        }
      }
    ],
    "tie_breaker" : 0.8
  }
}
}'
```

If you would look at the results for both of the preceding queries, you would notice the following:

```
{
  "took" : 1,
  "timed_out" : false,
  "_shards" : {
    "total" : 5,
    "successful" : 5,
    "failed" : 0
  },
  "hits" : {
    "total" : 1,
    "max_score" : 0.033352755,
    "hits" : [ {
      "_index" : "library",
      "_type" : "book",
      "_id" : "3",
      "_score" : 0.033352755,
      "_source":{ "title": "The Complete Sherlock
      Holmes","author": "Arthur Conan Doyle","year":
      1936,"characters": ["Sherlock Holmes","Dr. Watson", "G.
      Lestrade"],"tags": [],"copies": 0, "available" : false,
      "section" : 12}
```

        }]
      }
    }

Both queries resulted in exactly the same results and the same scores calculated for the document. One thing to remember is how the score is calculated. If the `tie_breaker` value is present, the score for each document is the sum of the score for the best matching field and the score of the other matching fields multiplied by the `tie_breaker` value. If the `tie_breaker` value is not present, the document is assigned the score equal to the score of the best matching field.

There is one more question when it comes to the `best_fields` matching: what happens when we would like to use the AND operator or the `minimum_should_match` property? The answer is simple: the `best_fields` matching is translated into many `match` queries and both the `operator` property and the `minimum_should_match` property are applied to each of the generated match queries. Because of that, a query as follows wouldn't return any documents in our case:

```
curl -XGET 'localhost:9200/library/_search?pretty' -d '{
 "query" : {
  "multi_match" : {
   "query" : "complete conan doyle",
   "fields" : [ "title", "author", "characters" ],
   "type" : "best_fields",
   "operator" : "and"
  }
 }
}'
```

This is because the preceding query would be translated into:

```
curl -XGET 'localhost:9200/library/_search?pretty' -d '{
 "query" : {
  "dis_max" : {
   "queries" : [
    {
     "match" : {
      "title" : {
       "query" : "complete conan doyle",
       "operator" : "and"
      }
```

```
          }
        },
        {
          "match" : {
            "author" : {
              "query" : "complete conan doyle",
              "operator" : "and"
            }
          }
        },
        {
          "match" : {
            "characters" : {
              "query" : "complete conan doyle",
              "operator" : "and"
            }
          }
        }
      ]
    }
  }
}'
```

And the preceding query looks as follows on the Lucene level:

```
(+title:complete +title:conan +title:doyle) | (+author:complete
  +author:conan +author:doyle) | (+characters:complete
  +characters:conan +characters:doyle)
```

We don't have any document in the index that has the `complete`, `conan`, and `doyle` terms in a single field. However, if we would like to match the terms in a different field, we can use the cross-field matching.

Cross fields matching

The `cross_fields` type matching is perfect when we want all the terms from the query to be found in the mentioned fields inside the same document. Let's recall our previous query, but this time instead of the `best_fields` matching, let's use the `cross_fields` matching type:

```
curl -XGET 'localhost:9200/library/_search?pretty' -d '{
```

```
  "query" : {
   "multi_match" : {
    "query" : "complete conan doyle",
    "fields" : [ "title", "author", "characters" ],
    "type" : "cross_fields",
    "operator" : "and"
   }
  }
}'
```

This time, the results returned by Elasticsearch were as follows:

```
{
   "took" : 1,
   "timed_out" : false,
   "_shards" : {
     "total" : 5,
     "successful" : 5,
     "failed" : 0
   },
   "hits" : {
     "total" : 1,
     "max_score" : 0.08154379,
     "hits" : [ {
       "_index" : "library",
       "_type" : "book",
       "_id" : "3",
       "_score" : 0.08154379,
       "_source":{ "title": "The Complete Sherlock
       Holmes","author": "Arthur Conan Doyle","year":
       1936,"characters": ["Sherlock Holmes","Dr. Watson", "G.
       Lestrade"],"tags": [],"copies": 0, "available" : false,
       "section" : 12}
     } ]
   }
}
```

This is because our query was translated into the following Lucene query:

```
+(title:complete author:complete characters:complete)
  +(title:conan author:conan characters:conan) +(title:doyle
  author:doyle characters:doyle)
```

The results will only contain documents having all the terms in any of the mentioned fields. Of course, this is only the case when we use the AND Boolean operator. With the OR operator, we will get documents having at least a single match in any of the fields.

One more thing that is taken care of when using the `cross_fields` type is the problem of different term frequencies for each field. Elasticsearch handles that by blending the term frequencies for all the fields that are mentioned in a query. To put it simply, Elasticsearch gives almost the same weight to all the terms in the fields that are used in a query.

Most fields matching

Another type of `multi_field` configuration is the `most_fields` type. As the official documentation states, it was designed to help run queries against documents that contain the same text analyzed in different ways. One of the examples is having multiple languages in different fields. For example, if we would like to search for books that have `die leiden` terms in their title or original title, we could run the following query:

```
curl -XGET 'localhost:9200/library/_search?pretty' -d '{
 "query" : {
  "multi_match" : {
   "query" : "Die Leiden",
   "fields" : [ "title", "otitle" ],
   "type" : "most_fields"
  }
 }
}'
```

Internally, the preceding request would be translated to the following query:

```
curl -XGET 'localhost:9200/library/_search?pretty' -d '{
 "query" : {
  "bool" : {
   "should" : [
    {
     "match" : {
      "title" : "die leiden"
     }
    },
```

```
        {
          "match" : {
            "otitle" : "die leiden"
          }
        }
      ]
    }
  }
}'
```

The resulting documents are given a score equal to the sum of scores from each match query divided by the number of matching match clauses.

Phrase matching

The `phrase` matching is very similar to the `best_fields` matching we already discussed. However, instead of translating the query using match queries, it uses `match_phrase` queries. Let's take a look at the following query:

```
curl -XGET 'localhost:9200/library/_search?pretty' -d '{
  "query" : {
    "multi_match" : {
      "query" : "sherlock holmes",
      "fields" : [ "title", "author" ],
      "type" : "phrase"
    }
  }
}'
```

Because we use the `phrase` matching, it would be translated into the following:

```
curl -XGET 'localhost:9200/library/_search?pretty' -d '{
  "query" : {
    "dis_max" : {
      "queries" : [
        {
          "match_phrase" : {
            "title" : "sherlock holmes"
          }
```

```
      },
      {
       "match_phrase" : {
        "author" : "sherlock holmes"
       }
      }
     ]
    }
   }
}'
```

Phrase with prefixes matching

This is exactly the same as the phrase matching, but instead of using `match_phrase` query, the `match_phrase_prefix` query is used. Let's assume we run the following query:

```
curl -XGET 'localhost:9200/library/_search?pretty' -d '{
 "query" : {
  "multi_match" : {
   "query" : "sherlock hol",
   "fields" : [ "title", "author" ],
   "type" : "phrase_prefix"
  }
 }
}'
```

What Elasticsearch would do internally is run a query similar to the following one:

```
curl -XGET 'localhost:9200/library/_search?pretty' -d '{
 "query" : {
  "dis_max" : {
   "queries" : [
    {
     "match_phrase_prefix" : {
      "title" : "sherlock hol"
     }
    },
    {
```

```
      "match_phrase_prefix" : {
       "author" : "sherlock hol"
      }
     }
    ]
   }
  }
}'
```

As you can see, by using the `type` property of the `multi_match` query, you can achieve different results without the need of writing complicated queries. What's more, Elasticsearch will also take care of the scoring and problems related to it.

Significant terms aggregation

One of the aggregations introduced after the release of Elasticsearch 1.0 is the `significant_terms` aggregation that we can use starting from release 1.1. It allows us to get the terms that are relevant and probably the most significant for a given query. The good thing is that it doesn't only show the top terms from the results of the given query, but also shows the one that seems to be the most important one.

The use cases for this aggregation type can vary from finding the most troublesome server working in your application environment to suggesting nicknames from the text. Whenever Elasticsearch can see a significant change in the popularity of a term, such a term is a candidate for being significant.

> Please remember that the `significant_terms` aggregation is marked as experimental and can change or even be removed in the future versions of Elasticsearch.

An example

The best way to describe the `significant_terms` aggregation type will be through an example. Let's start with indexing 12 simple documents, which represent reviews of work done by interns (commands are also provided in a `significant.sh` script for easier execution on Linux-based systems):

```
curl -XPOST 'localhost:9200/interns/review/1' -d '{"intern" : "Richard", "grade" : "bad", "type" : "grade"}'
curl -XPOST 'localhost:9200/interns/review/2' -d '{"intern" : "Ralf", "grade" : "perfect", "type" : "grade"}'
```

```
curl -XPOST 'localhost:9200/interns/review/3' -d '{"intern" :
  "Richard", "grade" : "bad", "type" : "grade"}'
curl -XPOST 'localhost:9200/interns/review/4' -d '{"intern" :
  "Richard", "grade" : "bad", "type" : "review"}'
curl -XPOST 'localhost:9200/interns/review/5' -d '{"intern" :
  "Richard", "grade" : "good", "type" : "grade"}'
curl -XPOST 'localhost:9200/interns/review/6' -d '{"intern" : "Ralf",
  "grade" : "good", "type" : "grade"}'
curl -XPOST 'localhost:9200/interns/review/7' -d '{"intern" : "Ralf",
  "grade" : "perfect", "type" : "review"}'
curl -XPOST 'localhost:9200/interns/review/8' -d '{"intern" :
  "Richard", "grade" : "medium", "type" : "review"}'
curl -XPOST 'localhost:9200/interns/review/9' -d '{"intern" :
  "Monica", "grade" : "medium", "type" : "grade"}'
curl -XPOST 'localhost:9200/interns/review/10' -d '{"intern" :
  "Monica", "grade" : "medium", "type" : "grade"}'
curl -XPOST 'localhost:9200/interns/review/11' -d '{"intern" :
  "Ralf", "grade" : "good", "type" : "grade"}'
curl -XPOST 'localhost:9200/interns/review/12' -d '{"intern" :
  "Ralf", "grade" : "good", "type" : "grade"}'
```

Of course, to show the real power of the significant_terms aggregation, we should use a way larger dataset. However, for the purpose of this book, we will concentrate on this example, so it is easier to illustrate how this aggregation works.

Now let's try finding the most significant grade for Richard. To do that we will use the following query:

```
curl -XGET 'localhost:9200/interns/_search?pretty' -d '{
 "query" : {
  "match" : {
   "intern" : "Richard"
  }
 },
 "aggregations" : {
  "description" : {
   "significant_terms" : {
    "field" : "grade"
   }
  }
 }
}'
```

Not Only Full Text Search

The result of the preceding query looks as follows:

```
{
  "took" : 2,
  "timed_out" : false,
  "_shards" : {
    "total" : 5,
    "successful" : 5,
    "failed" : 0
  },
  "hits" : {
    "total" : 5,
    "max_score" : 1.4054651,
    "hits" : [ {
      "_index" : "interns",
      "_type" : "review",
      "_id" : "4",
      "_score" : 1.4054651,
      "_source":{"intern" : "Richard", "grade" : "bad"}
    }, {
      "_index" : "interns",
      "_type" : "review",
      "_id" : "3",
      "_score" : 1.0,
      "_source":{"intern" : "Richard", "grade" : "bad"}
    }, {
      "_index" : "interns",
      "_type" : "review",
      "_id" : "8",
      "_score" : 1.0,
      "_source":{"intern" : "Richard", "grade" : "medium"}
    }, {
      "_index" : "interns",
      "_type" : "review",
      "_id" : "1",
      "_score" : 1.0,
      "_source":{"intern" : "Richard", "grade" : "bad"}
    }, {
      "_index" : "interns",
      "_type" : "review",
      "_id" : "5",
      "_score" : 1.0,
      "_source":{"intern" : "Richard", "grade" : "good"}
    } ]
```

```
    },
    "aggregations" : {
      "description" : {
        "doc_count" : 5,
        "buckets" : [ {
          "key" : "bad",
          "doc_count" : 3,
          "score" : 0.84,
          "bg_count" : 3
        } ]
      }
    }
}
```

As you can see, for our query, Elasticsearch informed us that the most significant grade for Richard is bad. Maybe it wasn't the best internship for him, who knows.

Choosing significant terms

To calculate significant terms, Elasticsearch looks for data that reports significant changes in their popularity between two sets of data: the **foreground** set and the **background** set. The foreground set is the data returned by our query, while the background set is the data in our index (or indices, depending on how we run our queries). If a term exists in 10 documents out of 1 million indexed documents, but appears in five documents from 10 returned, such a term is definitely significant and worth concentrating on.

Let's get back to our preceding example now to analyze it a bit. Richard got three grades from the reviewers: bad three times, medium one time, and good one time. From those three, the bad value appears in three out of five documents matching the query. In general, the bad grade appears in three documents (the bg_count property) out of the 12 documents in the index (this is our background set). This gives us 25 percent of the indexed documents. On the other hand, the bad grade appears in three out of five documents matching the query (this is our foreground set), which gives us 60 percent of the documents. As you can see, the change in popularity is significant for the bad grade and that's why Elasticsearch have chosen it to be returned in the significant_terms aggregation results.

Multiple values analysis

Of course, the `significant_terms` aggregation can be nested and provide us with nice data analysis capabilities that connect two multiple sets of data. For example, let's try to find a significant grade for each of the interns that we have information about. To do that, we will nest the `significant_terms` aggregation inside the `terms` aggregation and the query that does that looks as follows:

```
curl -XGET 'localhost:9200/interns/_search?size=0&pretty' -d '{
 "aggregations" : {
  "grades" : {
   "terms" : {
    "field" : "intern"
   },
   "aggregations" : {
    "significantGrades" : {
     "significant_terms" : {
      "field" : "grade"
     }
    }
   }
  }
 }
}'
```

The results returned by Elasticsearch for that query are as follows:

```
{
  "took" : 71,
  "timed_out" : false,
  "_shards" : {
    "total" : 5,
    "successful" : 5,
    "failed" : 0
  },
  "hits" : {
    "total" : 12,
    "max_score" : 0.0,
    "hits" : [ ]
  },
  "aggregations" : {
```

Chapter 3

```
      "grades" : {
        "doc_count_error_upper_bound" : 0,
        "sum_other_doc_count" : 0,
        "buckets" : [ {
          "key" : "ralf",
          "doc_count" : 5,
          "significantGrades" : {
            "doc_count" : 5,
            "buckets" : [ {
              "key" : "good",
              "doc_count" : 3,
              "score" : 0.21000000000000002,
              "bg_count" : 4
            } ]
          }
        }, {
          "key" : "richard",
          "doc_count" : 5,
          "significantGrades" : {
            "doc_count" : 5,
            "buckets" : [ {
              "key" : "bad",
              "doc_count" : 3,
              "score" : 0.6,
              "bg_count" : 3
            } ]
          }
        }, {
          "key" : "monica",
          "doc_count" : 2,
          "significantGrades" : {
            "doc_count" : 2,
            "buckets" : [ ]
          }
        } ]
      }
    }
  }
}
```

As you can see, we got the results for interns Ralf (`key` property equals `ralf`) and Richard (`key` property equals `richard`). We didn't get information for Monica though. That's because there wasn't a significant change for the term in the `grade` field associated with the `monica` value in the `intern` field.

Significant terms aggregation and full text search fields

Of course, the `significant_terms` aggregation can also be used on full text search fields, practically useful for identifying text keywords. The thing is that, running this aggregation of analyzed fields may require a large amount of memory because Elasticsearch will attempt to load every term into the memory.

For example, we could run the `significant_terms` aggregation against the title field in our library index like the following:

```
curl -XGET 'localhost:9200/library/_search?size=0&pretty' -d '{
 "query" : {
  "term" : {
   "available" : true
  }
 },
 "aggregations" : {
  "description" : {
   "significant_terms" : {
    "field" : "title"
   }
  }
 }
}'
```

However, the results wouldn't bring us any useful insight in this case:

```
    {
      "took" : 2,
      "timed_out" : false,
      "_shards" : {
        "total" : 5,
        "successful" : 5,
        "failed" : 0
      },
      "hits" : {
        "total" : 4,
        "max_score" : 0.0,
        "hits" : [ ]
      },
```

```
    "aggregations" : {
      "description" : {
        "doc_count" : 4,
        "buckets" : [ {
          "key" : "the",
          "doc_count" : 3,
          "score" : 1.125,
          "bg_count" : 3
        } ]
      }
    }
  }
```

The reason for this is that we don't have large enough data for the results to be meaningful. However, from a logical point of view, the `the` term is significant for the `title` field.

Additional configuration options

We could stop here and let you play with the `significant_terms` aggregation, but we will not. Instead, we will show you a few of the vast configuration options available for this aggregation type so that you can configure internal calculations and adjust it to your needs.

Controlling the number of returned buckets

Elasticsearch allows, how many buckets at maximum we want to have returned in the results. We can control it by using the `size` property. However, the final bucket list may contain more buckets than we set the `size` property to. This is the case when the number of unique terms is larger than the specified `size` property.

If you want to have even more control over the number of returned buckets, you can use the `shard_size` property. This property specifies how many candidates for significant terms will be returned by each shard. The thing to consider is that usually the low-frequency terms are the ones turning out to be the most interested ones, but Elasticsearch can't see that before merging the results on the aggregation node. Because of this, it is good to keep the `shard_size` property value higher than the value of the `size` property.

There is one more thing to remember: if you set the `shard_size` property lower than the `size` property, then Elasticsearch will replace the `shard_size` property with the value of the `size` property.

Please note that starting from Elasticsearch 1.2.0, if the `size` or `shard_size` property is set to `0`, Elasticsearch will change that and set it to `Integer.MAX_VALUE`.

Background set filtering

If you remember, we said that the background set of term frequencies used by the `significant_terms` aggregation is the whole index or indices. We can alter that behavior by using filter (using the `background_filter` property) to narrow down the background set. This is useful when we want to find significant terms in a given context.

For example, if we would like to narrow down the background set from our first example only to documents that are the real grades, not reviews, we would add the following `term` filter to our query:

```
curl -XGET 'localhost:9200/interns/_search?pretty&size=0' -d '{
 "query" : {
  "match" : {
   "intern" : "Richard"
  }
 },
 "aggregations" : {
  "description" : {
   "significant_terms" : {
    "field" : "grade",
    "background_filter" : {
     "term" : {
      "type" : "grade"
     }
    }
   }
  }
 }
}'
```

If you would look more closely at the results, you would notice that Elasticsearch calculated the significant terms for a smaller number of documents:

```
{
  "took" : 4,
  "timed_out" : false,
  "_shards" : {
    "total" : 5,
    "successful" : 5,
    "failed" : 0
  },
  "hits" : {
    "total" : 5,
    "max_score" : 0.0,
    "hits" : [ ]
  },
  "aggregations" : {
    "description" : {
      "doc_count" : 5,
      "buckets" : [ {
        "key" : "bad",
        "doc_count" : 3,
        "score" : 1.02,
        "bg_count" : 2
      } ]
    }
  }
}
```

Notice that `bg_count` is now 2 instead of 3 in the initial example. That's because there are only two documents having the `bad` value in the `grade` field and matching our filter specified in `background_filter`.

Minimum document count

A good thing about the `significant_terms` aggregation is that we can control the minimum number of documents a term needs to be present in to be included as a bucket. We do that by adding the `min_doc_count` property with the count of our choice.

Not Only Full Text Search

For example, let's add this parameter to our query that resulted in significant grades for each of our interns. Let's lower the default value of 3 that the `min_doc_count` property is set to and let's set it to 2. Our modified query would look as follows:

```
curl -XGET 'localhost:9200/interns/_search?size=0&pretty' -d '{
 "aggregations" : {
  "grades" : {
   "terms" : {
    "field" : "intern"
   },
   "aggregations" : {
    "significantGrades" : {
     "significant_terms" : {
      "field" : "grade",
      "min_doc_count" : 2
     }
    }
   }
  }
 }
}'
```

The results of the preceding query would be as follows:

```
    {
      "took" : 3,
      "timed_out" : false,
      "_shards" : {
        "total" : 5,
        "successful" : 5,
        "failed" : 0
      },
      "hits" : {
        "total" : 12,
        "max_score" : 0.0,
        "hits" : [ ]
      },
      "aggregations" : {
        "grades" : {
          "doc_count_error_upper_bound" : 0,
```

```
      "sum_other_doc_count" : 0,
      "buckets" : [ {
        "key" : "ralf",
        "doc_count" : 5,
        "significantGrades" : {
          "doc_count" : 5,
          "buckets" : [ {
            "key" : "perfect",
            "doc_count" : 2,
            "score" : 0.3200000000000001,
            "bg_count" : 2
          }, {
            "key" : "good",
            "doc_count" : 3,
            "score" : 0.21000000000000002,
            "bg_count" : 4
          } ]
        }
      }, {
        "key" : "richard",
        "doc_count" : 5,
        "significantGrades" : {
          "doc_count" : 5,
          "buckets" : [ {
            "key" : "bad",
            "doc_count" : 3,
            "score" : 0.6,
            "bg_count" : 3
          } ]
        }
      }, {
        "key" : "monica",
        "doc_count" : 2,
        "significantGrades" : {
          "doc_count" : 2,
          "buckets" : [ {
            "key" : "medium",
            "doc_count" : 2,
            "score" : 1.0,
            "bg_count" : 3
          } ]
        }
      } ]
    }
  }
}
```

Not Only Full Text Search

As you can see, the results differ from the original example—this is because the constraints on the significant terms have been lowered. Of course, that also means that our results may be worse now. Setting this parameter to 1 may result in typos and strange words being included in the results and is generally not advised.

There is one thing to remember when it comes to using the `min_doc_count` property. During the first phase of aggregation calculation, Elasticsearch will collect the highest scoring terms on each shard included in the process. However, because shard doesn't have the information about the global term frequencies, the decision about term being a candidate to a significant terms list is based on shard term frequencies. The `min_doc_count` property is applied during the final stage of the query, once all the results are merged from the shards. Because of this, it may happen that high-frequency terms are missing in the significant terms list and the list is populated by high-scoring terms instead. To avoid this, you can increase the `shard_size` property and the cost of memory consumption and higher network usage.

Execution hint

Elasticsearch allows us to specify execution mode, which should be used to calculate the `significant_terms` aggregation. Depending on the situation, we can either set the `execution_hint` property to `map` or to `ordinal`. The first execution type tells Elasticsearch to aggregate the data per bucket using the values themselves. The second value tells Elasticsearch to use ordinals of the values instead of the values themselves. In most situations, setting the `execution_hint` property to `ordinal` should result in slightly faster execution, but the data we are working on must expose the ordinals. However, if the fields you calculate the `significant_terms` aggregation on is high cardinality one (if it contains a high number of unique terms), then using `map` is, in most cases, a better choice.

> Please note that Elasticsearch will ignore the `execution_hint` property if it can't be applied.

More options

Because Elasticsearch is constantly being developed and changed, we decided not to include all the options that are possible to set. We also omitted the options that we think are very rarely used by the users so that we are able to write in further detail about more commonly used features. See the full list of options at http://www.elasticsearch.org/guide/en/elasticsearch/reference/current/search-aggregations-bucket-significantterms-aggregation.html.

[318]

There are limits

While we were working on this book, there were a few limitations when it comes to the `significant_terms` aggregation. Of course, those are no showstoppers that will force you to totally forget about that aggregation, but it is useful to know about them.

Memory consumption

Because the `significant_terms` aggregation works on indexed values, it needs to load all the unique terms into the memory to be able to do its job. Because of this, you have to be careful when using this aggregation on large indices and on fields that are analyzed. In addition to this, we can't lower the memory consumption by using doc values fields because the `significant_terms` aggregation doesn't support them.

Shouldn't be used as top-level aggregation

The `significant_terms` aggregation shouldn't be used as a top-level aggregation whenever you are using the `match_all` query, its equivalent returning all the documents or no query at all. In such cases, the foreground and background sets will be the same, and Elasticsearch won't be able to calculate the differences in frequencies. This means that no significant terms will be found.

Counts are approximated

Elasticsearch approximates the counts of how many documents contain a term based on the information returned for each shard. You have to be aware of that because this means that those counts can be miscalculated in certain situations (for example, count can be approximated too low when shards didn't include data for a given term in the top samples returned). As the documentation states, this was a design decision to allow faster execution at the cost of potentially small inaccuracies.

Floating point fields are not allowed

Fields that are floating point type-based ones are not allowed as the subject of calculation of the `significant_terms` aggregation. You can use the `long` or `integer` based fields though.

Documents grouping

One of the most desired functionalities in Elasticsearch was always a feature called document folding or document grouping. This functionality was the most +1 marked issue for Elasticsearch. It is not surprising at all. It is sometimes very convenient to show a list of documents grouped by a particular value, especially when the number of results is very big. In this case, instead of showing all the documents one by one, we would return only one (or a few) documents from every group. For example, in our library, we could prepare a query returning all the documents about wildlife sorted by publishing date, but limit the list to two books from every year. The other useful use case, where grouping can become very handy, is counting and showing distinct values in a field. An example of such behavior is returning only a single book that had many editions.

Top hits aggregation

The `top_hits` aggregation was introduced in Elasticsearch 1.3 along with the changes to scripting about which we will talk in the *Scripting changes* section later in this chapter. What is interesting is that we can force Elasticsearch to provide grouping functionality with this aggregation. In fact, it seems that a document folding is more or less a side effect and only one of the possible usage examples of the `top_hits` aggregation. In this section, we will only focus on how this particular aggregation works, and we assumed that you already know the basic rules that rule the world of the Elasticsearch aggregation framework.

> If you don't have any experience with this Elasticsearch functionality, please considering looking at *Elasticsearch Server Second Edition* published by *Packt Publishing* or reading the Elasticsearch documentation page available at http://www.elasticsearch.org/guide/en/elasticsearch/reference/current/search-aggregations.html.

The idea behind the `top_hits` aggregation is simple. Every document that is assigned to a particular bucket can be also remembered. By default, only three documents per bucket are remembered. Let's see how it works using our example `library` index.

An example

To show you a potential use case that leverages the `top_hits` aggregation, we decided to use the following query:

```
curl -XGET "http://127.0.0.1:9200/library/_search?pretty" -d'
{
  "size": 0,
  "aggs": {
    "when": {
      "histogram": {
        "field": "year",
        "interval": 100
      },
      "aggs": {
        "book": {
          "top_hits": {
            "_source": {
              "include": [
                "title",
                "available"
              ]
            },
            "size": 1
          }
        }
      }
    }
  }
}'
```

In the preceding example, we did the `histogram` aggregation on year ranges. Every bucket is created for every 100 years. The nested `top_hits` aggregations will remember a single document with the greatest score from each bucket (because of the `size` property set to 1). We added the `include` option only for simplicity of the results, so that we only return the `title` and `available` fields for every aggregated document. The response returned by Elasticsearch should be similar to the following one:

```
{
   "took": 2,
   "timed_out": false,
```

```
"_shards": {
   "total": 5,
   "successful": 5,
   "failed": 0
},
"hits": {
   "total": 4,
   "max_score": 0,
   "hits": []
},
"aggregations": {
   "when": {
      "buckets": [
         {
            "key_as_string": "1800",
            "key": 1800,
            "doc_count": 1,
            "book": {
               "hits": {
                  "total": 1,
                  "max_score": 1,
                  "hits": [
                     {
                        "_index": "library",
                        "_type": "book",
                        "_id": "4",
                        "_score": 1,
                        "_source": {
                           "title": "Crime and Punishment",
                           "available": true
                        }
                     }
                  ]
               }
            }
         },
         {
            "key_as_string": "1900",
            "key": 1900,
            "doc_count": 3,
            "book": {
               "hits": {
                  "total": 3,
```

```
                        "max_score": 1,
                        "hits": [
                            {
                                "_index": "library",
                                "_type": "book",
                                "_id": "3",
                                "_score": 1,
                                "_source": {
                                    "title": "The Complete Sherlock
                                    Holmes",
                                    "available": false
                                }
                            }
                        ]
                    }
                }
            }
        ]
    }
  }
}
```

The interesting parts of the response are highlighted. We can see that because of the `top_hits` aggregation, we have the most scoring document (from each bucket) included in the response. In our particular case, the query was the `match_all` one and all the documents have the same score, so the top scoring document for every bucket is more or less random. Elasticsearch used the `match_all` query because we didn't specify any query at all—this is the default behavior. If we want to have a custom sorting, this is not a problem for Elasticsearch. For example, we can return the first book from a given century. What we just need to do is add a proper sorting option, just like in the following query:

```
curl -XGET 'http://127.0.0.1:9200/library/_search?pretty' -d '{
  "size": 0,
  "aggs": {
    "when": {
      "histogram": {
        "field": "year",
        "interval": 100
      },
      "aggs": {
        "book": {
```

```
                "top_hits": {
                    "sort": {
                        "year": "asc"
                    },
                    "_source": {
                        "include": [
                            "title",
                            "available"
                        ]
                    },
                    "size": 1
                }
            }
          }
        }
      }
    }
}'
```

Please take a look at the highlighted fragment of the preceding query. We've added sorting to the top_hits aggregation, so the results are sorted on the basis of the year field. This means that the first document will be the one with the lowest value in that field and this is the document that is going to be returned for each bucket.

Additional parameters

However, sorting and field inclusion is not everything that we can we do inside the top_hits aggregation. Elasticsearch allows using several other functionalities related to documents retrieval. We don't want to discuss them all in detail because you should be familiar with most of them if you are familiar with the Elasticsearch aggregation module. However, for the purpose of this chapter, let's look at the following example:

```
curl -XGET 'http://127.0.0.1:9200/library/_search?pretty' -d '{
    "query": {
        "filtered": {
            "query": {
                "match": {
                    "_all": "quiet"
                }
```

```
            },
            "filter": {
               "term": {
                  "copies": 1,
                  "_name": "copies_filter"
               }
            }
         }
      },
      "size": 0,
      "aggs": {
         "when": {
            "histogram": {
               "field": "year",
               "interval": 100
            },
            "aggs": {
               "book": {
                  "top_hits": {
                     "highlight": {
                        "fields": {
                           "title": {}
                        }
                     },
                     "explain": true,
                     "version": true,
                     "_source": {
                        "include": [
                           "title",
                           "available"
                        ]
                     },
                     "fielddata_fields" : ["title"],
                     "script_fields": {
                        "century": {
```

```
                    "script": "(doc[\"year\"].value /
                    100).intValue()"
                }
            },
            "size": 1
        }
    }
}
}'
```

As you can see, our query contains the following functionalities:

- Named filters and queries (in our example the filter is named `copies_filter`)
- Document version inclusion
- Document source filtering (choosing fields that should be returned)
- Using field-data fields and script fields
- Inclusion of explained information that tells us why a given document was matched and included
- Highlighting usage

Relations between documents

While Elasticsearch is gaining more and more attention, it is no longer used as a search engine only. It is seen as a data analysis solution and sometimes as a primary data store. Having a single data store that enables fast and efficient full text searching often seems like a good idea. We not only can store documents, but we can also search them and analyze their contents bringing meaning to the data. This is usually more than we could expect from traditional SQL databases. However, if you have any experience with SQL databases, when dealing with Elasticsearch, you soon realize the necessity of modeling relationships between documents. Unfortunately, it is not easy and many of the habits and good practices from relation databases won't work in the world of the inverted index that Elasticsearch uses. You should already be familiar with how Elasticsearch handles relationships because we already mentioned nested objects and parent–child functionality in our *Elasticsearch Server Second Edition* book, but let's go through available possibilities and look closer at the traps connected with them.

The object type

Elasticsearch tries to interfere as little as possible when modeling your data and turning it into an inverted index. Unlike the relation databases, Elasticsearch can index structured objects and it is natural to it. It means that if you have any JSON document, you can index it without problems and Elasticsearch adapts to it. Let's look at the following document:

```
{
    "title": "Title",
    "quantity": 100,
    "edition": {
        "isbn": "1234567890",
        "circulation": 50000
    }
}
```

As you can see, the preceding document has two simple properties and a nested object inside it (the `edition` one) with additional properties. The mapping for our example is simple and looks as follows (it is also stored in the `relations.json` file provided with the book):

```
{
  "book" : {
    "properties" : {
      "title" : {"type": "string" },
      "quantity" : {"type": "integer" },
      "edition" : {
        "type" : "object",
        "properties" : {
          "isbn" : {"type" : "string", "index" : "not_analyzed" },
          "circulation" : {"type" : "integer" }
        }
      }
    }
  }
}
```

Unfortunately, everything will work only when the inner object is connected to its parent with a one-to-one relation. If you add the second object, for example, like the following:

```
{
    "title": "Title",
    "quantity": 100,
    "edition": [
        {
            "isbn": "1234567890",
            "circulation": 50000
        },
        {
            "isbn": "9876543210",
            "circulation": 2000
        }
    ]
}
```

Elasticsearch will flatten it. To Elasticsearch, the preceding document will look more or less like the following one (of course, the `_source` field will still look like the preceding document):

```
{
    "title": "Title",
    "quantity": 100,
    "edition": {
        "isbn": [ "1234567890", "9876543210" ],
         "circulation": [50000, 2000 ]
      }
}
```

This is not exactly what we want, and such representation will cause problems when you search for books containing editions with given ISBN numbers and given circulation. Simply, cross-matches will happen—Elasticsearch will return books containing editions with given ISBNs and any circulation.

We can test this by indexing our document by using the following command:

```
curl -XPOST 'localhost:9200/object/doc/1' -d '{
 "title": "Title",
 "quantity": 100,
 "edition": [
```

```
  {
    "isbn": "1234567890",
    "circulation": 50000
  },
  {
    "isbn": "9876543210",
    "circulation": 2000
  }
 ]
}'
```

Now, if we would run a simple query to return documents with the `isbn` field equal to `1234567890` and the `circulation` field equal to `2000`, we shouldn't get any documents. Let's test that by running the following query:

```
curl -XGET 'localhost:9200/object/_search?pretty' -d '{
 "fields" : [ "_id", "title" ],
 "query" : {
  "bool" : {
   "must" : [
    {
     "term" : {
      "isbn" : "1234567890"
     }
    },
    {
     "term" : {
      "circulation" : 2000
     }
    }
   ]
  }
 }
}'
```

Not Only Full Text Search

What we got as a result from Elasticsearch is as follows:

```
{
  "took" : 5,
  "timed_out" : false,
  "_shards" : {
    "total" : 5,
    "successful" : 5,
    "failed" : 0
  },
  "hits" : {
    "total" : 1,
    "max_score" : 1.0122644,
    "hits" : [ {
      "_index" : "object",
      "_type" : "doc",
      "_id" : "1",
      "_score" : 1.0122644,
      "fields" : {
        "title" : [ "Title" ]
      }
    } ]
  }
}
```

This cross-finding can be avoided by rearranging the mapping and document so that the source document looks like the following:

```
{
  "title": "Title",
  "quantity": 100,
  "edition": {
      "isbn": ["1234567890", "9876543210"],
       "circulation_1234567890": 50000,
       "circulation_9876543210": 2000
   }
}
```

[330]

Now, you can use the preceding mentioned query, which use the relationships between fields by the cost of greater complexity of query building. The important problem is that the mappings would have to contain information about all the possible values of the fields—this is not something that we would like to go for when having more than a couple of possible values. From the other side, this still does not allow us to create more complicated queries such as all books with a circulation of more than `10 000` and `ISBN` number starting with `23`. In such cases, a better solution would be to use nested objects.

To summarize, the `object` type could be handy only for the simplest cases when problems with cross-field searching does not exist—for example, when you don't want to search inside nested objects or you only need to search on one of the fields without matching on the others.

The nested documents

From the mapping point of view, the definition of a nested document differs only in the use of `nested` type instead of `object` (which Elasticsearch will use by default when guessing types). For example, let's modify our previous example so that it uses nested documents:

```
{
  "book" : {
    "properties" : {
      "title" : {"type": "string" },
      "quantity" : {"type": "integer" },
      "edition" : {
        "type" : "nested",
        "properties" : {
          "isbn" : {"type" : "string", "index" : "not_analyzed" },
          "circulation" : {"type" : "integer" }
        }
      }
    }
  }
}
```

When we are using the nested documents, Elasticsearch, in fact, creates one document for the main object (we can call it a parent one, but that can bring confusion when talking about the parent–child functionality) and additional documents for inner objects. During normal queries, these additional documents are automatically filtered out and not searched or displayed. This is called a block join in Apache Lucene (you can read more about Apache Lucene block join queries at a blog post written by Lucene committer Mike McCandless, available at `http://blog.mikemccandless.com/2012/01/searching-relational-content-with.html`). For performance reasons, Lucene keeps these documents together with the main document, in the same segment block.

This is why the nested documents have to be indexed at the same time as the main document. Because both sides of the relation are prepared before storing them in the index and both sides are indexed at the same time. Some people refer to nested objects as an index-time join. This strong connection between documents is not a big problem when the documents are small and the data are easily available from the main data store. But what if documents are quite big, one of the relationship parts changes a lot, and reindexing the second part is not an option? The next problem is what if a nested document belongs to more than one main document? These problems do not exist in the parent–child functionality.

If we would get back to our example, and we would change our index to use the `nested` objects and we would change our query to use the `nested` query, no documents would be returned because there is no match for such a query in a single nested document.

Parent–child relationship

When talking about the parent–child functionality, we have to start with its main advantage — the true separation between documents — and each part of the relation can be indexed independently. The first cost of this advantage is more complicated queries and thus slower queries. Elasticsearch provides special query and filter types, which allow us to use this relation. This is why it is sometimes called a query-time join. The second disadvantage, which is more significant, is present in the bigger applications and multi-node Elasticsearch setups. Let's see how the parent–child relationship works in the Elasticsearch cluster that contains multiple nodes.

 Please note that unlike nested documents, the children documents can be queried without the context of the parent document, which is not possible with nested documents.

Parent–child relationship in the cluster

To better show the problem, let's create two indices: the `rel_pch_m` index holding documents being the parents and the `rel_pch_s` index with documents that are children:

```
curl -XPUT localhost:9200/rel_pch_m -d '{ "settings" : {
  "number_of_replicas" : 0 } }'
curl -XPUT localhost:9200/rel_pch_s -d '{ "settings" : {
  "number_of_replicas" : 0 } }'
```

Our mappings for the `rel_pch_m` index are simple and they can be sent to Elasticsearch by using the following command:

```
curl -XPOST localhost:9200/rel_pch_m/book/_mapping?pretty -d '{
  "book" : {
    "properties" : {
      "title" : { "type": "string" },
      "quantity" : { "type": "integer" }
    }
  }
}'
```

The mappings for the `rel_pch_s` index are simple as well, but we have to inform Elasticsearch what type of documents should be treated as parents. We can use the following command to send the mappings for the second index to Elasticsearch:

```
curl -XPOST localhost:9200/rel_pch_s/edition/_mapping?pretty -d '{
  "edition" : {
    "_parent" : {
      "type" : "book"
    },
    "properties" : {
      "isbn" : { "type" : "string", "index" : "not_analyzed" },
      "circulation" : { "type" : "integer" }
    }
  }
}'
```

Not Only Full Text Search

The last step is to import data to these indices. We generated about `10000` records; an example document looks as follows:

```
{"index": {"_index": "rel_pch_m", "_type": "book", "_id": "1"}}
{"title" : "Doc no 1", "quantity" : 101}
{"index": {"_index": "rel_pch_s", "_type": "edition", "_id": "1",
  "_parent": "1"}}
{"isbn" : "no1", "circulation" : 501}
```

 If you are curious and want to experiment, you will find the simple bash script `create_relation_indices.sh` used to generate the example data.

The assumption is simple: we have `10000` documents of each type (`book` and `edition`). The key is the `_parent` field. In our example, it will always be set to `1`, so we have `10 000` books but our `10 000` edition belongs to that one particular book. This example is rather extreme, but it lets us point out an important thing.

 For visualization, we have used the ElasticHQ plugin available at http://www.elastichq.org/.

First let's look at the parent part of the relation and the index storing the parent documents, as shown in the following screenshot:

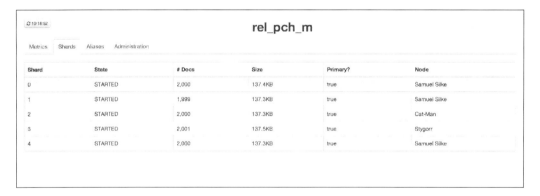

As we can see, the five shards of the index are located on three different nodes. Every shard has more or less the same number of documents. This is what we would expect—Elasticsearch used hashing to calculate the shard on which documents should be placed.

Now, let's look at the second index, which contains our children documents, as shown in the following screenshot:

Shard	State	# Docs	Size	Primary?	Node
0	STARTED	0	123.0B	true	Samuel Silke
1	STARTED	0	123.0B	true	Cat-Man
2	STARTED	10,000	594.7KB	true	Samuel Silke
3	STARTED	0	123.0B	true	Stygorr
4	STARTED	0	123.0B	true	Samuel Silke

The situation is different. We still have five shards, but four of them are empty and the last one contains all the 10,000 documents! So something is not right—all the documents we indexed are located in one particular shard. This is because Elasticsearch will always put documents with the same parent in the same shard (in other words, the `routing` parameter value for children documents is always equal to the `parent` parameter value). Our example shows that in situations when some parent documents have substantially more children, we can end up with uneven shards, which may cause performance and storage issues—for example, some shards may be idling, while others will be constantly overloaded.

A few words about alternatives

As we have seen, the handling of relations between documents can cause different problems to Elasticsearch. Of course, this is not only the case with Elasticsearch because full text search solutions are extremely valuable for searching and data analysis, and not for modeling relationships between data. If it is a big problem for your application, and the full text capability is not a core part of it, you may consider using an SQL database that allows full text searching to some extent. Of course, these solutions won't be as flexible and fast as Elasticsearch, but we have to pay the price if we need full relationship support. However, in most other cases, the change of data architecture and the elimination of relations by de-normalization will be sufficient.

Scripting changes between Elasticsearch versions

One of the great things in Elasticsearch is its scripting capabilities. You can use script for calculating score, text-based scoring, data filtering, and data analysis. Although scripting can be slow in some cases, such as calculating the score for each document, we think that this part of Elasticsearch is important. Because of this, we decided that this section should bring you the information about the changes and will extend the information present in the *Elasticsearch Server Second Edition* book.

Scripting changes

Elasticsearch scripting has gone through a lot of refactoring in version 1.0 and in the versions that came after that. Because of those changes, some users were lost as to why their scripts stopped working when upgrading to version 1.2 of Elasticsearch and what is happening in general. This section will try to give you an insight on what to expect.

Security issues

During the lifetime of Elasticsearch 1.1, an exploit was published (see `http://bouk.co/blog/elasticsearch-rce/`): it showed that with the default configuration, Elasticsearch was not fully secure. Because of that, dynamic scripting was disabled by default in Elasticsearch 1.2. Although, disabling dynamic scripting was enough to make Elasticsearch secure, it made script usage far more complicated.

Groovy – the new default scripting language

With the release of Elasticsearch 1.3, we can use a new scripting language that will become default in the next version: Groovy (see `http://groovy.codehaus.org/`). The reason for this is that it can be closed in its own sandbox, preventing dynamic scripts from doing any harm to the cluster and the operating system. In addition to that, because Groovy can be sandboxed, Elasticsearch allows us to use dynamic scripting when using it. Generally speaking, starting from version 1.3, if a scripting language can be sandboxed, it can be used in dynamic scripts. However, Groovy is not everything: Elasticsearch 1.3 allows us to use Lucene expressions, which we will cover in this section. However, with the release of Elasticsearch 1.3.8 and 1.4.3 dynamic scripting was turned off even for Groovy. Because of that, if you still want to use dynamic scripting for Groovy you need to add `script.groovy.sandbox.enabled` property to `elasticsearch.yml` and set it to `true` or make your Elasticsearch a bit less dynamic with stored scripts. Please be aware that enabling dynamic scripting exposes security issues though and should be used with caution.

Removal of MVEL language

Because of the security issues and introduction of Groovy, starting from Elasticsearch 1.4, MVEL will no longer be available by default with Elasticsearch distribution. The default language will be Groovy, and MVEL will only be available as a plugin installed on demand. Remember that if you want to drop MVEL scripts, it is really easy to port them to Groovy. Of course, you will be able to install the MVEL plugin, but still dynamic scripting will be forbidden.

Short Groovy introduction

Groovy is a dynamic language for the Java Virtual Machine. It was built on top of Java, with some inspiration from languages such as Python, Ruby, or Smalltalk. Even though Groovy is out of the context of this book, we decided to describe it because, as you know, it is the default scripting language starting from Elasticsearch 1.4. If you already know Groovy and you know how to use it in Elasticsearch, you can easily skip this section and move to the *Scripting in full text context* section of this book.

> The thing to remember is that Groovy is only sandboxed up to Elasticsearch 1.3.8 and 1.4.3. Starting from the mentioned versions it is not possible to run dynamic Groovy scripts unless Elasticsearch is configured to allow such. All the queries in the examples that we will show next require you to add `script.groovy.sandbox.enabled` property to `elasticsearch.yml` and set it to `true`.

Using Groovy as your scripting language

Before we go into an introduction to Groovy, let's learn how to use it in Elasticsearch scripts. To do this, check the version you are using. If you are using Elasticsearch older than 1.4, you will need to add the `lang` property with the value `groovy`. For example:

```
curl -XGET 'localhost:9200/library/_search?pretty' -d '{
 "fields" : [ "_id", "_score", "title" ],
 "query" : {
  "function_score" : {
   "query" : {
    "match_all" : {}
   },
   "script_score" : {
    "lang" : "groovy",
    "script" : "_index[\"title\"].docCount()"
   }
  }
 }
}'
```

If you are using Elasticsearch 1.4 or newer, you can easily skip the scripting language definition because Elasticsearch will use Groovy by default.

Variable definition in scripts

Groovy allows us to define variables in scripts used in Elasticsearch. To define a new variable, we use the `def` keyword followed by the variable name and its value. For example, to define a variable named `sum` and assign an initial value of `0`, to it we would use the following snippet of code:

```
def sum = 0
```

Of course, we are not only bound to simple variables definition. We can define lists, for example, a list of four values:

```
def listOfValues = [0, 1, 2, 3]
```

We can define a range of values, for example, from 0 to 9:

```
def rangeOfValues = 0..9
```

Finally, we can define maps:

```
def map = ['count':1, 'price':10, 'quantity': 12]
```

The preceding line of code will result in defining a map with three keys (`count`, `price`, and `quantity`) and three values corresponding to those keys (`1`, `10`, and `12`).

Conditionals

We are also allowed to use conditional statements in scripts. For example, we can use standard if - else if - else structures:

```
if (count > 1) {
  return count
} else if (count == 1) {
  return 1
} else {
  return 0
}
```

We can use the ternary operator:

```
def isHigherThanZero = (count > 0) ? true : false
```

The preceding code will assign a `true` value to the `isHigherThanZero` variable if the `count` variable is higher than `0`. Otherwise, the value assigned to the `isHigherThanZero` variable will be `false`.

Of course, we are also allowed to use standard switch statements that allow us to use an elegant way of choosing the execution path based on the value of the statement:

```
def isEqualToTenOrEleven = false;
switch (count) {
  case 10:
    isEqualToTenOrEleven = true
    break
  case 11:
    isEqualToTenOrEleven = true
    break
  default:
    isEqualToTenOrEleven  = false
}
```

The preceding code will set the value of the `isEqualToTenOrEleven` variable to `true` if the `count` variable is equal to `10` or `11`. Otherwise, the value of the `isEqualToTenOrEleven` variable will be set to `false`.

Loops

Of course, we can also use loops when using Elasticsearch scripts and Groovy as the language in which scripts are written. Let's start with the `while` loop that is going to be executed until the statement in the parenthesis is true:

```
def i = 2
def sum = 0
while (i > 0) {
  sum = sum + i
  i--
}
```

The preceding loop will be executed twice and ended. In the first iteration, the `i` variable will have the value of `2`, which means that the `i > 0` statement is true. In the second iteration, the value of the `i` variable will be `1`, which again makes the `i > 0` statement true. In the third iteration, the `i` variable will be `0`, which will cause the `while` loop not to execute its body and exit.

We can also use the `for` loop, which you are probably familiar with if you've used programming languages before. For example, to iterate 10 times over the for loop body, we could use the following code:

```
def sum = 0
for ( i = 0; i < 10; i++) {
   sum += i
}
```

We can also iterate over a range of values:

```
def sum = 0
for ( i in 0..9 ) {
   sum += i
}
```

Or iterate over a list of values:

```
def sum = 0
for ( i in [0, 1, 2, 3, 4, 5, 6, 7, 8, 9] ) {
   sum += i
}
```

If we have a map, we can iterate over its entries:

```
def map = ['quantity':2, 'value':1, 'count':3]
def sum = 0
for ( entry in map ) {
   sum += entry.value
}
```

An example

Now after seeing some basics of Groovy, let's try to run an example script that will modify the score of our documents. We will implement the following algorithm for score calculation:

- if the year field holds the value lower than 1800, we will give the book a score of 1.0
- if the year field is between 1800 and 1900, we will give the book a score of 2.0
- the rest of the books should have the score equal to the value of the year field minus 1000

Chapter 3

The query that does the preceding example looks as follows:

```
curl -XGET 'localhost:9200/library/_search?pretty' -d '{
 "fields" : [ "_id", "_score", "title", "year" ],
 "query" : {
  "function_score" : {
   "query" : {
    "match_all" : {}
   },
   "script_score" : {
    "lang" : "groovy",
    "script" : "def year = doc[\"year\"].value; if (year < 1800) {
    return 1.0 } else if (year < 1900) { return 2.0 } else { return
    year - 1000 }"
   }
  }
 }
}'
```

> You may have noticed that we've separated the def year = doc[\"year\"].value statement in the script from the rest of it using the ; character. We did it because we have the script in a single line and we need to tell Groovy where our assign statement ends and where another statement starts.

The result returned by Elasticsearch for the preceding query is as follows:

```
{
   "took" : 4,
   "timed_out" : false,
   "_shards" : {
     "total" : 5,
     "successful" : 5,
     "failed" : 0
   },
   "hits" : {
     "total" : 6,
     "max_score" : 961.0,
     "hits" : [ {
       "_index" : "library",
       "_type" : "book",
```

```
      "_id" : "2",
      "_score" : 961.0,
      "fields" : {
        "title" : [ "Catch-22" ],
        "year" : [ 1961 ],
        "_id" : "2"
      }
    }, {
      "_index" : "library",
      "_type" : "book",
      "_id" : "3",
      "_score" : 936.0,
      "fields" : {
        "title" : [ "The Complete Sherlock Holmes" ],
        "year" : [ 1936 ],
        "_id" : "3"
      }
    }, {
      "_index" : "library",
      "_type" : "book",
      "_id" : "1",
      "_score" : 929.0,
      "fields" : {
        "title" : [ "All Quiet on the Western Front" ],
        "year" : [ 1929 ],
        "_id" : "1"
      }
    }, {
      "_index" : "library",
      "_type" : "book",
      "_id" : "6",
      "_score" : 904.0,
      "fields" : {
        "title" : [ "The Peasants" ],
        "year" : [ 1904 ],
        "_id" : "6"
      }
    }, {
      "_index" : "library",
      "_type" : "book",
      "_id" : "4",
      "_score" : 2.0,
      "fields" : {
        "title" : [ "Crime and Punishment" ],
```

```
        "year" : [ 1886 ],
        "_id" : "4"
      }
    }, {
      "_index" : "library",
      "_type" : "book",
      "_id" : "5",
      "_score" : 1.0,
      "fields" : {
        "title" : [ "The Sorrows of Young Werther" ],
        "year" : [ 1774 ],
        "_id" : "5"
      }
    } ]
  }
}
```

As you can see, our script worked as we wanted it to.

There is more

Of course, the information we just gave is not a comprehensive guide to Groovy and was never intended to be one. Groovy is out of the scope of this book and we wanted to give you a glimpse of what to expect from it. If you are interested in Groovy and you want to extend your knowledge beyond what you just read, we suggest going to the official Groovy web page and reading the documentation available at http://groovy.codehaus.org/.

Scripting in full text context

Of course, scripts are not only about modifying the score on the basis of data. In addition to this, we can use full text-specific statistics in our scripts, such as document frequency or term frequency. Let's look at these possibilities.

Field-related information

The first text-related information we can use in scripts we would like to talk about is field-related statistics. The field-related information Elasticsearch allows us to use is as follows:

- `_index['field_name'].docCount()`: **Number of documents that contain a given field. This statistic doesn't take deleted documents into consideration.**

- `_index['field_name'].sumttf()`: Sum of the number of times all terms appear in all documents in a given field.
- `_index['field_name'].sumdf()`: Sum of document frequencies. This shows the sum of the number of times all terms appear in a given field in all documents.

 Please remember that the preceding information is given for a single shard, not for the whole index, so they may differ between shards.

For example, if we would like to give our documents a score equal to the number of documents having the `title` field living in a given shard, we could run the following query:

```
curl -XGET 'localhost:9200/library/_search?pretty' -d '{
 "fields" : [ "_id", "_score", "title" ],
 "query" : {
  "function_score" : {
   "query" : {
    "match_all" : {}
   },
   "script_score" : {
    "lang" : "groovy",
    "script" : "_index[\"title\"].docCount()"
   }
  }
 }
}'
```

If we would look at the response, we would see the following:

```
{
  "took" : 3,
  "timed_out" : false,
  "_shards" : {
    "total" : 5,
    "successful" : 5,
    "failed" : 0
  },
  "hits" : {
```

```
      "total" : 6,
      "max_score" : 2.0,
      "hits" : [ {
        "_index" : "library",
        "_type" : "book",
        "_id" : "1",
        "_score" : 2.0,
        "fields" : {
          "title" : [ "All Quiet on the Western Front" ],
          "_id" : "1"
        }
      }, {
        "_index" : "library",
        "_type" : "book",
        "_id" : "6",
        "_score" : 2.0,
        "fields" : {
          "title" : [ "The Peasants" ],
          "_id" : "6"
        }
      }, {
        "_index" : "library",
        "_type" : "book",
        "_id" : "4",
        "_score" : 1.0,
        "fields" : {
          "title" : [ "Crime and Punishment" ],
          "_id" : "4"
        }
      }, {
        "_index" : "library",
        "_type" : "book",
        "_id" : "5",
        "_score" : 1.0,
        "fields" : {
          "title" : [ "The Sorrows of Young Werther" ],
          "_id" : "5"
        }
      }, {
        "_index" : "library",
        "_type" : "book",
        "_id" : "2",
        "_score" : 1.0,
```

```
        "fields" : {
          "title" : [ "Catch-22" ],
          "_id" : "2"
        }
      }, {
        "_index" : "library",
        "_type" : "book",
        "_id" : "3",
        "_score" : 1.0,
        "fields" : {
          "title" : [ "The Complete Sherlock Holmes" ],
          "_id" : "3"
        }
      } ]
    }
  }
```

As you can see, we have five documents that were queried to return the preceding results. The first two documents have a score of 2.0, which means that they are probably living in the same shard because the four remaining documents have a score of 1.0, which means that are alone in their shard.

Shard level information

The shard level information that we are allowed to use are as follows:

- `_index.numDocs()`: Number of documents in a shard
- `_index.maxDoc()`: Internal identifier of the maximum number of documents in a shard
- `_index.numDeletedDocs()`: Number of deleted documents in a given shard

 Please remember that the preceding information is given for a single shard, not for the whole index, so they may differ between shards.

For example, if we would like to sort documents on the basis of the highest internal identifier each shard has, we could send the following query:

```
curl -XGET 'localhost:9200/library/_search?pretty' -d '{
 "fields" : [ "_id", "_score", "title" ],
 "query" : {
  "function_score" : {
   "query" : {
```

```
      "match_all" : {}
    },
    "script_score" : {
      "lang" : "groovy",
      "script" : "_index.maxDoc()"
    }
   }
  }
}'
```

Of course, it doesn't make much sense to use those statistics alone, like we just did, but with addition to other text-related information, they can be very useful.

Term level information

The next type of information that we can use in scripts is term level information. Elasticsearch allows us to use the following:

- `_index['field_name']['term'].df()`: Returns the number of documents the term appears in a given field
- `_index['field_name']['term'].ttf()`: Returns the sum of the number of times a given term appears in all documents in a given field
- `_index['field_name']['term'].tf()`: Returns the information about the number of times a given term appears in a given field in a document

To give a good example of how we can use the preceding statistics, let's index two documents by using the following commands:

```
curl -XPOST 'localhost:9200/scripts/doc/1' -d '{"name":"This is a
   document"}'
curl -XPOST 'localhost:9200/scripts/doc/2' -d '{"name":"This is a
   second document after the first document"}'
```

Now, let's try filtering documents on the basis of how many times a given term appears in the `name` field. For example, let's match only those documents that have in the `name` field the `document` term appearing at least twice. To do this, we could run the following query:

```
curl -XGET 'localhost:9200/scripts/_search?pretty' -d '{
  "query" : {
   "filtered" : {
```

```
  "query" : {
   "match_all" : {}
  },
  "filter" : {
   "script" : {
    "lang" : "groovy",
    "script": "_index[\"name\"][\"document\"].tf() > 1"
   }
  }
 }
}'
```

The result of the query would be as follows:

```
{
  "took" : 1,
  "timed_out" : false,
  "_shards" : {
    "total" : 5,
    "successful" : 5,
    "failed" : 0
  },
  "hits" : {
    "total" : 1,
    "max_score" : 1.0,
    "hits" : [ {
      "_index" : "scripts",
      "_type" : "doc",
      "_id" : "2",
      "_score" : 1.0,
      "_source":{"name":"This is a second document after the first document"}
    } ]
  }
}
```

As we can see, Elasticsearch did exactly what we wanted.

More advanced term information

In addition to already presented information, we can also use term positions, offsets, and payloads in our scripts. To get those, we can use one the `_index['field_name'].get('term', OPTION)` expression, where OPTION is one of the following:

- `_OFFSETS`: Term offsets
- `_PAYLOADS`: Term payloads
- `_POSITIONS`: Term positions

 Please remember that the field you want to get offsets or positions for needs to have this enabled during indexing.

In addition to this, we can also use the `_CACHE` option. It allows us to iterate multiple times over all the term positions. Options can also be combined using the | operator; for example, if you would like to get term offsets and positions for the document term in the `title` field, you could use the following expression in your script:

`_index['title'].get('document', _OFFSETS | _POSITIONS)`.

One thing to remember is that all the preceding options return an object called that, depending on the options we have chosen, contains the following information:

- `startOffset`: Start offset for the term
- `endOffset`: End offset for the term
- `payload`: Payload for the term
- `payloadAsInt(value)`: Returns payload for the term converted to integer or the value in case the current position doesn't have a payload
- `payloadAsFloat(value)`: Returns payload for the term converted to float or the value in case the current position doesn't have a payload
- `payloadAsString(value)`: Returns payload for the term converted to string or the value in case the current position doesn't have a payload
- `position`: Position of a term

To illustrate an example, let's create a new index with the following mappings:

```
curl -XPOST 'localhost:9200/scripts2' -d '{
 "mappings" : {
  "doc" : {
   "properties" : {
```

```
        "name" : { "type" : "string", "index_options" : "offsets" }
      }
    }
  }
}'
```

After this, we index two documents using the following commands:

```
curl -XPOST 'localhost:9200/scripts2/doc/1' -d '{"name":"This is the
  first document"}'
curl -XPOST 'localhost:9200/scripts2/doc/2' -d '{"name":"This is a
  second simple document"}'
```

Now, let's set the score of our documents to the sum of all the start positions for the document term in the name field. To do this, we run the following query:

```
curl -XGET 'localhost:9200/scripts2/_search?pretty' -d '{
 "query" : {
  "function_score" : {
   "query" : {
    "match_all" : {}
   },
   "script_score" : {
    "lang" : "groovy",
"script": "def termInfo = _index[\"name\"].get(\"document\",_OFFSETS);
def sum = 0; for (offset in termInfo) { sum += offset.startOffset; };
return sum;"
   }
  }
 }
}'
```

The results returned by Elasticsearch would be as follows:

```
    {
      "took" : 3,
      "timed_out" : false,
      "_shards" : {
        "total" : 5,
        "successful" : 5,
        "failed" : 0
      },
```

Chapter 3

```
    "hits" : {
      "total" : 2,
      "max_score" : 24.0,
      "hits" : [ {
        "_index" : "scripts2",
        "_type" : "doc",
        "_id" : "2",
        "_score" : 24.0,
        "_source":{"name":"This is a second simple document"}
      }, {
        "_index" : "scripts2",
        "_type" : "doc",
        "_id" : "1",
        "_score" : 18.0,
        "_source":{"name":"This is the first document"}
      } ]
    }
  }
```

As we can see, it works. If we look at the formatted script, we would see something like the following:

```
def termInfo = _index['name'].get('document',_OFFSETS);
def sum = 0;
for (offset in termInfo) {
  sum += offset.startOffset;
};
return sum;
```

As you can see, it is nothing sophisticated. First, we get the information about the offsets in an object; next, we create a variable to hold our offsets sum. Then, we have a loop for all the offsets information (we can have multiple instances of offsets for different occurrences of the same term in a field) and, finally, we return the sum that makes our score for the document to be set to the returned value.

> In addition to all what we talked about in the preceding section, we are also able to get information about term vectors if we turned them on during indexing. To do that, we can use the _index.termVectors() expression, which will return Apache Lucene Fields object instance. You can find more about the Fields object in Lucene Javadocs available at https://lucene.apache.org/core/4_9_0/core/org/apache/lucene/index/Fields.html.

Lucene expressions explained

Although marked as experimental, we decided to talk about it because this is a new and very good feature. The reason that makes Lucene expressions very handy is using them is very fast—their execution is as fast as native scripts, but yet they are like dynamic scripts with some limitations. This section will show you what you can do with Lucene expressions.

The basics

Lucene provides functionality to compile a JavaScript expression to a Java bytecode. This is how Lucene expressions work and this is why they are as fast as native Elasticsearch scripts. Lucene expressions can be used in the following Elasticsearch functionalities:

- Scripts responsible for sorting
- Aggregations that work on numeric fields
- In the `function_score` query in the `script_score` query
- In queries using `script_fields`

In addition to this, you have to remember that:

- Lucene expressions can be only used on numeric fields
- Stored fields can't be accessed using Lucene expressions
- Missing values for a field will be given a value of 0
- You can use `_score` to access the document score and `doc['field_name'].value` to access the value of a single valued numeric field in the document
- No loops are possible, only single statements

An example

Knowing the preceding information, we can try using Lucene expressions to modify the score of our documents. Let's get back to our `library` index and try to increase the score of the given document by 10% of the year it was originally released. To do this, we could run the following query:

```
curl -XGET 'localhost:9200/library/_search?pretty' -d '{
 "fields" : [ "_id", "_score", "title" ],
 "query" : {
  "function_score" : {
```

```
    "query" : {
     "match_all" : {}
    },
    "script_score" : {
     "lang" : "expression",
     "script" : "_score + doc[\"year\"].value * percentage",
     "params" : {
      "percentage" : 0.1
     }
    }
   }
  }
}'
```

The query is very simple, but let's discuss its structure. First, we are using the `match_all` query wrapped in the `function_score` query because we want all documents to match and we want to use script for scoring. We are also setting the script language to `expression` (by setting the `lang` property to `expression`) to tell Elasticsearch that our script is a Lucene expressions script. Of course, we provide the script and we parameterize it, just like we would with any other script. The results of the preceding query look as follows:

```
{
   "took" : 4,
   "timed_out" : false,
   "_shards" : {
     "total" : 5,
     "successful" : 5,
     "failed" : 0
   },
   "hits" : {
     "total" : 6,
     "max_score" : 197.1,
     "hits" : [ {
       "_index" : "library",
       "_type" : "book",
       "_id" : "2",
       "_score" : 197.1,
       "fields" : {
         "title" : [ "Catch-22" ],
         "_id" : "2"
```

```
            }
        }, {
            "_index" : "library",
            "_type" : "book",
            "_id" : "3",
            "_score" : 194.6,
            "fields" : {
              "title" : [ "The Complete Sherlock Holmes" ],
              "_id" : "3"
            }
        }, {
            "_index" : "library",
            "_type" : "book",
            "_id" : "1",
            "_score" : 193.9,
            "fields" : {
              "title" : [ "All Quiet on the Western Front" ],
              "_id" : "1"
            }
        }, {
            "_index" : "library",
            "_type" : "book",
            "_id" : "6",
            "_score" : 191.4,
            "fields" : {
              "title" : [ "The Peasants" ],
              "_id" : "6"
            }
        }, {
            "_index" : "library",
            "_type" : "book",
            "_id" : "4",
            "_score" : 189.6,
            "fields" : {
              "title" : [ "Crime and Punishment" ],
              "_id" : "4"
            }
        }, {
            "_index" : "library",
            "_type" : "book",
            "_id" : "5",
            "_score" : 178.4,
            "fields" : {
```

```
            "title" : [ "The Sorrows of Young Werther" ],
            "_id" : "5"
          }
        } ]
      }
    }
```

As we can see, Elasticsearch did what it was asked to do.

There is more

Of course, the provided example is a very simple one. If you are interested in what Lucene expressions provide, please visit the official Javadocs available at `http://lucene.apache.org/core/4_9_0/expressions/index.html?org/apache/lucene/expressions/js/package-summary.html`. The documents available at the given URL provide more information about what Lucene exposes in expressions module.

Summary

In this chapter, we extended our knowledge about query handling and data analysis. First of all, we discussed query rescore, which can help us when we need to recalculate the score of the top documents returned by a query. We also learned how to control multimatching queries. After that, we looked at two new aggregation types—one allowing us to get significant terms from a set of results and the other allowing documents grouping: a highly anticipated feature. We also discussed differences in relationship handling and approaches we can take when using Elasticsearch. Finally, we extended our knowledge about the Elasticsearch scripting module and we've learned what changes were introduced after Elasticsearch 1.0.

In the next chapter, we will try to improve our user query experience. We will start with user spelling mistakes and how Elasticsearch can help us by turning mistakes into good queries. We will also see what approaches we can take to handle user spelling mistake situations. After that, we will discuss improving query relevance on a given example. We will show you a query returning poor results and we will tune the query to match our needs.

4
Improving the User Search Experience

In the previous chapter, we extended our knowledge about query handling and data analysis. We started by looking at the query rescore that can help us when we need to recalculate the score of the top documents returned by a query. We controlled multi matching in Elasticsearch queries and looked at two new exciting aggregation types: significant terms aggregation and top hits aggregation. We discussed the differences in relationship handling and, finally, we extended our knowledge about the Elasticsearch scripting module and learned what the changes introduced were after the release of Elasticsearch 1.0. By the end of this chapter, we will have covered the following topics:

- Using the Elasticsearch Suggest API to correct user spelling mistakes
- Using the term suggester to suggest single words
- Using the phrase suggester to suggest whole phrases
- Configuring suggest capabilities to match your needs
- Using the completion suggester for the autocomplete functionality
- Improving query relevance by using different Elasticsearch functionalities

Correcting user spelling mistakes

One of the simplest ways to improve the user search experience is to correct their spelling mistakes either automatically or by just showing the correct query phrase and allowing the user to use it. For example, this is what **Google** shows us when we type in `elasticsaerch` instead of `Elasticsearch`:

Starting from 0.90.0 Beta1, Elasticsearch allows us to use the Suggest API to correct the user spelling mistakes. With the newer versions of Elasticsearch, the API was changed, bringing new features and becoming more and more powerful. In this section, we will try to bring you a comprehensive guide on how to use the Suggest API provided by Elasticsearch, both in simple use cases and in ones that require more configuration.

Testing data

For the purpose of this section, we decided that we need a bit more data than a few documents. In order to get the data we need, we decided to use the *Wikipedia* river plugin (https://github.com/elasticsearch/elasticsearch-river-wikipedia) to index some public documents from *Wikipedia*. First, we need to install the plugin by running the following command:

```
bin/plugin -install elasticsearch/elasticsearch-river-wikipedia/2.4.1
```

After that, we run the following command:

```
curl -XPUT 'localhost:9200/_river/wikipedia_river/_meta' -d '{
 "type" : "wikipedia",
 "index" : {
  "index" : "wikipedia"
 }
}'
```

Chapter 4

After that, Elasticsearch will start indexing the latest English dump from Wikipedia. If you look at the logs, you should see something like this:

```
[2014-08-28 22:35:01,566][INFO ][river.wikipedia          ] [Thing]
    [wikipedia][Wikipedia_river] creating wikipedia stream river for
    [http://download.wikimedia.org/enwiki/latest/enwiki-latest-pages-
    articles.xml.bz2]
[2014-08-28 22:35:01,568][INFO ][river.wikipedia          ] [Thing]
    [wikipedia][Wikipedia_river] starting wikipedia stream
```

As you can see, the river has started its work. After some time, you will have the data indexed in the index called `wikipedia`. If you want all data from the latest English Wikipedia dump to be indexed, you have to be patient, and we are not. The number of documents when we decided to cancel the indexation was 7080049. The index had about 19 GB in total size (without replicas).

Getting into technical details

Introduced in Version 0.90.3, the Suggest API is not the simplest one available in Elasticsearch. In order to get the desired suggest, we can either add a new `suggest` section to the query, or we can use a specialized REST endpoint that Elasticsearch exposes. In addition to this, we have multiple suggest implementations that allow us to correct user spelling mistakes, create the autocomplete functionality, and so on. All this gives us a powerful and flexible mechanism that we can use in order to make our search better.

Of course, the suggest functionality works on our data, so if we have a small set of documents in the index, the proper suggestion may not be found. When dealing with a smaller data set, Elasticsearch has fewer words in the index and, because of that, it has fewer candidates for suggestions. On the other hand, the more data, the bigger the possibility that we will have data that has some mistakes; however, we can configure Elasticsearch internals to handle such situations.

> Please note that the layout of this chapter is a bit different. We start by showing you a simple example on how to query for suggestions and how to interpret the Suggest API response without getting too much into all the configuration options. We do this because we don't want to overwhelm you with technical details, but we want to show you what you can achieve. The nifty configuration parameters come later.

Suggesters

Before we continue with querying and analyzing the responses, we would like to write a few words about the available suggester types—the functionality responsible for finding suggestions when using the Elasticsearch Suggest API. Elasticsearch allows us to use three suggesters currently: the term one, the phrase one, and the completion one. The first two allow us to correct spelling mistakes, while the third one allows us to develop a very fast autocomplete functionality. However, for now, let's not focus on any particular suggester type, but let's look on the query possibilities and the responses returned by Elasticsearch. We will try to show you the general principles, and then we will get into more details about each of the available suggesters.

Using the _suggest REST endpoint

There is a possibility that we can get suggestions for a given text by using a dedicated _suggest REST endpoint. What we need to provide is the text to analyze and the type of used suggester (term or phrase). So if we would like to get suggestions for the words graphics desiganer (note that we've misspelled the word on purpose), we would run the following query:

```
curl -XPOST 'localhost:9200/wikipedia/_suggest?pretty' -d '{
 "first_suggestion" : {
  "text" : "wordl war ii",
  "term" : {
   "field" : "_all"
  }
 }
}'
```

As you can see, each suggestion request is send to Elasticsearch in its own object with the name we chose (in the preceding case, it is first_suggestion). Next, we specify the text for which we want the suggestion to be returned using the text parameter. Finally, we add the suggester object, which is either term or phrase currently. The suggester object contains its configuration, which for the term suggester used in the preceding command, is the field we want to use for suggestions (the field property).

We can also send more than one suggestion at a time by adding multiple suggestion names. For example, if in addition to the preceding suggestion, we would also include a suggestion for the word raceing, we would use the following command:

```
curl -XPOST 'localhost:9200/wikipedia/_suggest?pretty' -d '{
 "first_suggestion" : {
```

```
    "text" : "wordl war ii",
    "term" : {
     "field" : "_all"
    }
  },
  "second_suggestion" : {
    "text" : "raceing",
    "term" : {
     "field" : "text"
    }
  }
}'
```

Understanding the REST endpoint suggester response

Let's now look at the example response we can expect from the `_suggest` REST endpoint call. Although the response will differ for each suggester type, let's look at the response returned by Elasticsearch for the first command we've sent in the preceding code that used the `term` suggester:

```
{
   "_shards" : {
      "total" : 5,
      "successful" : 5,
      "failed" : 0
   },
   "first_suggestion" : [ {
      "text" : "wordl",
      "offset" : 0,
      "length" : 5,
      "options" : [ {
         "text" : "world",
         "score" : 0.8,
         "freq" : 130828
      }, {
         "text" : "words",
         "score" : 0.8,
         "freq" : 20854
      }, {
```

```
          "text" : "wordy",
          "score" : 0.8,
          "freq" : 210
        }, {
          "text" : "woudl",
          "score" : 0.8,
          "freq" : 29
        }, {
          "text" : "worde",
          "score" : 0.8,
          "freq" : 20
        } ]
      }, {
        "text" : "war",
        "offset" : 6,
        "length" : 3,
        "options" : [ ]
      }, {
        "text" : "ii",
        "offset" : 10,
        "length" : 2,
        "options" : [ ]
      } ]
    }
```

As you can see in the preceding response, the `term` suggester returns a list of possible suggestions for each term that was present in the `text` parameter of our `first_suggestion` section. For each term, the `term` suggester will return an array of possible suggestions with additional information. Looking at the data returned for the `wordl` term, we can see the original word (the `text` parameter), its offset in the original `text` parameter (the `offset` parameter), and its length (the `length` parameter).

The `options` array contains suggestions for the given word and will be empty if Elasticsearch doesn't find any suggestions. Each entry in this array is a suggestion and is characterized by the following properties:

- `text`: This is the text of the suggestion.
- `score`: This is the suggestion score; the higher the score, the better the suggestion will be.
- `freq`: This is the frequency of the suggestion. The frequency represents how many times the word appears in documents in the index we are running the suggestion query against. The higher the frequency, the more documents will have the suggested word in its fields and the higher the chance that the suggestion is the one we are looking for.

Chapter 4

 Please remember that the phrase suggester response will differ from the one returned by the terms suggester, and we will discuss the response of the phrase suggester later in this section.

Including suggestion requests in query

In addition to using the _suggest REST endpoint, we can include the suggest section in addition to the query section in the normal query sent to Elasticsearch. For example, if we would like to get the same suggestion we've got in the first example but during query execution, we could send the following query:

```
curl -XGET 'localhost:9200/wikipedia/_search?pretty' -d '{
 "query" : {
  "match_all" : {}
 },
 "suggest" : {
  "first_suggestion" : {
   "text" : "wordl war ii",
   "term" : {
    "field" : "_all"
   }
  }
 }
}'
```

As you would expect, the response for the preceding query would be the query results and the suggestions as follows:

```
{
   "took" : 5,
   "timed_out" : false,
   "_shards" : {
     "total" : 5,
     "successful" : 5,
     "failed" : 0
   },
   "hits" : {
     "total" : 7080049,
     "max_score" : 1.0,
     "hits" : [
```

[363]

Improving the User Search Experience

```
            ...
        ]
      },
      "suggest" : {
        "first_suggestion" : [ {
          "text" : "wordl",
          "offset" : 0,
          "length" : 5,
          "options" : [ {
            "text" : "world",
            "score" : 0.8,
            "freq" : 130828
          }, {
            "text" : "words",
            "score" : 0.8,
            "freq" : 20854
          }, {
            "text" : "wordy",
            "score" : 0.8,
            "freq" : 210
          }, {
            "text" : "woudl",
            "score" : 0.8,
            "freq" : 29
          }, {
            "text" : "worde",
            "score" : 0.8,
            "freq" : 20
          } ]
        }, {
          "text" : "war",
          "offset" : 6,
          "length" : 3,
          "options" : [ ]
        }, {
          "text" : "ii",
          "offset" : 10,
          "length" : 2,
          "options" : [ ]
        } ]
      }
    }
```

Chapter 4

As we can see, we've got both search results and the suggestions whose structure we've already discussed earlier in this section.

There is one more possibility—if we have the same suggestion text, but we want multiple suggestion types, we can embed our suggestions in the `suggest` object and place the `text` property as the `suggest` object option. For example, if we would like to get suggestions for the `wordl war ii` text for the `text` field and for the `_all` field, we could run the following command:

```
curl -XGET 'localhost:9200/wikipedia/_search?pretty' -d '{
 "query" : {
  "match_all" : {}
 },
 "suggest" : {
  "text" : "wordl war ii",
  "first_suggestion" : {
   "term" : {
    "field" : "_all"
   }
  },
  "second_suggestion" : {
   "term" : {
    "field" : "text"
   }
  }
 }
}'
```

We now know how to make a query with suggestions returned or how to use the `_suggest` REST endpoint. Let's now get into more details of each of the available suggester types.

The term suggester

The `term` suggester works on the basis of the edit distance, which means that the suggestion with fewer characters that needs to be changed or removed to make the suggestion look like the original word is the best one. For example, let's take the words `worl` and `work`. In order to change the `worl` term to `work`, we need to change the `l` letter to `k`, so it means a distance of one. Of course, the text provided to the suggester is analyzed and then terms are chosen to be suggested. Let's now look at how we can configure the Elasticsearch `term` suggester.

Configuration

The Elasticsearch term suggester supports multiple configuration properties that allow us to tune its behavior to match our needs and to work with our data. Of course, we've already seen how it works and what it can give us, so we will concentrate on configuration now.

Common term suggester options

The common term suggester options can be used for all the suggester implementations that are based on the term suggester. Currently, these are the `phrase` suggester and, of course, the base `term` suggester. The available options are:

- `text`: This is the text we want to get the suggestions for. This parameter is required in order for the suggester to work.
- `field`: This is another required parameter. The field parameter allows us to set which field the suggestions should be generated for. For example, if we only want to consider title field terms in suggestions, we should set this parameter value to the title.
- `analyzer`: This is the name of the analyzer that should be used to analyze the text provided in the text parameter. If not set, Elasticsearch will use the analyzer used for the field provided by the field parameter.
- `size`: This is the maximum number of suggestions that are allowed to be returned by each term provided in the text parameter. It defaults to 5.
- `sort`: This allows us to specify how suggestions are sorted in the result returned by Elasticsearch. By default, this is set to a score, which tells Elasticsearch that the suggestions should be sorted by the suggestion score first, suggestion document frequency next, and finally, by the term. The second possible value is the frequency, which means that the results are first sorted by the document frequency, then by score, and finally, by the term.

- `suggest_mode`: This is another suggestion parameter that allows us to control which suggestions will be included in the Elasticsearch response. Currently, there are three values that can be passed to this parameter: `missing`, `popular`, and `always`. The default `missing` value will tell Elasticsearch to generate suggestions to only those words that are provided in the `text` parameter that doesn't exist in the index. If this property will be set to `popular`, then the term suggester will only suggest terms that are more popular (exist in more documents) than the original term for which the suggestion is generated. The last value, which is `always`, will result in a suggestion generated for each of the words in the `text` parameter.

Additional term suggester options

In addition to the common term suggester options, Elasticsearch allows us to use additional ones that will only make sense for the term suggester itself. These options are as follows:

- `lowercase_terms`: When set to `true`, this will tell Elasticsearch to make all terms that are produced from the `text` field after analysis, lowercase.
- `max_edits`: This defaults to 2 and specifies the maximum edit distance that the suggestion can have for it to be returned as a term suggestion. Elasticsearch allows us to set this value to 1 or 2. Setting this value to 1 can result in fewer suggestions or no suggestions at all for words with many spelling mistakes. In general, if you see many suggestions that are not correct, because of errors, you can try setting `max_edits` to 1.
- `prefix_length`: Because spelling mistakes usually don't appear at the beginning of the word, Elasticsearch allows us to set how much of the suggestion's initial characters must match with the initial characters of the original term. By default, this property is set to 1. If we are struggling with the suggester performance increasing, this value will improve the overall performance, because less suggestions will be needed to be processed by Elasticsearch.
- `min_word_length`: This defaults to 4 and specifies the minimum number of characters a suggestion must have in order to be returned on the suggestions list.
- `shard_size`: This defaults to the value specified by the `size` parameter and allows us to set the maximum number of suggestions that should be read from each shard. Setting this property to values higher than the `size` parameter can result in more accurate document frequency (this is because of the fact that terms are held in different shards for our indices unless we have a single shard index created) being calculated but will also result in degradation of the spellchecker's performance.

- `max_inspections`: This defaults to 5 and specifies how many candidates Elasticsearch will look at in order to find the words that can be used as suggestions. Elasticsearch will inspect a maximum of `shard_size` multiplied by the `max_inspections` candidates for suggestions. Setting this property to values higher than the default 5 may improve the suggester accuracy but can also decrease the performance.
- `min_doc_freq`: This defaults to 0, which means not enabled. It allows us to limit the returned suggestions to only those that appear in the number of documents higher than the value of this parameter (this is a per-shard value and not a globally counted one). For example, setting this parameter to 2 will result in suggestions that appear in at least two documents in a given shard. Setting this property to values higher than 0 can improve the quality of returned suggestions; however, it can also result in some suggestion not being returned because it has a low shard document frequency. This property can help us with removing suggestions that come from a low number of documents and may be erroneous. This parameter can be specified as a percentage; if we want to do this, its value must be less than 1. For example, 0.01 means 1 percent, which again means that the minimum frequency of the given suggestion needs to be higher than 1 percent of the total term frequency (of course, per shard).
- `max_term_freq`: This defaults to 0.01 and specifies the maximum number of documents the term from the `text` field can exist for it to be considered a candidate for spellchecking. Similar to the `min_doc_freq` parameter, it can be either provided as an absolute number (such as 4 or 100), or it can be a percentage value if it is beyond 1 (for example, 0.01 means 1 percent). Please remember that this is also a per-shard frequency. The higher the value of this property, the better the overall performance of the spellchecker will be. In general, this property is very useful when we want to exclude terms that appear in many documents from spellchecking, because they are usually correct terms.
- `accuracy`: This defaults to 0.5 and can be a number from 0 to 1. It specifies how similar the term should be when compared to the original one. The higher the value, the more similar the terms need to be. This value is used in comparison during string distance calculation for each of the terms from the original input.

- `string_distance`: This specifies which algorithm should be used to compare how similar terms are when comparing them to each other. This is an expert setting. These options are available: `internal`, which is the default comparison algorithm based on an optimized implementation of the Damerau Levenshtein similarity algorithm; `damerau_levenshtein`, which is the implementation of the Damerau Levenshtein string distance algorithm (http://en.wikipedia.org/wiki/Damerau%E2%80%93Levenshtein_distance); `levenstein`, which is the implementation of the Levenshtein distance (http://en.wikipedia.org/wiki/Levenshtein_distance), `jarowinkler`, which is an implementation of the Jaro-Winkler distance algorithm (http://en.wikipedia.org/wiki/Jaro%E2%80%93Winkler_distance), and finally, `ngram`, which is an N-gram based distance algorithm.

> Because of the fact that we've used the `terms` suggester during the initial examples, we decided to skip showing you how to query term suggesters and how the response looks. If you want to see how to query this suggester and what the response looks like, please refer to the beginning of the *Suggesters* section in this chapter.

The phrase suggester

The `term` suggester provides a great way to correct user spelling mistakes on a per-term basis. However, if we would like to get back phrases, it is not possible to do that when using this suggester. This is why the `phrase` suggester was introduced. It is built on top of the `term` suggester and adds additional phrase calculation logic to it so that whole phrases can be returned instead of individual terms. It uses N-gram based language models to calculate how good the suggestion is and will probably be a better choice to suggest whole phrases instead of the `term` suggester. The N-gram approach divides terms in the index into grams—word fragments built of one or more letters. For example, if we would like to divide the word `mastering` into bi-grams (a two letter N-gram), it would look like this: `ma as st te er ri in ng`.

> If you want to read more about N-gram language models, refer to the Wikipedia article available at http://en.wikipedia.org/wiki/Language_model#N-gram_models and continue from there.

Usage example

Before we continue with all the possibilities, we have to configure the phrase suggester; let's start with showing you an example of how to use it. This time, we will run a simple query to the `_search` endpoint with only the `suggests` section in it. We do this by running the following command:

```
curl -XGET 'localhost:9200/wikipedia/_search?pretty' -d '{
 "suggest" : {
  "text" : "wordl war ii",
  "our_suggestion" : {
   "phrase" : {
    "field" : "_all"
   }
  }
 }
}'
```

As you can see in the preceding command, it is almost the same as we sent when using the `term` suggester, but instead of specifying the `term` suggester type, we've specified the `phrase` type. The response to the preceding command will be as follows:

```
{
   "took" : 58,
   "timed_out" : false,
   "_shards" : {
     "total" : 5,
     "successful" : 5,
     "failed" : 0
   },
   "hits" : {
     "total" : 7080049,
     "max_score" : 1.0,
     "hits" : [
     ...
     ]
   },
   "suggest" : {
     "our_suggestion" : [ {
       "text" : "wordl war ii",
       "offset" : 0,
```

```
      "length" : 12,
      "options" : [ {
        "text" : "world war ii",
        "score" : 7.055394E-5
      }, {
        "text" : "words war ii",
        "score" : 2.3738032E-5
      }, {
        "text" : "wordy war ii",
        "score" : 3.575829E-6
      }, {
        "text" : "worde war ii",
        "score" : 1.1586584E-6
      }, {
        "text" : "woudl war ii",
        "score" : 1.0753317E-6
      } ]
    } ]
  }
}
```

As you can see, the response is very similar to the one returned by the term suggester, but instead of a single word being returned as the suggestion for each term from the text field, it is already combined and Elasticsearch returns whole phrases. Of course, we can configure additional parameters in the phrase section and, now, we will look at what parameters are available for usage. Of course, the returned suggestions are sorted by their score by default.

Configuration

The phrase suggester configuration parameter can be divided into three groups: basic parameters that define the general behavior, the smoothing models configuration to balance N-grams' weights, and candidate generators that are responsible for producing the list of terms suggestions that will be used to return final suggestions.

> Because the phrase suggester is based on the term suggester, it can also use some of the configuration options provided by it. These options are text, size, analyzer, and shard_size. Refer to the term suggester description earlier in this chapter to find out what they mean.

Basic configuration

In addition to properties mentioned in the preceding phrase, the suggester exposes the following basic options:

- `highlight`: This allows us to use suggestions highlighting. With the use of the `pre_tag` and `post_tag` properties, we can configure what prefix and postfix should be used to highlight suggestions. For example, if we would like to surround suggestions with the `<b>` and `</b>` tags, we should set `pre_tag` to `<b>` and `post_tag` to `</b>`.

- `gram_size`: This is the maximum size of the N-gram that is stored in the field and is specified by the `field` property. If the given field doesn't contain N-grams, this property should be set to `1` or not passed with the suggestion request at all. If not set, Elasticsearch will try to detect the proper value of this parameter by itself. For example, for fields using a `shingle` filter (http://www.elasticsearch.org/guide/en/elasticsearch/reference/current/analysis-shingle-tokenfilter.html), the value of this parameter will be set to the `max_shingle_size` property (of course, if not set explicitly).

- `confidence`: This is the parameter that allows us to limit the suggestion based on its score. The value of this parameter is applied to the score of the input phrase (the score is multiplied by the value of this parameter), and this score is used as a threshold for generated suggestions. If the suggestion score is higher than the calculated threshold, it will be included in the returned results; if not, then it will be dropped. For example, setting this parameter to `1.0` (which is the default value of it) will result in suggestions that are scored higher than the original phrase. On the other hand, setting it to `0.0` will result in the suggester returning all the suggestions (limited by the `size` parameter) no matter what their score is.

- `max_errors`: This is the property that allows us to specify the maximum number (or the percentage) of terms that can be erroneous (not correctly spelled) in order to create a correction using it. The value of this property can be either an integer number such as `1` or `5`, or it can be a float between 0 and 1, which will be treated as a percentage value. If we will set it as a float, it will specify the percentage of terms that can be erroneous. For example, a value of `0.5` will mean `50` percent. If we specify an integer number, such as `1` or `5`, Elasticsearch will treat it as a maximum number of erroneous terms. By default, it is set to `1`, which means that at most, a single term can be misspelled in a given correction.

- `separator`: This defaults to a whitespace character and specifies the separator that will be used to divide terms in the resulting bigram field.

- `force_unigrams`: This defaults to `true` and specifies whether the spellchecker should be forced to use a gram size of `1` (**unigram**).
- `token_limit`: This defaults to `10` and specifies the maximum number of tokens the corrections list can have in order for it to be returned. Setting this property to a value higher than the default one may improve the suggester accuracy at the cost of performance.
- `collate`: This allows us to check each suggestion against a specified query (using the `query` property inside the `collate` object) or filter (using the `filter` property inside the `collate` object). The provided query or filter is run as a template query and exposes the `{{suggestion}}` variable that represents the currently processed suggestion. By including an additional parameter called `prune` (in the `collate` object) and setting it to `true`, Elasticsearch will include the information if the suggestion matches the query or filter (this information will be included in the `collate_match` property in the results). In addition to this, the query preference can be included by using the `preference` property (which can take the same values as the ones used during the normal query processing).
- `real_word_error_likehood`: This is a percentage value, which defaults to `0.95` and specifies how likely it is that a term is misspelled even though it exists in the dictionary (built of the index). The default value of `0.95` tells Elasticsearch that `5%` of all terms that exist in its dictionary are misspelled. Lowering the value of this parameter will result in more terms being taken as misspelled ones even though they may be correct.

Let's now look at an example of using some of the preceding mentioned parameters, for example, suggestions highlighting. If we modify our initial phrase suggestion query and add highlighting, the command would look as follows:

```
curl -XGET 'localhost:9200/wikipedia/_search?pretty' -d '{
 "suggest" : {
  "text" : "wordl war ii",
  "our_suggestion" : {
   "phrase" : {
    "field" : "_all",
    "highlight" : {
     "pre_tag" : "<b>",
     "post_tag" : "</b>"
    },
    "collate" : {
```

```
      "prune" : true,
      "query" : {
       "match" : {
        "title" : "{{suggestion}}"
       }
      }
     }
    }
   }
  }
}'
```

The result returned by Elasticsearch for the preceding query would be as follows:

```
{
  "took" : 3,
  "timed_out" : false,
  "_shards" : {
    "total" : 5,
    "successful" : 5,
    "failed" : 0
  },
  "hits" : {
    "total" : 7080049,
    "max_score" : 1.0,
    "hits" : [
    ...
    ]
  },
    "suggest" : {
    "our_suggestion" : [ {
      "text" : "wordl war ii",
      "offset" : 0,
      "length" : 12,
      "options" : [ {
        "text" : "world war ii",
        "highlighted" : "<b>world</b> war ii",
        "score" : 7.055394E-5,
        "collate_match" : true
      }, {
        "text" : "words war ii",
```

```
          "highlighted" : "<b>words</b> war ii",
          "score" : 2.3738032E-5,
          "collate_match" : true
        }, {
          "text" : "wordy war ii",
          "highlighted" : "<b>wordy</b> war ii",
          "score" : 3.575829E-6,
          "collate_match" : true
        }, {
          "text" : "worde war ii",
          "highlighted" : "<b>worde</b> war ii",
          "score" : 1.1586584E-6,
          "collate_match" : true
        }, {
          "text" : "woudl war ii",
          "highlighted" : "<b>woudl</b> war ii",
          "score" : 1.0753317E-6,
          "collate_match" : true
        } ]
      } ]
    }
  }
```

As you can see, the suggestions were highlighted.

Configuring smoothing models

A **Smoothing model** is a functionality of the phrase suggester whose responsibility is to measure the balance between the weight of infrequent N-grams that don't exist in the index and the frequent ones that exist in the index. It is rather an expert option and if you want to modify these N-grams, you should check suggester responses for your queries in order to see whether your suggestions are proper for your case. Smoothing is used in language models to avoid situations where the probability of a given term is equal to zero. The Elasticsearch phrase suggester supports multiple smoothing models.

You can find out more about language models at http://en.wikipedia.org/wiki/Language_model.

In order to set which smoothing model we want to use, we need to add an object called smoothing and include a smoothing model name we want to use inside of it. Of course, we can include the properties we need or want to set for the given smoothing model. For example, we could run the following command:

```
curl -XGET 'localhost:9200/wikipedia/_search?pretty&size=0' -d '{
 "suggest" : {
  "text" : "wordl war ii",
  "generators_example_suggestion" : {
   "phrase" : {
    "analyzer" : "standard",
    "field" : "_all",
    "smoothing" : {
     "linear" : {
      "trigram_lambda" : 0.1,
      "bigram_lambda" : 0.6,
      "unigram_lambda" : 0.3
     }
    }
   }
  }
 }
}'
```

There are three smoothing models available in Elasticsearch. Let's now look at them.

Stupid backoff is the default smoothing model used by the Elasticsearch phrase suggester. In order to alter it or force its usage, we need to use the stupid_backoff name. The stupid backoff smoothing model is an implementation that will use a lower ordered N-gram (and will give it a discount equal to the value of the discount property) if the higher order N-gram count is equal to 0. To illustrate the example, let's assume that we use the ab bigram and the c unigram, which are common and exist in our index used by the suggester. However, we don't have the abc trigram present. What the stupid backoff model will do is that it will use the ab bigram model, because abc doesn't exist and, of course, the ab bigram model will be given a discount equal to the value of the discount property.

The stupid backoff model provides a single property that we can alter: discount. By default, it is set to 0.4, and it is used as a discount factor for the lower ordered N-gram model.

You can read more about N-gram smoothing models by looking at http://en.wikipedia.org/wiki/N-gram#Smoothing_techniques and http://en.wikipedia.org/wiki/Katz's_back-off_model (which is similar to the `stupid backoff` model described).

The **Laplace** smoothing model is also called additive smoothing. When used (to use it, we need to use the `laplace` value as its name), a constant value equal to the value of the `alpha` parameter (which is by `0.5` default) will be added to counts to balance weights of frequent and infrequent N-grams. As mentioned, the Laplace smoothing model can be configured using the `alpha` property, which is set to `0.5` by default. The usual values for this parameter are typically equal or below `1.0`.

You can read more about additive smoothing at http://en.wikipedia.org/wiki/Additive_smoothing.

Linear interpolation, the last smoothing model, takes the values of the lambdas provided in the configuration and uses them to calculate weights of trigrams, bigrams, and unigrams. In order to use the linear interpolation smoothing model, we need to provide the name of `linear` in the `smoothing` object in the suggester query and provide three parameters: `trigram_lambda`, `bigram_lambda`, and `unigram_lambda`. The sum of the values of the three mentioned parameters must be equal to `1`. Each of these parameters is a weight for a given type of N-gram; for example, the `bigram_lambda` parameter value will be used as a weights for bigrams.

Configuring candidate generators

In order to return possible suggestions for a term from the text provided in the `text` parameter, Elasticsearch uses so-called **candidate generators**. You can think of candidate generators as term suggesters although they are not exactly the same — they are similar, because they are used for every single term in the query provided to suggester. After the candidate terms are returned, they are scored in combination with suggestions for other terms from the text, and this way, the phrase suggestions are built.

Currently, **direct generators** are the only candidate generators available in Elasticsearch, although we can expect more of them to be present in the future. Elasticsearch allows us to provide multiple direct generators in a single phrase suggester request. We can do this by providing the list named `direct_generators`. For example, we could run the following command:

```
curl -XGET 'localhost:9200/wikipedia/_search?pretty&size=0' -d '{
  "suggest" : {
    "text" : "wordl war ii",
```

```
    "generators_example_suggestion" : {
      "phrase" : {
        "analyzer" : "standard",
        "field" : "_all",
        "direct_generator" : [
          {
            "field" : "_all",
            "suggest_mode" : "always",
            "min_word_len" : 2
          },
          {
            "field" : "_all",
            "suggest_mode" : "always",
            "min_word_len" : 3
          }
        ]
      }
    }
}'
```

The response should be very similar to the one previously shown, so we decided to omit it.

Configuring direct generators

Direct generators allow us to configure their behavior by using a parameter similar to that exposed by the terms suggester. These common configuration parameters are `field` (which is required), `size`, `suggest_mode`, `max_edits`, `prefix_length`, `min_word_length` (in this case, it defaults to 4), `max_inspections`, `min_doc_freq`, and `max_term_freq`. Refer to the `term` suggester description to see what these parameters mean.

In addition to the mentioned properties, direct generators allow us to use the `pre_filter` and `post_filter` properties. These two properties allow us to provide an analyzer name that Elasticsearch will use. The analyzer specified by the `pre_filter` property will be used for each term passed to the direct generator, and the filter specified by the `post_filter` property will be used after it is returned by the direct generator, just before these terms are passed to the phrase scorer for scoring.

For example, we could use the filtering functionality of the direct generators to include synonyms just before the suggestions are passed to the direct generator using the `pre_filter` property. For example, let's update our `wikipedia` index settings to include simple synonyms, and let's use them in filtering. To do this, we start with updating the settings with the following commands:

```
curl -XPOST 'localhost:9200/wikipedia/_close'
curl -XPUT 'localhost:9200/wikipedia/_settings' -d '{
  "settings" : {
   "index" : {
    "analysis": {
     "analyzer" : {
      "sample_synonyms_analyzer": {
       "tokenizer": "standard",
       "filter": [
        "sample_synonyms"
       ]
      }
     },
     "filter": {
      "sample_synonyms": {
       "type" : "synonym",
       "synonyms" : [
        "war => conflict"
       ]
      }
     }
    }
   }
  }
}'
curl -XPOST 'localhost:9200/wikipedia/_open'
```

Improving the User Search Experience

First, we need to close the index, update the setting, and then open it again because Elasticsearch won't allow us to change analysis settings on opened indices. Now we can test our direct generator with synonyms with the following command:

```
curl -XGET 'localhost:9200/wikipedia/_search?pretty&size=0' -d '{
 "suggest" : {
  "text" : "wordl war ii",
  "generators_with_synonyms" : {
   "phrase" : {
    "analyzer" : "standard",
    "field" : "_all",
    "direct_generator" : [
     {
      "field" : "_all",
      "suggest_mode" : "always",
      "post_filter" : "sample_synonyms_analyzer"
     }
    ]
   }
  }
 }
}'
```

The response to the preceding command should be as follows:

```
{
    "took" : 47,
    "timed_out" : false,
    "_shards" : {
      "total" : 5,
      "successful" : 5,
      "failed" : 0
    },
    "hits" : {
      "total" : 7080049,
      "max_score" : 0.0,
      "hits" : [ ]
    },
    "suggest" : {
      "generators_with_synonyms" : [ {
        "text" : "wordl war ii",
```

```
        "offset" : 0,
        "length" : 12,
        "options" : [ {
          "text" : "world war ii",
          "score" : 7.055394E-5
        }, {
          "text" : "words war ii",
          "score" : 2.4085322E-5
        }, {
          "text" : "world conflicts ii",
          "score" : 1.4253577E-5
        }, {
          "text" : "words conflicts ii",
          "score" : 4.8214292E-6
        }, {
          "text" : "wordy war ii",
          "score" : 4.1216194E-6
        } ]
      } ]
    }
  }
```

As you can see, instead of the war term, the conflict term was returned for some of the phrase suggester results. So, our synonyms' configuration was taken into consideration. However, please remember that the synonyms were taken before the scoring of the fragments, so it can happen that the suggestions with the synonyms are not the ones that are scored the most, and you will not be able to see them in the suggester results.

The completion suggester

With the release of Elasticsearch 0.90.3, we were given the possibility to use a prefix-based suggester. It allows us to create the autocomplete functionality in a very performance-effective way because of storing complicated structures in the index instead of calculating them during query time. Although this suggester is not about correcting user spelling mistakes, we thought that it will be good to show at least a simple example of this highly efficient suggester.

The logic behind the completion suggester

The prefix suggester is based on the data structure called **Finite State Transducer** (**FST**) (http://en.wikipedia.org/wiki/Finite_state_transducer). Although it is highly efficient, it may require significant resources to build on systems with large amounts of data in them: systems that Elasticsearch is perfectly suitable for. If we would like to build such a structure on the nodes after each restart or cluster state change, we may lose performance. Because of this, the Elasticsearch creators decided to use an FST-like structure during index time and store it in the index so that it can be loaded into the memory when needed.

Using the completion suggester

To use a prefix-based suggester we need to properly index our data with a dedicated field type called `completion`. It stores the FST-like structure in the index. In order to illustrate how to use this suggester, let's assume that we want to create an autocomplete feature to allow us to show book authors, which we store in an additional index. In addition to authors' names, we want to return the identifiers of the books they wrote in order to search for them with an additional query. We start with creating the `authors` index by running the following command:

```
curl -XPOST 'localhost:9200/authors' -d '{
 "mappings" : {
  "author" : {
   "properties" : {
    "name" : { "type" : "string" },
    "ac" : {
     "type" : "completion",
     "index_analyzer" : "simple",
     "search_analyzer" : "simple",
     "payloads" : true
    }
   }
  }
 }
}'
```

Our index will contain a single type called author. Each document will have two fields: the name field, which is the name of the author, and the ac field, which is the field we will use for autocomplete. The ac field is the one we are interested in; we've defined it using the completion type, which will result in storing the FST-like structure in the index. In addition to this, we've used the simple analyzer for both index and query time. The last thing is payload, which is the additional information we will return along with the suggestion; in our case, it will be an array of book identifiers.

The type property for the field we will use for autocomplete is mandatory and should be set to completion. By default, the search_analyzer and index_analyzer properties will be set to simple and the payloads property will be set to false.

Indexing data

To index the data, we need to provide some additional information in addition to what we usually provide during indexing. Let's look at the following commands that index two documents describing authors:

```
curl -XPOST 'localhost:9200/authors/author/1' -d '{
 "name" : "Fyodor Dostoevsky",
 "ac" : {
  "input" : [ "fyodor", "dostoevsky" ],
  "output" : "Fyodor Dostoevsky",
  "payload" : { "books" : [ "123456", "123457" ] }
 }
}'
curl -XPOST 'localhost:9200/authors/author/2' -d '{
 "name" : "Joseph Conrad",
 "ac" : {
  "input" : [ "joseph", "conrad" ],
  "output" : "Joseph Conrad",
  "payload" : { "books" : [ "121211" ] }
 }
}'
```

Notice the structure of the data for the `ac` field. We provide the `input`, `output`, and `payload` properties. The `payload` property is used to provide additional information that will be returned. The `input` property is used to provide input information that will be used to build the FST-like structure and will be used to match the user input to decide whether the document should be returned by the suggester. The `output` property is used to tell the suggester which data should be returned for the document.

> Please remember that the `payload` property must be a JSON object that starts with a { character and ends with a } character.

If the `input` and `output` property is the same in your case and you don't want to store payloads, you may index the documents just like you usually index your data. For example, the command to index our first document would look like this:

```
curl -XPOST 'localhost:9200/authors/author/3' -d '{
 "name" : "Stanislaw Lem",
 "ac" : [ "Stanislaw Lem" ]
}'
```

Querying data

Finally, let's look at how to query our indexed data. If we would like to find documents that have authors starting with `fyo`, we would run the following command:

```
curl -XGET 'localhost:9200/authors/_suggest?pretty' -d '{
 "authorsAutocomplete" : {
  "text" : "fyo",
  "completion" : {
   "field" : "ac"
  }
 }
}'
```

Before we look at the results, let's discuss the query. As you can see, we've run the command to the `_suggest` endpoint, because we don't want to run a standard query; we are just interested in autocomplete results. The rest of the query is exactly the same as the standard suggester query run against the `_suggest` endpoint, with the query type set to `completion`.

The results returned by Elasticsearch for the preceding query look as follows:

```
{
  "_shards" : {
    "total" : 5,
    "successful" : 5,
    "failed" : 0
  },
  "authorsAutocomplete" : [ {
    "text" : "fyo",
    "offset" : 0,
    "length" : 3,
    "options" : [ {
      "text" : "Fyodor Dostoevsky",
      "score" : 1.0,
      "payload":{"books":["123456","123457"]}
    } ]
  } ]
}
```

As you can see, in response, we've got the document we were looking for along with the payload information, which is the identifier of the books for that author.

Custom weights

By default, the term frequency will be used to determine the weight of the document returned by the prefix suggester. However, this may not be the best solution when you have multiple shards for your index, or your index is composed of multiple segments. In such cases, it is useful to define the weight of the suggestion by specifying the `weight` property for the field defined as `completion`; the `weight` property should be set to a positive integer value and not a float one like the boost for queries and documents. The higher the `weight` property value, the more important the suggestion is. This gives us plenty of opportunities to control how the returned suggestions will be sorted.

For example, if we would like to specify a weight for the first document in our example, we would run the following command:

```
curl -XPOST 'localhost:9200/authors/author/1' -d '{
 "name" : "Fyodor Dostoevsky",
 "ac" : {
  "input" : [ "fyodor", "dostoevsky" ],
  "output" : "Fyodor Dostoevsky",
```

```
    "payload" : { "books" : [ "123456", "123457" ] },
    "weight" : 80
  }
}'
```

Now, if we would run our example query, the results would be as follows:

```
{
  "_shards" : {
    "total" : 5,
    "successful" : 5,
    "failed" : 0
  },
  "authorsAutocomplete" : [ {
    "text" : "fyo",
    "offset" : 0,
    "length" : 3,
    "options" : [ {
      "text" : "Fyodor Dostoevsky",
      "score" : 80.0,
      "payload":{"books":["123456","123457"]}
    } ]
  } ]
}
```

See how the score of the result changed. In our initial example, it was `1.0` and, now, it is `80.0`; this is because we've set the weight parameter to `80` during the indexing.

Additional parameters

There are three additional parameters supported by the suggester that we didn't mention till now. They are `max_input_length`, `preserve_separators`, and `preserve_position_increments`. Both `preserve_separators` and `preserve_position_increments` can be set to `true` or `false`. When setting the `preserve_separators` parameter to `false`, the suggester will omit separators such as whitespace (of course, proper analysis is required). Setting the `preserve_position_increments` parameter to `false` is needed if the first word in the suggestion is a stop word and we are using an analyzer that throws stop words away. For example, if we have `The Clue` as our document and the `The` word will be discarded by the analyzer by setting `preserve_position_increments` to `false`, the suggester will be able to return our document by specifying `c` as `text`.

The `max_input_length` property is set to 50 by default and specifies the maximum input length in UTF-16 characters. This limit is used at indexing time to limit the total number of characters stored in the internal structures.

Improving the query relevance

Elasticsearch and search engines in general are used for searching. Of course, some use cases may require browsing some portion of the indexed data; sometimes, it is even needed to export whole query results. However, in most cases, scoring is one of the factors that play a major role in the search process. As we said in the *Default Apache Lucene scoring explained* section of *Chapter 2*, *Power User Query DSL*, Elasticsearch leverages the Apache Lucene library document scoring capabilities and allows you to use different query types to manipulate the score of results returned by our queries. What's more, we can change the low-level algorithm used to calculate the score that we will describe in the *Altering Apache Lucene scoring* section of *Chapter 6*, *Low-level Index Control*.

Given all this, when we start designing our queries, we usually go for the simplest query that returns the documents we want. However, given all the things we can do in Elasticsearch when it comes to scoring control, such queries return results that are not the best when it comes to the user search experience. This is because Elasticsearch can't guess what our business logic is and what documents are the ones that are the best from our point of view when running a query. In this section, we will try to follow a real-life example of query relevance tuning. We want to make this chapter a bit different compared to the other ones. Instead of only giving you an insight, we have decided to give you a full example of when the query tuning process may look like. Of course, remember that this is only an example and you should adjust this process to match your organization needs. Some of the examples you find in this section may be general purpose ones, and when using them in your own application, make sure that they make sense to you.

Just to give you a little insight into what is coming, we will start with a simple query that returns the results we want, we will alter the query by introducing different Elasticsearch queries to make the results better, we will use filters, we will lower the score of the documents we think of as garbage, and finally, we will introduce faceting to render drill-down menus for users to allow the narrowing of results.

Data

Of course, in order to show you the results of the query modifications that we perform, we need data. We would love to show you the real-life data we were working with, but we can't, as our clients wouldn't like this. However, there is a solution to that: for the purpose of this section, we have decided to index Wikipedia data. To do that, we will reuse the installed Wikipedia river plugin that we installed in the *Correcting user spelling mistakes* section earlier in this chapter.

Improving the User Search Experience

The Wikipedia river will create the `wikipedia` index for us if there is not an existing one. Because we already have such an index, we will delete it. We could go with the same index, but we know that we will need to adjust the index fields, because we need some additional analysis logic, and in order to not reindex the data, we create the index upfront.

> Remember to remove the old river before adding the new one. To remove the old river, you should just run the following command:
> `curl -XDELETE 'localhost:9200/_river/wikipedia_river'`

In order to reimport documents, we use the following commands:

```
curl -XDELETE 'localhost:9200/wikipedia'
curl -XPOST 'localhost:9200/wikipedia' -d'{
   "settings": {
      "index": {
         "analysis": {
            "analyzer": {
               "keyword_ngram": {
                  "filter": [
                     "lowercase"
                  ],
                  "tokenizer": "ngram"
               }
            }
         }
      }
   },
   "mappings": {
      "page": {
         "properties": {
            "category": {
               "type": "string",
               "fields": {
                  "untouched": {
```

```
                "type": "string",
                "index": "not_analyzed"
            }
        }
    },
    "disambiguation": {
        "type": "boolean"
    },
    "link": {
        "type": "string",
        "index": "not_analyzed"
    },
    "redirect": {
        "type": "boolean"
    },
    "redirect_page": {
        "type": "string"
    },
    "special": {
        "type": "boolean"
    },
    "stub": {
        "type": "boolean"
    },
    "text": {
        "type": "string"
    },
    "title": {
        "type": "string",
        "fields": {
            "ngram": {
                "type": "string",
                "analyzer": "keyword_ngram"
            },
            "simple": {
```

```
                    "type": "string",
                    "analyzer": "simple"
                }
            }
          }
        }
      }
    }
}'
```

For now, what we have to know is that we have a `page` type that we are interested in and whether that represents a Wikipedia page. We will use two fields for searching: the `text` and `title` fields. The first one holds the content of the page and the second one is responsible for holding its title.

What we have to do next is start the Wikipedia river. Because we were interested in the latest data in order to instantiate the river and start indexing, we've used the following command:

```
curl -XPUT 'localhost:9200/_river/wikipedia/_meta' -d '{
 "type" : "wikipedia"
}'
```

That's all; Elasticsearch will index the newest Wikipedia dump available to the index called `wikipedia`. All we have to do is wait. We were not patient, and we decided that we'll only index the first 10 million documents and, after our Wikipedia river hit that number of documents, we deleted it. We checked the final number of documents by running the following command:

```
curl -XGET 'localhost:9200/wikipedia/_search?q=*&size=0&pretty'
```

The response was as follows:

```
{
  "took" : 5,
  "timed_out" : false,
  "_shards" : {
    "total" : 5,
    "successful" : 5,
    "failed" : 0
  },
  "hits" : {
    "total" : 10425136,
```

```
    "max_score" : 0.0,
    "hits" : [ ]
  }
}
```

We can see that we have 10,425,136 documents in the index.

> When running examples from this chapter, please consider the fact that the data we've indexed changes over time, so the examples shown in this chapter may result in a different document if we run it after some time.

The quest for relevance improvement

After we have our indexed data, we are ready to begin the process of searching. We will start from the beginning using a simple query that will return the results we are interested in. After that, we will try to improve the query relevance. We will also try to pay attention to performance and notice the performance changes when they are most likely to happen.

The standard query

As you know, Elasticsearch includes the content of the documents in the _all field by default. So, why do we need to bother with specifying multiple fields in a query when we can use a single one, right? Going in that direction, let's assume that we've constructed the following query and now we send it to Elasticsearch to retrieve our precious documents using the following command:

```
curl -XGET 'localhost:9200/wikipedia/_search?fields=title&pretty' -d'
{
   "query": {
      "match": {
         "_all": {
            "query": "australian system",
            "operator": "OR"
         }
      }
   }
}'
```

Because we are only interested in getting the `title` field (Elasticsearch will use the `_source` field to return the title field, because the title field is not stored), we've added the `fields=title` request parameter and, of course, we want it to be in a human-friendly formatting, so we added the `pretty` parameter as well.

However, the results were not as perfect as we would like them to be. The first page of documents were as follows (the whole JSON response can be found in the `response_query_standard.json` file provided with the book):

```
Australian Honours System
List of Australian Awards
Australian soccer league
Australian football league system
AANBUS
Australia Day Honours
Australian rating system
TAAATS
Australian Arbitration system
Western Australian Land Information System (WALIS)
```

While looking at the title of the documents, it seems that some of these that contain both words from the query have a lower rank than the others. Let's try to improve things.

The multi match query

What we can do first is not use the `_all` field at all. The reason for this is that we need to tell Elasticsearch what importance each of the fields has. For example, in our case, the `title` field is more important than the content of the field, which is stored in the `text` field. In order to inform this to ElasticSearch, we will use the `multi_match` query. To send such a query to Elasticsearch, we will use the following command:

```
curl -XGET 'localhost:9200/wikipedia/_search?fields=title&pretty' -d'
{
   "query": {
      "multi_match": {
         "query": "australian system",
         "fields": [
            "title^100",
            "text^10",
            "_all"
         ]
```

                }
            }
}'

The first page of results of the preceding query was as follows (the whole JSON response can be found in the response_query_multi_match.json file provided with the book):

```
Australian Antarctic Building System
Australian rating system
Australian Series System
Australian Arbitration system
Australian university system
Australian Integrated Forecast System
Australian Education System
The Australian electoral system
Australian preferential voting system
Australian Honours System
```

Instead of running the query against a single _all field, we chose to run it against the title, text, and _all fields. In addition to this, we introduced boosting: the higher the boost value, the more important the field will be (the default boost value for a field is 1.0). So, we said that the title field is more important than the text field, and the text field is more important than _all.

If you look at the results now, they seem to be a bit more relevant but still not as good as we would like them to be. For example, look at the first and second documents on the results list. The first document's title is Australian Antarctic Building System, the second document's title is Australian rating system, and so on. I would like the second document to be higher than the first one.

Phrases comes into play

The next idea that should come into our minds is the introduction of phrase queries so that we can overcome the problem that was described previously. However, we still need the documents that don't have phrases included in the results just below the ones with the phrases present. So, we need to modify our query by adding the bool query on top. Our current query will come into the must section and the phrase query will go into the should section. An example command that sends the modified query would look as follows:

```
curl -XGET 'localhost:9200/wikipedia/_search?fields=title&pretty' -d'
{
    "query": {
```

```
        "bool": {
           "must": [
              {
                 "multi_match": {
                    "query": "australian system",
                    "fields": [
                       "title^100",
                       "text^10",
                       "_all"
                    ]
                 }
              }
           ],
           "should": [
              {
                 "match_phrase": {
                    "title": "australian system"
                 }
              },
              {
                 "match_phrase": {
                    "text": "australian system"
                 }
              }
           ]
        }
     }
}'
```

Now, if we look at the top results, they are as follows (the whole response can be found in the `response_query_phrase.json` file provided with the book):

```
        Australian honours system
        Australian Antarctic Building System
        Australian rating system
        Australian Series System
        Australian Arbitration system
```

```
              Australian university system
              Australian Integrated Forecast System
              Australian Education System
              The Australian electoral system
              Australian preferential voting system
```

We would really like to stop further query optimization, but our results are still not as good as we would like them to be, although they are a bit better. This is because we don't have all the phrases matched. What we can do is introduce the `slop` parameter, which will allow us to define how many words in between can be present for a match to be considered a phrase match. For example, our `australian system` query will be considered a phrase match for a document with the `australian education system` title and with a `slop` parameter of `1` or more. So, let's send our query with the `slop` parameter present by using the following command:

```
curl -XGET 'localhost:9200/wikipedia/_search?fields=title&pretty' -d'
{
   "query": {
      "bool": {
         "must": [
            {
               "multi_match": {
                  "query": "australian system",
                  "fields": [
                     "title^100",
                     "text^10",
                     "_all"
                  ]
               }
            }
         ],
         "should": [
            {
               "match_phrase": {
                  "title": {
                     "query": "australian system",
                     "slop": 1
                  }
               }
```

```
        },
        {
          "match_phrase": {
            "text": {
              "query": "australian system",
              "slop": 1
            }
          }
        }
      ]
    }
  }
}'
```

Now, let's look at the results (the whole response can be found in the `response_query_phrase_slop.json` file provided with the book):

```
Australian Honours System
Australian honours system
Wikipedia:Articles for deletion/Australian university system
Australian rating system
Australian Series System
Australian Arbitration system
Australian university system
Australian Education System
The Australian electoral system
Australian Legal System
```

It seems that the results are now better. However, we can always do some more tweaking and see whether we can get some more improvements.

Let's throw the garbage away

What we can do now is that we can remove the garbage from our results. We can do this by removing redirect documents and special documents (for example, the ones that are marked for deletion). To do this, we will introduce a filter so that it doesn't mess with the scoring of other results (because filters are not scored). What's more, Elasticsearch will be able to cache filter results and reuse them in our queries and speed up their execution. The command that sends our query with filters will look as follows:

```
curl -XGET 'localhost:9200/wikipedia/_search?fields=title&pretty' -d'
{
```

```
"query": {
   "filtered": {
      "query": {
         "bool": {
            "must": [
               {
                  "multi_match": {
                     "query": "australian system",
                     "fields": [
                        "title^100",
                        "text^10",
                        "_all"
                     ]
                  }
               }
            ],
            "should": [
               {
                  "match_phrase": {
                     "title": {
                        "query": "australian system",
                        "slop": 1
                     }
                  }
               },
               {
                  "match_phrase": {
                     "text": {
                        "query": "australian system",
                        "slop": 1
                     }
                  }
               }
            ]
         }
      },
```

```
            "filter": {
                "bool": {
                    "must_not": [
                        {
                            "term": {
                                "redirect": "true"
                            }
                        },
                        {
                            "term": {
                                "special": "true"
                            }
                        }
                    ]
                }
            }
        }
    }
}'
```

The results returned by it will look as follows:

```
Australian honours system
Australian Series System
Australian soccer league system
Australian Antarctic Building System
Australian Integrated Forecast System
Australian Defence Air Traffic System
Western Australian Land Information System
The Australian Advanced Air Traffic System
Australian archaeology
Australian Democrats
```

Isn't it better now? We think it is, but we can still make even more improvements.

Now, we boost

If you ever need to boost the importance of the phrase queries that we've introduced, we can do that by wrapping a phrase query with the `function_score` query. For example, if we want to have a phrase for the `title` field to have a boost of `1000`, we need to change the following part of the preceding query:

```
...
{
    "match_phrase": {
        "title": {
            "query": "australian system",
            "slop": 1
        }
    }
}
...
```

We need to replace the preceding part of the query with the following one:

```
...
{
    "function_score": {
        "boost_factor": 1000,
        "query": {
            "match_phrase": {
                "title": {
                    "query": "australian system",
                    "slop": 1
                }
            }
        }
    }
}
...
```

After introducing the preceding change, the documents with phrases will be scored even higher than before, but we will leave it for you to test.

Improving the User Search Experience

Performing a misspelling-proof search

If you look back at the mappings, you will see that we have the `title` field defined as multi field and one of the fields is analyzed with a defined `ngram` analyzer. By default, it will create bigrams, so from the `system` word, it will create the `sy ys st te em` bigrams. Imagine that we could drop some of them during searches to make our search misspelling-proof. For the purpose of showing how we can do this, let's take a simple misspelled query sent with the following command:

```
curl -XGET 'localhost:9200/wikipedia/_search?fields=title&pretty' -d'
{
    "query": {
        "query_string": {
            "query": "austrelia",
            "default_field": "title",
            "minimum_should_match": "100%"
        }
    }
}'
```

The results returned by Elasticsearch would be as follows:

```
{
  "took" : 10,
  "timed_out" : false,
  "_shards" : {
    "total" : 5,
    "successful" : 5,
    "failed" : 0
  },
  "hits" : {
    "total" : 0,
    "max_score" : null,
    "hits" : [ ]
  }
}
```

Chapter 4

We've sent a query that is misspelled against the `title` field and because there is no document with the misspelled term, we didn't get any results. So now, let's leverage the `title.ngram` field capabilities and omit some of the bigrams so that Elasticsearch can find some documents. Our command with a modified query looks as follows:

```
curl -XGET 'localhost:9200/wikipedia/_search?fields=title&pretty' -d'
{
    "query": {
        "query_string": {
            "query": "austrelia",
            "default_field": "title.ngram",
            "minimum_should_match": "85%"
        }
    }
}'
```

We changed the `default_field` property from `title` to `title.ngram` in order to inform Elasticsearch, the one with bigrams indexed. In addition to that, we've introduced the `minimum_should_match` property, and we've set it to 85 percent. This allows us to inform Elasticsearch that we don't want all the terms produced by the analysis process to match but only a percentage of them, and we don't care which terms these are.

> Lowering the value of the `minimum_should_match` property will give us more documents but a less accurate search. Setting the value of the `minimum_should_match` property to a higher one will result in the decrease of the documents returned, but they will have more bigrams similar to the query ones and, thus, they will be more relevant.

The top results returned by the preceding query are as follows (the whole result's response can be found in a file called `response_ngram.json` provided with the book):

```
Aurelia (Australia)
Australian Kestrel
Austrlia
Australian-Austrian relations
Australia-Austria relations
Australia–Austria relations
Australian religion
CARE Australia
Care Australia
Felix Austria
```

[401]

Improving the User Search Experience

If you would like to see how to use the Elasticsearch suggester to handle spellchecking, refer to the *Correcting user spelling mistakes* section in this chapter.

Drill downs with faceting

The last thing we want to mention is faceting and aggregations. You can do multiple things with it, for example, calculating histograms, statistics for fields, geo distance ranges, and so on. However, one thing that can help your users get the data they are interested in is terms faceting. For example, if you go to `amazon.com` and enter the `kids shoes` query, you would see the following screenshot:

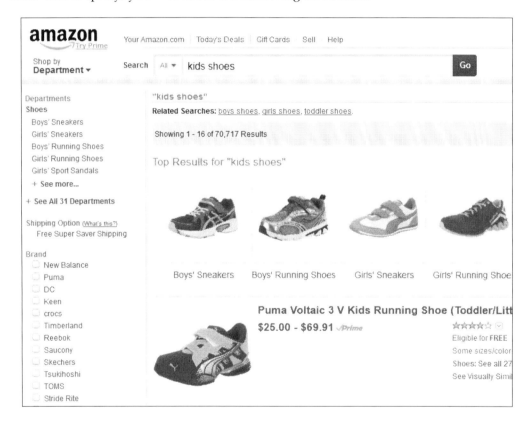

You can narrow down the results by the brand (the left-hand side of the page). The list of brands is not static and is generated on the basis of the results returned. We can achieve the same with terms faceting in Elasticsearch.

Chapter 4

 Please note that we are showing both queries with faceting and with aggregations. Faceting is deprecated and will be removed from Elasticsearch at some point. However, we know that our readers still use it and for that, we show different variants of the same query.

So now, let's get back to our Wikipedia data. Let's assume that we like to allow our users to choose the category of documents they want to see after the initial search. In order to do that, we add the facets section to our query (however, in order to simplify the example, let's use the match_all query instead of our complicated one) and send the new query with the following command:

```
curl -XGET 'localhost:9200/wikipedia/_search?fields=title&pretty' -d '{
    "query": {
        "match_all": {}
    },
    "facets": {
        "category_facet": {
            "terms": {
                "field": "category.untouched",
                "size": 10
            }
        }
    }
}'
```

As you can see, we've run the facet calculation on the category.untouched field, because terms faceting is calculated on the indexed data. If we run it on the category field, we will get a single term in the faceting result, and we want the whole category to be present. The faceting section of the results returned by the preceding query looks as follows (the entire result's response can be found in a file called response_query_facets.json provided with the book):

```
        "facets" : {
          "category_facet" : {
            "_type" : "terms",
            "missing" : 6175806,
            "total" : 16732022,
            "other" : 16091291,
            "terms" : [ {
              "term" : "Living people",
```

```
          "count" : 483501
        }, {
          "term" : "Year of birth missing (living people)",
          "count" : 39413
        }, {
          "term" : "English-language films",
          "count" : 22917
        }, {
          "term" : "American films",
          "count" : 16139
        }, {
          "term" : "Year of birth unknown",
          "count" : 15561
        }, {
          "term" : "The Football League players",
          "count" : 14020
        }, {
          "term" : "Main Belt asteroids",
          "count" : 13968
        }, {
          "term" : "Black-and-white films",
          "count" : 12945
        }, {
          "term" : "Year of birth missing",
          "count" : 12442
        }, {
          "term" : "English footballers",
          "count" : 9825
        } ]
      }
    }
```

By default, we've got the faceting results sorted on the basis of the count property, which tells us how many documents belong to that particular category. Of course, we can do the same with aggregations by using the following query:

```
curl -XGET 'localhost:9200/wikipedia/_search?fields=title&pretty' -d '{
  "query": {
    "match_all": {}
  },
  "aggs": {
    "category_agg": {
```

```
            "terms": {
                "field": "category.untouched",
                "size": 10
            }
        }
    }
}'
```

Now, if our user wants to narrow down its results to the `English-language films` category, we need to send the following query:

```
curl -XGET 'localhost:9200/wikipedia/_search?fields=title&pretty' -d '{
    "query": {
        "filtered": {
            "query" : {
                "match_all" : {}
            },
            "filter" : {
                "term": {
                    "category.untouched": "English-language films"
                }
            }
        }
    },
    "facets": {
        "category_facet": {
            "terms": {
                "field": "category.untouched",
                "size": 10
            }
        }
    }
}'
```

We've changed our query to include a filter and, thus, we've filtered down the documents set on which the faceting will be calculated.

Of course, we can do the same with aggregations by using the following query:

```
curl -XGET 'localhost:9200/wikipedia/_search?fields=title&pretty' -d '{
    "query": {
        "filtered": {
            "query" : {
                "match_all" : {}
            },
            "filter" : {
                "term": {
                    "category.untouched": "English-language films"
                }
            }
        }
    },
    "aggs": {
        "category_agg": {
            "terms": {
                "field": "category.untouched",
                "size": 10
            }
        }
    }
}'
```

Summary

In this chapter, we learned how to correct user spelling mistakes both by using the terms suggester and the phrase suggester, so now we know what to do in order to avoid empty pages that are a result of misspelling. In addition to that, we improved our users' query experience by improving the query relevance. We started with a simple query; we added multi match queries, phrase queries, boosts, and used query slops. We saw how to filter our garbage results and how to improve the phrase match importance. We used N-grams to avoid misspellings as an alternate method to using Elasticsearch suggesters. We've also discussed how to use faceting to allow our users to narrow down search results and thus simplify the way in which they can find the desired documents or products.

In the next chapter, we will finally get into performance-related topics, starting with discussions about Elasticsearch scaling. Then, we will discuss how to choose the right amount of shards and replicas for our deployment, and how routing can help us in our deployment. We will alter the default shard allocation logic, and we will adjust it to match our needs. Finally, we will see what Elasticsearch gives us when it comes to query execution logic and how we can control that to best match our deployment and indices architecture.

5
The Index Distribution Architecture

In the previous chapter, we were focused on improving the user search experience. We started with using the terms and phrase suggester to correct typos in user queries. In addition to that, we used the completion suggester to create an efficient, index time-calculated autocomplete functionality. Finally, we saw what Elasticsearch tuning may look like. We started with a simple query; we added multi match queries, phrase queries, boosts, and used query slops. We saw how to filter our garbage results and how to improve phrase match importance. We used n-grams to avoid misspellings as an alternate method to using Elasticsearch suggesters. We also discussed how to use faceting to allow our users to narrow down search results and thus simplify the way in which they can find the desired documents or products. By the end of this chapter, we will have covered:

- Choosing the right amount of shards and replicas
- Routing
- Shard allocation behavior adjustments
- Using query execution preference

Choosing the right amount of shards and replicas

In the beginning, when you started using Elasticsearch, you probably began by creating the index, importing your data to it and, after that, you started sending queries. We are pretty sure all worked well—at least in the beginning when the amount of data and the number of queries per second were not high. In the background, Elasticsearch created some shards and probably replicas as well (if you are using the default configuration, for example), and you didn't pay much attention to this part of the deployment.

When your application grows, you have to index more and more data and handle more and more queries per second. This is the point where everything changes. Problems start to appear (you can read about how we can handle the application's growth in *Chapter 8, Improving Performance*). It's now time to think about how you should plan your index and its configuration to rise with your application. In this chapter, we will give you some guidelines on how to handle this. Unfortunately, there is no exact recipe; each application has different characteristics and requirements, based on which, not only does the index structure depend, but also the configuration. For example, these factors can be ones like the size of the document or the whole index, query types, and the desired throughput.

Sharding and overallocation

You already know from the *Introducing Elasticsearch* section in *Chapter 1, Introduction to Elasticsearch*, what sharding is, but let's recall it. Sharding is the splitting of an Elasticsearch index to a set of smaller indices, which allows us to spread them among multiple nodes in the same cluster. While querying, the result is a sum of all the results that were returned by each shard of an index (although it's not really a sum, because a single shard may hold all the data we are interested in). By default, Elasticsearch creates five shards for every index even in a single-node environment. This redundancy is called overallocation: it seems to be totally not needed at this point and only leads to more complexity when indexing (spreading document to shards) and handling queries (querying shards and merging the results). Happily, this complexity is handled automatically, but why does Elasticsearch do this?

Let's say that we have an index that is built only of a single shard. This means that if our application grows above the capacity of a single machine, we will face a problem. In the current version of Elasticsearch, there is no possibility of splitting the index into multiple, smaller parts: we need to say how many shards the index should be built of when we create that index. What we can do is prepare a new index with more shards and reindex the data. However, such an operation requires additional time and server resources, such as CPU time, RAM, and mass storage. When it comes to the production environment, we don't always have the required time and mentioned resources. On the other hand, while using overallocation, we can just add a new server with Elasticsearch installed, and Elasticsearch will rebalance the cluster by moving parts of the index to the new machine without the additional cost of reindexing. The default configuration (which means five shards and one replica) chosen by the authors of Elasticsearch is the balance between the possibilities of growing and overhead resulting from the need to merge results from a different shard.

The default shard number of five is chosen for standard use cases. So now, this question arises: when should we start with more shards or, on the contrary, try to keep the number of shards as low as possible?

The first answer is obvious. If you have a limited and strongly defined data set, you can use only a single shard. If you do not, however, the rule of thumb dictates that the optimal number of shards be dependent on the target number of nodes. So, if you plan to use 10 nodes in the future, you need to configure the index to have 10 shards. One important thing to remember is that for high availability and query throughput, we should also configure replicas, and it also takes up room on the nodes just like the normal shard. If you have one additional copy of each shard (`number_of_replicas` equal to one), you end up with 20 shards—10 with the main data and 10 with its replicas.

To sum up, our simple formula can be presented as follows:

```
max number of nodes = number of shards * (number of replicas + 1)
```

In other words, if you have planned to use 10 shards and you like to have two replicas, the maximum number of nodes that will hold the data for this setup will be 30.

A positive example of overallocation

If you carefully read the previous part of this chapter, you will have a strong conviction that you should use the minimal number of shards. However, sometimes, having more shards is handy, because a shard is, in fact, an Apache Lucene index, and more shards means that every operation executed on a single, smaller Lucene index (especially indexing) will be faster. Sometimes, this is a good enough reason to use many shards. Of course, there is the possible cost of splitting a query into multiple requests to each and every shard and merge the response from it. This can be avoided for particular types of applications where the queries are always filtered by the concrete parameter. This is the case with multitenant systems, where every query is run in the context of the defined user. The idea is simple; we can index the data of this user in a single shard and use only that shard during querying. This is in place when routing should be used (we will discuss it in detail in the *Routing explained* section in this chapter).

Multiple shards versus multiple indices

You may wonder whether, if a shard is the *de-facto* of a small Lucene index, what about true Elasticsearch indices? What is the difference between having multiple small shards and having multiple indices? Technically, the difference is not that great and, for some use cases, having more than a single index is the right approach (for example, to store time-based data such as logs in time-sliced indices). When you are using a single index with many shards, you can limit your operations to a single shard when using routing, for example. When dealing with indices, you may choose which data you are interested in; for example, choose only a few of your time-based indices using the `logs_2014-10-10,logs_2014-10-11,...` notation. More differences can be spotted in the shard and index-balancing logic, although we can configure both balancing logics.

Replicas

While sharding lets us store more data than we can fit on a single node, replicas are there to handle increasing throughput and, of course, for high availability and fault tolerance. When a node with the primary shard is lost, Elasticsearch can promote one of the available replicas to be a new primary shard. In the default configuration, Elasticsearch creates a single replica for each of the shards in the index. However, the number of replicas can be changed at any time using the Settings API. This is very convenient when we are at a point where we need more query throughput; increasing the number of replicas allows us to spread the querying load on more machine, which basically allows us to handle more parallel queries.

The drawback of using more replicas is obvious: the cost of additional space used by additional copies of each shard, the cost of indexing on nodes that host the replicas, and, of course, the cost of data copy between the primary shard and all the replicas. While choosing the number of shards, you should also consider how many replicas need to be present. If you select too many replicas, you can end up using disk space and Elasticsearch resources, when in fact, they won't be used. On the other hand, choosing to have none of the replicas may result in the data being lost if something bad happens to the primary shard.

Routing explained

In the *Choosing the right amount of shards and replicas* section in this chapter, we mentioned routing as a solution for the shards on which queries will be executed on a single one. Now it's time to look closer at this functionality.

Shards and data

Usually, it is not important how Elasticsearch divides data into shards and which shard holds the particular document. During query time, the query will be sent to all the shards of a particular index, so the only crucial thing is to use the algorithm that spreads our data evenly so that each shard contains similar amounts of data. We don't want one shard to hold 99 percent of the data while the other shard holds the rest—it is not efficient.

The situation complicates slightly when we want to remove or add a newer version of the document. Elasticsearch must be able to determine which shard should be updated. Although it may seem troublesome, in practice, it is not a huge problem. It is enough to use the sharding algorithm, which will always generate the same value for the same document identifier. If we have such an algorithm, Elasticsearch will know which shard to point to when dealing with a document.

However, there are times when it would be nice to be able to hit the same shard for some portion of data. For example, we would like to store every book of a particular type only on a particular shard and, while searching for that kind of book, we could avoid searching on many shards and merging results from them. Instead, because we know the value we used for routing, we could point Elasticsearch to the same shard we used during indexing. This is exactly what routing does. It allows us to provide information that will be used by Elasticsearch to determine which shard should be used for document storage and for querying; the same routing value will always result in the same shard. It's basically something like saying "search for documents on the shard where you've put the documents by using the provided routing value".

Let's test routing

To show you an example that will illustrate how Elasticsearch allocates shards and which documents are placed on the particular shard, we will use an additional plugin. It will help us visualize what Elasticsearch did with our data. Let's install the Paramedic plugin using the following command:

```
bin/plugin -install karmi/elasticsearch-paramedic
```

After restarting Elasticsearch, we can point our browser to `http://localhost:9200/_plugin/paramedic/index.html` and we will able to see a page with various statistics and information about indices. For our example, the most interesting information is the cluster color that indicates the cluster state and the list of shards and replicas next to every index.

Let's start two Elasticsearch nodes and create an index by running the following command:

```
curl -XPUT 'localhost:9200/documents' -d '{
  "settings": {
    "number_of_replicas": 0,
    "number_of_shards": 2
  }
}'
```

We've created an index without replicas, which is built of two shards. This means that the largest cluster can have only two nodes, and each next node cannot be filled with data unless we increase the number of replicas (you can read about this in the *Choosing the right amount of shards and replicas* section of this chapter). The next operation is to index some documents; we will do that by using the following commands:

```
curl -XPUT localhost:9200/documents/doc/1 -d '{ "title" : "Document No. 1" }'
curl -XPUT localhost:9200/documents/doc/2 -d '{ "title" : "Document No. 2" }'
curl -XPUT localhost:9200/documents/doc/3 -d '{ "title" : "Document No. 3" }'
curl -XPUT localhost:9200/documents/doc/4 -d '{ "title" : "Document No. 4" }'
```

After that, if we would look at the installed Paramedic plugin, we would see our two primary shards created and assigned.

Chapter 5

In the information about nodes, we can also find the information that we are currently interested in. Each of the nodes in the cluster holds exactly two documents. This leads us to the conclusion that the sharding algorithm did its work perfectly, and we have an index that is built of shards that have evenly redistributed documents.

Now, let's create some chaos and let's shut down the second node. Now, using Paramedic, we should see something like this:

The Index Distribution Architecture

The first information we see is that the cluster is now in the red state. This means that at least one primary shard is missing, which tells us that some of the data is not available and some parts of the index are not available. Nevertheless, Elasticsearch allows us to execute queries; it is our decision as to what applications should do—inform the user about the possibility of incomplete results or block querying attempts. Let's try to run a simple query by using the following command:

```
curl -XGET 'localhost:9200/documents/_search?pretty'
```

The response returned by Elasticsearch will look as follows:

```
{
  "took" : 26,
  "timed_out" : false,
  "_shards" : {
    "total" : 2,
    "successful" : 1,
    "failed" : 0
  },
  "hits" : {
    "total" : 2,
    "max_score" : 1.0,
    "hits" : [ {
      "_index" : "documents",
      "_type" : "doc",
      "_id" : "2",
      "_score" : 1.0,
      "_source":{ "title" : "Document No. 2" }
    }, {
      "_index" : "documents",
      "_type" : "doc",
      "_id" : "4",
      "_score" : 1.0,
      "_source":{ "title" : "Document No. 4" }
    } ]
  }
}
```

As you can see, Elasticsearch returned the information about failures; we can see that one of the shards is not available. In the returned result set, we can only see the documents with identifiers of 2 and 4. Other documents have been lost, at least until the failed primary shard is back online. If you start the second node, after a while (depending on the network and gateway module settings), the cluster should return to the green state and all documents should be available. Now, we will try to do the same using routing, and we will try to observe the difference in the Elasticsearch behavior.

Indexing with routing

With routing, we can control the target shard Elasticsearch will choose to send the documents to by specifying the `routing` parameter. The value of the `routing` parameter is irrelevant; you can use whatever value you choose. The important thing is that the same value of the routing parameter should be used to place different documents together in the same shard. To say it simply, using the same routing value for different documents will ensure us that these documents will be placed in the same shard.

There are a few possibilities as to how we can provide the routing information to Elasticsearch. The simplest way is add the `routing` URI parameter when indexing a document, for example:

```
curl -XPUT localhost:9200/books/doc/1?routing=A -d '{ "title" : "Document" }'
```

Of course, we can also provide the routing value when using bulk indexing. In such cases, routing is given in the metadata for each document by using the `_routing` property, for example:

```
curl -XPUT localhost:9200/_bulk --data-binary '
{ "index" : { "_index" : "books", "_type" : "doc", "_routing" : "A" }}
{ "title" : "Document" }
'
```

Another option is to place a `_routing` field inside the document. However, this will work properly only when the `_routing` field is defined in the mappings. For example, let's create an index called `books_routing` by using the following command:

```
curl -XPUT 'localhost:9200/books_routing' -d '{
  "mappings": {
    "doc": {
```

```
      "_routing": {
        "required": true,
        "path": "_routing"
      },
      "properties": {
        "title" : {"type": "string" }
      }
    }
  }
}'
```

Now we can use `_routing` inside the document body, for example, like this:

```
curl -XPUT localhost:9200/books_routing/doc/1 -d '{ "title" :
"Document", "_routing" : "A" }'
```

In the preceding example, we used a `_routing` field. It is worth mentioning that the `path` parameter can point to any field that's not analyzed from the document. This is a very powerful feature and one of the main advantages of the routing feature. For example, if we extend our document with the `library_id` field's indicated library where the book is available, it is logical that all queries based on library can be more effective when we set up routing based on this `library_id` field. However, you have to remember that getting the routing value from a field requires additional parsing.

Routing in practice

Now let's get back to our initial example and do the same as what we did but now using routing. The first thing is to delete the old documents. If we do not do this and add documents with the same identifier, routing may cause that same document to now be placed in the other shard. Therefore, we run the following command to delete all the documents from our index:

```
curl -XDELETE 'localhost:9200/documents/_query?q=*:*'
```

After that, we index our data again, but this time, we add the routing information. The commands used to index our documents now look as follows:

```
curl -XPUT localhost:9200/documents/doc/1?routing=A -d '{ "title" :
"Document No. 1" }'
curl -XPUT localhost:9200/documents/doc/2?routing=B -d '{ "title" :
"Document No. 2" }'
```

```
curl -XPUT localhost:9200/documents/doc/3?routing=A -d '{ "title" :
"Document No. 3" }'
curl -XPUT localhost:9200/documents/doc/4?routing=A -d '{ "title" :
"Document No. 4" }'
```

As we said, the routing parameter tells Elasticsearch in which shard the document should be placed. Of course, it may happen that more than a single document will be placed in the same shard. That's because you usually have less shards than routing values. If we now kill one node, Paramedic will again show you the red cluster and the state. If we query for all the documents, Elasticsearch will return the following response (of course, it depends which node you kill):

```
curl -XGET 'localhost:9200/documents/_search?q=*&pretty'
```

The response from Elasticsearch would be as follows:

```
{
  "took" : 24,
  "timed_out" : false,
  "_shards" : {
    "total" : 2,
    "successful" : 1,
    "failed" : 0
  },
  "hits" : {
    "total" : 3,
    "max_score" : 1.0,
    "hits" : [ {
      "_index" : "documents",
      "_type" : "doc",
      "_id" : "1",
      "_score" : 1.0,
      "_source":{ "title" : "Document No. 1" }
    }, {
      "_index" : "documents",
      "_type" : "doc",
      "_id" : "3",
      "_score" : 1.0,
      "_source":{ "title" : "Document No. 3" }
    }, {
      "_index" : "documents",
      "_type" : "doc",
      "_id" : "4",
      "_score" : 1.0,
```

```
            "_source":{ "title" : "Document No. 4" }
        } ]
    }
}
```

In our case, the document with the identifier 2 is missing. We lost a node with the documents that had the routing value of B. If we were less lucky, we could lose three documents!

Querying

Routing allows us to tell Elasticsearch which shards should be used for querying. Why send queries to all the shards that build the index if we want to get data from a particular subset of the whole index? For example, to get the data from a shard where routing A was used, we can run the following query:

```
curl -XGET 'localhost:9200/documents/_search?pretty&q=*&routing=A'
```

We just added a routing parameter with the value we are interested in. Elasticsearch replied with the following result:

```
{
  "took" : 0,
  "timed_out" : false,
  "_shards" : {
    "total" : 1,
    "successful" : 1,
    "failed" : 0
  },
  "hits" : {
    "total" : 3,
    "max_score" : 1.0,
    "hits" : [ {
      "_index" : "documents",
      "_type" : "doc",
      "_id" : "1",
      "_score" : 1.0, "_source" : { "title" : "Document No. 1" }
    }, {
      "_index" : "documents",
      "_type" : "doc",
      "_id" : "3",
      "_score" : 1.0, "_source" : { "title" : "Document No. 3" }
    }, {
      "_index" : "documents",
```

```
            "_type" : "doc",
            "_id" : "4",
            "_score" : 1.0, "_source" : { "title" : "Document No. 4" }
        } ]
    }
}
```

Everything works like a charm. But look closer! We forgot to start the node that holds the shard with the documents that were indexed with the routing value of B. Even though we didn't have a full index view, the reply from Elasticsearch doesn't contain information about shard failures. This is proof that queries with routing hit only a chosen shard and ignore the rest. If we run the same query with routing=B, we will get an exception like the following one:

```
{
   "error" : "SearchPhaseExecutionException[Failed to execute phase
[query_fetch], all shards failed]",
   "status" : 503
}
```

We can test the preceding behavior by using the Search Shard API. For example, let's run the following command:

```
curl -XGET 'localhost:9200/documents/_search_shards?pretty&routing=A'
-d '{"query":"match_all":{}}'
```

The response from Elasticsearch would be as follows:

```
{
  "nodes" : {
    "QK5r_d5CSfaV1Wx78k633w" : {
      "name" : "Western Kid",
      "transport_address" : "inet[/10.0.2.15:9301]"
    }
  },
  "shards" : [ [ {
    "state" : "STARTED",
    "primary" : true,
    "node" : "QK5r_d5CSfaV1Wx78k633w",
    "relocating_node" : null,
    "shard" : 0,
    "index" : "documents"
  } ] ]
}
```

As we can see, only a single node will be queried.

There is one important thing that we would like to repeat. Routing ensures us that, during indexing, documents with the same routing value are indexed in the same shard. However, you need to remember that a given shard may have many documents with different routing values. Routing allows you to limit the number of shards used during queries, but it cannot replace filtering! This means that a query with routing and without routing should have the same set of filters. For example, if we use user identifiers as routing values if we search for that user's data, we should also include filters on that identifier.

Aliases

If you work as a search engine specialist, you probably want to hide some configuration details from programmers in order to allow them to work faster and not care about search details. In an ideal world, they should not worry about routing, shards, and replicas. Aliases allow us to use shards with routing as ordinary indices. For example, let's create an alias by running the following command:

```
curl -XPOST 'http://localhost:9200/_aliases' -d '{
  "actions" : [
    {
      "add" : {
        "index" : "documents",
        "alias" : "documentsA",
        "routing" : "A"
      }
    }
  ]
}'
```

In the preceding example, we created a named `documentsA` alias from the `documents` index. However, in addition to that, searching will be limited to the shard used when routing value A is used. Thanks to this approach, you can give information about the `documentsA` alias to developers, and they may use it for querying and indexing like any other index.

Multiple routing values

Elasticsearch gives us the possibility to search with several routing values in a single query. Depending on which shard documents with given routing values are placed, it could mean searching on one or more shards. Let's look at the following query:

```
curl -XGET 'localhost:9200/documents/_search?routing=A,B'
```

After executing it, Elasticsearch will send the search request to two shards in our index (which in our case, happens to be the whole index), because the routing value of A covers one of two shards of our index and the routing value of B covers the second shard of our index.

Of course, multiple routing values are supported in aliases as well. The following example shows you the usage of these features:

```
curl -XPOST 'http://localhost:9200/_aliases' -d '{
  "actions" : [
    {
      "add" : {
        "index" : "documents",
        "alias" : "documentsA",
        "search_routing" : "A,B",
        "index_routing" : "A"
      }
    }
  ]
}'
```

The preceding example shows you two additional configuration parameters we didn't talk about until now — we can define different values of routing for searching and indexing. In the preceding case, we've defined that during querying (the search_routing parameter) two values of routing (A and B) will be applied. When indexing (index_routing parameter), only one value (A) will be used. Note that indexing doesn't support multiple routing values, and you should also remember proper filtering (you can add it to your alias).

Altering the default shard allocation behavior

In *Elasticsearch Server Second Edition*, published by *Packt Publishing*, we talked about a number of things related to the shard allocation functionality provided by Elasticsearch. We discussed the Cluster Reroute API, shard rebalancing, and shard awareness. Although now very commonly used, these topics are very important if you want to be in full control of your Elasticsearch cluster. Because of that, we decided to extend the examples provided in *Elasticsearch Server Second Edition* and provide you with guidance on how to use Elasticsearch shards awareness and alter the default shard allocation mechanism.

Let's start with a simple example. We assume that we have a cluster built of four nodes that looks as follows:

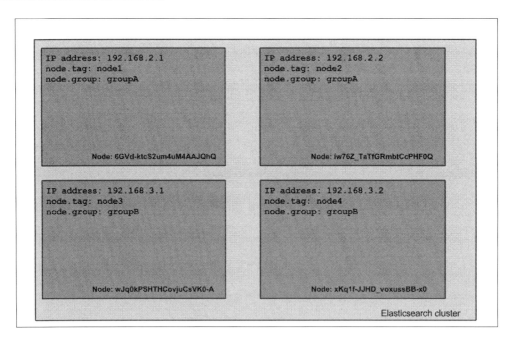

As you can see, our cluster is built of four nodes. Each node was bound to a specific IP address, and each node was given the `tag` property and a `group` property (added to `elasticsearch.yml` as `node.tag` and `node.group` properties). This cluster will serve the purpose of showing you how shard allocation filtering works. The `group` and `tag` properties can be given whatever names you want; you just need to prefix your desired property name with the `node` name; for example, if you would like to use a `party` property name, you would just add `node.party: party1` to your `elasticsearch.yml` file.

Allocation awareness

Allocation awareness allows us to configure shards and their replicas' allocation with the use of generic parameters. In order to illustrate how allocation awareness works, we will use our example cluster. For the example to work, we should add the following property to the `elasticsearch.yml` file:

```
cluster.routing.allocation.awareness.attributes: group
```

This will tell Elasticsearch to use the `node.group` property as the awareness parameter.

> One can specify multiple attributes when setting the `cluster.routing.allocation.awareness.attributes` property, for example:
> ```
> cluster.routing.allocation.awareness.attributes:
> group,
> node
> ```

After this, let's start the first two nodes, the ones with the `node.group` parameter equal to `groupA`, and let's create an index by running the following command:

```
curl -XPOST 'localhost:9200/mastering' -d '{
 "settings" : {
  "index" : {
   "number_of_shards" : 2,
   "number_of_replicas" : 1
  }
 }
}'
```

After this command, our two nodes' cluster will look more or less like this:

![Elasticsearch cluster diagram showing two nodes: Node 1 at IP 192.168.2.1 with node.tag node1, node.group groupA, containing Mastering Primary shard 0 and Mastering Replica shard 1 (Node: 6GVd-ktcS2urn4uM4AAJQhQ); Node 2 at IP 192.168.2.2 with node.tag node2, node.group groupA, containing Mastering Replica shard 0 and Mastering Primary shard 1 (Node: iw76Z_TaTfGRmbtCcPHF0Q).]

The Index Distribution Architecture

As you can see, the index was divided evenly between two nodes. Now let's see what happens when we launch the rest of the nodes (the ones with node.group set to groupB):

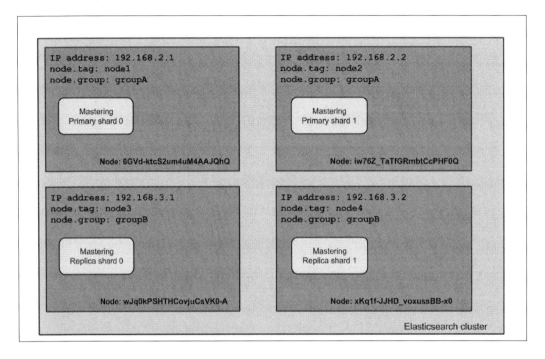

Notice the difference: the primary shards were not moved from their original allocation nodes, but the replica shards were moved to the nodes with a different node.group value. That's exactly right—when using shard allocation awareness, Elasticsearch won't allocate shards and replicas to the nodes with the same value of the property used to determine the allocation awareness (which, in our case, is node.group). One of the example usages of this functionality is to divide the cluster topology between virtual machines or physical locations in order to be sure that you don't have a single point of failure.

Please remember that when using allocation awareness, shards will not be allocated to the node that doesn't have the expected attributes set. So, in our example, a node without the node.group property set will not be taken into consideration by the allocation mechanism.

Forcing allocation awareness

Forcing allocation awareness can come in handy when we know, in advance, how many values our awareness attributes can take, and we don't want more replicas than needed to be allocated in our cluster, for example, not to overload our cluster with too many replicas. To do this, we can force allocation awareness to be active only for certain attributes. We can specify these values using the `cluster.routing.allocation.awareness.force.zone.values` property and providing a list of comma-separated values to it. For example, if we would like allocation awareness to only use the `groupA` and `groupB` values of the `node.group` property, we would add the following to the `elasticsearch.yml` file:

```
cluster.routing.allocation.awareness.attributes: group
cluster.routing.allocation.awareness.force.zone.values: groupA, groupB
```

Filtering

Elasticsearch allows us to configure the allocation for the whole cluster or for the index level. In the case of cluster allocation, we can use the properties prefixes:

- `cluster.routing.allocation.include`
- `cluster.routing.allocation.require`
- `cluster.routing.allocation.exclude`

When it comes to index-specific allocation, we can use the following properties prefixes:

- `index.routing.allocation.include`
- `index.routing.allocation.require`
- `index.routing.allocation.exclude`

The previously mentioned prefixes can be used with the properties that we've defined in the `elasticsearch.yml` file (our `tag` and `group` properties) and with a special property called `_ip` that allows us to match or exclude IPs using nodes' IP address, for example, like this:

```
cluster.routing.allocation.include._ip: 192.168.2.1
```

If we would like to include nodes with a `group` property matching the `groupA` value, we would set the following property:

```
cluster.routing.allocation.include.group: groupA
```

Notice that we've used the `cluster.routing.allocation.include` prefix, and we've concatenated it with the name of the property, which is `group` in our case.

What include, exclude, and require mean

If you look closely at the parameters mentioned previously, you would notice that there are three kinds:

- `include`: This type will result in the inclusion of all the nodes with this parameter defined. If multiple `include` conditions are visible, then all the nodes that match at least one of these conditions will be taken into consideration when allocating shards. For example, if we would add two `cluster.routing.allocation.include.tag` parameters to our configuration, one with a property to the value of `node1` and the second with the `node2` value, we would end up with indices (actually, their shards) being allocated to the first and second node (counting from left to right). To sum up, the nodes that have the `include` allocation parameter type will be taken into consideration by Elasticsearch when choosing the nodes to place shards on, but that doesn't mean that Elasticsearch will put shards on them.

- `require`: This was introduced in the Elasticsearch 0.90 type of allocation filter, and it requires all the nodes to have the value that matches the value of this property. For example, if we would add one `cluster.routing.allocation.require.tag` parameter to our configuration with the value of `node1` and a `cluster.routing.allocation.require.group` parameter, the value of `groupA` would end up with shards allocated only to the first node (the one with the IP address of `192.168.2.1`).

- `exclude`: This allows us to exclude nodes with given properties from the allocation process. For example, if we set `cluster.routing.allocation.include.tag` to `groupA`, we would end up with indices being allocated only to nodes with IP addresses `192.168.3.1` and `192.168.3.2` (the third and fourth node in our example).

> Property values can use simple wildcard characters. For example, if we would like to include all the nodes that have the `group` parameter value beginning with `group`, we could set the `cluster.routing.allocation.include.group` property to `group*`. In the example cluster case, it would result in matching nodes with the `groupA` and `groupB` `group` parameter values.

Runtime allocation updating

In addition to setting all discussed properties in the `elasticsearch.yml` file, we can also use the update API to update these settings in real-time when the cluster is already running.

Index level updates

In order to update settings for a given index (for example, our `mastering` index), we could run the following command:

```
curl -XPUT 'localhost:9200/mastering/_settings' -d '{
 "index.routing.allocation.require.group": "groupA"
}'
```

As you can see, the command was sent to the `_settings` end-point for a given index. You can include multiple properties in a single call.

Cluster level updates

In order to update settings for the whole cluster, we could run the following command:

```
curl -XPUT 'localhost:9200/_cluster/settings' -d '{
 "transient" : {
  "cluster.routing.allocation.require.group": "groupA"
 }
}'
```

As you can see, the command was sent to the `cluster/_settings` end-point. You can include multiple properties in a single call. Please remember that the `transient` name in the preceding command means that the property will be forgotten after the cluster restart. If you want to avoid this and set this property as a permanent one, use `persistent` instead of the `transient` one. An example command, which will keep the settings between restarts, could look like this:

```
curl -XPUT 'localhost:9200/_cluster/settings' -d '{
 "persistent" : {
  "cluster.routing.allocation.require.group": "groupA"
 }
}'
```

> Please note that running the preceding commands, depending on the command and where your indices are located, can result in shards being moved between nodes.

Defining total shards allowed per node

In addition to the previously mentioned properties, we are also allowed to define how many shards (primaries and replicas) for an index can by allocated per node. In order to do that, one should set the `index.routing.allocation.total_shards_per_node` property to a desired value. For example, in `elasticsearch.yml` we could set this:

```
index.routing.allocation.total_shards_per_node: 4
```

This would result in a maximum of four shards per index being allocated to a single node.

This property can also be updated on a live cluster using the Update API, for example, like this:

```
curl -XPUT 'localhost:9200/mastering/_settings' -d '{
 "index.routing.allocation.total_shards_per_node": "4"
}'
```

Now, let's see a few examples of what the cluster would look like when creating a single index and having the allocation properties used in the `elasticsearch.yml` file.

Defining total shards allowed per physical server

One of the properties that can be useful when having multiple nodes on a single physical server is `cluster.routing.allocation.same_shard.host`. When set to `true`, it prevents Elasticsearch from placing a primary shard and its replica (or replicas) on the same physical host. We really advise that you set this property to `true` if you have very powerful servers and that you go for multiple Elasticsearch nodes per physical server.

Inclusion

Now, let's use our example cluster to see how the allocation inclusion works. Let's start by deleting and recreating the `mastering` index by using the following commands:

```
curl -XDELETE 'localhost:9200/mastering'
curl -XPOST 'localhost:9200/mastering' -d '{
 "settings" : {
  "index" : {
```

```
    "number_of_shards" : 2,
    "number_of_replicas" : 0
  }
 }
}'
```

After this, let's try to run the following command:

```
curl -XPUT 'localhost:9200/mastering/_settings' -d '{
 "index.routing.allocation.include.tag": "node1",
 "index.routing.allocation.include.group": "groupA",
 "index.routing.allocation.total_shards_per_node": 1
}'
```

If we visualize the response of the index status, we would see that the cluster looks like the one in the following image:

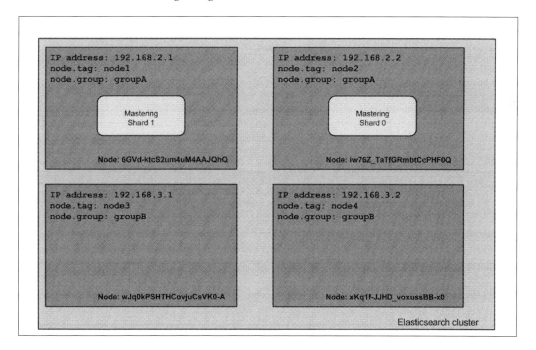

As you can see, the `mastering` index shards are allocated to nodes with the `tag` property set to `node1` or the `group` property set to `groupA`.

The Index Distribution Architecture

Requirement

Now, let's reuse our example cluster and try running the following command:

```
curl -XPUT 'localhost:9200/mastering/_settings' -d '{
 "index.routing.allocation.require.tag": "node1",
 "index.routing.allocation.require.group": "groupA"
}'
```

If we visualize the response of the index status command, we would see that the cluster looks like this:

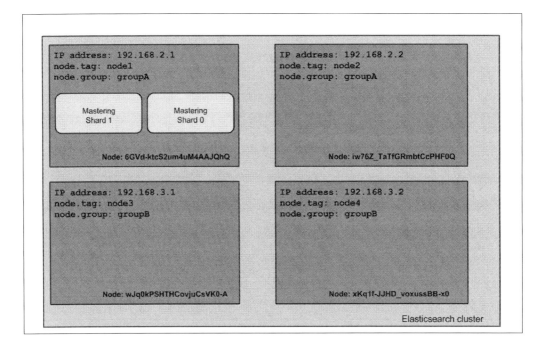

As you can see, the view is different than the one when using `include`. This is because we tell Elasticsearch to allocate shards of the `mastering` index only to the nodes that match both the `require` parameters, and in our case, the only node that matches both is the first node.

Exclusion

Let's now look at exclusions. To test it, we try to run the following command:

```
curl -XPUT 'localhost:9200/mastering/_settings' -d '{
 "index.routing.allocation.exclude.tag": "node1",
 "index.routing.allocation.require.group": "groupA"
}'
```

Again, let's look at our cluster now:

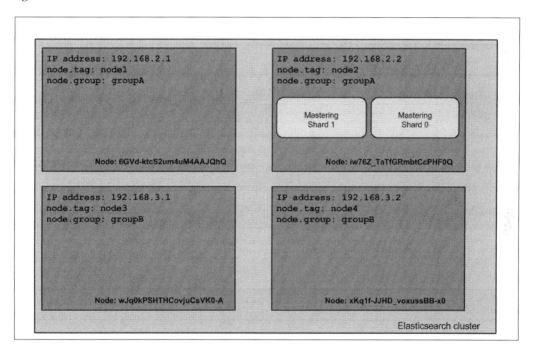

As you can see, we said that we require the `group` property to be equal to `groupA`, and we want to exclude the node with a `tag` equal to `node1`. This resulted in the shard of the `mastering` index being allocated to the node with the `192.168.2.2` IP address, which is what we wanted.

Disk-based allocation

Of course, the mentioned properties are not the only ones that can be used. With the release of Elasticsearch 1.3.0 we got the ability to configure awareness on the basis of the disk usage. By default, disk-based allocation is turned on, and if we want, we can turn it off by setting the `cluster.routing.allocation.disk.threshold_enabled` property to `false`.

There are three additional properties that can help us configure disk-based allocation. The `cluster.routing.allocation.disk.watermark.low` cluster controls when Elasticsearch does not allow you to allocate new shards on the node. By default, it is set to 85 percent and it means that when the disk usage is equal or higher than 85 percent, no new shards will be allocated on that node. The second property is `cluster.routing.allocation.disk.watermark.high`, which controls when Elasticsearch will try to move the shards out of the node and is set to 90 percent by default. This means that Elasticsearch will try to move the shard out of the node if the disk usage is `90` percent or higher.

Both `cluster.routing.allocation.disk.watermark.low` and `cluster.routing.allocation.disk.watermark.high` can be set to absolute values, for example, `1024mb`.

Query execution preference

Let's forget about the shard placement and how to configure it—at least for a moment. In addition to all the fancy stuff that Elasticsearch allows us to set for shards and replicas, we also have the possibility to specify where our queries (and other operations, for example, the real-time GET) should be executed.

Before we get into the details, let's look at our example cluster:

As you can see, we have three nodes and a single index called `mastering`. Our index is divided into two primary shards, and there is one replica for each primary shard.

Introducing the preference parameter

In order to control where the query (and other operations) we are sending will be executed, we can use the `preference` parameter, which can be set to one of the following values:

- `_primary`: Using this property, the operations we are sending will only be executed on primary shards. So, if we send a query against `mastering` index with the preference parameter set to the `_primary` value, we would have it executed on the nodes with the names `node1` and `node2`. For example, if you know that your primary shards are in one rack and the replicas are in other racks, you may want to execute the operation on primary shards to avoid network traffic.

- `_primary_first`: This option is similar to the `_primary` value's behavior but with a failover mechanism. If we ran a query against the `mastering` index with the preference parameter set to the `_primary_first` value, we would have it executed on the nodes with the names `node1` and `node2`; however, if one (or more) of the primary shards fails, the query will be executed against the other shard, which in our case is allocated to a node named `node3`. As we said, this is very similar to the `_primary` value but with additional fallback to replicas if the primary shard is not available for some reason.

- `_local`: Elasticsearch will prefer to execute the operation on a local node, if possible. For example, if we send a query to `node3` with the preference parameter set to `_local`, we would end up having that query executed on that node. However, if we send the same query to `node2`, we would end up with one query executed against the primary shard numbered 1 (which is located on that node) and the second part of the query will be executed against `node1` or `node3` where the shard numbered 0 resides. This is especially useful while trying to minimize the network latency; while using the `_local` preference, we ensure that our queries are executed locally whenever possible (for example, when running a client connection from a local node or sending a query to a node).

- `_only_node:wJq0kPSHTHCovjuCsVK0-A`: This operation will be only executed against a node with the provided identifier (which is `wJq0kPSHTHCovjuCsVK0-A` in this case). So in our case, the query would be executed against two replicas located on `node3`. Please remember that if there aren't enough shards to cover all the index data, the query will be executed against only the shard available in the specified node. For example, if we set the preference parameter to `_only_node:6GVd-ktcS2um4uM4AAJQhQ`, we would end up having our query executed against a single shard. This can be useful for examples where we know that one of our nodes is more powerful than the other ones and we want some of the queries to be executed only on that node.

- `_prefer_node:wJq0kPSHTHCovjuCsVK0-A`: This option sets the preference parameter to `_prefer_node:` the value followed by a node identifier (which is `wJq0kPSHTHCovjuCsVK0-A` in our case) will result in Elasticsearch preferring the mentioned node while executing the query, but if some shards are not available on the preferred node, Elasticsearch will send the appropriate query parts to nodes where the shards are available. Similar to the `_only_node` option, `_prefer_node` can be used while choosing a particular node, with a fall back to other nodes, however.

- `_shards:0,1`: This is the preference value that allows us to identify which shards the operation should be executed against (in our case, it will be all the shards, because we only have shards `0` and `1` in the `mastering` index). This is the only preference parameter value that can be combined with the other mentioned values. For example, in order to locally execute our query against the `0` and `1` shard, we should concatenate the `0,1` value with `_local` using the `;` character, so the final value of the preference parameter should look like this: `0,1;_local`. Allowing us to execute the operation against a single shard can be useful for diagnosis purposes.

- custom, string value: Setting the `_preference` parameter to a custom value will guarantee that the query with the same custom value will be executed against the same shards. For example, if we send a query with the `_preference` parameter set to the `mastering_elasticsearch` value, we would end up having the query executed against primary shards located on nodes named `node1` and `node2`. If we send another query with the same preference parameter value, then the second query will again be executed against the shards located on nodes named `node1` and `node2`. This functionality can help us in cases where we have different refresh rates and we don't want our users to see different results while repeating requests. There is one more thing missing, which is the default behavior. What Elasticsearch will do by default is that it will randomize the operation between shards and replicas. If we sent many queries, we would end up having the same (or almost the same) number of queries run against each of the shards and replicas.

Summary

In this chapter, we talked about general shards and the index architecture. We chose the right amount of shards and replicas for our deployment, and we used routing during indexing and querying and in conjunction with aliases. We also discussed shard-allocation behavior adjustments, and finally, we looked at what query execution preference can bring us.

In the next chapter, we will take a deeper look, altering the Apache Lucene scoring mechanism by providing different similarity models. We will adjust our inverted index format by using codecs. We will discuss near real-time indexing and querying, flush and refresh operations, and transaction log configuration. We will talk about throttling and segment merges. Finally, we will discuss Elasticsearch caching—field data, filter, and query shard caches.

6
Low-level Index Control

In the previous chapter, we talked about general shards and the index architecture. We started by learning how to choose the right amount of shards and replicas, and we used routing during indexing and querying, and in conjunction with aliases. We also discussed shard allocation behavior adjustments, and finally, we looked at what query execution preference can bring us.

In this chapter, we will take a deeper dive into more low-level aspects of handling shards in Elasticsearch. By the end of this chapter, you will have learned:

- Altering the Apache Lucene scoring by using different similarity models
- Altering index writing by using codes
- Near real-time indexing and querying
- Data flushing, index refresh, and transaction log handling
- I/O throttling
- Segment merge control and visualization
- Elasticsearch caching

Altering Apache Lucene scoring

With the release of Apache Lucene 4.0 in 2012, all the users of this great full text search library were given the opportunity to alter the default TF/IDF-based algorithm. The Lucene API was changed to allow easier modification and extension of the scoring formula. However, this was not the only change that was made to Lucene when it comes to documents' score calculation. Lucene 4.0 was shipped with additional similarity models, which basically allows us to use a different scoring formula for our documents. In this section, we will take a deeper look at what Lucene 4.0 brings and how these features were incorporated into Elasticsearch.

Available similarity models

As already mentioned, the original and default similarity model available before Apache Lucene 4.0 was the TF/IDF model. We already discussed it in detail in the *Default Apache Lucene scoring explained* section in *Chapter 2*, *Power User Query DSL*.

The five new similarity models that we can use are:

- **Okapi BM25**: This similarity model is based on a probabilistic model that estimates the probability of finding a document for a given query. In order to use this similarity in Elasticsearch, you need to use the BM25 name. The Okapi BM25 similarity is said to perform best when dealing with short text documents where term repetitions are especially hurtful to the overall document score.

- **Divergence from randomness (DFR)**: This similarity model is based on the probabilistic model of the same name. In order to use this similarity in Elasticsearch, you need to use the DFR name. It is said that the divergence from the randomness similarity model performs well on text similar to natural language text.

- **Information-based**: This is very similar to the model used by Divergence from randomness. In order to use this similarity in Elasticsearch, you need to use the IB name. Similar to the DFR similarity, it is said that the information-based model performs well on data similar to natural language text.

- **LM Dirichlet**: This similarity model uses Bayesian smoothing with Dirichlet priors. To use this similarity, we need to use the LMDirichlet name. More information about it can be found at https://lucene.apache.org/core/4_9_0/core/org/apache/lucene/search/similarities/LMDirichletSimilarity.html.

- **LM Jelinek Mercer**: This similarity model is based on the Jelinek Mercer smoothing method. To use this similarity, we need to use the LMJelinekMercer name. More information about it can be found at https://lucene.apache.org/core/4_9_0/core/org/apache/lucene/search/similarities/LMJelinekMercerSimilarity.html.

All the mentioned similarity models require mathematical knowledge to fully understand them and a deep explanation of these models is far beyond the scope of this book. However, if you would like to explore these models and increase your knowledge about them, please go to http://en.wikipedia.org/wiki/Okapi_BM25 for the Okapi BM25 similarity and http://terrier.org/docs/v3.5/dfr_description.html for divergence from the randomness similarity.

Setting a per-field similarity

Since Elasticsearch 0.90, we are allowed to set a different similarity for each of the fields we have in our mappings. For example, let's assume that we have the following simple mappings that we use in order to index blog posts (stored in the `posts_no_similarity.json` file):

```
{
 "mappings" : {
  "post" : {
   "properties" : {
    "id" : { "type" : "long", "store" : "yes" },
    "name" : { "type" : "string", "store" : "yes", "index" : "analyzed" },
    "contents" : { "type" : "string", "store" : "no", "index" : "analyzed" }
   }
  }
 }
}
```

What we would like to do is use the `BM25` similarity model for the `name` field and the `contents` field. In order to do this, we need to extend our field definitions and add the similarity property with the value of the chosen similarity name. Our changed mappings (stored in the `posts_similarity.json` file) would look like this:

```
{
 "mappings" : {
  "post" : {
   "properties" : {
    "id" : { "type" : "long", "store" : "yes" },
    "name" : { "type" : "string", "store" : "yes", "index" : "analyzed", "similarity" : "BM25" },
    "contents" : { "type" : "string", "store" : "no", "index" : "analyzed", "similarity" : "BM25" }
   }
  }
 }
}
```

That's all; nothing more is needed. After the preceding change, Apache Lucene will use the BM25 similarity to calculate the score factor for the `name` and `contents` fields.

Low-level Index Control

 Please note that in the case of the Divergence from randomness and Information-based similarities, we need to configure some additional properties to specify these similarities' behavior. How to do that is covered in the next part of the current section.

Similarity model configuration

As we now know how to set the desired similarity for each field in our index, it's time to see how to configure them if we need them, which is actually pretty easy. What we need to do is use the index settings section to provide an additional similarity section, for example, like this (this example is stored in the `posts_custom_similarity.json` file):

```
{
 "settings" : {
  "index" : {
   "similarity" : {
    "mastering_similarity" : {
     "type" : "default",
     "discount_overlaps" : false
    }
   }
  }
 },
 "mappings" : {
  "post" : {
   "properties" : {
    "id" : { "type" : "long", "store" : "yes" },
    "name" : { "type" : "string", "store" : "yes", "index" : "analyzed", "similarity" : "mastering_similarity" },
    "contents" : { "type" : "string", "store" : "no", "index" : "analyzed" }
   }
  }
 }
}
```

You can, of course, have more than one similarity configuration, but let's focus on the preceding example. We've defined a new similarity model named `mastering_similarity`, which is based on the default similarity, which is the TF/IDF one. We've set the `discount_overlaps` property to `false` for this similarity, and we've used it as the similarity for the `name` field. We'll talk about what properties can be used for different similarities further in this section. Now, let's see how to change the default similarity model Elasticsearch will use.

[442]

Choosing the default similarity model

In order to change the similarity model used by default, we need to provide a configuration of a similarity model that will be called `default`. For example, if we would like to use our `mastering_similarity` "name" as the default one, we would have to change the preceding configuration to the following one (the whole example is stored in the `posts_default_similarity.json` file):

```
{
 "settings" : {
  "index" : {
   "similarity" : {
    "default" : {
     "type" : "default",
     "discount_overlaps" : false
    }
   }
  }
 },
 ...
}
```

Because of the fact that the query norm and coordination factors (which were explained in the *Default Apache Lucene scoring explained* section in *Chapter 2, Power User Query DSL*) are used by all similarity models globally and are taken from the default similarity, Elasticsearch allows us to change them when needed. To do this, we need to define another similarity—one called base. It is defined exactly the same as what we've shown previously, but instead of setting its name to default, we set it to base, just like this (the whole example is stored in the `posts_base_similarity.json` file):

```
{
 "settings" : {
  "index" : {
   "similarity" : {
    "base" : {
     "type" : "default",
     "discount_overlaps" : false
    }
   }
  }
 },
 ...
}
```

If the base similarity is present in the index configuration, Elasticsearch will use it to calculate the `query norm` and `coord` factors when calculating the score using other similarity models.

Configuring the chosen similarity model

Each of the newly introduced similarity models can be configured to match our needs. Elasticsearch allows us to use the default and `BM25` similarities without any configuration, because they are preconfigured for us. In the case of `DFR` and `IB`, we need to provide the configuration in order to use them. Let's now see what properties each of the similarity models' implementation provides.

Configuring the TF/IDF similarity

In the case of the TF/IDF similarity, we are allowed to set only a single parameter – `discount_overlaps`, which defaults to `true`. By default, the tokens that have their position increment set to `0` (and therefore, are placed at the same position as the one before them) will not be taken into consideration when calculating the score. If we want them to be taken into consideration, we need to configure the similarity with the `discount_overlaps` property set to `false`.

Configuring the Okapi BM25 similarity

In the case of the Okapi BM25 similarity, we have these parameters: we can configure `k1` (controls the saturation – nonlinear term frequency normalization) as a float value, `b` (controls how the document length affects the term frequency values) as a float value, and `discount_overlaps`, which is exactly the same as in TF/IDF similarity.

Configuring the DFR similarity

In the case of the DFR similarity, we have these parameters that we can configure: `basic_model` (which can take the value `be`, `d`, `g`, `if`, `in`, or `ine`), `after_effect` (with values of `no`, `b`, and `l`), and the normalization (which can be `no`, `h1`, `h2`, `h3`, or `z`). If we choose a normalization other than `no`, we need to set the normalization factor. Depending on the chosen normalization, we should use `normalization.h1.c` (the float value) for the `h1` normalization, `normalization.h2.c` (the float value) for the `h2` normalization, `normalization.h3.c` (the float value) for the `h3` normalization, and `normalization.z.z` (the float value) for the `z` normalization. For example, this is what the example similarity configuration could look like:

```
"similarity" : {
 "esserverbook_dfr_similarity" : {
  "type" : "DFR",
  "basic_model" : "g",
```

```
    "after_effect" : "l",
    "normalization" : "h2",
    "normalization.h2.c" : "2.0"
  }
}
```

Configuring the IB similarity

In the case of the IB similarity, we have these parameters that we can configure: the distribution property (which can take the value of `ll` or `spl`) and the lambda property (which can take the value of `df` or `tff`). In addition to this, we can choose the normalization factor, which is the same as the one used for the DFR similarity, so we'll omit describing it for the second time. This is what the example IB similarity configuration could look like:

```
"similarity" : {
 "esserverbook_ib_similarity" : {
   "type" : "IB",
   "distribution" : "ll",
   "lambda" : "df",
   "normalization" : "z",
   "normalization.z.z" : "0.25"
  }
}
```

Configuring the LM Dirichlet similarity

In the case of the LM Dirichlet similarity, we have the `mu` property that we can configure the `mu` property, which is by default set to `2000`. An example configuration of this could look as follows:

```
"similarity" : {
 "esserverbook_lm_dirichlet_similarity" : {
   "type" : "LMDirichlet",
   "mu" : "1000"
  }
}
```

Configuring the LM Jelinek Mercer similarity

When it comes to the LM Jelinek Mercer similarity, we can configure the `lambda` property, which is set to `0.1` by default. An example configuration of this could look as follows:

```
"similarity" : {
 "esserverbook_lm_jelinek_mercer_similarity" : {
   "type" : "LMJelinekMercer",
```

```
    "lambda" : "0.7"
  }
}
```

 It is said that for short fields (like the document title) the optimal lambda value is around `0.1`, while for long fields the lambda should be set to `0.7`.

Choosing the right directory implementation – the store module

The store module is one of the modules that we usually don't pay much attention to when configuring our cluster; however, it is very important. It is an abstraction between the I/O subsystem and Apache Lucene itself. All the operation that Lucene does with the hard disk drive is done using the store module. Most of the store types in Elasticsearch are mapped to an appropriate Apache Lucene Directory class (http://lucene.apache.org/core/4_9_0/core/org/apache/lucene/store/Directory.html). The directory is used to access all the files the index is built of, so it is crucial to properly configure it.

The store type

Elasticsearch exposes five store types that we can use. Let's see what they provide and how we can leverage their features.

The simple filesystem store

The simplest implementation of the `Directory` class that is available is implemented using a random access file (Java `RandomAccessFile` – http://docs.oracle.com/javase/7/docs/api/java/io/RandomAccessFile.html) and maps to `SimpleFSDirectory` (http://lucene.apache.org/core/4_9_0/core/org/apache/lucene/store/SimpleFSDirectory.html) in Apache Lucene. It is sufficient for very simple applications. However, the main bottleneck will be multithreaded access, which has poor performance. In the case of Elasticsearch, it is usually better to use the new I/O-based system store instead of the Simple filesystem store. However, if you would like to use this system store, you should set `index.store.type` to `simplefs`.

The new I/O filesystem store

This store type uses the Directory class implementation based on the `FileChannel` class (http://docs.oracle.com/javase/7/docs/api/java/nio/channels/FileChannel.html) from `java.nio package` and maps to `NIOFSDirectory` in Apache Lucene (http://lucene.apache.org/core/4_9_0/core/org/apache/lucene/store/NIOFSDirectory.html). The discussed implementation allows multiple threads to access the same files concurrently without performance degradation. In order to use this store, one should set `index.store.type` to `niofs`.

> Please remember that because of some bugs that exist in the JVM machine for Microsoft Windows, it is very probable that the new I/O filesystem store will suffer from performance problems when running on Microsoft Windows. More information about this bug can be found at http://bugs.sun.com/bugdatabase/view_bug.do?bug_id=6265734.

The MMap filesystem store

This store type uses Apache Lucene's `MMapDirectory` (http://lucene.apache.org/core/4_9_0/core/org/apache/lucene/store/MMapDirectory.html) implementation. It uses the `mmap` system call (http://en.wikipedia.org/wiki/Mmap) for reading, and it uses random access files for writing. It uses a portion of the available virtual memory address space in the process equal to the size of the file being mapped. It doesn't have any locking, so it is scalable when it comes to multithread access. When using `mmap` to read index files for the operating system, it looks like it is already cached (it was mapped to the virtual space). Because of this, when reading a file from the Apache Lucene index, this file doesn't need to be loaded into the operating system cache and thus, the access is faster. This basically allows Lucene and thus Elasticsearch to directly access the I/O cache, which should result in fast access to index files.

It is worth noting that the MMap filesystem store works best on 64-bit environments and should only be used on 32-bit machines when you are sure that the index is small enough and the virtual address space is sufficient. In order to use this store, one should set `index.store.type` to `mmapfs`.

The hybrid filesystem store

Introduced in Elasticsearch 1.3.0, the hybrid file store uses both NIO and MMap access depending on the file type. A the time of writing this, only term dictionary and doc values were read and written using MMap, and all the other files of the index were opened using NIOFSDirectory. In order to use this store, one should set `index.store.type` to `default`.

The memory store

This is the second store type that is not based on the Apache Lucene Directory (the first one is the hybrid filesystem store). The memory store allows us to store all the index files in the memory, so the files are not stored on the disk. This is crucial, because it means that the index data is not persistent—it will be removed whenever a full cluster restart will happen. However, if you need a small, very fast index that can have multiple shards and replicas and can be rebuilt very fast, the memory store type may be the thing you are looking for. In order to use this store, one should set `index.store.type` to `memory`.

> The data stored in the memory store, like all the other stores, is replicated among all the nodes that can hold data.

Additional properties

When using the memory store type, we also have some degree of control over the caches, which are very important when using the memory store. Please remember that all the following settings are set per node:

- `cache.memory.direct`: This defaults to `true` and specifies whether the memory store should be allocated outside of the JVM heap memory. It is usually a good idea to leave it to the default value so that the heap is not overloaded with data.
- `cache.memory.small_buffer_size`: This defaults to `1kb` and defines a small buffer size—the internal memory structure used to hold segments' information and deleted documents' information.
- `cache.memory.large_buffer_size`: This defaults to `1mb` and defines a large buffer size—the internal memory structure used to hold index files other than segments' information and deleted documents.

- `cache.memory.small_cache_size`: The objects' small cache size—the internal memory structure used for the caching of index segments' information and deleted documents' information. It defaults to `10mb`.
- `cache.memory.large_cache_size`: The objects' large cache size—the internal memory structure used to cache information about the index other than the index segments' information and deleted documents' information. It defaults to `500mb`.

The default store type

There are differences when it comes to the default store of Elasticsearch 1.3.0 and the newer and older versions.

The default store type for Elasticsearch 1.3.0 and higher

Starting from Elasticsearch 1.3.0, the new default Elasticsearch store type is the hybrid one that we can choose by setting `index.store.type` to `default`.

The default store type for Elasticsearch versions older than 1.3.0

By default, Elasticsearch versions older than 1.3.0 use filesystem-based storage. However different store types are chosen for different operating systems. For example, for a 32-bit Microsoft Windows system, the `simplefs` type will be used; `mmapfs` will be used when Elasticsearch is running on Solaris and Microsoft Windows 64 bit, and `niofs` will be used for the rest of the world.

> If you are looking for some information from experts on how they see which Directory implementation to use, please look at the `http://blog.thetaphi.de/2012/07/use-lucenes-mmapdirectory-on-64bit.html` post written by Uwe Schindler and `http://jprante.github.io/lessons/2012/07/26/Mmap-with-Lucene.html` by Jörg Prante.

Usually, the default store type will be the one that you want to use. However, sometimes, it is worth considering using the MMap file system store type, especially when you have plenty of memory and your indices are big. This is because when using `mmap` to access the index file, it will cause the index files to be cached only once and be reused both by Apache Lucene and the operating system.

NRT, flush, refresh, and transaction log

In an ideal search solution, when new data is indexed, it is instantly available for searching. When you start Elasticsearch, this is exactly how it works even in distributed environments. However, this is not the whole truth, and we will show you why it is like this.

Let's start by indexing an example document to the newly created index using the following command:

```
curl -XPOST localhost:9200/test/test/1 -d '{ "title": "test" }'
```

Now, let's replace this document, and let's try to find it immediately. In order to do this, we'll use the following command chain:

```
curl -XPOST localhost:9200/test/test/1 -d '{ "title": "test2" }' ;
curl -XGET 'localhost:9200/test/test/_search?pretty'
```

The preceding command will probably result in a response that is very similar to the following one:

```
{"_index":"test","_type":"test","_id":"1","_version":2,"created":false}{
  "took" : 1,
  "timed_out" : false,
  "_shards" : {
    "total" : 5,
    "successful" : 5,
    "failed" : 0
  },
  "hits" : {
    "total" : 1,
    "max_score" : 1.0,
    "hits" : [ {
      "_index" : "test",
      "_type" : "test",
      "_id" : "1",
      "_score" : 1.0,
      "_source":{ "title": "test" }
    } ]
  }
}
```

We see two responses glued together. The first line starts with a response to the indexing command—the first command we've sent. As you can see, everything is correct—we've updated the document (look at `_version`). With the second command, our search query should return the document with the `title` field set to `test2`; however, as you can see, it returned the first document. What happened? Before we give you the answer to this question, we will take a step back and discuss how the underlying Apache Lucene library makes the newly indexed documents available for searching.

Updating the index and committing changes

As we already know from the *Introducing Apache Lucene* section in *Chapter 1, Introduction to Elasticsearch*, during the indexing process, new documents are written into segments. The segments are independent indices, which means that queries that are run in parallel to indexing should add newly created segments from time to time to the set of these segments that are used for searching. Apache Lucene does this by creating subsequent (because of the write-once nature of the index) `segments_N` files, which list segments in the index. This process is called committing. Lucene can do this in a secure way—we are sure that all changes or none of them hit the index. If a failure happens, we can be sure that the index will be in a consistent state.

Let's return to our example. The first operation adds the document to the index but doesn't run the `commit` command to Lucene. This is exactly how it works. However, a commit is not enough for the data to be available for searching. The Lucene library uses an abstraction class called `Searcher` to access the index, and this class needs to be refreshed.

After a commit operation, the `Searcher` object should be reopened in order for it to be able to see the newly created segments. This whole process is called refresh. For performance reasons, Elasticsearch tries to postpone costly refreshes and, by default, refresh is not performed after indexing a single document (or a batch of them), but the Searcher is refreshed every second. This happens quite often, but sometimes, applications require the refresh operation to be performed more often than once every second. When this happens, you can consider using another technology, or the requirements should be verified. If required, there is a possibility of forcing the refresh by using the Elasticsearch API. For example, in our example, we can add the following command:

```
curl -XGET localhost:9200/test/_refresh
```

If we add the preceding command before the search, Elasticsearch would respond as we had expected.

Changing the default refresh time

The time between automatic Searcher refresh operations can be changed by using the `index.refresh_interval` parameter either in the Elasticsearch configuration file or by using the Update Settings API, for example:

```
curl -XPUT localhost:9200/test/_settings -d '{
  "index" : {
    "refresh_interval" : "5m"
  }
}'
```

The preceding command will change the automatic refresh to be performed every 5 minutes. Please remember that the data that is indexed between refreshes won't be visible by queries.

> As we said, the refresh operation is costly when it comes to resources. The longer the period of the refresh, the faster your indexing will be. If you are planning for a very high indexing procedure when you don't need your data to be visible until the indexing ends, you can consider disabling the refresh operation by setting the `index.refresh_interval` parameter to `-1` and setting it back to its original value after the indexing is done.

The transaction log

Apache Lucene can guarantee index consistency and all or nothing indexing, which is great. However, this fact cannot ensure us that there will be no data loss when failure happens while writing data to the index (for example, when there isn't enough space on the device, the device is faulty, or there aren't enough file handlers available to create new index files). Another problem is that frequent commit is costly in terms of performance (as you may recall, a single commit will trigger a new segment creation, and this can trigger the segments to merge). Elasticsearch solves these issues by implementing the transaction log. The transaction log holds all uncommitted transactions and, from time to time, Elasticsearch creates a new log for subsequent changes. When something goes wrong, the transaction log can be replayed to make sure that none of the changes were lost. All of these tasks are happening automatically, so the user may not be aware of the fact that the commit was triggered at a particular moment. In Elasticsearch, the moment where the information from the transaction log is synchronized with the storage (which is the Apache Lucene index) and the transaction log is cleared is called **flushing**.

> Please note the difference between flush and refresh operations. In most of the cases, refresh is exactly what you want. It is all about making new data available for searching. On the other hand, the flush operation is used to make sure that all the data is correctly stored in the index and the transaction log can be cleared.

In addition to automatic flushing, it can be forced manually using the flush API. For example, we can run a command to flush all the data stored in the transaction log for all indices by running the following command:

`curl -XGET localhost:9200/_flush`

Or, we can run the `flush` command for the particular index, which in our case is the one called `library`:

`curl -XGET localhost:9200/library/_flush`

`curl -XGET localhost:9200/library/_refresh`

In the second example, we used it together with the refresh, which after flushing the data, opens a new searcher.

The transaction log configuration

If the default behavior of the transaction log is not enough, Elasticsearch allows us to configure its behavior when it comes to the transaction log handling. The following parameters can be set in the `elasticsearch.yml` file as well as using index settings' Update API to control the transaction log behavior:

- `index.translog.flush_threshold_period`: This defaults to 30 minutes (`30m`). It controls the time after which the flush will be forced automatically even if no new data was being written to it. In some cases, this can cause a lot of I/O operation, so sometimes it's better to perform the flush more often with less data stored in it.

- `index.translog.flush_threshold_ops`: This specifies the maximum number of operations after which the flush operation will be performed. By default, Elasticsearch does not limit these operations.

- `index.translog.flush_threshold_size`: This specifies the maximum size of the transaction log. If the size of the transaction log is equal to or greater than the parameter, the flush operation will be performed. It defaults to `200 MB`.

- `index.translog.interval`: This defaults to `5s` and describes the period between consecutive checks if the flush is needed. Elasticsearch randomizes this value to be greater than the defined one and less than double of it.
- `index.gateway.local.sync`: This defines how often the transaction log should be sent to the disk using the `fsync` system call. The default is `5s`.
- `index.translog.disable_flush`: This option allows us to disable the automatic flush. By default, flushing is enabled, but sometimes, it is handy to disable it temporarily, for example, during the import of a large amount of documents.

 All of the mentioned parameters are specified for an index of our choice, but they define the behavior of the transaction log for each of the index shards.

In addition to setting the previously mentioned properties in the `elasticsearch.yml` file, we can also set them by using the Settings Update API. For example, the following command will result in disabling flushing for the `test` index:

```
curl -XPUT localhost:9200/test/_settings -d '{
 "index" : {
   "translog.disable_flush" : true
  }
}'
```

The previous command was run before the import of a large amount of data, which gave us a performance boost for indexing. However, one should remember to turn on flushing when the import is done.

Near real-time GET

Transaction logs give us one more feature for free, that is, the real-time GET operation, which provides us with the possibility of returning the previous version of the document, including noncommitted versions. The real-time GET operation fetches data from the index, but first, it checks whether a newer version of this document is available in the transaction log. If there is no flushed document, the data from the index is ignored and a newer version of the document is returned—the one from the transaction log.

In order to see how it works, you can replace the search operation in our example with the following command:

`curl -XGET localhost:9200/test/test/1?pretty`

Elasticsearch should return a result similar to the following:

```
{
  "_index" : "test",
  "_type" : "test",
  "_id" : "1",
  "_version" : 2,
  "exists" : true, "_source" : { "title": "test2" }
}
```

If you look at the result, you would see that, again, the result was just as we expected and no trick with refresh was required to obtain the newest version of the document.

Segment merging under control

As you already know (we've discussed it throughout *Chapter 1, Introduction to Elasticsearch*), every Elasticsearch index is built out of one or more shards and can have zero or more replicas. You also know that each of the shards and replicas are actual Apache Lucene indices that are built of multiple segments (at least one segment). If you recall, the segments are written once and read many times, and data structures, apart from the information about the deleted documents that are held in one of the files, can be changed. After some time, when certain conditions are met, the contents of some segments can be copied to a bigger segment, and the original segments are discarded and thus deleted from the disk. Such an operation is called **segment merging**.

You may ask yourself, why bother about segment merging? There are a few reasons. First of all, the more segments the index is built of, the slower the search will be and the more memory Lucene will need. In addition to this, segments are immutable, so the information is not deleted from it. If you happen to delete many documents from your index, until the merge happens, these documents are only marked as deleted and are not deleted physically. So, when segment merging happens, the documents that are marked as deleted are not written into the new segment, and this way, they are removed, which decreases the final segment size.

 Many small changes can result in a large number of small segments, which can lead to problems with a large number of opened files. We should always be prepared to handle such situations, for example, by having the appropriate opened files' limit set.

Low-level Index Control

So, just to quickly summarize, segments merging takes place and from the user's point of view, it will result in two effects:

- It will reduce the number of segments in order to allow faster searching when a few segments are merged into a single one
- It will reduce the size of the index because of removing the deleted documents when the merge is finalized

However, you have to remember that segment merging comes with a price: the price of I/O operations, which can affect performance on slower systems. Because of this, Elasticsearch allows us to choose the merge policy and the store level throttling.

Choosing the right merge policy

Although segment merging is Apache Lucene's duty, Elasticsearch allows us to configure which merge policy we would like to use. There are three policies that we are currently allowed to use:

- `tiered` (the default one)
- `log_byte_size`
- `log_doc`

Each of the preceding mentioned policies have their own parameters, which define their behavior and the default values that we can override (please look at the section dedicated to the policy of your choice to see what those parameters are).

In order to tell Elasticsearch which merge policy we want to use, we should set `index.merge.policy.type` to the desired type, shown as follows:

```
index.merge.policy.type: tiered
```

> Once the index is created with the specified merge policy type, it can't be changed. However, all the properties defining the merge policy behavior can be changed using the Index Update API.

Let's now look at the different merge policies and the functionality that they provide. After this, we will discuss all the configuration options provided by the policies.

The tiered merge policy

The tiered merge policy is the default merge policy that Elasticsearch uses. It merges segments of approximately similar size, taking into account the maximum number of segments allowed per tier. It is also possible to differentiate the number of segments that are allowed to be merged at once from how many segments are allowed to be present per tier. During indexing, this merge policy will compute how many segments are allowed to be present in the index, which is called **budget**. If the number of segments the index is built of is higher than the computed budget, the tiered policy will first sort the segments by the decreasing order of their size (taking into account the deleted documents). After that, it will find the merge that has the lowest cost. The merge cost is calculated in a way that merges are reclaiming more deletions, and having a smaller size is favored.

If the merge produces a segment that is larger than the value specified by the `index.merge.policy.max_merged_segment` property, the policy will merge fewer segments to keep the segment size under the budget. This means that for indices that have large shards, the default value of the `index.merge.policy.max_merged_segment` property may be too low and will result in the creation of many segments, slowing down your queries. Depending on the volume of your data, you should monitor your segments and adjust the merge policy setting to match your needs.

The log byte size merge policy

The log byte size merge policy is a merge policy, which over time, will produce an index that will be built of a logarithmic size of indices. There will be a few large segments, then there will be a few merge factor smaller segments, and so on. You can imagine that there will be a few segments of the same level of size when the number of segments will be lower than the merge factor. When an extra segment is encountered, all the segments within that level are merged. The number of segments an index will contain is proportional to the logarithm of the next size in bytes. This merge policy is generally able to keep the low number of segments in your index while minimizing the cost of segments merging.

The log doc merge policy

The log doc merge policy is similar to the `log_byte_size` merge policy, but instead of operating on the actual segment size in bytes, it operates on the number of documents in the index. This merge policy will perform well when the documents are similar in terms of size or if you want segments of similar sizes in terms of the number of documents.

Merge policies' configuration

We now know how merge policies work, but we lack the knowledge about the configuration options. So now, let's discuss each of the merge policies and see what options are exposed to us. Please remember that the default values will usually be OK for most of the deployments and they should be changed only when needed.

The tiered merge policy

When using the `tiered` merge policy, the following options can be altered:

- `index.merge.policy.expunge_deletes_allowed`: This defaults to `10` and specifies the percentage of deleted documents in a segment in order for it to be considered to be merged when running `expungeDeletes`.

- `index.merge.policy.floor_segment`: This is a property that enables us to prevent the frequent flushing of very small segments. Segments smaller than the size defined by this property are treated by the merge mechanism, as they would have the size equal to the value of this property. It defaults to `2MB`.

- `index.merge.policy.max_merge_at_once`: This specifies the maximum number of segments that will be merged at the same time during indexing. By default, it is set to `10`. Setting the value of this property to higher values can result in multiple segments being merged at once, which will need more I/O resources.

- `index.merge.policy.max_merge_at_once_explicit`: This specifies the maximum number of segments that will be merged at the same time during the optimize operation or `expungeDeletes`. By default, this is set to `30`. This setting will not affect the maximum number of segments that will be merged during indexing.

- `index.merge.policy.max_merged_segment`: This defaults to `5GB` and specifies the maximum size of a single segment that will be produced during segment merging when indexing. This setting is an approximate value, because the merged segment size is calculated by summing the size of segments that are going to be merged minus the size of the deleted documents in these segments.

- `index.merge.policy.segments_per_tier`: This specifies the allowed number of segments per tier. Smaller values of this property result in less segments, which means more merging and lower indexing performance. It defaults to `10` and should be set to a value higher than or equal to `index.merge.policy.max_merge_at_once`, or you'll be facing too many merges and performance issues.

- `index.reclaim_deletes_weight`: This defaults to `2.0` and specifies how many merges that reclaim deletes are favored. When setting this value to `0.0`, the reclaim deletes will not affect the merge selection. The higher the value, the more favored the merge that reclaims deletes will be.
- `index.compund_format`: This is a Boolean value that specifies whether the index should be stored in a compound format or not. It defaults to `false`. If set to `true`, Lucene will store all the files that build the index in a single file. Sometimes, this is useful for systems running constantly out of file handlers, but it will decrease the searching and indexing performance.

The log byte size merge policy

When using the `log_byte_size` merge policy, the following options can be used to configure its behavior:

- `merge_factor`: This specifies how often segments are merged during indexing. With a smaller `merge_factor` value, the searches are faster and less memory is used, but this comes with the cost of slower indexing. With larger `merge_factor` values, it is the opposite—the indexing is faster (because of less merging being done), but the searches are slower and more memory is used. By default, `merge_factor` is given the value of `10`. It is advised to use larger values of `merge_factor` for batch indexing and lower values of this parameter for normal index maintenance.
- `min_merge_size`: This defines the size (the total size of the segment files in bytes) of the smallest segment possible. If a segment is lower in size than the number specified by this property, it will be merged if the `merge_factor` property allows us to do that. This property defaults to `1.6MB` and is very useful in order to avoid having many very small segments. However, one should remember that setting this property to a large value will increase the merging cost.
- `max_merge_size`: This defines the maximum size (the total size of the segment files in bytes) of the segment that can be merged with other segments. By default, it is not set, so there is no limit on the maximum size a segment can be in order to be merged.
- `maxMergeDocs`: This defines the maximum number of documents a segment can have in order to be merged with other segments. By default, it is not set, so there is no limit to the maximum number of documents a segment can have.
- `calibrate_size_by_deletes`: This is a Boolean value, which is set to `true` and specifies whether the size of the deleted documents should be taken into consideration when calculating the segment size.

Low-level Index Control

The mentioned properties we just saw should be prefixed with the `index.merge.policy` prefix. So if we would like to set the `min_merge_docs` property, we should use the `index.merge.policy.min_merge_docs` property.

In addition to this, the `log_byte_size` merge policy accepts the `index.merge.async` and `index.merge.async_interval` properties just like the `tiered` merge policy does.

The log doc merge policy

When using the `log_doc` merge policy, the following options can be used to configure its behavior:

- `merge_factor`: This is same as the property that is present in the `log_byte_size` merge policy, so please refer to this policy for the explanation.
- `min_merge_docs`: This defines the minimum number of documents for the smallest segment. If a segment contains a lower document count than the number specified by this property, it will be merged if the `merge_factor` property allows this. This property defaults to `1000` and is very useful in order to avoid having many very small segments. However, one should remember that setting this property to a large value will increase the merging cost.
- `max_merge_docs`: This defines the maximum number of documents a segment can have in order to be merged with other segments. By default, it is not set, so there is no limit to the maximum number of documents a segment can have.
- `calibrate_size_by_deletes`: This is a Boolean value that defaults to `true` and specifies whether the size of deleted documents should be taken into consideration when calculating the segment size.

Similar to the previous merge policy, the previously mentioned properties should be prefixed with the `index.merge.policy` prefix. So if we would like to set the `min_merge_docs` property, we should use the `index.merge.policy.min_merge_docs` property.

Scheduling

In addition to having control over how the merge policy is behaving, Elasticsearch allows us to define the execution of the merge policy once a merge is needed. There are two merge schedulers available, with the default being `ConcurrentMergeScheduler`.

The concurrent merge scheduler

This is a merge scheduler that will use multiple threads in order to perform segments' merging. This scheduler will create a new thread until the maximum number of threads is reached. If the maximum number of threads is reached and a new thread is needed (because segments' merge needs to be performed), all the indexing will be paused until at least one merge is completed.

In order to control the maximum threads allowed, we can alter the `index.merge.scheduler.max_thread_count` property. By default, it is set to the value calculated by the following equation:

```
maximum_value(1, minimum_value(3, available_processors / 2)
```

So, if our system has eight processors available, the maximum number of threads that the concurrent merge scheduler is allowed to use will be equal to four.

You should also remember that this is especially not good for spinning disks. You want to be sure that merging won't saturate your disks' throughput. Because of this, if you see extensive merging, you should lower the number of merging threads. It is usually said that for spinning disks, the number of threads used by the concurrent merge scheduler should be set to 1.

The serial merge scheduler

A simple merge scheduler uses the same thread for merging. It results in a merge that stops all the other document processing that was happening on the same thread, which in this case, means the stopping of indexing. This merge scheduler is only provided for backwards compatibility and, in fact, uses the concurrent merge scheduler with the number of threads equal to one.

Setting the desired merge scheduler

In order to set the desired merge scheduler, one should set the `index.merge.scheduler.type` property to the value of `concurrent` or `serial`. For example, in order to use the concurrent merge scheduler, one should set the following property:

```
index.merge.scheduler.type: concurrent
```

In order to use the serial merge scheduler, one should set the following property:

```
index.merge.scheduler.type: serial
```

Low-level Index Control

> When talking about the merge policy and merge schedulers, it would be nice to visualize them. If one needs to see how the merges are done in the underlying Apache Lucene library, we suggest that you visit Mike McCandless' blog post at `http://blog.mikemccandless.com/2011/02/visualizing-lucenes-segment-merges.html`.
>
> In addition to this, there is a plugin that allows us to see what is happening to the segments called SegmentSpy. Refer to the following URL for more information:
>
> `https://github.com/polyfractal/elasticsearch-segmentspy`

When it is too much for I/O – throttling explained

In the *Choosing the right directory implementation* section, we've talked about the store type, which means we are now able to configure the store module to match our needs. However, we didn't write everything about the store module – we didn't write about throttling.

Controlling I/O throttling

As you remember from the *Segment merging under control* section, Apache Lucene stores the data in immutable segment files that can be read many times but can be written only once. The merge process is asynchronous and, in general, it should not interfere with indexing and searching, looking from the Lucene point of view. However, problems may occur because merging is expensive when it comes to I/O – it requires you to read the segments that are going to be merged and write new ones. If searching and indexing happen concurrently, this can be too much for the I/O subsystem, especially on systems with low I/O. This is where throttling kicks in – we can control how much I/O Elasticsearch will use.

Configuration

Throttling can be configured both on a node-level and on the index-level, so you can either configure how many resources a node will use or how many resources will be used for the index.

The throttling type

In order to configure the throttling type on the node-level, one should use the `indices.store.throttle.type` property, which can take the value of `none`, `merge`, and `all`. The `none` value will tell Elasticsearch that no limiting should take place. The `merge` value tells Elasticsearch that we want to limit the I/O usage for the merging of nodes (and it is the default value) and the `all` value specifies that we want to limit all store module-based operations.

In order to configure the throttling type on the index-level, one should use the `index.store.throttle.type` property, which can take the same values as the `indices.store.throttle.type` property with an additional one – `node`. The `node` value will tell Elasticsearch that instead of using per-index throttling limiting, we will use the node-level configuration. This is the default value.

Maximum throughput per second

In both cases, when using index or node-level throttling, we are able to set the maximum bytes per second that I/O can use. For the value of this property, we can use `10mb`, `500mb`, or anything that we need. For the index-level configuration, we should use the `index.store.throttle.max_bytes_per_sec` property and for the node-level configuration, we should use `indices.store.throttle.max_bytes_per_sec`.

> The previously mentioned properties can be set both in the `elasticsearch.yml` file and can also be updated dynamically using the cluster update settings for the node-level configuration and using the index update settings for the index-level configuration.

Node throttling defaults

On the node-level, since Elasticsearch 0.90.1, throttling is enabled by default. The `indices.store.throttle.type` property is set to `merge` and the `indices.store.throttle.max_bytes_per_sec` property is set to `20mb`. Elasticsearch versions before 0.90.1 don't have throttling enabled by default.

Performance considerations

When using **SSD** (**solid state drives**) or when query speed matters only a little (or you are not searching when you index your data), it is worth considering disabling throttling completely. We can do this by setting the `indices.store.throttle.type` property to `none`. This causes Elasticsearch to not use any store-level throttling and use full disk throughput for store-based operations.

The configuration example

Now, let's imagine that we have a cluster that consists of four Elasticsearch nodes and we want to configure throttling for the whole cluster. By default, we want the merge operation not to process more than 50 megabytes per second for a node. We know that we can handle such operations without affecting the search performance, and this is what we are aiming at. In order to achieve this, we would run the following request:

```
curl -XPUT 'localhost:9200/_cluster/settings' -d '{
 "persistent" : {
  "indices.store.throttle.type" : "merge",
  "indices.store.throttle.max_bytes_per_sec" : "50mb"
 }
}'
```

In addition to this, we have a single index called `payments` that is very rarely used, and we've placed it in the smallest machine in the cluster. This index doesn't have replicas and is built of a single shard. What we would like to do for this index is limit the merges to process a maximum of 10 megabytes per second. So, in addition to the preceding command, we would run one like this:

```
curl -XPUT 'localhost:9200/payments/_settings' -d '{
 "index.store.throttle.type" : "merge",
 "index.store.throttle.max_bytes_per_sec" : "10mb"
}'
```

After running the preceding commands, we can check our index settings by running the following command:

```
curl -XGET 'localhost:9200/payments/_settings?pretty'
```

In response, we should get the following JSON:

```
    {
      "payments" : {
        "settings" : {
          "index" : {
            "creation_date" : "1414072648520",
            "store" : {
              "throttle" : {
                "type" : "merge",
                "max_bytes_per_sec" : "10mb"
```

```
            }
        },
        "number_of_shards" : "5",
        "number_of_replicas" : "1",
        "version" : {
          "created" : "1040001"
        },
        "uuid" : "M3lePTOvSN2jnDz1J0t4Uw"
      }
    }
  }
}
```

As you can see, after updating the index setting, closing the index, and opening it again, we've finally got our settings working.

Understanding Elasticsearch caching

One of the very important parts of Elasticsearch, although not always visible to the users, is caching. It allows Elasticsearch to store commonly used data in memory and reuse it on demand. Of course, we can't cache everything—we usually have way more data than we have memory, and creating caches may be quite expensive when it comes to performance. In this chapter, we will look at the different caches exposed by Elasticsearch, and we will discuss how they are used and how we can control their usage. Hopefully, such information will allow you to better understand how this great search server works internally.

The filter cache

The filter cache is the simplest of all the caches available in Elasticsearch. It is used during query time to cache the results of filters that are used in queries. We already talked about filters in section *Handling filters and why it matters* of *Chapter 2, Power User Query DSL*, but let's look at a simple example. Let's assume that we have the following query:

```
{
 "query" : {
  "filtered" : {
   "query" : {
    "match_all" : {}
   },
   "filter" : {
    "term" : {
```

```
            "category" : "romance"
          }
        }
      }
    }
}
```

The preceding query will return all the documents that have the `romance` term in the `category` field. As you can see, we've used the `match_all` query combined with a filter. Now, after the initial query, every query with the same filter present in it will reuse the results of our filter and save the precious I/O and CPU resources.

Filter cache types

There are two types of filter caches available in Elasticsearch: node-level and index-level filter caches. This gives us the possibility of choosing the filter cache to be dependent on the index or on a node (which is the default behavior). As we can't always predict where the given index will be allocated (actually, its shards and replicas), it is not recommended that you use the index-level filter cache because we can't predict the memory usage in such cases.

Node-level filter cache configuration

The default and recommended filter cache type is configured for all shards allocated to a given node (set using the `index.cache.filter.type` property to the `node` value or not setting that property at all). Elasticsearch allows us to use the `indices.cache.filter.size` property to configure the size of this cache. We can either use a percentage value as `10%` (which is the default value), or a static memory value as `1024mb`. If we use the percentage value, Elasticsearch will calculate it as a percentage of the maximum heap memory given to a node.

The node-level filter cache is a **Least Recently Used** cache type (**LRU**), which means that while removing cache entries, the ones that were used the least number of times will be thrown away in order to make place for the newer entries.

Index-level filter cache configuration

The second type of filter cache that Elasticsearch allows us to use is the index-level filter cache. We can configure its behavior by configuring the following properties:

- `index.cache.filter.type`: This property sets the type of the cache, which can take the values of `resident`, `soft`, `weak`, and `node` (the default one). By using this property, Elasticsearch allows us to choose the implementation of the cache. The entries in the `resident` cache can't be removed by JVM unless we want them to be removed (either by using the API or by setting the maximum size or expiration time) and is basically recommended because of this (filling up the filter cache can be expensive). The `soft` and `weak` filter cache types can be cleared by JVM when it lacks memory, with the difference that when clearing up memory, JVM will choose the weaker reference objects first and then choose the one that uses the soft reference. The `node` value tells Elasticsearch to use the node-level filter cache.

- `index.cache.filter.max_size`: This property specifies the maximum number of cache entries that can be stored in the filter cache (the default is `-1`, which means unbounded). You need to remember that this setting is not applied for the whole index but for a single segment of a shard for the index, so the memory usage will differ depending on how many shards (and replicas) there are (for the given index) and how many segments the index contains. Generally, the default, unbounded filter cache is fine with the `soft` type and the proper queries that are paying attention in order to make the caches reusable.

- `index.cache.filter.expire`: This property specifies the expiration time of an entry in the filter cache, which is unbounded (set to `-1`) by default. If we want our filter cache to expire if not accessed, we can set the maximum time of inactivity. For example, if we would like our cache to expire after 60 minutes, we should set this property to `60m`.

> If you want to read more about the soft and weak references in Java, please refer to the Java documentation, especially the Javadocs, for these two types: http://docs.oracle.com/javase/8/docs/api/java/lang/ref/SoftReference.html and http://docs.oracle.com/javase/8/docs/api/java/lang/ref/WeakReference.html.

The field data cache

The field data cache is used when we want to send queries that involve operations that work on uninverted data. What Elasticsearch needs to do is load all the values for a given field and store that in the memory—you can call this field data cache. This cache is used by Elasticsearch when we use faceting, aggregations, scripting, or sorting on the field value. When first executing an operation that requires data uninverting, Elasticsearch loads all the data for that field into the memory. Yes, that's right; all the data from a given field is loaded into the memory by default and is never removed from it. Elasticsearch does this to be able to provide fast document-based access to values in a field. Remember that the field data cache is usually expensive to build from the hardware resource's point of view, because the data for the whole field needs to be loaded into the memory, and this requires both I/O operations and CPU resources.

> One should remember that for every field that we sort on or use faceting on, the data needs to be loaded into the memory each and every term. This can be expensive, especially for the fields that are high cardinality ones: the ones with numerous different terms in them.

Field data or doc values

Lucene doc values and their implementation in Elasticsearch is getting better and better with each release. With the release of Elasticsearch 1.4.0, they are almost, or as fast as, the field data cache. The thing is that doc values are calculated during indexing time and are stored on the disk along with the index, and they don't require as much memory as the field data cache. In fact, they require very little heap space and are almost as fast as the field data cache. If you are using operations that require large amounts of field data cache, you should consider using doc values for such fields. You only need to add the `doc_values` property and set it to `true` for such fields, and Elasticsearch will do the rest.

> At the time of writing this, Elasticsearch does not allow using doc values on analyzed string fields. You can use doc values with all the other field types.

For example, if we would like to set our year field to use doc values, we would change its configuration to the following one:

```
"year" : {
 "type" : "long",
 "ignore_malformed" : false,
```

```
"index" : "analyzed",
"doc_values" : true
}
```

If you reindex your data, Elasticsearch would use the doc values (instead of the field data cache) for the operations that require uninverted data in the `year` field, for example, aggregations.

Node-level field data cache configuration

Since Elasticsearch 0.90.0, we are allowed to use the following properties to configure the node-level field data cache, which is the default field data cache if we don't alter the configuration:

- `indices.fielddata.cache.size`: This specifies the maximum size of the field data cache either as a percentage value such as `20%`, or an absolute memory size such as `10gb`. If we use the percentage value, Elasticsearch will calculate it as a percentage of the maximum heap memory given to a node. By default, the field data cache size is unbounded and should be monitored, as it can consume a vast amount of memory given to the JVM.

- `indices.fielddata.cache.expire`: This property specifies the expiration time of an entry in the field data cache, which is set to `-1` by default, which means that the entries in the cache won't be expired. If we want our field data cache to expire if not accessed, we can set the maximum time of inactivity. For example, if we like our cache to expire after 60 minutes, we should set this property to `60m`. Please remember that the field data cache is very expensive to rebuild, and the expiration should be considered with caution.

If we want to be sure that Elasticsearch will use the node-level field data cache, we should set the `index.fielddata.cache.type` property to the `node` value or not set that property at all.

Index-level field data cache configuration

Similar to index-level filter cache, we can also use the index-level field data cache, but again, it is not recommended that you do because of the same reasons: it is hard to predict which shards or which indices will be allocated to which nodes. Because of this, we can't predict the amount of memory that will be used for the field data cache for each index, and we can run into memory-related issues when Elasticsearch does the rebalancing, for example.

However, if you know what you are doing and what you want to use—resident or soft field data cache—you can use the `index.fielddata.cache.type` property and set it to `resident` or `soft`. As we already discussed during the filter cache's description, the entries in the resident cache can't be removed by JVM unless we want them to be, and it is basically recommended that you use this cache type when we want to use the index-level field data cache. Rebuilding the field data cache is expensive and will affect the Elasticsearch query's performance. The `soft` field data cache types can be cleared by JVM when it lacks memory.

The field data cache filtering

In addition to the previously mentioned configuration options, Elasticsearch allows us to choose which field values are loaded into the field data cache. This can be useful in some cases, especially if you remember that sorting, faceting, and aggregations use the field data cache to calculate the results. Elasticsearch allows us to use three types of field data loading filtering: by term frequency, by using `regex`, or a combination of both methods.

Let's talk about one of the examples where field data filtering can be useful and where you may want to exclude the terms with lower frequency from the results of faceting. For example, we may need to do this because we know that we have some terms in the index that have spelling mistakes, and these are lower cardinality terms for sure. We don't want to bother calculating aggregations for them, so we can remove them from the data, correct them in our data source, or remove them from the field data cache by filtering. This will not only exclude them from the results returned by Elasticsearch, but it will also make the field data memory footprint lower, because less data will be stored in the memory. Now let's look at the filtering possibilities.

Adding field data filtering information

In order to introduce the field data cache filtering information, we need to add an additional object to our mappings field definition: the `fielddata` object with its child object—`filter`. So our extended field definition for some abstract `tag` field would look as follows:

```
"tag" : {
 "type" : "string",
 "index" : "not_analyzed",
 "fielddata" : {
  "filter" : {
   ...
  }
 }
}
```

We will see what to put in the `filter` object in the upcoming sections.

Filtering by term frequency

Filtering by term frequency allows us to only load the terms that have a frequency higher than the specified minimum (the min parameter) and lower than the specified maximum (the max parameter). The term frequency bounded by the min and max parameters is not specified for the whole index but per segment, which is very important, because these frequencies will differ. The min and max parameters can be specified either as a percentage (for example, 1 percent is 0.01 and 50 percent is 0.5), or as an absolute number.

In addition to this, we can include the min_segment_size property that specifies the minimum number of documents a segment should contain in order to be taken into consideration while building the field data cache.

For example, if we would like to store only the terms that come from segments with at least 100 documents and the terms that have a segment term frequency between 1 percent to 20 percent in the field data cache, we should have mappings similar to the following ones:

```
{
 "book" : {
  "properties" : {
   "tag" : {
    "type" : "string",
    "index" : "not_analyzed",
    "fielddata" : {
     "filter" : {
      "frequency" : {
       "min" : 0.01,
       "max" : 0.2,
       "min_segment_size" : 100
      }
     }
    }
   }
  }
 }
}
```

Filtering by regex

In addition to filtering by the term frequency, we can also filter by the regex expression. In such a case, only the terms that match the specified regex will be loaded into the field data cache. For example, if we only want to load the data from the tag field, which probably has Twitter tags (starting with the # character), we should have the following mappings:

```
{
 "book" : {
  "properties" : {
   "tag" : {
    "type" : "string",
    "index" : "not_analyzed",
    "fielddata" : {
     "filter" : {
      "regex" : "^#.*"
     }
    }
   }
  }
 }
}
```

Filtering by regex and term frequency

Of course, we can combine the previously discussed filtering methods. So, if we want to have the field data cache responsible for holding the tag field data of only those terms that start with the # character, this comes from a segment with at least 100 documents and has a segment term frequency between 1 to 20 percent; we should have the following mappings:

```
{
 "book" : {
  "properties" : {
   "tag" : {
    "type" : "string",
    "index" : "not_analyzed",
    "fielddata" : {
     "filter" : {
      "frequency" : {
       "min" : 0.1,
       "max" : 0.2,
```

```
      "min_segment_size" : 100
    },
    "regex" : "^#.*"
   }
  }
 }
 }
}
}
```

> Remember that the field data cache is not built during indexing but can be rebuilt while querying and, because of that, we can change filtering during runtime by updating the `fielddata` section using the Mappings API. However, one has to remember that after changing the field data loading filtering settings, the cache should be cleared using the clear cache API described in the *Clearing the caches* section in this chapter.

The filtering example

So now, let's go back to the example from the beginning of the filtering section. What we want to do is exclude the terms with the lowest frequency from faceting results. In our case, the lowest ones are the ones that have the frequency lower than 50 percent. Of course, this frequency is very high, but in our example, we only use four documents. In production, you'd like to have different values: lower ones. In order to do this, we will create a `books` index with the following commands:

```
curl -XPOST 'localhost:9200/books' -d '{
  "settings" : {
   "number_of_shards" : 1,
   "number_of_replicas" : 0
  },
  "mappings" : {
   "book" : {
    "properties" : {
     "tag" : {
      "type" : "string",
      "index" : "not_analyzed",
      "fielddata" : {
       "filter" : {
        "frequency" : {
         "min" : 0.5,
         "max" : 0.99
```

```
            }
           }
          }
         }
        }
       }
      }
     }
    }'
```

Now, let's index some sample documents using the bulk API (the code is stored in the regex.json file provided with the book):

```
curl -s -XPOST 'localhost:9200/_bulk' --data-binary '
{ "index": {"_index": "books", "_type": "book", "_id": "1"}}
{"tag":["one"]}
{ "index": {"_index": "books", "_type": "book", "_id": "2"}}
{"tag":["one"]}
{ "index": {"_index": "books", "_type": "book", "_id": "3"}}
{"tag":["one"]}
{ "index": {"_index": "books", "_type": "book", "_id": "4"}}
{"tag":["four"]}
'
```

Now, let's check a simple term's faceting by running the following query (because as we already discussed, faceting and aggregations use the field data cache to operate):

```
curl -XGET 'localhost:9200/books/_search?pretty' -d ' {
 "query" : {
  "match_all" : {}
 },
 "aggregations" : {
  "tag" : {
   "terms" : {
    "field" : "tag"
   }
  }
 }
}'
```

The response for the preceding query would be as follows:

```
{
  "took" : 1,
  "timed_out" : false,
  "_shards" : {
    "total" : 1,
    "successful" : 1,
    "failed" : 0
  },
  .
  .
  .
  "aggregations" : {
  "tag" : {
        "doc_count_error_upper_bound" : 0,
        "sum_other_doc_count" : 0,
        "buckets" : [ {
           "key" : "one",
"doc_count" : 3 }]
}
}
```

As you can see, the terms aggregation was only calculated for the one term, and the four term was omitted. If we assume that the four term was misspelled, then we have achieved what we wanted.

Field data formats

Field data cache is not a simple functionality and is implemented to save as much memory as possible. Because of this, Elasticsearch exposes a few formats for the field data cache depending on the data type. We can set the format of the internal data stored in the field data cache by specifying the format property inside a fielddata object for a field, for example:

```
"tag" : {
 "type" : "string",
 "fielddata" : {
  "format" : "paged_bytes"
 }
}
```

Let's now look at the possible formats.

String-based fields

For string-based fields, Elasticsearch exposes three formats of the field data cache. The default format is `paged_bytes`, which stores unique occurrences of the terms sequentially and maps documents to these terms. This data is stored in the memory. The second format is `fst`, which stores the field data cache in a structure called **Finite State Transducer (FST** — http://en.wikipedia.org/wiki/Finite_state_transducer), which results in lower memory usage compared to the default format, but it is also slower compared to it. Finally, the third format is `doc_values`, which results in computing the field data cache entries during indexing and storing them on the disk along with the index files. This format is almost as fast as the default one, but its memory footprint is very low. However, it can't be used with analyzed string fields. Field data filtering is not supported for the `doc_values` format.

Numeric fields

For numeric-based fields, we have two options when it comes to the format of the field data cache. The default `array` format stores the data in an in-memory array. The second type of format is `doc_values`, which uses doc values to store the field data, which means that the field data cache entries will be computed during indexing and stored on the disk along with the index files. Field data filtering is not supported for the `doc_values` format.

Geographical-based fields

For geo-point based fields, we have options similar to the numeric fields: the default `array` format, which stores longitudes and latitudes in an array, or `doc_values`, which uses doc values to store the field data. Of course, field data filtering is not supported for the `doc_values` format.

Field data loading

In addition to what we wrote already, Elasticsearch allows us to configure how the field data cache is loaded. As we already mentioned, the field data cache is loaded by default when the cache is needed for the first time — during the first query execution that needs uninverted data. We can change this behavior by including the `loading` property and setting it to `eager`. This will make Elasticsearch load the field data cache eagerly whenever new data appears to be loaded into the cache. Therefore, to make the field data cache for the `tag` field to be loaded eagerly, we would configure it the following way:

```
"tag" : {
 "type" : "string",
 "fielddata" : {
```

```
    "loading" : "eager"
  }
}
```

We can also completely disable the field data cache loading by setting the `format` property to `disabled`. For example, to disable loading the field data cache for our `tag` field, we can change its configuration to the following one:

```
"tag" : {
 "type" : "string",
 "fielddata" : {
  "format" : "disabled"
 }
}
```

Please note that functionalities that require uninverted data (such as aggregations) won't work on such defined fields.

The shard query cache

A new cache introduced in Elasticsearch 1.4.0 can help with query performance. The shard query cache is responsible for caching local results for each shard. As you remember, when Elasticsearch executes a query, it is sent to all the relevant shards and is executed on them. The results are returned to the node that requested them and are combined. The shard query cache is about caching these partial results on the shard level.

> At the time of writing this, the only cached `search_type query` was `count`. Therefore, the documents returned by the query will not be cached, but the total number of hits, aggregations, and suggestions returned by each shard will be cached, speeding up proceeding queries. Note that this is likely to be changed in future versions of Elasticsearch.

The shard query cache is not enabled by default. However, we have two options that show you how to enable it. We can do this by adding the `index.cache.query.enable` property and setting it to `true` in the settings of our index or by updating the indices settings in real-time with a command like this:

```
curl -XPUT 'localhost:9200/mastering/_settings' -d '{
 "index.cache.query.enable" : true
}'
```

The second option is to enable the shard query cache per request. We can do this by using the `query_cache` URI parameter set to true on a per-query basis. The thing to remember is that passing this parameter overwrites the index-level settings. An example request could look as follows:

```
curl -XGET 'localhost:9200/books/_search?search_type=count&query_cache=true' -d
'{
 "query" : {
  "match_all" : {}
 },
 "aggregations" : {
  "tags" : {
   "terms" : {
    "field" : "tag"
   }
  }
 }
}'
```

The good thing about shard query cache is that it is invalidated and updated automatically. Whenever a shard's contents changes, Elasticsearch will update the contents of the cache automatically, so the results of the cached and not cached query will always be the same.

Setting up the shard query cache

By default, Elasticsearch will use up to 1 percent of the heap size given to a node for the shard query cache. This means that all indices present on a node can use up to 1 percent of the total heap memory for the query cache. We can change this by setting the `indices.cache.query.size` property in the `elasticsearch.yml` file.

In addition to this, we can control the expiration time of the cache by setting the `indices.cache.query.expire` property. For example, if we would like the cache to be automatically expired after 60 minutes, we should set the property to `60m`.

Using circuit breakers

Because queries can put a lot of pressure on Elasticsearch resources, they allow us to use so-called circuit breakers that prevent Elasticsearch from using too much memory in certain functionalities. Elasticsearch estimates the memory usage and rejects the query execution if certain thresholds are met. Let's look at the available circuit breakers and what they can help us with.

The field data circuit breaker

The field data circuit breaker will prevent request execution if the estimated memory usage for the request is higher than the configured values. By default, Elasticsearch sets `indices.breaker.fielddata.limit` to `60%`, which means that no more than 60 percent of the JVM heap is allowed to be used for the field data cache.

We can also configure the multiplier that Elasticsearch uses for estimates (the estimated values are multiplied by this property value) by using the `indices.breaker.fielddata.overhead` property. By default, it is set to `1.03`.

> Please note than before Elasticsearch 1.4.0, `indices.breaker.fielddata.limit` was called `indices.fielddata.breaker.limit` and `indices.breaker.fielddata.overhead` was called `indices.fielddatabreaker.overhead`.

The request circuit breaker

Introduced in Elasticsearch 1.4.0, the request circuit breaker allows us to configure Elasticsearch to reject the execution of the request if the total estimated memory used by it will be higher than the `indices.breaker.request.limit` property (set to `40%` of the total heap memory assigned to the JVM by default).

Similar to the field data circuit breaker, we can set the overhead by using the `indices.breaker.request.overhead` property, which defaults to `1`.

The total circuit breaker

In addition to the previously described circuit breakers, Elasticsearch 1.4.0 introduced a notion of the total circuit breaker, which defines the total amount of memory that can be used along all the other circuit breakers. We can configure it using `indices.breaker.total.limit`, and it defaults to `70%` of the JVM heap.

> Please remember that all the circuit breakers can be dynamically changed on a working cluster using the Cluster Update Settings API.

Clearing the caches

As we've mentioned earlier, sometimes it is necessary to clear the caches. Elasticsearch allows us to clear the caches using the `_cache` REST endpoint. Let's look at the usage possibilities.

Index, indices, and all caches clearing

The simplest thing we can do is just clear all the caches by running the following command:

```
curl -XPOST 'localhost:9200/_cache/clear'
```

Of course, as we are used to, we can choose a single index or multiple indices to clear the caches for them. For example, if we want to clear the cache for the `mastering` index, we should run the following command:

```
curl -XPOST 'localhost:9200/mastering/_cache/clear'
```

If we want to clear caches for the `mastering` and `books` indices, we should run the following command:

```
curl -XPOST 'localhost:9200/mastering,books/_cache/clear'
```

Clearing specific caches

By default, Elasticsearch clears all the caches when running the cache clear request. However, we are allowed to choose which caches should be cleared and which ones should be left alone. Elasticsearch allows us to choose the following behavior:

- Filter caches can be cleared by setting the `filter` parameter to `true`. In order to exclude this cache type from the clearing one, we should set this parameter to `false`. Note that the filter cache is not cleared immediately, but it is scheduled by Elasticsearch to be cleared in the next 60 seconds.
- The field data cache can be cleared by setting the `field_data` parameter to `true`. In order to exclude this cache type from the clearing one, we should set this parameter to `false`.

- To clear the caches of identifiers used for parent-child relationships, we can set the `id_cache` parameter to `true`. Setting this property to `false` will exclude that cache from being cleared.
- The shard query cache can be cleared by setting the `query_cache` parameter to `true`. Setting this parameter to `false` will exclude the shard query cache from being cleared.

For example, if we want all caches apart from the filter and shard query caches for the `mastering` index, we could run the following command:

```
curl -XPOST 'localhost:9200/mastering/_cache/clear?field_data=true&filter=false&query_cache=false'
```

Summary

In this chapter, we started by discussing how to alter the Apache Lucene scoring by using different similarity methods. We altered our index postings format writing by using codecs. We indexed and searched our data in a near real-time manner, and we also learned how to flush and refresh our data. We configured the transaction log and throttled the I/O subsystem. We talked about segment merging and how to visualize it. Finally, we discussed federated search and the usage of tribe nodes in Elasticsearch.

In the next chapter, we will focus on the Elasticsearch administration. We will configure discovery and recovery, and we will use the human-friendly Cat API. In addition to this, we will back up and restore our indices, finalizing what federated search is, and how to search and index data to multiple clusters while still using all the functionalities of Elasticsearch.

7
Elasticsearch Administration

In the previous chapter, we discussed how to alter the Apache Lucene scoring by using different similarity methods. We indexed and searched our data in a near real-time manner, and we also learned how to flush and refresh our data. We configured the transaction log and the throttled I/O subsystem. We talked about segment merging and how to visualize it. Finally, we discussed federated search and the usage of tribe nodes in Elasticsearch.

In this chapter, we will talk more about the Elasticsearch configuration and new features introduced in Elasticsearch 1.0 and higher. By the end of this chapter, you will have learned:

- Configuring the discovery and recovery modules
- Using the Cat API that allows a human-readable insight into the cluster status
- The backup and restore functionality
- Federated search

Discovery and recovery modules

When starting your Elasticsearch node, one of the first things that Elasticsearch does is look for a master node that has the same cluster name and is visible in the network. If a master node is found, the starting node gets joined into an already formed cluster. If no master is found, then the node itself is selected as a master (of course, if the configuration allows such behavior). The process of forming a cluster and finding nodes is called **discovery**. The module responsible for discovery has two main purposes—electing a master and discovering new nodes within a cluster.

Elasticsearch Administration

After the cluster is formed, a process called **recovery** is started. During the recovery process, Elasticsearch reads the metadata and the indices from the gateway, and prepares the shards that are stored there to be used. After the recovery of the primary shards is done, Elasticsearch should be ready for work and should continue with the recovery of all the replicas (if they are present).

In this section, we will take a deeper look at these two modules and discuss the possibilities of configuration Elasticsearch gives us and what the consequences of changing them are.

> Note that the information provided in the *Discovery and recovery modules* section is an extension of what we already wrote in *Elasticsearch Server Second Edition*, published by *Packt Publishing*.

Discovery configuration

As we have already mentioned multiple times, Elasticsearch was designed to work in a distributed environment. This is the main difference when comparing Elasticsearch to other open source search and analytics solutions available. With such assumptions, Elasticsearch is very easy to set up in a distributed environment, and we are not forced to set up additional software to make it work like this. By default, Elasticsearch assumes that the cluster is automatically formed by the nodes that declare the same `cluster.name` setting and can communicate with each other using multicast requests. This allows us to have several independent clusters in the same network.

There are a few implementations of the discovery module that we can use, so let's see what the options are.

Zen discovery

Zen discovery is the default mechanism that's responsible for discovery in Elasticsearch and is available by default. The default Zen discovery configuration uses multicast to find other nodes. This is a very convenient solution: just start a new Elasticsearch node and everything works—this node will be joined to the cluster if it has the same cluster name and is visible by other nodes in that cluster. This discovery method is perfectly suited for development time, because you don't need to care about the configuration; however, it is not advised that you use it in production environments. Relying only on the cluster name is handy but can also lead to potential problems and mistakes, such as the accidental joining of nodes. Sometimes, multicast is not available for various reasons or you don't want to use it for these mentioned reasons. In the case of bigger clusters, the multicast discovery may generate too much unnecessary traffic, and this is another valid reason why it shouldn't be used for production.

For these cases, Zen discovery allows us to use the unicast mode. When using the unicast Zen discovery, a node that is not a part of the cluster will send a ping request to all the addresses specified in the configuration. By doing this, it informs all the specified nodes that it is ready to be a part of the cluster and can be either joined to an existing cluster or can form a new one. Of course, after the node joins the cluster, it gets the cluster topology information, but the initial connection is only done to the specified list of hosts. Remember that even when using unicast Zen discovery, the Elasticsearch node still needs to have the same cluster name as the other nodes.

> If you want to know more about the differences between multicast and unicast ping methods, refer to these URLs: http://en.wikipedia.org/wiki/Multicast and http://en.wikipedia.org/wiki/Unicast.

If you still want to learn about the configuration properties of multicast Zen discovery, let's look at them.

Multicast Zen discovery configuration

The multicast part of the Zen discovery module exposes the following settings:

- `discovery.zen.ping.multicast.address` (the default: all available interfaces): This is the interface used for the communication given as the address or interface name.

- `discovery.zen.ping.multicast.port` (the default: `54328`): This port is used for communication.

- `discovery.zen.ping.multicast.group` (the default: `224.2.2.4`): This is the multicast address to send messages to.

- `discovery.zen.ping.multicast.buffer_size` (the default: `2048`): This is the size of the buffer used for multicast messages.

- `discovery.zen.ping.multicast.ttl` (the default: `3`): This is the time for which a multicast message lives. Every time a packet crosses the router, the TTL is decreased. This allows for the limiting area where the transmission can be received. Note that routers can have the threshold values assigned compared to TTL, which causes that TTL value to not match exactly the number of routers that a packet can jump over.

- `discovery.zen.ping.multicast.enabled` (the default: `true`): Setting this property to `false` turns off the multicast. You should disable multicast if you are planning to use the unicast discovery method.

The unicast Zen discovery configuration

The unicast part of Zen discovery provides the following configuration options:

- `discovery.zen.ping.unicats.hosts`: This is the initial list of nodes in the cluster. The list can be defined as a list or as an array of hosts. Every host can be given a name (or an IP address) or have a port or port range added. For example, the value of this property can look like this: `["master1", "master2:8181", "master3[80000-81000]"]`. So, basically, the hosts' list for the unicast discovery doesn't need to be a complete list of Elasticsearch nodes in your cluster, because once the node is connected to one of the mentioned nodes, it will be informed about all the others that form the cluster.

- `discovery.zen.ping.unicats.concurrent_connects` (the default: `10`): This is the maximum number of concurrent connections unicast discoveries will use. If you have a lot of nodes that the initial connection should be made to, it is advised that you increase the default value.

Master node

One of the main purposes of discovery apart from connecting to other nodes is to choose a master node—a node that will take care of and manage all the other nodes. This process is called **master election** and is a part of the discovery module. No matter how many master eligible nodes there are, each cluster will only have a single master node active at a given time. If there is more than one master eligible node present in the cluster, they can be elected as the master when the original master fails and is removed from the cluster.

Configuring master and data nodes

By default, Elasticsearch allows every node to be a master node and a data node. However, in certain situations, you may want to have worker nodes, which will only hold the data or process the queries and the master nodes that will only be used as cluster-managed nodes. One of these situations is to handle a massive amount of data, where data nodes should be as performant as possible, and there shouldn't be any delay in master nodes' responses.

Configuring data-only nodes

To set the node to only hold data, we need to instruct Elasticsearch that we don't want such a node to be a master node. In order to do this, we add the following properties to the `elasticsearch.yml` configuration file:

```
node.master: false
node.data: true
```

Configuring master-only nodes

To set the node not to hold data and only to be a master node, we need to instruct Elasticsearch that we don't want such a node to hold data. In order to do that, we add the following properties to the `elasticsearch.yml` configuration file:

```
node.master: true
node.data: false
```

Configuring the query processing-only nodes

For large enough deployments, it is also wise to have nodes that are only responsible for aggregating query results from other nodes. Such nodes should be configured as nonmaster and nondata, so they should have the following properties in the `elasticsearch.yml` configuration file:

```
node.master: false
node.data: false
```

> Please note that the `node.master` and the `node.data` properties are set to `true` by default, but we tend to include them for configuration clarity.

The master election configuration

We already wrote about the master election configuration in *Elasticsearch Server Section Edition*, but this topic is very important, so we decided to refresh our knowledge about it.

Imagine that you have a cluster that is built of 10 nodes. Everything is working fine until, one day, your network fails and three of your nodes are disconnected from the cluster, but they still see each other. Because of the Zen discovery and the master election process, the nodes that got disconnected elect a new master and you end up with two clusters with the same name with two master nodes. Such a situation is called a **split-brain** and you must avoid it as much as possible. When a split-brain happens, you end up with two (or more) clusters that won't join each other until the network (or any other) problems are fixed. If you index your data during this time, you may end up with data loss and unrecoverable situations when the nodes get joined together after the network split.

In order to prevent split-brain situations or at least minimize the possibility of their occurrences, Elasticsearch provides a `discovery.zen.minimum_master_nodes` property. This property defines a minimum amount of master eligible nodes that should be connected to each other in order to form a cluster. So now, let's get back to our cluster; if we set the `discovery.zen.minimum_master_nodes` property to 50 percent of the total nodes available plus one (which is six, in our case), we would end up with a single cluster. Why is that? Before the network failure, we would have 10 nodes, which is more than six nodes, and these nodes would form a cluster. After the disconnections of the three nodes, we would still have the first cluster up and running. However, because only three nodes disconnected and three is less than six, these three nodes wouldn't be allowed to elect a new master and they would wait for reconnection with the original cluster.

Zen discovery fault detection and configuration

Elasticsearch runs two detection processes while it is working. The first process is to send ping requests from the current master node to all the other nodes in the cluster to check whether they are operational. The second process is a reverse of that—each of the nodes sends ping requests to the master in order to verify that it is still up and running and performing its duties. However, if we have a slow network or our nodes are in different hosting locations, the default configuration may not be sufficient. Because of this, the Elasticsearch discovery module exposes three properties that we can change:

- `discovery.zen.fd.ping_interval`: This defaults to `1s` and specifies the interval of how often the node will send ping requests to the target node.
- `discovery.zen.fd.ping_timeout`: This defaults to `30s` and specifies how long the node will wait for the sent ping request to be responded to. If your nodes are 100 percent utilized or your network is slow, you may consider increasing that property value.
- `discovery.zen.fd.ping_retries`: This defaults to `3` and specifies the number of ping request retries before the target node will be considered not operational. You can increase this value if your network has a high number of lost packets (or you can fix your network).

There is one more thing that we would like to mention. The master node is the only node that can change the state of the cluster. To achieve a proper cluster state updates sequence, Elasticsearch master nodes process single cluster state update requests one at a time, make the changes locally, and send the request to all the other nodes so that they can synchronize their state. The master nodes wait for the given time for the nodes to respond, and if the time passes or all the nodes are returned, with the current acknowledgment information, it proceeds with the next cluster state update request processing. To change the time, the master node waits for all the other nodes to respond, and you should modify the default 30 seconds time by setting the `discovery.zen.publish_timeout` property. Increasing the value may be needed for huge clusters working in an overloaded network.

The Amazon EC2 discovery

Amazon, in addition to selling goods, has a few popular services such as selling storage or computing power in a pay-as-you-go model. So-called Amazon Elastic Compute Cloud (EC2) provides server instances and, of course, they can be used to install and run Elasticsearch clusters (among many other things, as these are normal Linux machines). This is convenient—you pay for instances that are needed in order to handle the current traffic or to speed up calculations, and you shut down unnecessary instances when the traffic is lower. Elasticsearch works well on EC2, but due to the nature of the environment, some features may work slightly differently. One of these features that works differently is discovery, because Amazon EC2 doesn't support multicast discovery. Of course, we can switch to unicast discovery, but sometimes, we want to be able to automatically discover nodes and, with unicast, we need to at least provide the initial list of hosts. However, there is an alternative— we can use the Amazon EC2 plugin, a plugin that combines the multicast and unicast discovery methods using the Amazon EC2 API.

> Make sure that during the set up of EC2 instances, you set up communication between them (on port `9200` and `9300` by default). This is crucial in order to have Elasticsearch nodes communicate with each other and, thus, cluster functioning is required. Of course, this communication depends on `network.bind_host` and `network.publish_host` (or `network.host`) settings.

The EC2 plugin installation

The installation of a plugin is as simple as with most of the plugins. In order to install it, we should run the following command:

```
bin/plugin install elasticsearch/elasticsearch-cloud-aws/2.4.0
```

The EC2 plugin's generic configuration

This plugin provides several configuration settings that we need to provide in order for the EC2 discovery to work:

- `cluster.aws.access_key`: Amazon access key – one of the credential values you can find in the Amazon configuration panel
- `cluster.aws.secret_key`: Amazon secret key – similar to the previously mentioned `access_key` setting, it can be found in the EC2 configuration panel

The last thing is to inform Elasticsearch that we want to use a new discovery type by setting the `discovery.type` property to `ec2` value and turn off multicast.

Optional EC2 discovery configuration options

The previously mentioned settings are sufficient to run the EC2 discovery, but in order to control the EC2 discovery plugin behavior, Elasticsearch exposes additional settings:

- `cloud.aws.region`: This region will be used to connect with Amazon EC2 web services. You can choose a region that's adequate for the region where your instance resides, for example, `eu-west-1` for Ireland. The possible values during the writing of the book were `eu-west`, `sa-east`, `us-east`, `us-west-1`, `us-west-2`, `ap-southeast-1`, and `ap-southeast-1`.
- `cloud.aws.ec2.endpoint`: If you are using EC2 API services, instead of defining a region, you can provide an address of the AWS endpoint, for example, `ec2.eu-west-1.amazonaws.com`.
- `cloud.aws.protocol`: This is the protocol that should be used by the plugin to connect to Amazon Web Services endpoints. By default, Elasticsearch will use the HTTPS protocol (which means setting the value of the property to `https`). We can also change this behavior and set the property to `http` for the plugin to use HTTP without encryption. We are also allowed to overwrite the `cloud.aws.protocol` settings for each service by using the `cloud.aws.ec2.protocol` and `cloud.aws.s3.protocol` properties (the possible values are the same – `https` and `http`).

- `cloud.aws.proxy_host`: Elasticsearch allows us to define a proxy that will be used to connect to AWS endpoints. The `cloud.aws.proxy_host` property should be set to the address to the proxy that should be used.

- `cloud.aws.proxy_port`: The second property related to the AWS endpoints proxy allows us to specify the port on which the proxy is listening. The `cloud.aws.proxy_port` property should be set to the port on which the proxy listens.

- `discovery.ec2.ping_timeout` (the default: `3s`): This is the time to wait for the response for the ping message sent to the other node. After this time, the nonresponsive node will be considered dead and removed from the cluster. Increasing this value makes sense when dealing with network issues or we have a lot of EC2 nodes.

The EC2 nodes scanning configuration

The last group of settings we want to mention allows us to configure a very important thing when building cluster working inside the EC2 environment—the ability to filter available Elasticsearch nodes in our Amazon Elastic Cloud Computing network. The Elasticsearch EC2 plugin exposes the following properties that can help us configure its behavior:

- `discovery.ec2.host_type`: This allows us to choose the host type that will be used to communicate with other nodes in the cluster. The values we can use are `private_ip` (the default one; the private IP address will be used for communication), `public_ip` (the public IP address will be used for communication), `private_dns` (the private hostname will be used for communication), and `public_dns` (the public hostname will be used for communication).

- `discovery.ec2.groups`: This is a comma-separated list of security groups. Only nodes that fall within these groups can be discovered and included in the cluster.

- `discovery.ec2.availability_zones`: This is array or command-separated list of availability zones. Only nodes with the specified availability zones will be discovered and included in the cluster.

- `discovery.ec2.any_group` (this defaults to `true`): Setting this property to `false` will force the EC2 discovery plugin to discover only those nodes that reside in an Amazon instance that falls into all of the defined security groups. The default value requires only a single group to be matched.

- `discovery.ec2.tag`: This is a prefix for a group of EC2-related settings. When you launch your Amazon EC2 instances, you can define tags, which can describe the purpose of the instance, such as the customer name or environment type. Then, you use these defined settings to limit discovery nodes. Let's say you define a tag named `environment` with a value of `qa`. In the configuration, you can now specify the following:
    - `discovery.ec2.tag.environment`: `qa` and only nodes running on instances with this tag will be considered for discovery.
    - `cloud.node.auto_attributes`: When this is set to `true`, Elasticsearch will add EC2-related node attributes (such as the availability zone or group) to the node properties and will allow us to use them, adjusting the Elasticsearch shard allocation and configuring the shard placement. You can find more about shard placement in the *Altering the default shard allocation behavior* section of *Chapter 5, The Index Distribution Architecture*.

Other discovery implementations

The Zen discovery and EC2 discovery are not the only discovery types that are available. There are two more discovery types that are developed and maintained by the Elasticsearch team, and these are:

- **Azure discovery**: https://github.com/elasticsearch/elasticsearch-cloud-azure
- **Google Compute Engine discovery**: https://github.com/elasticsearch/elasticsearch-cloud-gce

In addition to these, there are a few discovery implementations provided by the community, such as the ZooKeeper discovery for older versions of Elasticsearch (https://github.com/sonian/elasticsearch-zookeeper).

The gateway and recovery configuration

The gateway module allows us to store all the data that is needed for Elasticsearch to work properly. This means that not only is the data in Apache Lucene indices stored, but also all the metadata (for example, index allocation settings), along with the mappings configuration for each index. Whenever the cluster state is changed, for example, when the allocation properties are changed, the cluster state will be persisted by using the gateway module. When the cluster is started up, its state will be loaded using the gateway module and applied.

One should remember that when configuring different nodes and different gateway types, indices will use the gateway type configuration present on the given node. If an index state should not be stored using the gateway module, one should explicitly set the index gateway type to none.

The gateway recovery process

Let's say explicitly that the recovery process is used by Elasticsearch to load the data stored with the use of the gateway module in order for Elasticsearch to work. Whenever a full cluster restart occurs, the gateway process kicks in to load all the relevant information we've mentioned—the metadata, the mappings, and of course, all the indices. When the recovery process starts, the primary shards are initialized first, and then, depending on the replica state, they are initialized using the gateway data, or the data is copied from the primary shards if the replicas are out of sync.

Elasticsearch allows us to configure when the cluster data should be recovered using the gateway module. We can tell Elasticsearch to wait for a certain number of master eligible or data nodes to be present in the cluster before starting the recovery process. However, one should remember that when the cluster is not recovered, all the operations performed on it will not be allowed. This is done in order to avoid modification conflicts.

Configuration properties

Before we continue with the configuration, we would like to say one more thing. As you know, Elasticsearch nodes can play different roles—they can have a role of data nodes—the ones that hold data—they can have a master role, or they can be only used for request handing, which means not holding data and not being master eligible. Remembering all this, let's now look at the gateway configuration properties that we are allowed to modify:

- `gateway.recover_after_nodes`: This is an integer number that specifies how many nodes should be present in the cluster for the recovery to happen. For example, when set to 5, at least 5 nodes (doesn't matter whether they are data or master eligible nodes) must be present for the recovery process to start.

- `gateway.recover_after_data_nodes`: This is an integer number that allows us to set how many data nodes should be present in the cluster for the recovery process to start.

- `gateway.recover_after_master_nodes`: This is another gateway configuration option that allows us to set how many master eligible nodes should be present in the cluster for the recovery to start.
- `gateway.recover_after_time`: This allows us to set how much time to wait before the recovery process starts after the conditions defined by the preceding properties are met. If we set this property to `5m`, we tell Elasticsearch to start the recovery process 5 minutes after all the defined conditions are met. The default value for this property is `5m`, starting from Elasticsearch 1.3.0.

Let's imagine that we have six nodes in our cluster, out of which four are data eligible. We also have an index that is built of three shards, which are spread across the cluster. The last two nodes are master eligible and they don't hold the data. What we would like to configure is the recovery process to be delayed for 3 minutes after the four data nodes are present. Our gateway configuration could look like this:

```
gateway.recover_after_data_nodes: 4
gateway.recover_after_time: 3m
```

Expectations on nodes

In addition to the already mentioned properties, we can also specify properties that will force the recovery process of Elasticsearch. These properties are:

- `gateway.expected_nodes`: This is the number of nodes expected to be present in the cluster for the recovery to start immediately. If you don't need the recovery to be delayed, it is advised that you set this property to the number of nodes (or at least most of them) with which the cluster will be formed from, because that will guarantee that the latest cluster state will be recovered.
- `gateway.expected_data_nodes`: This is the number of expected data eligible nodes to be present in the cluster for the recovery process to start immediately.
- `gateway.expected_master_nodes`: This is the number of expected master eligible nodes to be present in the cluster for the recovery process to start immediately.

Now, let's get back to our previous example. We know that when all six nodes are connected and are in the cluster, we want the recovery to start. So, in addition to the preceeding configuration, we would add the following property:

```
gateway.expected_nodes: 6
```

So the whole configuration would look like this:

```
gateway.recover_after_data_nodes: 4
gateway.recover_after_time: 3m
gateway.expected_nodes: 6
```

The preceding configuration says that the recovery process will be delayed for 3 minutes once four data nodes join the cluster and will begin immediately after six nodes are in the cluster (doesn't matter whether they are data nodes or master eligible nodes).

The local gateway

With the release of Elasticsearch 0.20 (and some of the releases from 0.19 versions), all the gateway types, apart from the default `local gateway type`, were deprecated. It is advised that you do not use them, because they will be removed in future versions of Elasticsearch. This is still not the case, but if you want to avoid full data reindexation, you should only use the `local` gateway type, and this is why we won't discuss all the other types.

The `local` gateway type uses a local storage available on a node to store the metadata, mappings, and indices. In order to use this gateway type and the local storage available on the node, there needs to be enough disk space to hold the data with no memory caching.

The persistence to the local gateway is different from the other gateways that are currently present (but deprecated). The writes to this gateway are done in a synchronous manner in order to ensure that no data will be lost during the write process.

> In order to set the type of gateway that should be used, one should use the `gateway.type` property, which is set to `local` by default.

There is one additional thing regarding the local gateway of Elasticsearch that we didn't talk about—dangling indices. When a node joins a cluster, all the shards and indices that are present on the node, but are not present in the cluster, will be included in the cluster state. Such indices are called **dangling indices**, and we are allowed to choose how Elasticsearch should treat them.

Elasticsearch exposes the `gateway.local.auto_import_dangling` property, which can take the value of `yes` (the default value that results in importing all dangling indices into the cluster), `close` (results in importing the dangling indices into the cluster state but keeps them closed by default), and `no` (results in removing the dangling indices). When setting the `gateway.local.auto_import_dangling` property to `no`, we can also set the `gateway.local.dangling_timeout` property (defaults to `2h`) to specify how long Elasticsearch will wait while deleting the dangling indices. The dangling indices feature can be nice when we restart old Elasticsearch nodes, and we don't want old indices to be included in the cluster.

Low-level recovery configuration

We discussed that we can use the gateway to configure the behavior of the Elasticsearch recovery process, but in addition to that, Elasticsearch allows us to configure the recovery process itself. We mentioned some of the recovery configuration options already when talking about shard allocation in the *Altering The default shard allocation behavior* section of *Chapter 5, The Index Distribution Architecture*; however, we decided that it would be good to mention the properties we can use in the section dedicated to gateway and recovery.

Cluster-level recovery configuration

The recovery configuration is specified mostly on the cluster level and allows us to set general rules for the recovery module to work with. These settings are:

- `indices.recovery.concurrent_streams`: This defaults to `3` and specifies the number of concurrent streams that are allowed to be opened in order to recover a shard from its source. The higher the value of this property, the more pressure will be put on the networking layer; however, the recovery may be faster, depending on your network usage and throughput.

- `indices.recovery.max_bytes_per_sec`: By default, this is set to `20MB` and specifies the maximum number of data that can be transferred during shard recovery per second. In order to disable data transfer limiting, one should set this property to `0`. Similar to the number of concurrent streams, this property allows us to control the network usage of the recovery process. Setting this property to higher values may result in higher network utilization and a faster recovery process.

- `indices.recovery.compress`: This is set to `true` by default and allows us to define whether ElasticSearch should compress the data that is transferred during the recovery process. Setting this to `false` may lower the pressure on the CPU, but it will also result in more data being transferred over the network.

- `indices.recovery.file_chunk_size`: This is the chunk size used to copy the shard data from the source shard. By default, it is set to `512KB` and is compressed if the `indices.recovery.compress` property is set to `true`.
- `indices.recovery.translog_ops`: This defaults to `1000` and specifies how many transaction log lines should be transferred between shards in a single request during the recovery process.
- `indices.recovery.translog_size`: This is the chunk size used to copy the shard transaction log data from the source shard. By default, it is set to `512KB` and is compressed if the `indices.recovery.compress` property is set to `true`.

> In the versions prior to Elasticsearch 0.90.0, there was the `indices.recovery.max_size_per_sec` property that could be used, but it was deprecated, and it is suggested that you use the `indices.recovery.max_bytes_per_sec` property instead. However, if you are using an Elasticsearch version older than 0.90.0, it may be worth remembering this.

All the previously mentioned settings can be updated using the Cluster Update API, or they can be set in the `elasticsearch.yml` file.

Index-level recovery settings

In addition to the values mentioned previously, there is a single property that can be set on a per-index basis. The property can be set both in the `elasticsearch.yml` file and using the indices Update Settings API, and it is called `index.recovery.initial_shards`. In general, Elasticsearch will only recover a particular shard when there is a quorum of shards present and if that quorum can be allocated. A quorum is 50 percent of the shards for the given index plus one. By using the `index.recovery.initial_shards` property, we can change what Elasticsearch will take as a quorum. This property can be set to the one of the following values:

- `quorum`: 50 percent, plus one shard needs to be present and be allocable. This is the default value.
- `quorum-1`: 50 percent of the shards for a given index need to be present and be allocable.
- `full`: All of the shards for the given index need to be present and be allocable.
- `full-1`: 100 percent minus one shards for the given index need to be present and be allocable.

- **integer** value: Any integer such as 1, 2, or 5 specifies the number of shards that are needed to be present and that can be allocated. For example, setting this value to 2 will mean that at least two shards need to be present and Elasticsearch needs at least 2 shards to be allocable.

It is good to know about this property, but in most cases, the default value will be sufficient for most deployments.

The indices recovery API

With the introduction of the indices recovery API, we are no longer limited to only looking at the cluster state and the output similar to the following one:

```
curl 'localhost:9200/_cluster/health?pretty'
{
  "cluster_name" : "mastering_elasticsearch",
  "status" : "red",
  "timed_out" : false,
  "number_of_nodes" : 10,
  "number_of_data_nodes" : 10,
  "active_primary_shards" : 9,
  "active_shards" : 9,
  "relocating_shards" : 0,
  "initializing_shards" : 0,
  "unassigned_shards" : 1
}
```

By running an HTTP GET request to the _recovery endpoint (for all the indices or for a particular one), we can get the information about the state of the indices' recovery. For example, let's look at the following request:

`curl -XGET 'localhost:9200/_recovery?pretty'`

The preceding request will return information about ongoing and finished recoveries of all the shards in the cluster. In our case, the response was as follows (we had to cut it):

```
{
  "test_index" : {
    "shards" : [ {
      "id" : 3,
      "type" : "GATEWAY",
```

```
      "stage" : "START",
      "primary" : true,
      "start_time_in_millis" : 1414362635212,
      "stop_time_in_millis" : 0,
      "total_time_in_millis" : 175,
      "source" : {
        "id" : "3M_ErmCNTR-huTqOTv5smw",
        "host" : "192.168.1.10",
        "transport_address" : "inet[/192.168.1.10:9300]",
        "ip" : "192.168.10",
        "name" : "node1"
      },
      "target" : {
        "id" : "3M_ErmCNTR-huTqOTv5smw",
        "host" : "192.168.1.10",
        "transport_address" : "inet[/192.168.1.10:9300]",
        "ip" : "192.168.1.10",
        "name" : "node1"
      },
      "index" : {
        "files" : {
          "total" : 400,
          "reused" : 400,
          "recovered" : 400,
          "percent" : "100.0%"
        },
        "bytes" : {
          "total" : 2455604486,
          "reused" : 2455604486,
          "recovered" : 2455604486,
          "percent" : "100.0%"
        },
        "total_time_in_millis" : 28
      },
      "translog" : {
        "recovered" : 0,
        "total_time_in_millis" : 0
      },
      "start" : {
        "check_index_time_in_millis" : 0,
        "total_time_in_millis" : 0
      }
    }, {
      "id" : 9,
```

```
        "type" : "GATEWAY",
        "stage" : "DONE",
        "primary" : true,
        "start_time_in_millis" : 1414085189696,
        "stop_time_in_millis" : 1414085189729,
        "total_time_in_millis" : 33,
        "source" : {
          "id" : "nNw_k7_XSOivvPCJLHVE5A",
          "host" : "192.168.1.11",
          "transport_address" : "inet[/192.168.1.11:9300]",
          "ip" : "192.168.1.11",
          "name" : "node3"
        },
        "target" : {
          "id" : "nNw_k7_XSOivvPCJLHVE5A",
          "host" : "192.168.1.11",
          "transport_address" : "inet[/192.168.1.11:9300]",
          "ip" : "192.168.1.11",
          "name" : "node3"
        },
        "index" : {
          "files" : {
            "total" : 0,
            "reused" : 0,
            "recovered" : 0,
            "percent" : "0.0%"
          },
          "bytes" : {
            "total" : 0,
            "reused" : 0,
            "recovered" : 0,
            "percent" : "0.0%"
          },
          "total_time_in_millis" : 0
        },
        "translog" : {
          "recovered" : 0,
          "total_time_in_millis" : 0
        },
        "start" : {
          "check_index_time_in_millis" : 0,
          "total_time_in_millis" : 33
        },
         .
```

```
            .
            .
          ]
        }
    }
}
```

The preceding response contains information about two shards for `test_index` (the information for the rest of the shards was removed for clarity). We can see that one of the shards is during the recovery process (`"stage" : "START"`) and the second one already finished the recovery process (`"stage" : "DONE"`). We can see a lot of information about the recovery process, and the information is provided on the index shard level, which allows us to clearly see at what stage our Elasticsearch cluster is. We can also limit the information to only shards that are currently being recovered by adding the `active_only=true` parameter to our request, so it would look as follows:

```
curl -XGET 'localhost:9200/_recovery?active_only=true&pretty'
```

If we want to get even more detailed information, we can add the `detailed=true` parameter to our request, so it would look like this:

```
curl -XGET 'localhost:9200/_recovery?detailed=true&pretty'
```

The human-friendly status API – using the Cat API

The Elasticsearch Admin API is quite extensive and covers almost every part of its architecture—from low-level information about Lucene to high-level information about the cluster nodes and their health. All this information is available both using the Elasticsearch Java API as well as using the REST API; however, the data is returned in the JSON format. What's more—the returned data can sometimes be hard to analyze without further parsing. For example, try to run the following request on your Elasticsearch cluster:

```
curl -XGET 'localhost:9200/_stats?pretty'
```

On our local, single node cluster, Elasticsearch returns the following information (we cut it down drastically; the full response can be found in the `stats.json` file provided with the book):

```
{
  "_shards" : {
    "total" : 60,
```

```
      "successful" : 30,
      "failed" : 0
    },
    "_all" : {
      "primaries" : {
        .
        .
        .
      },
      "total" : {
        .
        .
        .
      }
    },
    "indices" : {
      .
      .
      .
    }
}
```

If you look at the provided `stats.json` file, you would see that the response is about 1,350 lines long. This isn't quite convenient for analysis by a human without additional parsing. Because of this, Elasticsearch provides us with a more human-friendly API—the Cat API. The special Cat API returns data in a simple text, tabular format, and what's more, it provides aggregated data that is usually usable without any further processing.

> Remember that we've told you that Elasticsearch allows you to get information not just in the JSON format? If you don't remember this, please try to add the `format=yaml` request parameter to your request.

The basics

The base endpoint for the Cat API is quite obvious—it is `/_cat`. Without any parameters, it shows us all the available endpoints for that API. We can check this by running the following command:

```
curl -XGET 'localhost:9200/_cat'
```

Chapter 7

The response returned by Elasticsearch should be similar or identical (depending on your Elasticsearch version) to the following one:

```
=^.^=
/_cat/allocation
/_cat/shards
/_cat/shards/{index}
/_cat/master
/_cat/nodes
/_cat/indices
/_cat/indices/{index}
/_cat/segments
/_cat/segments/{index}
/_cat/count
/_cat/count/{index}
/_cat/recovery
/_cat/recovery/{index}
/_cat/health
/_cat/pending_tasks
/_cat/aliases
/_cat/aliases/{alias}
/_cat/thread_pool
/_cat/plugins
/_cat/fielddata
/_cat/fielddata/{fields}
```

So, looking for the top Elasticsearch allows us to get the following information using the Cat API:

- Shard allocation-related information
- All shard-related information (limited to a given index)
- Nodes information, including elected master indication
- Indices' statistics (limited to a given index)
- Segments' statistics (limited to a given index)
- Documents' count (limited to a given index)
- Recovery information (limited to a given index)
- Cluster health
- Tasks pending execution
- Index aliases and indices for a given alias

- The thread pool configuration
- Plugins installed on each node
- The field data cache size and field data cache sizes for individual fields

Using the Cat API

Let's start using the Cat API through an example. We can start with checking the cluster health of our Elasticsearch cluster. To do this, we just run the following command:

`curl -XGET 'localhost:9200/_cat/health'`

The response returned by Elasticsearch to the preceding command should be similar to the following one:

```
1414347090 19:11:30 elasticsearch yellow 1 1 47 47 0 0 47
```

It is clean and nice. Because it is in a tabular format, it is also easier to use the response in tools such as `grep`, `awk`, or `sed` — a standard set of tools for every administrator. It is also more readable once you know what it is all about. To add a header describing each column purpose, we just need to add an additional v parameter just like this:

`curl -XGET 'localhost:9200/_cat/health?v'`

The response is very similar to what we've seen previously, but it now contains a header describing each column:

```
epoch      timestamp cluster        status node.total node.data shards pri relo init unassign
1414347107 19:11:47  elasticsearch yellow          1         1     47
47   0    0       47
```

Common arguments

Every Cat API endpoint has its own arguments, but there are a few common options that are shared among all of them:

- `v`: This adds a header line to response with names of presented items.
- `h`: This allows us to show only chosen columns (refer to the next section).
- `help`: This lists all possible columns that this particular endpoint is able to show. The command shows the name of the parameter, its abbreviation, and the description.

- `bytes`: This is the format for information representing values in bytes. As we said, the Cat API is designed to be used by humans and, because of that, these values are represented in a human-readable form by default, for example, `3.5kB` or `40GB`. The `bytes` option allows us to set the same base for all numbers, so sorting or numerical comparison will be easier. For example, `bytes=b` presents all values in bytes, `bytes=k` in kilobytes, and so on.

> For the full list of arguments for each Cat API endpoint, refer to the official Elasticsearch documentation available at http://www.elasticsearch.org/guide/en/elasticsearch/reference/current/cat.html.

The examples

When we wrote this book, the Cat API had 21 endpoints. We don't want to describe them all—it would be a repetition of information contained in the documentation or chapters about the administration API. However, we didn't want to leave this section without any example regarding the usage of the Cat API. Because of this, we decided to show you how easily you can get information using the Cat API compared to the standard JSON API exposed by Elasticsearch.

Getting information about the master node

The first example shows you how easy it is to get information about which node in our cluster is the master node. By calling the `/_cat/master` REST endpoint, we can get information about the nodes and which one of them is currently being elected as a master. For example, let's run the following command:

```
curl -XGET 'localhost:9200/_cat/master?v'
```

The response returned by Elasticsearch for my local two nodes cluster looks as follows:

```
id                     host           ip        node
8gfdQlV-SxKB0uUxkjbxSg Banshee.local  10.0.1.3  Siege
```

As you can see in the response, we've got the information about which node is currently elected as the master—we can see its identifier, IP address, and name.

Getting information about the nodes

The `/_cat/nodes` REST endpoint provides information about all the nodes in the cluster. Let's see what Elasticsearch will return after running the following command:

```
curl -XGET 'localhost:9200/_cat/nodes?v&h=name,node.role,load,uptime'
```

In the preceding example, we have used the possibility of choosing what information we want to get from the approximately 70 options for this endpoint. We have chosen to get only the node name, its role—whether a node is a data or client node— node load, and its uptime.

The response returned by Elasticsearch looks as follows:

```
name               node.role load uptime
Alicia Masters     d         6.09 6.7m
Siege              d         6.09 1h
```

As you can see the `/_cat/nodes` REST endpoint provides all requested information about the nodes in the cluster.

Backing up

One of the most important tasks for the administrator is to make sure that no data will be lost in the case of a system failure. Elasticsearch, in its assumptions, is a resistant and well-configured cluster of nodes and can survive even a few simultaneous disasters. However, even the most properly configured cluster is vulnerable to network splits and network partitions, which in some very rare cases can result in data corruption or loss. In such cases, being able to get data restored from the backup is the only solution that can save us from recreating our indices. You probably already know what we want to talk about: the snapshot / restore functionality provided by Elasticsearch. However, as we said earlier, we don't want to repeat ourselves—this is a book for more advanced Elasticsearch users, and basics of the snapshot and restore API were already described in *Elasticsearch Server Second Edition* by *Packt Publishing* and in the official documentation. Now, we want to focus on the functionalities that were added after the release of Elasticsearch 1.0 and thus omitted in the previous book—let's talk about the cloud capabilities of the Elasticsearch backup functionality.

Saving backups in the cloud

The central concept of the snapshot / restore functionality is a **repository**. It is a place where the data—our indices and the related meta information—is safely stored (assuming that the storage is reliable and highly available). The assumption is that every node that is a part of the cluster has access to the repository and can both write to it and read from it. Because of the need for high availability and reliability, Elasticsearch, with the help of additional plugins, allows us to push our data outside of the cluster—to the cloud. There are three possibilities where our repository can be located, at least using officially supported plugins:

- The **S3 repository**: Amazon Web Services
- The **HDFS repository**: Hadoop clusters
- The **Azure repository**: Microsoft's cloud platform

Because we didn't discuss any of the plugins related to the snapshot / restore functionality, let's get through them to see where we can push our backup data.

The S3 repository

The S3 repository is a part of the Elasticsearch AWS plugin, so to use S3 as the repository for snapshotting, we need to install the plugin first:

```
bin/plugin -install elasticsearch/elasticsearch-cloud-aws/2.4.0
```

After installing the plugin on every Elasticsearch node in the cluster, we need to alter their configuration (the `elasticsearch.yml` file) so that the AWS access information is available. The example configuration can look like this:

```
cloud:
  aws:
    access_key: YOUR_ACCESS_KEY
    secret_key: YOUT_SECRET_KEY
```

To create the S3 repository that Elasticsearch will use for snapshotting, we need to run a command similar to the following one:

```
curl -XPUT 'http://localhost:9200/_snapshot/s3_repository' -d '{
 "type": "s3",
 "settings": {
  "bucket": "bucket_name"
 }
}'
```

The following settings are supported when defining an S3-based repository:

- `bucket`: This is the required parameter describing the Amazon S3 bucket to which the Elasticsearch data will be written and from which Elasticsearch will read the data.
- `region`: This is the name of the AWS region where the bucket resides. By default, the `US Standard` region is used.
- `base_path`: By default, Elasticsearch puts the data in the root directory. This parameter allows you to change it and alter the place where the data is placed in the repository.
- `server_side_encryption`: By default, encryption is turned off. You can set this parameter to `true` in order to use the AES256 algorithm to store data.
- `chunk_size`: By default, this is set to `100m` and specifies the size of the data chunk that will be sent. If the snapshot size is larger than `chunk_size`, Elasticsearch will split the data into smaller chunks that are not larger than the size specified in `chunk_size`.
- `buffer_size`: The size of this buffer is set to `5m` (which is the lowest possible value) by default. When the chunk size is greater than the value of `buffer_size`, Elasticsearch will split it into `buffer_size` fragments and use the AWS multipart API to send it.
- `max_retries`: This specifies the number of retries Elasticsearch will take before giving up on storing or retrieving the snapshot. By default, it is set to `3`.

In addition to the preceding properties, we are allowed to set two additional properties that can overwrite the credentials stored in `elasticserch.yml`, which will be used to connect to S3. This is especially handy when you want to use several S3 repositories—each with its own security settings:

- `access_key`: This overwrites `cloud.aws.access_key` from `elasticsearch.yml`
- `secret_key`: This overwrites `cloud.aws.secret_key` from `elasticsearch.yml`

The HDFS repository

If you use Hadoop and its HDFS (http://wiki.apache.org/hadoop/HDFS) filesystem, a good alternative to back up the Elasticsearch data is to store it in your Hadoop cluster. As with the case of S3, there is a dedicated plugin for this. To install it, we can use the following command:

```
bin/plugin -i elasticsearch/elasticsearch-repository-hdfs/2.0.2
```

Note that there is an additional plugin version that supports Version 2 of Hadoop. In this case, we should append `hadoop2` to the plugin name in order to be able to install the plugin. So for Hadoop 2, our command that installs the plugin would look as follows:

```
bin/plugin -i elasticsearch/elasticsearch-repository-hdfs/2.0.2-hadoop2
```

There is also a lite version that can be used in a situation where Hadoop is installed on the system with Elasticsearch. In this case, the plugin does not contain Hadoop libraries and are already available to Elasticsearch. To install the lite version of the plugin, the following command can be used:

```
bin/plugin -i elasticsearch/elasticsearch-repository-hdfs/2.0.2-light
```

After installing the plugin on each Elasticsearch (no matter which version of the plugin was used) and restarting the cluster, we can use the following command to create a repository in our Hadoop cluster:

```
curl -XPUT 'http://localhost:9200/_snapshot/hdfs_repository' -d '{
 "type": "hdfs"
 "settings": {
  "path": "snapshots"
 }
}'
```

The available settings that we can use are as follows:

- `uri`: This is the optional parameter that tells Elasticsearch where HDFS resides. It should have a format like `hdfs://HOST:PORT/`.
- `path`: This is the information about the path where snapshot files should be stored. It is a required parameter.
- `load_default`: This specifies whether the default parameters from the Hadoop configuration should be loaded and set to `false` if the reading of the settings should be disabled.
- `conf_location`: This is the name of the Hadoop configuration file to be loaded. By default, it is set to `extra-cfg.xml`.
- `chunk_size`: This specifies the size of the chunk that Elasticsearch will use to split the snapshot data; by default, it is set to `10m`. If you want the snapshotting to be faster, you can use smaller chunks and more streams to push the data to HDFS.

- `conf.<key>`: This is where `key` is any Hadoop argument. The value provided using this property will be merged with the configuration.
- `concurrent_streams`: By default, this is set to `5` and specifies the number of concurrent streams used by a single node to write and read to HDFS.

The Azure repository

The last of the repositories we wanted to mention is Microsoft's Azure cloud. Just like Amazon S3, we are able to use a dedicated plugin to push our indices and metadata to Microsoft cloud services. To do this, we need to install a plugin, which we can do by running the following command:

```
bin/plugin -install elasticsearch/elasticsearch-cloud-azure/2.4.0
```

The configuration is also similar to the Amazon S3 plugin configuration. Our `elasticsearch.yml` file should contain the following section:

```
cloud:
  azure:
    storage_account: YOUR_ACCOUNT
    storage_key: YOUT_SECRET_KEY
```

After Elasticsearch is configured, we need to create the actual repository, which we do by running the following command:

```
curl -XPUT 'http://localhost:9200/_snapshot/azure_repository' -d '{
 "type": "azure"
}'
```

The following settings are supported by the Elasticsearch Azure plugin:

- `container`: As with the bucket in Amazon S3, every piece of information must reside in the container. This setting defines the name of the container in the Microsoft Azure space. The default value is `elasticserch-snapshots`.
- `base_path`: This allows us to change the place where Elasticsearch will put the data. By default, Elasticsearch puts the data in the root directory.
- `chunk_size`: This is the maximum chunk size used by Elasticsearch (set to `64m` by default, and this is also the maximum value allowed). You can change it to change the size when the data should be split into smaller chunks.

Federated search

Sometimes, having data in a single cluster is not enough. Imagine a situation where you have multiple locations where you need to index and search your data—for example, local company divisions that have their own clusters for their own data. The main center of your company would also like to search the data—not in each location but all at once. Of course, in your search application, you can connect to all these clusters and merge the results manually, but from Elasticsearch 1.0, it is also possible to use the so-called **tribe node** that works as a federated Elasticsearch client and can provide access to more than a single Elasticsearch cluster. What the tribe node does is fetch all the cluster states from the connected clusters and merge these states into one global cluster state available on the tribe node. In this section, we will take a look at tribe nodes and how to configure and use them.

> Remember that the described functionality was introduced in Elasticsearch 1.0 and is still marked as experimental. It can be changed or even removed in future versions of Elasticsearch.

The test clusters

For the purpose of showing you how tribe nodes work, we will create two clusters that hold data. The first cluster is named `mastering_one` (as you remember to set the cluster name, you need to specify the `cluster.name` property in the `elasticsearch.yml` file) and the second cluster is named `mastering_two`. To keep it as simple as it can get, each of the clusters contain only a single Elasticsearch node. The node in the cluster named `mastering_one` is available at the `192.168.56.10` IP address and the cluster named `mastering_one` is available at the `192.168.56.40` IP address.

Cluster one was indexed with the following documents:

```
curl -XPOST '192.168.56.10:9200/index_one/doc/1' -d '{"name" : "Test document 1 cluster 1"}'
curl -XPOST '192.168.56.10:9200/index_one/doc/2' -d '{"name" : "Test document 2 cluster 1"}'
```

For the second cluster the following data was indexed:

```
curl -XPOST '192.168.56.40:9200/index_two/doc/1' -d '{"name" : "Test document 1 cluster 2"}'
curl -XPOST '192.168.56.40:9200/index_two/doc/2' -d '{"name" : "Test document 2 cluster 2"}'
```

Creating the tribe node

Now, let's try to create a simple tribe node that will use the multicast discovery by default. To do this, we need a new Elasticsearch node. We also need to provide a configuration for this node that will specify which clusters our tribe node should connect together—in our case, these are our two clusters that we created earlier. To configure our tribe node, we need the following configuration in the `elasticsearch.yml` file:

```
tribe.mastering_one.cluster.name: mastering_one
tribe.mastering_two.cluster.name: mastering_two
```

All the configurations for the tribe node are prefixed with the `tribe` prefix. In the preceding configuration, we told Elasticsearch that we will have two tribes: one named `mastering_one` and the second one named `mastering_two`. These are arbitrary names that are used to distinguish the clusters that are a part of the tribe cluster.

We can start our tribe node, which we will start on a server with the `192.168.56.50` IP address. After starting Elasticsearch, we will try to use the default multicast discovery to find the `mastering_one` and `mastering_two` clusters and connect to them. You should see the following in the logs of the tribe node:

```
[2014-10-30 17:28:04,377][INFO ][cluster.service          ] 
[Feron] added {[mastering_one_node_1][mGF6HHoORQGYkVTzuPd4Jw]
[ragnar][inet[/192.168.56.10:9300]]{tribe.name=mastering_one},},
reason: cluster event from mastering_one, zen-disco-receive(from
master [[mastering_one_node_1][mGF6HHoORQGYkVTzuPd4Jw][ragnar]
[inet[/192.168.56.10:9300]]])
[2014-10-30 17:28:08,288][INFO ][cluster.service          ] 
[Feron] added {[mastering_two_node_1][ZqvDAsY1RmylH46hqCTEnw]
[ragnar][inet[/192.168.56.40:9300]]{tribe.name=mastering_two},},
reason: cluster event from mastering_two, zen-disco-receive(from
master [[mastering_two_node_1][ZqvDAsY1RmylH46hqCTEnw][ragnar]
[inet[/192.168.56.40:9300]]])
```

As we can see, our tribe node joins two clusters together.

Using the unicast discovery for tribes

Of course, multicast discovery is not the only possibility to connect multiple clusters together using the tribe node; we can also use the unicast discovery if needed. For example, to change our tribe node configuration to use unicast, we would change the `elasticsearch.yml` file to look as follows:

```
tribe.mastering_one.cluster.name: mastering_one
tribe.mastering_one.discovery.zen.ping.multicast.enabled: false
```

```
tribe.mastering_one.discovery.zen.ping.unicast.hosts:
["192.168.56.10:9300"]
tribe.mastering_two.cluster.name: mastering_two
tribe.mastering_two.discovery.zen.ping.multicast.enabled: false
tribe.mastering_two.discovery.zen.ping.unicast.hosts:
["192.168.56.40:9300"]
```

As you can see, for each tribe cluster, we disabled the multicast and we specified the unicast hosts. Also note the thing we already wrote about—each property for the tribe node is prefixed with the `tribe` prefix.

Reading data with the tribe node

We said in the beginning that the tribe node fetches the cluster state from all the connected clusters and merges it into a single cluster state. This is done in order to enable read and write operations on all the clusters when using the tribe node. Because the cluster state is merged, almost all operations work in the same way as they would on a single cluster, for example, searching.

Let's try to run a single query against our tribe now to see what we can expect. To do this, we use the following command:

```
curl -XGET '192.168.56.50:9200/_search?pretty'
```

The results of the preceding query look as follows:

```
{
  "took" : 9,
  "timed_out" : false,
  "_shards" : {
    "total" : 10,
    "successful" : 10,
    "failed" : 0
  },
  "hits" : {
    "total" : 4,
    "max_score" : 1.0,
    "hits" : [ {
      "_index" : "index_two",
      "_type" : "doc",
      "_id" : "1",
      "_score" : 1.0,
      "_source":{"name" : "Test document 1 cluster 2"}
    }, {
      "_index" : "index_one",
```

```
         "_type" : "doc",
         "_id" : "2",
         "_score" : 1.0,
         "_source":{"name" : "Test document 2 cluster 1"}
      }, {
         "_index" : "index_two",
         "_type" : "doc",
         "_id" : "2",
         "_score" : 1.0,
         "_source":{"name" : "Test document 2 cluster 2"}
      }, {
         "_index" : "index_one",
         "_type" : "doc",
         "_id" : "1",
         "_score" : 1.0,
         "_source":{"name" : "Test document 1 cluster 1"}
      } ]
   }
}
```

As you can see, we have documents coming from both clusters—yes, that's right; our tribe node was about to automatically get data from all the connected tribes and return the relevant results. We can, of course, do the same with more sophisticated queries; we can use percolation functionality, suggesters, and so on.

Master-level read operations

Read operations that require the master to be present, such as reading the cluster state or cluster health, will be performed on the tribe cluster. For example, let's look at what cluster health returns for our tribe node. We can check this by running the following command:

`curl -XGET '192.168.56.50:9200/_cluster/health?pretty'`

The results of the preceding command will be similar to the following one:

```
{
   "cluster_name" : "elasticsearch",
   "status" : "yellow",
   "timed_out" : false,
   "number_of_nodes" : 5,
   "number_of_data_nodes" : 2,
   "active_primary_shards" : 10,
   "active_shards" : 10,
   "relocating_shards" : 0,
```

```
    "initializing_shards" : 0,
    "unassigned_shards" : 10
}
```

As you can see, our tribe node reported 5 nodes to be present. We have a single node for each of the connected clusters: one tribe node and two internal nodes that are used to provide connectivity to the connected clusters. This is why there are 5 nodes and not three of them.

Writing data with the tribe node

We talked about querying and master-level read operations, so it is time to write some data to Elasticsearch using the tribe node. We won't say much; instead of talking about indexing, let's just try to index additional documents to one of our indices that are present on the connected clusters. We can do this by running the following command:

`curl -XPOST '192.168.56.50:9200/index_one/doc/3' -d '{"name" : "Test document 3 cluster 1"}'`

The execution of the preceding command will result in the following response:

```
{"_index":"index_one","_type":"doc","_id":"3","_version":1,"created":true}
```

As we can see, the document has been created and, what's more, it was indexed in the proper cluster. The tribe node just did its work by forwarding the request internally to the proper cluster. All the write operations that don't require the cluster state to change, such as indexing, will be properly executed using the tribe node.

Master-level write operations

Master-level write operations can't be executed on the tribe node — for example, we won't be able to create a new index using the tribe node. Operations such as index creation will fail when executed on the tribe node, because there is no global master present. We can test this easily by running the following command:

`curl -XPOST '192.168.56.50:9200/index_three'`

The preceding command will return the following error after about 30 seconds of waiting:

```
{"error":"MasterNotDiscoveredException[waited for [30s]]","status":503}
```

As we can see, the index was not created. We should run the master-level write commands on the clusters that are a part of the tribe.

Handling indices conflicts

One of the things that the tribe node can't handle properly is indices with the same names present in multiple connected clusters. What the Elasticsearch tribe node will do by default is that it will choose one and only one index with the same name. So, if all your clusters have the same index, only a single one will be chosen.

Let's test this by creating the index called `test_conflicts` on the `mastering_one` cluster and the same index on the `mastering_two` cluster. We can do this by running the following commands:

```
curl -XPOST '192.168.56.10:9200/test_conflicts'
curl -XPOST '192.168.56.40:9200/test_conflicts'
```

In addition to this, let's index two documents—one to each cluster. We do this by running the following commands:

```
curl -XPOST '192.168.56.10:9200/test_conflicts/doc/11' -d '{"name" : "Test conflict cluster 1"}'
curl -XPOST '192.168.56.40:9201/test_conflicts/doc/21' -d '{"name" : "Test conflict cluster 2"}'
```

Now, let's run our tribe node and try to run a simple search command:

```
curl -XGET '192.168.56.50:9202/test_conflicts/_search?pretty'
```

The output of the command will be as follows:

```
{
  "took" : 1,
  "timed_out" : false,
  "_shards" : {
    "total" : 5,
    "successful" : 5,
    "failed" : 0
  },
  "hits" : {
    "total" : 1,
    "max_score" : 1.0,
    "hits" : [ {
      "_index" : "test_conflicts",
      "_type" : "doc",
```

```
        "_id" : "11",
        "_score" : 1.0,
        "_source":{"name" : "Test conflict cluster 1"}
    } ]
  }
}
```

As you can see, we only got a single document in the result. This is because the Elasticsearch tribe node can't handle indices with the same names coming from different clusters and will choose only one index. This is quite dangerous, because we don't know what to expect.

The good thing is that we can control this behavior by specifying the `tribe.on_conflict` property in `elasticsearch.yml` (introduced in Elasticsearch 1.2.0). We can set it to one of the following values:

- `any`: This is the default value that results in Elasticsearch choosing one of the indices from the connected tribe clusters.
- `drop`: Elasticsearch will ignore the index and won't include it in the global cluster state. This means that the index won't be visible when using the cluster node (both for write and read operations) but still will be present on the connected clusters themselves.
- `prefer_TRIBE_NAME`: Elasticsearch allows us to choose the tribe cluster from which the indices should be taken. For example, if we set our property to `prefer_mastering_one`, it would mean that Elasticsearch will load the conflicting indices from the cluster named `mastering_one`.

Blocking write operations

The tribe node can also be configured to block all write operations and all the metadata change requests. To block all the write operations, we need to set the `tribe.blocks.write` property to `true`. To disallow metadata change requests, we need to set the `tribe.blocks.metadata` property to `true`. By default, these properties are set to `false`, which means that write and metadata altering operations are allowed. Disallowing these operations can be useful when our tribe node should only be used for searching and nothing else.

In addition to this, Elasticsearch 1.2.0 introduced the ability to block write operations on defined indices. We do this by using the `tribe.blocks.indices.write` property and setting its value to the name of the indices. For example, if we want our tribe node to block write operations on all the indices starting with `test` and `production`, we set the following property in the `elasticsearch.yml` file of the tribe node:

```
tribe.blocks.indices.write: test*, production*
```

Summary

In this chapter, we focused more on the Elasticsearch configuration and new features that were introduced in Elasticsearch 1.0. We configured discovery and recovery, and we used the human-friendly Cat API. In addition to that, we used the backup and restore functionality, which allowed easy backup and recovery of our indices. Finally, we looked at what federated search is and how to search and index data to multiple clusters, while still using all the functionalities of Elasticsearch and being connected to a single node.

In the next chapter, we will focus on the performance side of Elasticsearch. We will start by optimizing our queries with filters. We will discuss the garbage collector work, and we will benchmark our queries with the new benchmarking capabilities of Elasticsearch. We will use warming queries to speed up the query execution time, and we will use the Hot Threads API to see what is happening inside Elasticsearch. Finally, we will discuss Elasticsearch scaling and prepare Elasticsearch for high indexing and querying use cases.

8
Improving Performance

In the previous chapter, we looked at the discovery and recovery modules' configuration. We configured these modules and learned why they are important. We also saw additional discovery implementations available through plugins. We used the human-friendly Cat API to get information about the cluster in a human-readable form. We backed up our data to the external cloud storage, and we discussed tribe nodes—a federated search functionality allowing you to connect several Elasticsearch clusters together. By the end of this chapter, you will have learned the following things:

- What doc values can help us with when it comes to queries that are based on field data cache
- How garbage collector works
- How to benchmark your queries and fix performance problems before going to production
- What is the Hot Threads API and how it can help you with problems' diagnosis
- How to scale Elasticsearch and what to look at when doing that
- Preparing Elasticsearch for high querying throughput use cases
- Preparing Elasticsearch for high indexing throughput use cases

Using doc values to optimize your queries

In the *Understanding Elasticsearch caching* section of *Chapter 6, Low-level Index Control* we described caching: one of many ways that allow us to improve Elasticsearch's outstanding performance. Unfortunately, caching is not a silver bullet and, sometimes, it is better to avoid it. If your data is changing rapidly and your queries are very unique and not repeatable, then caching won't really help and can even make your performance worse sometimes.

The problem with field data cache

Every cache is based on a simple principle. The main assumption is that to improve performance, it is worth storing some part of the data in the memory instead of fetching from slow sources such as spinning disks, or to save the system a need to recalculate some processed data. However, caching is not free and it has its price—in terms of Elasticsearch, the cost of caching is mostly memory. Depending on the cache type, you may only need to store recently used data, but again, that's not always possible. Sometimes, it is necessary to hold all the information at once, because otherwise, the cache is just useless. For example, the field data cache used for sorting or aggregations—to make this functionality work, all values for a given field must be uninverted by Elasticsearch and placed in this cache. If we have a large number of documents and our shards are very large, we can be in trouble. The signs of such troubles may be something such as those in the response returned by Elasticsearch when running queries:

```
{
  "error": "ReduceSearchPhaseException[Failed to execute phase
  [fetch], [reduce] ; shardFailures {[vWD3FNVoTy-
  64r2vf6NwAw][dvt1][1]: ElasticsearchException[Java heap space];
  nested: OutOfMemoryError[Java heap space]; }{[vWD3FNVoTy-
  64r2vf6NwAw][dvt1][2]: ElasticsearchException[Java heap space];
  nested: OutOfMemoryError[Java heap space]; }]; nested:
  OutOfMemoryError[Java heap space]; ",
  "status": 500
}
```

The other indications of memory-related problems may be present in Elasticsearch logs and look as follows:

```
[2014-11-29 23:21:32,991][DEBUG][action.search.type       ]
  [Abigail Brand] [dvt1][2], node[vWD3FNVoTy-64r2vf6NwAw], [P],
  s[STARTED]: Failed to execute
  [org.elasticsearch.action.search.SearchRequest@49d609d3]
  lastShard [true]
```

```
org.elasticsearch.ElasticsearchException: Java heap space
  at org.elasticsearch.ExceptionsHelper.convertToRuntime
  (ExceptionsHelper.java:46)
  at org.elasticsearch.search.SearchService.executeQueryPhase
  (SearchService.java:304)
  at org.elasticsearch.search.action.
  SearchServiceTransportAction$5.call
  (SearchServiceTransportAction.java:231)
  at org.elasticsearch.search.action.
  SearchServiceTransportAction$5.call
  (SearchServiceTransportAction.java:228)
  at org.elasticsearch.search.action.
  SearchServiceTransportAction$23.run
  (SearchServiceTransportAction.java:559)
  at java.util.concurrent.ThreadPoolExecutor.runWorker
  (ThreadPoolExecutor.java:1145)
  at java.util.concurrent.ThreadPoolExecutor$Worker.run
  (ThreadPoolExecutor.java:615)
  at java.lang.Thread.run(Thread.java:744)
Caused by: java.lang.OutOfMemoryError: Java heap space
```

This is where doc values can help us. Doc values are data structures in Lucene that are column-oriented, which means that they do not store the data in inverted index but keep them in a document-oriented data structure that is stored on the disk and calculated during the indexation. Because of this, doc values allow us to avoid keeping uninverted data in the field data cache and instead use doc values that access the data from the index, and since Elasticsearch 1.4.0, values are as fast as you would use in the memory field data cache.

The example of doc values usage

To show you the difference in memory consumption between the doc values-based approach and the field data cache-based approach, we indexed some simple documents into Elasticsearch. We indexed the same data to two indices: dvt1 and dvt2. Their structure is identical; the only difference is highlighted in the following code:

```
{
  "t": {
    "properties": {
      "token": {
        "type": "string",
        "index": "not_analyzed",
```

```
            "doc_values": true
          }
        }
      }
    }
```

The `dvt2` index uses `doc_values`, while `dtv1` doesn't use it, so the queries run against them (if they use sorting or aggregations) will use the field data cache.

> For the purpose of the tests, we've set the JVM heap lower than the default values given to Elasticsearch. The example Elasticsearch instance was run using:
>
>   bin/elasticsearch -Xmx16m -Xms16m
>
> This seems somewhat insane for the first sight, but who said that we can't run Elasticsearch on the embedded device? The other way to simulate this problem is, of course, to index way more data. However, for the purpose of the test, keeping the memory low is more than enough.

Let's now see how Elasticsearch behaves when hitting our example indices. The query does not look complicated but shows the problem very well. We will try to sort our data on the basis of our single field in the document: the `token` type. As we know, sorting requires uninverted data, so it will use either the field data cache or doc values if they are available. The query itself looks as follows:

```
{
  "sort": [
    {
      "token": {
        "order": "desc"
      }
    }
  ]
}
```

It is a simple sort, but it is sufficient to take down our server when we try to search in the `dvt1` index. At the same time, a query run against the `dvt2` index returns the expected results without any sign of problems.

The difference in memory usage is significant. We can compare the memory usage for both indices after restarting Elasticsearch and removing the memory limit from the startup parameters. After running the query against both `dvt1` and `dvt2`, we use the following command to check the memory usage:

```
curl -XGET 'localhost:9200/dvt1,dvt2/_stats/fielddata?pretty'
```

Chapter 8

The response returned by Elasticsearch in our case was as follows:

```
{
  "_shards" : {
    "total" : 20,
    "successful" : 10,
    "failed" : 0
  },
  "_all" : {
    "primaries" : {
      "fielddata" : {
        "memory_size_in_bytes" : 17321304,
        "evictions" : 0
      }
    },
    "total" : {
      "fielddata" : {
        "memory_size_in_bytes" : 17321304,
        "evictions" : 0
      }
    }
  },
  "indices" : {
    "dvt2" : {
      "primaries" : {
        "fielddata" : {
          "memory_size_in_bytes" : 0,
          "evictions" : 0
        }
      },
      "total" : {
        "fielddata" : {
          "memory_size_in_bytes" : 0,
          "evictions" : 0
        }
      }
    },
    "dvt1" : {
      "primaries" : {
        "fielddata" : {
          "memory_size_in_bytes" : 17321304,
          "evictions" : 0
        }
      },
```

```
            "total" : {
              "fielddata" : {
                "memory_size_in_bytes" : 17321304,
                "evictions" : 0
              }
            }
          }
        }
      }
}
```

The most interesting parts are highlighted. As we can see, the indexes without `doc_values` use `17321304` bytes (16 MB) of memory for the field data cache. At the same time, the second index uses nothing; exactly no RAM memory is used to store the uninverted data.

Of course, as with most optimizations, doc values are not free to use when it comes to resources. Among the drawbacks of using doc values are speed—doc values are slightly slower compared to field data cache. The second drawback is the additional space needed for `doc_values`. For example, in our simple test case, the index with doc values was 41 MB, while the index without doc values was 34 MB. This gives us a bit more than 20 percent increase in the index size, but that usually depends on the data you have in your index. However, remember that if you have memory problems related to queries and field data cache, you may want to turn on doc values, reindex your data, and not worry about out-of-memory exceptions related to the field data cache anymore.

Knowing about garbage collector

You know that Elasticsearch is a Java application and, because of that, it runs in the Java Virtual Machine. Each Java application is compiled into a so-called **byte code**, which can be executed by the JVM. In the most general way of thinking, you can imagine that the JVM is just executing other programs and controlling their behavior. However, this is not what you will care about unless you develop plugins for Elasticsearch, which we will discuss in *Chapter 9*, *Developing Elasticsearch Plugins*. What you will care about is the **garbage collector**—the piece of JVM that is responsible for memory management. When objects are de-referenced, they can be removed from the memory by the garbage collector. When the memory is running, the low garbage collector starts working and tries to remove objects that are no longer referenced. In this section, we will see how to configure the garbage collector, how to avoid memory swapping, how to log the garbage collector behavior, how to diagnose problems, and how to use some Java tools that will show you how it all works.

> You can learn more about the architecture of JVM in many places you find on the World Wide Web, for example, on Wikipedia: http://en.wikipedia.org/wiki/Java_virtual_machine.

Java memory

When we specify the amount of memory using the `Xms` and `Xmx` parameters (or the `ES_MIN_MEM` and `ES_MAX_MEM` properties), we specify the minimum and maximum size of the JVM heap space. It is basically a reserved space of physical memory that can be used by the Java program, which in our case, is Elasticsearch. A Java process will never use more heap memory than what we've specified with the `Xmx` parameter (or the `ES_MAX_MEM` property). When a new object is created in a Java application, it is placed in the heap memory. After it is no longer used, the garbage collector will try to remove that object from the heap to free the memory space and for JVM to be able to reuse it in the future. You can imagine that if you don't have enough heap memory for your application to create new objects on the heap, then bad things will happen. JVM will throw an `OutOfMemory` exception, which is a sign that something is wrong with the memory—either we don't have enough of it, or we have some memory leak and we don't release the object that we don't use.

> When running Elasticsearch on machines that are powerful and have a lot of free RAM memory, we may ask ourselves whether it is better to run a single large instance of Elasticsearch with plenty of RAM given to the JVM or a few instances with a smaller heap size. Before we answer this question, we need to remember that the more the heap memory is given to the JVM, the harder the work for the garbage collector itself gets. In addition to this, when setting the heap size to more than 31 GB, we don't benefit from the compressed operators, and JVM will need to use 64-bit pointers for the data, which means that we will use more memory to address the same amount of data. Given these facts, it is usually better to go for multiple smaller instances of Elasticsearch instead of one big instance.

The JVM memory (in Java 7) is divided into the following regions:

- **eden space**: This is the part of the heap memory where the JVM initially allocates most of the object types.
- **survivor space**: This is the part of the heap memory that stores objects that survived the garbage collection of the eden space heap. The survivor space is divided into survivor space 0 and survivor space 1.

- **tenured generation**: This is the part of the heap memory that holds objects that were living for some time in the survivor space heap part.
- **permanent generation**: This is the non-heap memory that stores all the data for the virtual machine itself, such as classes and methods for objects.
- **code cache**: This is the non-heap memory that is present in the HotSpot JVM that is used for the compilation and storage of native code.

The preceding classification can be simplified. The eden space and the survivor space is called the **young generation** heap space, and the tenured generation is often called **old generation**.

The life cycle of Java objects and garbage collections

In order to see how the garbage collector works, let's go through the life cycle of a sample Java object.

When a new object is created in a Java application, it is placed in the young generation heap space inside the eden space part. Then, when the next young generation garbage collection is run and the object survives that collection (basically, if it was not a one-time used object and the application still needs it), it will be moved to the survivor part of the young generation heap space (first to survivor 0 and then, after another young generation garbage collection, to survivor 1).

After living for sometime in the survivor 1 space, the object is moved to the tenured generation heap space, so it will now be a part of the old generation. From now on, the young generation garbage collector won't be able to move that object in the heap space. Now, this object will be live in the old generation until our application decides that it is not needed anymore. In such a case, when the next full garbage collection comes in, it will be removed from the heap space and will make place for new objects.

There is one thing to remember: what you usually try to aim to do is smaller, but more garbage collections count rather than one but longer. This is because you want your application to be running at the same constant performance level and the garbage collector work to be transparent for Elasticsearch. When a big garbage collection happens, it can be a stop for the world garbage collection event, where Elasticsearch will be frozen for a short period of time, which will make your queries very slow and will stop your indexing process for some time.

Based on the preceding information, we can say (and it is actually true) that at least till now, Java used generational garbage collection; the more garbage collections our object survives, the further it gets promoted. Because of this, we can say that there are two types of garbage collectors working side by side: the young generation garbage collector (also called minor) and the old generation garbage collector (also called major).

> With the update 9 of Java 7, Oracle introduced a new garbage collector called G1. It is promised to be almost totally unaffected by stop the world events and should be working faster compared to other garbage collectors. To read more about G1, please refer to http://www.oracle.com/technetwork/tutorials/tutorials-1876574.html. Although Elasticsearch creators advise against using G1, numerous companies use it with success, and it allowed them to overcome problems with stop the world events when using Elasticsearch with large volumes of data and heavy queries.

Dealing with garbage collection problems

When dealing with garbage collection problems, the first thing you need to identify is the source of the problem. It is not straightforward work and usually requires some effort from the system administrator or the people responsible for handling the cluster. In this section, we will show you two methods of observing and identifying problems with the garbage collector; the first is to turn on logging for the garbage collector in Elasticsearch, and the second is to use the jstat command, which is present in most Java distributions.

In addition to the presented methods, please note that there are tools out there that can help you diagnose issues related to memory and the garbage collector. These tools are usually provided in the form of monitoring software solutions such as Sematext Group SPM (http://sematext.com/spm/index.html) or NewRelic (http://newrelic.com/). Such solutions provide sophisticated information not only related to garbage collection, but also the memory usage as a whole.

Improving Performance

An example dashboard from the mentioned SPM application showing the garbage collector work looks as follows:

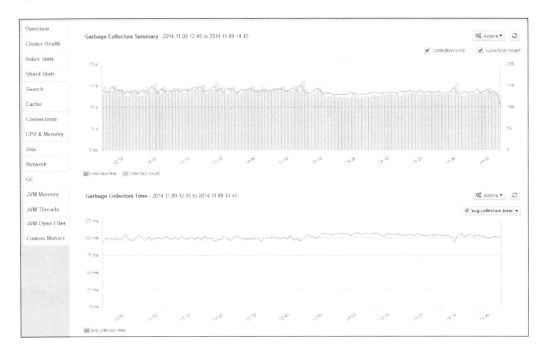

Turning on logging of garbage collection work

Elasticsearch allows us to observe periods when the garbage collector is working too long. In the default `elasticsearch.yml` configuration file, you can see the following entries, which are commented out by default:

```
monitor.jvm.gc.young.warn: 1000ms
monitor.jvm.gc.young.info: 700ms
monitor.jvm.gc.young.debug: 400ms
monitor.jvm.gc.old.warn: 10s
monitor.jvm.gc.old.info: 5s
monitor.jvm.gc.old.debug: 2s
```

As you can see, the configuration specifies three log levels and the thresholds for each of them. For example, for the `info` logging level, if the young generation collection takes 700 milliseconds or more, Elasticsearch will write the information to logs. In the case of the old generation, it will be written to logs if it will take more than five seconds.

> Please note that in older Elasticsearch versions (before 1.0), the prefix to log information related to young generation garbage collection was `monitor.jvm.gc.ParNew.*`, while the prefix to log old garbage collection information was `monitor.jvm.gc.ConcurrentMarkSweep.*`.

What you'll see in the logs is something like this:

```
[2014-11-09 15:22:52,355][WARN ][monitor.jvm              ]
  [Lizard] [gc][old][964][1] duration [14.8s], collections
  [1]/[15.8s], total [14.8s]/[14.8s], memory [8.6gb]-
  >[3.4gb]/[11.9gb], all_pools {[Code Cache] [8.3mb]-
  >[8.3mb]/[48mb]}{[young] [13.3mb]->[3.2mb]/[266.2mb]}{[survivor]
  [29.5mb]->[0b]/[33.2mb]}{[old] [8.5gb]->[3.4gb]/[11.6gb]}
```

As you can see, the preceding line from the log file says that it is about the old garbage collector work. We can see that the total collection time took 14.8 seconds. Before the garbage collection operation, there was 8.6 GB of heap memory used (out of 11.9 GB). After the garbage collection work, the amount of heap memory used was reduced to 3.4 GB. After this, you can see information in more detailed statistics about which parts of the heap were taken into consideration by the garbage collector: the code cache, young generation space, survivor space, or old generation heap space.

When turning on the logging of the garbage collector work at a certain threshold, we can see when things don't run the way we would like by just looking at the logs. However, if you would like to see more, Java comes with a tool for that: `jstat`.

Using JStat

Running the `jstat` command to look at how our garbage collector works is as simple as running the following command:

jstat -gcutil 123456 2000 1000

The `-gcutil` switch tells the command to monitor the garbage collector work, `123456` is the virtual machine identifier on which Elasticsearch is running, `2000` is the interval in milliseconds between samples, and `1000` is the number of samples to be taken. So, in our case, the preceding command will run for a little more than 33 minutes (`2000 * 1000 / 1000 / 60`).

Improving Performance

In most cases, the virtual machine identifier will be similar to your process ID or even the same but not always. In order to check which Java processes are running and what their virtual machines identifiers are, one can just run a `jps` command, which is provided with most JDK distributions. A sample command would be like this:

```
jps
```

The result would be as follows:

```
16232 Jps
11684 ElasticSearch
```

In the result of the `jps` command, we see that each line contains the JVM identifier, followed by the process name. If you want to learn more about the `jps` command, please refer to the Java documentation at `http://docs.oracle.com/javase/7/docs/technotes/tools/share/jps.html`.

> Please remember to run the `jstat` command from the same account that Elasticsearch is running, or if that is not possible, run `jstat` with administrator privileges (for example, using the `sudo` command on Linux systems). It is crucial to have access rights to the process running Elasticsearch, or the `jstat` command won't be able to connect to that process.

Now, let's look at a sample output of the `jstat` command:

S0	S1	E	O	P	YGC	YGCT	FGC	FGCT	GCT
12.44	0.00	27.20	9.49	96.70	78	0.176	5	0.495	0.672
12.44	0.00	62.16	9.49	96.70	78	0.176	5	0.495	0.672
12.44	0.00	83.97	9.49	96.70	78	0.176	5	0.495	0.672
0.00	7.74	0.00	9.51	96.70	79	0.177	5	0.495	0.673
0.00	7.74	23.37	9.51	96.70	79	0.177	5	0.495	0.673
0.00	7.74	43.82	9.51	96.70	79	0.177	5	0.495	0.673
0.00	7.74	58.11	9.51	96.71	79	0.177	5	0.495	0.673

The preceding example comes from the Java documentation and we decided to take it because it nicely shows us what `jstat` is all about. Let's start by saying what each of the columns mean:

- `S0`: This means that survivor space 0 utilization is a percentage of the space capacity
- `S1`: This means that survivor space 1 utilization is a percentage of the space capacity

- E: This means that the eden space utilization is a percentage of the space capacity
- O: This means that the old space utilization is a percentage of the space capacity
- YGC: This refers to the number of young garbage collection events
- YGCT: This is the time of young garbage collections in seconds
- FGC: This is the number of full garbage collections
- FGCT: This is the time of full garbage collections in seconds
- GCT: This is the total garbage collection time in seconds

Now, let's get back to our example. As you can see, there was a young garbage collection event after sample three and before sample four. We can see that the collection took 0.001 of a second (0.177 YGCT in the fourth sample minus 0.176 YGCT in the third sample). We also know that the collection promoted objects from the eden space (which is 0 percent in the fourth sample and was 83.97 percent in the third sample) to the old generation heap space (which was increased from 9.49 percent in the third sample to 9.51 percent in the fourth sample). This example shows you how you can analyze the output of jstat. Of course, it can be time consuming and requires some knowledge about how garbage collector works, and what is stored in the heap. However, sometimes, it is the only way to see why Elasticsearch is stuck at certain moments.

Remember that if you ever see Elasticsearch not working correctly—the S0, S1 or E columns at 100 percent and the garbage collector working and not being able to handle these heap spaces—then either your young is too small and you should increase it (of course, if you have sufficient physical memory available), or you have run into some memory problems. These problems can be related to memory leaks when some resources are not releasing the unused memory. On the other hand, when your old generation space is at 100 percent and the garbage collector is struggling with releasing it (frequent garbage collections) but it can't, then it probably means that you just don't have enough heap space for your Elasticsearch node to operate properly. In such cases, what you can do without changing your index architecture is to increase the heap space that is available for the JVM that is running Elasticsearch (for more information about JVM parameters, refer to http://www.oracle.com/technetwork/java/javase/tech/vmoptions-jsp-140102.html).

Improving Performance

Creating memory dumps

One additional thing that we didn't mention till now is the ability to dump the heap memory to a file. Java allows us to get a snapshot of the memory for a given point in time, and we can use that snapshot to analyze what is stored in the memory and find problems. In order to dump the Java process memory, one can use the `jmap` (http://docs.oracle.com/javase/7/docs/technotes/tools/share/jmap.html) command, for example, like this:

```
jmap -dump:file=heap.dump 123456
```

The `123456` heap dump, in our case, is the identifier of the Java process we want to get the memory dump for, and `-dump:file=heap.dump` specifies that we want the dump to be stored in the file named `heap.dump`. Such a dump can be further analyzed by specialized software, such as `jhat` (http://docs.oracle.com/javase/7/docs/technotes/tools/share/jhat.html), but the usage of such programs are beyond the scope of this book.

More information on the garbage collector work

Tuning garbage collection is not a simple process. The default options set for us in Elasticsearch deployment are usually sufficient for most cases, and the only thing you'll need to do is adjust the amount of memory for your nodes. The topic of tuning the garbage collector work is beyond the scope of the book; it is very broad and is called black magic by some developers. However, if you would like to read more about garbage collector, what the options are, and how they affect your application, I can suggest a great article that can be found at http://www.oracle.com/technetwork/java/javase/gc-tuning-6-140523.html. Although the article in the link is concentrated on Java 6, most of the options, if not all, can be successfully used with deployments running on Java 7.

Adjusting the garbage collector work in Elasticsearch

We now know how the garbage collector works and how to diagnose problems with it, so it would be nice to know how we can change Elasticsearch start up parameters to change how garbage collector works. It depends on how you run Elasticsearch. We will look at the two most common ones: standard start up script provided with the Elasticsearch distribution package and when using the service wrapper.

Using a standard start up script

When using a standard start up script in order to add additional JVM parameters, we should include them in the `JAVA_OPTS` environment property. For example, if we would like to include `-XX:+UseParNewGC -XX:+UseConcMarkSweepGC` in our Elasticsearch start up parameters in Linux-like systems, we would do the following:

```
export JAVA_OPTS="-XX:+UseParNewGC -XX:+UseConcMarkSweepGC"
```

In order to check whether the property was properly considered, we can just run another command:

```
echo $JAVA_OPTS
```

The preceding command should result in the following output in our case:

```
-XX:+UseParNewGC -XX:+UseConcMarkSweepGC
```

Service wrapper

Elasticsearch allows the user to install it as a service using the Java service wrapper (https://github.com/elasticsearch/elasticsearch-servicewrapper). If you are using the service wrapper, setting up JVM parameters is different when compared to the method shown previously. What we need to do is modify the `elasticsearch.conf` file, which will probably be located in `/opt/elasticsearch/bin/service/` (if your Elasticsearch was installed in `/opt/elasticsearch`). In the mentioned file, you will see properties such as:

```
set.default.ES_HEAP_SIZE=1024
```

You will see properties such as these as well:

```
wrapper.java.additional.1=-Delasticsearch-service
wrapper.java.additional.2=-Des.path.home=%ES_HOME%
wrapper.java.additional.3=-Xss256k
wrapper.java.additional.4=-XX:+UseParNewGC
wrapper.java.additional.5=-XX:+UseConcMarkSweepGC
wrapper.java.additional.6=-XX:CMSInitiatingOccupancyFraction=75
wrapper.java.additional.7=-XX:+UseCMSInitiatingOccupancyOnly
wrapper.java.additional.8=-XX:+HeapDumpOnOutOfMemoryError
wrapper.java.additional.9=-Djava.awt.headless=true
```

Improving Performance

The first property is responsible for setting the heap memory size for Elasticsearch, while the rest are additional JVM parameters. If you would like to add another parameter, you can just add another `wrapper.java.additional` property, followed by a dot and the next available number, for example:

```
wrapper.java.additional.10=-server
```

> One thing to remember is that tuning the garbage collector work is not something that you do once and forget. It requires experimenting, as it is very dependent on your data, queries and all that combined. Don't fear making changes when something is wrong, but also observe them and look how Elasticsearch works after making changes.

Avoid swapping on Unix-like systems

Although this is not strict about garbage collection and heap memory usage, we think that it is crucial to see how to disable swap. Swapping is the process of writing memory pages to the disk (swap partition in Unix-based systems) when the amount of physical memory is not sufficient or the operating system decides that for some reason, it is better to have some part of the RAM memory written into the disk. If the swapped memory pages will be needed again, the operating system will load them from the swap partition and allow processes to use them. As you can imagine, such processes take time and resources.

When using Elasticsearch, we want to avoid its process memory being swapped. You can imagine that having parts of memory used by Elasticsearch written to the disk and then again read from it can hurt the performance of both searching and indexing. Because of this, Elasticsearch allows us to turn off swapping for it. In order to do that, one should set `bootstrap.mlockall` to `true` in the `elasticsearch.yml` file.

However, the preceding setting is only the beginning. You also need to ensure that the JVM won't resize the heap by setting the `Xmx` and `Xms` parameters to the same values (you can do that by specifying the same values for the `ES_MIN_MEM` and `ES_MAX_MEM` environment variables for Elasticsearch). Also remember that you need to have enough physical memory to handle the settings you've set.

Now if we run Elasticsearch, we can run into the following message in the logs:

```
[2013-06-11 19:19:00,858][WARN ][common.jna               ]
  Unknown mlockall error 0
```

This means that our memory locking is not working. So now, let's modify two files on our Linux operating system (this will require administration rights). We assume that the user who will run Elasticsearch is `elasticsearch`.

First, we modify `/etc/security/limits.conf` and add the following entries:

```
elasticsearch - nofile 64000
elasticsearch - memlock unlimited
```

The second thing is to modify the `/etc/pam.d/common-session` file and add the following:

```
session required pam_limits.so
```

After re-logging to the `elasticsearch` user account, you should be able to start Elasticsearch and not see the `mlockall` error message.

Benchmarking queries

There are a few important things when dealing with search or data analysis. We need the results to be precise, we need them to be relevant, and we need them to be returned as soon as possible. If you are a person responsible for designing queries that are run against Elasticsearch, sooner or later, you will find yourself in a position where you will need to improve the performance of your queries. The reasons can vary from hardware-based problems to bad data architecture to poor query design. When writing this book, the benchmark API was only available in the trunk of Elasticsearch, which means that it was not a part of official Elasticsearch distribution. For now we can either use tools like jMeter or ab (the Apache benchmark is http://httpd.apache.org/docs/2.2/programs/ab.html) or use trunk version of Elasticsearch. Please also note that the functionality we are describing can change with the final release, so keeping an eye on http://www.elasticsearch.org/guide/en/elasticsearch/reference/master/search-benchmark.html is a good idea if you want to use benchmarking functionality.

Preparing your cluster configuration for benchmarking

By default, the benchmarking functionality is disabled. Any attempt to use benchmarking on the Elasticsearch node that is not configured properly will lead to an error similar to the following one:

```
{
  "error" : "BenchmarkNodeMissingException[No available nodes for executing benchmark [benchmark_name]]",
  "status" : 503
}
```

Improving Performance

This is okay; no one wants to take a risk of running potentially dangerous functionalities on production cluster. During performance testing and benchmarking, you will want to run many complicated and heavy queries, so running such benchmarks on the Elasticsearch cluster that is used by real users doesn't seem like a good idea. It will lead to the slowness of the cluster, and it could result in crashes and a bad user experience. To use benchmarking, you have to inform Elasticsearch which nodes can run the generated queries. Every instance we want to use for benchmarking should be run with the --node.bench option set to true. For example, we could run an Elasticsearch instance like this:

```
bin/elasticsearch --node.bench true
```

The other possibility is to add the node.bench property to the elasticsearch.yml file and, of course, set it to true. Whichever way we choose, we are now ready to run our first benchmark.

Running benchmarks

Elasticsearch provides the _bench REST endpoint, which allows you to define the task to run on benchmarking-enabled nodes in the cluster. Let's look at a simple example to learn how to do that. We will show you something practical; in the *Handling filters and why it matters* section in *Chapter 2, Power User Query DSL*, we talked about filtering. We tried to convince you that, in most cases, post filtering is bad. We can now check it ourselves and see whether the queries with post filtering are really slower. The command that allows us to test this looks as follows (we have used the Wikipedia database):

```
curl -XPUT 'localhost:9200/_bench/?pretty' -d '{
    "name": "firstTest",
    "competitors": [ {
        "name": "post_filter",
        "requests": [ {
            "post_filter": {
                "term": {
                    "link": "Toyota Corolla"
                }
            }
        }]
    },
    {
        "name": "filtered",
```

```
            "requests": [ {
                "query": {
                    "filtered": {
                        "query": {
                            "match_all": {}
                        },
                        "filter": {
                            "term": {
                                "link": "Toyota Corolla"
                            }
                        }
                    }
                }
            }]
        }]
}'
```

The structure of a request to the _bench REST endpoint is pretty simple. It contains a list of competitors—queries or sets of queries (because each competitor can have more than a single query)—that will be compared to each other by the Elasticsearch benchmarking functionality. Each competitor has its name to allow easier results analysis. Now, let's finally look at the results returned by the preceding request:

```
{
    "status": "COMPLETE",
    "errors": [],
    "competitors": {
        "filtered": {
            "summary": {
                "nodes": [
                    "Free Spirit"
                ],
                "total_iterations": 5,
                "completed_iterations": 5,
                "total_queries": 5000,
                "concurrency": 5,
                "multiplier": 1000,
                "avg_warmup_time": 6,
                "statistics": {
                    "min": 1,
```

```
                    "max": 5,
                    "mean": 1.9590000000000019,
                    "qps": 510.4645227156713,
                    "std_dev": 0.6143244085137575,
                    "millis_per_hit": 0.0009694501018329939,
                    "percentile_10": 1,
                    "percentile_25": 2,
                    "percentile_50": 2,
                    "percentile_75": 2,
                    "percentile_90": 3,
                    "percentile_99": 4
                }
            }
        },
        "post_filter": {
            "summary": {
                "nodes": [
                    "Free Spirit"
                ],
                "total_iterations": 5,
                "completed_iterations": 5,
                "total_queries": 5000,
                "concurrency": 5,
                "multiplier": 1000,
                "avg_warmup_time": 74,
                "statistics": {
                    "min": 66,
                    "max": 217,
                    "mean": 120.88000000000022,
                    "qps": 8.272667107875579,
                    "std_dev": 18.487886855778815,
                    "millis_per_hit": 0.05085254582484725,
                    "percentile_10": 98,
                    "percentile_25": 109.26595744680851,
                    "percentile_50": 120.32258064516128,
                    "percentile_75": 131.3181818181818,
                    "percentile_90": 143,
                    "percentile_99": 171.01000000000022
                }
            }
        }
    }
}
```

As you can see, the test was successful; Elasticsearch returned an empty `errors` table. For every test we've run with both `post_filter` and `filtered` queries, only a single node named `Free Spirit` was used for benchmarking. In both cases, the same number of queries was used (`5000`) with the same number of simultaneous requests (`5`). Comparing the warm-up time and statistics, you can easily draw conclusions about which query is better. We would like to choose the filtered query; what about you?

Our example was quite simple (actually it was very simple), but it shows you the usefulness of benchmarking. Of course, our initial request didn't use all the configuration options exposed by the Elasticsearch benchmarking API. To summarize all the options, we've prepared a list of the available global options for the `_bench` REST endpoint:

- `name`: This is the name of the benchmark, making it easy to distinguish multiple benchmarks (refer to the *Controlling currently run benchmarks* section).
- `competitors`: This is the definition of tests that Elasticsearch should perform. It is the array of objects describing each test.
- `num_executor_nodes`: This is the maximum number of Elasticsearch nodes that will be used during query tests as a source of queries. It defaults to `1`.
- `percentiles`: This is an array defining percentiles Elasticsearch should compute and return in results with the query execution time. The default value is `[10, 25, 50, 75, 90, 99]`.
- `iteration`: This defaults to `5` and defines the number of repetitions for each competitor that Elasticsearch should perform.
- `concurrency`: This is the concurrency for each iteration and it defaults to `5`, which means that five concurrent threads will be used by Elasticsearch.
- `multiplier`: This is the number of repetitions of each query in the given iteration. By default, the query is run `1000` times.
- `warmup`: This informs you that Elasticsearch should perform the warm-up of the query. By default, the warm-up is performed, which means that this value is set to `true`.

- `clear_caches`: By default, this is set to `false`, which means that before each iteration, Elasticsearch will not clean the caches. We can change this by setting the value to `true`. This parameter is connected with a series of parameters saying which cache should or should not be cleared. These additional parameters are `clear_caches.filter` (the filter cache), `clear_caches.field_data` (the field data cache), `clear_caches.id` (the ID cache), and `clear_caches.recycler` (the recycler cache). In addition, there are two parameters that can take an array of names: `clear_caches.fields` specifies the names of fields and which cache should be cleared and `clear_caches.filter_keys` specifies the names of filter keys to clear. For more information about caches, refer to the *Understanding Elasticsearch caching* section in *Chapter 6*, *Low-level Index Control*.

In addition to the global options, each competitor is an object that can contain the following parameters:

- `name`: Like its equivalent on the root level, this helps distinguish several competitors from each other.
- `requests`: This is a table of objects defining queries that should be run within given competitors. Each object is a standard Elasticsearch query that is defined using the query DSL.
- `num_slowest`: This is the number of the slowest queries tracked. It defaults to 1. If we want Elasticsearch to track and record more than one slow query, we should increase the value of that parameter.
- `search_type`: This indicates the type of searches that should be performed. Few of the options are `query_then_fetch`, `dfs_query_then_fetch`, and `count`. It defaults to `query_then_fetch`.
- `indices`: This is an array with indices names to which the queries should be limited.
- `types`: This is an array with type names to which the queries should be limited.
- `iteration`, `concurrency`, `multiplier`, `warmup`, `clear_caches`: These parameters override their version defined on the global level.

Controlling currently run benchmarks

Depending on the parameters we've used to execute our benchmark, a single benchmarking command containing several queries with thousands of repeats can run for several minutes or even hours. It is very handy to have a possibility to check how the tests run and estimate how long it will take for the benchmark command to end. As you can expect, Elasticsearch provides such information. To get this, the only thing we need to do is run the following command:

```
curl -XGET 'localhost:9200/_bench?pretty'
```

The output generated for the preceding command can look as follows (it was taken during the execution of our sample benchmark):

```
{
  "active_benchmarks" : {
    "firstTest" : {
      "status" : "RUNNING",
      "errors" : [ ],
      "competitors" : {
        "post_filter" : {
          "summary" : {
            "nodes" : [
            "James Proudstar" ],
            "total_iterations" : 5,
            "completed_iterations" : 3,
            "total_queries" : 3000,
            "concurrency" : 5,
            "multiplier" : 1000,
            "avg_warmup_time" : 137.0,
            "statistics" : {
              "min" : 39,
              "max" : 146,
              "mean" : 78.95077720207264,
              "qps" : 32.81378178835111,
              "std_dev" : 17.42543552392229,
              "millis_per_hit" : 0.031591310251188054,
              "percentile_10" : 59.0,
              "percentile_25" : 66.86363636363637,
              "percentile_50" : 77.0,
              "percentile_75" : 89.22727272727272,
              "percentile_90" : 102.0,
              "percentile_99" : 124.86000000000013
```

```
            }
           }
          }
         }
        }
       }
      }
```

Thanks to it, you can see the progress of tests and try to estimate how long you will have to wait for the benchmark to finish and return the results. If you would like to abort the currently running benchmark (for example, it takes too long and you already see that the tested query is not optimal), Elasticsearch has a solution. For example, to abort our benchmark called `firstTest`, we run a POST request to the `_bench/abort` REST endpoint, just like this:

```
curl -XPOST 'localhost:9200/_bench/abort/firstTest?pretty'
```

The response returned by Elasticsearch will show you a partial result of the test. It is almost the same as what we've seen in the preceding example, except that the status of the benchmark will be set to `ABORTED`.

Very hot threads

When you are in trouble and your cluster works slower than usual and uses large amounts of CPU power, you know you need to do something to make it work again. This is the case when the Hot Threads API can give you the information necessary to find the root cause of problems. A hot thread in this case is a Java thread that uses a high CPU volume and executes for longer periods of time. Such a thread doesn't mean that there is something wrong with Elasticsearch itself; it gives you information on what can be a possible hotspot and allows you to see which part of your deployment you need to look more deeply at, such as query execution or Lucene segments merging. The Hot Threads API returns information about which parts of the Elasticsearch code are hot spots from the CPU side or where Elasticsearch is stuck for some reason.

When using the Hot Threads API, you can examine all nodes, a selected few of them, or a particular node using the `/_nodes/hot_threads` or `/_nodes/{node or nodes}/hot_threads` endpoints. For example, to look at hot threads on all the nodes, we would run the following command:

```
curl 'localhost:9200/_nodes/hot_threads'
```

The API supports the following parameters:

- `threads` (the default: `3`): This is the number of threads that should be analyzed. Elasticsearch takes the specified number of the hottest threads by looking at the information determined by the `type` parameter.
- `interval` (the default: `500ms`): Elasticsearch checks threads twice to calculate the percentage of time spent in a particular thread on an operation defined by the `type` parameter. We can use the `interval` parameter to define the time between these checks.
- `type` (the default: `cpu`): This is the type of thread state to be examined. The API can check the CPU time taken by the given thread (`cpu`), the time in the blocked state (`block`), or the time in the waiting (`wait`) state. If you would like to know more about the thread states, refer to `http://docs.oracle.com/javase/7/docs/api/java/lang/Thread.State.html`.
- `snapshots` (the default: `10`): This is the number of stack traces (a nested sequence of method calls at a certain point of time) snapshots to take.

Using the Hot Threads API is very simple; for example, to look at hot threads on all the nodes that are in the waiting state with check intervals of one second, we would use the following command:

```
curl 'localhost:9200/_nodes/hot_threads?type=wait&interval=1s'
```

Usage clarification for the Hot Threads API

Unlike other Elasticsearch API responses where you can expect JSON to be returned, the Hot Threads API returns formatted text, which contains several sections. Before we discuss the response structure itself, we would like to tell you a bit about the logic that is responsible for generating this response. Elasticsearch takes all the running threads and collects various information about the CPU time spent in each thread, the number of times the particular thread was blocked or was in the waiting state, how long it was blocked or was in the waiting state, and so on. The next thing is to wait for a particular amount of time (specified by the `interval` parameter), and after that time passes, collect the same information again. After this is done, threads are sorted on the basis of time each particular thread was running. The sort is done in a descending order so that the threads running for the longest period of time are on top of the list. Of course, the mentioned time is measured for a given operation type specified by the `type` parameter. After this, the first N threads (where N is the number of threads specified by the `threads` parameter) are analyzed by Elasticsearch. What Elasticsearch does is that, at every few milliseconds, it takes a few snapshots (the number of snapshots is specified by the `snapshot` parameter) of stack traces of the threads that were selected in the previous step. The last thing that needs to be done is the grouping of stack traces in order to visualize changes in the thread state and return the response to the caller.

The Hot Threads API response

Now, let's go through the sections of the response returned by the Hot Threads API. For example, the following screenshot is a fragment of the Hot Threads API response generated for Elasticsearch that was just started:

```
> curl 'localhost:9200/_nodes/hot_threads'
::: [N'Gabthoth][aBb5552UQvyFCk1PNCaJnA][Banshee-3.local][inet[/10.0.1.3:9300]]

   1.4% (6.7ms out of 500ms) cpu usage by thread 'elasticsearch[N'Gabthoth][http_server_boss][T#1]{New I/O server boss #51}'
     10/10 snapshots sharing following 14 elements
       sun.nio.ch.KQueueArrayWrapper.kevent0(Native Method)
       sun.nio.ch.KQueueArrayWrapper.poll(KQueueArrayWrapper.java:200)
       sun.nio.ch.KQueueSelectorImpl.doSelect(KQueueSelectorImpl.java:103)
       sun.nio.ch.SelectorImpl.lockAndDoSelect(SelectorImpl.java:87)
       sun.nio.ch.SelectorImpl.select(SelectorImpl.java:98)
       sun.nio.ch.SelectorImpl.select(SelectorImpl.java:102)
       org.elasticsearch.common.netty.channel.socket.nio.NioServerBoss.select(NioServerBoss.java:163)
       org.elasticsearch.common.netty.channel.socket.nio.AbstractNioSelector.run(AbstractNioSelector.java:212)
       org.elasticsearch.common.netty.channel.socket.nio.NioServerBoss.run(NioServerBoss.java:42)
       org.elasticsearch.common.netty.util.ThreadRenamingRunnable.run(ThreadRenamingRunnable.java:108)
       org.elasticsearch.common.netty.util.internal.DeadLockProofWorker$1.run(DeadLockProofWorker.java:42)
       java.util.concurrent.ThreadPoolExecutor.runWorker(ThreadPoolExecutor.java:1145)
       java.util.concurrent.ThreadPoolExecutor$Worker.run(ThreadPoolExecutor.java:615)
       java.lang.Thread.run(Thread.java:744)

   0.7% (3.3ms out of 500ms) cpu usage by thread 'elasticsearch[N'Gabthoth][search][T#6]'
     10/10 snapshots sharing following 10 elements
       sun.misc.Unsafe.park(Native Method)
       java.util.concurrent.locks.LockSupport.park(LockSupport.java:186)
       java.util.concurrent.LinkedTransferQueue.awaitMatch(LinkedTransferQueue.java:735)
       java.util.concurrent.LinkedTransferQueue.xfer(LinkedTransferQueue.java:644)
       java.util.concurrent.LinkedTransferQueue.take(LinkedTransferQueue.java:1137)
       org.elasticsearch.common.util.concurrent.SizeBlockingQueue.take(SizeBlockingQueue.java:162)
       java.util.concurrent.ThreadPoolExecutor.getTask(ThreadPoolExecutor.java:1068)
       java.util.concurrent.ThreadPoolExecutor.runWorker(ThreadPoolExecutor.java:1130)
       java.util.concurrent.ThreadPoolExecutor$Worker.run(ThreadPoolExecutor.java:615)
       java.lang.Thread.run(Thread.java:744)

   0.5% (2.7ms out of 500ms) cpu usage by thread 'elasticsearch[N'Gabthoth][search][T#10]'
     10/10 snapshots sharing following 10 elements
       sun.misc.Unsafe.park(Native Method)
       java.util.concurrent.locks.LockSupport.park(LockSupport.java:186)
       java.util.concurrent.LinkedTransferQueue.awaitMatch(LinkedTransferQueue.java:735)
       java.util.concurrent.LinkedTransferQueue.xfer(LinkedTransferQueue.java:644)
       java.util.concurrent.LinkedTransferQueue.take(LinkedTransferQueue.java:1137)
       org.elasticsearch.common.util.concurrent.SizeBlockingQueue.take(SizeBlockingQueue.java:162)
       java.util.concurrent.ThreadPoolExecutor.getTask(ThreadPoolExecutor.java:1068)
       java.util.concurrent.ThreadPoolExecutor.runWorker(ThreadPoolExecutor.java:1130)
       java.util.concurrent.ThreadPoolExecutor$Worker.run(ThreadPoolExecutor.java:615)
       java.lang.Thread.run(Thread.java:744)
>
```

Now, let's discuss the sections of the response. To do that, we will use a slightly different response compared to the one shown previously. We do this to better visualize what is happening inside Elasticsearch. However, please remember that the general structure of the response will not change.

The first section of the Hot Threads API response shows us which node the thread is located on. For example, the first line of the response can look as follows:

```
::: [N'Gabthoth][aBb5552UQvyFCk1PNCaJnA][Banshee-3.local][inet[/10.0.1.3:9300]]
```

Thanks to it, we can see which node the Hot Threads API returns information about and which node is very handy when the Hot Threads API call goes to many nodes.

The next lines of the Hot Threads API response can be divided into several sections, each starting with a line similar to the following one:

```
0.5% (2.7ms out of 500ms) cpu usage by thread
  'elasticsearch[N'Gabthoth][search][T#10]'
```

In our case, we see a thread named `search`, which takes `0.5` percent of all the CPU time at the time when the measurement was done. The `cpu usage` part of the preceding line indicates that we are using `type` equal to `cpu` (other values you can expect here are `block usage` for threads in the blocked state and `wait usage` for threads in the waiting states). The thread name is very important here, because by looking at it, we can see which Elasticsearch functionality is the hot one. In our example, we see that this thread is all about searching (the `search` value). Other example values that you can expect to see are `recovery_stream` (for recovery module events), `cache` (for caching events), `merge` (for segments merging threads), `index` (for data indexing threads), and so on.

The next part of the Hot Threads API response is the section starting with the following information:

```
10/10 snapshots sharing following 10 elements
```

This information will be followed by a stack trace. In our case, `10/10` means that 10 snapshots have been taken for the same stack trace. In general, this means that all the examination time was spent in the same part of the Elasticsearch code.

Scaling Elasticsearch

As we already said multiple times both in this book and in *Elasticsearch Server Second Edition*, Elasticsearch is a highly scalable search and analytics platform. We can scale it both horizontally and vertically.

Vertical scaling

When we talk about **vertical scaling**, we often mean adding more resources to the server Elasticsearch is running on: we can add memory and we can switch to a machine with better CPU or faster disk storage. Of course, with better machines, we can expect increase in performance; depending on our deployment and its bottleneck, there can be smaller or higher improvement. However, there are limitations when it comes to vertical scaling. For example, one of such is the maximum amount of physical memory available for your servers or the total memory required by the JVM to operate. When you have large enough data and complicated queries, you can very soon run into memory issues, and adding new memory may not be helpful at all.

Improving Performance

For example, you may not want to go beyond 31 GB of physical memory given to the JVM because of garbage collection and the inability to use compressed ops, which basically means that to address the same memory space, JVM will need to use twice the memory. Even though it seems like a very big issue, vertical scaling is not the only solution we have.

Horizontal scaling

The other solution available to us Elasticsearch users is **horizontal scaling**. To give you a comparison, vertical scaling is like building a sky scrapper, while horizontal scaling is like having many houses in a residential area. Instead of investing in hardware and having powerful machines, we choose to have multiple machines and our data split between them. Horizontal scaling gives us virtually unlimited scaling possibilities. Even with the most powerful hardware time, a single machine is not enough to handle the data, the queries, or both of them. If a single machine is not able to handle the amount of data, we have such cases where we divide our indices into multiple shards and spread them across the cluster, just like what is shown in the following figure:

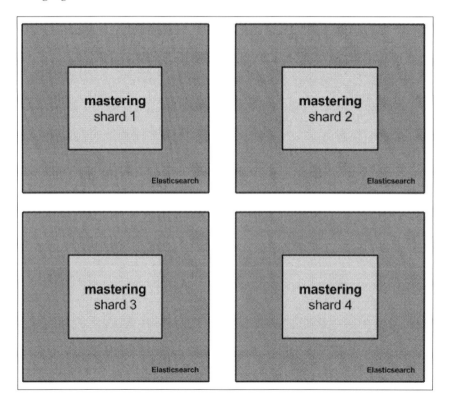

When we don't have enough processing power to handle queries, we can always create more replicas of the shards we have. We have our cluster: four Elasticsearch nodes with the `mastering` index created and running on it and built of four shards.

If we want to increase the querying capabilities of our cluster, we would just add additional nodes, for example, four of them. After adding new nodes to the cluster, we can either create new indices that will be built of more shards to spread the load more evenly, or add replicas to already existing shards. Both options are viable. We should go for more primary shards when our hardware is not enough to handle the amount of data it holds. In such cases, we usually run into out-of-memory situations, long shard query execution time, swapping, or high I/O waits. The second option—having replicas—is a way to go when our hardware is happily handling the data we have, but the traffic is so high that the nodes just can't keep up. The first option is simple, but let's look at the second case: having more replicas. So, with four additional nodes, our cluster would look as follows:

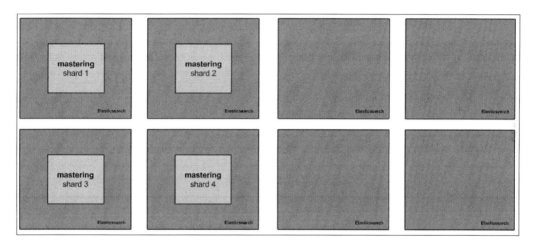

Now, let's run the following command to add a single replica:

```
curl -XPUT 'localhost:9200/mastering/_settings' -d '{
 "index" : {
  "number_of_replicas" : 1
 }
}'
```

Our cluster view would look more or less as follows:

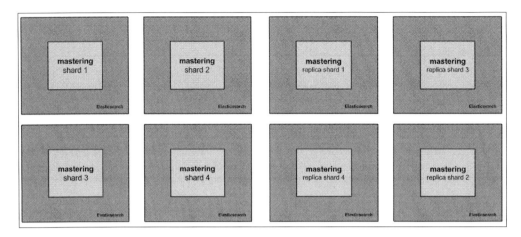

As you can see, each of the initial shards building the mastering index has a single replica stored on another node. Because of this, Elasticsearch is able to round robin the queries between the shard and its replicas so that the queries don't always hit one node. Because of this, we are able to handle almost double the query load compared to our initial deployment.

Automatically creating replicas

Elasticsearch allows us to automatically expand replicas when the cluster is big enough. You might wonder where such functionality can be useful. Imagine a situation where you have a small index that you would like to be present on every node so that your plugins don't have to run distributed queries just to get data from it. In addition to this, your cluster is dynamically changing; you add and remove nodes from it. The simplest way to achieve such a functionality is to allow Elasticsearch to automatically expand replicas. To do this, we would need to set index.auto_expand_replicas to 0-all, which means that the index can have 0 replicas or be present on all the nodes. So if our small index is called mastering_meta and we would like Elasticsearch to automatically expand its replicas, we would use the following command to create the index:

```
curl -XPOST 'localhost:9200/mastering_meta/' -d '{
 "settings" : {
  "index" : {
   "auto_expand_replicas" : "0-all"
  }
 }
}'
```

We can also update the settings of that index if it is already created by running the following command:

```
curl -XPUT 'localhost:9200/mastering_meta/_settings' -d '{
 "index" : {
  "auto_expand_replicas" : "0-all"
 }
}'
```

Redundancy and high availability

The Elasticsearch replication mechanism not only gives us the ability to handle higher query throughput, but also gives us redundancy and high availability. Imagine an Elasticsearch cluster hosting a single index called `mastering` that is built of 2 shards and 0 replicas. Such a cluster could look as follows:

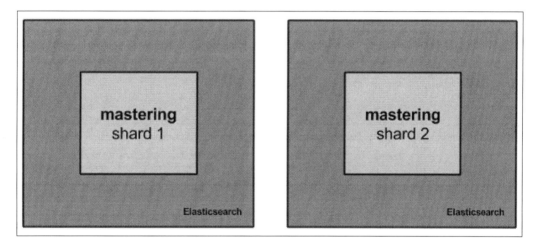

Now, what would happen when one of the nodes fails? The simplest answer is that we lose about 50 percent of the data, and if the failure is fatal, we lose that data forever. Even when having backups, we would need to spin up another node and restore the backup; this takes time. If your business relies on Elasticsearch, downtime means money loss.

Now let's look at the same cluster but with one replica:

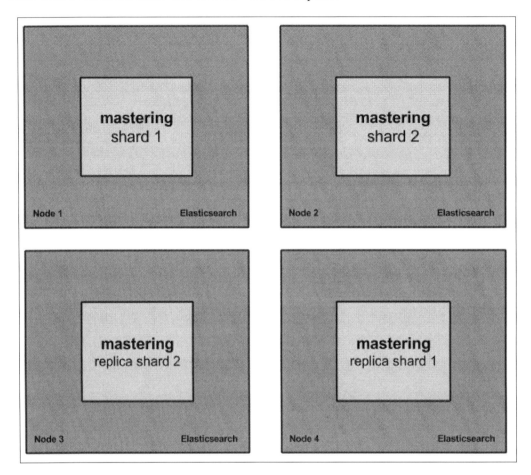

Now, losing a single Elasticsearch node means that we still have the whole data available and we can work on restoring the full cluster structure without downtime. What's more, with such deployment, we can live with two nodes failing at the same time in some cases, for example, Node 1 and Node 3 or Node 2 and Node 4. In both the mentioned cases, we would still be able to access all the data. Of course, this will lower performance because of less nodes in the cluster, but this is still better than not handling queries at all.

Because of this, when designing your architecture and deciding on the number of nodes, how many nodes indices will have, and the number of shards for each of them, you should take into consideration how many nodes' failure you want to live with. Of course, you can't forget about the performance part of the equation, but redundancy and high availability should be one of the factors of the scaling equation.

Cost and performance flexibility

The default distributed nature of Elasticsearch and its ability to scale horizontally allow us to be flexible when it comes to performance and costs that we have when running our environment. First of all, high-end servers with highly performant JVM disks, numerous CPU cores, and a lot of RAM are expensive. In addition to this, cloud computing is getting more and more popular and it not only allows us to run our deployment on rented machines, but it also allows us to scale on demand. We just need to add more machines, which is a few clicks away or can even be automated with some degree of work.

Getting this all together, we can say that having a horizontally scalable solution, such as Elasticsearch, allows us to bring down the costs of running our clusters and solutions. What's more, we can easily sacrifice performance if costs are the most crucial factor in our business plan. Of course, we can also go the other way. If we can afford large clusters, we can push Elasticsearch to hundreds of terabytes of data stored in the indices and still get decent performance (of course, with proper hardware and property distributed).

Continuous upgrades

High availability, cost, performance flexibility, and virtually endless growth are not the only things worth saying when discussing the scalability side of Elasticsearch. At some point in time, you will want to have your Elasticsearch cluster to be upgraded to a new version. It can be because of bug fixes, performance improvements, new features, or anything that you can think of. The thing is that when having a single instance of each shard, an upgrade without replicas means the unavailability of Elasticsearch (or at least its parts), and that may mean downtime of the applications that use Elasticsearch. This is another point why horizontal scaling is so important; you can perform upgrades, at least to the point where software such as Elasticsearch is supported. For example, you could take Elasticsearch 1.0 and upgrade it to Elasticsearch 1.4 with only rolling restarts, thus having all the data still available for searching and indexing happening at the same time.

Multiple Elasticsearch instances on a single physical machine

Although we previously said that you shouldn't go for the most powerful machines for different reasons (such as RAM consumption after going above 31 GB JVM heap), we sometimes don't have much choice. This is out of the scope of the book, but because we are talking about scaling, we thought it may be a good thing to mention what can be done in such cases.

Improving Performance

In cases such as the ones we are discussing, when we have high-end hardware with a lot of RAM memory, a lot of high speed disk, numerous CPU cores, among others, we should think about diving the physical server into multiple virtual machines and running a single Elasticsearch server on each of the virtual machines.

> There is also a possibility of running multiple Elasticsearch servers on a single physical machine without running multiple virtual machines. Which road to take—virtual machines or multiple instances—is really your choice; however, we like to keep things separate and, because of that, we are usually going to divide any large server into multiple virtual machines. When dividing a large server into multiple smaller virtual machines, remember that the I/O subsystem will be shared across these smaller virtual machines. Because of this, it may be good to wisely divide the disks between virtual machines.

To illustrate such a deployment, please look at the following provided figure. It shows how you could run Elasticsearch on three large servers, each divided into four separate virtual machines. Each virtual machine would be responsible for running a single instance of Elasticsearch.

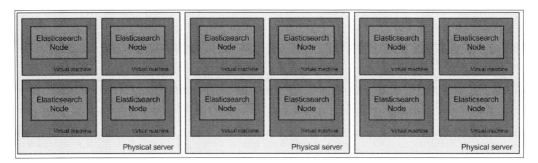

Preventing the shard and its replicas from being on the same node

There is one additional thing worth mentioning. When having multiple physical servers divided into virtual machines, it is crucial to ensure that the shard and its replica won't end up on the same physical machine. This would be tragic if a server crashes or is restarted. We can tell Elasticsearch to separate shards and replicas using cluster allocation awareness. In our preceding case, we have three physical servers; let's call them `server1`, `server2`, and `server3`.

Now for each Elasticsearch on a physical server, we define the `node.server_name` property and we set it to the identifier of the server. So, for the example of all Elasticsearch nodes on the first physical server, we would set the following property in the `elasticsearch.yml` configuration file:

```
node.server_name: server1
```

In addition to this, each Elasticsearch node (no matter on which physical server) needs to have the following property added to the `elasticsearch.yml` configuration file:

```
cluster.routing.allocation.awareness.attributes: server_name
```

It tells Elasticsearch not to put the primary shard and its replicas on the nodes with the same value in the `node.server_name` property. This is enough for us, and Elasticsearch will take care of the rest.

Designated nodes' roles for larger clusters

There is one more thing that we wanted to tell you; actually, we already mentioned that both in the book you are holding in your hands and in *Elasticsearch Server Second Edition*, *Packt Publishing*. To have a fully fault-tolerant and highly available cluster, we should divide the nodes and give each node a designated role. The roles we can assign to each Elasticsearch node are as follows:

- The master eligible node
- The data node
- The query aggregator node

By default, each Elasticsearch node is master eligible (it can serve as a master node), can hold data, and can work as a query aggregator node, which means that it can send partial queries to other nodes, gather and merge the results, and respond to the client sending the query. You may wonder why this is needed. Let's give you a simple example: if the master node is under a lot of stress, it may not be able to handle the cluster state-related command fast enough and the cluster can become unstable. This is only a single, simple example, and you can think of numerous others.

Because of this, most Elasticsearch clusters that are larger than a few nodes usually look like the one presented in the following figure:

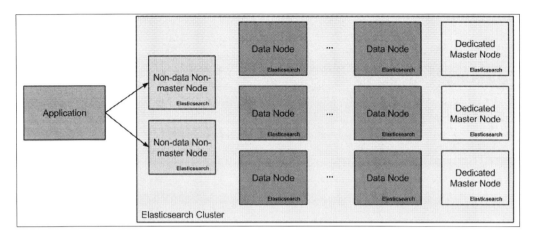

As you can see, our hypothetical cluster contains two aggregator nodes (because we know that there will not be too many queries, but we want redundancy), a dozen of data nodes because the amount of data will be large, and at least three master eligible nodes that shouldn't be doing anything else. Why three master nodes when Elasticsearch will only use a single one at any given time? Again, this is because of redundancy and to be able to prevent split brain situations by setting the `discovery.zen.minimum_master_nodes` to 2, which would allow us to easily handle the failure of a single master eligible node in the cluster.

Let's now give you snippets of the configuration for each type of node in our cluster. We already talked about this in the *Discovery and recovery modules* section in *Chapter 7, Elasticsearch Administration*, but we would like to mention it once again.

Query aggregator nodes

The query aggregator nodes' configuration is quite simple. To configure them, we just need to tell Elasticsearch that we don't want these nodes to be master eligible and hold data. This corresponds to the following configuration in the `elasticsearch.yml` file:

```
node.master: false
node.data: false
```

Data nodes

Data nodes are also very simple to configure; we just need to say that they should not be master eligible. However, we are not big fans of default configurations (because they tend to change) and, thus, our Elasticsearch data nodes' configuration looks as follows:

```
node.master: false
node.data: true
```

Master eligible nodes

We've left the master eligible nodes for the end of the general scaling section. Of course, such Elasticsearch nodes shouldn't be allowed to hold data, but in addition to that, it is good practice to disable the HTTP protocol on such nodes. This is done in order to avoid accidentally querying these nodes. Master eligible nodes can be smaller in resources compared to data and query aggregator nodes, and because of that, we should ensure that they are only used for master-related purposes. So, our configuration for master eligible nodes looks more or less as follows:

```
node.master: true
node.data: false
http.enabled: false
```

Using Elasticsearch for high load scenarios

Now that we know the theory (and some examples of Elasticsearch scaling), we are ready to discuss the different aspects of Elasticsearch preparation for high load. We decided to split this part of the chapter into three sections: one dedicated to preparing Elasticsearch for a high indexing load, one dedicated for the preparation of Elasticsearch for a high query load, and one that can be taken into consideration in both cases. This should give you an idea of what to think about when preparing your cluster for your use case.

Please consider that performance testing should be done after preparing the cluster for production use. Don't just take the values from the book and go for them; try them with your data and your queries and try altering them, and see the differences. Remember that giving general advices that works for everyone is not possible, so treat the next two sections as general advices instead of ready for use recipes.

General Elasticsearch-tuning advices

In this section, we will look at the general advices related to tuning Elasticsearch. They are not connected to indexing performance only or querying performance only but to both of them.

Choosing the right store

One of the crucial aspects of this is that we should choose the right store implementation. This is mostly important when running an Elasticsearch version older than 1.3.0. In general, if you are running a 64-bit operating system, you should again go for `mmapfs`. If you are not running a 64-bit operating system, choose the `niofs` store for Unix-based systems and `simplefs` for Windows-based ones. If you can allow yourself to have a volatile store, but a very fast one, you can look at the `memory` store: it will give you the best index access performance but requires enough memory to handle not only all the index files, but also to handle indexing and querying.

With the release of Elasticsearch 1.3.0, we've got a new store type called `default`, which is the new default store type. As Elasticsearch developers said, it is a hybrid store type. It uses memory-mapped files to read term dictionaries and doc values, while the rest of the files are accessed using the `NIOFSDirectory` implementation. In most cases, when using Elasticsearch 1.3.0 or higher, the `default` store type should be used.

The index refresh rate

The second thing we should pay attention to is the index refresh rate. We know that the refresh rate specifies how fast documents will be visible for search operations. The equation is quite simple: the faster the refresh rate, the slower the queries will be and the lower the indexing throughput. If we can allow ourselves to have a slower refresh rate, such as `10s` or `30s`, it may be a good thing to set it. This puts less pressure on Elasticsearch, as the internal objects will have to be reopened at a slower pace and, thus, more resources will be available both for indexing and querying. Remember that, by default, the refresh rate is set to `1s`, which basically means that the index searcher object is reopened every second.

To give you a bit of an insight into what performance gains we are talking about, we did some performance tests, including Elasticsearch and a different refresh rate. With a refresh rate of `1s`, we were able to index about 1.000 documents per second using a single Elasticsearch node. Increasing the refresh rate to `5s` gave us an increase in the indexing throughput of more than 25 percent, and we were able to index about 1280 documents per second. Setting the refresh rate to `25s` gave us about 70 percent of throughput more compared to a `1s` refresh rate, which was about 1700 documents per second on the same infrastructure. It is also worth remembering that increasing the time indefinitely doesn't make much sense, because after a certain point (depending on your data load and the amount of data you have), the increase in performance is negligible.

Thread pools tuning

This is one of the things that is very dependent on your deployment. By default, Elasticsearch comes with a very good default when it comes to all thread pools' configuration. However, there are times when these defaults are not enough. You should remember that tuning the default thread pools' configuration should be done only when you really see that your nodes are filling up the queues and they still have processing power left that could be designated to the processing of the waiting operations.

For example, if you did your performance tests and you see your Elasticsearch instances not being saturated 100 percent, but on the other hand, you've experienced rejected execution errors, then this is a point where you should start adjusting the thread pools. You can either increase the amount of threads that are allowed to be executed at the same time, or you can increase the queue. Of course, you should also remember that increasing the number of concurrently running threads to very high numbers will lead to many CPU context switches (http://en.wikipedia.org/wiki/Context_switch), which will result in a drop in performance. Of course, having massive queues is also not a good idea; it is usually better to fail fast rather than overwhelm Elasticsearch with several thousands of requests waiting in the queue. However, this all depends on your particular deployment and use case. We would really like to give you a precise number, but in this case, giving general advice is rarely possible.

Adjusting the merge process

Lucene segments' merging adjustments is another thing that is highly dependent on your use case and several factors related to it, such as how much data you add, how often you do that, and so on. There are two things to remember when it comes to Lucene segments and merging. Queries run against an index with multiple segments are slower than the ones with a smaller number of segments. Performance tests show that queries run against an index built of several segments are about 10 to 15 percent slower than the ones run against an index built of only a single segment. On the other hand, though, merging is not free and the fewer segments we want to have in our index, the more aggressive a merge policy should be configured.

Generally, if you want your queries to be faster, aim for fewer segments for your indices. For example, for `log_byte_size` or `log_doc` merge policies, setting the `index.merge.policy.merge_factor` property to a value lower than the default of `10` will result in less segments, lower RAM consumption, faster queries, and slower indexing. Setting the `index.merge.policy.merge_factor` property to a value higher than `10` will result in more segments building the index, higher RAM consumption, slower queries, and faster indexing.

There is one more thing: throttling. By default, Elasticsearch will throttle merging to `20mb/s`. Elasticsearch uses throttling so that your merging process doesn't affect searching too much. What's more, if merging is not fast enough, Elasticsearch will throttle the indexing to be single threaded so that the merging could actually finish and not have an extensive number of segments. However, if you are running SSD drives, the default `20mb/s` throttling is probably too much and you can set it to 5 to 10 times more (at least). To adjust throttling, we need to set the `indices.store.throttle.max_bytes_per_sec` property in `elasticsearch.yml` (or using the Cluster Settings API) to the desired value, such as `200mb/s`.

In general, if you want indexing to be faster, go for more segments for indices. If you want your queries to be faster, your I/O can handle more work because of merging, and you can live with Elasticsearch consuming a bit more RAM memory, go for more aggressive merge policy settings. If you want Elasticsearch to index more documents, go for a less aggressive merge policy, but remember that this will affect your queries' performance. If you want both of these things, you need to find a golden spot between them so that the merging is not too often but also doesn't result in an extensive number of segments.

Data distribution

As we know, each index in the Elasticsearch world can be divided into multiple shards, and each shard can have multiple replicas. In cases where you have multiple Elasticsearch nodes and indices divided into shards, proper data distribution may be crucial to even the load the cluster and not have some nodes doing more work than the other ones.

Chapter 8

Let's take the following example—imagine that we have a cluster that is built of four nodes, and it has a single index built of three shards and one replica allocated. Such deployment could look as follows:

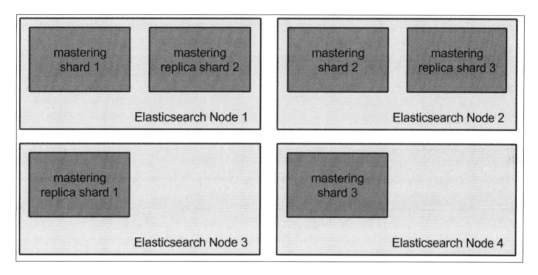

As you can see, the first two nodes have two physical shards allocated to them, while the last two nodes have one shard each. So the actual data allocation is not even. When sending the queries and indexing data, we will have the first two nodes do more work than the other two; this is what we want to avoid. We could make the `mastering` index have two shards and one replica so that it would look like this:

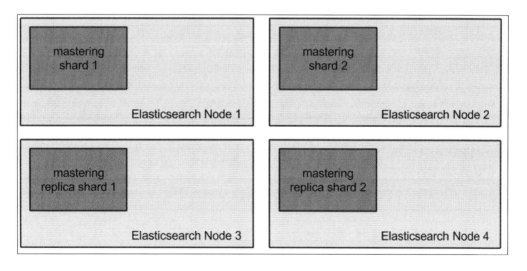

Or, we could have the mastering index divided into four shards and have one replica.

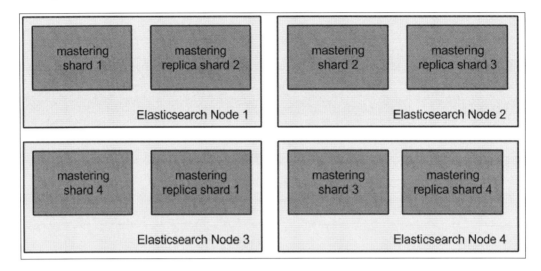

In both cases, we will end up with an even distribution of shards and replicas, with Elasticsearch doing a similar amount of work on all the nodes. Of course, with more indices (such as having daily indices), it may be trickier to get the data evenly distributed, and it may not be possible to have evenly distributed shards, but we should try to get to such a point.

One more thing to remember when it comes to data distribution, shards, and replicas is that when designing your index architecture, you should remember what you want to achieve. If you are going for a very high indexing use case, you may want to spread the index into multiple shards to lower the pressure that is put on the CPU and the I/O subsystem of the server. This is also true in order to run expensive queries, because with more shards, you can lower the load on a single server. However, with queries, there is one more thing: if your nodes can't keep up with the load caused by queries, you can add more Elasticsearch nodes and increase the number of replicas so that physical copies of the primary shards are placed on these nodes. This will make the indexing a bit slower but will give you the capacity to handle more queries at the same time.

Advices for high query rate scenarios

One of the great features of Elasticsearch is its ability to search and analyze the data that was indexed. However, sometimes, the user is needed to adjust Elasticsearch, and our queries to not only get the results of the query, but also get them fast (or in a reasonable amount of time). In this section, we will not only look at the possibilities but also prepare Elasticsearch for high query throughput use cases. We will also look at general performance tips when it comes to querying.

Filter caches and shard query caches

The first cache that can help with query performance is the filter cache (if our queries use filters, and if not, they should probably use filters). We talked about filters in the *Handling filters and why it matters* section in *Chapter 2*, *Power User Query DSL*. What we didn't talk about is the cache that is responsible for storing results of the filters: the filter cache. By default, Elasticsearch uses the filter cache implementation that is shared among all the indices on a single node, and we can control its size using the `indices.cache.filter.size` property. It defaults to `10` percent by default and specifies the total amount of memory that can be used by the filter cache on a given node. In general, if your queries are already using filters, you should monitor the size of the cache and evictions. If you see that you have many evictions, then you probably have a cache that's too small, and you should consider having a larger one. Having a cache that's too small may impact the query performance in a bad way.

The second cache that has been introduced in Elasticsearch is the shard query cache. It was added to Elasticsearch in Version 1.4.0, and its purpose is to cache aggregations, suggester results, and the number of hits (it will not cache the returned documents and, thus, it only works with `search_type=count`). When your queries are using aggregations or suggestions, it may be a good idea to enable this cache (it is disabled by default) so that Elasticsearch can reuse the data stored there. The best thing about the cache is that it promises the same near real-time search as search that is not cached.

To enable the shard query cache, we need to set the `index.cache.query.enable` property to `true`. For example, to enable the cache for our mastering index, we could issue the following command:

```
curl -XPUT 'localhost:9200/mastering/_settings' -d '{
 "index.cache.query.enable": true
}'
```

Please remember that using the shard query cache doesn't make sense if we don't use aggregations or suggesters.

One more thing to remember is that, by default, the shard query cache is allowed to take no more than 1 percent of the JVM heap given to the Elasticsearch node. To change the default value, we can use the `indices.cache.query.size` property. By using the `indices.cache.query.expire` property, we can specify the expiration date of the cache, but it is not needed, and in most cases, results stored in the cache are invalidated with every index refresh operation.

Think about the queries

This is the most general advice we can actually give: you should always think about optimal query structure, filter usage, and so on. We talked about it extensively in the *Handling filters and why it matters* section in *Chapter 2*, *Power User Query DSL*, but we would like to mention that once again, because we think it is very important. For example, let's look at the following query:

```
{
  "query" : {
    "bool" : {
      "must" : [
        {
          "query_string" : {
            "query" : "name:mastering AND department:it AND
            category:book"
          }
        },
        {
          "term" : {
            "tag" : "popular"
          }
        },
        {
          "term" : {
            "tag" : "2014"
          }
        }
      ]
    }
  }
}
```

It returns the book name that matches a few conditions. However, there are a few things we can improve in the preceding query. For example, we could move a few things to filtering so that the next time we use some parts of the query, we save CPU cycles and reuse the information stored in the cache. For example, this is what the optimized query could look like:

```
{
  "query" : {
    "filtered" : {
      "query" : {
        "match" : {
          "name" : "mastering"
        }
      },
      "filter" : {
        "bool" : {
          "must" : [
            {
              "term" : {
                "department" : "it"
              }
            },
            {
              "term" : {
                "category" : "book"
              }
            },
            {
              "terms" : {
                "tag" : [ "popular", "2014" ]
              }
            }
          ]
        }
      }
    }
  }
}
```

As you can see, there are a few things that we did. First of all, we used the `filtered` query to introduce filters and we moved most of the static, non-analyzed fields to filters. This allows us to easily reuse the filters in the next queries that we execute. Because of such query restructuring, we were able to simplify the main query, so we changed `query_string_query` to the `match` query, because it is enough for our use case. This is exactly what you should be doing when optimizing your queries or designing them—have optimization and performance in mind and try to keep them as optimal as they can be. This will result in faster query execution, lower resource consumption, and better health of the whole Elasticsearch cluster.

However, performance is not the only difference when it comes to the outcome of queries. As you know, filters don't affect the score of the documents returned and are not taken into consideration when calculating the score. Because of this, if you compare the scores returned by the preceding queries for the same documents, you would notice that they are different. This is worth remembering.

Using routing

If your data allows routing, you should consider using it. The data with the same routing value will always end up in the same shard. Because of this, we can save ourselves the need to query all the shards when asking for certain data. For example, if we store the data of our clients, we may use a client identifier as the routing value. This will allow us to store the data of a single client inside a single shard. This means that during querying, Elasticsearch needs to fetch data from only a single shard, as shown in the following figure:

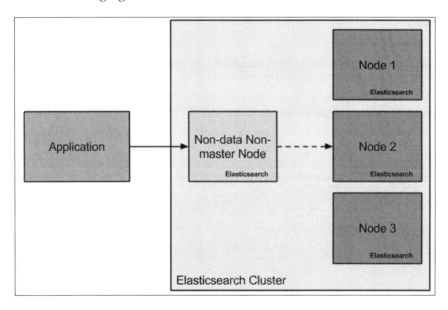

If we assume that the data lives in a shard allocated to Node 2, we can see that Elasticsearch only needed to run the query against that one particular node to get all the data for the client. If we don't use routing, the simplified query execution could look as follows:

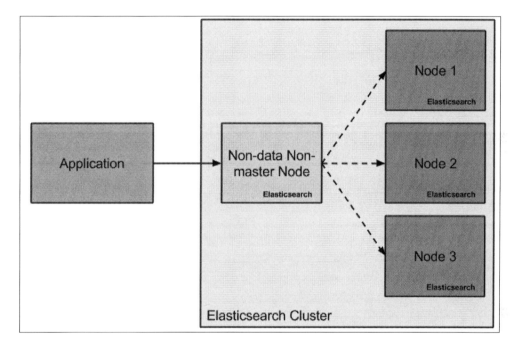

In the case of nonrouting, Elasticsearch first needs to query all the index shards. If your index contains dozen of shards, the performance improvement will be significant as long as a single Elasticsearch instance can handle the shard size.

> Please remember that not every use case is eligible to use routing. To be able to use it, your data needs to be virtually divided so that it is spread across the shards. For example, it usually doesn't make sense to have dozens of very small shards and one massive one, because for the massive one, performance may not be decent.

Parallelize your queries

One thing that is usually forgotten is the need to parallelize queries. Imagine that you have a dozen nodes in your cluster, but your index is built of a single shard. If the index is large, your queries will perform worse than you would expect. Of course, you can increase the number of replicas, but that won't help; a single query will still go to a single shard in that index, because replicas are not more than the copies of the primary shard, and they contain the same data (or at least they should).

One thing that will actually help is dividing your index into multiple shards—the number of shards depends on the hardware and deployment. In general, it is advised to have the data evenly divided so that nodes are equally loaded. For example, if you have four Elasticsearch nodes and two indices, you may want to have four shards for each index, just like what is shown in the following figure:

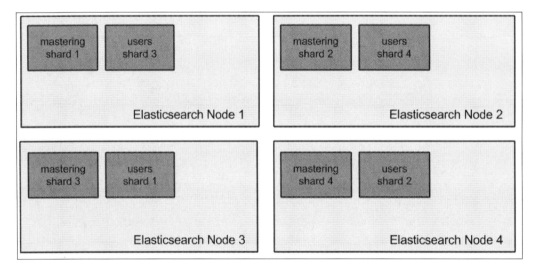

Field data cache and breaking the circuit

By default, the field data cache in Elasticsearch is unbounded. This can be very dangerous, especially when you are using faceting and sorting on many fields. If these fields are high cardinality ones, then you can run into even more trouble. By trouble, we mean running out of memory.

We have two different factors we can tune to be sure that we won't run into out-of-memory errors. First of all, we can limit the size of the field data cache. The second thing is the circuit breaker, which we can easily configure to just throw an exception instead of loading too much data. Combining these two things will ensure that we don't run into memory issues.

However, we should also remember that Elasticsearch will evict data from the field data cache if its size is not enough to handle faceting request or sorting. This will affect the query performance, because loading field data information is not very efficient. However, we think that it is better to have our queries slower rather than having our cluster blown up because of out-of-memory errors.

Finally, if your queries are using field data cache extensively (such as aggregations or sorting) and you are running into memory-related issues (such as OutOfMemory exceptions or GC pauses), consider using doc values that we already talked about. Doc values should give you performance that's similar to field data cache, and support for doc values is getting better and better with each Elasticsearch release (improvements to doc values are made in Lucene itself).

Keeping size and shard_size under control

When dealing with queries that use aggregations, for some of them, we have the possibility of using two properties: size and shard_size. The size parameter defines how many buckets should be returned by the final aggregation results; the node that aggregates the final results will get the top buckets from each shard that returns the result and will only return the top size of them to the client. The shard_size parameter tells Elasticsearch about the same but on the shard level. Increasing the value of the shard_size parameter will lead to more accurate aggregations (such as in the case of significant terms' aggregation) at the cost of network traffic and memory usage. Lowering this parameter will cause aggregation results to be less precise, but we will benefit from lower memory consumption and lower network traffic. If we see that the memory usage is too large, we can lower the size and shard_size properties of problematic queries and see whether the quality of the results is still acceptable.

High indexing throughput scenarios and Elasticsearch

In this section, we will discuss some optimizations that will allow us to concentrate on the indexing throughput and speed. Some use cases are highly dependent on the amount of data you can push to Elasticsearch every second, and the next few topics should cover some information regarding indexing.

Improving Performance

Bulk indexing

This is very obvious advice, but you would be surprised by how many Elasticsearch users forget about indexing data in bulk instead of sending the documents one by one. The thing to remember, though, is to not overload Elasticsearch with too many bulk requests. Remember about the bulk thread pool and its size (equal to the number of CPU cores in the system by default with a queue of 50 requests), and try to adjust your indexers so that they don't to go beyond it. Or, you will first start to queue their requests and if Elasticsearch is not able to process them, you will quickly start seeing rejected execution exceptions, and your data won't be indexed. On the other hand, remember that your bulk requests can't be too large, or Elasticsearch will need a lot of memory to process them.

Just as an example, I would like to show you two types of indexing happening. In the first figure, we have indexing throughput when running the indexation one document by one. In the second figure, we do the same, but instead of indexing documents one by one, we index them in batches of 10 documents.

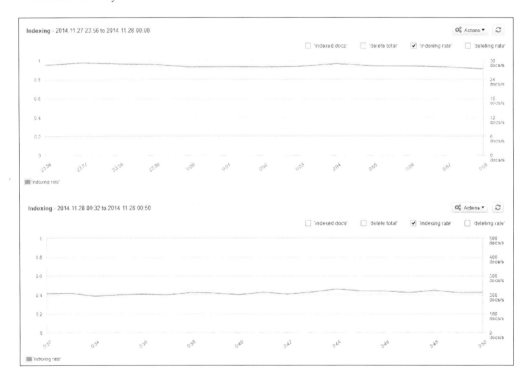

As you can see, when indexing documents one by one, we were able to index about 30 documents per second and it was stable. The situation changed with bulk indexing and batches of 10 documents. We were able to index slightly more than 200 documents per second, so the difference can be clearly seen.

Of course, this is a very basic comparison of indexing speed, and in order to show you the real difference, we should use dozens of threads and push Elasticsearch to its limits. However, the preceding comparison should give you a basic view of the indexing throughput gains when using bulk indexing.

Doc values versus indexing speed

When talking about indexing speed, we have to talk about doc values. As we already said a few times in the book, doc values allows us to fight gigantic JVM heap requirements when Elasticsearch needs to uninvert fields for functionalities such as sorting, aggregations, or faceting. However, writing doc values requires some additional work during the indexation. If we are all about the highest indexing speed and the most indexing throughput, you should consider not going for doc values. On the other hand, if you have a lot of data—and you probably have when you are indexing fast—using doc values may be the only way that will allow using aggregations or sorting on field values without running into memory-related problems.

Keep your document fields under control

The amount of data you index makes the difference, which is understandable. However, this is not the only factor; the size of the documents and their analysis matters as well. With larger documents, you can expect not only your index to grow, but also make the indexation slightly slower. This is why you may sometimes want to look at all the fields you are indexing and storing. Keep your stored fields to a minimum or don't use them at all; the only stored field you need in most cases is the `_source` field.

There is one more thing—apart from the `_source` field, Elasticsearch indexes the `_all` field by default. Let's remind you: the `_all` field is used by Elasticsearch to gather data from all the other textual fields. In some cases, this field is not used at all and because of that, it is nice to turn it off. Turning it off is simple and the only thing to do is add the following entry to the type mappings:

```
"_all" : {"enabled" : false}
```

We can do this during the index creation, for example, like this:

```
curl -XPOST 'localhost:9200/disabling_all' -d '{
 "mappings" : {
  "test_type" : {
   "_all" : { "enabled" : false },
   "properties" : {
    "name" : { "type" : "string" },
    "tag" : { "type" : "string", "index" : "not_analyzed" }
   }
  }
 }
}'
```

The indexing should be slightly faster depending on the size of your documents and the number of textual fields in it.

There is an additional thing, which is good practice when disabling the `_all` field: setting a new default search field. We can do this by setting the `index.query.default_field` property. For example, in our case, we can set it in the `elasticsearch.yml` file and set it to the `name` field from our preceding mappings:

```
index.query.default_field: name
```

The index architecture and replication

When designing the index architecture, one of the things you need to think about is the number of shards and replicas that the index is built of. During that time, we also need to we think about data distribution among Elasticsearch nodes, optimal performance, high availability, reliability, and so on. First of all, distributing primary shards of the index across all nodes we have will parallelize indexing operations and will make them faster.

The second thing is data replication. What we have to remember is that too many replicas will cause the indexation speed to drop. This is because of several reasons. First of all, you need to transfer the data between primary shards and replicas. The second thing is that, usually, replicas and primary shards may live on the same nodes (not primary shards and its replicas, of course, but replicas of other primaries). For example, take a look at what is shown in the following figure:

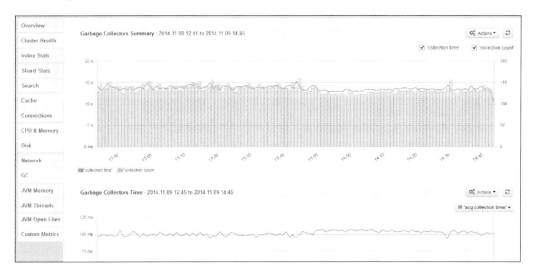

Because of this, Elasticsearch will need the data for both primary shards and replicas and, thus, it will use the disk. Depending on the cluster setup, the indexing throughput may drop in such cases (depends on the disks, number of documents indexed at the same time, and so on).

Tuning write-ahead log

We already talked about transaction logs in the *Data flushing, index refresh and transaction log handling* section of *Chapter 6, Low-level Index Control*. Elasticsearch has an internal module called translog (http://www.elasticsearch.org/guide/en/elasticsearch/reference/current/index-modules-translog.html). It is a per-shard structure that serves the purpose of write-ahead logging (http://en.wikipedia.org/wiki/Write-ahead_logging). Basically, it allows Elasticsearch to expose the newest updates for GET operations, ensure data durability, and optimize writing to Lucene indices.

By default, Elasticsearch keeps a maximum of `5000` operations in the transaction log with a maximum size of 200 MB. However, if we can pay the price of data not being available for search operations for longer periods of time but we want more indexing throughput, we can increase these defaults. By specifying the `index.translog.flush_threshold_ops` and `index.translog.flush_threshold_size` properties (both are set per index and can be updated in real time using the Elasticsearch API), we can set the maximum number of operations allowed to be stored in the transaction log and its maximum size. We've seen deployments having this property values set to 10 times the default values.

One thing to remember is that in case of failure, shard initialization will be slower — of course on the ones that had large transaction logs. This is because Elasticsearch needs to process all the information from the transaction log before the shard is ready for use.

Think about storage

One of the crucial things when it comes to high indexing use cases is the storage type and its configuration. If your organization can afford SSD disks (solid state drives), go for them. They are superior in terms of speed compared to the traditional spinning disks, but of course, that comes at the cost of price. If you can't afford SSD drives, configure your spinning disks to work in RAID 0 (http://en.wikipedia.org/wiki/RAID) or point Elasticsearch to use multiple data paths.

What's more, don't use shared or remote filesystems for Elasticsearch indices; use local storage instead. Remote and shared filesystems are usually slower compared to local disk drives and will cause Elasticsearch to wait for read and write, and thus result in a general slowdown.

RAM buffer for indexing

Remember that the more the available RAM for the indexing buffer (the `indices.memory.index_buffer_size` property), the more documents Elasticsearch can hold in the memory, but of course, we don't want to occupy 100 percent of the available memory only to Elasticsearch. By default, this is set to 10 percent, but if you really need a high indexing rate, you can increase it. It is advisable to have approximately 512 MB of RAM for each active shard that takes part in the indexing process, but remember that the `indices.memory.index_buffer_size` property is per node and not per shard. So, if you have 20 GB of heap given to the Elasticsearch node and 10 shards active on the node, Elasticsearch will give each shard about 200 MB of RAM for indexing buffering (10 percent of 20 GB / 10 shards) by default.

Summary

In this chapter, we were focused on the performance and scaling of Elasticsearch. We looked at how doc values can help us with improving the query performance, how garbage collector works, and what to look at when changing its configuration. We benchmarked our queries and we saw what the Hot Threads API is. Finally, we discussed how to scale Elasticsearch and how to prepare it for high querying and indexing use cases.

In the next chapter, we will write some code. We will create the Apache Maven project used to write Elasticsearch plugins. We will write a custom REST action to extend the Elasticsearch functionality. In addition to this, we will learn what needs to be done in order to introduce new analysis plugins for Elasticsearch, and we will create such plugins.

9
Developing Elasticsearch Plugins

In the previous chapter, we were focused on the performance and scaling of our Elasticsearch clusters. We looked at how doc values can help us improve query performance and lower the memory for queries, which deals with field data cache at the cost of slightly slower indexing. We looked at how garbage collector works and what to look at when changing its configuration. We've benchmarked our queries, and we've seen what Hot Threads API gives us. Finally, we discussed how to scale Elasticsearch. By the end of this chapter, you will have learned:

- How to set up the Apache Maven project for Elasticsearch plugins' development
- How to develop a custom REST action plugin
- How to develop a custom analysis plugin extending Elasticsearch analysis capabilities

Creating the Apache Maven project structure

Before we start with showing you how to develop a custom Elasticsearch plugin, we would like to discuss a way to package it so that it can be installed by Elasticsearch using the `plugin` command. In order to do that, we will use Apache Maven (http://maven.apache.org/), which is designed to simplify software projects' management. It aims to make your build process easier, provide a unifying build system, manage dependencies, and so on.

Please note that the chapter you are currently reading was written and tested using Elasticsearch 1.4.1.

Also remember that the book you are holding in your hands is not about Maven but Elasticsearch, and we will keep Maven-related information to the required minimum.

 Installing Apache Maven is a straightforward task; we assume that you already have it installed. However, if you have problems with it, please consult http://maven.apache.org/ for more information.

Understanding the basics

The result of a Maven build process is an artifact. Each artifact is defined by its identifier, its group, and its version. This is crucial when working with Maven, because every dependency you'll use will need to be identified by these three mentioned properties.

The structure of the Maven Java project

The idea behind Maven is quite simple—you create a project structure that looks something like this:

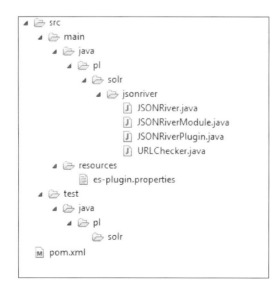

You can see that the code is placed in the `src` folder—the code is in the `main` folder and the unit tests are located in the `test` folder. Although you can change the default layout, Maven tends to work best with the default layout.

The idea of POM

In addition to the code, you can see a file named `pom.xml` that is located in the root directory in the previous image. This is a project object model file that describes the project, its properties, and its dependencies. That's right—you don't need to manually download dependencies if they are present in one of the available Maven repositories—during its work, Maven will download them, put them in your local repository on your hard disk, and use it when needed. All you need to care about is writing an appropriate `pom.xml` section that will inform Maven which dependencies should be used.

For example, this is an example Maven `pom.xml` file:

```xml
<project xmlns="http://maven.apache.org/POM/4.0.0" xmlns:xsi="http://www.w3.org/2001/XMLSchema-instance"
    xsi:schemaLocation="http://maven.apache.org/POM/4.0.0 http://maven.apache.org/xsd/maven-4.0.0.xsd">
    <modelVersion>4.0.0</modelVersion>

    <groupId>pl.solr</groupId>
    <artifactId>analyzer</artifactId>
    <version>1.0-SNAPSHOT</version>
    <packaging>jar</packaging>

    <name>analyzer</name>
    <url>http://solr.pl</url>

    <properties>
        <elasticsearch.version>1.4.1</elasticsearch.version>
        <project.build.sourceEncoding>UTF-8</project.build.sourceEncoding>
    </properties>

    <dependencies>
        <dependency>
            <groupId>org.elasticsearch</groupId>
            <artifactId>elasticsearch</artifactId>
            <version>${elasticsearch.version}</version>
        </dependency>
```

```
            </dependencies>
</project>
```

This is a simplified version of a `pom.xml` file that we will extend in the rest of the chapter. You can see that it starts with the root `project` tag and then defines the group identifier, the artifact identifier, the version, and the packaging method (in our case, the standard build command will create a jar file). In addition to this, we've specified a single dependency — the Elasticsearch library Version 1.4.1.

Running the build process

In order to run the build process, what we need to do is simply run the following command in the directory where the `pom.xml` file is present:

```
mvn clean package
```

It will result in running Maven. It will clean all the generated content in the working directory, compile and package our code. Of course, if we have unit tests, they will have to pass in order for the package to be built. The built package will be written into the `target` directory created by Maven.

> If you want to learn more about the Maven life cycle, please refer to http://maven.apache.org/guides/introduction/introduction-to-the-lifecycle.html.

Introducing the assembly Maven plugin

In order to build the ZIP file that will contain our plugin code, we need to package it. By default, Maven doesn't support pure ZIP files' packaging, so in order to make it all work, we will use the Maven Assembly plugin (you can find more about the plugin at http://maven.apache.org/plugins/maven-assembly-plugin/). In general, the described plugin allows us to aggregate the project output along with its dependencies, documentations, and configuration files into a single archive.

In order for the plugin to work, we need to add the `build` section to our `pom.xml` file that will contain information about the assembly plugin, the jar plugin (which is responsible for creating the proper jar), and the compiler plugin, because we want to be sure that the code will be readable by Java 7. In addition to this, let's assume that we want our archive to be put into the `target/release` directory of our project. The relevant section of the `pom.xml` file should look as follows:

```
<build>
  <plugins>
    <plugin>
```

```xml
        <groupId>org.apache.maven.plugins</groupId>
        <artifactId>maven-jar-plugin</artifactId>
        <version>2.3</version>
        <configuration>
          <finalName>elasticsearch-${project.name}-${elasticsearch.version}</finalName>
        </configuration>
      </plugin>

      <plugin>
        <groupId>org.apache.maven.plugins</groupId>
        <artifactId>maven-assembly-plugin</artifactId>
        <version>2.2.1</version>
        <configuration>
         <finalName>elasticsearch-${project.name}-${elasticsearch.version}</finalName>
          <appendAssemblyId>false</appendAssemblyId>
            <outputDirectory>${project.build.directory}/release/</outputDirectory>
          <descriptors>
            <descriptor>assembly/release.xml</descriptor>
          </descriptors>
        </configuration>
        <executions>
         <execution>
         <id>generate-release-plugin</id>
          <phase>package</phase>
          <goals>
           <goal>single</goal>
          </goals>
         </execution>
        </executions>
      </plugin>

      <plugin>
       <artifactId>maven-compiler-plugin</artifactId>
       <configuration>
        <source>1.7</source>
        <target>1.7</target>
   </configuration>
      </plugin>
 </plugins>
</build>
```

Developing Elasticsearch Plugins

If you look closely at the assembly plugin configuration, you'll notice that we specify the assembly descriptor called `release.xml` in the `assembly` directory. This file is responsible for specifying what kind of archive we want to have as the output. Let's put the following `release.xml` file in the `assembly` directory of our project:

```xml
<?xml version="1.0"?>
<assembly>
 <id>bin</id>
 <formats>
  <format>zip</format>
 </formats>
 <includeBaseDirectory>false</includeBaseDirectory>
 <dependencySets>
  <dependencySet>
   <unpack>false</unpack>
   <outputDirectory>/</outputDirectory>
   <useProjectArtifact>false</useProjectArtifact>
   <useTransitiveFiltering>true</useTransitiveFiltering>
   <excludes>
    <exclude>org.elasticsearch:elasticsearch</exclude>
   </excludes>
  </dependencySet>
 </dependencySets>
 <fileSets>
  <fileSet>
   <directory>${project.build.directory}/</directory>
   <outputDirectory>/</outputDirectory>
   <includes>
    <include>elasticsearch-${project.name}-${elasticsearch.version}.jar</include>
   </includes>
  </fileSet>
 </fileSets>
</assembly>
```

Again, we don't need to know all the details; however, it is nice to understand what is going on, even on the general level. The preceding code file tells the Maven Assembly plugin that we want our archive to be packed with ZIP (`<format>zip</format>`), and we want Elasticsearch libraries to be excluded (the `exclude` section), because they will already be present in Elasticsearch, where we will install the plugin. In addition to this, we've specified that we want our project jar to be included (the `includes` section).

If you want to see the full project structure with the full pom.xml file and all the needed files, please look at the code provided with the book for *Chapter 9, Developing Elasticsearch Plugins*.

Creating custom REST action

Let's start the journey of extending Elasticsearch by creating a custom REST action. We've chosen this as the first extension, because we wanted to take the simplest approach as the introduction to extending Elasticsearch.

We assume that you already have a Java project created and that you are using Maven, just like we did in the *Creating the Apache Maven project structure* section in the beginning of this chapter. If you would like to use an already created and working example and start from there, please look at the code for *Chapter 9, Developing Elasticsearch Plugins* that is available with the book.

The assumptions

In order to illustrate how to develop a custom REST action, we need to have an idea of how it should work. Our REST action will be really simple – it should return names of all the nodes or names of the nodes that start with the given prefix if the prefix parameter is passed to it. In addition to that, it should only be available when using the HTTP GET method, so POST requests, for example, shouldn't be allowed.

Implementation details

We will need to develop two Java classes:

- A class that extends the BaseRestHandler Elasticsearch abstract class from the org.elasticsearch.rest package that will be responsible for handling the REST action code – we will call it a CustomRestAction.

- A class that will be used by Elasticsearch to load the plugin – this class needs to extend the Elasticsearch AbstractPlugin class from the org.elasticsearch.plugin package – we will call it CustomRestActionPlugin.

In addition to the preceding two, we will need a simple text file that we will discuss after implementing the two mentioned Java classes.

Using the REST action class

The most interesting class is the one that will be used to handle the user's requests—we will call it `CustomRestAction`. In order to work, it needs to extend the `BaseRestHandler` class from the `org.elasticsearch.rest` package—the base class for REST actions in Elasticsearch. In order to extend this class, we need to implement the `handleRequest` method in which we will process the user request and a three argument constructor that will be used to initialize the base class and register the appropriate handler under which our REST action will be visible.

The whole code for the `CustomRestAction` class looks as follows:

```
public class CustomRestAction extends BaseRestHandler {
  @Inject
  public CustomRestAction(Settings settings, RestController
  controller, Client client) {
    super(settings, controller, client);
    controller.registerHandler(Method.GET,"/_mastering/nodes", this);
  }
  @Override
  public void handleRequest(RestRequest request, RestChannel
  channel, Client client) {
    final String prefix = request.param("prefix", "");
    client.admin().cluster().prepareNodesInfo().all().execute(new
    RestBuilderListener<NodesInfoResponse>(channel) {
      @Override
      public RestResponse buildResponse(
      NodesInfoResponse response, XContentBuilder builder)
      throws Exception {
        List<String> nodes = new ArrayList<String>();
        for (NodeInfo nodeInfo : response.getNodes()) {
          String nodeName = nodeInfo.getNode().getName();
          if (prefix.isEmpty()) {
            nodes.add(nodeName);
          } else if (nodeName.startsWith(prefix)) {
            nodes.add(nodeName);
          }
        }
        builder.startObject()
        .field("nodes", nodes)
```

```
        .endObject();
        return new BytesRestResponse(RestStatus.OK, builder);
      }
    });
  }
}
```

The constructor

For each custom REST class, Elasticsearch will pass three arguments when creating an object of such type: the `Settings` type object, which holds the settings; the `RestController` type object that we will use to bind our REST action to the REST endpoint; and the `Client` type object, which is an Elasticsearch client and entry point for cooperation with it. All of these arguments are also required by the super class, so we invoke the base class constructor and pass them.

There is one more thing: the `@Inject` annotation. It allows us to inform Elasticsearch that it should put the objects in the constructor during the object creation. For more information about it, please refer to the Javadoc of the mentioned annotation, which is available at https://github.com/elasticsearch/elasticsearch/blob/master/src/main/java/org/elasticsearch/common/inject/Inject.java.

Now, let's focus on the following code line:

```
controller.registerHandler(Method.GET, "/_mastering/nodes", this);
```

What it does is that it registers our custom REST action implementation and binds it to the endpoint of our choice. The first argument is the HTTP method type, the REST action will be able to work with. As we said earlier, we only want to respond to GET requests. If we would like to respond to multiple types of HTTP methods, we should just include multiple `registerHandler` method invocations with each HTTP method. The second argument specifies the actual REST endpoint our custom action will be available at; in our case, it will available under the `/_mastering/nodes` endpoint. The third argument tells Elasticsearch which class should be responsible for handling the defined endpoint; in our case, this is the class we are developing, thus we are passing `this`.

Handling requests

Although the `handleRequest` method is the longest one in our code, it is not complicated. We start by reading the request parameter with the following line of code:

```
String prefix = request.param("prefix", "");
```

We store the prefix request parameter in the variable called `prefix`. By default, we want an empty `String` object to be assigned to the `prefix` variable if there is no prefix parameter passed to the request (the default value is defined by the second parameter of the `param` method of the `request` object).

Next, we retrieve the `NodesInfoResponse` object using the Elasticsearch client object and its abilities to run administrative commands. In this case, we have used the possibility of sending queries to Elasticsearch in an asynchronous way. Instead of the call `execute().actionGet()` part, which waits for a response and returns it, we have used the `execute()` call, which takes a future object that will be informed when the query finishes. So, the rest of the method is in the `buildResponse()` callback of the `RestBuilderListener` object. The `NodesInfoResponse` object will contain an array of `NodeInfo` objects, which we will use to get node names. What we need to do is return all the node names that start with a given prefix or all if the `prefix` parameter was not present in the request. In order to do this, we create a new array:

```
List<String> nodes = new ArrayList<String>();
```

We iterate over the available nodes using the following `for` loop:

```
for (NodeInfo nodeInfo : response.getNodes())
```

We get the node name using the `getName` method of the `DiscoveryNode` object, which is returned after invoking the `getNode` method of `NodeInfo`:

```
String nodeName = nodeInfo.getNode().getName();
```

If `prefix` is empty or if it starts with the given prefix, we add the name of the node to the array we've created. After we iterate through all the `NodeInfo` objects, we call the are starting build the response and sent it through the HTTP.

Writing response

The last thing regarding our `CustomRestAction` class is the response handling, which is the responsibility of the last part of the `buildResponse()` method that we created. It is simple because an appropriate response builder is already provided by Elasticsearch under the `builder` argument. It takes into consideration the `format` parameter used by the client in the call, so by default, we send the response in a proper JSON format just like Elasticsearch does and also take the YAML (http://en.wikipedia.org/wiki/YAML) format for free.

Now, we use the `builder` object we got to start the response object (using the `startObject` method) and start a `nodes` field (because the value of the field is a collection, it will automatically be formatted as an array). The `nodes` field is created inside the initial object, and we will use it to return matching nodes names. Finally, we close the object using the `endObject` method.

After we have our object ready to be sent as a response, we return the `BytesRestResponse` object. We do this in the following line:

```
return new BytesRestResponse(RestStatus.OK, builder);
```

As you can see, to create the object, we need to pass two parameters: `RestStatus` and the `XContentBuilder`, which holds our response. The `RestStatus` class allows us to specify the response code, which is `RestStatus.OK` in our case, because everything went smoothly.

The plugin class

The `CustomRestActionPlugin` class will hold the code that is used by Elasticsearch to initialize the plugin itself. It extends the `AbstractPlugin` class from the `org.elasticsearch.plugin` package. Because we are creating an extension, we are obliged to implement the following code parts:

- constructor: This is a standard constructor that will take a single argument; in our case, it will be empty
- The `onModule` method: This is the method that includes the code that will add our custom REST action so that Elasticsearch will know about it
- The `name` method: This is the name of our plugin
- The `description` method: This is a short description of our plugin

The code of the whole class looks as follows:

```
public class CustomRestActionPlugin extends AbstractPlugin {
  @Inject
  public CustomRestActionPlugin(Settings settings) {
  }

  public void onModule(RestModule module) {
    module.addRestAction(CustomRestAction.class);
  }

  @Override
  public String name() {
    return "CustomRestActionPlugin";
  }

  @Override
  public String description() {
    return "Custom REST action";
  }
}
```

The constructor, `name`, and `description` methods are very simple, and we will just skip discussing them, and we will focus on the `onModule` method. This method takes a single argument: the `RestModule` class object, which is the class that allows us to register our custom REST action. Elasticsearch will call the `onModule` method for all the modules that are available and eligible (all REST actions). What we do is just a simple call to the `RestModule` `addRestAction` method, passing in our `CustomRestAction` class as an argument. That's all when it comes to Java development.

Informing Elasticsearch about our REST action

We have our code ready, but we need one additional thing; we need to let Elasticsearch know what the class registering our plugin is—the one we've called `CustomRestActionPlugin`. In order to do this, we create an `es-plugin.properties` file in the `src/main/resources` directory with the following content:

```
plugin=pl.solr.rest.CustomRestActionPlugin
```

We just specify the `plugin` property there, which should have a value of the class we use to register our plugins (the one that extends the Elasticsearch `AbstractPlugin` class). This file will be included in the jar file that will be created during the build process and will be used by Elasticsearch during the plugin load process.

Chapter 9

Time for testing

Of course, we could leave it now and say that we are done, but we won't. We would like to show you how to build each of the plugins, install it, and finally, test it to see whether it actually works. Let's start with building our plugin.

Building the REST action plugin

We start with the easiest part—building our plugin. In order to do this, we run a simple command:

```
mvn compile package
```

We tell Maven that we want the code to be compiled and packaged. After the command finishes, we can find the archive with the plugin in the `target/release` directory (assuming you are using a project setup similar to the one we've described at the beginning of the chapter).

Installing the REST action plugin

In order to install the plugin, we will use the `plugin` command that is located in the `bin` directory of the Elasticsearch distributable package. Assuming that we have our plugin archive stored in the `/home/install/es/plugins` directory, we will run the following command (we run it from the Elasticsearch home directory):

```
bin/plugin --install rest --url file:/home/install/es/plugins/elasticsearch-rest-1.4.1.zip
```

We need to install the plugin on all the nodes in our cluster, because we want to be able to run our custom REST action on each Elasticsearch instance.

In order to learn more about installing Elasticsearch plugins, please refer to our previous book, *Elasticsearch Server Second Edition*, or check out the official Elasticsearch documentation at http://www.elasticsearch.org/guide/reference/modules/plugins/.

After we have the plugin installed, we need to restart our Elasticsearch instance we were making the installation on. After the restart, we should see something like this in the logs:

```
[2014-12-12 21:04:48,348][INFO ][plugins                  ]
[Archer] loaded [CustomRestActionPlugin], sites []
```

As you can see, Elasticsearch informed us that the plugin named `CustomRestActionPlugin` was loaded.

Checking whether the REST action plugin works

We can finally check whether the plugin works. In order to do that, we will run the following command:

```
curl -XGET 'localhost:9200/_mastering/nodes?pretty'
```

As a result, we should get all the nodes in the cluster, because we didn't provide the `prefix` parameter and this is exactly what we've got from Elasticsearch:

```
{
  "nodes" : [ "Archer" ]
}
```

Because we only had one node in our Elasticsearch cluster, we've got the `nodes` array with only a `single` entry.

Now, let's test what will happen if we add the `prefix=Are` parameter to our request. The exact command we've used was as follows:

```
curl -XGET 'localhost:9200/_mastering/nodes?prefix=Are&pretty'
```

The response from Elasticsearch was as follows:

```
{
  "nodes" : [ ]
}
```

As you can see, the `nodes` array is empty, because we don't have any node in the cluster that would start with the `Are` prefix. At the end, let's check another format of response:

```
curl -XGET 'localhost:9200/_mastering/nodes?pretty&format=yaml'
```

Now the response is not in a JSON format. Look at the example output for a cluster consisting of two nodes:

```
---
nodes:
- "Atalon"
- "Slapstick"
```

As we can see, our REST plugin is not so complicated but already has several features.

Creating the custom analysis plugin

The last thing we want to discuss when it comes to custom Elasticsearch plugins is the analysis process extension. We've chosen to show how to develop a custom analysis plugin because this is sometimes very useful, for example, when you want to have the custom analysis process that you use in your company introduced, or when you want to use the Lucene analyzer or filter that is not present in Elasticsearch itself or as a plugin for it. Because creating an analysis extension is more complicated compared to what we've seen when developing a custom REST action, we decided to leave it until the end of the chapter.

Implementation details

Because developing a custom analysis plugin is the most complicated, at least from the Elasticsearch point of view and the number of classes we need to develop, we will have more things to do compared to previous examples. We will need to develop the following things:

- The TokenFilter class extension (from the org.apache.lucene.analysis package) implementation that will be responsible for handling token reversing; we will call it CustomFilter

- The AbstractTokenFilterFactory extension (from the org.elasticsearch.index.analysis package) that will be responsible for providing our CustomFilter instance to Elasticsearch; we will call it CustomFilterFactory

- The custom analyzer, which will extend the org.apache.lucene.analysis.Analyzer class and provide the Lucene analyzer functionality; we will call it CustomAnalyzer

- The analyzer provider, which we will call CustomAnalyzerProvider, which extends AbstractIndexAnalyzerProvider from the org.elasticsearch.index.analysis package, and which will be responsible for providing the analzyer instance to Elasticsearch

- An extension of AnalysisModule.AnalysisBinderProcessor from the org.elasticsearch.index.analysis package, which will have information about the names under which our analyzer and token filter will be available in Elasticsearch; we will call it CustomAnalysisBinderProcessor

- An extension of the AbstractComponent class from the org.elasticsearch.common.component package, which will inform Elasticsearch which factories should be used for our custom analyzer and token filter; we will call it CustomAnalyzerIndicesComponent

- The `AbstractModule` extension (from the `org.elasticsearch.common.inject` package) that will inform Elasticsearch that our `CustomAnalyzerIndicesComponent module` should be a singleton; we will call it `CustomAnalyzerModule`
- Finally, the usual `AbstractPlugin` extension (from the `org.elasticsearch.plugins` package) that will register our plugin; we will call it `CustomAnalyzerPlugin`

So let's start discussing the code.

Implementing TokenFilter

The funniest thing about the currently discussed plugin is that the whole analysis work is actually done on a Lucene level, and what we need to do is write the `org.apache.lucene.analysis.TokenFilter` extension, which we will call `CustomFilter`. In order to do this, we need to initialize the super class and override the `incrementToken` method. Our class will be responsible for reversing the tokens, so that's the logic we want our analyzer and filter to have. The whole implementation of our `CustomFilter` class looks as follows:

```
public class CustomFilter extends TokenFilter {
  private final CharTermAttribute termAttr = addAttribute(CharTermAttribute.class);

  protected CustomFilter(TokenStream input) {
    super(input);
  }

  @Override
  public boolean incrementToken() throws IOException {
    if (input.incrementToken()) {
      char[] originalTerm = termAttr.buffer();
      if (originalTerm.length > 0) {
        StringBuilder builder = new StringBuilder(new String(originalTerm).trim()).reverse();
        termAttr.setEmpty();
        termAttr.append(builder.toString());
      }
      return true;
    } else {
      return false;
    }
  }
}
```

The first thing we see in the implementation is the following line:

```
private final CharTermAttribute termAttr =
addAttribute(CharTermAttribute.class);
```

It allows us to retrieve the text of the token we are currently processing. In order to get access to the other token information, we need to use other attributes. The list of attributes can be found by looking at the classes implementing Lucene's `org.apache.lucene.util.Attribute` interface (http://lucene.apache.org/core/4_10_0/core/org/apache/lucene/util/Attribute.html). What you need to know now is that by using the static `addAttribute` method, we can bind different attributes and use them during token processing.

Then, we have the constructor, which is only used for super class initialization, so we can skip discussing it.

Finally, there is the `incrementToken` method, which returns `true` when there is a token in the token stream left to be processed, and `false` if there is no token left to be processed. So, what we do first is we check whether there is a token to be processed by calling the `incrementToken` method of input, which is the `TokenStream` instance stored in the super class. Then, we get the term text by calling the `buffer` method of the attribute we bind in the first line of our class. If there is text in the term (its length is higher than zero), we use a `StringBuilder` object to reverse the text, we clear the term buffer (by calling `setEmpty` on the attribute), and we append the reversed text to the already emptied term buffer (by calling the `append` method of the attribute). After this, we return `true`, because our token is ready to be processed further—on a token filter level, we don't know whether the token will be processed further or not, so we need to be sure we return the correct information, just in case.

Implementing the TokenFilter factory

The factory for our token filter implementation is one of the simplest classes in the case of the discussed plugins. What we need to do is create an `AbstractTokenFilterFactory` (from the `org.elasticsearch.index.analysis` package) extension that overrides a single `create` method in which we create our token filter. The code of this class looks as follows:

```
public class CustomFilterFactory extends
AbstractTokenFilterFactory {
  @Inject
  public CustomFilterFactory(Index index, @IndexSettings Settings
indexSettings, @Assisted String name, @Assisted Settings settings)
{
    super(index, indexSettings, name, settings);
  }
```

```
    @Override
    public TokenStream create(TokenStream tokenStream) {
      return new CustomFilter(tokenStream);
    }
}
```

As you can see, the class is very simple. We start with the constructor, which is needed, because we need to initialize the parent class. In addition to this, we have the `create` method, in which we create our `CustomFilter` class with the provided `TokenStream` object.

Before we go on, we would like to mention two more things: the `@IndexSettings` and `@Assisted` annotations. The first one will result in index settings being injected as the `Settings` class object to the constructor; of course, this is done automatically. The `@Assisted keyword` results in the annotated parameter value to be injected from the argument of the factory method.

Implementing the class custom analyzer

We wanted to keep the example implementation as simple as possible and, because of that, we've decided not to complicate the analyzer implementation. To implement our analyzer, we need to extend an abstract `Analyzer` class from Lucene's `org.apache.lucene.analysis` package, and we did that. The whole code of our `CustomAnalyzer` class looks as follows:

```
public class CustomAnalyzer extends Analyzer {
  public CustomAnalyzer() {
  }

  @Override
  protected TokenStreamComponents createComponents(String field,
Reader reader) {
    final Tokenizer src = new WhitespaceTokenizer(reader);
    return new TokenStreamComponents(src, new CustomFilter(src));
  }
}
```

If you want to see more complicated analyzer implementations, please look at the source code of Apache Lucene, Apache Solr, and Elasticsearch.

The `createComponent` method is the one we need to implement, and it should return a `TokenStreamComponents` object (from the `org.apache.lucene.analysis` package) for a given field name (the `String` type object—the first argument of the method) and data (the `Reader` type object—the second method argument). What we do is create a `Tokenizer object` using the `WhitespaceTokenizer` class available in Lucene. This will result in the input data to be tokenized on whitespace characters. Then, we create a Lucene `TokenStreamComponents` object, to which we give the source of tokens (our previously created `Tokenizer object`) and our `CustomFilter object`. This will result in our `CustomFilter object` to be used by `CustomAnalyzer`.

Implementing the analyzer provider

Let's talk about another provider implementation in addition to the token filter factory we've created earlier. This time, we need to extend `AbstractIndexAnalyzerProvider` from the `org.elasticsearch.index.analysis` package in order for Elasticsearch to be able to create our analyzer. The implementation is very simple, as we only need to implement the `get` method in which we should return our analyzer. The `CustomAnalyzerProvider` class code looks as follows:

```
public class CustomAnalyzerProvider extends
AbstractIndexAnalyzerProvider<CustomAnalyzer> {
  private final CustomAnalyzer analyzer;

  @Inject
  public CustomAnalyzerProvider(Index index, @IndexSettings
Settings indexSettings, Environment env, @Assisted String name,
@Assisted Settings settings) {
      super(index, indexSettings, name, settings);
      analyzer = new CustomAnalyzer();
  }

  @Override
  public CustomAnalyzer get() {
      return this.analyzer;
  }
}
```

As you can see, we've implemented the constructor in order to be able to initialize the super class. In addition to that, we are creating a single instance of our analyzer, which we will return when Elasticsearch requests it. We do this because we don't want to create an analyzer every time Elasticsearch requests it; this is not efficient. We don't need to worry about multithreading because our analyzer is thread-safe and, thus, a single instance can be reused. In the `get` method, we are just returning our analyzer.

Implementing the analysis binder

The binder is a part of our custom code that informs Elasticsearch about the names under which our analyzer and token filter will be available. Our `CustomAnalysisBinderProcessor` class extends `AnalysisModule.AnalysisBinderProcessor` from `org.elasticsearch.index.analysis`, and we override two methods of this class: `processAnalyzers` in which we will register our analyzer and `processTokenFilters` in which we will register our token filter. If we had only an analyzer or only a token filter, we would only override a single method. The code of `CustomAnalysisBinderProcessor` looks as follows:

```
public class CustomAnalysisBinderProcessor extends
AnalysisModule.AnalysisBinderProcessor {
  @Override
  public void processAnalyzers(AnalyzersBindings
analyzersBindings) {
     analyzersBindings.processAnalyzer("mastering_analyzer",
CustomAnalyzerProvider.class);
  }

  @Override
  public void processTokenFilters(TokenFiltersBindings
tokenFiltersBindings) {
     tokenFiltersBindings.processTokenFilter("mastering_filter",
CustomFilterFactory.class);
  }
}
```

The first method—`processAnalyzers`—takes a single `AnalysisBinding` object type, which we can use to register our analyzer under a given name. We do this by calling the `processAnalyzer` method of the `AnalysisBinding` object and pass in the name under which our analyzer will be available and the implementation of `AbstractIndexAnalyzerProvider`, which is responsible for creating our analyzer, which in our case, is the `CustomAnalyzerProvider` class.

The second method—procesTokenFilters—again takes a single TokenFiltersBindings class, which enables us to register our token filter. We do this by calling the processTokenFilter method and passing the name under which our token filter will be available and the token filter factory class, which in our case, is CustomFilterFactory.

Implementing the analyzer indices component

Now, we need to implement a node level component that will allow our analyzer and token filter to be reused. However, we will tell Elasticsearch that our analyzer should be reusable only on the indices level and not globally (just to show you how to do it). What we need to do is extend the AbstractComponent class from the org.elasticsearch.common.component package. In fact, we only need to develop a constructor for the class we called CustomAnalyzerIndicesComponent. The whole code for the mentioned class looks as follows:

```
public class CustomAnalyzerIndicesComponent extends
AbstractComponent {
  @Inject
  public CustomAnalyzerIndicesComponent(Settings settings,
IndicesAnalysisService indicesAnalysisService) {
    super(settings);
    indicesAnalysisService.analyzerProviderFactories().put(
        "mastering_analyzer",
        new PreBuiltAnalyzerProviderFactory("mastering_analyzer",
AnalyzerScope.INDICES, new CustomAnalyzer()));

    indicesAnalysisService.tokenFilterFactories().put("mastering_filter",
        new PreBuiltTokenFilterFactoryFactory(new
TokenFilterFactory() {
          @Override
          public String name() {
            return "mastering_filter";
          }

          @Override
          public TokenStream create(TokenStream tokenStream) {
            return new CustomFilter(tokenStream);
          }
        }));
  }
}
```

First of all, we pass the constructor arguments to the super class in order to initialize it. After that, we create a new analyzer, which is our `CustomAnalyzer` class, by using the following code snippet:

```
indicesAnalysisService.analyzerProviderFactories().put(
        "mastering_analyzer",
        new PreBuiltAnalyzerProviderFactory("mastering_analyzer",
AnalyzerScope.INDICES, new CustomAnalyzer()));
```

As you can see, we've used the `IndicesAnalysisService` object and its `analyzerProviderFactories` method to get the map of `PreBuiltAnalyzerProviderFactory` (as a value and the name as a key in the map), and we've put a newly created `PreBuiltAnalyzerProviderFactory` object with the name of `mastering_analyzer`. In order to create the `PreBuiltAnalyzerProviderFactory` we've used our `CustomAnalyzer` and `AnalyzerScope.INDICES` enum values (from the `org.elasticsearch.index.analysis` package). The other values of `AnalyzerScope` enum are `GLOBAL` and `INDEX`. If you would like the analyzer to be globally shared, you should use `AnalyzerScope.GLOBAL` and `AnalyzerScope.INDEX`, both of which should be created for each index separately.

In a similar way, we add our token filter, but this time, we use the `tokenFilterFactories` method of the `IndicesAnalysisService` object, which returns a `Map` of `PreBuiltTokenFilterFactoryFactory` as a value and a name (a `String` object) as a key. We put a newly created `TokenFilterFactory` object with the name of `mastering_filter`.

Implementing the analyzer module

A simple class called `CustomAnalyzerModule` extends `AbstractModule` from the `org.elasticsearch.common.inject` package. It is used to tell Elasticsearch that our `CustomAnalyzerIndicesComponent` class should be used as a singleton; we do this because it's enough to have a single instance of that class. Its code looks as follows:

```
public class CustomAnalyzerModule extends AbstractModule {
  @Override
  protected void configure() {
    bind(CustomAnalyzerIndicesComponent.class).asEagerSingleton();
  }
}
```

As you can see, we implement a single configure method, which tells you to bind the `CustomAnalyzerIndicesComponent` class as a singleton.

Implementing the analyzer plugin

Finally, we need to implement the plugin class so that Elasticsearch knows that there is a plugin to be loaded. It should extend the `AbstractPlugin` class from the `org.elasticsearch.plugins` package and thus implement at least the `name` and `descriptions` methods. However, we want our plugin to be registered, and that's why we implement two additional methods, which we can see in the following code snippet:

```
public class CustomAnalyzerPlugin extends AbstractPlugin {
  @Override
  public Collection<Class<? extends Module>> modules() {
      return ImmutableList.<Class<? extends
Module>>of(CustomAnalyzerModule.class);
  }

  public void onModule(AnalysisModule module) {
      module.addProcessor(new CustomAnalysisBinderProcessor());
  }

  @Override
  public String name() {
    return "AnalyzerPlugin";
  }

  @Override
  public String description() {
    return "Custom analyzer plugin";
  }
}
```

The `name` and `description` methods are quite obvious, as they are returning the name of the plugin and its description. The `onModule` method adds our `CustomAnalysisBinderProcessor` object to the `AnalysisModule` object provided to it.

The last method is the one we are not yet familiar with: the `modules` method:

```
public Collection<Class<? extends Module>> modules() {
  return ImmutableList.<Class<? extends
Module>>of(CustomAnalyzerModule.class);
}
```

We override this method from the super class in order to return a collection of modules that our plugin is registering. In this case, we are registering a single module class—`CustomAnalyzerModule`—and we are returning a list with a single entry.

Informing Elasticsearch about our custom analyzer

Once we have our code ready, we need to add one additional thing: we need to let Elasticsearch know what the class registering our plugin is—the one we've called `CustomAnalyzerPlugin`. In order to do that, we create an `es-plugin.properties` file in the `src/main/resources` directory with the following content:

```
plugin=pl.solr.analyzer.CustomAnalyzerPlugin
```

We just specify the `plugin` property there, which should have a value of the class we use to register our plugins (the one that extends the Elasticsearch `AbstractPlugin` class). This file will be included in the JAR file that will be created during the build process and will be used by Elasticsearch during the plugin load process.

Testing our custom analysis plugin

Now, we want to test our custom analysis plugin just to be sure that everything works. In order to do that, we need to build our plugin, install it on all nodes in our cluster, and finally, use the Admin Indices Analyze API to see how our analyzer works. Let's do that.

Building our custom analysis plugin

We start with the easiest part: building our plugin. In order to do that, we run a simple command:

```
mvn compile package
```

We tell Maven that we want the code to be compiled and packaged. After the command finishes, we can find the archive with the plugin in the `target/release` directory (assuming you are using a project setup similar to the one we've described at the beginning of the chapter).

Installing the custom analysis plugin

To install the plugin, we will use the `plugin` command, just like we did previously. Assuming that we have our plugin archive stored in the `/home/install/es/plugins` directory, would run the following command (we run it from the Elasticsearch home directory):

```
bin/plugin --install analyzer --url
file:/home/install/es/plugins/elasticsearch-analyzer-1.4.1.zip
```

We need to install the plugin on all the nodes in our cluster, because we want Elasticsearch to be able to find our analyzer and filter no matter on which node the analysis process is done. If we don't install the plugin on all nodes, we can be certain that we will run into issues.

> In order to learn more about installing Elasticsearch plugins, please refer to our previous book, *Elasticsearch Server Section Edition*, by *Packt Publishing* or refer to the official Elasticsearch documentation.

After we have the plugin installed, we need to restart our Elasticsearch instance we were creating the installation on. After the restart, we should see something like this in the logs:

```
[2014-12-03 22:39:11,231][INFO ][plugins                  ]
[Tattletale] loaded [AnalyzerPlugin], sites []
```

With the preceding log line, Elasticsearch informs us that the plugin named `AnalyzerPlugin` was successfully loaded.

Checking whether our analysis plugin works

We can finally check whether our custom analysis plugin works as it should. In order to do that, we start with creating an empty index called `analyzetest` (the index name doesn't matter). We do this by running the following command:

```
curl -XPOST 'localhost:9200/analyzetest/'
```

After this we use the Admin Indices Analyze API (http://www.elasticsearch.org/guide/en/elasticsearch/reference/current/indices-analyze.html) to see how our analyzer works. We do that by running the following command:

```
curl -XGET 'localhost:9200/analyzetest/_analyze?analyzer=mastering_analyzer&pretty' -d 'mastering elasticsearch'
```

So, what we should see in response is two tokens: one that should be reversed—mastering—`gniretsam` and another one that should also be reversed—elasticsearch—`hcraescitsale`. The response Elasticsearch returns looks as follows:

```
{
  "tokens" : [ {
    "token" : "gniretsam",
    "start_offset" : 0,
    "end_offset" : 9,
    "type" : "word",
    "position" : 1
  }, {
    "token" : "hcraescitsale",
    "start_offset" : 10,
    "end_offset" : 23,
    "type" : "word",
    "position" : 2
  } ]
}
```

As you can see, we've got exactly what we expected, so it seems that our custom analysis plugin works as intended.

Summary

In this chapter, we were focused on developing custom plugins for Elasticsearch. We learned how to properly set up your Maven project to be able to automatically build your Elasticsearch plugins. You saw how to develop a custom REST action plugin, and we extended Elasticsearch analysis capabilities by creating a plugin that included a custom token filter and new analyzer.

We've reached the end of the book, and we wanted to write a small summary and say a few words to the brave reader who managed to get to the end. We decided to write the second edition of *Mastering Elasticsearch* after writing *Elasticsearch Server Second Edition*. We thought that we had left a number of topics uncovered, and we wanted to write them in this book. We went from introducing Apache Lucene and Elasticsearch to querying and data handling—both on the Lucene index and the Elasticsearch level. We hope that, by now, you know how Lucene works and how Elasticsearch uses it, and you will find this knowledge worthy in your journey with this great search engine. We talked about some topics that can be useful when things are hot, such as I/O throttling, Hot Threads API, and how to speed up your queries. We also concentrated on things such as choosing the right query for the use case and Elasticsearch scaling.

Finally, we dedicated one chapter to discussing Java development on how to extend Elasticsearch with your own plugins. In the first version of the book, we also described the Java API briefly, but we decided it doesn't make sense. The API would require its own book and showing only some things regarding them just feels wrong. Hopefully, you'll be able to write your own plugins and even though we didn't write about all the possibilities, we hope that you'll be able to find the things we didn't write about.

Thank you for reading the book; we hope that you like it and that it brought you some knowledge that you were seeking, and that you'll be able to use it whether you use Elasticsearch professionally or just as a hobby.

Finally, please stop by at `http://elasticsearchserverbook.com/` from time to time. In addition to the usual posts we make, we will publish the book fragments that didn't make it to the book or were cut down because the book would be too broad.

Module 3

Learning ELK Stack

Build mesmerizing visualizations, analytics, and logs from your data using Elasticsearch, Logstash, and Kibana

1
Introduction to ELK Stack

This chapter explains the importance of log analysis in today's data-driven world and what are the challenges associated with log analysis. It introduces ELK stack as a complete log analysis solution, and explains what ELK stack is and the role of each of the open source components of the stack, namely, Elasticsearch, Logstash, and Kibana. Also, it briefly explains the key features of each of the components and describes the installation and configuration steps for them.

The need for log analysis

Logs provide us with necessary information on how our system is behaving. However, the content and format of the logs varies among different services or say, among different components of the same system. For example, a scanner may log error messages related to communication with other devices; on the other hand, a web server logs information on all incoming requests, outgoing responses, time taken for a response, and so on. Similarly, application logs for an e-commerce website will log business-specific logs.

As the logs vary by their content, so will their uses. For example, the logs from a scanner may be used for troubleshooting or for a simple status check or reporting while the web server log is used to analyze traffic patterns across multiple products. Analysis of logs from an e-commerce site can help figure out whether packages from a specific location are returned repeatedly and the probable reasons for the same.

The following are some common use cases where log analysis is helpful:

- Issue debugging
- Performance analysis
- Security analysis
- Predictive analysis
- **Internet of things** (**IoT**) and logging

Issue debugging

Debugging is one of the most common reasons to enable logging within your application. The simplest and most frequent use for a debug log is to grep for a specific error message or event occurrence. If a system administrator believes that a program crashed because of a network failure, then he or she will try to find a `connection dropped` message or a similar message in the server logs to analyze what caused the issue. Once the bug or the issue is identified, log analysis solutions help capture application information and snapshots of that particular time can be easily passed across development teams to analyze it further.

Performance analysis

Log analysis helps optimize or debug system performance and give essential inputs around bottlenecks in the system. Understanding a system's performance is often about understanding resource usage in the system. Logs can help analyze individual resource usage in the system, behavior of multiple threads in the application, potential deadlock conditions, and so on. Logs also carry with them timestamp information, which is essential to analyze how the system is behaving over time. For instance, a web server log can help know how individual services are performing based on response times, HTTP response codes, and so on.

Security analysis

Logs play a vital role in managing the application security for any organization. They are particularly helpful to detect security breaches, application misuse, malicious attacks, and so on. When users interact with the system, it generates log events, which can help track user behavior, identify suspicious activities, and raise alarms or security incidents for breaches.

The intrusion detection process involves session reconstruction from the logs itself. For example, `ssh` login events in the system can be used to identify any breaches on the machines.

Predictive analysis

Predictive analysis is one of the hot trends of recent times. Logs and events data can be used for very accurate predictive analysis. Predictive analysis models help in identifying potential customers, resource planning, inventory management and optimization, workload efficiency, and efficient resource scheduling. It also helps guide the marketing strategy, user-segment targeting, ad-placement strategy, and so on.

Internet of things and logging

When it comes to IoT devices (devices or machines that interact with each other without any human intervention), it is vital that the system is monitored and managed to keep downtime to a minimum and resolve any important bugs or issues swiftly. Since these devices should be able to work with little human intervention and may exist on a large geographical scale, log data is expected to play a crucial role in understanding system behavior and reducing downtime.

Challenges in log analysis

The current log analysis process mostly involves checking logs at multiple servers that are written by different components and systems across your application. This has various problems, which makes it a time-consuming and tedious job. Let's look at some of the common problem scenarios:

- Non-consistent log format
- Decentralized logs
- Expert knowledge requirement

Non-consistent log format

Every application and device logs in its own special way, so each format needs its own expert. Also, it is difficult to search across because of different formats.

Let's take a look at some of the common log formats. An interesting thing to observe will be the way different logs represent different timestamp formats, different ways to represent INFO, ERROR, and so on, and the order of these components with logs. It's difficult to figure out just by seeing logs what is present at what location. This is where tools such as Logstash help.

Tomcat logs

A typical tomcat server startup log entry will look like this:

```
May 24, 2015 3:56:26 PM org.apache.catalina.startup.HostConfig deployWAR
INFO: Deployment of web application archive \soft\apache-tomcat-7.0.62\webapps\sample.war has finished in 253 ms
```

Apache access logs – combined log format

A typical Apache access log entry will look like this:

```
127.0.0.1 - - [24/May/2015:15:54:59 +0530] "GET /favicon.ico HTTP/1.1"
200 21630
```

IIS logs

A typical IIS log entry will look like this:

```
2012-05-02 17:42:15 172.24.255.255 - 172.20.255.255 80 GET /images/
favicon.ico - 200 Mozilla/4.0+(compatible;MSIE+5.5;+Windows+2000+Server)
```

Variety of time formats

Not only log formats, but timestamp formats are also different among different types of applications, different types of events generated across multiple devices, and so on. Different types of time formats across different components of your system also make it difficult to correlate events occurring across multiple systems at the same time:

- 142920788
- Oct 12 23:21:45
- [5/May/2015:08:09:10 +0000]
- Tue 01-01-2009 6:00
- 2015-05-30 T 05:45 UTC
- Sat Jul 23 02:16:57 2014
- 07:38, 11 December 2012 (UTC)

Decentralized logs

Logs are mostly spread across all the applications that may be across different servers and different components. The complexity of log analysis increases with multiple components logging at multiple locations. For one or two servers' setup, finding out some information from logs involves running `cat` or `tail` commands or piping these results to `grep` command. But what if you have `10`, `20`, or say, `100` servers? These kinds of searches are mostly not scalable for a huge cluster of machines and need a centralized log management and an analysis solution.

Expert knowledge requirement

People interested in getting the required business-centric information out of logs generally don't have access to the logs or may not have the technical expertise to figure out the appropriate information in the quickest possible way, which can make analysis slower, and sometimes, impossible too.

The ELK Stack

The ELK platform is a complete log analytics solution, built on a combination of three open source tools—Elasticsearch, Logstash, and Kibana. It tries to address all the problems and challenges that we saw in the previous section. ELK utilizes the open source stack of Elasticsearch for deep search and data analytics; Logstash for centralized logging management, which includes shipping and forwarding the logs from multiple servers, log enrichment, and parsing; and finally, Kibana for powerful and beautiful data visualizations. ELK stack is currently maintained and actively supported by the company called Elastic (formerly, Elasticsearch).

Let's look at a brief overview of each of these systems:

- Elasticsearch
- Logstash
- Kibana

Elasticsearch

Elasticsearch is a distributed open source search engine based on Apache Lucene, and released under an Apache 2.0 license (which means that it can be downloaded, used, and modified free of charge). It provides horizontal scalability, reliability, and multitenant capability for real-time search. Elasticsearch features are available through JSON over a RESTful API. The searching capabilities are backed by a schema-less Apache Lucene Engine, which allows it to dynamically index data without knowing the structure beforehand. Elasticsearch is able to achieve fast search responses because it uses indexing to search over the texts.

Elasticsearch is used by many big companies, such as GitHub, SoundCloud, FourSquare, Netflix, and many others. Some of the use cases are as follows:

- **Wikipedia**: This uses Elasticsearch to provide a full text search, and provide functionalities, such as *search-as-you-type*, and *did-you-mean* suggestions.

- **The Guardian**: This uses Elasticsearch to process 40 million documents per day, provide real-time analytics of site-traffic across the organization, and help understand audience engagement better.
- **StumbleUpon**: This uses Elasticsearch to power intelligent searches across its platform and provide great recommendations to millions of customers.
- **SoundCloud**: This uses Elasticsearch to provide real-time search capabilities for millions of users across geographies.
- **GitHub**: This uses Elasticsearch to index over 8 million code repositories, and index multiple events across the platform, hence providing real-time search capabilities across it.

Some of the key features of Elasticsearch are:

- It is an open source distributed, scalable, and highly available real-time document store
- It provides real-time search and analysis capabilities
- It provides a sophisticated RESTful API to play around with lookup, and various features, such as multilingual search, geolocation, autocomplete, contextual did-you-mean suggestions, and result snippets
- It can be scaled horizontally easily and provides easy integrations with cloud-based infrastructures, such as AWS and others

Logstash

Logstash is a data pipeline that helps collect, parse, and analyze a large variety of structured and unstructured data and events generated across various systems. It provides plugins to connect to various types of input sources and platforms, and is designed to efficiently process logs, events, and unstructured data sources for distribution into a variety of outputs with the use of its output plugins, namely file, `stdout` (as output on console running Logstash), or Elasticsearch.

It has the following key features:

- **Centralized data processing**: Logstash helps build a data pipeline that can centralize data processing. With the use of a variety of plugins for input and output, it can convert a lot of different input sources to a single common format.

- **Support for custom log formats**: Logs written by different applications often have particular formats specific to the application. Logstash helps parse and process custom formats on a large scale. It provides support to write your own filters for tokenization and also provides ready-to-use filters.
- **Plugin development**: Custom plugins can be developed and published, and there is a large variety of custom developed plugins already available.

Kibana

Kibana is an open source Apache 2.0 licensed data visualization platform that helps in visualizing any kind of structured and unstructured data stored in Elasticsearch indexes. Kibana is entirely written in HTML and JavaScript. It uses the powerful search and indexing capabilities of Elasticsearch exposed through its RESTful API to display powerful graphics for the end users. From basic business intelligence to real-time debugging, Kibana plays its role through exposing data through beautiful histograms, geomaps, pie charts, graphs, tables, and so on.

Kibana makes it easy to understand large volumes of data. Its simple browser-based interface enables you to quickly create and share dynamic dashboards that display changes to Elasticsearch queries in real time.

Some of the key features of Kibana are as follows:

- It provides flexible analytics and a visualization platform for business intelligence.
- It provides real-time analysis, summarization, charting, and debugging capabilities.
- It provides an intuitive and user friendly interface, which is highly customizable through some drag and drop features and alignments as and when needed.
- It allows saving the dashboard, and managing more than one dashboard. Dashboards can be easily shared and embedded within different systems.
- It allows sharing snapshots of logs that you have already searched through, and isolates multiple problem transactions.

ELK data pipeline

A typical ELK stack data pipeline looks something like this:

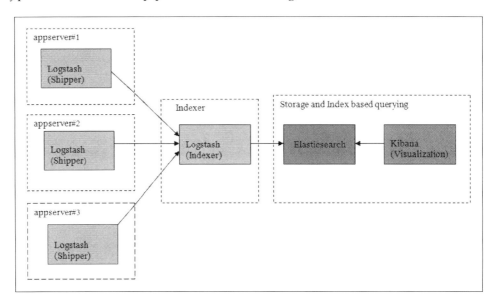

In a typical ELK Stack data pipeline, logs from multiple application servers are shipped through Logstash shipper to a centralized Logstash indexer. The Logstash indexer will output data to an Elasticsearch cluster, which will be queried by Kibana to display great visualizations and build dashboards over the log data.

ELK Stack installation

A Java runtime is required to run ELK Stack. The latest version of Java is recommended for the installation. At the time of writing this book, the minimum requirement is Java 7. You can use the official Oracle distribution, or an open source distribution, such as OpenJDK.

You can verify the Java installation by running the following command in your shell:

```
> java -version
java version "1.8.0_40"
Java(TM) SE Runtime Environment (build 1.8.0_40-b26)
Java HotSpot(TM) 64-Bit Server VM (build 25.40-b25, mixed mode)
```

If you have verified the Java installation in your system, we can proceed with the ELK installation.

Installing Elasticsearch

When installing Elasticsearch during production, you can use the method described below, or the Debian or RPM packages provided on the download page.

> You can download the latest version of Elasticsearch from `https://www.elastic.co/downloads/elasticsearch`.

```
curl -O https://download.elastic.co/elasticsearch/elasticsearch/elasticsearch-1.5.2.tar.gz
```

> If you don't have cURL, you can use the following command to install it:
> `sudo apt-get install curl`

Then, unpack the zip file on your local filesystem:

```
tar -zxvf elasticsearch-1.5.2.tar.gz
```

And then, go to the installation directory:

```
cd  elasticsearch-1.5.2
```

> Elastic, the company behind Elasticsearch, recently launched Elasticsearch 2.0 with some new aggregations, better compression options, simplified query DSL by merging query and filter concepts, and improved performance.
> More details can be found in the official documentation:
> `https://www.elastic.co/guide/en/elasticsearch/reference/current/index.html`.

Running Elasticsearch

In order to run Elasticsearch, execute the following command:

```
$ bin/elasticsearch
```

Add the `-d` flag to run it in the background as a daemon process.

We can test it by running the following command in another terminal window:

```
curl 'http://localhost:9200/?pretty'
```

This shows you an output similar to this:

```
{
  "status" : 200,
  "name" : "Master",
  "cluster_name" : "elasticsearch",
  "version" : {
    "number" : "1.5.2",
    "build_hash" : "c88f77ffc81301dfa9dfd81ca2232f09588bd512",
    "build_timestamp" : "2015-05-13T13:05:36Z",
    "build_snapshot" : false,
    "lucene_version" : "4.10.3"
  },
  "tagline" : "You Know, for Search"
}
```

We can shut down Elasticsearch through the API as follows:

`curl -XPOST 'http://localhost:9200/_shutdown'`

Elasticsearch configuration

Elasticsearch configuration files are under the `config` folder in the Elasticsearch installation directory. The `config` folder has two files, namely `elasticsearch.yml` and `logging.yml`. The former will be used to specify configuration properties of different Elasticsearch modules, such as network address, paths, and so on, while the latter will specify logging-related configurations.

The configuration file is in the YAML format and the following sections are some of the parameters that can be configured.

Network Address

To specify the address where all network-based modules will bind and publish to:

```
network :
    host : 127.0.0.1
```

Paths

To specify paths for data and log files:

```
path:
  logs: /var/log/elasticsearch
  data: /var/data/elasticsearch
```

The cluster name

To give a name to a production cluster, which is used to discover and auto join nodes:

```
cluster:
  name: <NAME OF YOUR CLUSTER>
```

The node name

To change the default name of each node:

```
node:
  name: <NAME OF YOUR NODE>
```

Elasticsearch plugins

Elasticsearch has a variety of plugins that ease the task of managing indexes, cluster, and so on. Some of the mostly used ones are the Kopf plugin, Marvel, Sense, Shield, and so on, which will be covered in the subsequent chapters. Let's take a look at the Kopf plugin here.

Kopf is a simple web administration tool for Elasticsearch that is written in JavaScript, AngularJS, jQuery and Twitter bootstrap. It offers an easy way of performing common tasks on an Elasticsearch cluster. Not every single API is covered by this plugin, but it does offer a REST client, which allows you to explore the full potential of the Elasticsearch API.

In order to install the `elasticsearch-kopf` plugin, execute the following command from the Elasticsearch installation directory:

bin/plugin -install lmenezes/elasticsearch-kopf

Now, go to this address to see the interface: `http://localhost:9200/_plugin/kopf/`.

Introduction to ELK Stack

You can see a page similar to this, which shows Elasticsearch nodes, shards, a number of documents, size, and also enables querying the documents indexed.

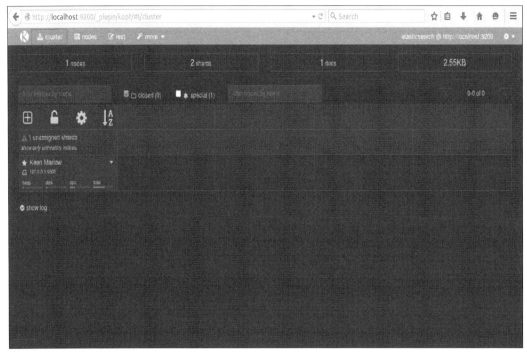

Elasticsearch Kopf UI

Installing Logstash

First, download the latest Logstash TAR file from the download page.

Check for the latest Logstash release version at
https://www.elastic.co/downloads/logstash.

```
curl -O http://download.elastic.co/logstash/logstash/logstash-1.5.0.tar.gz
```

Then, unpack the GZIP file on your local filesystem:

```
tar -zxvf logstash-1.5.0.tar.gz
```

Now, you can run Logstash with a basic configuration.

Running Logstash

Run Logstash using `-e` flag, followed by the configuration of standard input and output:

`cd logstash-1.5.0`

`bin/logstash -e 'input { stdin { } } output { stdout {} }'`

Now, when we type something in the command prompt, we will see its output in Logstash as follows:

`hello logstash`

`2015-05-15T03:34:30.111Z 0.0.0.0 hello logstash`

Here, we are running Logstash with the `stdin` input and the `stdout` output as this configuration prints whatever you type in a structured format as the output. The `-e` flag allows you to quickly test the configuration from the command line.

Now, let's try the `codec` setting for output for a pretty formatted output. Exit from the running Logstash by issuing a *Ctrl + C* command, and then we need to restart Logstash with the following command:

`bin/logstash -e 'input { stdin { } } output { stdout { codec => rubydebug } }'`

Now, enter some more test input:

```
Hello PacktPub

{
   "message" => " Hello PacktPub",
   "@timestamp" => "2015-05-20T23:48:05.335Z",
   "@version" => "1",
   "host" => "packtpub"
}
```

The output that you see is the most common output that we generally see from Logstash:

- `"message"` includes the complete input message or the event line
- `"@timestamp"` will include the timestamp of the time when the event was indexed; or if date filter is used, this value can also use one of the fields in the message to get a timestamp specific to the event
- `"host"` will generally represent the machine where this event was generated

Logstash with file input

Logstash can be easily configured to read from a log file as input.

For example, to read Apache logs from a file and output to a standard output console, the following configuration will be helpful:

```
input {
  file {
    type => "apache"
    path => "/user/packtpub/intro-to-elk/elk.log"
  }
}
output {
  stdout {
    codec => rubydebug
  }
}
```

Logstash with Elasticsearch output

Logstash can be configured to output all inputs to an Elasticsearch instance. This is the most common scenario in an ELK platform:

```
bin/logstash -e 'input { stdin { } } output { elasticsearch { host = localhost } }'
```

Then type 'you know, for logs

You will be able to see indexes in Elasticsearch through `http://localhost:9200/_search`.

Configuring Logstash

Logstash configuration files are in the JSON format. A Logstash config file has a separate section for each type of plugin that you want to add to the event processing pipeline. For example:

```
# This is a comment. You should use comments to describe
# parts of your configuration.
input {
  ...
}

filter {
  ...
```

```
}

output {
  ...
}
```

Each section contains the configuration options for one or more plugins. If you specify multiple filters, they are applied in the order of their appearance in the configuration file.

When you run `logstash`, you use the `-flag` to read configurations from a configuration file or even from a folder containing multiple configuration files for each type of plugin—input, filter, and output:

`bin/logstash -f ../conf/logstash.conf`

> If you want to test your configurations for syntax errors before running them, you can simply check with the following command:
> `bin/logstash –configtest ../conf/logstash.conf`
> This command just checks the configuration without running `logstash`.

Logstash runs on JVM and consumes a hefty amount of resources to do so. Logstash, at times, has significant memory consumption. Obviously, this could be a great challenge when you want to send logs from a small machine without harming application performance.

In order to save resources, you can use the Logstash forwarder (previously known as Lumberjack). The forwarder uses Lumberjack's protocol, enabling you to securely ship compressed logs, thus reducing resource consumption and bandwidth. The sole input is file/s, while the output can be directed to multiple destinations.

Other options do exist as well, to send logs. You can use `rsyslog` on Linux machines, and there are other agents for Windows machines, such as `nxlog` and `syslog-ng`. There is another lightweight tool to ship logs called `Log-Courier` (`https://github.com/driskell/log-courier`), which is an enhanced fork of the Logstash forwarder with some improvements.

Installing Logstash forwarder

Download the latest Logstash forwarder release from the download page.

 Check for the latest Logstash forwarder release version at `https://www.elastic.co/downloads/logstash`.

Prepare a configuration file that contains input plugin details and ssl certificate details to establish a secure communication between your forwarder and indexer servers, and run it using the following command:

```
Logstash forwarder -config Logstash forwarder.conf
```

And in Logstash, we can use the Lumberjack plugin to get data from the forwarder:

```
input {
  lumberjack {
    # The port to listen on
    port => 12345

    # The paths to your ssl cert and key
    ssl_certificate => "path/to/ssl.crt"
    ssl_key => "path/to/ssl.key"

    # Set the type of log.
    type => "log type"
  }
}
```

Logstash plugins

Some of the most popular Logstash plugins are:

- Input plugin
- Filters plugin
- Output plugin

Input plugin

Some of the most popular Logstash input plugins are:

- **file**: This streams log events from a file
- **redis**: This streams events from a redis instance
- **stdin**: This streams events from standard input

- **syslog**: This streams syslog messages over the network
- **ganglia**: This streams ganglia packets over the network via udp
- **lumberjack**: This receives events using the lumberjack protocol
- **eventlog**: This receives events from Windows event log
- **s3**: This streams events from a file from an s3 bucket
- **elasticsearch**: This reads from the Elasticsearch cluster based on results of a search query

Filters plugin

Some of the most popular Logstash filter plugins are as follows:

- **date**: This is used to parse date fields from incoming events, and use that as Logstash timestamp fields, which can be later used for analytics
- **drop**: This drops everything from incoming events that matches the filter condition
- **grok**: This is the most powerful filter to parse unstructured data from logs or events to a structured format
- **multiline**: This helps parse multiple lines from a single source as one Logstash event
- **dns**: This filter will resolve an IP address from any fields specified
- **mutate**: This helps rename, remove, modify, and replace fields in events
- **geoip**: This adds geographic information based on IP addresses that are retrieved from `Maxmind` database

Output plugin

Some of the most popular Logstash output plugins are as follows:

- **file**: This writes events to a file on disk
- **e-mail**: This sends an e-mail based on some conditions whenever it receives an output
- **elasticsearch**: This stores output to the Elasticsearch cluster, the most common and recommended output for Logstash
- **stdout**: This writes events to standard output
- **redis**: This writes events to redis queue and is used as a broker for many ELK implementations
- **mongodb**: This writes output to mongodb
- **kafka**: This writes events to Kafka topic

Installing Kibana

Before we can install and run Kibana, it has certain prerequisites:

- Elasticsearch should be installed, and its HTTP service should be running on port `9200` (default).
- Kibana must be configured to use the host and port on which Elasticsearch is running (check out the following *Configuring Kibana* section).

Download the latest Kibana release from the download page.

Check for the latest Kibana release version at
https://www.elastic.co/downloads/kibana.

```
curl -O https://download.elastic.co/kibana/kibana/kibana-4.0.2-linux-x64.tar.gz
```

Then, unpack `kibana-4.0.2-linux-x64.tar.gz` on your local file system and create a soft link to use a short name.

```
tar -zxvf kibana-4.0.2-linux-x64.tar.gz

ln -s kibana-4.0.2-linux-x64 kibana
```

Then, you can explore the `kibana` folder:

```
cd kibana
```

Configuring Kibana

The Kibana configuration file is present in the `config` folder inside the `kibana` installation:

`config/kibana.yml`

Following are some of the important configurations for Kibana.

This controls which port to use.

`port: 5601`.

Chapter 1

Property to set the host to bind the server is:

`host: "localhost".`

Set the `elasticsearch_url` to point at your Elasticsearch instance, which is `localhost` by default.

`elasticsearch_url: http://localhost:9200`

Running Kibana

Start Kibana manually by issuing the following command:

`bin/kibana`

You can verify the running Kibana instance on port `5601` by placing the following URL in the browser:

`http://localhost:5601`

This should fire up the Kibana UI for you.

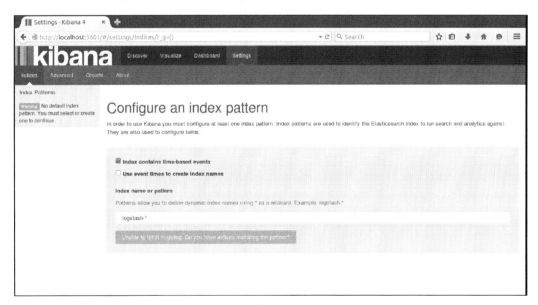

Kibana UI

> We need to specify **Index name or pattern** that has to be used to show data indexed in Elasticsearch. By default, Kibana assumes the default index as `logstash-*` as it is assuming that data is being fed to Elasticsearch through Logstash. If you have changed the name of the index in Logstash output plugin configuration, then we need to change that accordingly.
>
> **Kibana 3** versus **Kibana 4**
>
>
>
> Kibana 4 is a major upgrade over Kibana 3. Kibana 4 offers some advanced tools, which provides more flexibility in visualization and helps us use some of the advanced features of Elasticsearch. Kibana 3 had to be installed on a web server; Kibana 4 is released as a standalone application. Some of the new features in Kibana 4 as compared to Kibana 3 are as follows:
>
> - Search results highlighting
> - Shipping with its own web server and using Node.js on the backend
> - Advanced aggregation-based analytics features, for example, unique counts, non-date histograms, ranges, and percentiles

Kibana interface

As you saw in the preceding screenshot of the Kibana UI, the Kibana interface consists of four main components—**Discover**, **Visualize**, **Dashboard**, and **Settings**.

Discover

The **Discover** page helps to interactively explore the data matching the selected index pattern. This page allows submitting search queries, filtering the search results, and viewing document data. Also, it gives us the count of matching results and statistics related to a field. If the **timestamp** field is configured in the indexed data, it will also display, by default, a histogram showing distribution of documents over time.

Chapter 1

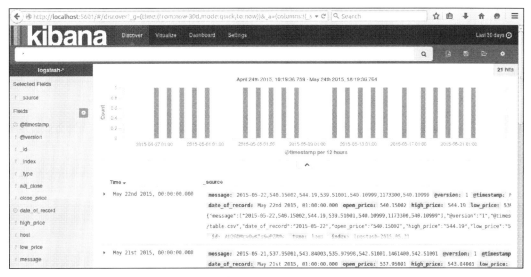

Kibana Discover Page

Visualize

The **Visualize** page is used to create new visualizations based on different data sources—a new interactive search, a saved search, or an existing saved visualization. Kibana 4 allows you to create the following visualizations in a new visualization wizard:

- Area chart
- Data table
- Line chart
- Markdown widget
- Metric
- Pie chart
- Tile map
- Vertical bar chart

These visualizations can be saved, used individually, or can be used in dashboards.

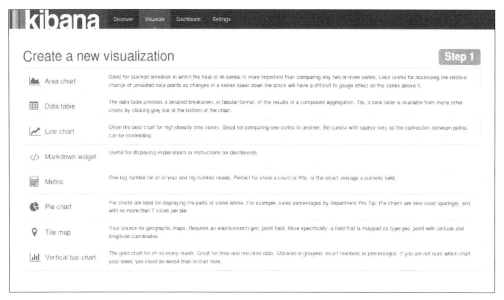

Kibana Visualize Page

Dashboard

Dashboard is a collection of saved visualizations in different groups. These visualizations can be arranged freely with a drag and drop kind of feature, and can be ordered as per the importance of the data. Dashboards can be easily saved, shared, and loaded at a later point in time.

Settings

The **Settings** page helps configure Elasticsearch indexes that we want to explore and configures various index patterns. Also, this page shows various indexed fields in one index pattern and data types of those fields. It also helps us create scripted fields, which are computed on the fly from the data.

Summary

In this chapter, we gathered a basic understanding of ELK stack, and also figured out why we need log analysis, and why ELK stack specifically. We also set up Elasticsearch, Logstash, and Kibana.

In the next chapter, we will look at how we can use our ELK stack installation to quickly build a data pipeline for analysis.

Building Your First Data Pipeline with ELK

In the previous chapter, we got familiar with each component of ELK Stack—Elasticsearch, Logstash, and Kibana. We got the components installed and configured. In this chapter, we will build our first basic data pipeline using ELK Stack. This will help us understand how easy it is to get together the components of ELK Stack to build an end-to-end analytics pipeline.

While running the example in this chapter, we assume that you already installed Elasticsearch, Logstash, and Kibana as described in *Chapter 1, Introduction to ELK Stack*.

Input dataset

For our example, the dataset that we are going to use here is the daily Google (GOOG) Quotes price dataset over a 6 month period from July 1, 2014 to December 31, 2014. This is a good dataset to understand how we can quickly analyze simple datasets, such as these, with ELK.

This dataset can be easily downloaded from the following source:
`http://finance.yahoo.com/q/hp?s=GOOG`

Data format for input dataset

The most significant fields of this dataset are `Date`, `Open Price`, `Close Price`, `High Price`, `Volume`, and `Adjusted Price`.

The following table shows some of the sample data from the dataset. The actual dataset is in the CSV format.

Date	Open	High	Low	Close	Volume	Adj Close
Dec 31, 2014	531.25	532.60	525.80	526.40	1,368,200	526.40
Dec 30, 2014	528.09	531.15	527.13	530.42	876,300	530.42
Dec 29, 2014	532.19	535.48	530.01	530.33	2,278,500	530.33
Dec 26, 2014	528.77	534.25	527.31	534.03	1,036,000	534.03
Dec 24, 2014	530.51	531.76	527.02	528.77	705,900	528.77
Dec 23, 2014	527.00	534.56	526.29	530.59	2,197,600	530.59
Dec 22, 2014	516.08	526.46	516.08	524.87	2,723,800	524.87
Dec 19, 2014	511.51	517.72	506.91	516.35	3,690,200	516.35
Dec 18, 2014	512.95	513.87	504.70	511.10	2,926,700	511.10
Dec 17, 2014	497.00	507.00	496.81	504.89	2,883,200	504.89
Dec 16, 2014	511.56	513.05	489.00	495.39	3,964,300	495.39
Dec 15, 2014	522.74	523.10	513.27	513.80	2,813,400	513.80
Dec 12, 2014	523.51	528.50	518.66	518.66	1,994,600	518.66
Dec 11, 2014	527.80	533.92	527.10	528.34	1,610,800	528.34
Dec 10, 2014	533.08	536.33	525.56	526.06	1,712,300	526.06

We need to put this data into a location from where ELK Stack can access it for further analysis.

We will look at some of the top entries of the CSV file using the Unix `head` command as follows:

```
$ head GOOG.csv
2014-12-31,531.25244,532.60236,525.80237,526.4024,1368200,526.4024
2014-12-30,528.09241,531.1524,527.13239,530.42242,876300,530.42242
2014-12-29,532.19244,535.48242,530.01337,530.3324,2278500,530.3324
2014-12-26,528.7724,534.25244,527.31238,534.03247,1036000,534.03247
2014-12-24,530.51245,531.76141,527.0224,528.7724,705900,528.7724
2014-12-23,527.00238,534.56244,526.29236,530.59241,2197600,530.59241
2014-12-22,516.08234,526.4624,516.08234,524.87238,2723800,524.87238
2014-12-19,511.51233,517.72235,506.9133,516.35229,3690200,516.35229
2014-12-18,512.95233,513.87231,504.7023,511.10233,2926700,511.10233
```

Each row represents the Quote price data for a particular date separated by a comma.

Now, when we are familiar with the data, we will set up the ELK Stack where we can parse and process the data using Logstash, index it in Elasticsearch, and then build beautiful visualizations in Kibana.

Configuring Logstash input

As we already know, Logstash has a rich set of plugins for different types of inputs, outputs and filters, which can read, parse, and filter data as per our needs. We will utilize the `file` input plugin to read the source file.

A `file` input plugin streams events from the input file, and each event is assumed as a single line. It automatically detects file rotation and handles it. It maintains the location where it left reading, and will automatically detect the new data if configured correctly. It reads files in a similar manner:

```
tail -0f
```

In general, a `file` input plugin configuration will look as follows:

```
input {

file {
    path => #String (path of the files) (required)
    start_position => #String (optional, default "end")
    tags => #array (optional)
    type => #string (optional)
}

}
```

- `path`: The `path` field is the only required field in `file` input plugin, which represents the path of the file from where input events have to be processed.
- `start_position`: This defines from where Logstash starts reading input files. Values can be `"beginning"` or `"end"`. The default value is `"end"` which caters to the needs of reading live streams. If we need to read some historic data, it can be set to `"beginning"`.
- `tags`: `tags` represents any number of strings as an array that can be utilized later to filter and process events based on tags assigned to them.
- `type`: The `type` field can be used to mark a specific type of events, which helps to filter and search them later. Type is added to the document that is stored in Elasticsearch, and can later be viewed in Kibana under the `_type` field. For example, we can assign type as `"error_logs"` or `"info_logs"`.

Let's configure Logstash for our input dataset:

```
input{
file{
path =>"/opt/logstash/input/GOOG.csv"
```

```
        start_position =>"beginning"
    }
}
```

We will provide the path of the CSV file in the `path` attribute, and as our dataset is historic, we will use `start_position` as `"beginning"`.

Filtering and processing input

Once we configure the input file, we need to filter the input based on our needs so that we can identify which fields we need, and process them as per the required analysis.

A `filter` plugin will perform the intermediary processing on the input event. We can apply the filter conditionally based on certain fields.

Since our input file is a CSV file, we will use the `csv` filter for the same. The `csv` filter takes an event field that contains CSV formatted data, parses it, and stores it as individual fields. It can also parse data with any separator other than commas. A typical `csv` filter is as follows:

```
    filter {
        csv {
            columns => #Array of column names.
            separator => #String ; default -","
        }
    }
```

The `attribute` columns take the name of fields in our CSV file, which is optional. By default, the columns will be named as `column 1`, `column 2`, and so on.

The `attribute` separator defines what character is used to separate the different columns in the file. The default is a comma, but it can be any other separator too.

In our example, we can specify a simple `csv` filter as follows:

```
    filter {
        csv {
        columns =>
["date_of_record","open","high","low","close","volume","adj_close"
]
            separator => ","
        }
    }
```

Here, we specified the column names as defined in our CSV file, and explicitly defined the separator as a comma just to make it clear.

Now, we are done with `csv` filter configuration, but we still need to do some intermediary processing on the columns to associate specific data types with our columns.

First of all, we need to specify which column represents the `date` field so that it can be explicitly indexed as date type and can be used to filter based on date. Logstash has a specific filter called `date` for the same. A typical `date` filter looks as follows:

```
filter {
  date {
    match =>   # array (optional), default: []
    target =>  # string (optional), default: "@timestamp"
    timezone => # string (optional)
  }

}
```

Here, in the `match` attribute, we define an array, which is in the `[field, formats]` format; that is, field, followed by a set of time formats that can be applied to that field. For example, if our log file has multiple formats, we can use the the following code:

```
match => [ "date_field", "MMM dd YYY HH:mm:ss",
           "MMM  d YYY HH:mm:ss",  "MMddYYYY","ISO8601" ]
```

> **Date formats in Logstash**: Date formats allowed are as per the allowed JodaTime `DateTimeFormat` library:
> http://joda-time.sourceforge.net/apidocs/org/joda/time/format/DateTimeFormat.html

As per our `date` format, our `date` filter will be as follows:

```
date{
match => ["date_of_record", "yyyy-MM-dd"]
target => "@timestamp"
}
```

The `target` filter defines where to map the matching timestamp. By default, it maps to `@timestamp` (the field that represents the time stamp of the event, which defaults to the time when the event was captured). In our case, since we are taking some historic data, we don't want the event captured time to be in `@timestamp`, but the date of record. We will map our `date` field to `@timestamp`. It is not mandatory to define this, but recommended to use.

After updating the data type of `date` fields, the next operation we require is updating the data type of fields, which we need for numeric comparisons or operations. By default, the value will be of `string` data type. We will convert them to integers so that we can perform some aggregations and comparisons on the data.

We will use `mutate` filter for the conversion of fields to a specific data type. This filter helps perform general mutations on the fields, which includes modifications of data types, renaming, replacing fields, and removing fields. It can also help merge two fields, perform uppercase and lowercase conversions, split and strip fields, and so on.

A typical `mutate` filter looks like this:

```
filter {
  mutate {

    convert => # hash of field and data type (optional)
    join =>    # hash of fields to be joined (optional)
    lowercase => # array of fields to be converted (optional)
    merge =>   # hash  of fields to be merged (optional)
    rename =>  # hash of original and rename field (optional)
    replace => # hash of fields to replaced with (optional)
    split =>   # hash of fields to be split (optional)
    strip => # array of fields (optional)
    uppercase =>  # array of fields (optional)
  }

}
```

Let's see what our `mutate` filter looks like:

```
mutate {

convert => ["open","float"]

convert => ["high ","float"]

convert => ["low ","float"]
convert => ["close ","float"]

convert => ["volume","integer"]
convert => ["adj_close","float"]


}
```

We are using the `convert` functionality to convert our `price` and `volume` fields to `integer`. Valid data types are `"integer"`, `"float"`, and `"string"`.

Putting data to Elasticsearch

Now that we have set up the data to be consumed by a CSV file into Logstash, followed by parsing and processing based on the data type needed, we now need to put the data in Elasticsearch so that we can index the different fields and consume them later via the Kibana interface.

We will use the `output` plugin of Logstash for an `elasticsearch` output.

A typical `elasticsearch` plugin configuration looks like this:

```
output {

  elasticsearch {

    action =>  # string (optional), default: "index"

    cluster =>  # string (optional)

    host =>  # string (optional)

    document_id =>  # string (optional), default: nil


    index =>  # string (optional), default: "logstash-%{+YYYY.MM.dd}"
    index_type =>  # string (optional)
    port =>  # string (optional)
    protocol =>  # string, one of ["node", "transport", "http"] (optional)
  }
}
```

- `action`: This specifies what action to perform on incoming documents. The default is `"index"` and possible values are `"index"` or `"delete"`. The `"index"` value will index a document and `"delete"` will delete a document based on document ID.
- `cluster`: This is the name of the cluster set in `elasticsearch`.
- `host`: This is the hostname or IP address of the `elasticsearch`.
- `document_id`: This is the document ID of the index; it is useful to delete or overwrite the existing entries.
- `index`: This is the index name to which the incoming events have to be written. By default, it is indexed based on each day, and named as `"logstash-%{+YYYY.MM.dd}"`.

- **`index_type`**: This specifies the index type to write events to. This is to ensure that you write similar types of events to the same index type.
- **`port`**: This specifies the port to be used for the `elasticsearch` service.
- **`protocol`**: This specifies the protocol to be used to connect with Elasticsearch. The values are `"http"`, `"node"`, and `"transport"`.

Now, let's take a look at our `elasticsearch` output configuration:

```
output{

elasticsearch {

host => "localhost"

}
}
```

We used the default value for index and most of the other settings.

Now, when we have seen how individual plugins are configured, let's take a look at what the overall Logstash configuration looks like:

```
input{
file{

path =>"/opt/logstash/input/GOOG.csv"
start_position =>"beginning"

}

}

filter{
csv{

columns => ["date_of_record","open","high","low","close","volume","adj_close"]

separator => ","
}

date {

match => ["date_of_record","yyyy-MM-dd"]
```

```
    }

    mutate {

    convert => ["open","float"]

    convert => ["high","float"]

    convert => ["low","float"]

    convert => ["close","float"]

    convert => ["volume","integer"]

    convert => ["adj_close","float"]
    }

}
output{

    elasticsearch {

    host => "localhost"

    }

}
```

We will save this configuration in the Logstash installation folder with the name logstash.conf, and as we saw earlier, we can run Logstash with this configuration using the following command:

> Before running Logstash with this configuration, make sure the Elasticsearch is running as per the instructions in the previous chapter.

```
$ bin/logstash -f logstash.conf
```

Logstash will start to run with the defined configuration and keep on indexing all incoming events to the elasticsearch indexes. You may see an output similar to this on the console:

```
May 31, 2015 4:04:54 PM org.elasticsearch.node.internal.InternalNode start
INFO: [logstash-4004-9716] started
Logstash startup completed
```

At this point, we can open the `elasticsearch Kopf` plugin console to verify whether we have some documents indexed already, and we can also query the documents.

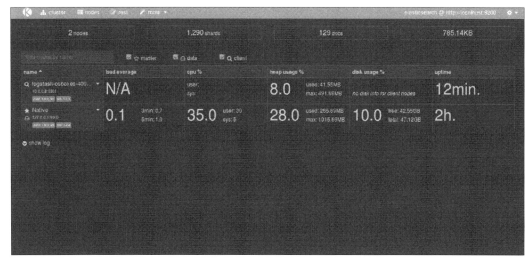

Elasticsearch Kopf interface

As we can see that there are 129 documents indexed already, we verified that our Logstash configuration worked well.

Visualizing with Kibana

Now when you verify that your data is indexed successfully in Elasticsearch, we can go ahead and look at the Kibana interface to get some useful analytics from the data.

Running Kibana

As described in the previous chapter, we will start the Kibana service from the Kibana installation directory.

```
$ bin/kibana
```

Now, let's see Kibana up and running similar to the following screenshot on the browser, by going to the following URL:

```
http://localhost:5601
```

Kibana Discover page

As we already set up Kibana to take **logstash-*** indexes by default, it displays the indexed data as a histogram of counts, and the associated data as fields in the JSON format.

First of all, we need to set the `date` filter to filter based on our date range so that we can build our analysis on the same. Since we took data from July 1, 2014 to December 31, 2014, we will configure our `date` filter for the same.

Clicking on the **Time Filter** icon at the extreme top-right corner, we can set an Absolute **Time Filter** based on our range as follows:

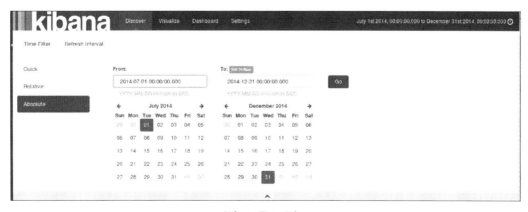

Kibana Time Filter

[637]

Building Your First Data Pipeline with ELK

Now, we are all set to build beautiful visualizations on the collected dataset using the rich set of visualization features that Kibana provides.

Before we build the visualization, let's confirm whether all fields are indexed properly with their associated data types so that we can perform the appropriate operations on them.

For this, let's click on the **Settings** page at the top of the screen and select the **logstash-*** index pattern on the left of the screen. The page looks something like this:

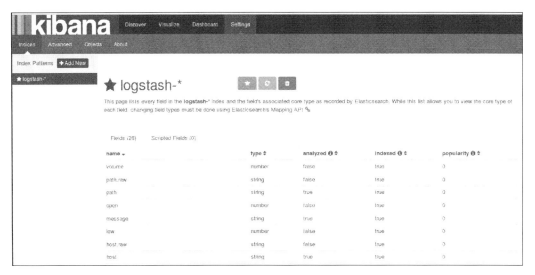

Kibana Settings page

It shows all our fields that were indexed, their data types, index status, and popularity value.

Kibana visualizations

Let's build some basic visualizations from the Kibana visualizations page, and we will use them later in dashboard.

Click on the visualization page link at the top of the Kibana home page, and click on the new visualization icon.

Kibana visualization menu

Building a line chart

The first visualization that we will build is a line chart showing weekly close price index movement for the GOOG script over a six month period.

Select **Line Chart** from the visualization menu, and then we'll select **Y-Axis** metrics as **Max**, and **Field** as **close**. In the **buckets** section, select **Aggregation** as **Date Histogram** based on the **@timestamp** field, and **Interval** as **Weekly**, and click on **Apply**.

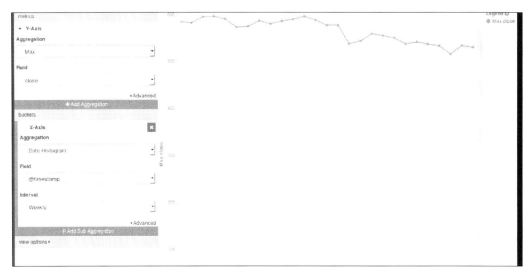

Kibana Line chart

Now, save the visualization using some name for the line chart, which we will pull into the dashboard later.

Building a bar chart

We will build a vertical bar chart representing the movement of weekly traded volumes over a six month period.

Select **Vertical Bar Chart** from the visualization menu, and select **Y-Axis** **Aggregation** as **Sum**, and **Field** as **volume**. In the **buckets** section, select **X-Axis** **Aggregation** as **Date Histogram**, and **Field** as **@timestamp**, and **Interval** as **Weekly**. Click on **Apply** to see a vertical bar chart representing the weekly total volume traded over a six month period.

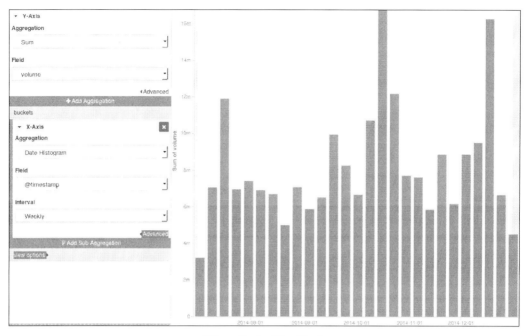

Kibana Vertical Bar Chart

Now, save the visualization using some name for the bar chart, which we will pull into the dashboard later.

Building a Metric

Metric represents one big number that we want to show as something special about data.

We will show the **Highest Volume Traded** in a single day in a six month period using Metric.

Click on **Metric** in the visualization menu, and select **Metric Aggregation** as **Max**, **Field** as **volume**. Click on **Apply** to see the result of visualization on the right as follows:

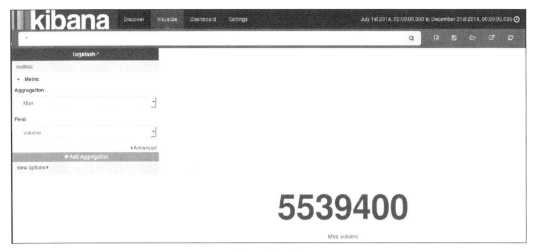

Kibana Metric

Now, save the visualization using some name for the **Metric**, which we will pull into the dashboard later.

Building a data table

Data tables are meant to show detailed breakdowns in a tabular format for results of some composed aggregations.

We will create a data table of **Monthly Average** volume traded over six months.

Select **Data table** from the visualization menu, click on **split rows** and select **Aggregation** as **Average** and **Fields** as **volume**. In the **buckets** section, select **Aggregation** as **Date Histogram**, **Fields** as **@timestamp**, and **Interval** as **Monthly**. Click on **Apply** to see the image as in the following screenshot:

Kibana Data table

Now, save the visualization using some name for the data table, which we will pull into the dashboard later.

After we have built some visualizations, let's build a dashboard that includes these visualizations.

Select the dashboard page link at top of the page, and click on the **Add Visualization** link to select visualizations from your saved visualizations and arrange them.

Building Your First Data Pipeline with ELK

The Dashboard, after including a line chart, bar chart, data table, and Metric, looks like this:

Kibana Dashboard

Now, we can save this dashboard using the save button, and it can be pulled later and shared easily.

Dashboards can be embedded as an IFrame in other systems or can be directly shared as links.

Click on the **share** button to see the options to share:

Kibana Share options

If you have completed everything up to this point, then you have successfully set up your first ELK data pipeline.

Summary

In this chapter, we saw how you can utilize different input, filter, and output plugins in Logstash to gather, parse, and index data to Elasticsearch, and later utilize the Kibana interface to query and visualize over Elasticsearch indexes. We also built some visualizations, and a dashboard using those visualizations. We successfully built our first data pipeline using ELK Stack. In the coming chapters, we will look at individual components in more detail.

3
Collect, Parse and Transform Data with Logstash

By now, we should have a basic understanding of ELK Stack and what role it plays in log analysis or event analysis systems. In *Chapter 2, Building Your First Data Pipeline with ELK*, we built analytics over the GOOG stock price data with the ELK Stack configuration, and also understood role of each component of the stack in the pipeline.

In this chapter, we will get into more detail on Logstash, the most important component of the ELK Stack, and see how Logstash helps collect, parse, and transform any format and any type of data to a common format, which can be used to build a wide variety of analytics systems across many applications.

We saw in *Chapter 1, Introduction to ELK Stack*, the importance of log analysis and problem with log analysis methods. Also, there are a variety of log formats, and date and time formats in logs. Often these logs are customized to each application and require expert knowledge to gather essential information out of them. Now, we will see how Logstash provides us with a variety of plugins that help us overcome all of these problems and build easily-configurable and manageable visualizations on top of it.

In this chapter, while explaining various configurations of Logstash plugins, we assume that you have installed Logstash, as explained in *Chapter 1, Introduction to ELK Stack*, and have the basic configuration set up and running. If you do not, you should get Logstash installed and run a basic `stdin`, `stdout` configuration and then resume this chapter so that you can try out some configuration options based on the explanations.

Configuring Logstash

As we have seen in previous chapters, a general Logstash plugin configuration looks like this:

```
input {

}

filter {

}

output {

}
```

A Logstash configuration consists of a series of `input`, `filter`, and `output` plugins and their corresponding properties. Each plugin plays an important role towards parsing, processing, and finally putting the data in the required format. Input plugins generate the event, filters modify them, and output will ship them to other systems.

Logstash plugins

Logstash plugins

Logstash has a variety of plugins to help integrate it with a variety of input and output sources. Let's explore the various plugins available.

Listing all plugins in Logstash

You can execute the following command to list all available plugins in your installed Logstash version:

```
bin/plugin list
```

Also, you can list all plugins containing a name fragment by executing this command:

```
bin/plugin list <namefragment>
```

To list all plugins for group names, input, output, or filter, we can execute this command:

```
bin/plugin list --group <group name>
bin/plugin list --group output
```

Before exploring various plugin configurations, let's take a look at the data types and conditional expressions used in various Logstash configurations.

Data types for plugin properties

A Logstash plugin requires certain settings or properties to be set. Those properties have certain values that belong to one of the following important data types.

Array

An array is collection of values for a property.

An example can be seen as follows:

```
path => ["value1","value2"]
```

The => sign is the assignment operator that is used for all properties of configuration values in Logstash configuration.

Boolean

A boolean value is either `true` or `false` (without quotes).

An example can be seen as follows:

```
periodic_flush => false
```

Codec

Codec is actually not a data type but a way to encode or decode data at input or output.

An example can be seen as follows:

```
codec => "json"
```

This instance specifies that this codec, at output, will encode all output in JSON format.

Hash

Hash is basically a key value pair collection. It is specified as `"key" => "value"` and multiple values in a collection are separated by a space.

An example can be seen as follows:

```
match => {
"key1" => "value1" "key2" => "value2"}
```

String

String represents a sequence of characters enclosed in quotes.

An example can be seen as follows:

```
value => "Welcome to ELK"
```

Comments

Comments begin with the # character.

An example can be seen as follows:

```
#this represents a comment
```

Field references

Fields can be referred to using [`field_name`] or nested fields using [`level1`][`level2`].

Logstash conditionals

Logstash conditionals are used to filter events or log lines under certain conditions. Conditionals in Logstash are handled like other programming languages and work with `if`, `if else` and `else` statements. Multiple `if else` blocks can be nested.

Syntax for conditionals is as follows:

```
if  <conditional expression1>{
#some statements here.
}
else if   <conditional expression2>{
#some statements here.
}
else{
#some statements here.
}
```

Conditionals work with comparison operators, boolean operators and unary operators:

Comparison operators include:

- **Equality operators**: `==, !=, <, >, <=, >=`
- **Regular expressions**: `=~, !~`
- **Inclusion**: `in, not in`
- Boolean operators include `and, or, nand, xor`
- Unary operators include `!`

Let's take a look at this with an example:

```
filter {
  if [action] == "login" {
    mutate { remove => "password" }
  }
}
```

Multiple expressions can be specified in a single statement using boolean operators.

An example can be seen as follows:

```
output {
  # Send Email on Production Errors
  if [loglevel] == "ERROR" and [deployment] == "production" {
   email{

     }

   }
}
```

Types of Logstash plugins

The following are types of Logstash plugins:

- Input
- Filter
- Output
- Codec

Now let's take a look at some of the most important input, output, filter and codec plugins, which will be useful for building most of the log analysis pipeline use cases.

Input plugins

An input plugin is used to configure a set of events to be fed to Logstash. Some of the most important input plugins are:

file

The `file` plugin is used to stream events and log lines files to Logstash. It automatically detects file rotations, and reads from the point last read by it.

> The Logstash `file` plugin maintains `sincedb` files to track the current positions in files being monitored. By default it writes `sincedb` files at `$HOME/.sincedb*` path. The location and frequency can be altered using `sincedb_path` and `sincedb_write_interval` properties of the plugin.

A most basic file configuration looks like this:

```
input{
file{
path => "/path/to/logfiles"
}
```

The only required configuration property is the *path* to the files. Let's look at how we can make use of some of the configuration properties of the file plugin to read different types of files.

Configuration options

The following configuration options are available for the file input plugin:

add_field

It is used to add a field to incoming events, its value type is `Hash`, and default value is `{}`.

Let's take the following instance as an example:

```
add_field => { "input_time" => "%{@timestamp}" }
```

codec

It is used to specify a codec, which can decode a specific type of input.

For example: `codec => "json"` is used to decode the `json` type of input.

The default value of codec is `"plain"`.

delimiter

It is used to specify a delimiter, which identifies separate lines. By default, it is `"\n"`.

exclude

To exclude certain types of files from the input path, the data type is `array`.

Let's take the following instance as an example:

```
path =>["/app/packtpub/logs/*"]
exclude => "*.gz"
```

This will exclude all gzip files from input.

path

This is the only required configuration for the file plugin. It specifies an array of path locations from where to read logs and events.

sincedb_path

It specifies the location where to write the `sincedb` files, which keeps track of the current position of files being monitored. The default is `$HOME/.sincedb*`

sincedb_write_interval

It specifies how often (number in seconds), the `sincedb` files that keep track of the current position of monitored files, are to be written. The default is 15 seconds.

start_position

It has two values: `"beginning"` and `"end"`. It specifies where to start reading incoming files from. The default value is `"end"`, as in most situations this is used for live streaming data. Although, if you are working on old data, it can be set to `"beginning"`.

> This option has impact only when a file is being read for the first time, called `"first contact"`, as it maintains the location in the `"sincedb"` location. So for the next setting, this option has no impact unless you decide to remove the `sincedb` files.

tags

It specifies the array of tags that can be added to incoming events. Adding tags to your incoming events helps with processing later, when using conditionals. It is often helpful to tag certain data as `"processed"` and use those tags to decide a future course of action.

For example, if we specify `"processed"` in tags:

```
tags =>["processed"]
```

In filter, we can check in conditionals:

```
filter{
if  "processed" in tags[]{

}
}
```

type

The `type` option is really helpful to process the different type of incoming streams using Logstash. You can configure multiple input paths for different type of events, just give a `type` name, and then you can filter them separately and process.

Let's take the following instance as an example:

```
input {
file{
path => ["var/log/syslog/*"]
type => "syslog"
}
file{
path => ["var/log/apache/*"]
type => "apache"
}
}
```

In `filter`, we can filter based on type:

```
filter {
if [type] == "syslog" {
grok {

}

}
if [type] == "apache" {
grok {

}
}
}
```

As in the preceding example, we have configured a separate type for incoming files; `"syslog"` and `"apache"`. Later in filtering the stream, we can specify conditionals to filter based on this type.

stdin

The `stdin` plugin is used to stream events and log lines from standard input.

A basic configuration for `stdin` looks like this:

```
stdin {

}
```

When we configure `stdin` like this, whatever we type in the console will go as input to the Logstash event pipeline. This is mostly used as the first level of testing of configuration before plugging in the actual file or event input.

Configuration options

The following configuration options are available for the `stdin` input plugin:

add_field

The `add_field` configuration for `stdin` is the same as `add_field` in the `file` input plugin and is used for similar purposes.

codec

It is used to decode incoming data before passing it on to the data pipeline. The default value is `"line"`.

tags

The `tags` configuration for `stdin` is the same as `tags` in the `file` input plugin and is used for similar purposes.

type

The `type` configuration for `stdin` is the same as `type` in the `file` input plugin and is used for similar purposes.

twitter

You may need to analyze a Twitter stream based on a topic of interest for various purposes, such as sentiment analysis, trending topics analysis, and so on. The `twitter` plugin is helpful to read events from the Twitter streaming API. This requires a consumer key, consumer secret, keyword, oauth token, and oauth token secret to work.

These details can be obtained by registering an application on the Twitter developer API page (https://dev.twitter.com/apps/new):

```
twitter {
    consumer_key => "your consumer key here"
    keywords => "keywords which you want to filter on streams"
    consumer_secret => "your consumer secret here"
    oauth_token => "your oauth token here"
    oauth_token_secret => "your oauth token secret here"
}
```

Configuration options

The following configuration options are available for the `twitter` input plugin:

add_field

The `add_field` configuration for the `twitter` plugin is the same as `add_field` in the `file` input plugin and is used for similar purposes.

codec

The `codec` configuration for `twitter` is the same as the `codec` plugin in the `file` input plugin and is used for similar purposes.

consumer_key

This is a required configuration with no default value. Its value can be obtained from the Twitter app registration page. Its value is the `String` type.

consumer_secret

The same as `consumer_key`, its value can be obtained from the Twitter dev app registration.

full_tweet

This is a boolean configuration with the default value; `false`. It specifies whether to record a full tweet object obtained from the Twitter streaming API.

keywords

This is an `array` type required configuration, with no default value. It specifies a set of `keywords` to track from the Twitter stream.

An example can be seen as follows:

```
keywords    => ["elk","packtpub"]
```

oauth_token

The `oauth_token` option is also obtained from the Twitter dev API page.

> After you get your consumer key and consumer secret, click on **Create My Access Token** to create your oauth token and oauth token secret.

oauth_token_secret

The `oauth_token_secret` option is obtained from the Twitter dev API page.

tags

The `tags` configuration for the `twitter` input plugin is the same as `tags` in the `file` input plugin and is used for similar purposes.

type

`type` configuration for `twitter` input plugins is the same as `type` in the `file` input plugin and is used for similar purposes.

lumberjack

The `lumberjack` plugin is useful to receive events via the `lumberjack` protocol that is used in Logstash forwarder.

The basic required configuration option for the `lumberjack` plugin looks like this:

```
lumberjack {
    port =>
    ssl_certificate =>
    ssl_key =>
}
```

> Lumberjack or Logstash forwarder is a light weight log shipper used to ship log events from source systems. Logstash is quite a memory consuming process, so installing it on every node from where you want to ship data is not recommended. Logstash forwarder is a light weight version of Logstash, which provides low latency, secure and reliable transfer, and provides low resource usage.
>
> More details about Lumberjack or Logstash forwarder can be found from here:
>
> https://github.com/elastic/logstash-forwarder

Configuration options

The following configuration options are available for the `lumberjack` input plugin:

add_field

The `add_field` configuration for the `lumberjack` plugin is the same as `add_field` in the `file` input plugin and is used for similar purposes.

codec

The `codec` configuration for the `lumberjack` plugin is the same as the `codec` plugin in the `file` input plugin and is used for similar purposes.

host

It specifies the host on which to listen to. The default value: `"0.0.0.0"`.

port

This is a number type required configuration and it specifies the port to listen to. There is no default value.

ssl_certificate

It specifies the path to the SSL certificate to be used for the connection. It is a required setting.

An example is as follows:

```
ssl_certificate => "/etc/ssl/logstash.pub"
```

ssl_key

It specifies the path to the SSL key that has to be used for the connection. It is also a required setting.

An example is as follows:

```
ssl_key => "/etc/ssl/logstash.key"
```

ssl_key_passphrase

It specifies the SSL key passphrase that has to be used for the connection.

tags

The `tags` configuration for the `lumberjack` input plugin is the same as `tags` in the `file` input plugin and is used for similar purposes.

type

The `type` configuration for the `lumberjack` input plugins is the same as `type` in the `file` input plugin and is used for similar purposes.

redis

The `redis` plugin is used to read events and logs from the `redis` instance.

> Redis is often used in ELK Stack as a broker for incoming log data from the Logstash forwarder, which helps to queue data until the time the indexer is ready to ingest logs. This helps to keep the system in check under heavy load.

The basic configuration of the `redis` input plugin looks like this:

```
redis {
}
```

Configuration options

The following configuration options are available for the `redis` input plugin:

add_field

The `add_field` configuration for `redis` is the same as `add_field` in the `file` input plugin and is used for similar purposes.

codec

The `codec` configuration for `redis` is the same as `codec` in the `file` input plugin and is used for similar purposes.

data_type

The `data_type` option can have a value as either `"list"`, `"channel"` or `"pattern_channel"`.

From the Logstash documentation for the `redis` plugin (https://www.elastic.co/guide/en/logstash/current/plugins-inputs-redis.html):

> "If `redis_type` is `list`, then we will BLPOP the key. If `redis_type` is `channel`, then we will SUBSCRIBE to the key. If `redis_type` is `pattern_channel`, then we will PSUBSCRIBE to the key."

While using `redis` on the consumer and publisher side, `key` and `data_type` should be the same on both sides.

host

It specifies the hostname of the `redis` server. The default value is `"127.0.0.1"`.

key

It specifies the key for redis; `"list"` or `"channel"`.

password

It is a `password` type configuration that specifies the password to be used for connection.

port

It specifies the port on which the `redis` instance is running. The default is `6379`.

An extensive list and latest documentation on all available Logstash input plugins is available at https://www.elastic.co/guide/en/logstash/current/input-plugins.html.

Now that we have seen some of the most important input plugins for Logstash, let's have a look at some output plugins.

Output plugins

Logstash provides a wide variety of output plugins that help integrate incoming events with almost any type of destination. Let's look at some of the most used output plugins in detail.

csv

The `csv` plugin is used to write a CSV file as output, specifying the fields in `csv` and the path of the file.

The basic configuration of the `csv` output plugin looks like this:

```
csv {
    fields => ["date","open_price","close_price"]
    path => "/path/to/file.csv"
}
```

Configuration options

The following are the configuration options available for the `csv` plugin:

codec

It is used to encode the data before it goes out of Logstash. The default value is `"plain"`, which will output data as it is.

csv_options

The `csv_options` option is used to specify advanced options for the `csv` output. It includes changing the default column and row separator.

An example is as follows:

```
csv_options => {"col_sep" => "\t" "row_sep" => "\r\n"}
```

fields

The `fields` setting is a required setting that is used to specify the fields for the output CSV file. It is specified as an array of field names and written in the same order as in the array. There is no default value for this setting.

gzip

The `gzip` setting is a boolean type of setting that specifies whether to output as a gzip compressed format or not. The default is `false`.

path

The `path` setting is a required setting and is used to specify the path to the CSV file.

file

The `file` output plugin, just like the `file` input plugin, will be used to write events to a file in the file system.

The basic configuration of the `file` output plugin looks like this:

```
file
{
path = > "path/to/file"
}
```

Configuration options

The available configuration options are:

- `codec`
- `gzip`
- `max_size`
- `path`

Most of these configuration options have been covered earlier and are well understood by their name.

email

The `email` plugin is a very important output plugin as it is very useful to send e-mails for certain events and failure scenarios.

The basic required configuration looks like this:

```
email {
    to => "abc@example.com"
}
```

Configuration options

The following configuration options are available for the `email` plugin:

attachments

The `attachments` option is an array of file paths to be attached with the e-mail. The default value is `[]`

body

The `body` option specifies the body of the e-mail in plain text format. The default value is `""`.

cc

The `cc` option specifies the list of e-mails to be included as the cc addresses in the e-mail. It accepts multiple e-mail IDs in a comma separated format.

from

The `from` option specifies the e-mail address to be used as the sender address in the e-mail. The default value is `"logstash.alert@nowhere.com"` and must be overridden as per the type of alerts or system.

to

The `to` option is a required setting that specifies the receiver address for the e-mail. It can also be expressed as a string of comma separated e-mail addresses.

htmlbody

The `htmlbody` option specifies the body of the e-mail in HTML format. It includes HTML mark-up tags in the e-mail body.

replyto

The `replyto` option specifies the e-mail address to be used for the `Reply-To` field for the e-mail.

subject

The `subject` option specifies the subject for the e-mail. The default value is `""`.

elasticsearch

The `elasticsearch` plugin is the most important plugin used in ELK Stack, because it is where you will want to write your output to be stored to analyze later in Kibana.

We will take a look at ElasticSearch in more detail in *Chapter 5*, *Why Do We Need Elasticsearch in ELK?*, but let's look at the configuration options for this plugin here:

The basic configuration for the `elasticsearch` plugin looks like this:

```
elasticsearch {
}
```

Configuration options

Some of the most important configuration options are mentioned as follows:

option	data type	required	default value
action	string	N	"index"
bind_host	string	N	
bind_port	number	N	
cacert	a valid system path	N	
cluster	string	N	
document_id	string	N	
document_type	string	N	
host	array	N	
index	string	N	"logstash-%{+YYYY.MM.dd}"
max_retries	number	N	3
node_name	string	N	
password	password	N	
port	string	N	
user	string	N	

ganglia

Ganglia is a monitoring tool that is used to monitor the performance of a cluster of machines in a distributed computing environment. Ganglia makes uses of a daemon called Gmond, which is a small service that is installed on each machine that needs to be monitored.

The `ganglia` output plugin in Logstash is used to send metrics to the `gmond` service based on events in logs.

The basic `ganglia` output plugin configuration looks like this:

```
ganglia {
    metric =>
    value =>
}
```

Configuration options

The following configuration options are available for the `ganglia` plugin

metric

The `metric` option specifies the metric that is to be used for performance monitoring. It can even take values from the event fields.

unit

The `unit` option specifies the unit like kb/s, ms for the metric used.

value

The `value` option specifies the value of metric used.

jira

The `jira` plugin doesn't come by default in Logstash installation but can be easily installed by a plugin `install` command like this:

`bin/plugin install logstash-output-jira`

The `jira` plugin is used to send events to a JIRA instance, which can create JIRA tickets based on certain events in your logs. To use this, the JIRA instance must accept REST API calls, since it internally makes use of JIRA REST API to pass the output events from Logstash to JIRA.

The basic configuration of the `jira` output plugin looks like this:

```
jira {
    issuetypeid =>
    password =>
    priority =>
    projectid =>
    summary =>
    username =>
}
```

Configuration options

The following are the configuration options and their corresponding data types available for the `jira` plugin:

Option	Data type	Required
`assignee`	string	N
`issuetypeid`	string	Y
`password`	string	Y
`priority`	string	Y
`projectid`	string	Y
`reporter`	string	N
`summary`	string	Y
`username`	string	Y

kafka

As explained on the Hortonworks Kafka page (`http://hortonworks.com/hadoop/kafka/`):

> "Apache™ Kafka is a fast, scalable, durable, and fault-tolerant publish-subscribe messaging system."

The `kafka` output plugin is used to write certain events to a topic on `kafka`. It uses the Kafka Producer API to write messages to a topic on the broker.

The basic `kafka` configuration looks like this:

```
kafka {
    topic_id =>
}
```

Configuration options

There are many `kafka` specific configuration options that can be obtained from official documentation, but the only required configuration is `topic_id`.

topic_id

The `topic_id` option defines the topic to send messages to.

lumberjack

The `lumberjack` plugin is used to write output to a Logstash forwarder or lumberjack.

The basic configuration for the `lumberjack` plugin looks like this:

```
lumberjack {
    hosts =>
    port =>
    ssl_certificate =>
}
```

Configuration options

The following configuration options are available for the `lumberjack` plugin:

hosts

The `hosts` option specifies the list of addresses where `lumberjack` can send messages to.

port

The `port` option specifies the port to connect to the `lumberjack` communication.

ssl_certificate

It specifies the path to `ssl_certificate` to be used for communication.

redis

The `redis` plugin is used to send events to a `redis` instance.

Configuration options

Configuration options are similar to the ones defined for the `redis` input plugin.

rabbitmq

RabbitMQ is an open source message broker software (sometimes called message-oriented middleware) that implements the **Advanced Message Queuing Protocol** (**AMQP**). More information is available in the official documentation at http://www.rabbitmq.com.

In RabbitMQ, the producer always sends messages to an exchange, and the exchange decides what to do with the messages. There are various exchange types that defines a further course of action for the messages, namely `direct`, `topic`, `headers` and `fanout`.

The `rabbitmq` plugin pushes the events from logs to the RabbitMQ exchange.

The basic configuration of the `rabbitmq` plugin looks like this:

```
rabbitmq {
    exchange =>
    exchange_type =>
    host =>
}
```

stdout

The `stdout` plugin writes the output events to the console. It is used to debug the configuration to test the event output from Logstash before integrating with other systems.

The basic configuration looks like this:

```
output {
  stdout {}
}
```

mongodb

MongoDB is a document-oriented NoSQL database, which stores data as JSON documents.

Like the `jira` plugin, this is also a community maintained plugin and doesn't ship with Logstash. It can be easily installed using the following plugin `install` command:

`bin/plugin install logstash-output-mongodb`

The basic configuration for the `mongodb` output plugin is:

```
mongodb {
    collection =>
    database =>
    uri =>
}
```

Configuration options

The following configuration options are available for the `mongodb` plugin:

collection

The `collection` option specifies which `mongodb` collection has to be used to write data.

database

The `database` option specifies the `mongodb` database to be used to store the data.

uri

The `uri` option specifies the connection string to be used to connect to `mongodb`.

An extensive list and latest documentation on all available Logstash output plugins is available at https://www.elastic.co/guide/en/logstash/current/output-plugins.html.

Filter plugins

Filter plugins are used to do intermediate processing on events read from an input plugin and before passing them as output via an output plugin. They are often used to identify the fields in input events, and to conditionally process certain parts of input events.

Let's take a look at some of the most important filter plugins.

csv

The `csv` filter is used to parse the data from an incoming CSV file and assign values to fields.

Configuration options

Configuration options for the `csv` filter plugin were covered in an example in *Chapter 2, Building Your First Data Pipeline with ELK*.

date

In ELK, it is very important to assign the correct timestamp to an event so that it can be analyzed on the `time` filter in Kibana. The `date` filter is meant to assign the appropriate timestamp based on fields in logs, or events, and assign a proper format to the timestamp.

If the `date` filter is not set, Logstash will assign a timestamp as the first time it sees the event or when the file is read.

The basic configuration of the `date` filter looks like this:

```
date {
}
```

Configuration options

Configuration options for the `date` filter are already covered in an example in *Chapter 2, Building Your First Data Pipeline with ELK*.

drop

The `drop` filter is used to drop everything that matches the conditionals for this filter.

Let's take the following instance as an example:

```
filter {
if [fieldname == "test"] {
drop {
}
}
}
```

The preceding filter will cause all events having the `test` fieldname to be dropped. This is very helpful to filter out non useful information out of the incoming events.

Configuration options

The following configuration options are present for this filter:

- `add_field`
- `add_tag`
- `remove_field`
- `remove_tag`

geoip

The `geoip` filter is used to add the geographical location of the IP address present in the incoming event. It fetches this information from the Maxmind database.

> Maxmind is a company that specializes in products built to get useful information from IP addresses. GeoIP is their IP intelligence product that is used to trace the location of an IP address. All Logstash releases have a Maxmind's GeoLite city database shipped with them. It is also available at http://dev.maxmind.com/geoip/legacy/geolite/.

The basic configuration of the `geoip` filter looks like this:

```
geoip {
    source =>
}
```

Configuration options

The following configuration option is available for the `geoip` plugin.

source

The `source` option is a required setting that is of the `string` type. It is used to specify an IP address or a hostname that has to be mapped via the `geoip` service. Any field from events that contains the IP address or hostname can be provided, and if the field is of the `array` type, only the first value is taken.

grok

The `grok` option is by far the most popular and most powerful plugin that Logstash has. It can parse any unstructured log event and convert it into a structured set of fields that can be processed further and used in analysis.

It is used to parse any type of logs, whether it be apache logs, mysql logs, custom application logs, or just any unstructured text in events.

Logstash, by default, comes with a set of `grok` patterns that can be directly used to tag certain types of fields, and custom regular expressions are also supported.

All available `grok` patterns are available at:

https://github.com/logstash-plugins/logstash-patterns-core/tree/master/patterns

Some examples of the `grok` patterns are as follows:

```
HOSTNAME \b(?:[0-9A-Za-z][0-9A-Za-z]{0,62})(?:\.(?:[0-9A-Za-z][0-9A-Za-z]{0,62}))*(\.?|\b)
DAY (?:Mon(?:day)?|Tue(?:sday)?|Wed(?:nesday)?|Thu(?:rsday)?|Fri(?:day)?|Sat(?:urday)?|Sun(?:day)?)
YEAR (?>\d\d){1,2}
HOUR (?:2[0123]|[01]?[0-9])
MINUTE (?:[0-5][0-9])
```

The preceding `grok` patterns can be directly used to tag fields of those types with an operator like this:

```
%{HOSTNAME:host_name}
```

Here, `host_name` is the field name that we want to assign to the part of the log event that represents the hostname like `string`.

Let's try to look at `grok` in more detail:

The `grok` patterns in logs are represented by this general format:
`%{SYNTAX:SEMANTIC}`

Here, `SYNTAX` is the name of the pattern that matches the text in log, and `SEMANTIC` is the field name that we want to assign to that pattern.

Let's take the following instance as an example:

Let's say you want to represent the number of bytes transferred in one event:

```
%{NUMBER:bytes_transferred}
```

Here, `bytes_transferred` will refer to the actual value of bytes transferred in the log event.

Let's take a look at how we can represent a line from HTTP logs:

```
54.3.245.1 GET /index.html 14562 0.056
```

The `grok` pattern would be represented as:

```
%{IP:client_ip} %{WORD: request_method } %{URIPATHPARAM:uri_path} %{NUMBER:bytes_transferred} %{NUMBER:duration}
```

The basic `grok` configuration for the preceding event will look like this:

```
filter{
grok{
match => { "message" =>"%{IP:client_ip} %{WORD:request_method} %{URIPATHPARAM:uri_path} %{NUMBER:bytes_transferred} %{NUMBER:duration}"}
}
}
```

After being processed with this `grok` filter, we can see the following fields added to the event with the values:

- `client_ip : 54.3.245.1`
- `request_method : GET`
- `uri_path :/index.html`
- `bytes_transferred :14562`
- `duration :0.056`

Custom grok patterns

Custom `grok` patterns can be created based on a regular expression if not found in the list of `grok` patterns available.

These URLs are useful to design and test `grok` patterns for the matching text as required:

`http://grokdebug.herokuapp.com` and `http://grokconstructor.appspot.com/`

mutate

The `mutate` filter is an important filter plugin that helps rename, remove, replace, and modify fields in an incoming event. It is also specially used to convert the data type of fields, merge two fields, and convert text from lower case to upper case and vice versa.

The basic configuration of the `mutate` filter looks like this:

```
filter {
mutate {
}
}
```

Configuration options

There are various configuration options for `mutate` and most of them are understood by the name:

Option	Data type	Required	Default value
add_field	hash	N	{}
add_tag	array	N	[]
convert	hash	N	
join	hash	N	
lowercase	array	N	
merge	hash	N	
remove_field	array	N	[]
remove_tag	array	N	[]
rename	hash	N	
replace	hash	N	
split	hash	N	
strip	array	N	
update	hash	N	
uppercase	array	N	

sleep

The `sleep` option is used to put Logstash in sleep mode for the amount of time specified. We can also specify the frequency of sleep intervals based on the number of events.

Let's take the following instance as an example:

If we want to let Logstash sleep for `1` sec for every fifth event processed, we can configure it like this:

```
filter {
  sleep {
    time => "1"    # Sleep 1 second
    every => 5     # Sleep on every 5th event.
  }
}
```

An extensive list and the latest documentation on all available Logstash filter plugins is available at https://www.elastic.co/guide/en/logstash/current/filter-plugins.html.

Codec plugins

Codec plugins are used to encode or decode incoming or outgoing events from Logstash. They act as stream filters in input and output plugins.

Some of the most important codec plugins are:

- avro
- json
- line
- multiline
- plain
- rubydebug
- spool

Let's take a look at some details about some of the most commonly used ones.

json

If your input event or output event consists of full JSON documents, then the `json` codec plugin is helpful. It can be defined as:

```
input{
  stdin{
```

```
codec => json{
}
}
}
```

Or it can be simply defined as:

```
input{
stdin{
codec => "json"
}
}
```

line

The `line` codec is used to read each line in an input as an event or to decode each outgoing event as a line. It can be defined as:

```
input{
stdin{
codec => line{
}
}
}
```

Or it can be simply defined as:

```
input{
stdin{
codec => "line"
}
}
```

multiline

The `multiline` codec is very helpful for certain types of events where you like to take more than one line as one event. This is really helpful in cases such as Java Exceptions or stack traces.

For example, the following configuration can take a full stack trace as one event:

```
input {
  file {
    path => "/var/log/someapp.log"
    codec => multiline {
      pattern => "^%{TIMESTAMP_ISO8601} "
      negate => true
```

```
            what => previous
        }
    }
}
```

This will take all lines that don't start with a timestamp as a part of the previous line and consider everything as a single event.

plain

The `plain` plugin is used to specify that there is no encoding or decoding required for events as it will be taken care of by corresponding input or output plugin types itself. For many plugins, such as `redis`, `mongodb` and so on, this is the default codec type.

rubydebug

The `rubydebug` plugin is used only with output event data, and it prints output event data using the Ruby Awesome Print library.

An extensive list and latest documentation on all available Logstash codec plugins is available at https://www.elastic.co/guide/en/logstash/current/codec-plugins.html.

Summary

In this chapter, we saw various configuration options for Logstash plugins, namely input, filter, output and codec plugins, and how these various plugins available with Logstash can be used to help collect, parse, and transform various types of events generated from multiple types of sources.

In the next chapter, we will see how we can create our own plugin to cater to the needs for custom format or to handle special type of events not handled through existing plugins.

4
Creating Custom Logstash Plugins

In the previous chapter, we saw how we could use the various available Logstash plugins for various types of input, processing and output requirements. But, if you need to create your own plugins for some custom needs, we can do that too. In this chapter, we will look at some of the following advanced concepts for Logstash plugins:

- Plugin management in Logstash.
- Downloading and installing community managed plugins.
- Creating custom Logstash plugins.

Logstash plugin management

From 1.5.0+ version onwards, Logstash plugins are separated from the core package and are maintained as separate self-contained packages using **RubyGems**. It facilitates the release of plugin updates separately from Logstash releases. Also, it reduces the overall size of the Logstash core package.

Logstash plugins are developed in Ruby.

 RubyGems is a package manager for the Ruby programming language that provides a standard format to distribute Ruby programs and libraries (in a self-contained format called a "gem"). It is a tool designed to easily manage the installation of gems, and a server to distribute them.

Creating Custom Logstash Plugins

Logstash core plugins and community plugins are published on `https://rubygems.org/`, and can be easily downloaded from here and installed.

All Logstash plugins are stored in GitHub at the following repository:

`https://github.com/logstash-plugins`

Plugin lifecycle management

Logstash plugin management is done through the install script that is shipped with the Logstash installation:

`$LOGSTASH_HOME/bin/plugin`

Installing a plugin

To install a plugin, we can issue the following command:

`$bin/plugin install <plug_in_name>`

`plug_in_name` is the name of the plugin as mentioned in the gem name in `https://rubygems.org/` or in the Logstash plugin repository.

Let's take the following command as an example:

`$bin/plugin install logstash-input-rabbitmq`

The preceding command will install the `rabbitmq` input plugin to the Logstash installation. You can also specify the `--version` parameter to install a specific version of the plugin.

> RabbitMQ (`https://www.rabbitmq.com`) is a messaging broker, a common platform to send and receive messages, which holds messages until received.

Also, plugins downloaded from `https://rubygems.org/` can be installed using the file path as follows:

`$bin/plugin install path/to/logstash-input-rabbitmq-0.1.0.gem`

You can also explore all available Logstash plugins by searching https://rubygems.org/ for "logstash".

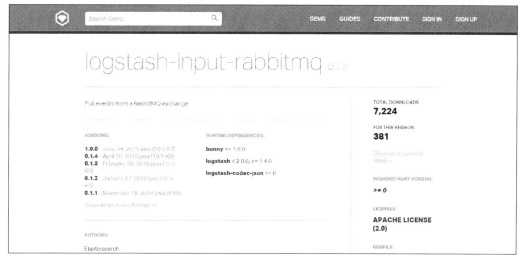

Plugin download page at https://rubygems.org/

Updating a plugin

To update a previously installed plugin, we can issue the command:

`$bin/plugin update <plug_in_name>`

Let's take the following command as an example:

`$bin/plugin update logstash-input-rabbitmq`

The preceding command will update the `logstash-input-rabbitmq` plugin to the latest version. Please make sure to test the updates well before moving on to the production environment.

Uninstalling a plugin

To uninstall a plugin, we can issue the following command:

`$bin/plugin uninstall <plug_in_name>`

Let's take the following command as an example:

`$bin/plugin uninstall logstash-input-rabbitmq`

Structure of a Logstash plugin

The preceding command will uninstall the `logstash-input-rabbitmq` plugin from the Logstash installation.

Structure of a Logstash plugin

As already mentioned in Logstash plugin management, Logstash plugins are self-contained RubyGems.

> This section requires a little bit knowledge of the Ruby programming language. If you are looking for a quick overview, you can look at the official Ruby tutorial here: https://www.ruby-lang.org/en/documentation/quickstart/

As extensive knowledge of Ruby is not expected from the readers, we will take a look at some simple illustrations of how a plugin works, and how we can design one simple plugin on our own. We will also cover some details of how the plugins are bundled to gems. More information is available at https://www.elastic.co/guide/en/logstash/current/contributing-to-logstash.html.

Let's look at the structure of a `drop filter` plugin, which is used to drop certain events on certain conditions (https://github.com/logstash-plugins/logstash-filter-drop):

```
# encoding: utf-8
require "logstash/filters/base"
require "logstash/namespace"

# Drop filter.
#
# Drops everything that gets to this filter.
#
# This is best used in combination with conditionals, for example:
# [source,ruby]
#     filter {
#        if [loglevel] == "debug" {
#          drop { }
#        }
#     }
#
# The above will only pass events to the drop filter if the loglevel
field is
# `debug`. This will cause all events matching to be dropped.
class LogStash::Filters::Drop < LogStash::Filters::Base
```

```
    config_name "drop"
    # Drop all the events within a pre-configured percentage.
    #
    # This is useful if you just need a percentage but not the whole.
    #
    # Example, to only drop around 40% of the events that have the field
loglevel wiht value "debug".
    #
    #     filter {
    #       if [loglevel] == "debug" {
    #         drop {
    #           percentage => 40
    #         }
    #       }
    #     }
    config :percentage, :validate => :number, :default => 100
    public
    def register
      # nothing to do.
    end

    public
    def filter(event)
      event.cancel if (@percentage == 100 || rand < (@percentage /
100.0))
    end # def filter
end # class LogStash::Filters::Drop
```

Now, let's try to break it down and look at each component of a plugin.

Required dependencies

The first requirement actually loads the `logstash/namespace.rb` file, which defines the modules namespaces for the input, filter, output, and codec plugins.

```
require "logstash/namespace"
```

Then, since this is a `filter` plugin, we will add dependency for the filter:

```
require "logstash/filters/base"
```

Similarly, for input, we can add `/logstash/inputs/base`, and for output `/logstash/outputs/base`.

Class declaration

Next, for each plugin, we need to declare a class for it, and it should include the required `Base` class for the `filter` plugin as well:

    class LogStash::Filters::Drop < LogStash::Filters::Base

So, as we have a `drop` filter, we will declare a class by its name.

Configuration name

Next, we need to specify the name of the plugin that will be used in the Logstash configuration. We do this by declaring `config_name`:

    config_name "drop"

So, it will be used like this:

    filter {
    drop {
    }
    }

Configuration options setting

We can define as many configuration options as we need for the plugin with this setting. It allows us to set the name of the option, its data type and default value, and specify if it is required:

    config :percentage, :validate => :number, :default => 100

The following are the configurations:

- `:validate`: It allows us to enforce the data type for the option. The possible values can be `:string`, `:number`, `:array`, `:hash`, `:boolean`, and so on.

    For the `drop` filter, we have a specified validation for the `percentage` option to be of type `:number`.

- `:default`: It allows us to specify the default value for the option.

    For the `drop` filter, we have specified the value `100` as the default for the option named `percentage`.

- `:required`: It takes a boolean value as either `true` or `false` and specifies whether the option is required or not.

Plugin methods

Every plugin type (input, filter, output, and codec) has certain methods that they need to implement to initialize instance variables and to execute actual operations inside the plugin.

Plugin type	Methods
Input plugin	register and run(queue)
Filter plugin	register and filter(event)
Output plugin	register and receive
Codec plugin	register, encode, decode

Input plugin

For the input plugin, the register and run(queue) methods need to be implemented.

The register method is used to initialize the instance variables if any.

The run method converts the stream of incoming messages to events that can be further transformed:

```
public
def run(queue)
  #Code which converts messages to event here.
end # def run
```

Filter plugin

For the filter plugin, the register and filter (event) methods need to be implemented:

```
public
def register
  # nothing to do.
end
```

The register method is used to initialize instance variables if any. For drop filter, we don't need to use any instance variables, so we will keep it empty.

```
public
def filter(event)
  event.cancel if (@percentage == 100 || rand < (@percentage / 100.0))
  end # def filter
```

The `filter` method does the actual work of filtering the events. Inside the `filter` method, we can use the `config` parameters set using an `'@'` prefix, and we have event properties available using event `hashmap`.

For example, we can get the message as `event["message"]`.

Also, certain operations, such as `event.cancel`, are also available.

For example, in the `drop` filter, we will use `event.cancel` to cancel the event matching this filter.

Output plugin

For the output plugin, the `register` and `receive` methods need to be implemented.

The `register` method is used to initialize the instance variables, if any.

The `receive` method processes the events before sending them to the output destination, depending on the type of plugin.

```
public
def receive(event)
end # def event
```

Codec plugin

The codec plugin is used with input and output plugins to decode an input event or encoding an outgoing event.

For the codec plugin, `register`, `encode` or `decode` methods need to be implemented.

The `register` method is used to initialize instance variables, if any.

The `encode` method is used to encode an event to another format.

An example is the `json` codec plugin, which transforms the events to `json` format:

```
public
  def encode(event)
    @on_event.call(event, event.to_json)
  end
```

The `decode` method decodes the incoming data to an event. This method needs a `yield` statement to return decoded events to a pipeline.

For example, in the `spool` codec plugin, to send the messages to some buffer:

```
  public
  def decode(data)
    data.each do |event|
      yield event
    end
  end
```

Writing a Logstash filter plugin

Now, we have seen the structure of a plugin, which gives us a head start on developing one of our own.

In this section, we will demonstrate building a simple filter plugin using the knowledge of the structure of a plugin that we acquired in the previous section.

In this illustration, we will assume that we have a sequence of numbers coming in a stream, and we want to denote them with certain currencies based on a name, which we will pass as a parameter to the plugin. Let's see what our simple `currency` filter plugin looks like:

```
# Adds a Currency Symbol to price field
#
#filter {
#    currency{
#        name => "$"
#    }
#}

require "logstash/filters/base"
require "logstash/namespace"

class LogStash::Filters::Currency < LogStash::Filters::Base

config_name "currency"

config :name, :validate => :string, :default => "$"

public
def register
#do nothing
end

public
```

```
    def filter(event)
        if @name
            msg = @name + event["message"]
            event["message"] = msg
        end
    end

end
```

Let's take a look at how the preceding filter is structured.

First, we have added the dependency for the required classes:

```
require "logstash/filters/base"
require "logstash/namespace"
```

Then, we have defined a class for the filter:

```
class LogStash::Filters::Currency < LogStash::Filters::Base
```

Next, we named the filter using `config_name`:

```
config_name "currency"
```

Now, we will specify the configuration option needed for this filter as we need the name of the currency to be specified so we can add it to the message. We will define it as follows:

```
config :name, :validate => :string, :default => "$"
```

Then, as we don't need to set any instance variables, we have provided an empty `register` method for the filter:

```
public
def register
#do nothing
end
```

Next, we will implement the `filter` method for the `filter` plugin, which will take an event and apply the logic for `currency`:

```
public
def filter(event)
    if @name
        msg = @name + event["message"]
        event["message"] = msg
    end
end
```

Here, we will first check the value of the `name` filter and if it is present, we will add the value in front of the message; otherwise, the filter will be ignored.

Now, `filter` can be used as follows:

```
filter {
    currency{
        name => "$"
    }
}
```

Let's say if your input is `200` after using this filter, each incoming event's output from the Logstash filter plugin will look like this:

```
{

"@timestamp" => "2015-06-21T14:21:54.123Z",
"message" => "$200",
}
```

Building the plugin

Now, when we have successfully created a plugin, save it as `currency.rb` in the following folder structure:

```
logstash-filter-currency
└──lib
│    └──logstash
│           └──filters
│    └──currency.rb
Gemfile
logstash-filter-currency.gemspec
```

Now, to create the RubyGem for the folder, we will require a gemfile and a gemspec file present in the `logstash-filter-currency` top folder.

> **gemfile**: A gemfile describes the `gem` dependencies required to execute associated Ruby code.
>
> **gemspec file**: A gemspec file defines the specification of the RubyGem that will be built.

Creating Custom Logstash Plugins

Let's add some specifications to our gemspec file:

```
Gem::Specification.new do |s|
  s.name = 'logstash-filter-currency'
  s.version         = '0.1.0'
  s.licenses = ['Apache License (2.0)']
  s.summary = "This plugin adds a currency name before message."
  s.description = "This plugin is used to add core logstash available plugin, to define a new functionality of adding currency symbols for certain messages"
  s.authors = ["Saurabh Chhajed"]
  s.email = 'saurabh.chhajed@gmail.com'
  s.homepage = "http://saurzcode.in"
  s.require_paths = ["lib"]

  # Files
  s.files = ["lib/logstash/filters/currency.rb"]


  # Special flag to let us know this is actually a logstash plugin
  s.metadata = { "logstash_plugin" => "true", "logstash_group" => "filter" }

  # Gem dependencies
  s.add_runtime_dependency "logstash-core", '>= 1.4.0', '< 2.0.0'
  s.add_development_dependency 'logstash-devutils'
end
```

Save this `logstash-filter-currency.gemspec` file under the root plugin folder as shown in the folder structure.

It requires Ruby gem bundlers to build gems based on these files, which can be easily installed on the Ruby console using:

`$ gem install bundler`

More information on using bundler can be found at `http://bundler.io/`.

Now, we can build the gem using:

`$gem build logstash-filter-currency.gemspec`

That's it! This should have created a gem named `logstash-filter-currency-0.1.0.gem` in the same folder.

It can be installed to the existing Logstash installation easily:

```
$ bin/plugin install /path/to/ logstash-filter-currency-0.1.0.gem
```

If successful, you should see the plugin listed in:

```
$bin/plugin list
```

We can quickly test the plugin using the `logstash -e` flag option:

```
bin/logstash -e 'input { stdin{} } filter { currency { name => "$" } } output {stdout { codec => rubydebug }}'
```

For the `filter` plugin, any number that we write will be appended by the $ currency name:

```
200
{
    "message" => "$200"
    "@version" => "1",
    "@timestamp" => "2015-06-27T19:17:20.230Z",
    "host" => "saurzcode"
}
```

We can see $ being added to the number `200` that we entered as standard input.

Now, we have successfully created our first Logstash filter plugin and tested it successfully.

Similarly, plugins of input and output types can be created and deployed.

Summary

In this chapter, we saw how to create a custom Logstash plugin for requirements that were not fulfilled through the available plugins. By now, we've seen all the different types of features and plugins supported by Logstash and how we can extend Logstash for varying needs of input and output sources.

Next, we will take a detailed look at the features of the other two components of ELK stack—Elasticsearch, and Kibana.

5
Why Do We Need Elasticsearch in ELK?

In this chapter, we will look at the role of Elasticsearch in ELK Stack. It covers the features of Elasticsearch, and why it is such a wonderful technology to enable fast search responses for real time analytics. In the end, we will also briefly look at some of the plugins available for Elasticsearch, which make our lives much easier while dealing with the Elasticsearch cluster.

Why Elasticsearch?

Elasticsearch is a search and analytics engine that enables fast and scalable searches in a distributed environment. As we have already covered in *Chapter 1, Introduction to ELK Stack*, some of the biggest distributed architectures, such as GitHub, StackOverflow, and Wikipedia, make use of the Elasticsearch full-text search, structured search, and analytics capabilities for fast and relevant searches.

Elasticsearch is built on Apache Lucene. The definition of Lucene from its Apache page (`https://lucene.apache.org`) is:

> "Apache LuceneTM is a high-performance, full-featured text search engine library written entirely in Java. It is a technology suitable for nearly any application that requires full-text search, especially cross-platform"

Elasticsearch hides the complexity behind Lucene by providing a powerful RESTful API built on top of it, which makes querying the indexed data easier, and makes it available to any programming language. It extends the capabilities of Lucene by providing real-time analytics built on structured and unstructured data of petabytes of size distributed across many servers.

Before taking a deep dive into the various APIs that Elasticsearch provides, let's understand some of the basic concepts of Elasticsearch.

Elasticsearch basic concepts

Let's look at some of the basic concepts of Elasticsearch, which explain how it stores the indexed data.

Index

Index in Elasticsearch is a collection of documents that share some common characteristics.

Each index contains multiple types, which in turn contains multiple documents, and each document contains multiple fields. An index consists of multiple JSON documents in Elasticsearch. There can be any number of indices in a cluster in Elasticsearch.

In ELK, when Logstash JSON documents are sent to Elasticsearch, they are sent as the default index pattern `"logstash-%{+YYYY.MM.dd}"`. It partitions indices by day so that it can easily be searched and deleted if required. This pattern can be changed in the Logstash output plugin configuration.

The URL to search and query the indices looks like this:

`http://localhost:9200/[index]/[type]/[operation]`

Document

A document in Elasticsearch is a JSON document stored in an index. Each document has a type and corresponding ID, which represents it uniquely.

For example, a document stored in Elasticsearch would look similar to this:

```
{
  "_index" : "packtpub",
  "_type" : "elk",
  "_id" : "1",
  "_version" : 1,
  "found" : true,
  "_source":{
book_name : "learning elk"
}
}
```

Field

A field is a basic unit inside a document. As in the preceding example, a basic field is a key value pair as follows:

```
book_name : "learning elk"
```

Type

Type is used to provide a logical partition inside the indices. It basically represents a class of similar types of documents. An index can have multiple types and we can define them as per the context.

For example, the index for Facebook can have `post` as one of the index types, `comments` as another.

Mapping

Mapping is used to map each field of the document with its corresponding data type, such as `string`, `integer`, `float`, `double`, `date`, and so on. Elasticsearch creates a mapping for the fields automatically during index creation, and those mappings can be easily queried or modified based on specific types of needs.

Shard

A shard is the actual physical entity where the data for each index is stored. Each index can have a number of primary and replica shards where it stores the data. Shards are distributed among all the nodes in the cluster and can be moved from one node to another in case of node failures or the addition of new nodes.

Primary shard and replica shard

Each document in an Elasticsearch index is stored on one primary shard and a number of replica shards. While indexing, the document is first stored on a primary shard and then on the corresponding replica shard. By default, the number of primary shards for each index is five and can be configured as per our needs.

Replica shards will typically reside on a different node than the primary shard and help in case of failover and load balancing to cater to multiple requests.

Cluster

A cluster is a collection of nodes that stores the indexed data. Elasticsearch provides horizontal scalability with the help of data stored in the cluster. Each cluster is represented by a cluster name, which different nodes join. The cluster name is set by a property called `cluster.name` in the Elasticsearch configuration `elasticsearch.yml`, which defaults to `"elasticsearch"`:

```
cluster.name: elasticsearch
```

Node

A node is a single running instance of Elasticsearch, which belongs to one of the clusters. By default, every node in Elasticsearch joins the cluster named `"elasticsearch"`. Each node can have its own configuration defined in `elasticsearch.yml`, they can have different settings regarding memory and resource allocations.

In Elasticsearch, nodes can play three types of roles:

- **Data node**: Data nodes index documents and perform searches on indexed documents. It is always recommended to add more data nodes in order to increase performance or scale the cluster. A node can be made a data node by setting these properties in the `elasticsearch.yml` configuration for the node:

    ```
    node.master = false
    node.data=true
    ```

- **Master node**: Master nodes are responsible for management of a cluster. For large clusters, it is recommended to have three dedicated master nodes (one primary and two backup), which only act as master nodes and do not store indices or perform searches. A node can be configured to be a dedicated master node with this configuration in `elasticsearch.yml`:

    ```
    node.master =true
    node.data=false
    ```

- **Routing node or load balancer node**: These nodes do not play the role of either a master or data node, but just perform load balancing, or routing of requests for searches, or indexing the document to appropriate nodes. This is useful for high volume searches or index operations. A node can be configured to be a routing node with this configuration in `elasticsearch.yml`:

    ```
    node.master =false
    node.data=false
    ```

Exploring the Elasticsearch API

In ELK, although Logstash and Kibana act as an interface to talk to Elasticsearch indices, it's still necessary to understand how Logstash and Kibana makes use of Elasticsearch RESTful APIs to perform various operations, such as creating and managing indices, storing and retrieving the documents, and forming various types of search queries around the indices. It is also often useful to know how to delete indices.

As we already know, Elasticsearch provides an extensive API to perform various operations. The generic syntax of querying the cluster from the command line is as follows:

```
$curl -X<VERB> '<PROTOCOL>://<HOST>:<PORT>/<PATH>/<OPERATION_NAME>?<QUERY_STRING>' -d '<BODY>'
```

Let's understand various parts of this command:

- `VERB`: This can take values for the request method type: `GET`, `POST`, `PUT`, `DELETE`, `HEAD`.
- `PROTOCOL`: This is either `http` or `https`.
- `HOST`: This is the hostname of the node in the cluster. For local installations, this can be `'localhost'` or `'127.0.0.1'`.
- `PORT`: This is the port on which the Elasticsearch instance is currently running. The default is `9200`.
- `PATH`: This corresponds to the name of the index, type, and ID to be queried, for example: `/index/type/id`.
- `OPERATION_NAME`: This corresponds to the name of the operation to be performed, for example: `_search`, `_count`, and so on.
- `QUERY_STRING`: This is an optional parameter to be specified for query string parameters. For example, `?pretty` for pretty print of JSON documents.
- `BODY`: This makes a request for body text.

Let's take the following command as an example:

```
curl -XGET 'http://localhost:9200/logstash-2014.08.04/_search?pretty'
```

This URL will search in the index named `logstash-2014.08.04`.

For the upcoming sections, it is assumed that you have already installed Elasticsearch as explained in *Chapter 1, Introduction to ELK Stack*, and it is running.

In this section, we will make use of the indices created in our example in *Chapter 2, Building Your First Data Pipeline with ELK*, and will try to perform some operations on them.

Listing all available indices

Let's first try to see all available indices in our cluster by executing the following command:

```
curl -XGET 'localhost:9200/_cat/indices?v'
```

Why Do We Need Elasticsearch in ELK?

Upon executing this, we will get the following response:

```
health status index              pri rep docs.count docs.deleted store.
size pri.store.size
green  open   logstash-2014.12.19  5   1      1            0
6.1kb         6.1kb
green  open   logstash-2014.12.08  5   1      1            0
6.1kb         6.1kb
green  open   logstash-2014.07.17  5   1      1            0
6kb           6kb
green  open   logstash-2014.08.04  5   1      1            0
6.1kb         6.1kb
green  open   logstash-2014.11.05  5   1      1            0
6.1kb         6.1kb
green  open   logstash-2014.07.27  5   1      1            0
6.1kb         6.1kb
green  open   logstash-2014.09.16  5   1      1            0
6.1kb         6.1kb
green  open   logstash-2014.12.15  5   1      1            0
6.1kb         6.1kb
green  open   logstash-2014.12.10  5   1      1            0
6.1kb         6.1kb
green  open   logstash-2014.09.18  5   1      1            0
6kb           6kb
green  open   logstash-2014.12.18  5   1      1            0
6.1kb         6.1kb
green  open   logstash-2014.07.08  5   1      1            0
6.1kb         6.1kb
```

This will show all the indices that are stored among all nodes in the cluster, and some information about them such as health, index name, size, count of documents, number of primary shards, and so on.

For example, the first row in the preceding text shows that we have `5` primary and `1` replica shards of the index named `logstash-2014.12.19` and it has `1` document in it and `0` deleted documents.

Listing all nodes in a cluster

We can also see all nodes in a cluster by invoking the following command:

```
curl -XGET 'http://localhost:9200/_cat/nodes?v'
```

The response is as follows:

```
host       ip              heap.percent   ram.percent load node.role
master name
packtpub 127.0.1.1              18              35       0.27      d
*       Animus
```

Since ours is a single node cluster on `localhost`, it shows one node and the memory related characteristics of this node.

Checking the health of the cluster

We can check the health of a cluster by invoking the following command:

```
curl -XGET 'http://localhost:9200/_cluster/health?pretty=true'
{
  "cluster_name" : "elasticsearch",
  "status" : "yellow",
  "timed_out" : false,
  "number_of_nodes" : 1,
  "number_of_data_nodes" : 1,
  "active_primary_shards" : 11,
  "active_shards" : 11,
  "relocating_shards" : 0,
  "initializing_shards" : 0,
  "unassigned_shards" : 11
}
```

Health can be checked at cluster level, shard level, or indices level, using URLs that are similar to the following ones:

```
curl -XGET 'http://localhost:9200/_cluster/health?level=cluster&pretty=true'
curl -XGET 'http://localhost:9200/_cluster/health?level=shards&pretty=true'
curl -XGET 'http://localhost:9200/_cluster/health?level=indices&pretty=true'
```

Health status of the cluster

Elasticsearch cluster health is indicated in three parameters:

- **Red** indicates that some or all primary shards are not ready to serve the requests.
- **Yellow** indicates that all primary shards are allocated but some or all of the replicas have not been allocated. Normally, single node clusters will have their health status as yellow as no other node is available for replication.
- **Green** indicates that all shards and their replicas are well allocated and the cluster is fully operational.

Creating an index

In ELK, index creation is automatically handled by providing the index name in the Logstash `elasticsearch` output plugin. Still, let's take a look at how we can create an index:

`curl -XPUT 'localhost:9200/<index_name>?pretty'`

For example, to create an index named `packtpub`, we can issue the following command:

`curl -XPUT 'localhost:9200/packtpub/?pretty'`

We can also directly create an index while putting the document inside the index as follows:

```
curl -xPUT 'localhost:9200/packtpub/elk/1?pretty' -d '
{
book_name : "learning elk"
}'
```

The response of the preceding command is:

```
{
  "_index" : "packtpub",
  "_type" : "elk",
  "_id" : "1",
  "_version" : 1,
  "created" : true
}
```

With the preceding command, a new index named `packtpub` was created along with type `elk`, and a document with ID `1` was stored in it.

Retrieving the document

We will now retrieve the document that we just indexed:

```
curl -XGET 'localhost:9200/packtpub/elk/1?pretty'
```

The response of the preceding query will be:

```
{
  "_index" : "packtpub",
  "_type" : "elk",
  "_id" : "1",
  "_version" : 1,
  "found" : true,
  "_source":{
book_name : "learning elk"
}
}
```

The _source field will contain a full document, which was indexed with ID as 1.

From our GOOG price indices example from *Chapter 2, Building Your First Data Pipeline with ELK*, let's try to query for a document:

```
curl -XGET 'localhost:9200/logstash-2014.08.04/logs/_search?pretty'
```

This will give us the following response:

```
{
  "took" : 3,
  "timed_out" : false,
  "_shards" : {
    "total" : 5,
    "successful" : 5,
    "failed" : 0
  },
  "hits" : {
    "total" : 1,
    "max_score" : 1.0,
    "hits" : [ {
      "_index" : "logstash-2014.08.04",
      "_type" : "logs",
      "_id" : "AU2qgZixPoayDyQnreXd",
      "_score" : 1.0,
```

```
        "_source":{"message":["2014-08-05,570.05255,571.9826,562.61255,
   565.07257,1551200,565.07257"],"@version":"1","@timestamp":"2014-08-
   04T23:00:00.000Z","host":"packtpub","path":"/opt/logstash/input/
   GOOG.csv","date_of_record":"2014-08-05","open":570.05255,"high":5
   71.9826,"low":562.61255,"close":565.07257,"volume":1551200,"adj_
   close":"565.07257"}
      } ]
    }
}
```

We got the complete message stored as the _source field, which contains JSON emitted from Logstash.

Deleting documents

In order to delete a document inside one index, we can issue the following command:

```
curl -XDELETE 'localhost:9200/packtpub/elk/1?pretty'
```

Deleting an index

Let's delete the index that we created:

```
curl -XDELETE 'localhost:9200/packtpub?pretty'
```

The response is as follows:

```
{
   "acknowledged" : true
}
```

This indicates that the index was successfully deleted.

Elasticsearch Query DSL

The queries that we saw until now were basic commands that were used to retrieve data, but the actual power of Elasticsearch's querying lies in a robust Query Domain Specific Language based on JSON also called Query DSL. Kibana makes extensive use of Query DSL in order to get results in a desired format for you. You almost never really have to worry about writing the query JSON, as Kibana will automatically create and put the results in a nice format.

Chapter 5

For example, in order to get only three results out of all the matching ones, we can specify it like this:

```
curl -XPOST 'localhost:9200/logstash-*/_search' -d '
{
  "query": { "match_all": {} },
  "size": 3
}'
```

The response is as follows, which contains three documents matching the search:

```
{
    "took" : 390,
    "timed_out" : false,
    "_shards" : {
      "total" : 640,
      "successful" : 640,
      "failed" : 0
    },
    "hits" : {
      "total" : 128,
      "max_score" : 1.0,
      "hits" : [{
          "_index" : "logstash-2014.07.01",
          "_type" : "logs",
          "_id" : "AU2qge3cPoayDyQnreX0",
          "_score" : 1.0,
          "_source" : {
            "message" : ["2014-07-02,583.3526,585.44269,580.39264,582.33765,1056400,582.33765"],
            "@version" : "1",
            "@timestamp" : "2014-07-01T23:00:00.000Z",
            "host" : "packtpub",
            "path" : "/opt/logstash/input/GOOG.csv",
            "date_of_record" : "2014-07-02",
            "open" : 583.3526,
            "high" : 585.44269,
            "low" : 580.39264,
            "close" : 582.33765,
            "volume" : 1056400,
            "adj_close" : "582.33765"
          }
        }, {
          "_index" : "logstash-2014.07.09",
```

```
          "_type" : "logs",
          "_id" : "AU2qge3cPoayDyQnreXv",
          "_score" : 1.0,
          "_source" : {
            "message" : ["2014-07-
  10,565.91254,576.59265,565.01257,571.10254,1356700,571.10254"],
            "@version" : "1",
            "@timestamp" : "2014-07-09T23:00:00.000Z",
            "host" : "packtpub",
            "path" : "/opt/logstash/input/GOOG.csv",
            "date_of_record" : "2014-07-10",
            "open" : 565.91254,
            "high" : 576.59265,
            "low" : 565.01257,
            "close" : 571.10254,
            "volume" : 1356700,
            "adj_close" : "571.10254"
          }
        }, {
          "_index" : "logstash-2014.07.21",
          "_type" : "logs",
          "_id" : "AU2qgZixPoayDyQnreXn",
          "_score" : 1.0,
          "_source" : {
            "message" : ["2014-07-
  22,590.72266,599.65271,590.60266,594.74268,1699200,594.74268"],
            "@version" : "1",
            "@timestamp" : "2014-07-21T23:00:00.000Z",
            "host" : "packtpub",
            "path" : "/opt/logstash/input/GOOG.csv",
            "date_of_record" : "2014-07-22",
            "open" : 590.72266,
            "high" : 599.65271,
            "low" : 590.60266,
            "close" : 594.74268,
            "volume" : 1699200,
            "adj_close" : "594.74268"
          }
        }
      ]
    }
  }
```

Similarly, the query to get results sorted by a field will look similar to this:

```
curl -XPOST 'localhost:9200/logstash-*/_search' -d '
{
"query" : {
"match_all" :{}
},
"sort" : {"open" : { "order":"desc"}},
"size" :3
}'
```

You can see the response of the preceding query, sorted by the `"open"` field in a `desc` manner:

```
{
    "took" : 356,
    "timed_out" : false,
    "_shards" : {
      "total" : 640,
      "successful" : 640,
      "failed" : 0
    },
    "hits" : {
      "total" : 128,
      "max_score" : null,
      "hits" : [{
          "_index" : "logstash-2014.07.23",
          "_type" : "logs",
          "_id" : "AU2qgZixPoayDyQnreXl",
          "_score" : null,
          "_source" : {
            "message" : ["2014-07-
24,596.4527,599.50269,591.77271,593.35266,1035100,593.35266"],
            "@version" : "1",
            "@timestamp" : "2014-07-23T23:00:00.000Z",
            "host" : "packtpub",
            "path" : "/opt/logstash/input/GOOG.csv",
            "date_of_record" : "2014-07-24",
            "open" : 596.4527,
            "high" : 599.50269,
            "low" : 591.77271,
            "close" : 593.35266,
            "volume" : 1035100,
```

```
          "adj_close" : "593.35266"
        },
        "sort" : [596.4527]
      }, {
        "_index" : "logstash-2014.09.21",
        "_type" : "logs",
        "_id" : "AU2qgZioPoayDyQnreW8",
        "_score" : null,
        "_source" : {
          "message" : ["2014-09-
22,593.82269,593.95166,583.46271,587.37262,1689500,587.37262"],
          "@version" : "1",
          "@timestamp" : "2014-09-21T23:00:00.000Z",
          "host" : "packtpub",
          "path" : "/opt/logstash/input/GOOG.csv",
          "date_of_record" : "2014-09-22",
          "open" : 593.82269,
          "high" : 593.95166,
          "low" : 583.46271,
          "close" : 587.37262,
          "volume" : 1689500,
          "adj_close" : "587.37262"
        },
        "sort" : [593.82269]
      }, {
        "_index" : "logstash-2014.07.22",
        "_type" : "logs",
        "_id" : "AU2qgZixPoayDyQnreXm",
        "_score" : null,
        "_source" : {
          "message" : ["2014-07-
23,593.23267,597.85266,592.50269,595.98267,1233200,595.98267"],
          "@version" : "1",
          "@timestamp" : "2014-07-22T23:00:00.000Z",
          "host" : "packtpub",
          "path" : "/opt/logstash/input/GOOG.csv",
          "date_of_record" : "2014-07-23",
          "open" : 593.23267,
          "high" : 597.85266,
          "low" : 592.50269,
          "close" : 595.98267,
          "volume" : 1233200,
          "adj_close" : "595.98267"
        },
```

```
      "sort" : [593.23267]
    }
  ]
 }
}
```

 More details on Query DSL can be found at the Elasticsearch official documentation here: https://www.elastic.co/guide/en/elasticsearch/reference/current/query-dsl.html

Now when we have an understanding of Query DSL in Elasticsearch, let's look at one of the queries automatically created by Kibana, in our example from *Chapter 2*, *Building Your First Data Pipeline with ELK*.

Go to the Kibana **Visualize** page and open the *Highest Traded Volume Visualization* that we created earlier. If we click on the arrow button at the bottom, it opens up buttons for **Request**, **Response** like this:

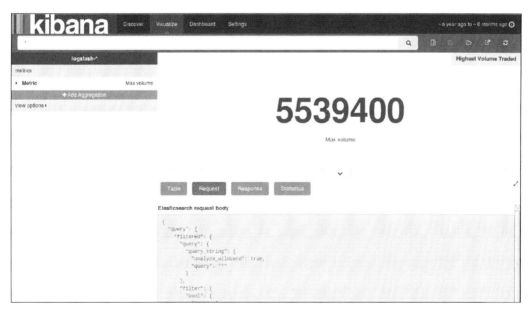

Elasticsearch Request Body on Kibana UI

Here, we can easily see the request sent by Kibana to Elasticsearch as **Elasticsearch request body**:

```
{
  "query": {
    "filtered": {
      "query": {
        "query_string": {
          "analyze_wildcard": true,
          "query": "*"
        }
      },
      "filter": {
        "bool": {
          "must": [
            {
              "range": {
                "@timestamp": {
                  "gte": 1403880285618,
                  "lte": 1419472695417
                }
              }
            }
          ],
          "must_not": []
        }
      }
    }
  },
  "size": 0,
  "aggs": {
    "1": {
      "max": {
        "field": "volume"
      }
    }
  }
}
```

The preceding query makes use of query filters to apply range on the `@timestamp` field, along with aggregations to find the maximum value of the `"Volume"` field. Similarly, we can also check for other visualizations created. Kibana takes care of creating queries for all the types of visualizations that you create.

Elasticsearch plugins

Elasticsearch has a very rich set of plugins, mainly community driven, which are really helpful to analyze the cluster, and execute full-text structural queries easily.

Let's look at a few of the plugins.

Bigdesk plugin

This plugin was developed by Lukas Vlcek. It helps analyze the nodes across the cluster with the help of live charts and various statistics related to JVM, CPU, and OS, and about shards and their replicas.

> More information is available at https://github.com/lukas-vlcek/bigdesk.

The following screenshot shows the Bigdesk plugin:

BigDesk plugin

Why Do We Need Elasticsearch in ELK?

Elastic-Hammer plugin

The Elastic-Hammer plugin acts as a frontend for Elasticsearch. It helps query the cluster and provides syntax checking while typing queries as well.

 More details can be found here: `https://github.com/andrewvc/elastic-hammer`.

Elasticsearch Elastic-Hammer plugin

Head plugin

Head plugins are capable of generating statistics of the cluster, as well as providing browsing, and performing structured queries on Elasticsearch indices.

 More details can be found here: `https://github.com/mobz/elasticsearch-head`.

Chapter 5

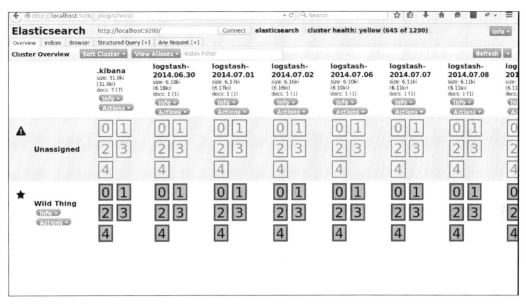

Elasticsearch head plugin

There are many more plugins available that are supported by Elasticsearch or by the community and they play an important role while interacting with Elasticsearch.

 You can easily check the list of available plugins here:

https://www.elastic.co/guide/en/elasticsearch/reference/current/modules-plugins.html#_plugins

Summary

In this chapter, we learned the basic concepts of Elasticsearch. We also figured out how querying on a Elasticsearch index works, and how Kibana makes use of Elasticsearch queries to efficiently analyze indexed data and show beautiful visualizations on top of it.

In the next chapter, we will look at Kibana's features in more detail to understand how it helps perform some searches on data with querying on its **Discover** page.

6
Finding Insights with Kibana

In the previous chapter, we saw how Elasticsearch plays a role in ELK Stack to support fast searches and a variety of aggregations. In this chapter, we will take a look at how Kibana acts as the frontend of ELK, where it hides all the complexities of data and presents beautiful visualizations, charts, and dashboards built over the data, which helps gain essential insights into the data.

Kibana makes it easy to create and share dashboards consisting of various types of charts and graphs. Kibana visualizations automatically display changes in data over time based on Elasticsearch queries. It's easy to install and set up, and helps us quickly explore and discover many aspects of data.

Kibana 4 features

Some of the unique features in Kibana 4 are as follows:

Search highlights

Search terms are highlighted in the list of documents shown after the search:

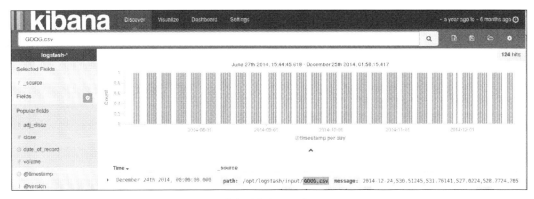

Search highlight in Kibana 4

Elasticsearch aggregations

Kibana 4 makes extensive use of Elasticsearch aggregations and sub aggregations to provide more than one aggregation for visualizations. There are mainly two types of aggregations—Bucketing and Metrics. Bucketing produces a list of buckets, each one with a set of documents belonging to it, for example, terms, range, histograms, and so on. Metrics calculate the compute metrics for a set of documents, for example, min, max, sum, average, and so on. These types of computations can only be done on numeric type of fields.

Scripted fields

Scripted fields are used to make computations on the fly on indexed data.
For example, for a certain field you always want to multiply by `100` before you show it. You can save it as a scripted field. Scripted fields, though, can't be searched.

Let's take the following script as an example: `doc['volume'].value * 100`.

This script will always multiply the value of volume by `100` before it shows it.

Dynamic dashboards

Dashboards are very flexible and dynamic as individual visualizations can be easily arranged as per convenience, and data can be refreshed automatically.

Kibana interface

A Kibana interface consists of four main tabs:

- **Discover**: The **Discover** page enables free text searches, field-based searches, range-based searches, and so on.
- **Visualize**: The **Visualize** page enables building many visualizations, such as pie charts, bar charts, line charts, and so on, which can be saved and used in dashboards later.
- **Dashboard**: The **Dashboard** represents collections of multiple visualizations and searches, which can be used to easily apply filters based on click interaction, and draw conclusions based on multiple data aggregations.
- **Settings**: **Settings** enables the configuration of index patterns, scripted fields, the data types of fields, and so on.

Let's take a look at the **Discover** page in more detail.

Discover page

The **Discover** page is used to perform interactive searches on your indexed data. It allows you to perform ad hoc searches based on fields, the filtering of data, and allows you to view indexed documents as well.

Finding Insights with Kibana

A typical Kibana home page, which defaults to the **Discover** page, looks as follows:

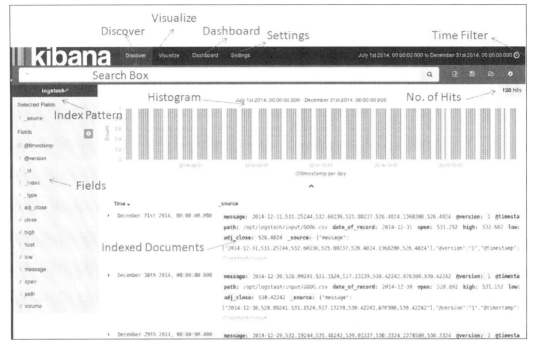

Kibana Discover page

The **Discover** page shows all the indexed fields in the **Index Pattern** on the left, a **Time Filter** at the top, and a **Search Box** to enter your search queries. Also, it shows a default **Histogram** based on the **@timestamp** field in the documents and displays **No. of Hits** in the document corresponding to your search. It shows **500** documents by default with the latest based on the timestamp at the top.

Time filter

Remember the time when your boss asked to find some statistics from your data for a specific time? The time filter is the answer for these kinds of searches. You can filter data on any specific time period selected from the calendar, called **Absolute**, or make it **Relative** based on current time. There are also some quick time filters available for use.

Quick time filter

A quick time filter helps filter quickly based on some already available time ranges:

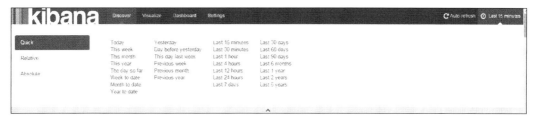

Kibana Time Filter – Quick

Relative time filter

A relative time filter helps filter based on relative time from the current time. By default, the time filter is set to **Relative** with **15 Minutes ago** from **Now**:

Kibana Time Filter - Relative

Absolute time filter

The absolute time filter helps filter based on a range of dates selected for **From** and **To** a date and time:

Kibana Time Filter – Absolute

Kibana Auto-refresh setting

The **Auto-refresh** setting can be set to set a refresh interval:

Kibana Auto-refresh setting

The time filter can also be specified using click and drag on an area of a histogram or other charts:

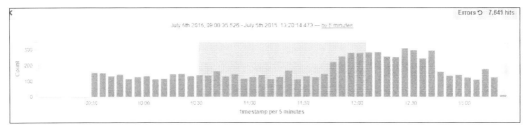

Zoom-in to Set Time Filter

Querying and searching data

Kibana uses Lucene query syntax to search among indices stored in index patterns. You can also specify an Elasticsearch query DSL, like we explained in *Chapter 5*, *Why Do We Need Elasticsearch in ELK?* The field list, index documents lists, and the histogram are automatically refreshed based on the search and time filter settings.

>
> **Analyzed and Not Analyzed Fields**
>
> As mentioned in the Logstash index template for Elasticsearch (https://github.com/logstash-plugins/logstash-output-elasticsearch/blob/master/lib/logstash/outputs/elasticsearch/elasticsearch-template.json), when we index string fields, both analyzed (tokenized) and non-analyzed versions are saved in indexes. All non-analyzed fields appear with the .raw extension in the **Discover** or **Visualize** pages.

Let's look at some examples of searches.

Freetext search

The freetext search is aimed at filtering documents containing the search term. It searches in all the documents for all the fields containing the searched term.

Let's take the following instance as an example:

You want to search for all the ELK books from an index pattern consisting of PacktPub books collections. You can write `'ELK'` in the search box, and it filters all documents containing the term `ELK`.

> Search syntax can be looked up here:
> `https://lucene.apache.org/core/2_9_4/queryparsersyntax.html`

Boolean searches can be performed on the following terms:

AND

`"Learning" AND "ELK"`

The preceding query will search for all documents that contain both terms: `"Learning"` and `"ELK"`.

OR

`"Logstash" OR "ELK`

The preceding query will search for all documents that contain the terms `"Logstash"` or `"ELK"`.

NOT

`"Logstash" NOT "ELK"`

The preceding query will search for documents that contain the term `Logstash` but not `"ELK"`.

Groupings

`("Logstash" OR "ELK")  AND "Kibana"`

The preceding query will search for documents that contain `"Kibana"` and can contain either `"ELK"` or `"Logstash"`.

Wildcard searches

You can also perform wildcard searches using the following terms:

- `plan*`: will search for all documents that have terms, such as `plans`, or `plant`, or `planting`, and so on
- `plan?`: will search for `plant` or `plans`
- `?` and `*`: cannot be used as the first character in a search

Field searches

Field searches aim to search for specific values or ranges of values for fields in your indexed document that displays on the left-hand side of the **Discover** page.

Field searches can be performed using the field name and the `:` character, followed by a value for the field we want to filter on.

```
<field_name>: <field_value>
```

Let's take a look at some examples of field searches:

```
title : "Learning ELK"
title : "Learning ELK" AND  category : "technology"
```

Range searches

Range searches are used to search for a range of values for a field.

For example, to search for a specific date range:

```
date_of_record : [20140701 TO 20141231]
```

To search for a range of values for the `volume` field:

```
volume : [ 100000 TO 200000]
```

Range and field searches can be combined using boolean operators like this:

```
publish_date : [20150701 TO 20151231] AND title : "Learning ELK"
```

Special characters escaping

The following is the list of special characters, which if we want to search for, need to be escaped using the `\` operator:

```
+ - && || ! ( ) { } [ ] ^ " ~ * ? : \
```

For example, to search for `1:2` it needs to be escaped as `1\:2`.

New search

You can start a new search by clicking on the **New Search** button on the **Discover** toolbar:

Kibana New Search option

Saving the search

Searches can be saved and used in visualizations later using the **Save Search** option on the **Discover** toolbar. Saved searches can also be added to a dashboard in order to show the information in a traditional table format. This is very important for real-world applications in identifying issues:

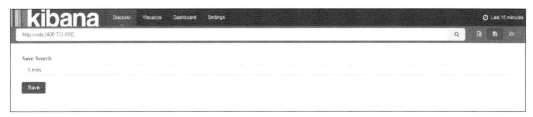

Kibana Save Search option

Loading a search

Previously saved searches can be loaded using the **Load Saved Search** option on the **Discover** toolbar:

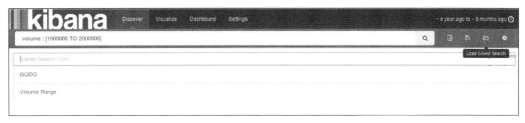

Loading a Saved Search

Finding Insights with Kibana

Field searches using field list

Field searches can also be performed by clicking on the *positive* or *negative* filter icon on certain values on the field.

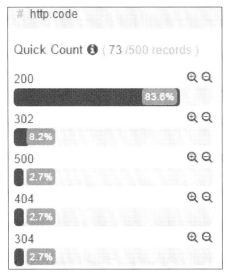

Positive and negative filter on fields using field list

In the preceding figure, if you click on the *positive filter* icon, it will filter all documents having the `http.code` value as `200`, and if you click on *negative filter*, it will show all documents having the `http.code` value other than `200`.

You can also add certain fields on the right-hand side panel by clicking on the *add* button on the field name in the field list. This enables an easy view of fields as tables based on your searches.

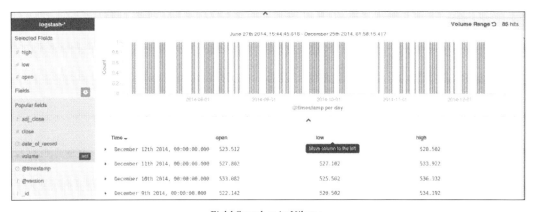

Field Searches in Kibana

In this way, fields can be quickly added and documents can be sorted in fields, and fields can be arranged in any order. This is especially helpful to build a table for a quick search.

Summary

In this chapter, we saw how we can use Kibana's **Discover** page to gain insights into the data with some quick searches, which can be saved and used later.

In the next chapter, we will see the **Visualize**, **Dashboard**, and **Settings** pages in Kibana in detail.

7
Kibana – Visualization and Dashboard

In the last chapter, we looked at the **Discover** page and how we could make some quick searches across indexed documents. In this chapter, we will look at the **Visualize** and **Dashboard** features in Kibana. We will see how we can leverage the power of Kibana, built over Elasticsearch indexes, to build various types of charts and graphs, and awesome dashboards covering various analytics, which can be easily embedded or shared with others.

Visualize page

The **Visualize** page helps create visualizations in the form of graphs and charts. These visualizations can be saved and viewed individually or can be used in multiple dashboards, which act as a collection of visualizations.

Kibana – Visualization and Dashboard

All visualizations in Kibana are based on the aggregation feature of Elasticsearch. Kibana also supports multilevel aggregations to come up with various useful data analytics. Let's take a look at what a **Visualize** page looks like:

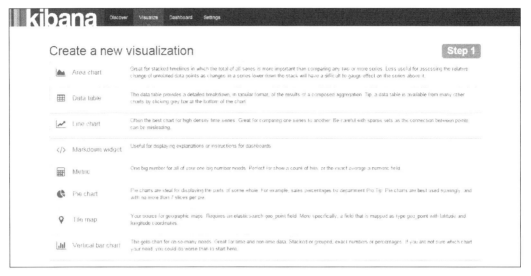

Kibana Visualize page

The **Visualize** page has two parts—either you can create a new visualization or open an existing one from your saved list.

Creating a visualization

To create a new visualization, select **Visualize** from the top menu bar, which opens a new **Visualize** page, and then click on the **New Visualization** button on tool bar.

Creating a new visualization is a three step process on the **Visualize** page:

1. Select a visualization type.
2. Select a data source (from a new search or an existing saved search).
3. Configure the aggregations (metrics and buckets) that are to be used for the visualization on the **Edit** page.

Visualization types

Kibana supports the following visualizations:

- Area chart
- Data table
- Line chart
- Markdown widget
- Metric
- Pie chart
- Tile map
- Vertical bar chart

Before we start building visualizations of various types, let's understand a bit about Elasticsearch aggregations, which forms the backbone of the visualizations in Kibana.

Metrics and buckets aggregations

The metrics and buckets concepts come from the aggregation functionality of Elasticsearch, and they play a vital role when designing a visualization for your dataset in Kibana.

Buckets

Buckets help distribute documents among multiple buckets containing a subset of indexed documents. Buckets are very similar to the GROUP BY functionality in SQL. They help group documents based on specified criteria, and metrics can be applied on these documents.

Buckets usually represent the **X-axis** in Kibana charts and it is possible to add sub-buckets to a bucket.

The following buckets are available for the **X-axis** in Kibana:

- **Date Histogram**
- **Histogram**
- **Range**
- **Date Range**

- **IPV4 Range**
- **Terms**
- **Filters**
- **Significant Terms**

Let's take a look at a few important visualizations here.

Date Histogram

Date Histogram requires a field name of type date and interval for the configuration. It groups documents as per the specified field and interval specified. For example, if you specify the field **bucket** as **@timestamp** and **Interval** as **weekly**, documents will be grouped based on weekly data, and then you can apply some metrics, such as **Count**, **Average**, and so on, on top of the grouped documents.

Histogram

Histogram is similar to **Date Histogram**, except that it requires the field of type numbers and a numeric interval to be specified. It will bucket documents for the particular interval specified in the chosen field. This is like a range aggregation with equal intervals.

Range

Range is like **Histogram**, but it allows you to configure different ranges as per the requirements, manually. For example, for a field count, you can choose the bucketing range to be `0-1000`, `1000-5000`, `5000-15000`, and so on.

Date Range

Date Range requires a date field and a custom range to be specified for each bucket.

Terms

Terms help group documents by the value of any field, which is very similar to the `GROUP BY` statement in SQL. The **Terms** aggregation also lets you choose whether you want **Top N** or **Bottom N**, or you can specify the order based on metrics too. For example, you can choose to group by a product type and get the top five spends in that product type.

Chapter 7

Buckets in visualizations

Metrics

Metrics represents computations performed on values of fields in each bucket, for example, computing the count, average, minimum, or maximum of a field in the document. Metrics usually represent the **Y-axis** in **Area chart**, **Vertical bar chart**, and **Line chart**. The types of metrics available in Kibana are:

- **Count**
- **Average**
- **Sum**
- **Unique Count**
- **Min**
- **Max**
- **Percentile**
- **Percentile Ranks**

Let's take a look at a few of them.

Count

The **Count** metric aggregation is very important, and its main purpose is to calculate the count of the number of fields in each bucket in a bucket aggregation.

[727]

For example, to count the number of visitors for each of the product categories, you can specify the product category field as bucket aggregation and count metric aggregation.

Average, Sum, Min, and Max

Similar to **Count** aggregation, **Average**, **Sum**, **Min**, and **Max** provide the average, sum, minimum, and maximum, respectively, of all the values of a numeric field provided in the aggregation.

Unique Count

Unique Count is similar to the COUNT (DISTINCT fieldname) functionality in SQL, which counts number of unique values for a field.

Kibana visualization metrics

Advanced options

Buckets and metrics aggregations have **Advanced** options, which can take JSON input as scripted fields, as described in *Chapter 6, Finding Insights with Kibana*. The following script is an example:

```
{ "script" : "doc['volume'].value * 100"}
```

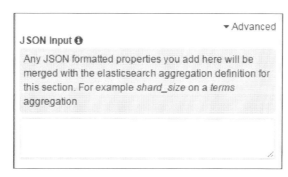

JSON Input Advanced option

Overall, a **New Visualization** page looks like this, with the toolbar at the top, **metrics** and **buckets** configuration on the left and the preview pane on right-hand side:

Kibana New Visualization page

The toolbar at the top has the options to create a new visualization, save a visualization, open a saved visualization, share a visualization, and refresh it.

Kibana Visualization toolbar

When creating a visualization, Kibana provides two options as a search source:

- **From a saved search**
- **From a new search**

Kibana search source selection

From a saved search uses searches that you saved in the **Discover** page.

From a new search is used to create a new visualization based on a new search.

Visualizations

Now, let's take a look at various visualization types and how they can be used.

Area chart

Area chart is especially useful to create stacked timelines or distribute data.

Area chart uses **metrics** as **Y-axis** and **buckets** for **X-axis**. We can also define sub-aggregations in **buckets**, which give you the functionality of **Split Charts** (multiple charts based on different aggregations) or **Split Area** (Area chart split based on different aggregations).

Chapter 7

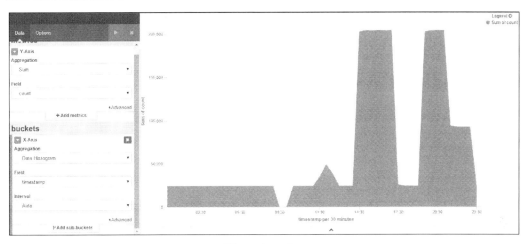

Kibana Area chart

Data table

Data table is used to present aggregated data in a tabular format and helps identify **Top N** kinds of aggregations.

For example, to get the top five clients by the number of hits, the following data table visualization can be used:

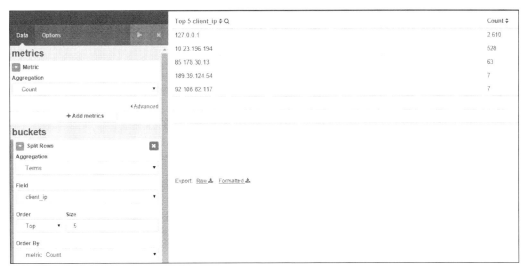

Kibana Data table

Line chart

Line charts are used for high density time series, and are often helpful when comparing one series with another:

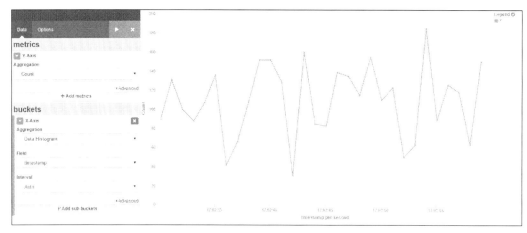

Kibana Line chart

Markdown widget

Markdown widget is used to display information or instructions on **Dashboard** and can be used for any requirements for text on **Dashboard**.

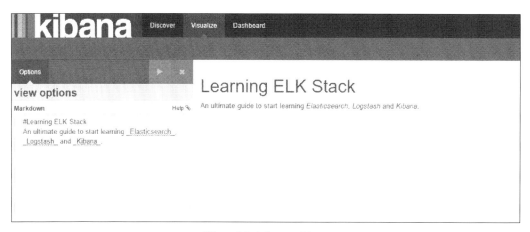

Kibana Markdown widget

Metric

Metric is used to show a one number kind of analysis for your field. It can be used to compute the total number of hits or the sum or average of a field.

For example, the following metric can be used to show the average response time of the application over a period of time:

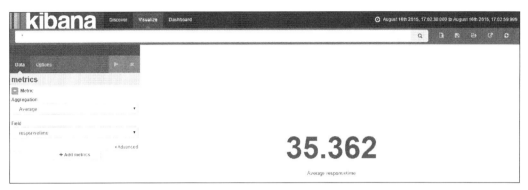

Kibana Metric

Pie chart

Pie charts are often used to show parts of a whole or a percentage relationship. It represents the distribution of data over multiple slices in a pie chart.

A slice of the pie chart is determined by metrics aggregations, which can have the values **Count**, **Sum**, or **Unique Count**. Bucket aggregation defines the type of data that has to be represented in one chart.

For example, the following pie chart can be used to show the distribution of the different response codes of an application:

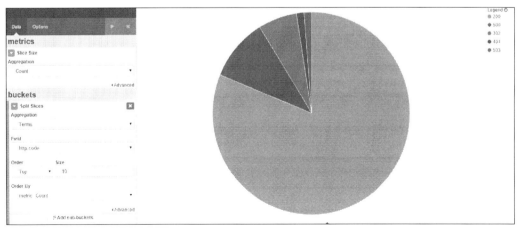

Kibana Pie chart

Tile map

Tile maps are used to locate geographic locations based on geo coordinates. It works on the **Geohash** bucket aggregation, which groups multiple coordinates into one bucket.

Kibana Tile map

Vertical bar chart

Vertical bar chart is a chart that can be used for a variety of purposes and works well with time- and non-time-based fields. It can be used as single bar or stacked as well.

Y-axis is **metrics** and **X-axis** is **buckets** aggregation.

For example, the following Vertical bar chart can be used to show a count of HTTP response codes:

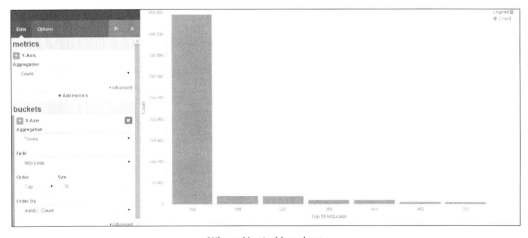

Kibana Vertical bar chart

Dashboard page

Kibana **Dashboard** is just a collection of saved visualizations or saved searches, which can be arranged in any order. Visualizations can be used on multiple dashboards and changes will reflect to all of them automatically. A dashboard can be saved and shared easily.

Let's look at what **Dashboard** will look like:

Building a new dashboard

When you click on the Kibana **Dashboard** page link at the top of the page for the first time, it displays an empty Kibana dashboard that is ready to add visualizations to:

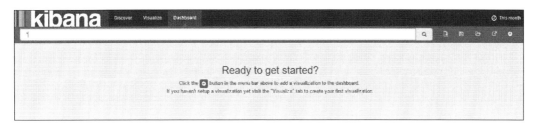

Kibana New Dashboard screen

You can click on the **+** button with a circle on the extreme right-hand side toolbar to add any saved visualizations or searches that you saved in the **Discover** page in a tabular format. After you have added the visualizations, you can move the individual visualizations around, edit them, or remove them. You can even resize or drag and drop them as per your requirements.

Setting a refresh interval on the time filter at the top automatically refreshes the dashboard with the latest values.

The *click to filter* feature in Kibana dashboards is very useful in scenarios where you would like all visualizations and searches to reflect events at a particular time. For example, you can click on a specific bar in a histogram and all the other visualizations and searches will reflect the same automatically.

Saving and loading a dashboard

Once you are done with the arrangement of visualizations, to save a dashboard, click on the **Save Dashboard** button on the toolbar and enter a name for the dashboard and save.

Kibana provides the facility to save a dashboard, which reflects values at a particular time. To do this, there is an option to save time with the dashboard. This is useful to provide snapshots of the system at a particular time.

Kibana Save Dashboard

To load a saved dashboard, click on the **Load Dashboard** button on the toolbar and choose among a list of saved dashboards.

Sharing a dashboard

Once completed and saved, you can share a link to a dashboard or embed it within another application using the IFrame tag. To do so, click on the **Share** button on the toolbar, which shows both a code to embed within another application, and a direct link to the dashboard, which can be copied and shared.

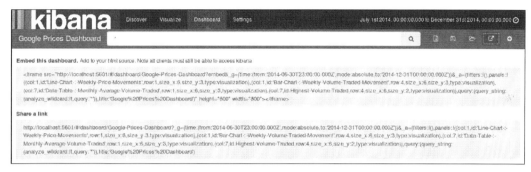

Kibana Share screen

Summary

In this chapter, we've seen how to create different types of visualizations in Kibana based on aggregations. We also saw how to arrange and share them using Kibana **Dashboards**. In the next chapter, we'll see how we can put all the components of ELK together to build a powerful data pipeline.

8
Putting It All Together

In the previous chapters, we looked at the basics of Elasticsearch, Kibana, and Logstash. We saw the configurations and properties of each of them, and tried to understand what role each of the components plays in building a data pipeline for your data.

Now we will apply everything that we have learnt so far. We'll create an end-to-end running solution to analyze logs using ELK Stack.

For demo purposes, we will use a sample web application that runs on the Tomcat server. We'll set up ELK Stack, where we'll use Logstash to collect, parse and index access logs to Elasticsearch. Finally, we'll see various searches and visualizations on it in the Kibana interface.

Input dataset

The input dataset is a continuous stream of Tomcat access logs in the following format:

```
10.0.0.2 - - [08/Sep/2015:17:39:46 +0100] "GET /elk/demo/10 HTTP/1.1" 200 40
10.0.0.2 - - [08/Sep/2015:17:39:47 +0100] "GET /elk/demo/11 HTTP/1.1" 200 39
10.0.0.3 - - [08/Sep/2015:17:39:48 +0100] "GET /elk/demo/12 HTTP/1.1" 200 39
10.0.0.2 - - [08/Sep/2015:17:39:49 +0100] "GET /elk/demo/13 HTTP/1.1" 200 39
10.0.0.2 - - [08/Sep/2015:17:39:50 +0100] "GET /elk/demo/14 HTTP/1.1" 200 39
10.0.0.4 - - [08/Sep/2015:17:39:51 +0100] "GET /elk/demo/15 HTTP/1.1" 200 40
10.0.0.2 - - [08/Sep/2015:17:39:52 +0100] "GET /elk/demo/16 HTTP/1.1" 200 39
```

Putting It All Together

```
10.0.0.2 - - [08/Sep/2015:17:39:53 +0100] "GET /elk/demo/17 HTTP/1.1" 200 39
10.0.0.5 - - [08/Sep/2015:17:39:54 +0100] "GET /elk/demo/18 HTTP/1.1" 200 39
10.0.0.2 - - [08/Sep/2015:17:39:55 +0100] "GET /elk/demo/19 HTTP/1.1" 200 39
10.0.0.2 - - [08/Sep/2015:17:39:56 +0100] "GET /elk/demo/20 HTTP/1.1" 200 40
10.0.0.6 - - [08/Sep/2015:17:39:57 +0100] "GET /elk/demo/21 HTTP/1.1" 200 38
10.0.0.2 - - [08/Sep/2015:17:39:58 +0100] "GET /elk/demo/22 HTTP/1.1" 200 40
10.0.0.2 - - [08/Sep/2015:17:39:59 +0100] "GET /elk/demo/23 HTTP/1.1" 200 39
```

The preceding log format is a Common Apache log format, defined in the Tomcat `server.xml` file in `conf` folder as follows:

```
<Valve className="org.apache.catalina.valves.AccessLogValve"
directory="logs"
       prefix="localhost_access_log." suffix=".txt"
       pattern="%h %l %u %t &quot;%r&quot; %s %b" />
```

The log pattern is in the following format:

```
%h %l %u %t "%r" %s %b
```

- `%h`: This represents the remote hostname (or IP address)
- `%l`: This represents the remote logical username
- `%u`: This represents the remote user that was authenticated
- `%t`: This specifies the date and time in common log format
- `%r`: This represents the request
- `%s`: This represents the response HTTP code
- `%b`: This represents the bytes sent in response, excluding HTTP headers

Configuring Logstash input

In this section, we'll configure Logstash to read data from access logs located on Tomcat, and index it in Elasticsearch, making filters and tokenization of terms in logs as per the grok pattern.

Grok pattern for access logs

As we already saw, some of the commonly used grok patterns are already included with the Logstash installation. Check out the list of Logstash grok patterns on GitHub at https://github.com/logstash-plugins/logstash-patterns-core/tree/master/patterns.

There is already a grok pattern for the Common Apache log format in the Logstash installation as follows:

```
COMMONAPACHELOG %{IPORHOST:clientip} %{USER:ident} %{USER:auth}
\[%{HTTPDATE:timestamp}\] "(?:%{WORD:verb} %{NOTSPACE:request}(?:
HTTP/%{NUMBER:httpversion})?|%{DATA:rawrequest})"
%{NUMBER:response} (?:%{NUMBER:bytes}|-)
```

We can directly use `COMMONAPACHELOG` as a matching pattern for our incoming messages to Logstash as follows:

```
input{
file{
path =>"/var/lib/tomcat7/logs/localhost_access_logs.txt"
start_position =>"beginning"
}
}
```

Next, we need to specify our grok pattern matching with the incoming message, assign a timestamp field from our message, and convert the data types of some of the fields as per our needs:

```
filter{
 grok {
      match => { "message" => "%{COMMONAPACHELOG}" }
    }

date{
    match => ["timestamp","dd/MMM/yyyy:HH:mm:ss Z"]
}
mutate{
convert => ["response","integer"]
convert => ["bytes","integer"]
}
}
```

Finally, to configure the output plugin to send filtered messages to Elasticsearch, we will not specify any port here as we are using the default port for Elasticsearch, that is, `9200`:

```
output{
elasticsearch {
host => "localhost"
}
}
```

Now that we have understood the individual configuration, let's see what the overall configuration for Tomcat looks like:

```
input{
file{
path =>"/var/lib/tomcat7/logs/localhost_access_log.txt"
start_position =>"beginning"
}
}

filter{
 grok {
      match => { "message" => "%{COMMONAPACHELOG}" }
    }

date{
    match => ["timestamp","dd/MMM/yyyy:HH:mm:ss Z"]
}
mutate{
convert => ["response","integer"]
convert => ["bytes","integer"]
}
}
output{
elasticsearch {
host => "localhost"
}
}


*
```

Now, lets start `logstash` with this configuration:

`$ bin/logstash -f logstash.conf`

Chapter 8

Logstash will start to run with the defined configuration and keep on indexing all incoming events to the Elasticsearch indexes. You may see an output that is similar to this one on the console:

```
May 31, 2015 4:04:54 PM org.elasticsearch.node.internal.InternalNode
start
INFO: [logstash-4004-9716] started
Logstash startup completed
```

Now, you will see your Apache access logs data in Elasticsearch. Logstash was able to parse the input line and break it into different pieces of information, based on the grok patterns, for the Apache access logs. Now, we can easily set up analytics on HTTP response codes, request methods, and different URLs.

At this point, we can open the Elasticsearch Kopf plugin console that we installed in *Chapter 1, Introduction to ELK Stack*, to verify whether we have some documents indexed already, and we can also query these documents.

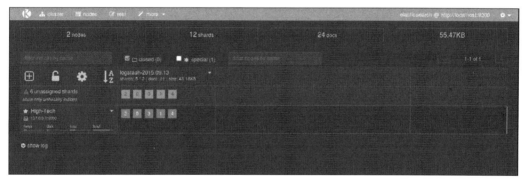

Elasticsearch Kopf UI

If we can see some indexes for Logstash already in Elasticsearch, we have verified that our Logstash configuration worked well.

Visualizing with Kibana

Now that you have verified that your data is indexed successfully in Elasticsearch, we can go ahead and look at the Kibana interface to get some useful analytics from the data.

Running Kibana

As described in *Chapter 1, Introduction to ELK Stack*, we will start the Kibana service from the Kibana installation directory:

```
$ bin/kibana
```

Putting It All Together

Now, let's see Kibana up and running with a screen similar to the following screenshot on the browser with this URL:

`http://localhost:5601`

We can verify our index and fields in the **Settings** page under the indices tab as follows:

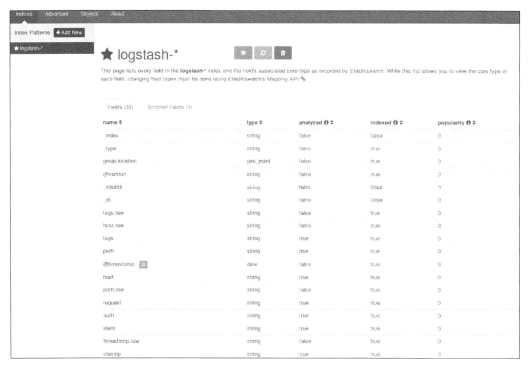

Kibana Settings page

It shows all our fields that were indexed, their data types, index status, and popularity value.

As we have already set up Kibana to take the `logstash-*` indexes by default, it starts to display the indexed data as a histogram of counts, and the associated data as fields in the JSON format as follows:

[744]

Chapter 8

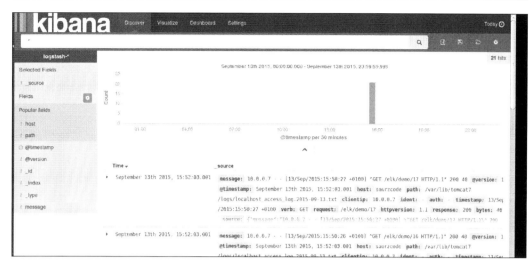

The Kibana Discover page showing indexed values

Searching on the Discover page

After our data is indexed, we can perform some quick searches on our fields to analyze some data.

To search for a specific client IP, we can type search command as `clientip: 10.0.0.7` and the indexed document on the page displays matching highlighted values:

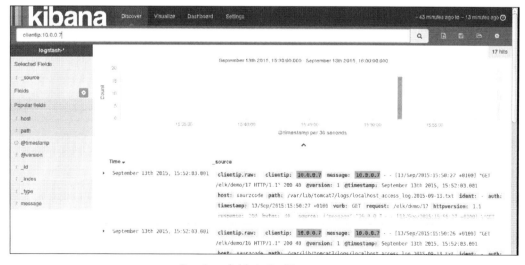

Search on fields in the Discover page

Putting It All Together

To search all GET requests coming from specific client IP, we can issue a query like this:

```
clientip:10.0.0.7 AND  verb:GET
```

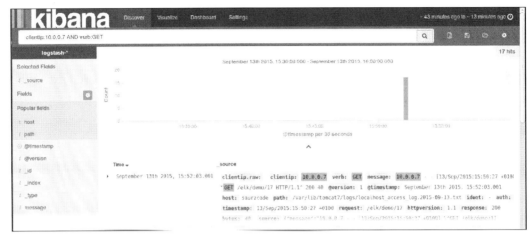

Searching on fields

To search all instances of a particular GET request coming from a specific client IP we can issue a query like the one shown in the following screenshot:

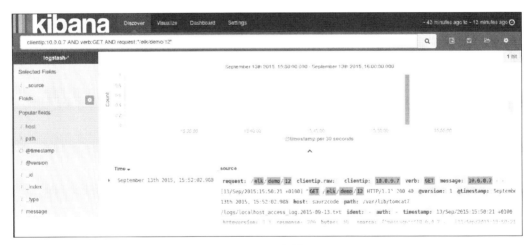

Searching on fields II

Once our data is fully indexed, the **Discover** page will look something like this, with a default histogram based on the count of documents over time:

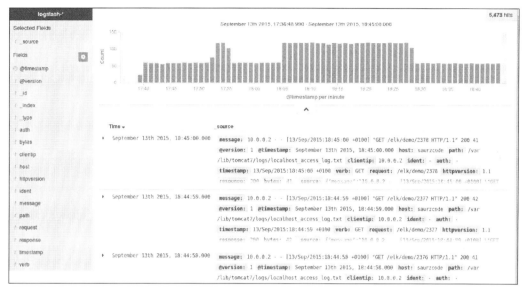

The Discover page after full indexing

Visualizations – charts

Let's build some basic visualizations from the Kibana **Visualize** page, and we will use them later in dashboard.

Click on the **Visualize** page link at the top of the Kibana home page and click on the new visualization icon.

Putting It All Together

This page shows various types of visualizations that are possible with the Kibana interface:

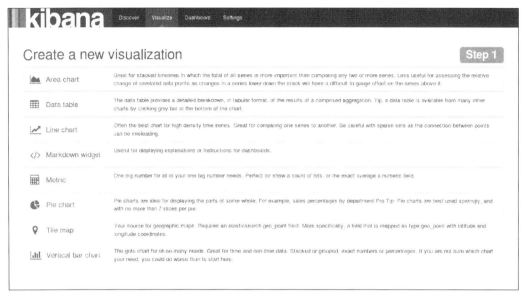

Kibana visualization menu

Building a Line chart

The first visualization that we will build is a **Line chart** showing the number of hits over time for the application. To do this, we'll choose the **Y-axis metrics** as **Count** and the **X-axis bucket** as **Date Histogram**, and then click on **Apply**. The resulting **Line chart** looks like this:

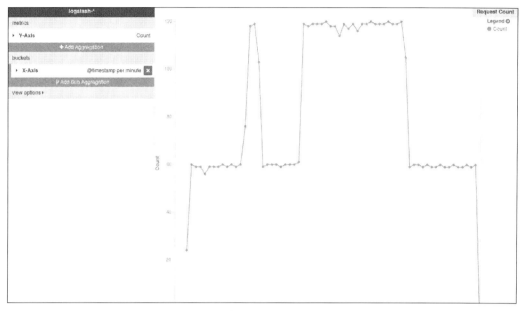

Line Chart – Request Count

Now, save the visualization using any name for the **Line chart**, which we will pull in **Dashboard** later.

Putting It All Together

Building an Area chart

We can build an **Area chart** based on the number of bytes transferred over time as follows. To do this, we'll choose the **Y-axis metrics** as **Average** and choose **Field** as **bytes**. The resulting **Area chart** looks like this:

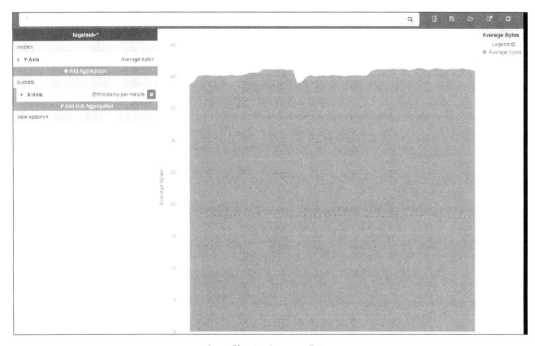

Area Chart – Average Bytes

Now, save the visualization using any name for the **Area chart**, which we will pull in **Dashboard** later.

Building a Bar chart

We'll build a vertical split bar chart showing the number of requests split across multiple clients. For the **Y-axis metrics**, we will use **Count**, and for the **X-axis aggregation**, we'll use **Date Histogram**. We'll use sub aggregation using the **Split Bars** feature, and split it using the **clientip** term:

Chapter 8

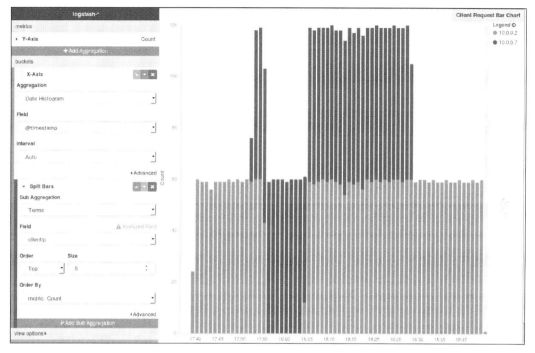

Bar Chart – Requests by Clients

Now, save the visualization using any name for the **Bar chart**, which we will pull in **Dashboard** later.

Building a Markdown

Markdown is lightweight markup language that has a simple formatting syntax for various documentation needs. We'll build one Markdown to give an explanation of our **Dashboard**:

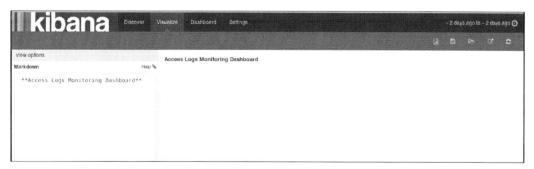

Markdown

Dashboard page

On the **Dashboard** page, we can choose from our list of saved visualizations or searches to include them in our **Dashboard**:

Add visualization or searches to Dashboard

After we have selected the visualizations that we want to include in our dashboard, we can drag and drop and arrange them accordingly. The resulting dashboard looks like this:

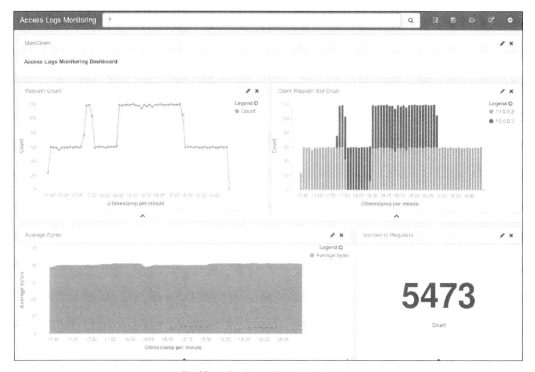

Dashboard – Access Logs Monitoring

Chapter 8

Once completed, we can choose to share the dashboard using the share button, which also gives us the code to be used if we want to include it as an embedded dashboard in some other application:

Share Dashboard

Summary

In this chapter, we saw how we could build an end-to-end data pipeline built over our logs using ELK Stack, which helps us get useful analysis from our data. This chapter helped us understand how the features of Elasticsearch, Logstash, and Kibana come together to help build our own analytics pipeline.

In the next chapter, we'll take a look at some of the practical implementations of ELK Stack and how it is helping the industry.

9
ELK Stack in Production

So far in the book, we saw how we could use ELK stack to figure out useful information out of our logs, and build a centralized logging solution for multiple data sources of an application.

In our end-to-end log pipeline, we configured ELK on our local machine to use local Elasticsearch, Logstash, and Kibana instances.

In this chapter, we will take a look at how ELK Stack can be used in production with huge amounts of data and a variety of data sources. Some of the biggest companies, such as Bloomberg, LinkedIn, Netflix, and so on, are successfully using ELK Stack in production and ELK Stack is gaining popularity day by day.

When we talk about the production level implementation of ELK Stack, some of the perquisites are:

- Prevention of data loss
- Data protection
- Scalability of the solution
- Data retention

Prevention of data loss

Data loss prevention is critical for a production system, as monitoring and debugging is largely dependent on each and every log event to be present in the system; otherwise, whole analytics or the debugging system will fail, and we end up losing some of the important events in our system.

Data loss can be prevented using a message broker in front of the Logstash indexers. Message brokers, such as Redis, prove to be useful when dealing with a large stream of data, as Logstash may slow down while indexing data to Elasticsearch. Redis can help in these situations where it can buffer the data while Logstash is busy indexing to Elasticsearch. It also adds a layer of resiliency where if indexing fails, events are held in a queue instead of getting lost. ZeroMQ, RabbitMQ, AMQP can also be used as a broker in place of Redis.

For example, the following architecture can be useful:

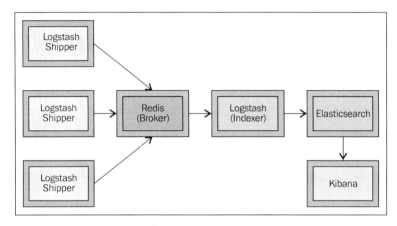

ELK Architecture with message broker

Data protection

Since data is of immense value and carries a lot of confidential information, it is extremely important to protect the data at various points while in ELK Stack. Elasticsearch indices must be prevented from unauthorized access, and Kibana Dashboard should be protected too. We can also set up an Nginx reverse proxy to access Kibana instances, which will put your Kibana console behind an authentication page that requires a username and password.

Kibana supports SSL encryption for both client requests and the requests the Kibana server sends to Elasticsearch.

To encrypt communications between the browser and the Kibana server, we can configure the `ssl_key_file` and `ssl_cert_file` properties in `kibana.yml`:

The following are SSL for outgoing requests from the Kibana server (PEM formatted):

- `ssl_key_file`: /path/to/your/server.key
- `ssl_cert_file`: /path/to/your/server.crt

Elasticsearch shield can be used to provide index level access control to your data in Elasticsearch. We can create a role for Kibana in shield, and determine what access we want to grant to users of Kibana, as follows:

```
kibana4:
  cluster:
      - cluster:monitor/nodes/info
      - cluster:monitor/health
  indices:
    '*':
      - indices:admin/mappings/fields/get
      - indices:admin/validate/query
      - indices:data/read/search
      - indices:data/read/msearch
      - indices:admin/get
    '.kibana':
      - indices:admin/exists
      - indices:admin/mapping/put
      - indices:admin/mappings/fields/get
      - indices:admin/refresh
      - indices:admin/validate/query
      - indices:data/read/get
      - indices:data/read/mget
      - indices:data/read/search
      - indices:data/write/delete
      - indices:data/write/index
      - indices:data/write/update
      - indices:admin/create
```

We can also give the Kibana server level roles, which gives access to the `.kibana` index as follows:

```
kibana4_server:
  cluster:
      - cluster:monitor/nodes/info
      - cluster:monitor/health
  indices:
    '.kibana':
      - indices:admin/create
      - indices:admin/exists
      - indices:admin/mapping/put
      - indices:admin/mappings/fields/get
      - indices:admin/refresh
      - indices:admin/validate/query
      - indices:data/read/get
      - indices:data/read/mget
      - indices:data/read/search
      - indices:data/write/dclctc
      - indices:data/write/index
      - indices:data/write/update
```

Please note that shield is not free and is a part of a paid service provided by Elastic. Search Guard is another tool that is free and works well to secure your Elasticsearch installation. More details are available at `http://floragunn.com/searchguard`.

System scalability

As the data in the application grows, it is essential that the log analytics system should scale well with the system. Also, there are times when your systems are under a heavy load, and you need your log analytics systems to analyze what is going on with the application. ELK Stack provides that capability where you can easily scale each component as per your needs. You can always add more Elasticsearch nodes (master nodes and data nodes) in the cluster. It is recommended that you have three master nodes (one primary and two backup) for large clusters. Also, load balancing or routing nodes can be added for high volume searches and indexing requirements. You can also get more Logstash and Redis instances, and add more than one Kibana instance too. A typical scaled architecture may look like this:

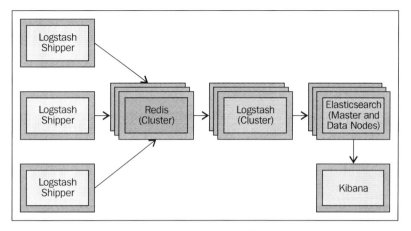

ELK Architecture with Cluster

Data retention

When setting up a log analytics system, it is extremely important to define your data retention policy as Elasticsearch can't hold all the data that you have, which may result in data loss. There should be a process to automatically delete old indices after a certain defined period.

The Elasticsearch Curator (https://github.com/elasticsearch/curator) is especially useful to manage your indices. You can schedule Curator to delete old indices based on your need. For example, the following command can be set up in a crontab to delete indices older than 10 days at a specified time, daily:

```
curator --host 10.0.0.7 delete indices --older-than 10 --time-unit days \
--timestring '%Y.%m.%d'
```

ELK Stack implementations

The ELK community is quite large, and it's growing rapidly as it is gaining more and more attention. Let's take a look at some of the already existing successful ELK Stack implementations.

ELK Stack at LinkedIn

LinkedIn is a business oriented social networking site, which is mainly used for professional networking. LinkedIn was launched in May 5, 2003. As of March 2015, LinkedIn reports more than 364 million acquired users, in more than 200 countries and territories.

Refer to `http://www.slideshare.net/TinLe1/elk-atlinked-in`.

Problem statement

LinkedIn has millions of multiple data centers, tens of thousands of servers, hundreds of billions of log records. It is a challenge to log, index, search, store, visualize, and analyze all of these logs all day, every day. Also, security in terms of access control, storage, and transport has to be maintained. As data grows, the system will scale to more data centers, more servers, and will produce even more logs. It needs an efficient log analytics pipeline that can handle data at this scale.

Criteria for solution

The log analytics solution that LinkedIn is looking for, must meet the following:

- It is horizontally scalable, so that more nodes can be added when needed
- It is fast, and quick, and as close to real-time as possible
- It is inexpensive
- It is flexible
- It has a large user community and supports availability
- It is open source

Solution

ELK Stack proved to match all these criteria. ELK is currently used across many teams in LinkedIn. This is what the current ELK Stack implementation at LinkedIn looks like:

- 100 plus ELK clusters across 20 plus teams and six data centers
- Some of the larger clusters have:
    - Greater than 32 billion docs (30+ TB)
    - Daily indices that average 3.0 billion docs (~3 TB)

The current architecture for ELK Stack at LinkedIn uses Elasticsearch, Logstash, Kibana, and Kafka.

> **Apache Kafka**: Kafka is a high throughput distributed messaging system, which was invented by LinkedIn, and open sourced in 2011. It is a fast, scalable, distributed, and durable messaging system which proves useful for systems that produce huge amounts of data. More details can be found at the Kafka site `http://kafka.apache.org`.

Kafka at LinkedIn

Kafka is a common data-transport layer across LinkedIn. Kafka handles around 1.1 trillion messages per day, a 200 TB per day input, and a 700 TB per day output. The architecture is spread across 1100 brokers, over 50 plus clusters, which includes around 32000 topics and 350 thousands partitions.

Operational challenges

LinkedIn generates lots of data, so reliable transport, queuing, storing, and indexing is very essential. It has to take data from various sources, such as Java, Scala, Python, Node.js, Go, and so on. Obviously, the data format was different across these sources so transformations were needed.

Logging using Kafka at LinkedIn

LinkedIn uses dedicated clusters for logs in each data center. They have individual Kafka topics per application, and it acts as a common logging transport for all services, languages, and frameworks. To ingest logs from Kafka to Logstash, they used their own Kafka input plugin; later, they started using KCC (Kafka console consumer) using a pipe input plugin.

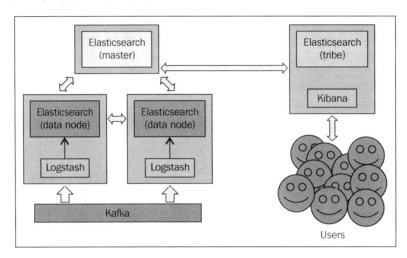

ELK at LinkedIn

An example configuration of a Logstash pipe plugin using KCC is as follows:

```
pipe {
    type => "mobile"
    command => "/opt/bin/kafka-console-consumer/kafka-console-consumer.sh \
        --formatter com.linkedin.avro.KafkaMessageJsonWithHexFormatter \
        --property schema.registry.url=http://schema-server.example.com:12250/schemaRegistry/schemas \
        --autocommit.interval.ms=60000 \
        --zookeeper zk.example.com:12913/kafka-metrics \
        --topic log_stash_event \
        --group logstash1"
    codec => "json"
}
```

ELK at SCA

SCA is a leading global hygiene and forest products company. The SCA group companies develop and produce sustainable personal care, tissue, and forest products. As we can see at `https://www.elastic.co/blog/improving-user-intelligence-with-the-elk-stack-at-sca`:

> "At SCA we use Elasticsearch, Logstash, and Kibana to record searches, clicks on result documents and user feedback, on both the intranet and external sites. We also collect qualitative metrics by asking our public users a question after showing search results: "Did you find what you were looking for?" The user has the option to give a thumbs up or down and also write a comment."

How is ELK used in SCA?

All search parameters and results information are recorded for each search event: the query string, paging, sorting, facets, the number of hits, search response time, the date and time of the search, and so on. Clicking a result document also records a multitude of information: the position of the document in the result list, the time it took from search to click, and various document metadata (such as URL, source, format, last modified, author, and more). A click event also gets connected with the search event that generated it. This is also the case for feedback events.

Each event is written to a log file that is being monitored by Logstash, which then creates a document from each event, and pushes them to Elasticsearch where the data is visualized in Kibana.

How is it helping in analytics?

Since a lot of information is being indexed in the stack, a variety of analytics can be performed from simple queries, such as "What are the ten most frequent queries during the past week?" and "Users who click on document X, what do they search for?", to the more complex ones, such as "What is the distribution of clicked documents' last modified dates, coming from source S, on Wednesdays?"

Analysis like this helps them tune the search to meet the needs of the users and deliver value to them. It helps adjust the relevance model, add new facets or remove old ones, or change the layout of search and result pages.

What this means for SCA is that they get a search that is ever improving. The direct feedback loop between the users and administrators of the system creates a sense of community, especially when users see that their grievances are being tended to. Users find what they are looking for to a greater and greater extent, saving them time and frustration.

ELK for monitoring at SCA

This setup is not only used to record information about user behavior, but also used to monitor the health of the servers. In that context Elasticsearch, Logstash, and Kibana are being used as a *Time Series Database*. Every few seconds, information about each server's CPU, memory, and disk usage (time series data) is being indexed. It also helps gain access to the historic aspect of data and to find trends in the system. This can, of course, be correlated with the user statistics. For example, a rise in CPU usage can be correlated to an increase in query volume.

Refer to: `https://www.elastic.co/blog/improving-user-intelligence-with-the-elk-stack-at-sca`.

ELK at Cliffhanger Solutions

Cliffhanger Solutions is an application and service provider for the utility and telecom industry. It helps customers and utility companies with preventative maintenance and reducing outage restoration times.

> *"At Cliffhanger Solutions, we index data in real time from various sources using Elasticsearch and Logstash. Sources include GPS location data from maintenance trucks or from tablets running our app, readings from smart meters and facility data from* **GIS (geographical information systems)***."*

Chapter 9

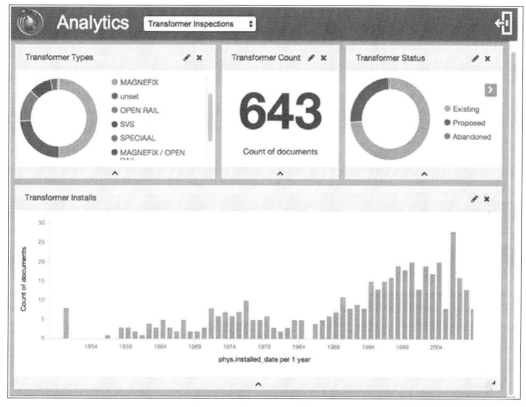

Kibana dashboard at Cliffhanger

Operators can now quickly get answers to questions such as "Can I safely close this switch and restore power to these 1500 customers?" or "A storm is coming in from the South, how fast can I get my bucket trucks to the area where the storm will hit?" As for preventative maintenance, engineers can seek answers to questions such as "Transformers from vendor X have a higher than average **MTBF (mean time between failures)**. Find all of them and sort them by installation date, then send them to the work order system for inspection or replacement." While it might not sound like a big deal, this is actually pretty incredible, and this wasn't possible until now without a heavy investments in consultancy or getting locked in with the few *one stop shop* large vendors that offer a total solution. As we can see at `https://www.elastic.co/blog/using-elk-to-keep-the-lights-on`:

"Cliffhanger Solutions is a small company, but the flexibility of Elasticsearch allowed us to focus on creating value for our customers instead of getting stuck in maintaining different systems for different clients. And our clients are getting it as well. For example, we serve a tiny utility on a Caribbean island, with only 1 guy in the IT department. By using ATLAS (+Kibana) out of the box, we built them a dashboard to show them outages on a map, color coded by customer density. This would never have been possible even a few years ago. The ELK stack is pretty incredible at making data searchable even if the source data is not clearly defined. Unlike traditional databases you don't need to know your questions in advance, you can explore and find correlations you didn't even know existed. It reduces a lot of overhead.

Internally, at the Cliffhanger office, we use the ELK stack to monitor the status of our clients' applications. We use it to improve search relevance, performance, find errors and prevent hack attacks. We share this data with our clients. They like this level of transparency and it gives them confidence that their data is safe."

Refer to `https://www.elastic.co/blog/using-elk-to-keep-the-lights-on`.

Kibana demo – Packetbeat dashboard

Finally, from ELK itself, there is a very good demo for the Kibana dashboard, which shows various aspects of the stack, and shows the power and breadth of information it gives. It is available at `http://demo.elastic.co`.

Packetbeat is a real-time network packet analytics provider, and an open source data shipper that integrates with Elasticsearch and Kibana to provide real-time analytics for web, database, and other network protocols.

This demo is spread across multiple dashboards based on Packetbeat, such as the MySQL dashboard, the MongoDB dashboard, the Web Transactions dashboard, the Thrift-RPC and PostgreSQL dashboard. It helps us understand many advanced searches and visualizations built on the Kibana platform. Here is what the dashboard looks like:

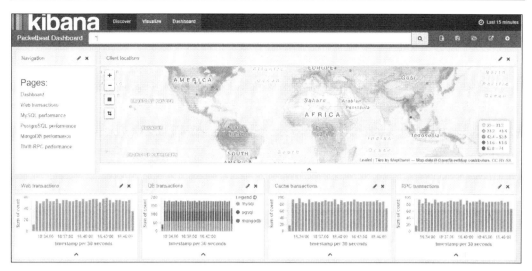

Kibana Packetbeat Demo dashboard

As we can see on the left-hand side of the preceding screenshot, it displays links to various dashboards. A MySQL performance dashboard, which displays the various queries used, performance of queries, and so on, looks like this:

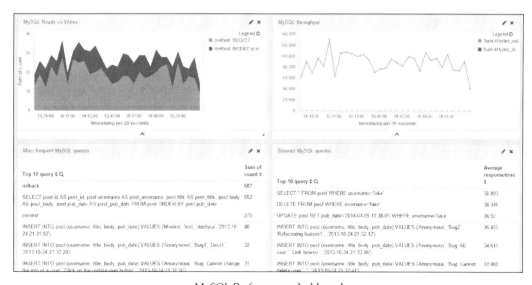

MySQL Performance dashboard

A Web Transactions dashboard, which displays various web transactions, which includes the various HTTP methods used, total number of requests, error codes, and so on, looks like this:

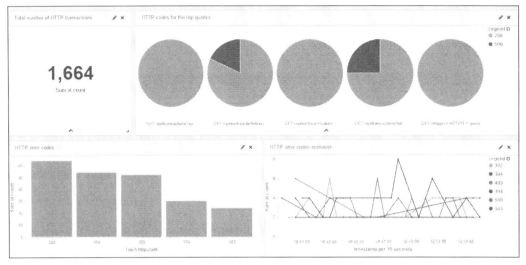

Web Transactions dashboard

A MongoDB dashboard, which dispays MongoDB throughput, errors, errors per collections, input and output throughput, and so on, looks like this:

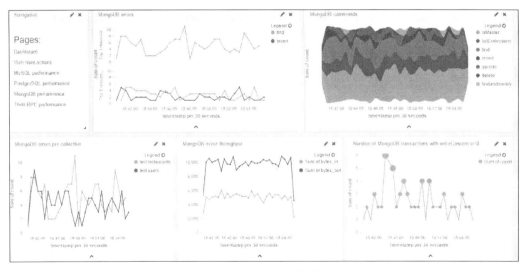

MongoDB Performance dashboard

Chapter 9

We can also explore multiple visualizations built in each of these dashboards. For example, a configuration of a GeoIP visualization, which plots clients across the geography, looks like this:

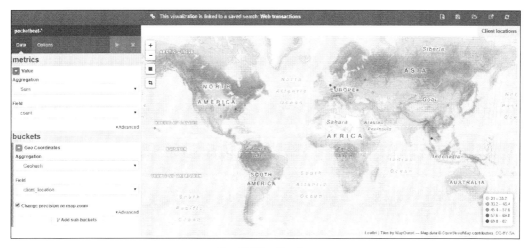

Geo IP Visualization

Summary

In this chapter, we looked at some of the production level strategies for ELK Stack and also looked at some of the implementations of the stack. ELK Stack is gaining more popularity as the community of users evolves, and with a multitude of use cases, which get benefits from the stack.

10
Expanding Horizons with ELK

In all the previous chapters, we explored all the capabilities of ELK Stack, and how it makes your life easier to analyze logs. Now, we will explore some of the plugins and utilities that extend the capability of the stack and make it more wonderful, secure, and easy to maintain. We'll also take a look at the roadmap for the components of ELK Stack.

The following topics are covered in this chapter:

- Elasticsearch plugins and utilities
    - Curator for index management
    - Shield for security
    - Marvel to monitor
- ELK roadmap

Elasticsearch plugins and utilities

Elasticsearch is a very important component of ELK Stack, so it's very important to have a good management of the Elasticsearch cluster, and to maintain security. There are a few plugins and utilities that are available.

Curator for index management

Curator is an important utility that helps manage the Elasticsearch indices. As your data grows, it becomes important to manage the kind of information that you want to retain and what information you can remove from your system. Curator can help remove old indices and optimize the system.

The following are some of the high level tasks that Curator can perform for your Elasticsearch indices:

- Delete indices and snapshots
- Close indices
- Open closed indices
- Show indices and snapshots
- Add or remove indices from an alias
- Optimize indices
- Change the number of replicas per shard for indices

Curator commands

Curator can be easily configured as cron entries in your system, where you can schedule the cleanup of indices regularly. Let's take a look at the command-line syntax of Curator:

```
curator [FLAGS] COMMAND [FLAGS] SUBCOMMAND [FLAGS]
```

All available options can be explored using the `help` command:

```
curator --help
```

Let's look at some examples of how Curator can be used:

- Deleting the indices older than a certain period:
    ```
    curator --host 10.0.0.X delete indices --older-than 180 --time-unit days \ --timestring '%Y.%m.%d'
    ```
- Show all the indices matching a timestring:
    ```
    curator --host 10.0.0.x show indices --timestring '%Y.%m.%d'
    ```
- Add indices older than 30 days to `alias last_month`:
    ```
     curator alias --alias-older-than 30 --alias last_month
    ```
- Remove indices older than `60` days from `alias last_month`:
    ```
     curator alias --unalias-older-than 60 --alias last_month
    ```

Curator installation

Curator installation is very easy and quick; it can be done via the python pip utility:

```
pip install elasticsearch-curator
```

Curator is hosted at https://github.com/elastic/curator, and detailed information about Curator can be found in its official documentation at https://www.elastic.co/guide/en/elasticsearch/client/curator/current/index.html.

Shield for security

Shield is an Elasticsearch plugin from Elastic that adds security to your Elasticsearch cluster. Shield helps protect the data by adding a secure authentication or role-based authorization process.

The following are high-level capabilities of shield:

- It adds authorization control to cluster by enabling password protection, role-based access control, and IP filtering techniques
- It adds SSL/TLS encryption, and message authentication capability
- It adds auditing capabilities to maintain an audit trail of changes in data

> More details on shield can be found in its official documentation here:
> https://www.elastic.co/guide/en/shield/current/index.html

Shield is available for 30 days with a trial license, and a subscription needs to be purchased after that. There are open sources alternatives for shield for Elasticsearch security, such as Search Guard (https://github.com/floragunncom/search-guard).

Shield installation

To install shield, you need to follow these steps from the Elasticsearch installation directory:

1. Install the license plugin:

   ```
   bin/plugin -i elasticsearch/license/latest

   -> Installing elasticsearch/license/latest...
   Trying http://download.elasticsearch.org/elasticsearch/license/license-latest.zip...
   Downloading ....................................................
   DONE
   Installed elasticsearch/license/latest into /usr/share/elasticsearch/plugins/license
   ```

2. Install the shield plugin:

   ```
   bin/plugin -i elasticsearch/shield/latest

   -> Installing elasticsearch/shield/latest...
   Trying http://download.elasticsearch.org/elasticsearch/shield/
   shield-latest.zip...
   Downloading

   DONE
   Installed elasticsearch/shield/latest into /usr/share/
   elasticsearch/plugins/shield
   ```

3. After installing plugin, start your Elasticsearch instance and check in the start up logs for references of shield:

   ```
   [2015-10-17 07:46:27,508][INFO ][transport                ]
   [Witchfire] Using [org.elasticsearch.shield.transport.
   ShieldServerTransportService] as transport service, overridden by
   [shield]
   [2015-10-17 07:46:27,510][INFO ][transport                ]
   [Witchfire] Using [org.elasticsearch.shield.transport.netty.
   ShieldNettyTransport] as transport, overridden by [shield]
   [2015-10-17 07:46:27,511][INFO ][http                     ]
   [Witchfire] Using [org.elasticsearch.shield.transport.netty.
   ShieldNettyHttpServerTransport] as http transport, overridden by
   [shield]
   ```

Once the shield plugin is added, your access to Elasticsearch at `http://localhost:9200` is restricted without a valid authentication.

Adding users and roles

You need to add users and roles in shield to access Elasticsearch. The following simple command can help you add users with a role, and you can set a password for each user:

```
bin/shield/esusers useradd es_admin -r admin
```

```
packtpub@saurzcode:/usr/share/elasticsearch/bin/shield$ sudo ./esusers useradd es_admin -r admin
Enter new password:
Retype new password:
```

Adding roles in shield

Once added, you can verify the user through a `list` command, or you can delete users, change the password, and so on.

```
packtpub@saurzcode:/usr/share/elasticsearch/bin/shield$ sudo ./esusers list
es_admin      : admin
packtpub@saurzcode:/usr/share/elasticsearch/bin/shield$ sudo ./esusers userdel es_admin
packtpub@saurzcode:/usr/share/elasticsearch/bin/shield$ sudo ./esusers list
No users found
```

Listing and removing roles in shield

Please note that the license plugin that we installed enables the 30 day trial version of shield, beyond which it is degraded to limited functionalities and the license needs to be purchased to enable full functionality.

Using Kibana4 on shield protected Elasticsearch

If we need to use Kibana on top of Elasticsearch that is now protected using shield, we need to add a `kibana4-server` role in shield, and provide a corresponding configuration in the Kibana configuration file in the Kibana installation at `config/kibana.yml`.

The following is the Kibana server role:

```
esusers useradd kibana4-server -r kibana4_server -p password
```

The following is the Kibana configuration:

```
kibana_elasticsearch_username: kibana4-server
kibana_elasticsearch_password: password
```

Marvel to monitor

Marvel is a product that helps monitor an Elasticsearch cluster. It provides a single interface to view aggregated analytics on the cluster. You can view the essential metrics for your cluster, such as health, state of nodes, and indices. Marvel can help perform a root cause analysis of cluster-related issues so that you can anticipate problems before they occur and fix them. You can also analyze historical or real-time data with it.

Marvel 2.0, supporting Elasticsearch 2.0, is a complete rewrite as a Kibana plugin. It is free for use by everyone, but multicluster support comes as a commercial feature. More on Marvel 2.0 can be found here `https://www.elastic.co/guide/en/marvel/current/index.html`.

Marvel installation

Just like shield, the Marvel installation is also a one step process. We need to execute the following command from the Elasticsearch installation directory:

```
bin/plugin -i elasticsearch/marvel/latest
```

Marvel installation

The following are some of the features that Marvel provides.

Marvel dashboards

Looking quite similar to Kibana dashboards, Marvel dashboard gives you various metrics about your Elasticsearch cluster, and various nodes and indices. Values in *yellow* need your attention and have to be taken care of.

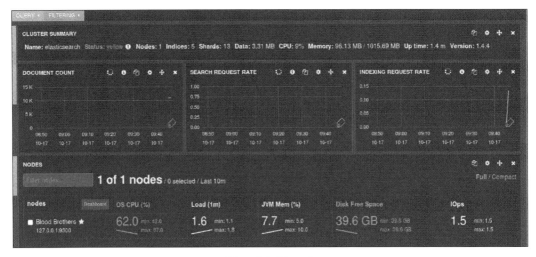

Marvel dashboard

Chapter 10

It gives you the **DOCUMENT COUNT, SEARCH REQUEST RATE, INDEXING REQUEST RATE**, various statistics on nodes and indexes, such as **OS CPU, Load, JVM Mem, Disk Free Space** and **IOps** operations, as shown in the following screenshots:

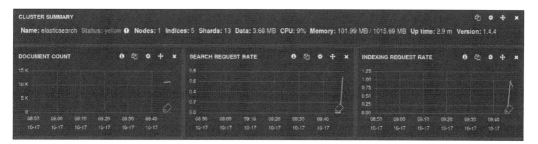

Marvel dashboard statistics

Marvel node metrics

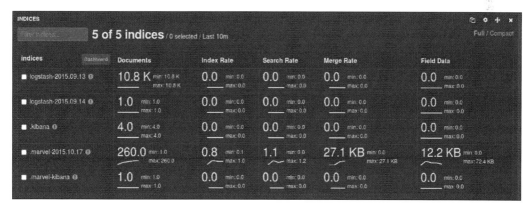

Marvel indices metrics

Expanding Horizons with ELK

There is also a very good dashboard that represents the Shard Allocation in your cluster, and where different indices sit on various shards and replicas. It displays all primary nodes and replica nodes with different color codes along with the state of various nodes.

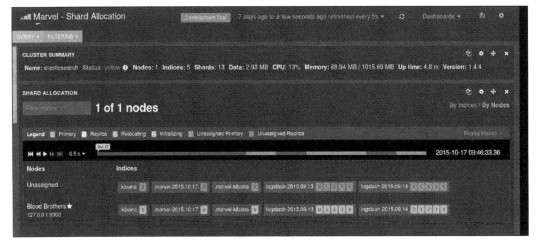

Marvel Shard Allocation dashboard

ELK roadmap

All the tools in ELK Stack and its ecosystem are in an active development phase, and new updates are being pushed regularly. It's evolving rapidly to suit the needs of modern enterprise applications.

Elasticsearch roadmap

Elasticsearch is widely used across companies in various use cases, and its ecosystem and plugins are evolving very rapidly. With a wide range of plugins available for various tasks involving Elasticsearch, it is becoming more and more adaptable to a variety of use cases.

 All plugins and integrations are documented here: https://www.elastic.co/guide/en/elasticsearch/plugins/current/index.html

Chapter 10

Logstash roadmap

Logstash is probably the most active development among ELK Stack tools. The development team and community are working hard to make the tool more enterprise grade by adding more resiliency, robustness, and maintainability features.

Logstash 1.5.x has already made significant changes related to plugin management and development. The following are the capabilities being added in coming versions of Logstash.

Event persistence capability

Currently we need to use a message broker, such as Redis, and so on, to throttle the event queue or to save losing the events in the pipeline. The upcoming versions of Logstash are going to add the capability of persisting the events queue to disk to avoid loss of data in case of plugin crash or restart.

End-to-end message acknowledgement

The current Logstash implementation lacks the capability of acknowledging the message across end-to-end systems. The upcoming versions of Logstash are planned to include notification of failed events, and so on, so that events can be replayed or handled.

Logstash monitoring and management API

The Logstash process currently lacks the support to monitor the installation, and to track event successes and failures, in the pipeline. Monitoring API planned in future releases is aimed at providing these capabilities.

Also, currently, if you need to change any configuration, you need to change the Logstash configuration file, and the system needs a restart to take the change in to effect. The Logstash management API is planned to overcome this limitation so that configuration can be updated dynamically without interrupting the pipeline.

> More capabilities that are being added to Logstash can be tracked at https://github.com/elastic/logstash/labels/roadmap.

[779]

Kibana roadmap

Kibana is getting more and more useful with a variety of use cases now utilizing the tool with ELK Stack, and also the integration with many other systems. With increasing use of analysis on a variety of data, new chart types, and aggregations are being added. The following are some of the recent capabilities added to the platform in version 4.1:

- The ability to build a bubble chart, derived from **Line chart**
- Field formatting options in **Settings**.
- Kibana objects (dashboards, charts and searches) can now be imported and exported as well.

You can track more new enhancements in Kibana here `https://www.elastic.co/guide/en/kibana/current/releasenotes.html`.

Summary

In this chapter, we saw some of the tools and utilities that make your life easy while using ELK Stack. Also, we explored how ELK Stack and its ecosystem are evolving to the needs of modern enterprises to extend its support to multiple systems and data sources.

Bibliography

This course is a blend of text and quizzes, all packaged up keeping your journey in mind. It includes content from the following Packt products:

- *Elasticsearch Essentials, Bharvi Dixit*
- *Mastering Elasticsearch - Second Edition, Rafał Kuć, and Marek Rogoziński*
- *Learning ELK Stack, Saurabh Chhajed*

Index

A

absolute time filter 715
access logs
  grok pattern 741-743
**additional configuration options,
    significant terms aggregation**
  about 313
  background set filtering 314, 315
  execution hint 318
  minimum document count 315-318
  more options 318
additional term suggester options
  about 367
  accuracy 368
  lowercase_terms 367
  max_edits 367
  max_inspections 368
  max_term_freq 368
  min_doc_freq 368
  min_word_length 367
  prefix_length 367
  shard_size 367
  string_distance 369
additive smoothing
  reference 377
**Advanced Message Queuing Protocol
    (AMQP)** 667
advices, for high query rate scenarios
  about 561
  circuit, breaking 566, 567
  field data cache 566, 567
  filter caches 561
  optimal query structure 562-564
  queries, parallelizing 566
  routing, using 564, 565

  shard query caches 561
  size and shard_size properties,
    controlling 567
aggregation
  buckets 74
  combining 96, 97
  metrics 74
  syntax 74, 75
  values, extracting 76
aggregation framework 73
aggregation results
  returning 77
aggregation types
  avg 80
  max 80
  min 79
  sum 80
  value_count 79
allocation awareness
  about 425, 426
  forcing 427
Amazon EC2 discovery
  about 489
  generic configuration 490
  nodes scanning configuration 491, 492
  optional configuration options 490, 491
  plugin installation 490
analysis 217
analysis binder
  implementing 594, 595
analyzer indices component
  implementing 595, 596
analyzer module
  implementing 596
analyzer plugin
  implementing 597, 598

analyzer provider
  implementing 593, 594
AND operator 218
Apache Kafka
  about 761
  reference 761
Apache Lucene
  about 214, 691
  architecture 214
  data analysis 217
  inverted index 214
  reference 691
Apache Lucene scoring
  altering 439
  default similarity model, selecting 443, 444
  per-field similarity, setting 441
  similarity model configuration 442
  similarity models 440
Apache Lucene scoring mechanism
  about 233
  document, returning by Lucene 234
  Elasticsearch point of view 236, 237
  example 237-240
  TF/IDF scoring formula 235
Apache Maven
  reference 575
Apache Maven project structure
  about 576
  assembly Maven plugin 580
  basics 576
  build process, running 578
  creating 575, 576
  Maven assembly plugin 578
  pom.xml 577, 578
Application Program Interface (API) 227
architecture, Apache Lucene
  about 214
  document 214
  field 214
  term 214
  token 214
architecture, Elasticsearch
  features 224
area chart 730
arrays 38
ASCII folding filter 217

attributes, core data types
  boost 35
  index 35
  null_value 35
  store 35
attributes, string-based fields
  analyzer 36
  ignore_above 36
  index_analyzer 36
  omit_norms 36
  search_analyzer 36
  term_vector 35
avg aggregation 81
Azure repository 510

B

background set 309
backup mechanism
  about 506
  Azure repository 510
  HDFS repository 508, 509
  implementing 195
  performing 506
  performing, snapshots API used 195, 196
  S3 repository 507, 508
  saving, in cloud 507
bar chart
  building 640, 641
basic concepts, Elasticsearch
  cluster 223
  document 222
  index 222
  mapping 222
  node 223
  replica 224
  shard 223
  type 222
basic HTTP authentication
  setting up 205
basic operations, with Elasticsearch
  about 15
  document, deleting 21
  document existence, checking 22
  document, fetching 18
  document, indexing 16-18

document, updating 19
index, creating 16
basic options, phrase suggester
  collate 373
  confidence 372
  force_unigrams 373
  gram_size 372
  highlight 372
  max_errors 372
  real_word_error_likehood 373
  separator 372
  token_limit 373
basic parameters
  configuring 11, 12
basic queries
  about , 56, 265
  examples 266
basic queries use cases
  lower scoring partial queries,
    ignoring 274-277
  simplified query, for multiple terms 273
  values, searching in range 272
benchmarking queries
  about 535
  benchmarks, controlling 541, 542
  benchmarks, running 536-539
  cluster configuration, preparing 535, 536
best fields matching 298-301
Bigdesk plugin
  about 707
  reference 707
Boolean model 164
Boolean operators
  - 219
  + 219
  AND 218
  NOT 219
  OR 219
Boolean type field 37
bool query
  about 64
  boost 64
  disable_coord 65
  filter 64
  minimum_should_match 64
  must 64
  must_not 64

  should 64
bounding boxes
  about 110
  using, with geo distance
    aggregation 115, 116
bucket aggregations 84, 85
buckets
  about 74, 725
  advanced options 729, 730
  aggregations 725
  Date Histogram 726
  Date Range 726
  Histogram 726
  Range 726
  Terms 726
budget 457
bulk create
  about 147
  Java example 148, 149
  Python example 147, 148
bulk delete
  about 151
  Java example 151
  Python example 151
bulk index 149
bulk processing
  practical considerations 161, 162
BulkProcessor
  parameters 158
bulk update
  about 149
  Python example 150
bundler
  reference 688
byte code 524

C

caches
  all caches, clearing 480
  clearing 480
  specific caches, clearing 480, 481
candidate generators
  about 377
  configuring 377, 378
Cat API
  about 501, 502

basics 502, 503
common arguments 504, 505
examples 505
using 504
Centos
Elasticsearch, installing on 10
character filters 26
cheaper bulk operations
about 147
bulk create 147-149
bulk delete 151
bulk index 149
bulk update 149, 150
circle 118
circuit breakers
field data circuit breaker 479
request circuit breaker 479
total circuit breaker 479
using 479
class custom analyzer
implementing 592, 593
client node 180
cloud
references 196
cluster
about 6
creating 188, 189
node, adding in 13
scaling 190, 194
snapshot, restoring to 203
cluster, Elasticsearch 693
cluster health
checking 697
checking, status 698
status, indication parameters 698
cluster-level recovery configuration
about 496
indices.recovery.compress 496
indices.recovery.concurrent_streams 496
indices.recovery.file_chunk_size 497
indices.recovery.max_bytes_per_sec 496
indices.recovery.translog_ops 497
indices.recovery.translog_size 497
codec plugin
methods 684, 685
plugin methods 684

codec plugins, Logstash plugins
about 674
json codec plugin 674
line codec 675
multiline codec 675
plain plugin 676
reference 676
rubydebug plugin 676
common terms, Elasticsearch
cluster 6
doc type 7
document 6
index 7
node 6
replica 7
shard 7
common term suggester options
about 366
analyzer 366
field 366
size 366
sort 366
suggest_mode 367
text 366
communication, Elasticsearch
about 227
data indexing 228
data querying 229
complete document
fetching 18, 19
completion suggester
about 381
additional parameters 386
custom weights 385, 386
data indexing 383, 384
data, querying 384, 385
logic 382
using 382, 383
compound queries
about 56, 63
bool query 64, 65
examples 267
not query 65
compound queries use cases
matched documents, boosting 273
concurrent merge scheduler 461

configuration, Elasticsearch
  cluster name 615
  network address 614
  node name 615
  paths, specifying 614
configuration options, csv plugin
  about 661
  codec 661
  csv_options 661
  fields 662
  gzip 662
  path 662
configuration options, email plugin
  about 663
  attachments 663
  body 663
  cc 663
  from 663
  htmlbody 663
  replyto 663
  subject 663
  to 663
configuration options, file input plugin
  about 653
  add_field 653
  codec 653
  delimiter 653
  exclude 653
  path 654
  sincedb_path 654
  sincedb_write_interval 654
  start_position 654
  tags 654
  type 655
configuration options, ganglia plugin
  about 665
  metric 665
  unit 665
  value 665
configuration options, geoip filter
  about 671
  source 671
configuration options, kafka plugin
  about 666
  topic_id 666

configuration options, log byte size
    merge policy
  calibrate_size_by_deletes 459
  maxMergeDocs 459
  max_merge_size 459
  merge_factor 459
  min_merge_size 459
configuration options, log doc merge policy
  calibrate_size_by_deletes 460
  max_merge_docs 460
  merge_factor 460
  min_merge_docs 460
configuration options, lumberjack plugin
  about 658, 667
  add_field 658
  codec 658
  host 659
  hosts 667
  port 659, 667
  ssl_certificate 659, 667
  ssl_key 659
  ssl_key_passphrase 659
  tags 659
  type 659
configuration options, mongodb plugin
  about 668
  collection 668
  database 669
  uri 669
configuration options, redis plugin
  about 660
  add_field 660
  codec 660
  data_type 660
  host 660
  key 660
  password 660
  port 661
configuration options setting
  * default 682
  * required 682
  * validate 682
configuration options, stdin plugin
  about 656
  add_field 656
  codec 656

[787]

tags 656
type 656
configuration options, tiered merge policy
  index.compund_format 459
  index.merge.policy.expunge_deletes_
    allowed 458
  index.merge.policy.floor_segment 458
  index.merge.policy.max_merge_at_
    once 458
  index.merge.policy.max_merge_at_once_
    explicit 458
  index.merge.policy.max_merged_
    segment 458
  index.merge.policy.segments_per_tier 458
  index.reclaim_deletes_weight 459
configuration options, twitter plugin
  about 657
  add_field 657
  codec 657
  consumer_key 657
  consumer_secret 657
  full_tweet 657
  keywords 657
  oauth_token 657
  oauth_token_secret 657
  tags 658
  type 658
core data types
  attributes 35
critical access
  securing 207
cross fields matching 301-303
CRUD operations, with elasticsearch-py
  about 43, 45
  document existence, checking 49
  documents, deleting 49
  documents, indexing 47
  documents, retrieving 48
  documents, updating 48
  global timeout 45
  indexes, creating with mappings 46, 47
  indexes, creating with settings 46, 47
  per-request timeout 45
  request timeouts 45
  updates, with docs 49
  value, appending in array 49
  value of field, replacing 48

CRUD operations, with Java
  about 50
  document, deleting 53
  document, fetching 52
  document, indexing 51
  document, updating 52
  document, updating with doc 52
  document, updating with script 52, 53
  Elasticsearch connection 50, 51
csv filter
  about 669
  configuration options 669
csv plugin
  about 661
  configuration options 661
Curator
  commands 772
  installation 772, 773
  reference 773
  used, for index management 771, 772
curl tool
  reference 228
custom analysis plugin
  analysis binder, implementing 594, 595
  analyzer indices component,
    implementing 595, 596
  analyzer module, implementing 596
  analyzer plugin, implementing 597, 598
  analyzer provider, implementing 593, 594
  building 598
  checking 599, 600
  class custom analyzer,
    implementing 592, 593
  creating 589
  implementation details 589
  installing 599
  testing 598
  TokenFilter factory, implementing 591, 592
  TokenFilter, implementing 590, 591
custom analyzers
  creating 29
  working 31
custom REST action
  assumptions 581
  creating 581
  implementation 581

custom scoring
  relevancy, controlling with 167

D

Dashboard page
  about 735, 752, 753
  dashboard, building 735, 736
  dashboard, loading 736
  dashboard, saving 736
  dashboard, sharing 737
data
  sorting 69
data analysis
  about 217
  indexing 218
  querying 218
data field caches
  issues 520, 521
data loss
  prevention 755, 756
data node
  about 181, **555**
  configuring 486
data-only nodes
  configuring 486
data pagination
  about 156
  without scoring 157
  with scoring 156
data protection 756-758
data retention 759
data table
  about 731
  building 642-644
data types
  about 34
  complex data types 34
  configuring 34
  core types 34
data types, Elasticsearch
  geo_point 104
data types, for plugin properties
  array 649
  boolean 650
  codec 650
  comments 650
  field references 651
  hash 650
  string 650
Date data type 37
date filter
  about 669
  configuration options 670
date formats
  about 631
  reference 631
date histogram aggregation
  about 93
  building 93
date histogram aggregation response
  building 94
date range aggregation
  about 89
  building 90
date range aggregation
  parsing 90
debian package
  Elasticsearch, installing on Ubuntu 9
decay functions, function_score query
  exp 175, 176
  gauss 175, 176
  linear 175, 176
default analyzer
  changing 30
default shard allocation behavior
  allocation awareness 425, 426
  altering 424
  filtering 427
  runtime allocation, updating 428
  total shards allowed per node, defining 430
  total shards allowed per physical server, defining 430
default similarity model
  selecting 443, 444
default store type
  about 449
  for Elasticsearch 1.3.0 449
  for Elasticsearch versions older than 1.3.0 449
DELETE requests
  restricting 207

desired merge scheduler
  setting 461
DFR similarity
  configuring 444
direct generators
  about 377
  configuring 378-381
Discover page 713, 714
discovery module
  about 483
  configuration 484
  Zen discovery configuration 484, 485
Divergence from Randomness (DFR) 164
divergence from randomness similarity
       model 440
doc type 7
document
  about 6
  complete document, fetching 18, 19
  deleting 21
  existence, checking 22
  fetching 18
  indexing, in Elasticsearch 16-18
  part of document, fetching 19
  re-indexing, scan-scroll used 157-160
  relations 326
  scrolling, scan-scroll used 157-160
  sorting, by field values 69, 70
  updating 19
  updating, partially 20
  whole document, updating 20
document analysis 26
document metadata fields
  about 32
  _all 33
  dynamic 34
  _id 32
  _source 32
  _ttl 33
document relationships
  considerations 142
document routing 71
documents, Elasticsearch 692
documents, Elasticsearch API
  deleting 700
  retrieving 699

documents grouping
  about 320
  additional parameters 324, 326
  example 321-324
  top hits aggregation 320
document types 222
doc values 217
  example, of usage 521-524
  used, for optimizing queries 520
doc_values
  advantages 101
drop filter
  about 670
  configuration options 670

E

EC2 discovery configuration options
  cloud.aws.ec2.endpoint 490
  cloud.aws.protocol 490
  cloud.aws.proxy_host 491
  cloud.aws.proxy_port 491
  cloud.aws.region 490
  discovery.ec2.ping_timeout 491
EC2 nodes scanning configuration
  discovery.ec2.any_group 491
  discovery.ec2.availability_zones 491
  discovery.ec2.groups 491
  discovery.ec2.host_type 491
  discovery.ec2.tag 492
EC2 plugin's generic configuration
  cluster.aws.access_key 490
  cluster.aws.secret_key 490
Elastic-Hammer plugin
  about 708
  reference 708
Elasticsearch
  about 3, 691
  basic concepts 222
  best practices, in production 186-188
  cluster 693
  communicating with 227
  concepts 692
  configuration 614
  configuring 9
  data, inserting 633-636
  document 692

document, indexing in 16-18
failure detection 226
features 4
field 692
filters 255
Head plugin, installing for 14
index 692
informing, about custom analyzer 598
informing, about REST action 586
installation directory layout 10, 11
installing 9, 613
installing, on Centos 10
installing, on Ubuntu 9
key concepts 224
key features 610
mapping 693
node 694
node types 180
out-of-the-box tools 164
overview 609
plugins 615, 707
plugins and utilities 771
plugins, reference 778
primary shard 693
Query DSL Language 700-706
query rewrite 240
reference 613
relational data, managing in 126-128
replica shard 693
roadmap 778
running 613, 614
scaling 545
search types 145, 146
securing 204
Sense, installing for 15
shard 693
startup process 225, 226
type 693
use cases 609, 610
workings 225
Elasticsearch API
  about 694, 695
  available indices, listing 695, 696
  cluster health, checking 697
  document, retrieving 699, 700
  documents, deleting 700
  index, creating 698
  index, deleting 700
  nodes in cluster, listing 696
Elasticsearch Azure plugin, settings
  base_path 510
  chunk_size 510
  container 510
Elasticsearch caching
  about 465
  all caches, clearing 480
  caches, clearing 480
  circuit breakers, using 479
  field data cache 468
  filter cache 465
  shard query cache 477
Elasticsearch curator
  reference 759
Elasticsearch mapping 31
elasticsearch plugin
  about 663
  configuration options 664
Elasticsearch plugins
  about 707
  Bigdesk plugin 707
  Elastic-Hammer plugin 708
  head plugin 708, 709
  installed plugins, checking 14
  installing 13
  Java plugins 13
  reference 709
  site plugins 13
elasticsearch-py
  installing 45
  reference 43
Elasticsearch queries
  basic queries 56
  compound queries 56
Elasticsearch structure
  relational databases 7-9
Elasticsearch, using for high load scenarios
  about 555
  advices, for high query rate scenarios 561
  general Elasticsearch-tuning advices 556
  high indexing throughput scenarios 567
Elasticsearch version
  upgrading 185

ELK roadmap
  about 778
  Elasticsearch roadmap 778
  Kibana roadmap 780
  Logstash roadmap 779
ELK stack
  about 609
  data pipeline 612
  Elasticsearch 609, 610
  implementing, at Cliffhanger Solutions 764
  installation 612
  Kibana 611
  Logstash 610, 611
ELK stack, at Cliffhanger Solutions
  about 764-766
  reference 766
ELK stack, at LinkedIn
  about 760
  criteria 760
  problem statement 760
  reference 760
  solution 761
  with Kafka 761
ELK stack, at SCA
  about 763
  for analytics 763
  for monitoring 764
  reference 764
  usage 763
email plugin
  about 662
  configuration options 663
endpoints
  restricting 208
envelope 118
exact term search 24
examples, Cat API
  master node information, obtaining 505
  node information, obtaining 506
exclude parameter 428
exists queries 62
expectations on nodes, gateway module
  gateway.expected_data_nodes 494
  gateway.expected_master_nodes 494
  gateway.expected_nodes 494

F

factors, for calculating score property of document
  coordination factor 234
  document boost 234
  filter boost 234
  inverse document frequency 234
  length norm 234
  query norm 235
  term frequency 234
failure detection, Elasticsearch 226
features, Elasticsearch
  distributed 4
  High Availability 4
  powerful Query DSL 4
  REST-based 4
  schemaless 4
federated search
  about 511
  indices conflicts, handling 516, 517
  test clusters 511
  tribe node, creating 512
  write operation, blocking 517
field
  indexing 39
field data cache
  about 468
  doc values 468
  field data 468
  field data formats 475
  field data loading 476, 477
  index-level field data cache configuration 469
  node-level field data cache configuration 469
field data cache filtering
  about 470
  example 473-475
  filtering, by regex 472
  filtering by regex and term frequency 472
  filtering, by term frequency 471
  information, adding 470
field data circuit breaker 479
field data formats
  about 475

geographical-based fields 476
numeric-based fields 476
string-based fields 476
field, Elasticsearch 692
fields
  querying 219
  sorting 70
field searches
  performing 718
  with field list 720
field values
  documents, sorting by 69, 70
file input plugin
  about 629, 652
  configuration options 653
file output plugin
  about 662
  configuration options 662
file plugin
  methods 683
filter based aggregation
  about 94
  building 95
filter-based aggregation response
  parsing 95
filter cache
  about 465, 466
  index-level filter cache configuration 467
  node-level filter cache configuration 466
  types 466
filter input plugin, Logstash plugins
  about 669
  csv filter 669
  date filter 669
  drop filter 670
  geoip filter 670
  grok option 671, 672
  mutate filter 673
  sleep option 674
filter plugin
  plugin methods 683, 684
filter plugins, Logstash
  date 621
  dns 621
  drop 621
  geoip 621

grok 621
multiline 621
mutate 621
filters
  about 63
  and filter 261
  bool filter 261
  comparing, with query 255-259
  filtered query 262-264
  filtering method, selecting 264
  not filter 261
  or filter 261
  performance considerations 261
  post filtering 262-264
  working 259, 260
flushing 452
foreground set 309
freetext search
  about 717
  AND 717
  Groupings 717
  NOT 717
  OR 717
  wildcard searches 718
full text search
  about 24
  examples 24
full text search queries
  about 57, 265, 268
  examples 268
  match_all 57
  match_query 58
  multi match 59
  query_string 59
full text search queries use cases
  Lucene query syntax, using 279
  user queries, handling without
    errors 279, 280
function_score query
  about 167
  decay functions 175, 176
  field_value_factor 170, 171
  parameters 168
  script_score 172-174
  weight function 169

G

ganglia plugin
  about 664
  configuration options 665
garbage collection problems
  dealing with 527
garbage collector
  about 524, 532
  adjusting 532
  collection problems, dealing with 527, 528
  Java memory 525
  JStat using 529-531
  life cycle 526
  logging, turning on 528, 529
  memory dumps, creating 532
  service wrapper 533
  standard start up script, using 533
  swapping on Unix-like systems,
      avoiding 534, 535
gateway configuration properties
  gateway.recover_after_data_nodes 493
  gateway.recover_after_master_nodes 494
  gateway.recover_after_nodes 493
  gateway.recover_after_time 494
gateway module
  about 492
  configuration properties 493, 494
  expectations on nodes 494
  gateway recovery process 493
  local gateway 495
  low-level recovery configuration 496
gemfile 687
gemspec file 687
general Elasticsearch-tuning advices
  data distribution 558-560
  index refresh rate 556, 557
  merge process, adjusting 558
  store, selecting 556
  thread pools tuning 557
geo-aggregations 112, 113
geo bounding box query 109
geo distance aggregation
  about 113, 114
  bounding boxes, using with 115, 116
geo distance query 106, 107
geo distance range query 108

geographical information systems (GIS) 764
Geohashes
  versus Quadtree 119
geoip filter
  about 670
  configuration options 671
  reference 670
geo-point data
  indexing 104, 105
  querying 106
  sorting, by distance 111, 112
  working with 104
geo-point fields
  mapping 104
geo-shape data
  indexing 119
  querying 120-122
geo-shape fields
  mapping 119
geo-shapes
  about 116
  circle 118
  envelope 118
  linestring 117
  point 117
  polygon 118
geo-spatial data 103
global options, _bench REST endpoint
  clear_caches 540
  competitors 539
  concurrency 539
  iteration 539
  multiplier 539
  name 539
  num_executor_nodes 539
  percentiles 539
  warmup 539
grok option
  about 671, 672
  Custom grok patterns 672
  reference 671
grok pattern
  for access logs 741, 743
  reference 741
Groovy
  about 337
  conditional statements 338, 339

example 340-343
loops 339, 340
using, as scripting language 337
variable, defining in scripts 338

H

Hadoop plugins
  references 196
HDFS repository
  about 508, 509
  settings 509
head plugin
  about 708, 709
  reference 708
high indexing throughput scenarios
  about 567
  bulk indexing 568, 569
  document fields, controlling 569, 570
  doc values, versus indexing speed 569
  index architecture 570, 571
  RAM buffer, for indexing 572
  replication 570, 571
  storage type 572
  write-ahead log, tuning 571, 572
histogram aggregation
  about 91
  building 92
histogram aggregation response
  parsing 92
horizontal scaling
  about 546-548
  continuous upgrades 551
  cost 551
  high availability 549
  multiple Elasticsearch instances, on single
    physical machine 551, 552
  nodes' roles, for larger clusters 553, 554
  performance flexibility 551
  redundancy 549
  replicas, creating automatically 548, 549
Hortonworks Kafka
  reference 666
Hot Threads API
  about 542
  interval parameter 543
  response 544, 545

snapshots parameter 543
threads parameter 543
type parameter 543
usage clarification 543
human-friendly status API
  Cat API 501
hybrid filesystem store 448

I

IB similarity
  configuring 445
IDF (term) 24
implementation, custom analysis plugin
  AbstractComponent class 589
  AbstractModule extension 590
  AbstractPlugin extension 590
  AbstractTokenFilterFactory extension 589
  AnalysisModule.AnalysisBinder
    Processor 589
  analyzer provider 589
  custom analyzer 589
  TokenFilter class extension 589
implementation, custom REST action
  about 581
  Elasticsearch, informing 586
  plugin class 585, 586
  REST action class, using 582
implications 100, 101
include parameter 428
index
  about 7
  building, with sample documents 165, 166
  changes, committing 451
  creating 16
  default refresh time, changing 452
  mappings, inserting in 40
  transaction log 452, 453
  updating 451
index analysis options 34
index distribution architecture
  about 409
  example, over allocation 412
  multiple shards, versus multiple
    indices 412
  over allocation 410, 411
  replicas 412, 413

[795]

right amount of shards and replicas,
    selecting 410
sharding 410, 411
index, Elasticsearch
    about 692
    search and query, reference 692
index, Elasticsearch API
    creating 698
    deleting 700
indexing
    altering 450
index-level filter cache configuration
    about 467
    index.cache.filter.expire 467
    index.cache.filter.max_size 467
    index.cache.filter.type 467
index-level recovery settings
    about 497
    full 497
    full-1 497
    integer value 498
    quorum 497
    quorum-1 497
index settings
    modifying, during restore 202, 203
indices
    renaming 201
indices conflicts
    handling 516, 517
indices recovery API 498, 501
Information Based (IB) 164
input dataset
    about 627, 739, 740
    data format 627, 628
    log pattern 740
    reference 627
input plugin
    methods 683
input plugin, Logstash plugins
    file plugin 652
    lumberjack plugin 658
    redis plugin 659
    stdin plugin 655
    twitter 656
input plugins, Logstash
    configuring 629, 630

elasticsearch 621
eventlog 621
file 620
filtering 630-632
ganglia 621
lumberjack 621
processing 630-632
redis 620
s3 621
stdin 620
syslog 621
installation directory layout,
    Elasticsearch 10, 11
installation, ELK stack
    Elasticsearch, installing 613
    Kibana, installing 622
    Logstash, installing 616
    performing 612
installing
    Elasticsearch, on Centos 10
    Elasticsearch, on Ubuntu 9
    Elasticsearch plugins 13
    elasticsearch-py 45
    Head plugin, for Elasticsearch 14
    Pip 44
    Sense, for Elasticsearch 15
    virtualenv 44
interface, Kibana
    Dashboard 626, 713
    Discover 624, 713, 714
    Settings 626, 713
    Visualize 625, 626, 713
Internet of things (IoT) 605
inverted index 25, 26, 214, 215
I/O throttling
    about 462
    controlling 462
I/O throttling configuration
    about 462
    example 464, 465
    maximum throughput per second 463
    node throttling defaults 463
    performance considerations 463
    throttling type, configuring 463

J

Java memory
  about 525
  code cache 526
  eden space 525
  permanent generation 526
  survivor space 525
  tenured generation 526
Java objects
  life cycle 526
Java plugins 13
JavaScript Object Notation (JSON) 6
Java service wrapper
  reference 533
Java Virtual Machine (JVM) 227
jira plugin
  about 665
  configuration options 666
JSON document
  reference 227
JSON object
  example 6
JVM and OS dependencies, of Elasticsearch
  reference 8

K

Kafka, at LinkedIn
  about 761
  logging with 762
  operational challenges 761
kafka plugin
  about 666
  configuration options 666
keyword analyzer 27
Kibana
  configuring 622
  enhancements, reference 780
  installing 622
  interface 624, 713
  key features 611
  overview 611
  Packetbeat dashboard 766-769
  reference 622
  roadmap 780
  running 623, 624, 636-638
  visualization, building 638

Kibana 3
  versus Kibana 4 624
Kibana 4, features
  dynamic dashboards 713
  Elasticsearch aggregations 712
  scripted fields 712
  search highlights 712

L

language analyzer
  about 28
  reference 28
language plugin
  reference 173
Laplace smoothing model 377
Least Recently Used cache type (LRU) 466
limitations, significant terms aggregation
  about 319
  approximated counts 319
  avoiding, as top level aggregation 319
  floating point fields, avoiding 319
  memory consumption 319
linear interpolation smoothing model 377
line chart
  about 732
  building 639
linestring 117
LM Dirichlet similarity
  configuring 445
LM Jelinek Mercer similarity
  configuring 445
load balancing, Nginx
  about 209
  reference 210
log analysis
  need for 605
log analysis, challenges
  about 607
  expert knowledge requirement 609
  non-consistent log format 607
  variety of time formats 608
log analysis, use cases
  Internet of things (IoT) 607
  issue debugging 606
  logging 607
  performance analysis 606

predictive analysis 606
log byte size merge policy
  about 457
  configuration options 459
Log-Courier
  reference 619
log doc merge policy
  about 457
  configuration options 460
Logstash
  comparison operators 651
  conditionals 651
  configuring 618, 619, 648
  data types, for plugin properties 649
  filter plugins, reference 674
  input plugins, configuring 629, 630
  input plugins, reference 661
  installing 616
  key features 610, 611
  Logstash forwarder, installing 620
  output plugins, reference 669
  overview 610
  plugin management 677
  plugins 620, 649
  reference 616
  roadmap 779
  roadmap, reference 779
  running 617
  with Elasticsearch output 618
  with file input 618
Logstash, capabilities
  end-to-end message acknowledgement 779
  event persistence capability 779
  management API 779
  monitoring API 779
Logstash filter plugin
  building 687, 688
  writing 685, 686
Logstash forwarder
  reference 658
Logstash index template
  reference 716
Logstash input
  configuring 740
  grok pattern, for access logs 741, 743

Logstash plugins
  about 649
  download link 678
  installing 678
  lifecycle management 678, 679
  listing 649
  management 677
  references 678, 679
  structure 680
  types 652
  uninstalling 679
  updating 679
Logstash plugins, types
  about 652
  codec plugins 674
  filter plugins 669
  input plugins 652
  output plugins 661
lowercase filter 217
low-level recovery configuration
  about 496
  cluster-level recovery configuration 496
  index-level recovery settings 497
Lucene analyzers
  about 27, 28, **217**
  keyword analyzer 27
  language analyzer 28
  simple analyzer 27
  standard analyzer 27
  whitespace analyzer 27
Lucene expressions
  about 352
  basics 352
  example 352-355
Lucene index
  about 216
  doc values 217
  norm 216
  posting formats 216
  term vectors 216
Lucene query language
  about 218
  basics 218
  Boolean operators 218
  fields, querying 219, 220
  special characters, handling 221
  term modifiers 220, 221

lumberjack plugin
  about 658, 666
  configuration options 658, 667

M

manual backups 204
manual restoration 204
mapping, Elasticsearch 693
mappings
  about **222**
  inserting, in index 40
  updating 41
  viewing 41
markdown widget 732
Marvel
  dashboards 776-778
  installation 776
  used, for monitoring 775
master election
  about 486
  configuration 487, 488
  Zen discovery configuration 488
  Zen discovery fault detection 488
master eligible nodes 555
master node
  about 223, 181
  Amazon EC2 discovery 489
  configuring 486
  discovery implementations 492
master-only nodes
  configuring 487
match query
  about 58
  phrase search option 58
Maven Assembly plugin
  about 578
  reference 578
  using 578, 580
max aggregation 81
mean time between failures (MTBF) 765
memory pressure 100, 101
memory store
  about 448
  properties 448
merge
  tiered merge policy 457

merge policy
  log byte size merge policy 457
  log doc merge policy 457
  selecting 456
merge schedulers
  about 460
  concurrent merge scheduler 461
  desired merge scheduler, selecting 461
  serial merge scheduler 461
methods, for codec plugin
  decode method 684
  encode method 684
  register method 684
methods, for filter plugin
  filter method 684
  register method 683
methods, for input plugin
  register method 683
  run method 683
methods, for output plugin
  receive method 684
  register method 684
Metric
  building 641, 642
metric aggregations
  about 77
  basic stats, computing 78
  combined stats, computing 78, 79
  distinct counts, finding 83, 84
  extended stats, computing 82, 83
  multi-value metric 77
  single-value metric 77
  stats, computing separately 79, 80
metrics
  about 74, 727, **732**
  Advanced options 729, 730
  aggregations 725
  Average 728
  Count 727
  Max 728
  Min 728
  Sum 728
  Unique Count 728
Metrics to Watch
  about 191
  CPU utilization 191
  disk I/O utilization 193

disk low utilization 193
memory utilization 192
min aggregation 81
missing queries 62
MMap filesystem store 447
mongodb plugin
  about 668
  configuration options 668
most fields matching 303, 304
multi buckets 84
multicasting discovery 182
multicast Zen discovery configuration
  about 485
  discovery.zen.ping.multicast.address 485
  discovery.zen.ping.multicast.buffer_
      size 485
  discovery.zen.ping.multicast.enabled 485
  discovery.zen.ping.multicast.group 485
  discovery.zen.ping.multicast.port 485
  discovery.zen.ping.multicast.ttl 485
  discovery.zen.ping.unicats.concurrent_
      connects 486
multi get
  about 152
  Java example 153
  Python example 153
multilevel aggregation response
  parsing 99, 100
multimatch
  best fields matching 298-301
  controlling 297
  cross fields matching 301-303
  most fields matching 303, 304
  phrase matching 304
  phrase with prefixes matching 305, 306
  types 298
multi match query 59
**multiple Elasticsearch instances, on single
      physical machine**
  about 551, 552
  shard and its replicas, preventing from
      being on same node 552, 553
multiple indices
  restoring 201
multiple language stemming filters 217
multiple shards
  versus multiple indices 412

multi search APIs
  about 152, 154
  Java example 155
  Python example 155
multivalued fields
  sorting 70
Mustache template engine
  about 251
  referenced 251
mutate filter
  about 673
  configuration options 673

N

near real-time GET 454, 455
nested aggregations
  about 133
  syntax 134, 135
nested data
  indexing 132
nested documents 331, 332
nested field
  querying 132, 133
nested mappings
  creating 131
nested objects
  working with 129, 130
network file system drive (NFS drive)
  about 196
  client machines, configuring 198
  creating 196
new I/O filesystem store 447
NFS Exports 197
NFS host server
  configuring 197
Nginx
  setting up 205-207
N-gram smoothing models
  reference 377
node
  about 6
  adding, in cluster 13
  data node 223
  master node 223
  tribe node 223

[800]

node, Elasticsearch
  about 694
  data nodes 694
  load balancer node 694
  master node 694
  routing node 694
node-level filter cache configuration 466
nodes' roles
  about 553
  data node 553
  master eligible node 553
  query aggregator node 553
node types, Elasticsearch
  about 180
  client node 180
  data node 181
  master node 181
node upgrade
  without downtime 184
non-consistent log format
  about 607
  Apache access log 608
  IIS logs 608
  tomcat logs 607
norms 216
not analyzed queries
  about 265, 268
  examples 268
not analyzed queries use cases
  efficient query time stopwords
      handling 278
  results, limiting to given tags 277
NOT operator 219
not query 65
number data types 36

O

objects 38
object type 327-331
Okapi BM25 similarity
  configuring 444
Okapi BM25 similarity model 440
old generation 526
online book store
  implementing 231, 232

OpenStreetMap
  reference 110
options array, properties
  freq 362
  score 362
  text 362
OR operator 219
output plugin
  methods 684
output plugin, Logstash plugins
  about 661
  csv plugin 661
  elasticsearch plugin 663
  email plugin 662
  file output plugin 662
  ganglia plugin 665
  jira plugin 665
  kafka plugin 666
  lumberjack plugin 666
  mongodb plugin 668
  rabbitmq plugin 667
  redis plugin 667
  stdout plugin 668
output plugins, Logstash
  elasticsearch 621
  e-mail 621
  file 621
  kafka 621
  mongodb 621
  redis 621
  stdout 621
over allocation
  about 410
  example 412

P

Packetbeat dashboard
  about 766-769
  reference 766
parameters, for transaction log configuration
  about 453
  index.gateway.local.sync 454
  index.translog.disable_flush 454
  index.translog.flush_threshold_ops 453
  index.translog.flush_threshold_period 453

index.translog.flush_threshold_size 453
index.translog.interval 454
parameters, functions_score query
 boost 168
 boost_mode 168
 max_boost 168
 min_score 168
 score_mode 168
parameters, Query-DSL
 _source 56
 from 56
 query 56
 size 56
parent-child documents
 has_child query 140, 141
 has_parent query 141
 indexing 139, 140
 querying 140
parent-child mappings
 creating 138
parent-child relationship
 about 137, 332
 in cluster 333-335
partial restore 202
pattern queries 266, 269
pattern queries use cases
 autocomplete functionality,
  using prefixes 280
 matching phrases 285
 pattern matching 281
 spans 285, 287
per-field similarity
 setting 441
phrase matching 304
phrase suggester
 about 369
 basic configuration 372-375
 basic options 372
 candidate generators, configuring 377, 378
 configuration 371
 direct generators, configuring 378-381
 smoothing models, configuring 375, 376
 usage example 370, 371
phrase with prefixes matching 305, 306
pie chart 733
Pip
 installing 44

plugin class, custom REST action
 about 585, 586
 constructor 585
 description method 585
 name method 585
 onModule method 585
plugin methods 683
plugins and utilities, Elasticsearch
 about 771
 Curator 771, 772
 Marvel 775
 Shield 773
plugins, Logstash
 about 649
 filter plugins 621
 input plugins 620, 621
 listing 649
 output plugins 621
point 117
polygon 118
position aware queries 266, 270
posting formats 216
practical considerations, for bulk processing
 about 161
 bulk indexing 162
 bulk updates 162
 multisearch 162
 scan-scroll 162
preference parameter
 _local property 435
 _only_node:wJq0kPSHTHCovjuCsVK0-A
  property 436
 _prefer_node:wJq0kPSHTHCovjuCsVK0-A
  property 436
 _primary_first property 435
 _primary property 435
 _shards:0,1 property 436
 about 435
 custom, string value property 436
Python environments
 setting up 44

Q

Quadtree
 versus Geohash 119

query
  about 63
  performing, on data 716
query aggregator nodes 554
Query API 229
query categorization
  about 265
  basic queries 265, 266
  compound queries 265, 267
  full text search queries 265, 268
  not analyzed queries 265
  pattern queries 266, 269
  position aware queries 266, 270
  score altering queries 266, 269
  similarity supporting queries 266, 269
  structure aware queries 266, 270
Query-DSL
  about 55, **233**, 265
  parameters 56
  syntax 55
Query DSL Language, Elasticsearch
  about 700-706
  reference 705
query execution preference
  about 434, 435
  preference parameter 435
query processing-only nodes
  configuring 487
query relevance improvement
  about 387
  data 387-391
  faceting 402-406
  garbage, removing 396-398
  misspelling-proof search, making 400-402
  multi match query 392, 393
  phrase queries, boosting 399
  phrases 393-396
  quest 391
  standard query 391, 392
query rescoring
  about 291, 292
  example query 292
  rescore parameters 295, 296
  scoring mode, selecting 296
  structure, rescore query 292-295

query rewrite
  about 240
  Apache Lucene 243-245
  prefix query example 241-243
  properties 245-248
  working 240
query_string query 59
query templates
  about 248-250
  conditional expressions 252
  default values 253
  loops 252
  Mustache template engine 251
  providing, as string value 251
  storing, in files 254
quick time filter 715

R

RabbitMQ
  about 667
  references 667, 678
range aggregation
  about 87, 88
  building 88
range aggregation response
  parsing 89
range query 61
range searches
  performing 718
real-time GET operation 454
recovery module 484
redis plugin
  about 659, 667
  configuration options 660, 667
  reference 660
relational data
  managing, in Elasticsearch 126-128
relational data, in document-oriented
    NoSQL world 126
relations, between documents
  about 326
  alternatives 335
  nested documents 331, 332
  object type 327-331
  parent-child relationship 332
relative time filter 715

relevancy
   about 163
   controlling, with custom scoring 167
relevant search 163, 164
replicas 412, 413
repository 507
request circuit breaker 479
require parameter 428
rescore parameters
   query_weight 296
   rescore_query_weight 296
   window_size 295
REST 5
REST action class
   constructor 583
   requests, handling 584
   response, writing 585
   using 582
REST action plugin
   building 587
   checking 588
   installing 587
restore
   index settings, modifying during 202, 203
restore mechanism
   implementing 195
reverse nested aggregation 136, 137
rewrite property
   about 245
   constant_score_boolean 246
   constant_score_filter 246
   scoring_boolean 245
   top_terms_boost_N 246
   top_terms_N 246
routing
   about 413
   aliases 422
   implementing 418-420
   indexing with 417, 418
   multiple routing values 423
   querying 420-422
   shards and data 413
   testing 414-417
RPM package
   Elasticsearch, installing on Centos 10
Ruby
   reference 680

RubyGem
   about 677
   reference 678
runtime allocation
   cluster level updates 429
   index level updates 429
   updating 428

S

S3 repository
   about 507
   creating 507
scaling
   about 545
   horizontal scaling 546-548
   vertical scaling 545, 546
scan-scroll
   used, for re-indexing documents 157-160
   used, for scrolling documents 157-160
score 233
score altering queries 266, 269
score altering queries use cases
   importance of books, decreasing with
       certain value 284
   newer books, favoring 283, 284
score_mode parameter
   values 296
scoring 233
scripting
   reference 53
scripting changes
   Groovy 336
   MVEL language, removing 337
   security issues 336
scripting changes, Elasticsearch versions
   about 336
   scripting changes 336
scripting, in full text context
   about 343
   advanced term information 349-351
   field-related information 343-346
   shard level information 346, 347
   term level information 347, 348
search 3, 24
search database
   creating 53, 54

searches
　field searches 718
　field searches, using field list 720
　field searches, with field list 720
　freetext search 717
　loading 719
　new search, starting 719
　performing, on data 716
　range searches 718
　reference, for syntax 717
　saving 719
　special characters, escaping 718
Search Guard
　about 758
　references 758, 773
search requests
　reference 68
search requests, with Java
　about 67
　search responses, parsing 68
search requests, with Python 66, 67
search types, Elasticsearch
　dfs_query_then_fetch 146
　query_then_fetch 145
　scan 146
segment merging
　about 455, 456
　merge policy, selecting 456
　scheduling 460
segments merge 215
Sense
　installing, for Elasticsearch 15
serial merge scheduler 461
settings, HDFS repository
　chunk_size 509
　concurrent_streams 510
　conf.<key> 510
　conf_location 509
　load_default 509
　path 509
　uri 509
settings, memory store
　about 448
　cache.memory.direct 448
　cache.memory.large_buffer_size 448
　cache.memory.large_cache_size 449
　cache.memory.small_buffer_size 448

　cache.memory.small_cache_size 449
settings, S3 repository
　about 508
　base_path 508
　bucket 508
　buffer_size 508
　chunk_size 508
　max_retries 508
　region 508
　server_side_encryption 508
shard 7
shard, Elasticsearch
　about 693
　primary shards 693
　replica shard 693
sharding 410
shard query cache
　about 477, 478
　setting up 478
Shield
　installation 773, 774
　Kibana4, using on shield protected
　　　Elasticsearch 775
　reference 773
　roles, adding 774, 775
　used, for security 773
　users, adding 774, 775
significant terms aggregation
　about 306
　additional configuration options 313
　example 306-309
　limitations 319
　multiple values analysis 310, 311
　significant terms, selecting 309
　using, on full text search fields 312, 313
similarity models
　configuration 442
　configuring 444
　DFR similarity, configuring 444
　divergence from randomness (DFR) 440
　IB similarity, configuring 445
　information-based model 440
　LM Dirichlet 440
　LM Dirichlet similarity, configuring 445
　LM Jelinek Mercer 440
　LM Jelinek Mercer similarity,
　　　configuring 445

Okapi BM25 440
Okapi BM25 similarity, configuring 444
TF/IDF similarity, configuring 444
similarity supporting queries 266, 269
similarity supporting queries use cases
  documents with similar field values,
      searching 282, 283
  similar terms, searching 281
simple analyzer 27
simple filesystem store 446
single buckets 84
single point of failure (SPOF) 224
site plugins 13
sleep option 674
smoothing models
  about 375
  configuring 375, 376
  Laplace smoothing model 377
  linear interpolation smoothing model 377
  stupid backoff model 376
snapshot
  deleting 200
  information, obtaining of 200
  restoring 200
  restoring, to cluster 203
snapshot, creating
  about 199
  repository path, registering 199
  shared file system repository, registering in
      Elasticsearch 199
snapshots API
  used, for performing backup 195, 196
special characters
  handling 221
split-brain
  about 183, **487**
  avoiding 183
SSD (solid state drives) 463
standard analyzer 27
startup process, Elasticsearch 225, 226
stdin plugin
  about 655
  configuration options 656
stdout plugin 668
store module 446
store types
  about 446

default store type 449
hybrid filesystem store 448
memory store 448
MMap filesystem store 447
new I/O filesystem store 447
simple filesystem store 446
string 35
string-based fields
  attributes 35, 36
string fields
  sorting 70
structure aware queries 266, 270
structure aware queries use cases
  parent document score, affecting with
      nested document score 288
  parent documents with nested document,
      returning 287
structure, Logstash plugins
  about 680, 681
  class declaration 682
  configuration name 682
  configuration options setting 682
  drop filter plugin, reference 680
  plugin methods 683
  reference 680
  required dependencies 681
stupid backoff smoothing model 376
suggester
  _suggest REST endpoint 360
  about **360**
  completion suggester 381
  phrase suggester 369
  REST endpoint suggester response 361, 362
  suggestion requests, including
      in query 363, 365
  term suggester 366
sum aggregation 81
system scalability 758

T

Term-Based Search Queries
  about 60
  exists query 62
  missing queries 62
  range query 61
  term query 60

terms query 60
term frequencies-inverse document
    frequencies (TF-IDF) 24, 25, 233
term modifiers 220, 221
term query 60
terms aggregation 86, 87
terms query 60
term suggester
    common options 366
    configuration 366
term vectors
    about 216
    reference 35
text search
    about 24
    exact term search 24
    full text search 24
TF/IDF scoring formula
    about 235
    Lucene conceptual scoring formula 235
    Lucene practical scoring formula 235, 236
TF/IDF similarity
    configuring 444
TF (term) 24
tiered merge policy
    about 457
    configuration options 458
tile map 734
time filter
    about 714
    absolute time filter 715
    Auto-refresh setting 716
    quick time filter 715
    relative time filter 715
time formats
    decentralized logs 608
TokenFilter
    implementing 590, 591
TokenFilter factory
    implementing 591, 592
token filters
    about 27
    reference 27
tokenizers
    about 27
    reference 27

total circuit breaker 479
total shards allowed per node
    defining 430
total shards allowed per physical server
    defining 430
    disk-based allocation 433, 434
    exclusion 433
    inclusion 430, 431
    requirement 432
transaction log
    about 452
    configuration 453
tribe node
    about 223, **511**
    creating 512
    data, reading with 513, 514
    data, writing with 515
    master-level read operations 514, 515
    master-level write operations 515, 516
    unicast discovery, using 512, 513
Twitter API access token keys
    reference 53
twitter plugin
    about 656
    configuration options 657
    reference 656
type, Elasticsearch 693

U

Ubuntu
    Elasticsearch, installing on 9
unicasting discovery
    about 183
    configuring 183
unicast Zen discovery configuration
    about 486
    discovery.zen.ping.unicats.hosts 486
use cases, queries
    about 270
    basic queries use cases 272
    compound queries use cases 273
    example data 271
    full text search queries use cases 279
    not analyzed queries use cases 277
    pattern queries use cases 280, 285
    score altering queries use cases 283

similarity supporting queries use cases 281
structure aware queries use cases 287
user spelling mistakes, correcting
about 358
data, testing 358, 359
technical details 359

V

Vector Space Model (VSM) 24, 164
vertical bar chart 734
vertical scaling 545, 546
virtualenv
installing 44
visualization types
about 730
area chart 730
data table 731
line chart 732
markdown widget 732
metric 732
pie chart 733
tile map 734
vertical bar chart 734
visualization, with Kibana
about 636, 743
area chart, building 750
bar chart, building 640, 641, 750, 751
charts, creating 747
Dashboard page 752, 753
data table, building 642-644
Discover page, searching on 745-747
Kibana, running 636-744
line chart, building 639, 749
Markdown, building 751
Metric, building 641, 642
visualization, building 638

Visualize page
about 723, 724
buckets aggregations 725
metrics aggregations 725
visualization, creating 724
visualization types 725

W

whitespace analyzer 27
whole document
updating 20
write operations
blocking 517

Y

YAML
reference 585
young generation heap space 526

Z

Zen discovery
about 484
multicast Zen discovery configuration 485
unicast Zen discovery configuration 486
Zookeeper 182

Thank you for buying
Elasticsearch: A Complete Guide

About Packt Publishing

Packt, pronounced 'packed', published its first book, *Mastering phpMyAdmin for Effective MySQL Management*, in April 2004, and subsequently continued to specialize in publishing highly focused books on specific technologies and solutions.

Our books and publications share the experiences of your fellow IT professionals in adapting and customizing today's systems, applications, and frameworks. Our solution-based books give you the knowledge and power to customize the software and technologies you're using to get the job done. Packt books are more specific and less general than the IT books you have seen in the past. Our unique business model allows us to bring you more focused information, giving you more of what you need to know, and less of what you don't.

Packt is a modern yet unique publishing company that focuses on producing quality, cutting-edge books for communities of developers, administrators, and newbies alike. For more information, please visit our website at www.packtpub.com.

Writing for Packt

We welcome all inquiries from people who are interested in authoring. Book proposals should be sent to author@packtpub.com. If your book idea is still at an early stage and you would like to discuss it first before writing a formal book proposal, then please contact us; one of our commissioning editors will get in touch with you.

We're not just looking for published authors; if you have strong technical skills but no writing experience, our experienced editors can help you develop a writing career, or simply get some additional reward for your expertise.

Please check www.PacktPub.com for information on our titles

Printed in Germany
by Amazon Distribution